Garfield
FAT CAT 3-PACK
VOLUME 9

BY
JIM DAVIS

BALLANTINE BOOKS • NEW YORK

2015 Ballantine Books Trade Paperback Edition

Published in the United States by Ballantine Books, an imprint of Random House,
a division of Penguin Random House LLC, New York.

BALLANTINE and the HOUSE colophon are registered trademarks of Penguin Random House LLC.

Originally published as three separate volumes, in both black and white and colorized editions, by Ballantine Books, an imprint of Random House, a division of Penguin Random House LLC as *Garfield Hits the Big Time* in 1993 (black and white) and 2013 (colorized), *Garfield Pulls His Weight* in 1994 (black and white) and 2013 (colorized), and *Garfield Dishes It Out* in 1994 (black and white) and 2014 (colorized). This compilation was originally published in black and white in 1998.

ISBN 978-0-345-52607-6

Printed in China

www.ballantinebooks.com

9 8 7 6 5 4

Garfield
hits the
big time

BY JIM DAVIS

Ballantine Books • **New York**

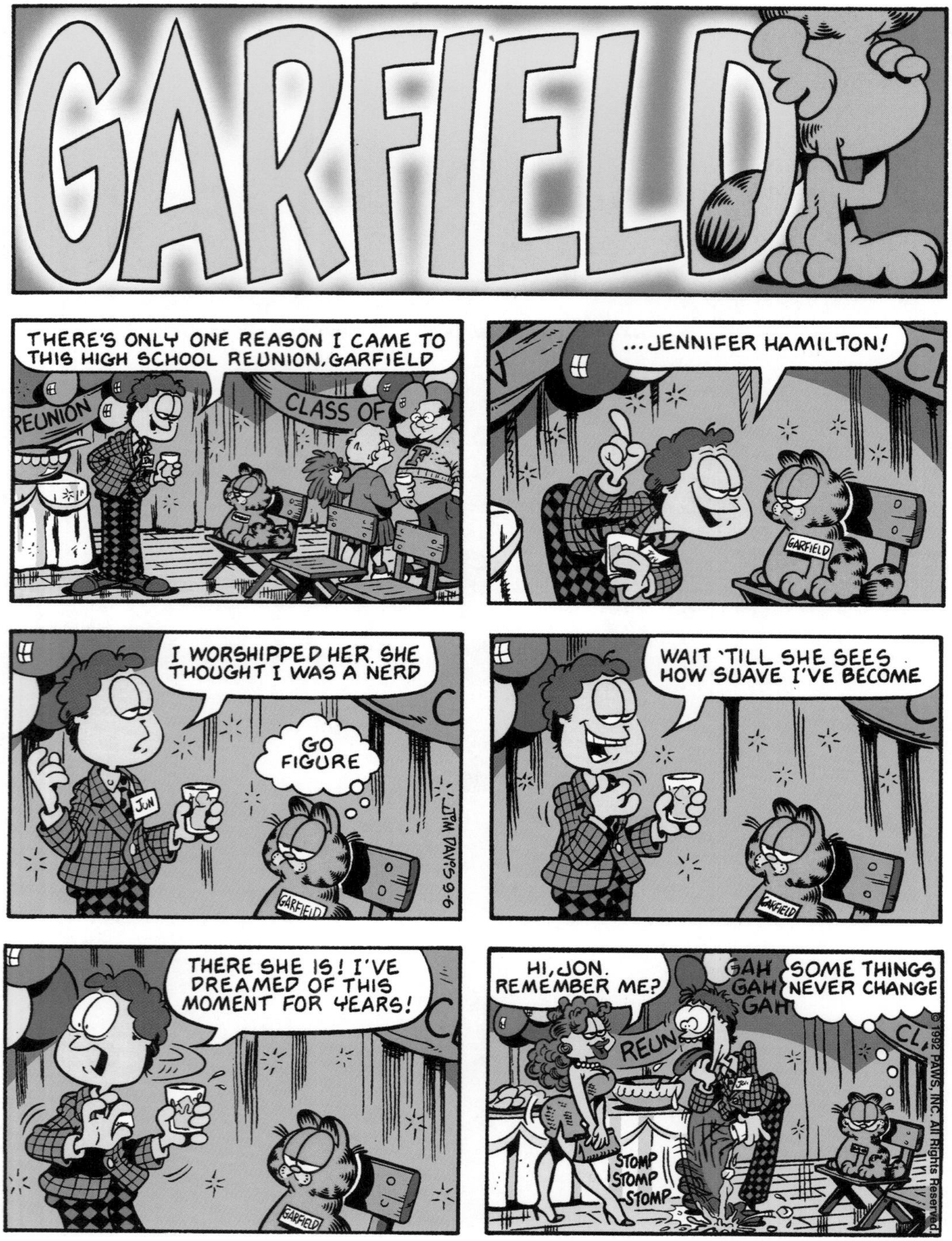
GARFIELD
THERE'S ONLY ONE REASON I CAME TO THIS HIGH SCHOOL REUNION, GARFIELD
REUNION
CLASS OF
...JENNIFER HAMILTON!
GARFIELD
I WORSHIPPED HER. SHE THOUGHT I WAS A NERD
GO FIGURE
JON
GARFIELD
JIM DAVIS 9-6
WAIT 'TILL SHE SEES HOW SUAVE I'VE BECOME
GARFIELD
THERE SHE IS! I'VE DREAMED OF THIS MOMENT FOR YEARS!
GARFIELD
HI, JON. REMEMBER ME?
GAH GAH GAH
SOME THINGS NEVER CHANGE
REUN
STOMP STOMP STOMP
© 1992 PAWS, INC. All Rights Reserved

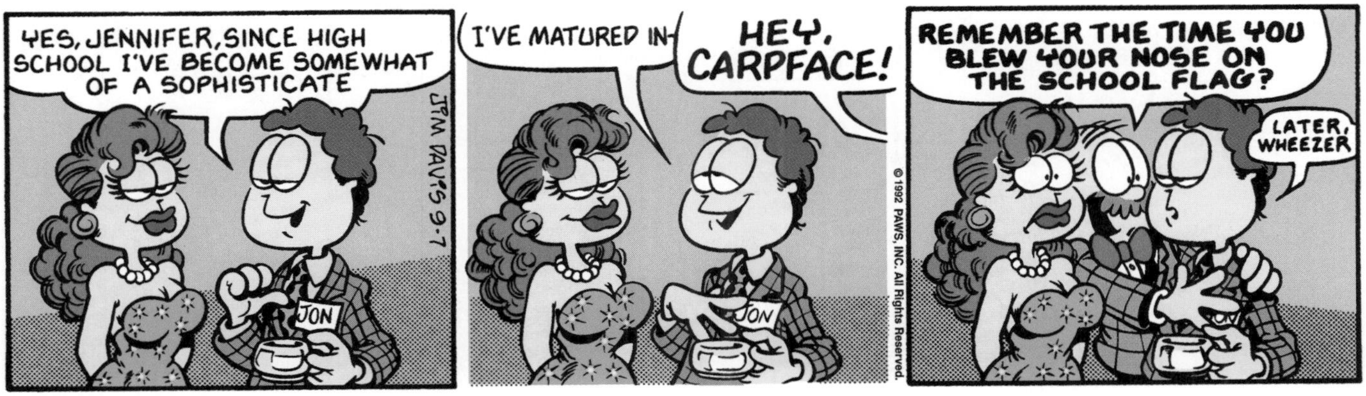
YES, JENNIFER, SINCE HIGH SCHOOL I'VE BECOME SOMEWHAT OF A SOPHISTICATE
JIM DAVIS 9-7
I'VE MATURED IN-
HEY, CARPFACE!
© 1992 PAWS, INC. All Rights Reserved.
REMEMBER THE TIME YOU BLEW YOUR NOSE ON THE SCHOOL FLAG?
LATER, WHEEZER
JON

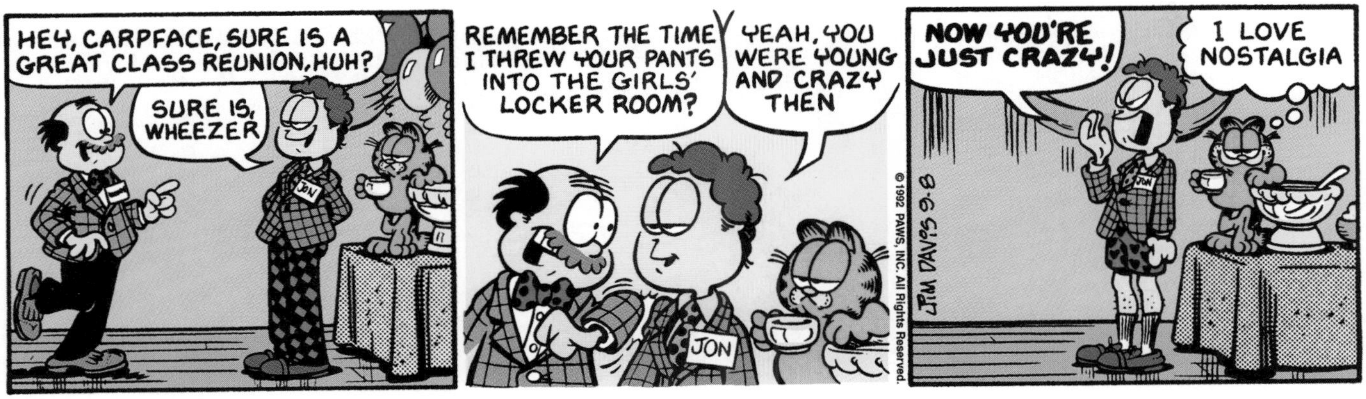
HEY, CARPFACE, SURE IS A GREAT CLASS REUNION, HUH?
SURE IS, WHEEZER
REMEMBER THE TIME I THREW YOUR PANTS INTO THE GIRLS' LOCKER ROOM?
YEAH, YOU WERE YOUNG AND CRAZY THEN
© 1992 PAWS, INC. All Rights Reserved.
JIM DAVIS 9-8
NOW YOU'RE JUST CRAZY!
I LOVE NOSTALGIA
JON

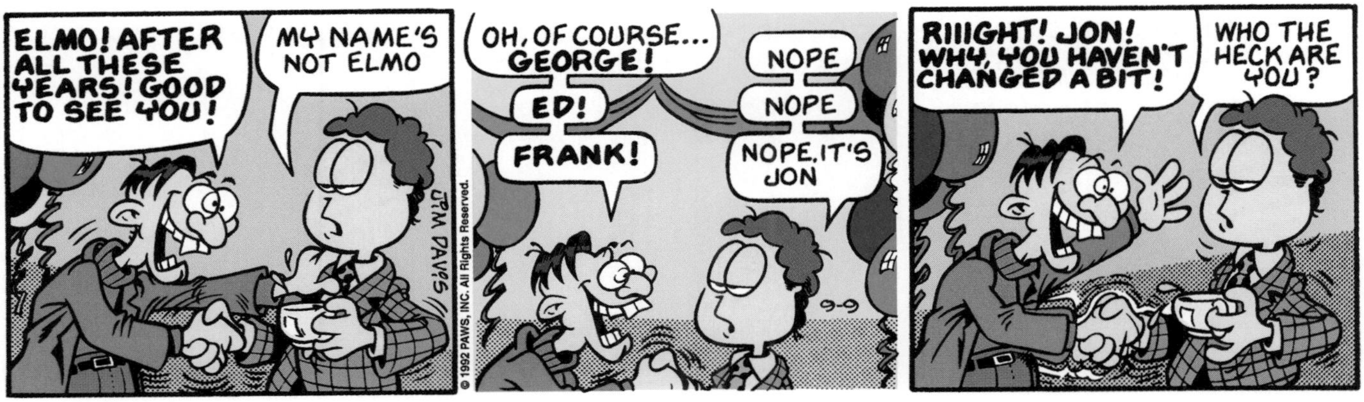
ELMO! AFTER ALL THESE YEARS! GOOD TO SEE YOU!
MY NAME'S NOT ELMO
JIM DAVIS
© 1992 PAWS, INC. All Rights Reserved.
OH, OF COURSE... GEORGE!
NOPE
ED!
NOPE
FRANK!
NOPE, IT'S JON
9-9
RIIIGHT! JON! WHY, YOU HAVEN'T CHANGED A BIT!
WHO THE HECK ARE YOU?

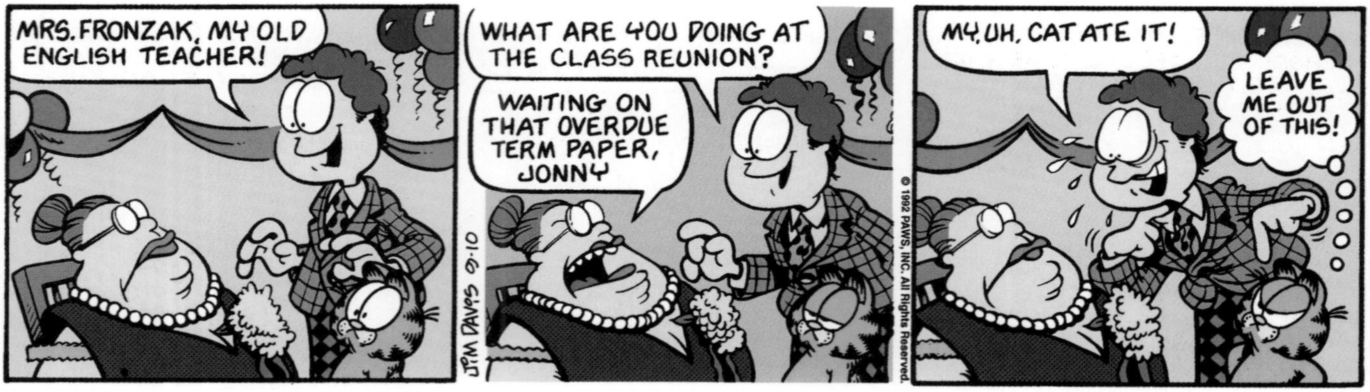
MRS. FRONZAK, MY OLD ENGLISH TEACHER!
JIM DAVIS 9-10
WHAT ARE YOU DOING AT THE CLASS REUNION?
WAITING ON THAT OVERDUE TERM PAPER, JONNY
© 1992 PAWS, INC. All Rights Reserved.
MY, UH, CAT ATE IT!
LEAVE ME OUT OF THIS!

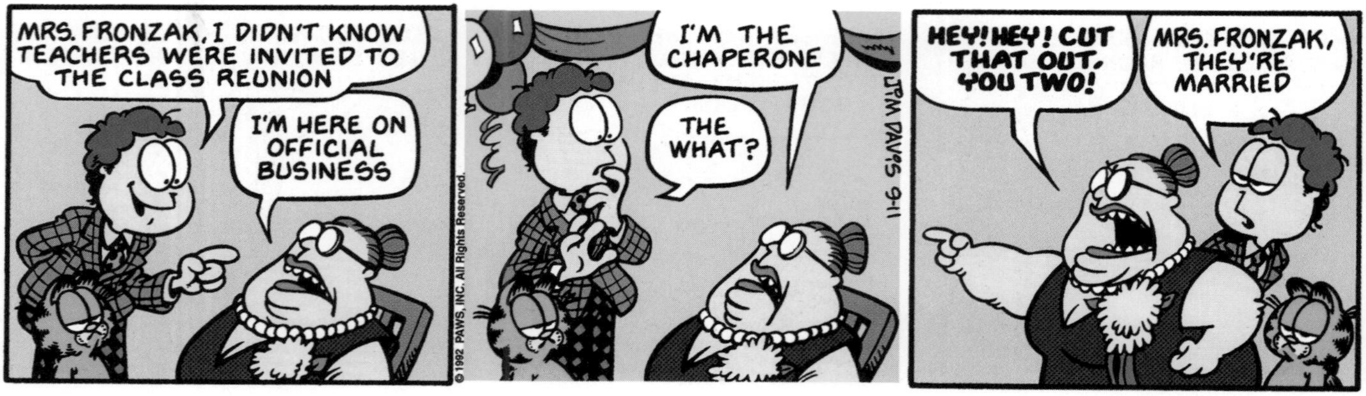
MRS. FRONZAK, I DIDN'T KNOW TEACHERS WERE INVITED TO THE CLASS REUNION
I'M HERE ON OFFICIAL BUSINESS
© 1992 PAWS, INC. All Rights Reserved.
I'M THE CHAPERONE
THE WHAT?
JIM DAVIS 9-11
HEY! HEY! CUT THAT OUT, YOU TWO!
MRS. FRONZAK, THEY'RE MARRIED

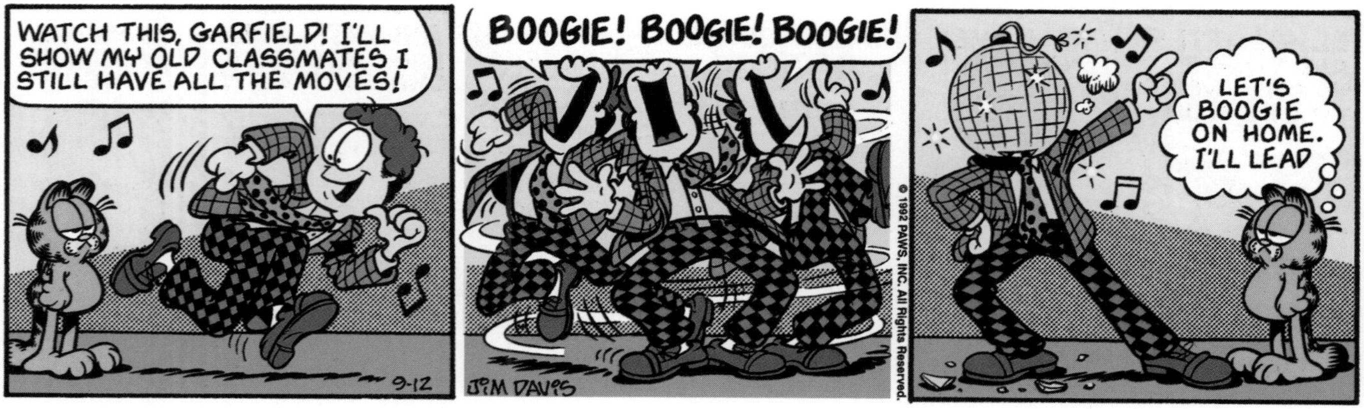
WATCH THIS, GARFIELD! I'LL SHOW MY OLD CLASSMATES I STILL HAVE ALL THE MOVES!
9-12
BOOGIE! BOOGIE! BOOGIE!
JIM DAVIS
© 1992 PAWS, INC. All Rights Reserved.
LET'S BOOGIE ON HOME. I'LL LEAD

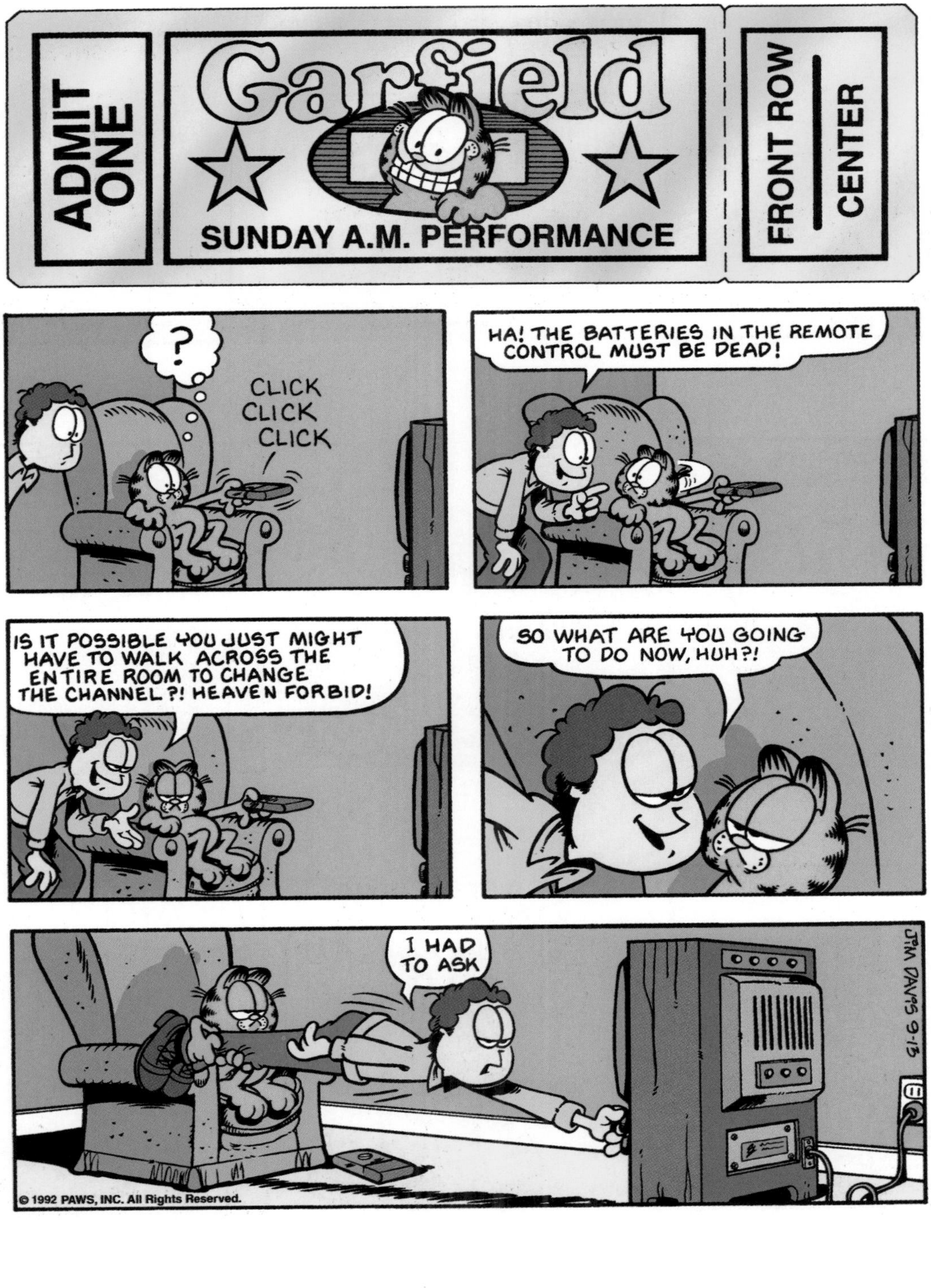
ADMIT ONE
Garfield
SUNDAY A.M. PERFORMANCE
FRONT ROW
CENTER
?
CLICK CLICK CLICK
HA! THE BATTERIES IN THE REMOTE CONTROL MUST BE DEAD!
IS IT POSSIBLE YOU JUST MIGHT HAVE TO WALK ACROSS THE ENTIRE ROOM TO CHANGE THE CHANNEL?! HEAVEN FORBID!
SO WHAT ARE YOU GOING TO DO NOW, HUH?!
I HAD TO ASK
JIM DAVIS 9-13
© 1992 PAWS, INC. All Rights Reserved.

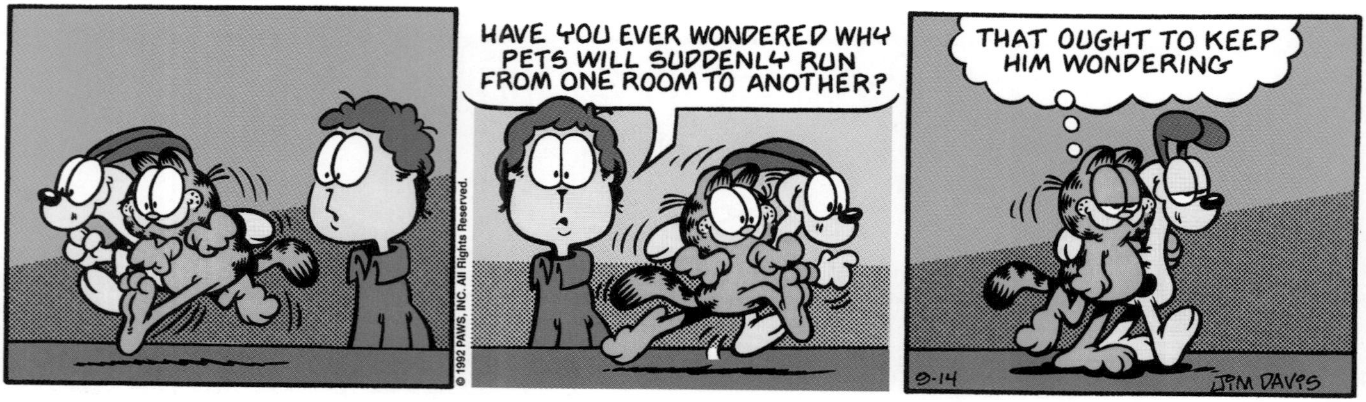
HAVE YOU EVER WONDERED WHY PETS WILL SUDDENLY RUN FROM ONE ROOM TO ANOTHER?
THAT OUGHT TO KEEP HIM WONDERING
9-14
JIM DAVIS
© 1992 PAWS, INC. All Rights Reserved.

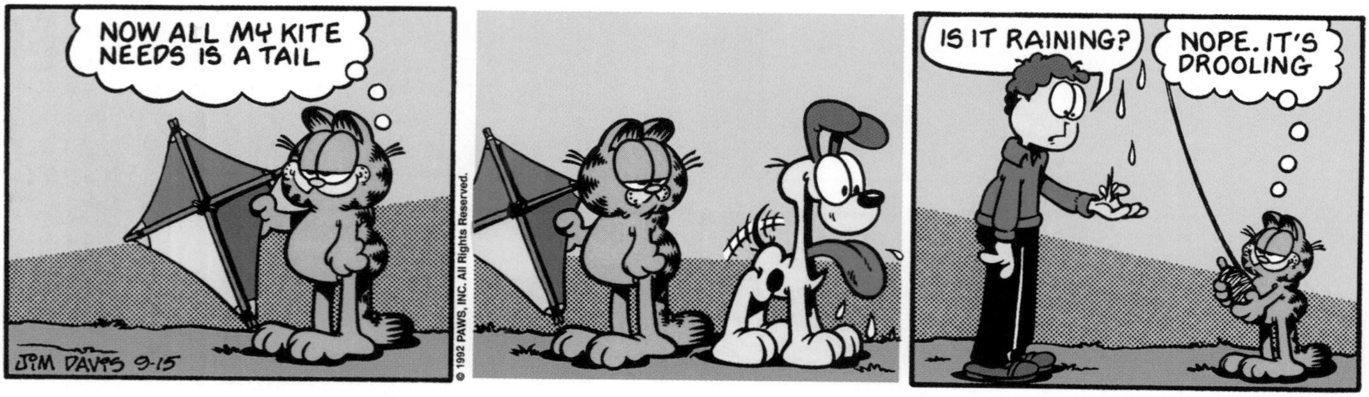
NOW ALL MY KITE NEEDS IS A TAIL
JIM DAVIS 9-15
IS IT RAINING?
NOPE. IT'S DROOLING
© 1992 PAWS, INC. All Rights Reserved.

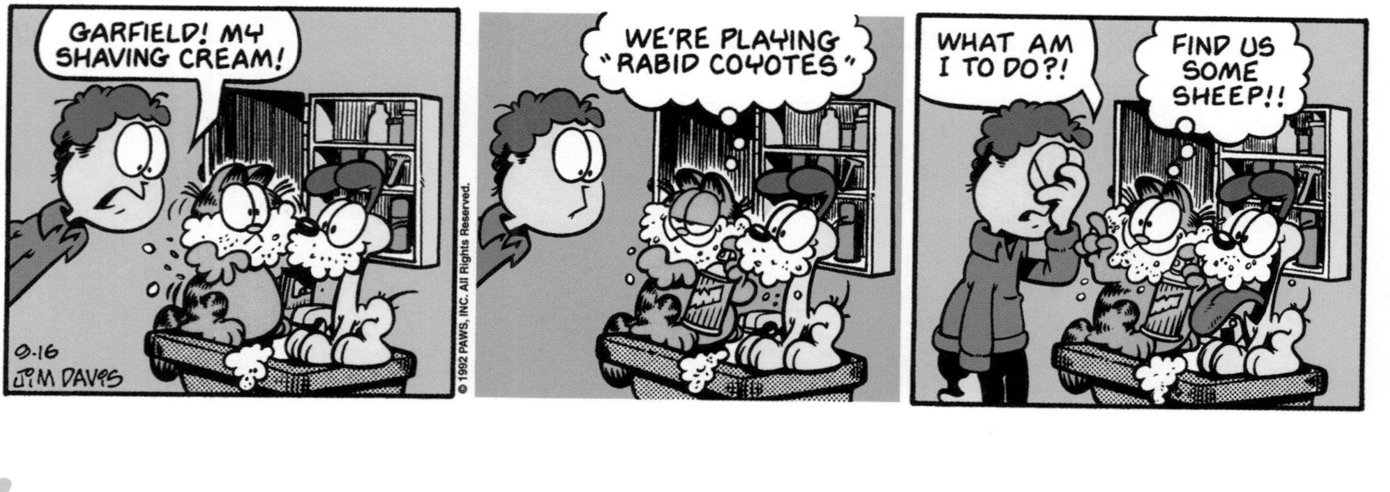
GARFIELD! MY SHAVING CREAM!
9-16
JIM DAVIS
WE'RE PLAYING "RABID COYOTES"
WHAT AM I TO DO?!
FIND US SOME SHEEP!!
© 1992 PAWS, INC. All Rights Reserved.

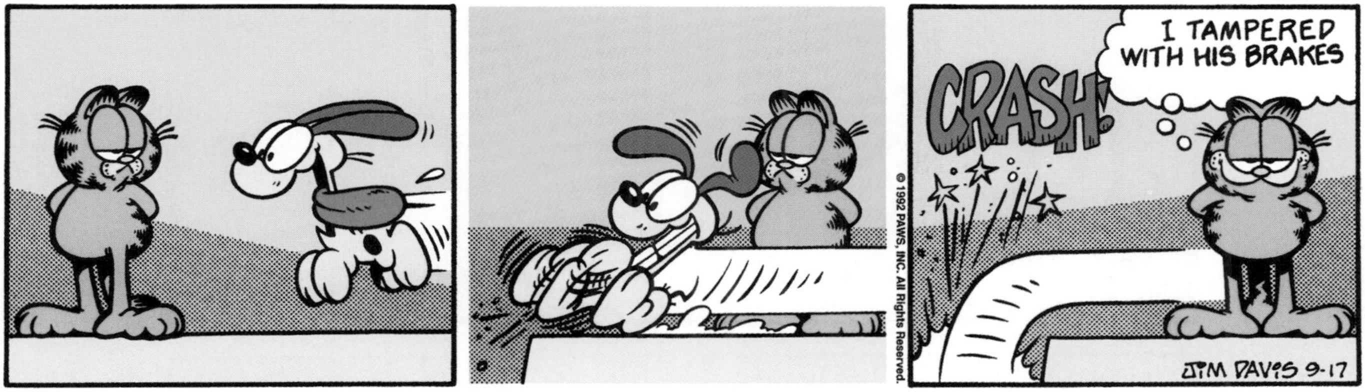
CRASH!
I TAMPERED WITH HIS BRAKES
© 1992 PAWS, INC. All Rights Reserved.
JIM DAVIS 9-17

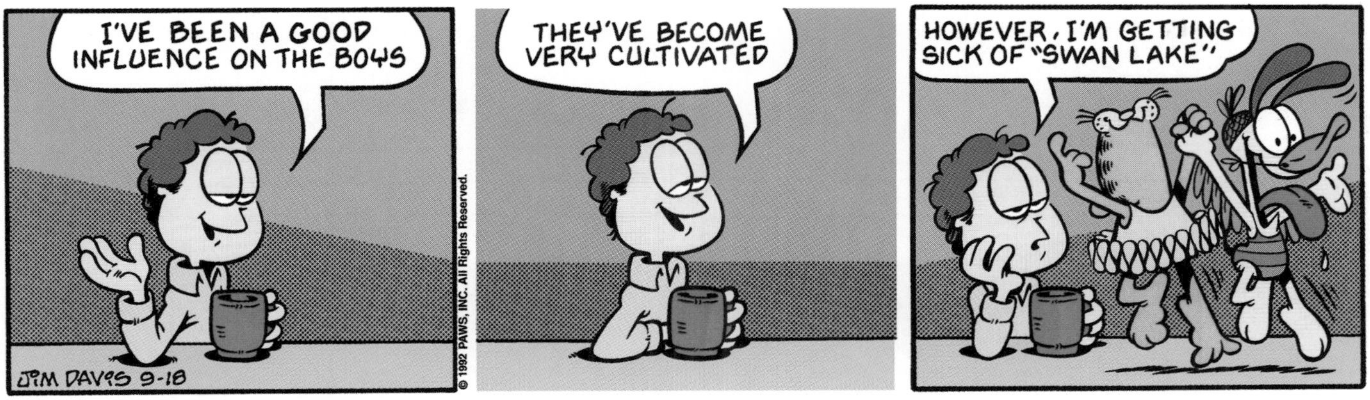
I'VE BEEN A GOOD INFLUENCE ON THE BOYS
THEY'VE BECOME VERY CULTIVATED
HOWEVER, I'M GETTING SICK OF "SWAN LAKE"
© 1992 PAWS, INC. All Rights Reserved.
JIM DAVIS 9-18

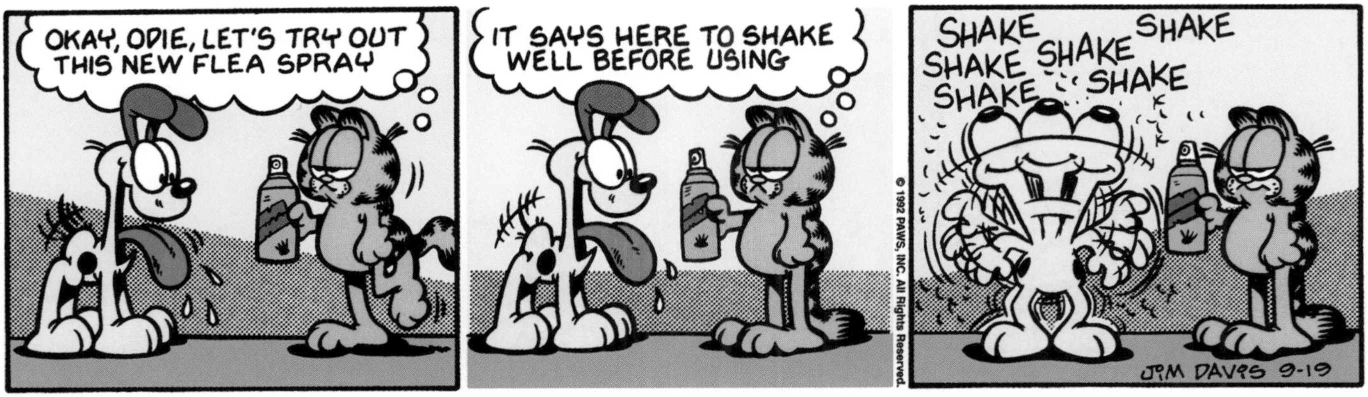
OKAY, ODIE, LET'S TRY OUT THIS NEW FLEA SPRAY
IT SAYS HERE TO SHAKE WELL BEFORE USING
SHAKE SHAKE SHAKE SHAKE SHAKE SHAKE SHAKE
© 1992 PAWS, INC. All Rights Reserved.
JIM DAVIS 9-19

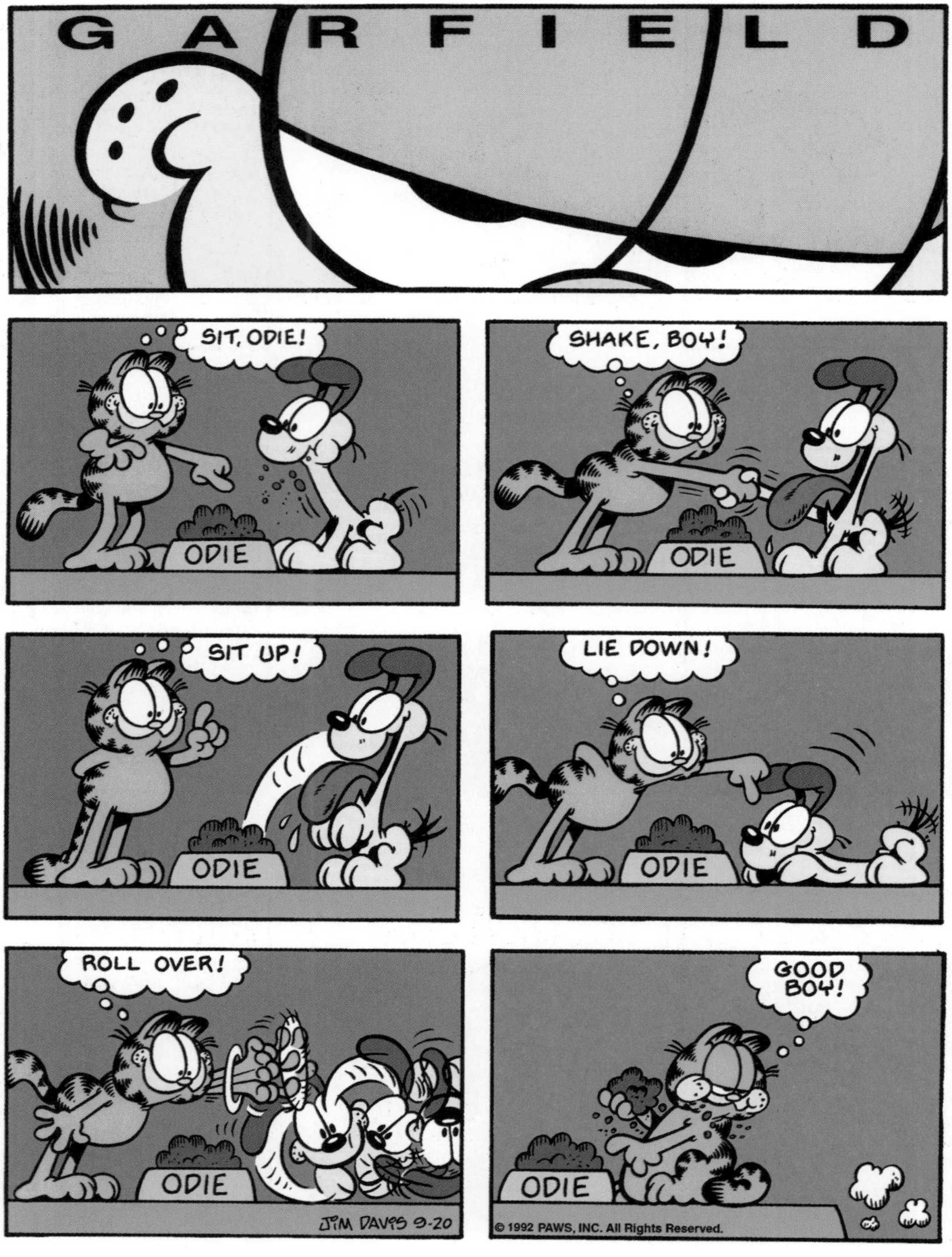
GARFIELD
SIT, ODIE!
ODIE
SHAKE, BOY!
ODIE
SIT UP!
ODIE
LIE DOWN!
ODIE
ROLL OVER!
ODIE
JIM DAVIS 9-20
GOOD BOY!
ODIE
© 1992 PAWS, INC. All Rights Reserved.

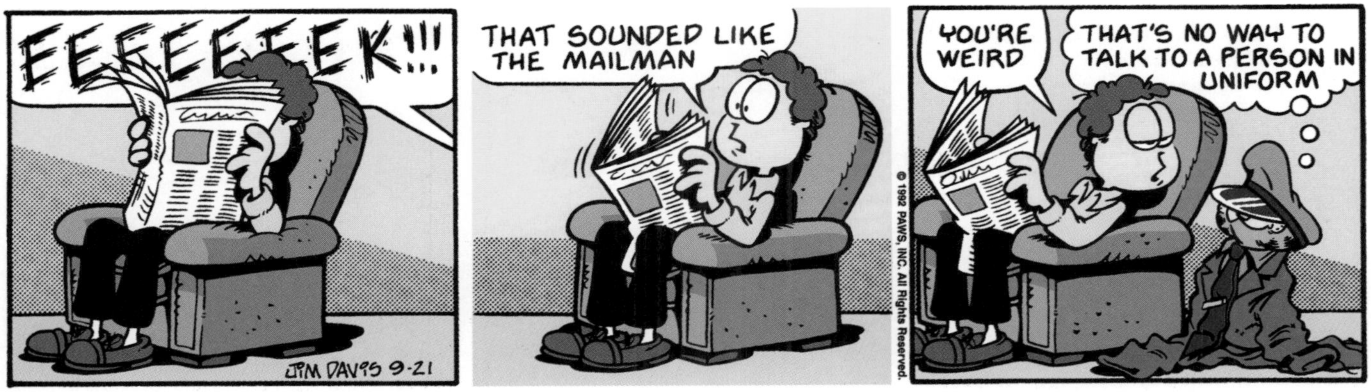
EEEEEEEEK!!!
JIM DAVIS 9-21
THAT SOUNDED LIKE THE MAILMAN
© 1992 PAWS, INC. All Rights Reserved.
YOU'RE WEIRD
THAT'S NO WAY TO TALK TO A PERSON IN UNIFORM

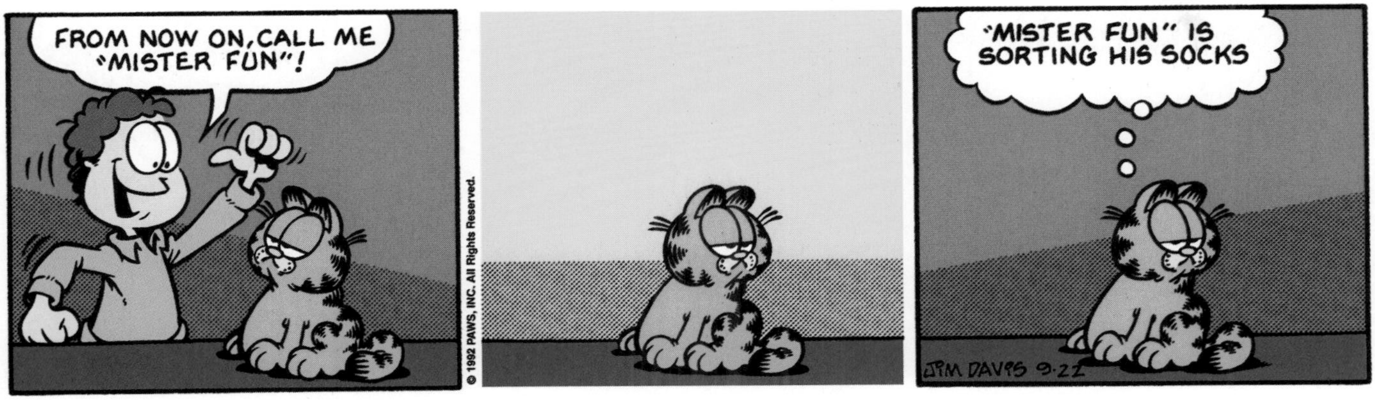
FROM NOW ON, CALL ME "MISTER FUN"!
© 1992 PAWS, INC. All Rights Reserved.
"MISTER FUN" IS SORTING HIS SOCKS
JIM DAVIS 9-22

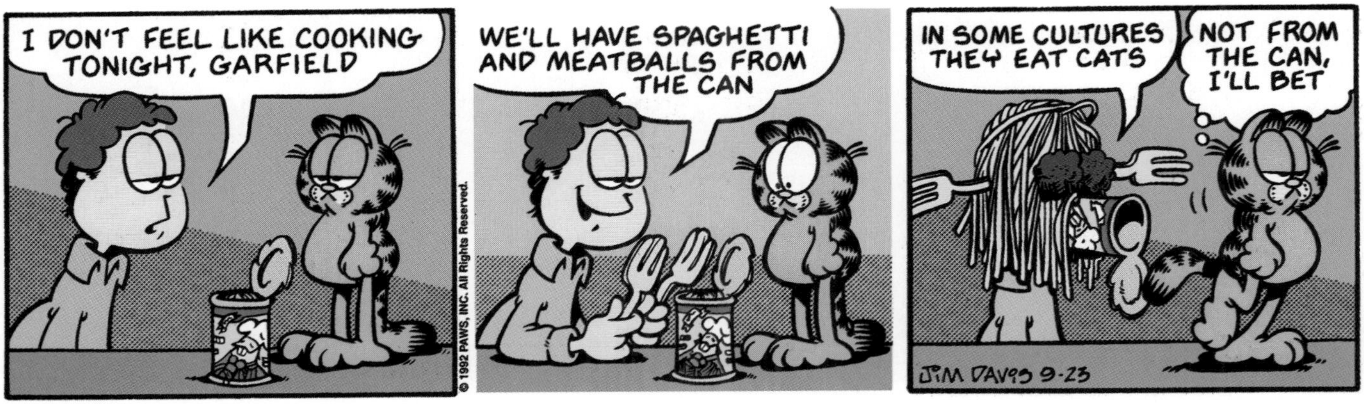
I DON'T FEEL LIKE COOKING TONIGHT, GARFIELD
© 1992 PAWS, INC. All Rights Reserved.
WE'LL HAVE SPAGHETTI AND MEATBALLS FROM THE CAN
IN SOME CULTURES THEY EAT CATS
NOT FROM THE CAN, I'LL BET
JIM DAVIS 9-23

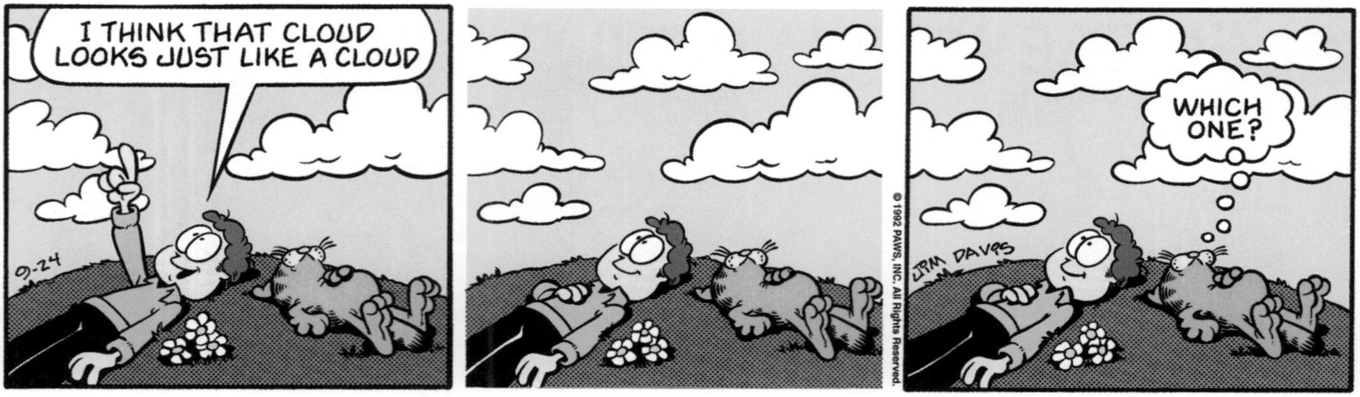
I THINK THAT CLOUD LOOKS JUST LIKE A CLOUD
9-24
WHICH ONE?
JIM DAVIS
© 1992 PAWS, INC. All Rights Reserved.

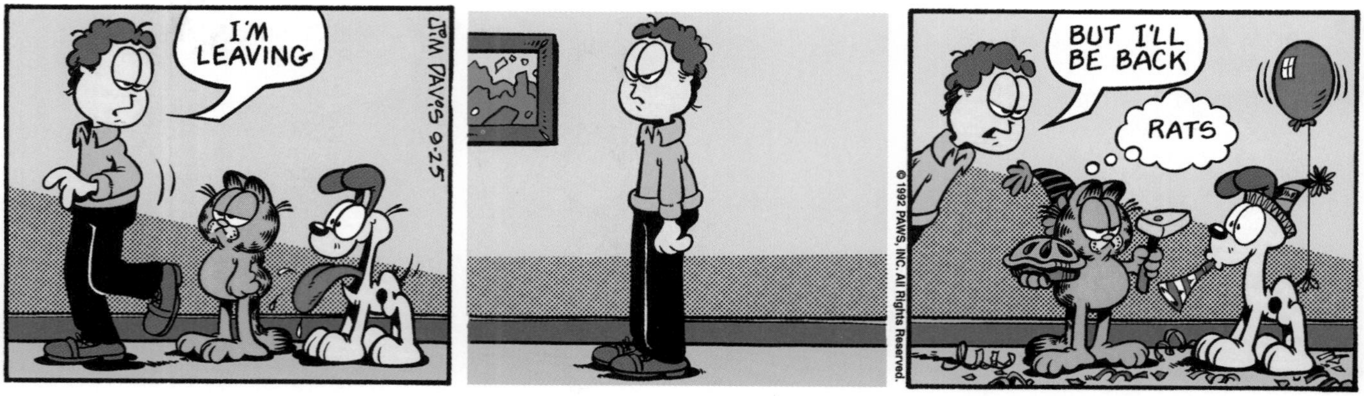
I'M LEAVING
JIM DAVIS 9-25
BUT I'LL BE BACK
RATS
© 1992 PAWS, INC. All Rights Reserved.

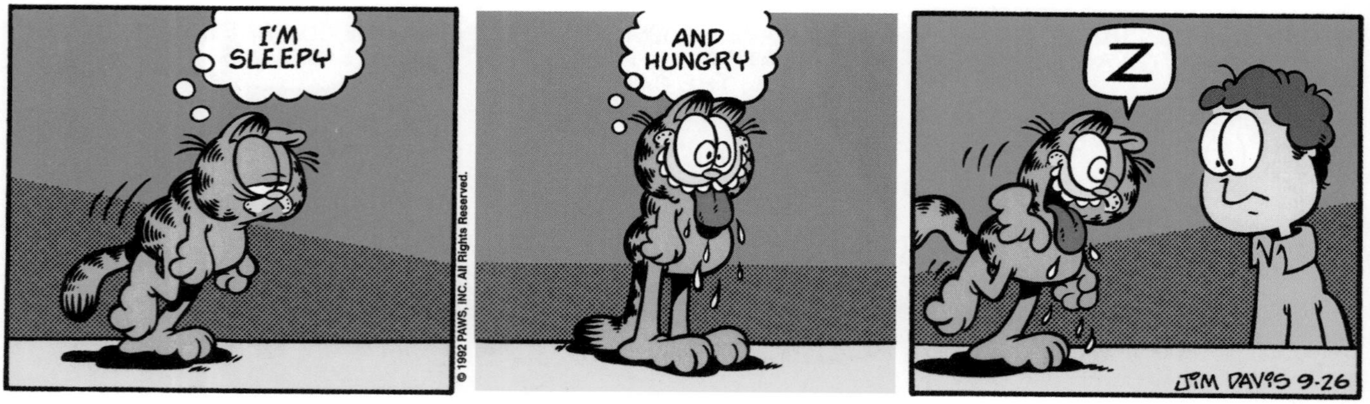
I'M SLEEPY
AND HUNGRY
Z
JIM DAVIS 9-26
© 1992 PAWS, INC. All Rights Reserved.

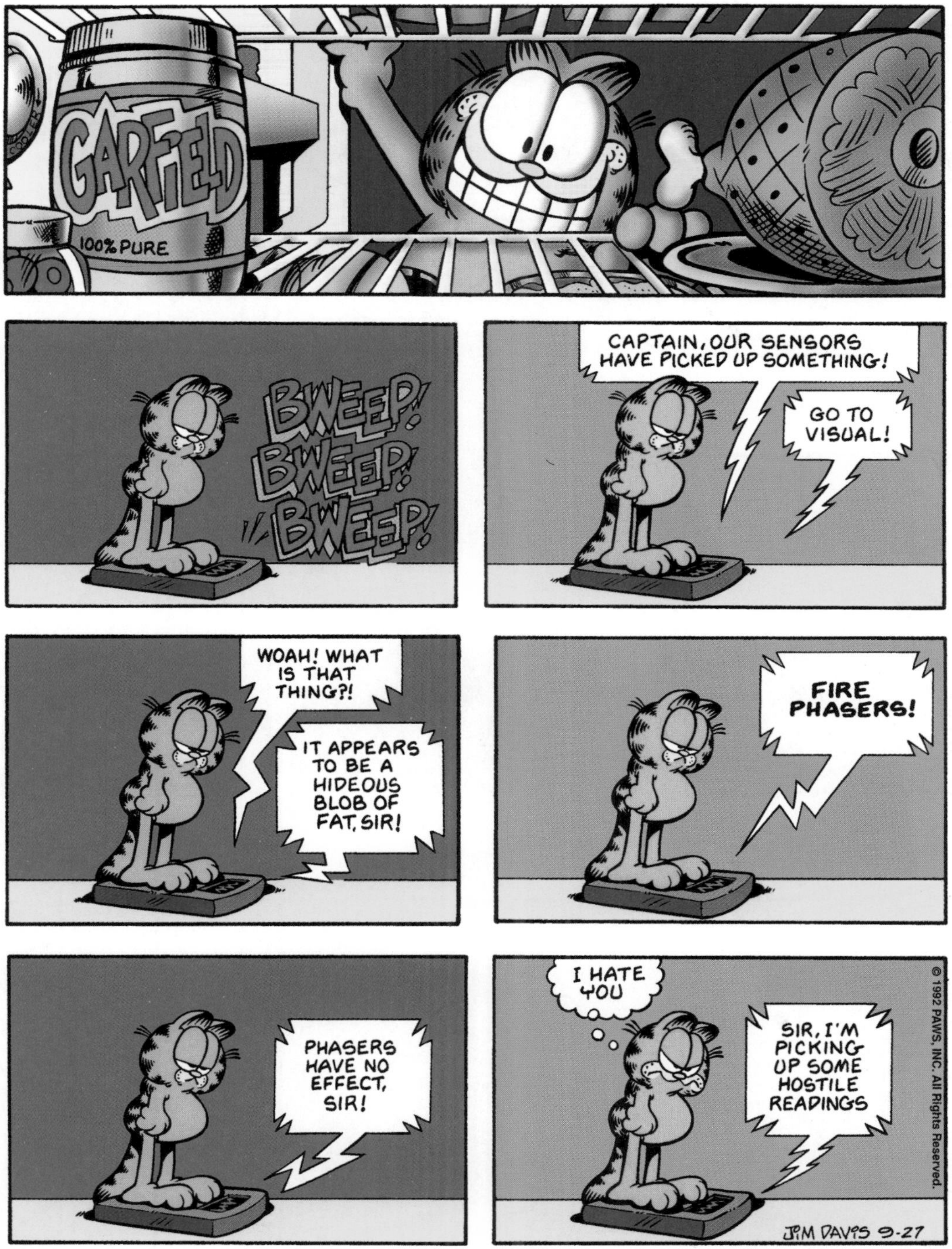
GARFIELD
100% PURE
BWEEP! BWEEP! BWEEP!
CAPTAIN, OUR SENSORS HAVE PICKED UP SOMETHING!
GO TO VISUAL!
WOAH! WHAT IS THAT THING?!
IT APPEARS TO BE A HIDEOUS BLOB OF FAT, SIR!
FIRE PHASERS!
PHASERS HAVE NO EFFECT, SIR!
I HATE YOU
SIR, I'M PICKING UP SOME HOSTILE READINGS
JIM DAVIS 9-27
© 1992 PAWS, INC. All Rights Reserved.

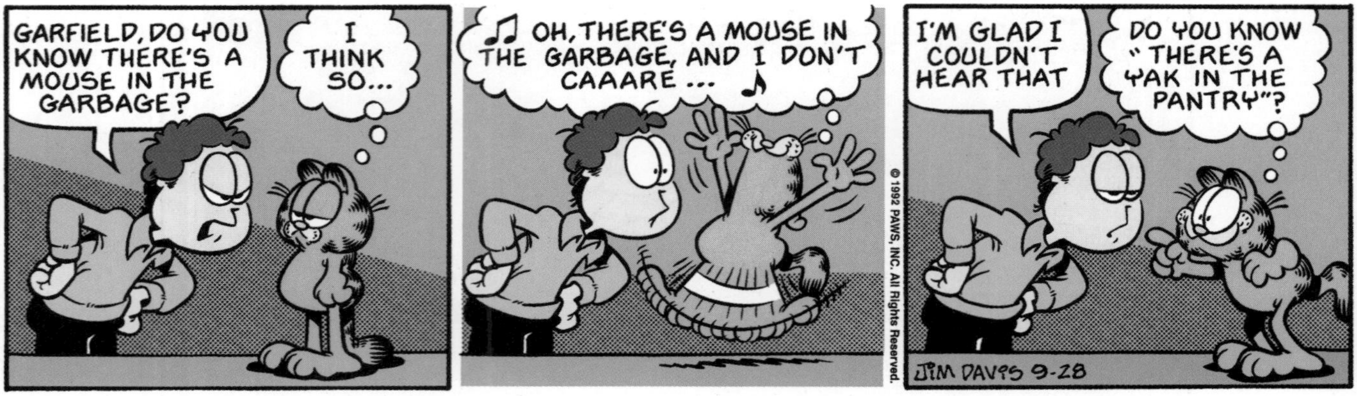
GARFIELD, DO YOU KNOW THERE'S A MOUSE IN THE GARBAGE?
I THINK SO...
OH, THERE'S A MOUSE IN THE GARBAGE, AND I DON'T CAAARE ...
I'M GLAD I COULDN'T HEAR THAT
DO YOU KNOW "THERE'S A YAK IN THE PANTRY"?
© 1992 PAWS, INC. All Rights Reserved.
JIM DAVIS 9-28

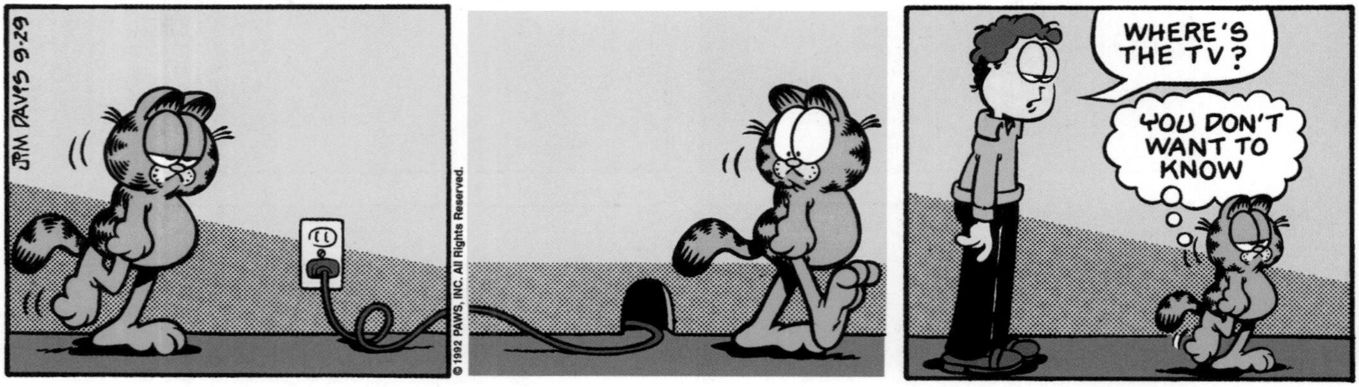
JIM DAVIS 9-29
© 1992 PAWS, INC. All Rights Reserved.
WHERE'S THE TV?
YOU DON'T WANT TO KNOW

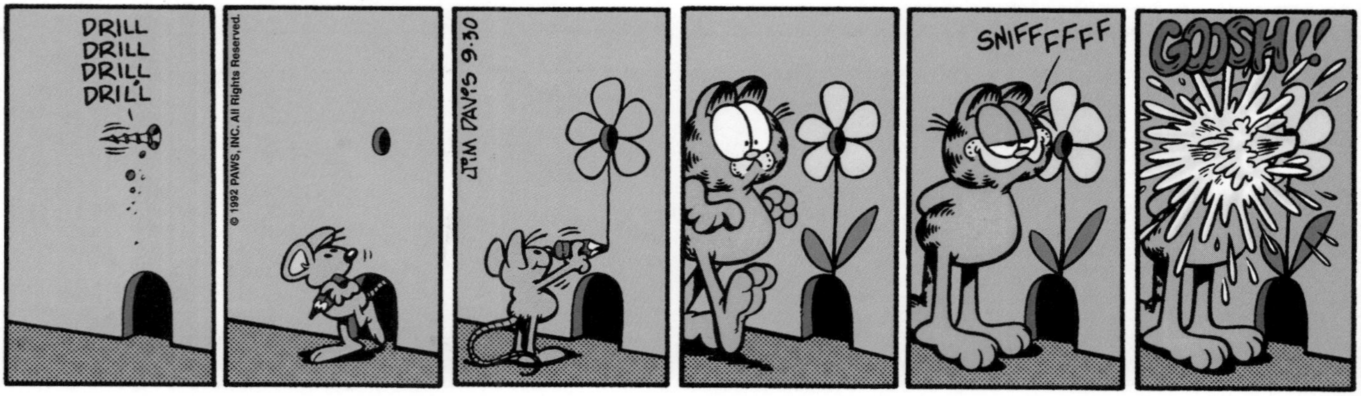
DRILL DRILL DRILL DRILL
© 1992 PAWS, INC. All Rights Reserved.
JIM DAVIS 9-30
SNIFFFFFF
GOOSH!!

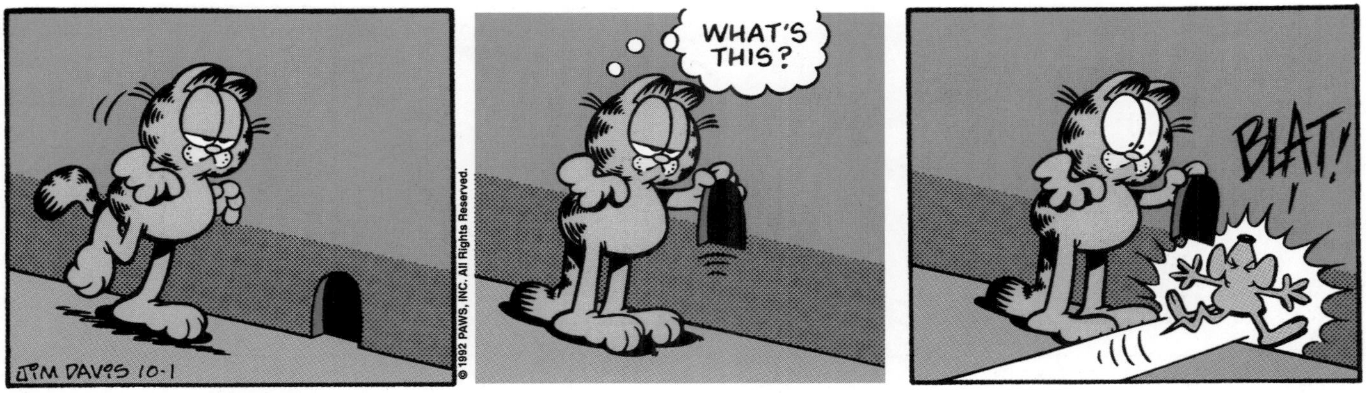
JIM DAVIS 10-1
© 1992 PAWS, INC. All Rights Reserved.
WHAT'S THIS?
BLAT!

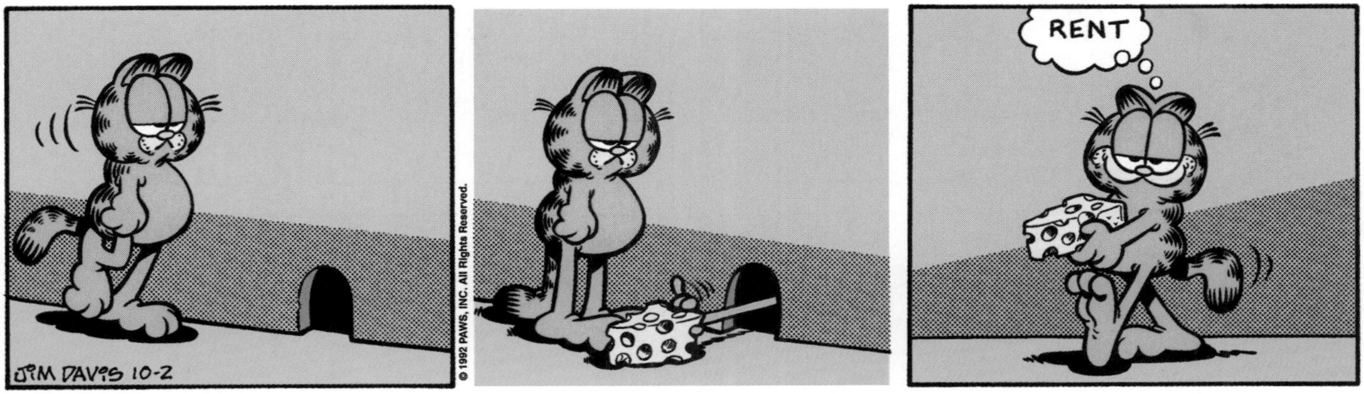
JIM DAVIS 10-2
© 1992 PAWS, INC. All Rights Reserved.
RENT

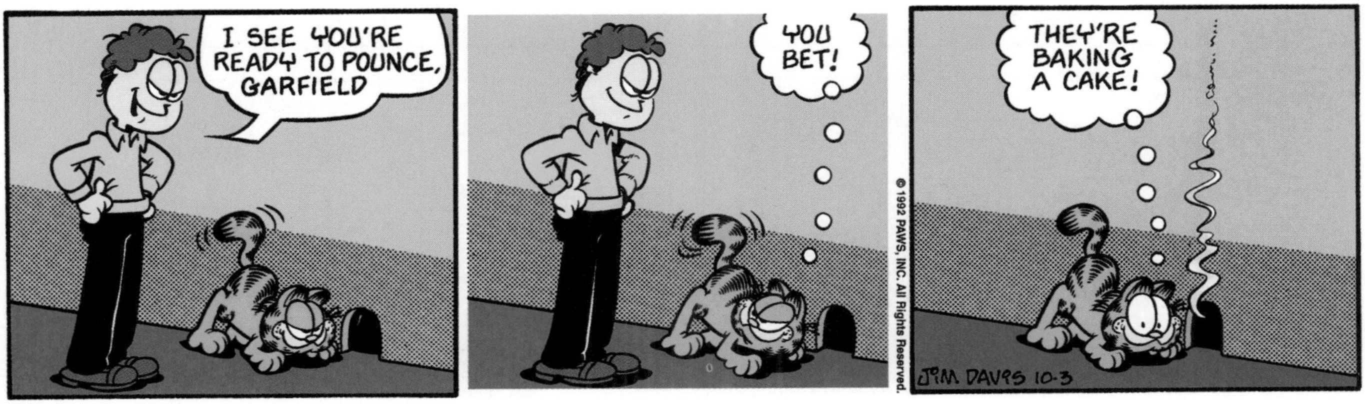
I SEE YOU'RE READY TO POUNCE, GARFIELD
YOU BET!
© 1992 PAWS, INC. All Rights Reserved.
THEY'RE BAKING A CAKE!
JIM DAVIS 10-3

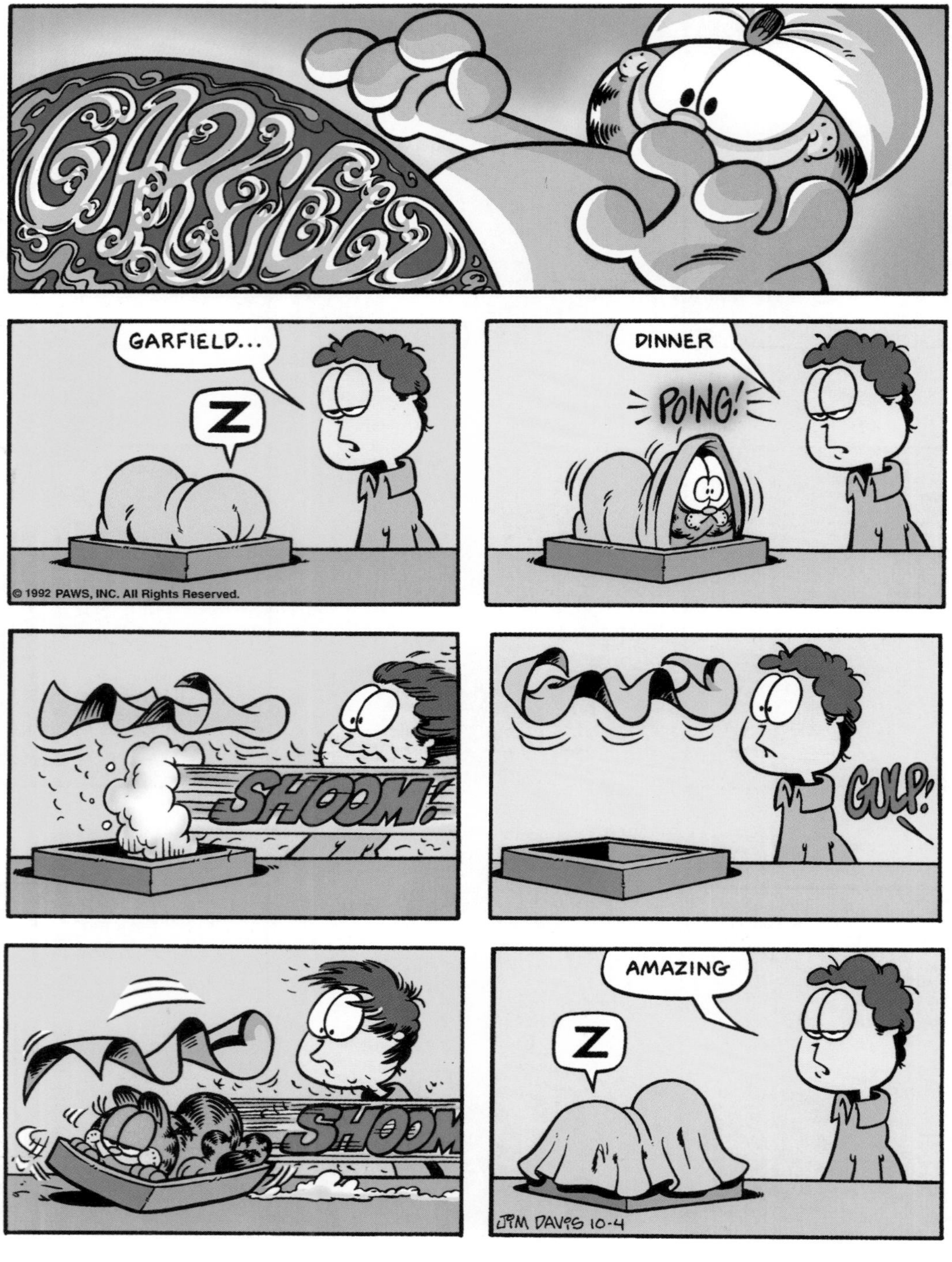
GARFIELD...
Z
© 1992 PAWS, INC. All Rights Reserved.
DINNER
POING!
SHOOM!
GULP!
SHOOM
AMAZING
Z
JIM DAVIS 10-4

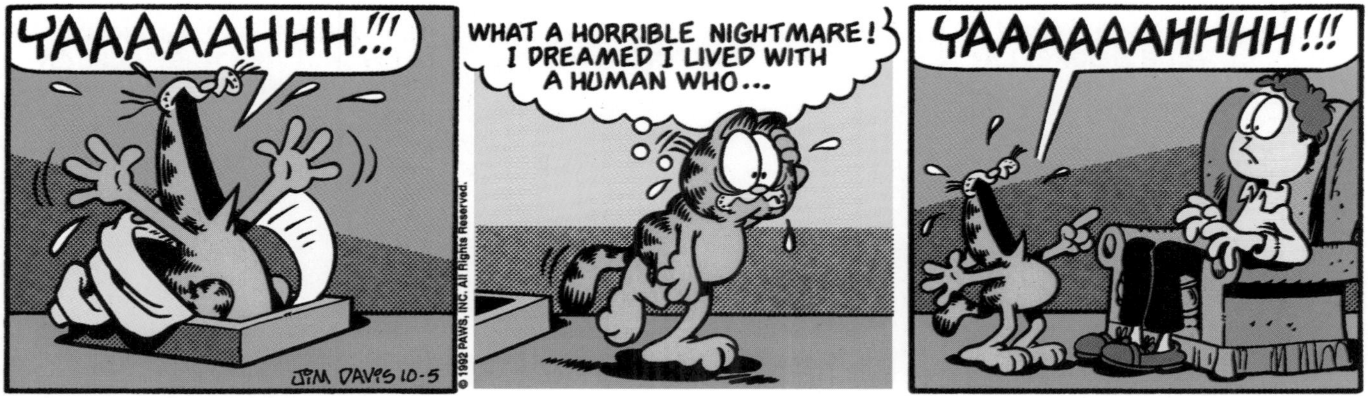
YAAAAAHHH!!!
JIM DAVIS 10-5
© 1992 PAWS, INC. All Rights Reserved.
WHAT A HORRIBLE NIGHTMARE! I DREAMED I LIVED WITH A HUMAN WHO...
YAAAAAAHHHH!!!

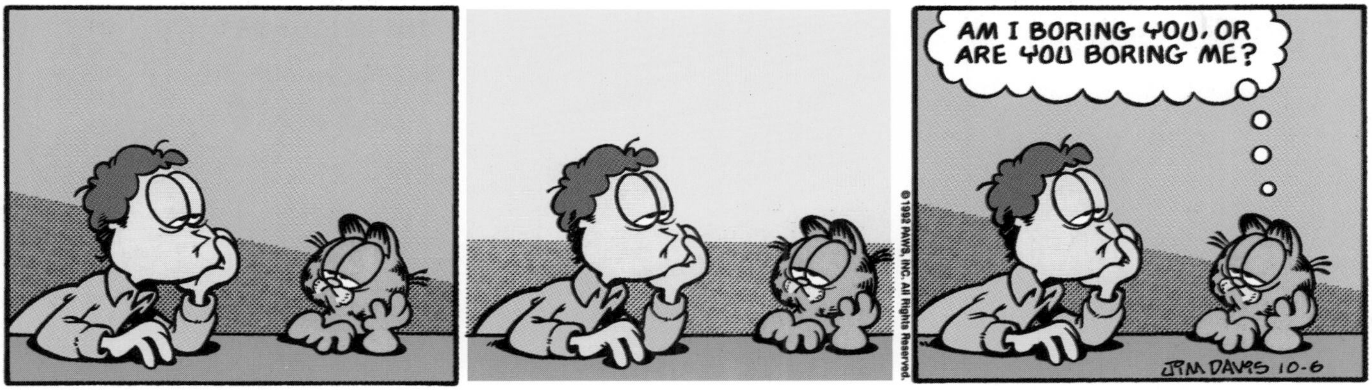
© 1992 PAWS, INC. All Rights Reserved.
AM I BORING YOU, OR ARE YOU BORING ME?
JIM DAVIS 10-6

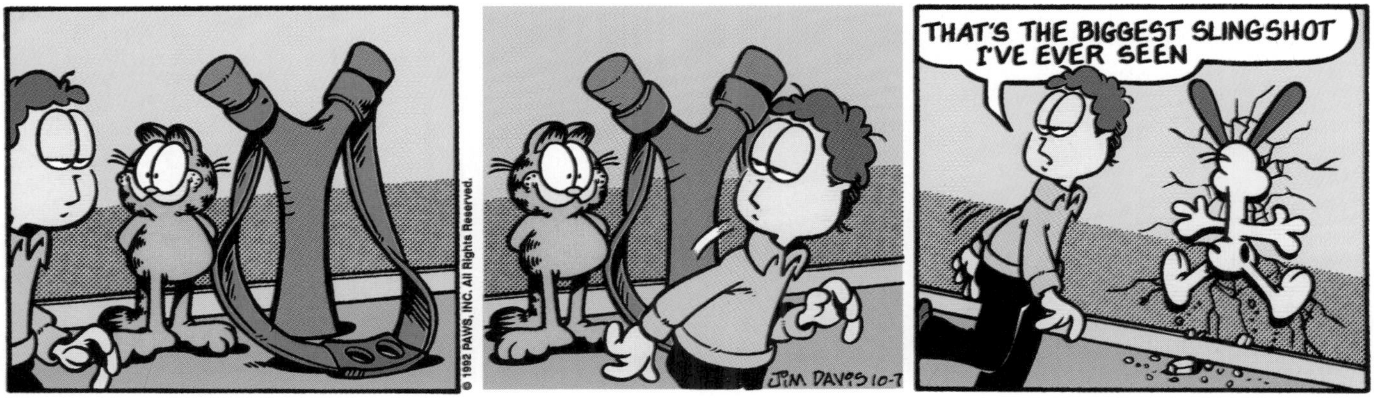
© 1992 PAWS, INC. All Rights Reserved.
JIM DAVIS 10-7
THAT'S THE BIGGEST SLINGSHOT I'VE EVER SEEN

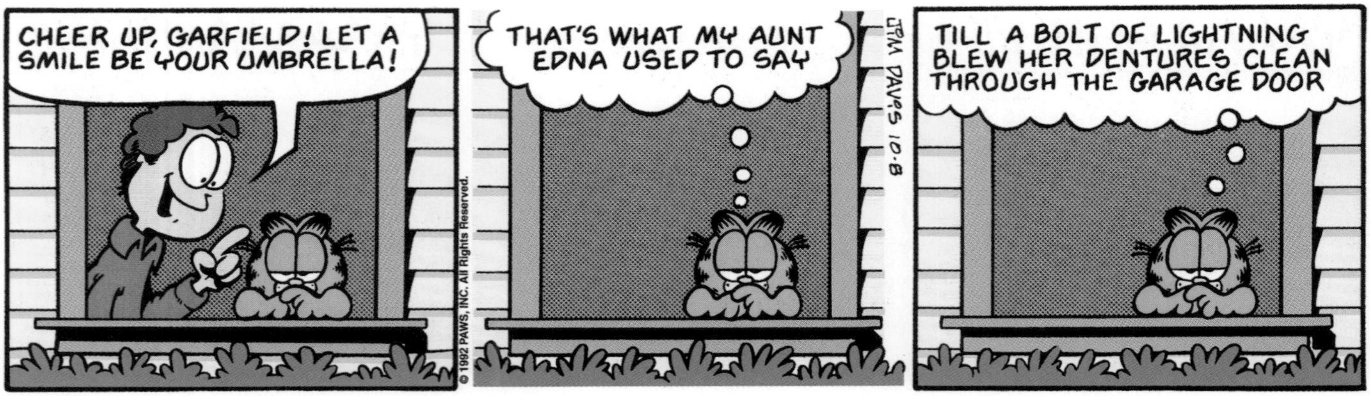
CHEER UP, GARFIELD! LET A SMILE BE YOUR UMBRELLA!
© 1992 PAWS, INC. All Rights Reserved.
THAT'S WHAT MY AUNT EDNA USED TO SAY
JIM DAVIS 10-8
TILL A BOLT OF LIGHTNING BLEW HER DENTURES CLEAN THROUGH THE GARAGE DOOR

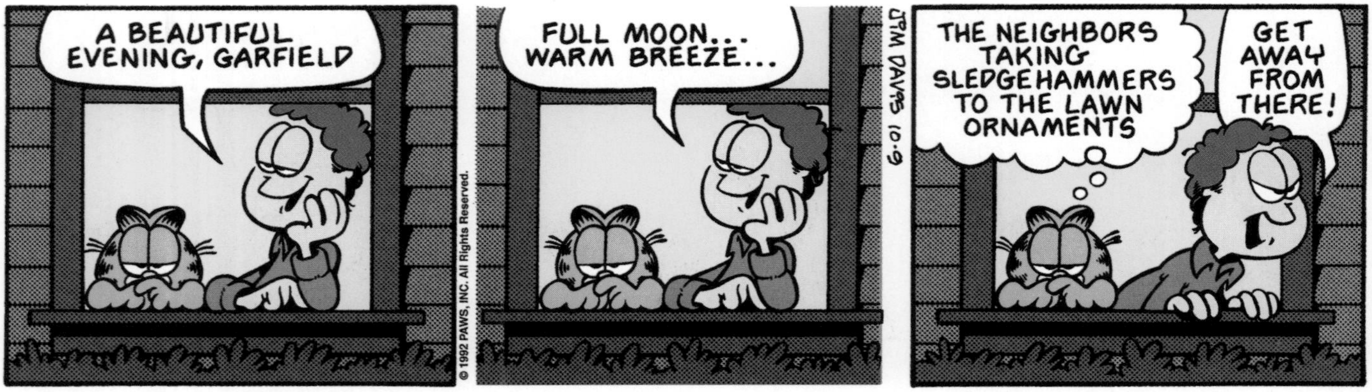
A BEAUTIFUL EVENING, GARFIELD
© 1992 PAWS, INC. All Rights Reserved.
FULL MOON... WARM BREEZE...
JIM DAVIS 10-9
THE NEIGHBORS TAKING SLEDGEHAMMERS TO THE LAWN ORNAMENTS
GET AWAY FROM THERE!

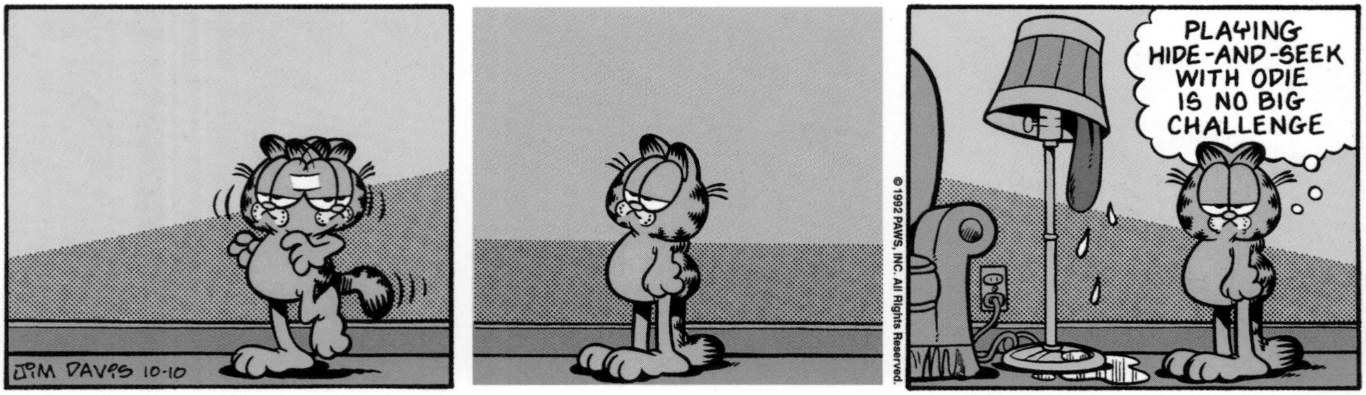
JIM DAVIS 10-10
© 1992 PAWS, INC. All Rights Reserved.
PLAYING HIDE-AND-SEEK WITH ODIE IS NO BIG CHALLENGE

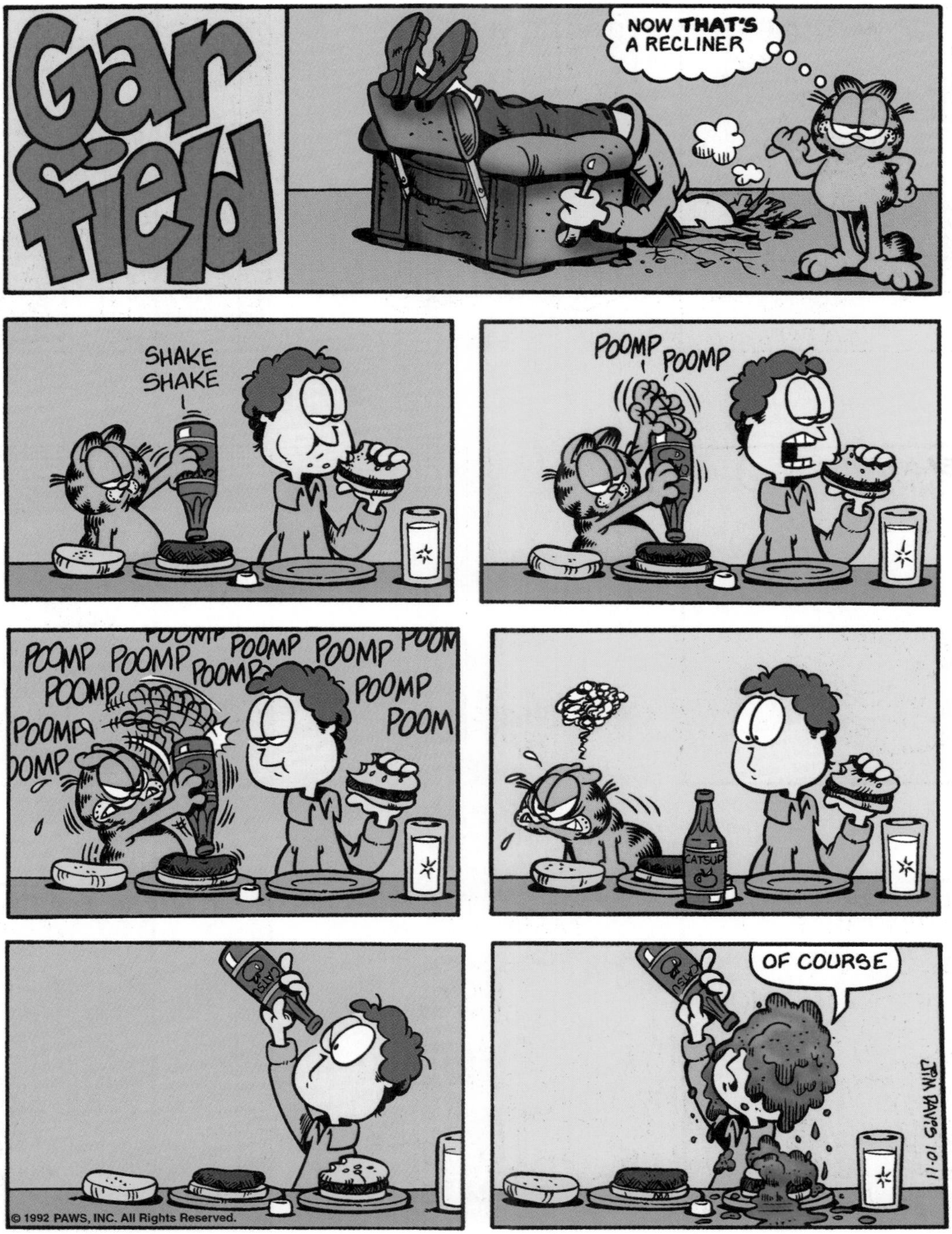
Garfield
NOW THAT'S A RECLINER
SHAKE SHAKE
POOMP POOMP
POOMP POOMP POOMP POOMP POOMP POOMP POOMP POOMP POOMP POOM
CATSUP
OF COURSE
JIM DAVIS 10-11
© 1992 PAWS, INC. All Rights Reserved.

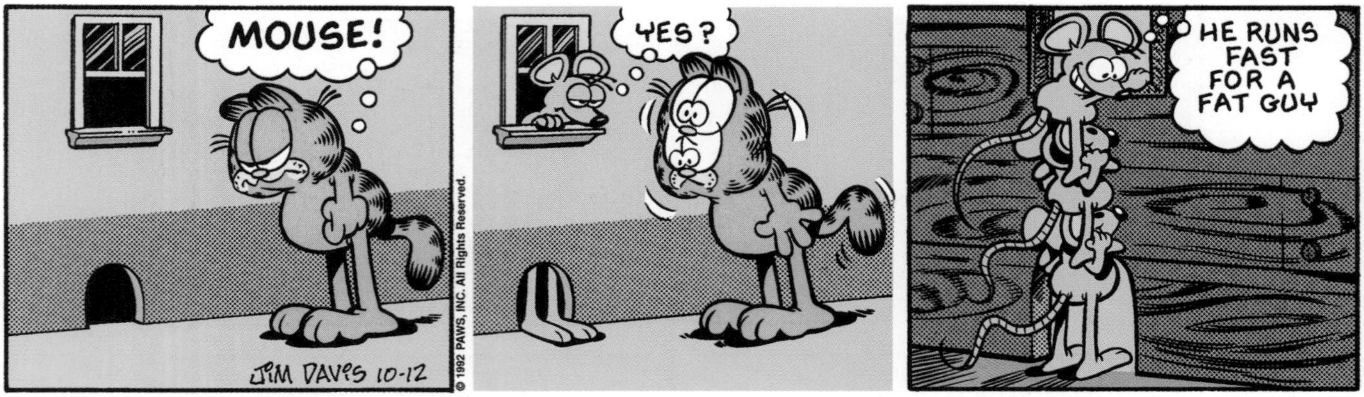
MOUSE!
JIM DAVIS 10-12
© 1992 PAWS, INC. All Rights Reserved.
YES?
HE RUNS FAST FOR A FAT GUY

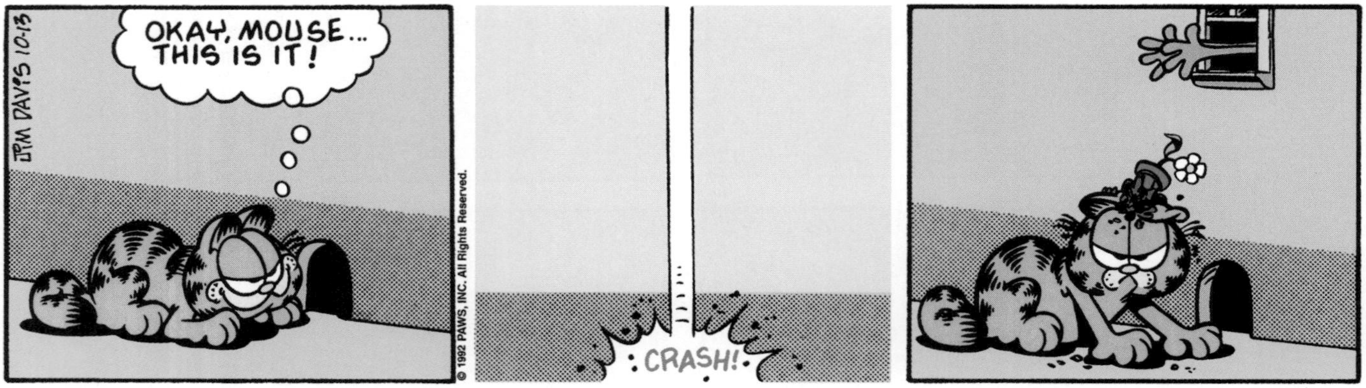
JIM DAVIS 10-13
OKAY, MOUSE... THIS IS IT!
© 1992 PAWS, INC. All Rights Reserved.
CRASH!

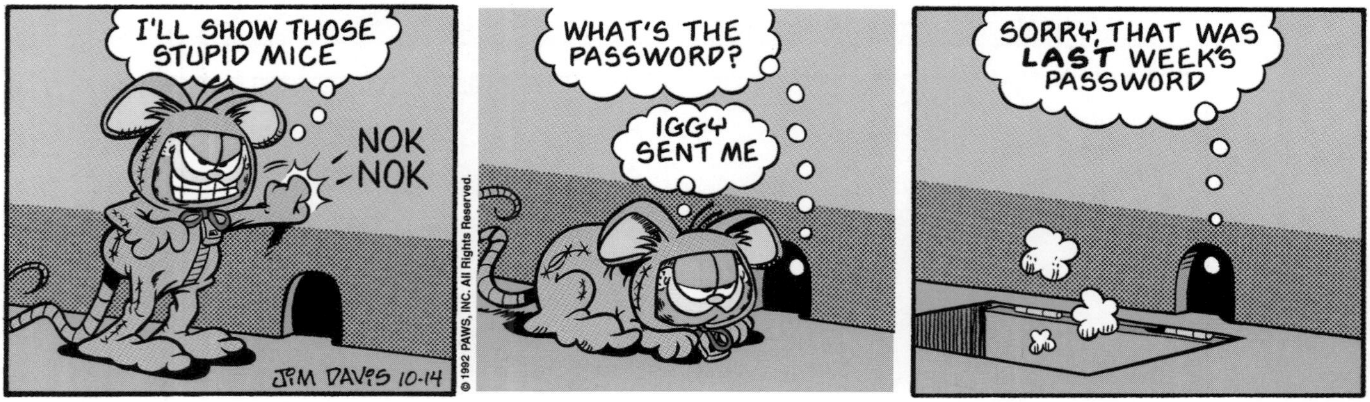
I'LL SHOW THOSE STUPID MICE
NOK NOK
JIM DAVIS 10-14
© 1992 PAWS, INC. All Rights Reserved.
WHAT'S THE PASSWORD?
IGGY SENT ME
SORRY, THAT WAS LAST WEEK'S PASSWORD

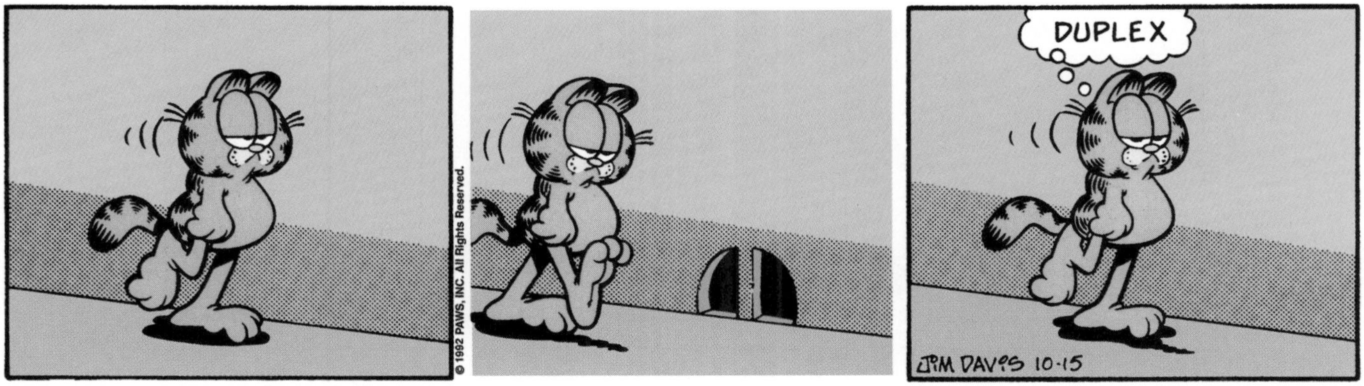
© 1992 PAWS, INC. All Rights Reserved.
DUPLEX
JIM DAVIS 10-15

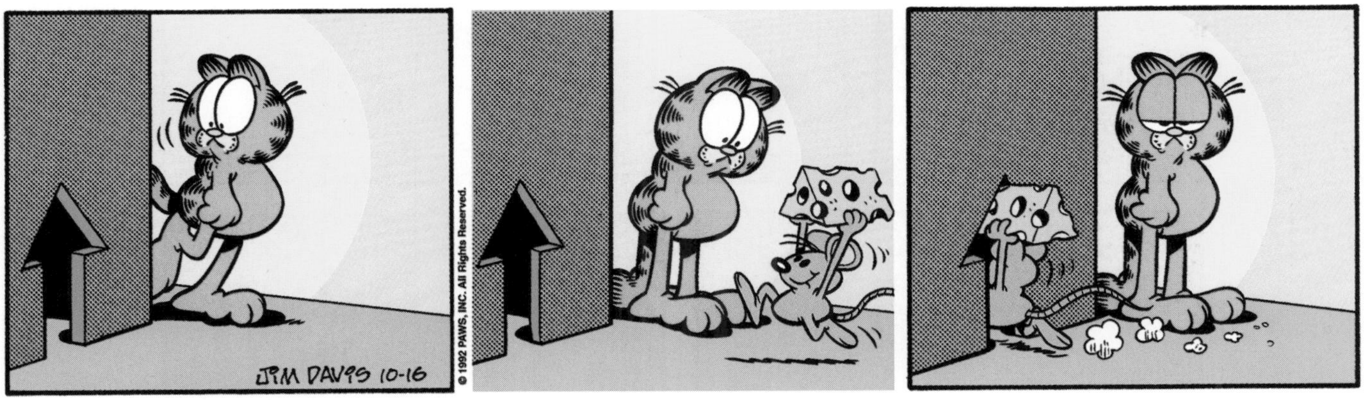
JIM DAVIS 10-16
© 1992 PAWS, INC. All Rights Reserved.

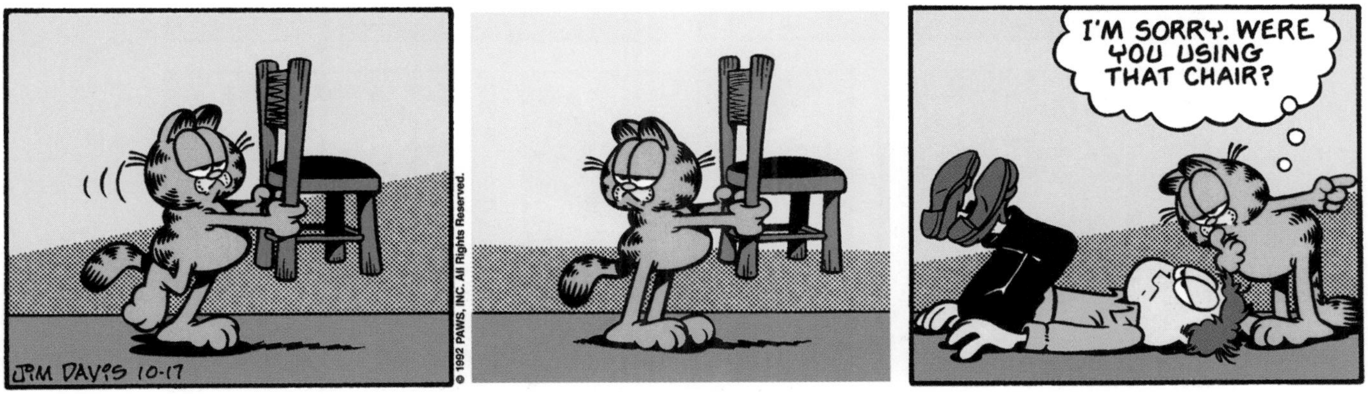
JIM DAVIS 10-17
© 1992 PAWS, INC. All Rights Reserved.
I'M SORRY. WERE YOU USING THAT CHAIR?

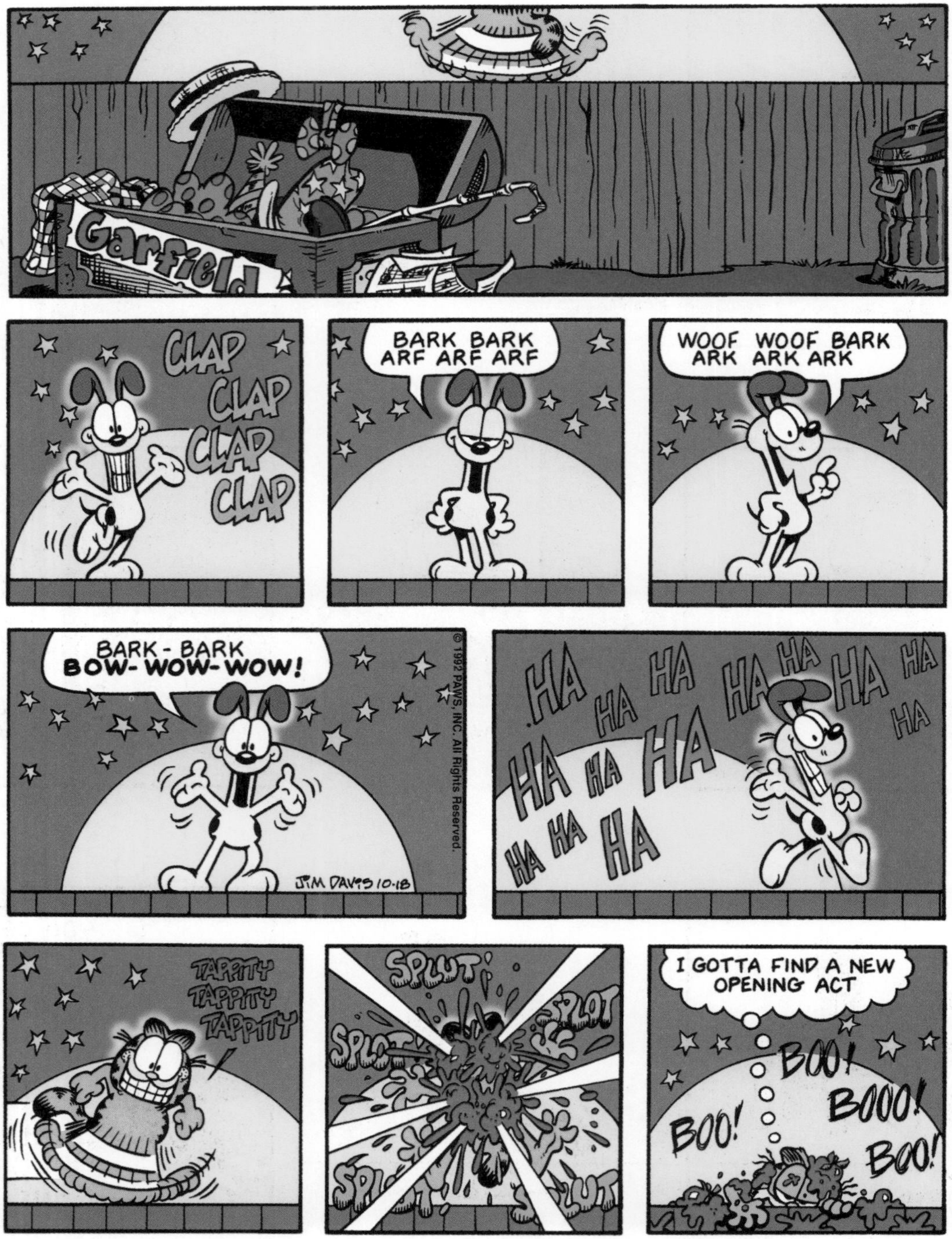
Garfield
CLAP
CLAP
CLAP
CLAP
BARK BARK
ARF ARF ARF
WOOF WOOF BARK
ARK ARK ARK
BARK - BARK
BOW- WOW- WOW!
© 1992 PAWS, INC. All Rights Reserved.
JIM DAVIS 10-18
HA HA HA HA HA HA HA HA HA HA HA HA HA HA HA HA HA
TAPPITY
TAPPITY
TAPPITY
SPLUT!
SPLOT
SPLOT
SPLUT
I GOTTA FIND A NEW
OPENING ACT
BOO!
BOOO!
BOO!
BOO!

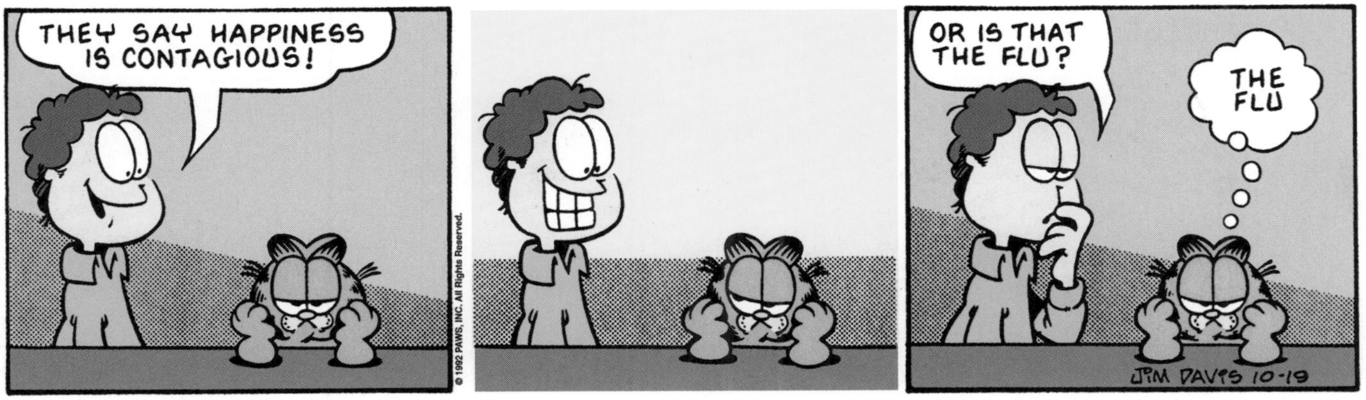
THEY SAY HAPPINESS IS CONTAGIOUS!
© 1992 PAWS, INC. All Rights Reserved.
OR IS THAT THE FLU?
THE FLU
JIM DAVIS 10-19

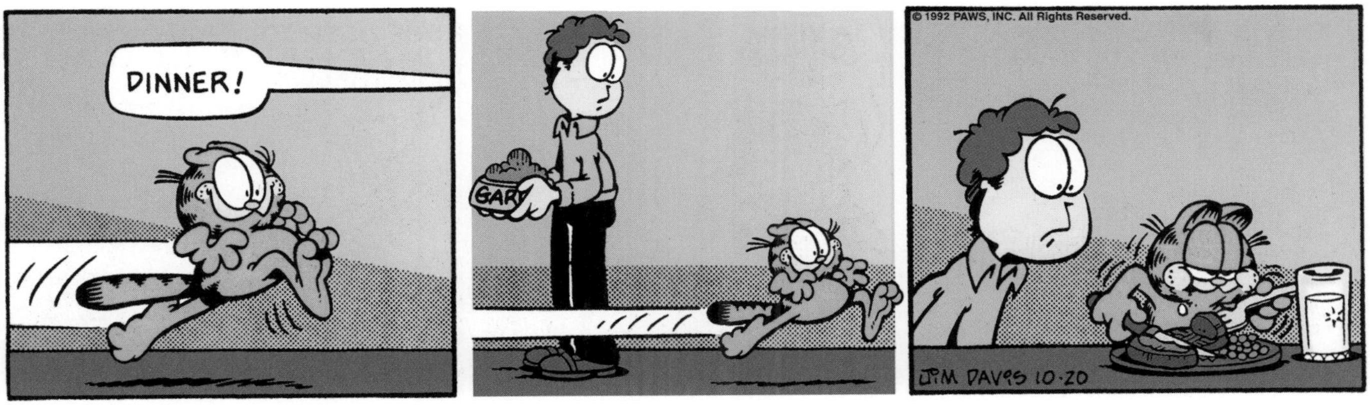
DINNER!
GAR
© 1992 PAWS, INC. All Rights Reserved.
JIM DAVIS 10-20

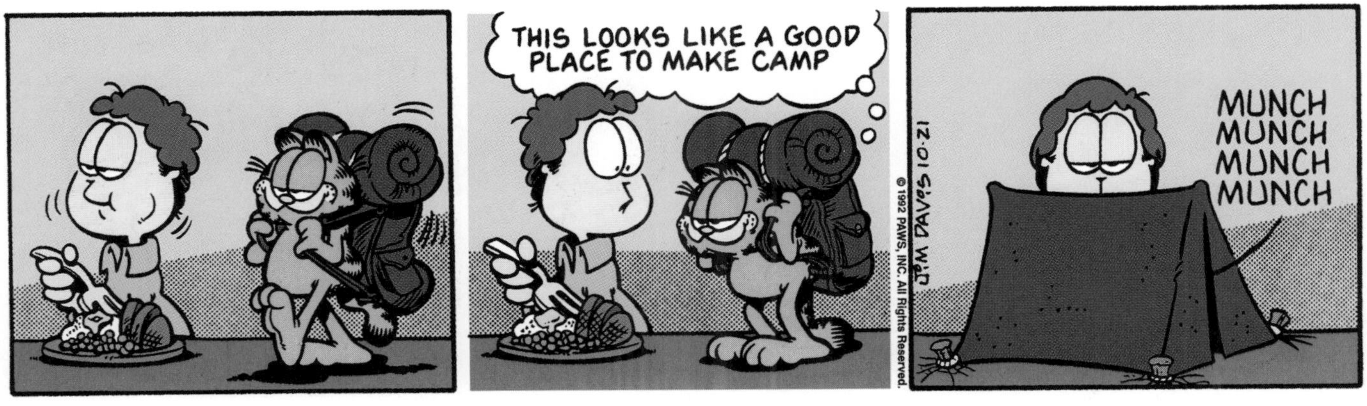
THIS LOOKS LIKE A GOOD PLACE TO MAKE CAMP
JIM DAVIS 10-21
© 1992 PAWS, INC. All Rights Reserved.
MUNCH
MUNCH
MUNCH
MUNCH

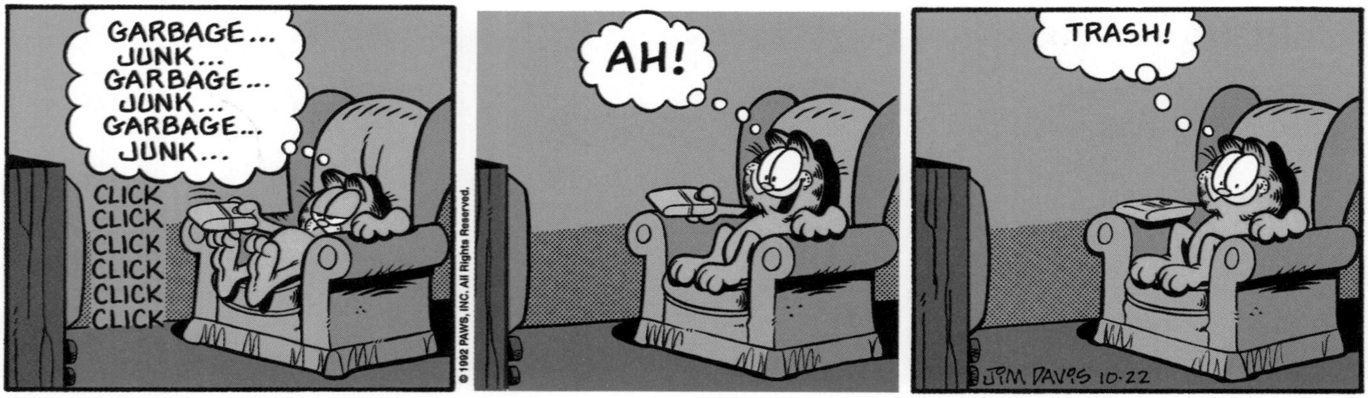
GARBAGE... JUNK... GARBAGE... JUNK... GARBAGE... JUNK...
CLICK CLICK CLICK CLICK CLICK CLICK
© 1992 PAWS, INC. All Rights Reserved.
AH!
TRASH!
JIM DAVIS 10-22

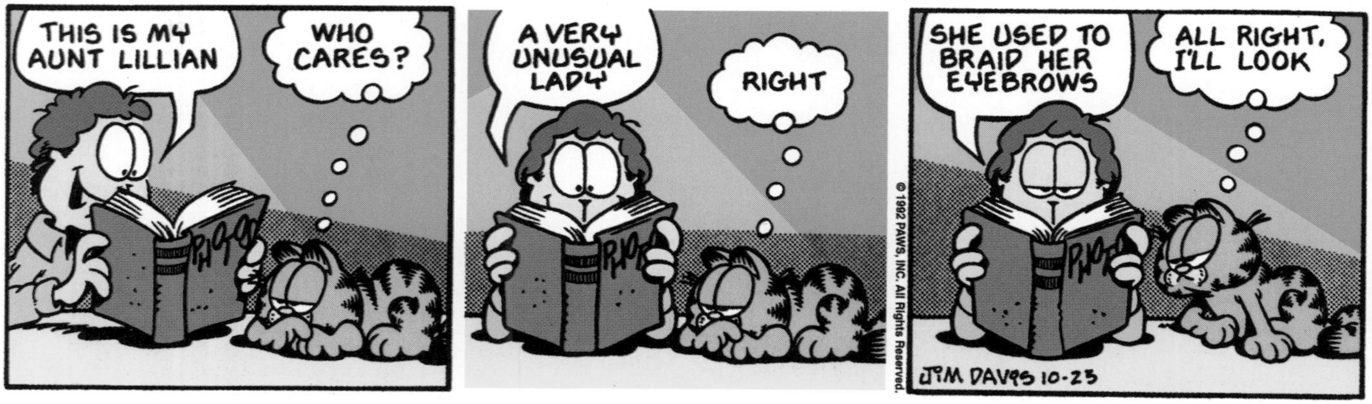
THIS IS MY AUNT LILLIAN
WHO CARES?
A VERY UNUSUAL LADY
RIGHT
© 1992 PAWS, INC. All Rights Reserved.
SHE USED TO BRAID HER EYEBROWS
ALL RIGHT, I'LL LOOK
JIM DAVIS 10-23

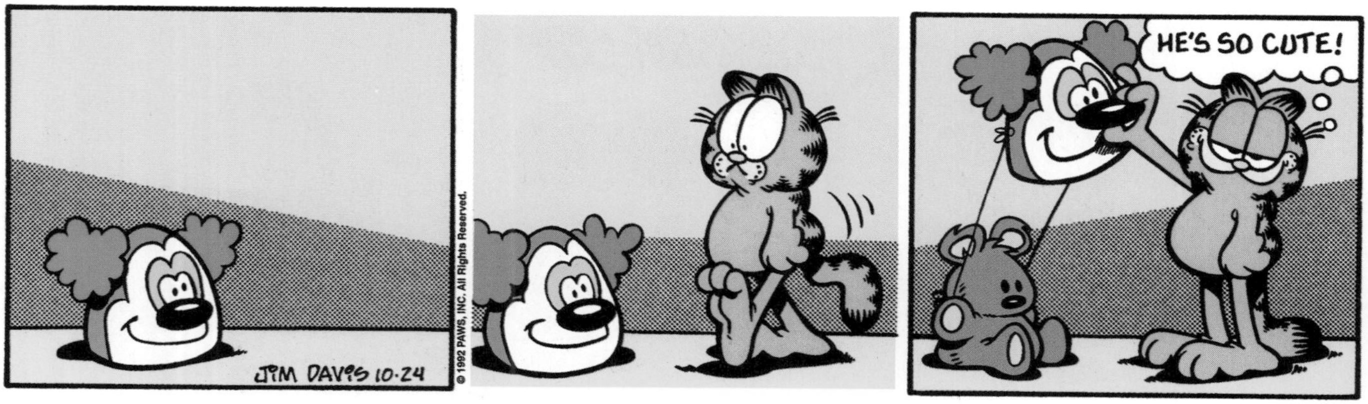
JIM DAVIS 10-24
© 1992 PAWS, INC. All Rights Reserved.
HE'S SO CUTE!

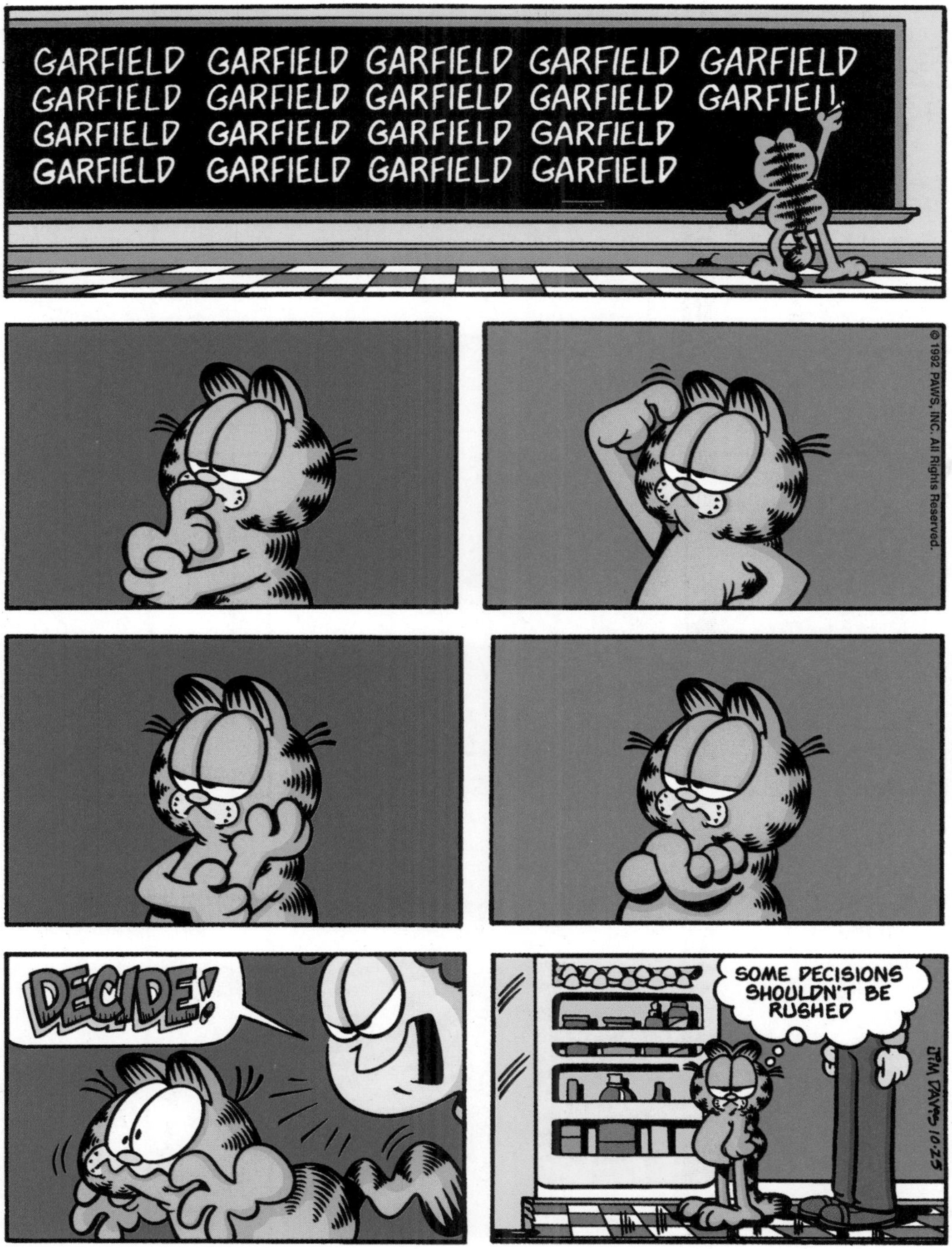
GARFIELD GARFIELD GARFIELD GARFIELD GARFIELD
GARFIELD GARFIELD GARFIELD GARFIELD GARFIELD
GARFIELD GARFIELD GARFIELD GARFIELD
GARFIELD GARFIELD GARFIELD GARFIELD
© 1992 PAWS, INC. All Rights Reserved.
DECIDE!
SOME DECISIONS SHOULDN'T BE RUSHED

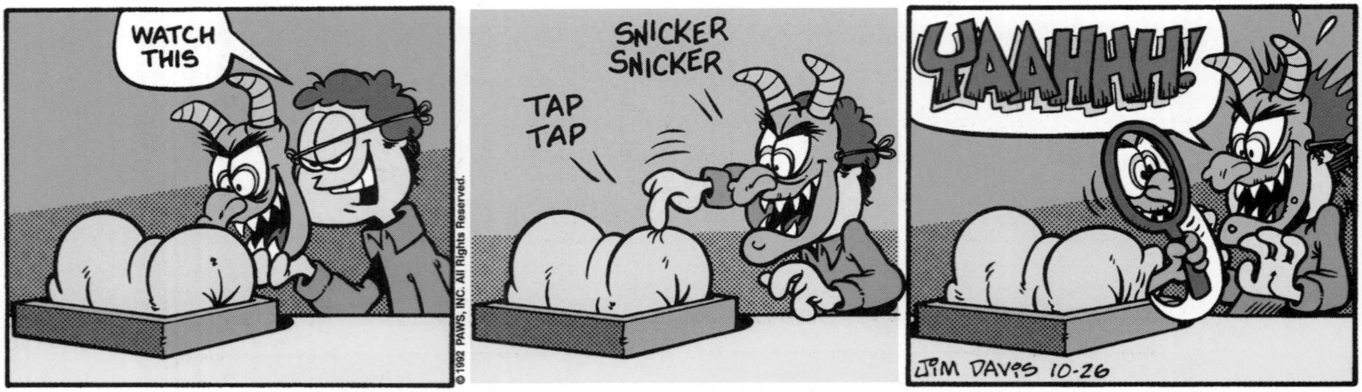
WATCH THIS
TAP TAP
SNICKER SNICKER
YAAHHH!
JIM DAVIS 10-26
© 1992 PAWS, INC. All Rights Reserved.

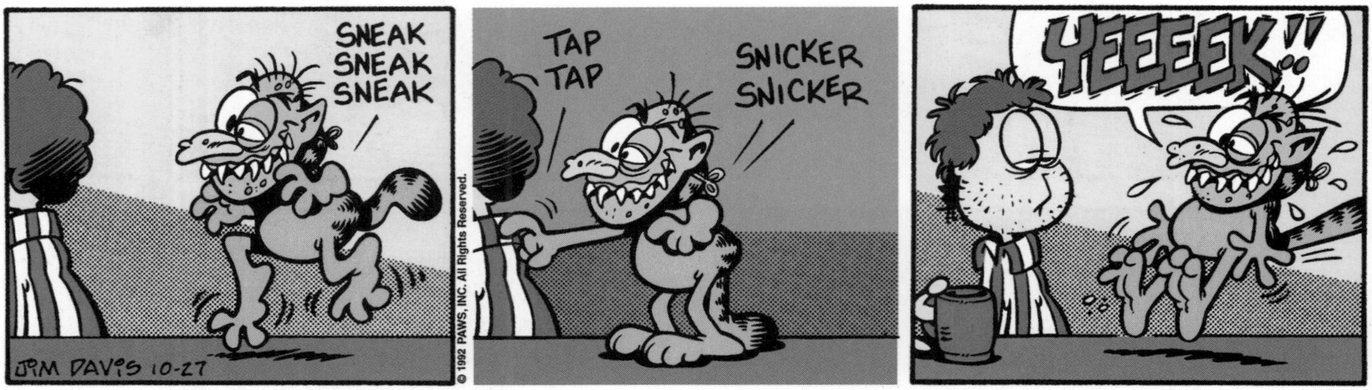
SNEAK SNEAK SNEAK
JIM DAVIS 10-27
TAP TAP
SNICKER SNICKER
YEEEEK!!
© 1992 PAWS, INC. All Rights Reserved.

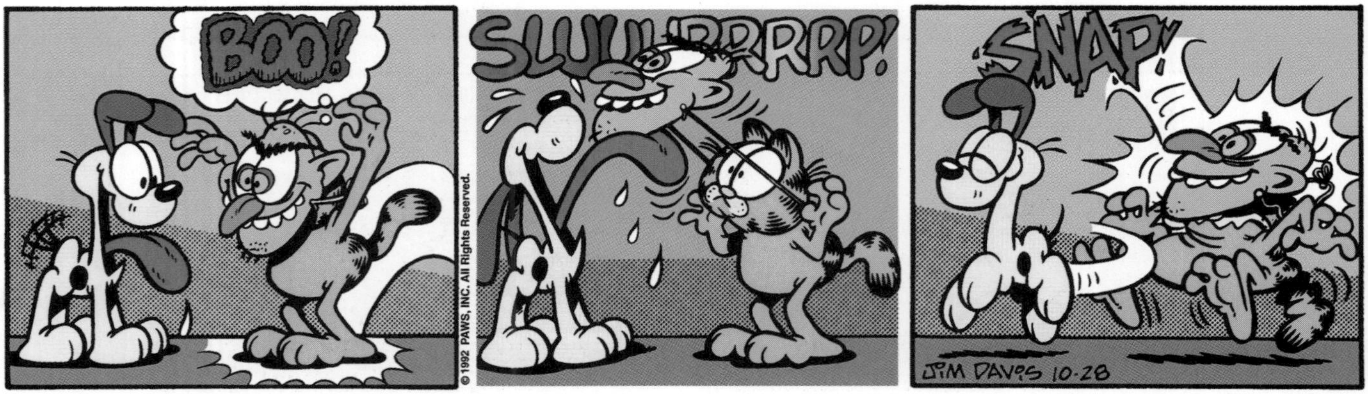
BOO!
SLUUURRRRP!
SNAP!
JIM DAVIS 10-28
© 1992 PAWS, INC. All Rights Reserved.

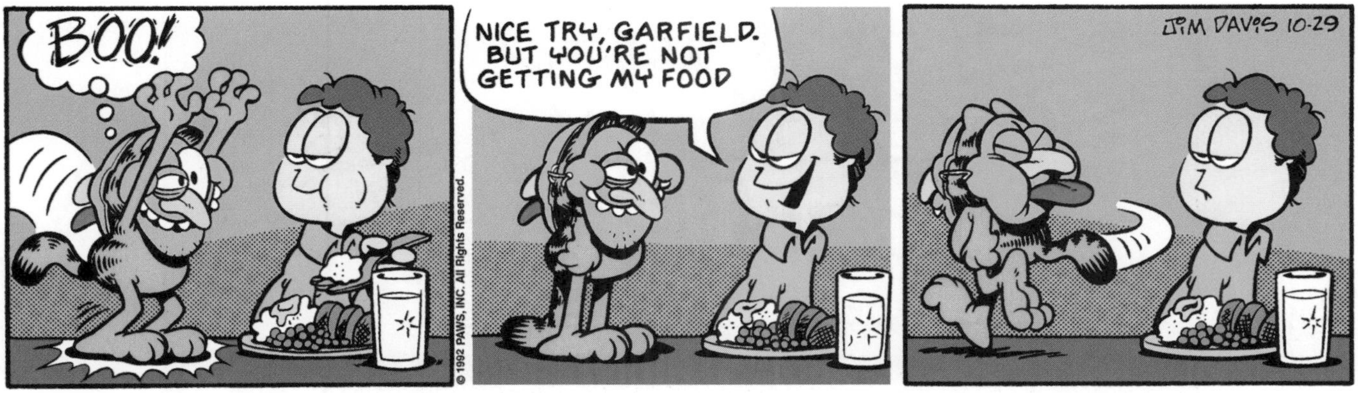
BOO!
NICE TRY, GARFIELD. BUT YOU'RE NOT GETTING MY FOOD
JIM DAVIS 10-29

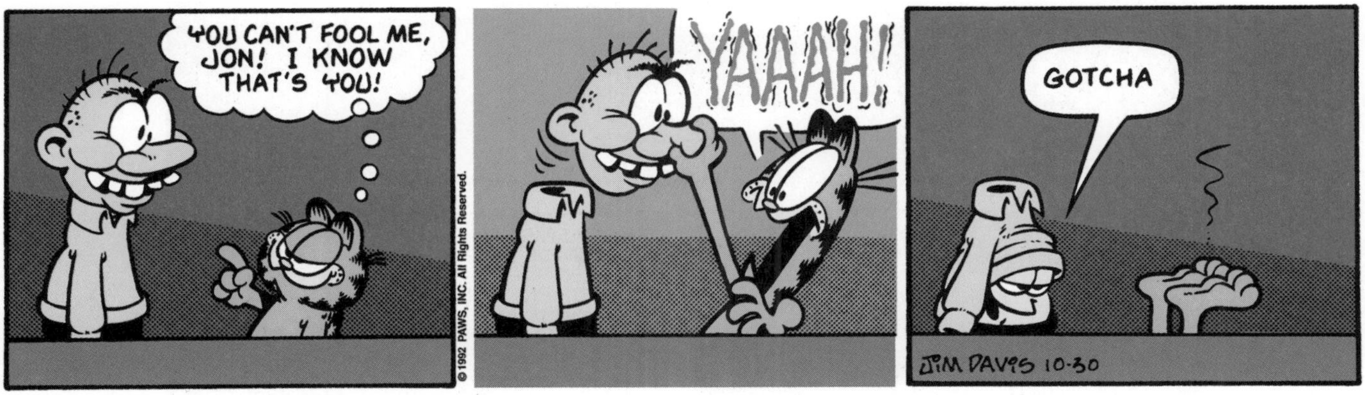
YOU CAN'T FOOL ME, JON! I KNOW THAT'S YOU!
YAAAH!
GOTCHA
JIM DAVIS 10-30

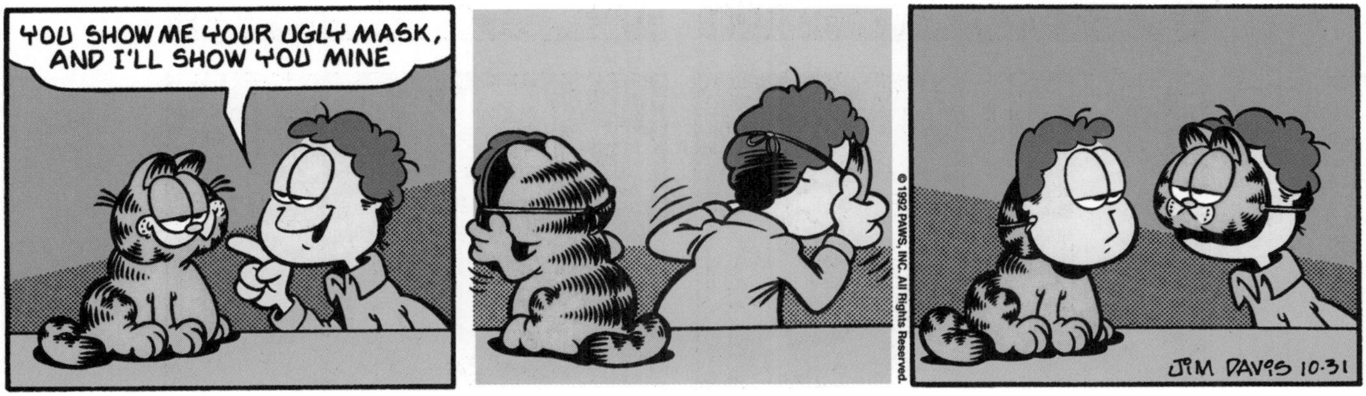
YOU SHOW ME YOUR UGLY MASK, AND I'LL SHOW YOU MINE
JIM DAVIS 10-31

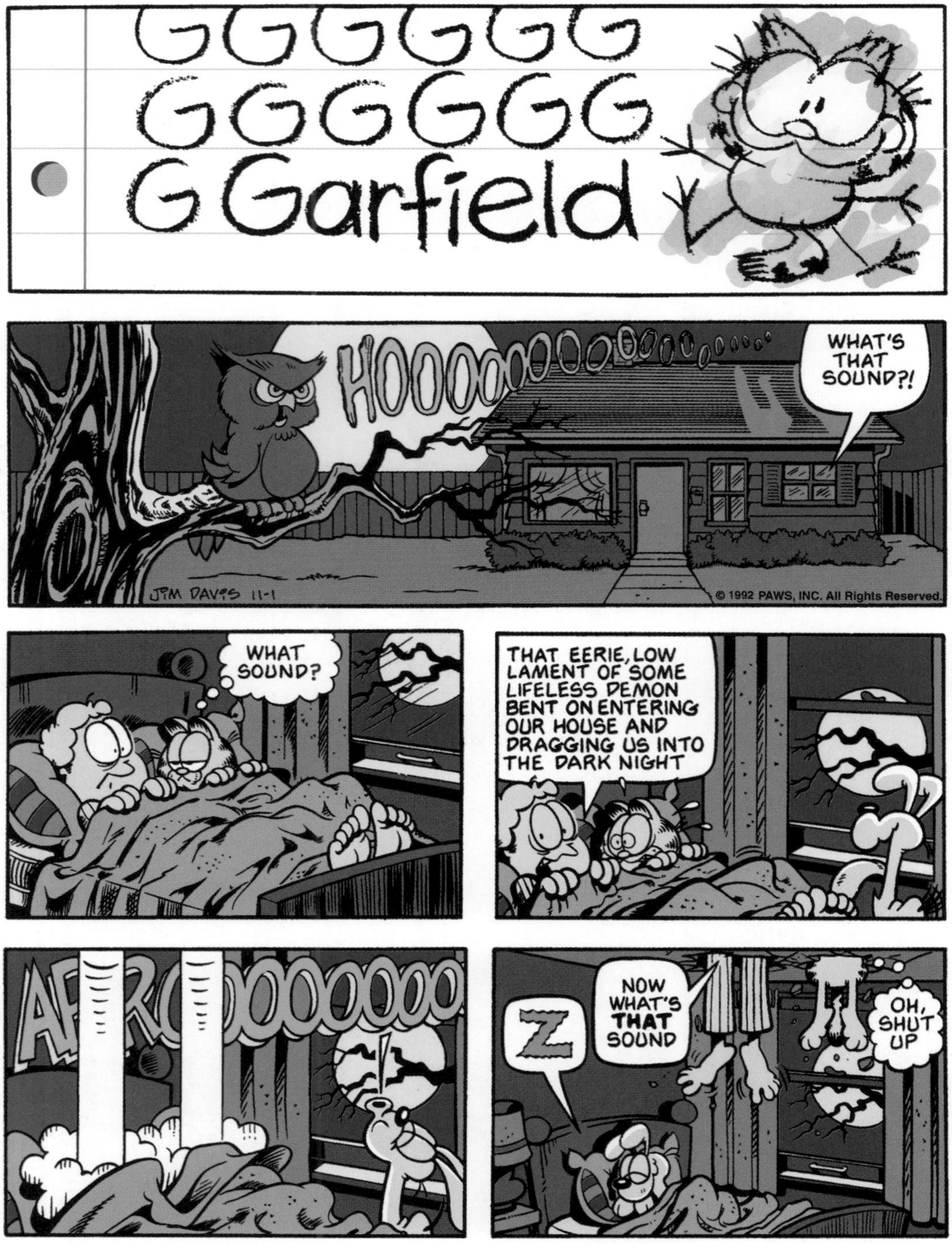
GGGGGG
GGGGGG
G Garfield
HOOOOOOOOOOOOOOOOOOO
WHAT'S THAT SOUND?!
JIM DAVIS 11-1
© 1992 PAWS, INC. All Rights Reserved.
WHAT SOUND?
THAT EERIE, LOW LAMENT OF SOME LIFELESS DEMON BENT ON ENTERING OUR HOUSE AND DRAGGING US INTO THE DARK NIGHT
AROOOOOOOOO
Z
NOW WHAT'S **THAT** SOUND
OH, SHUT UP

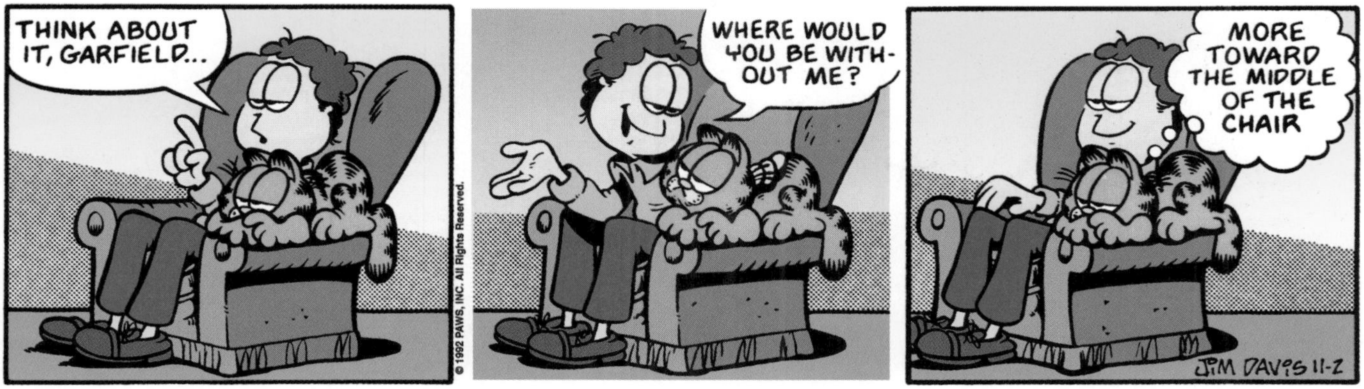
THINK ABOUT IT, GARFIELD...
© 1992 PAWS, INC. All Rights Reserved.
WHERE WOULD YOU BE WITH-OUT ME?
MORE TOWARD THE MIDDLE OF THE CHAIR
JIM DAVIS 11-2

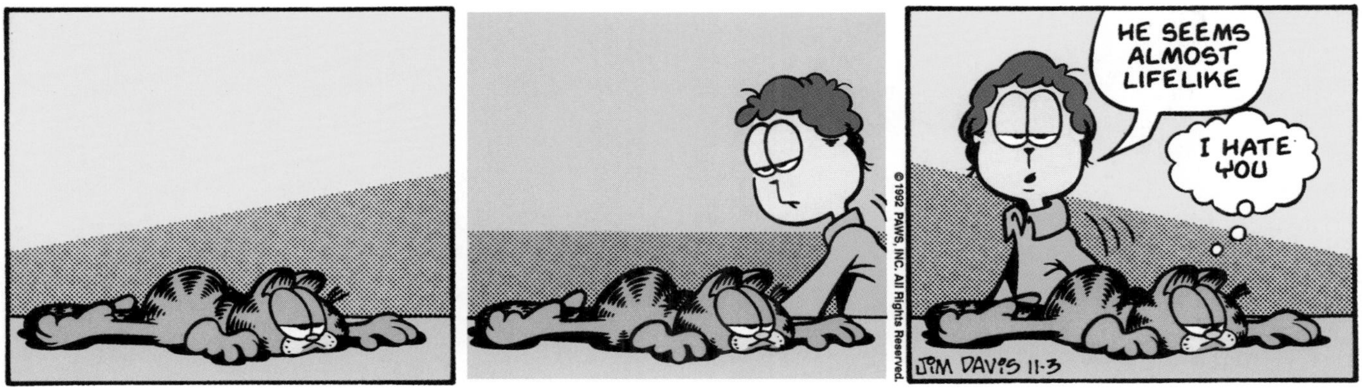
© 1992 PAWS, INC. All Rights Reserved.
HE SEEMS ALMOST LIFELIKE
I HATE YOU
JIM DAVIS 11-3

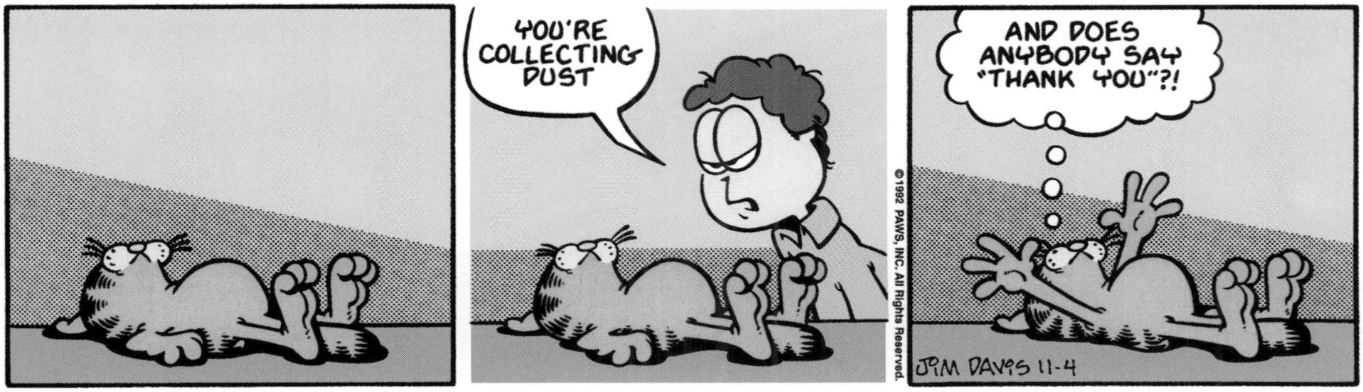
YOU'RE COLLECTING DUST
© 1992 PAWS, INC. All Rights Reserved.
AND DOES ANYBODY SAY "THANK YOU"?!
JIM DAVIS 11-4

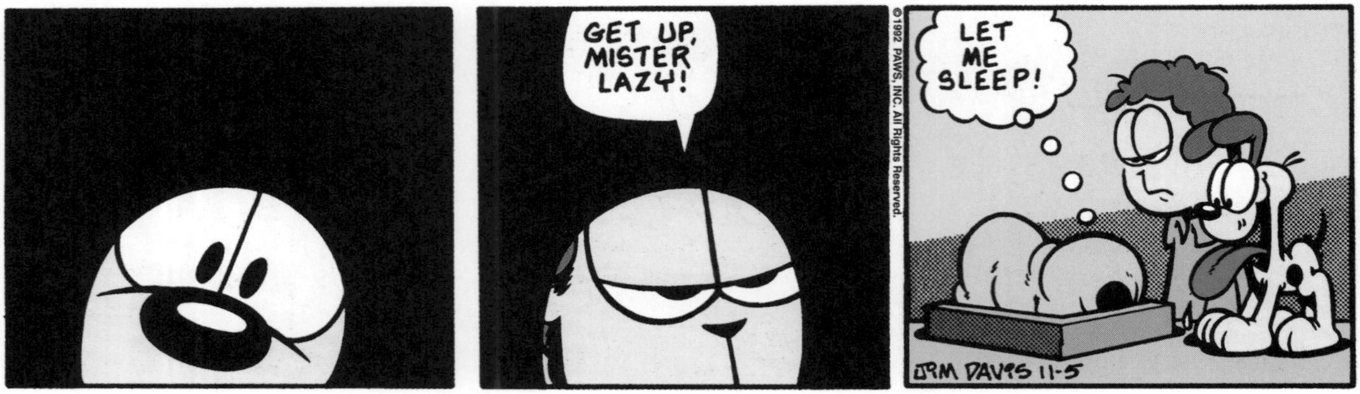
GET UP, MISTER LAZY!
©1992 PAWS, INC. All Rights Reserved.
LET ME SLEEP!
JIM DAVIS 11-5

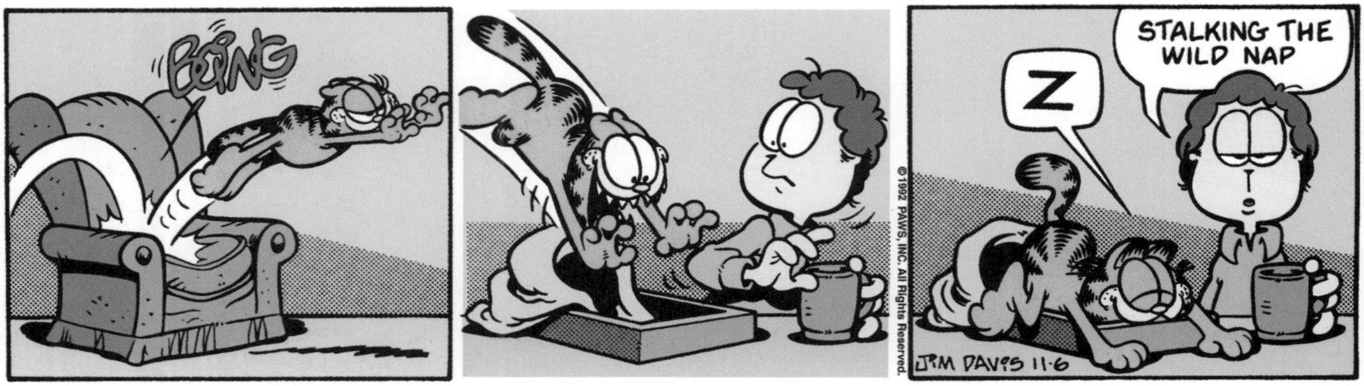
BOING
©1992 PAWS, INC. All Rights Reserved.
Z
STALKING THE WILD NAP
JIM DAVIS 11-6

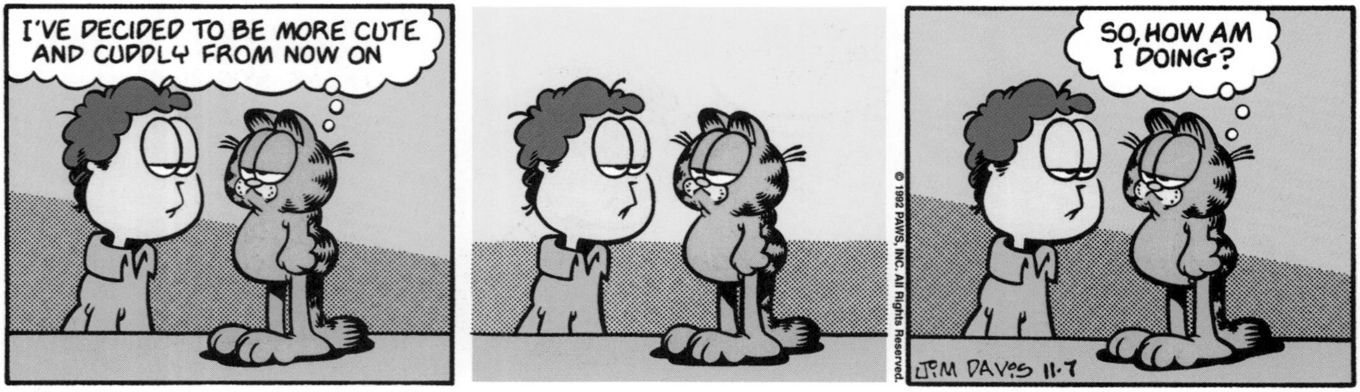
I'VE DECIDED TO BE MORE CUTE AND CUDDLY FROM NOW ON
© 1992 PAWS, INC. All Rights Reserved.
SO, HOW AM I DOING?
JIM DAVIS 11-7

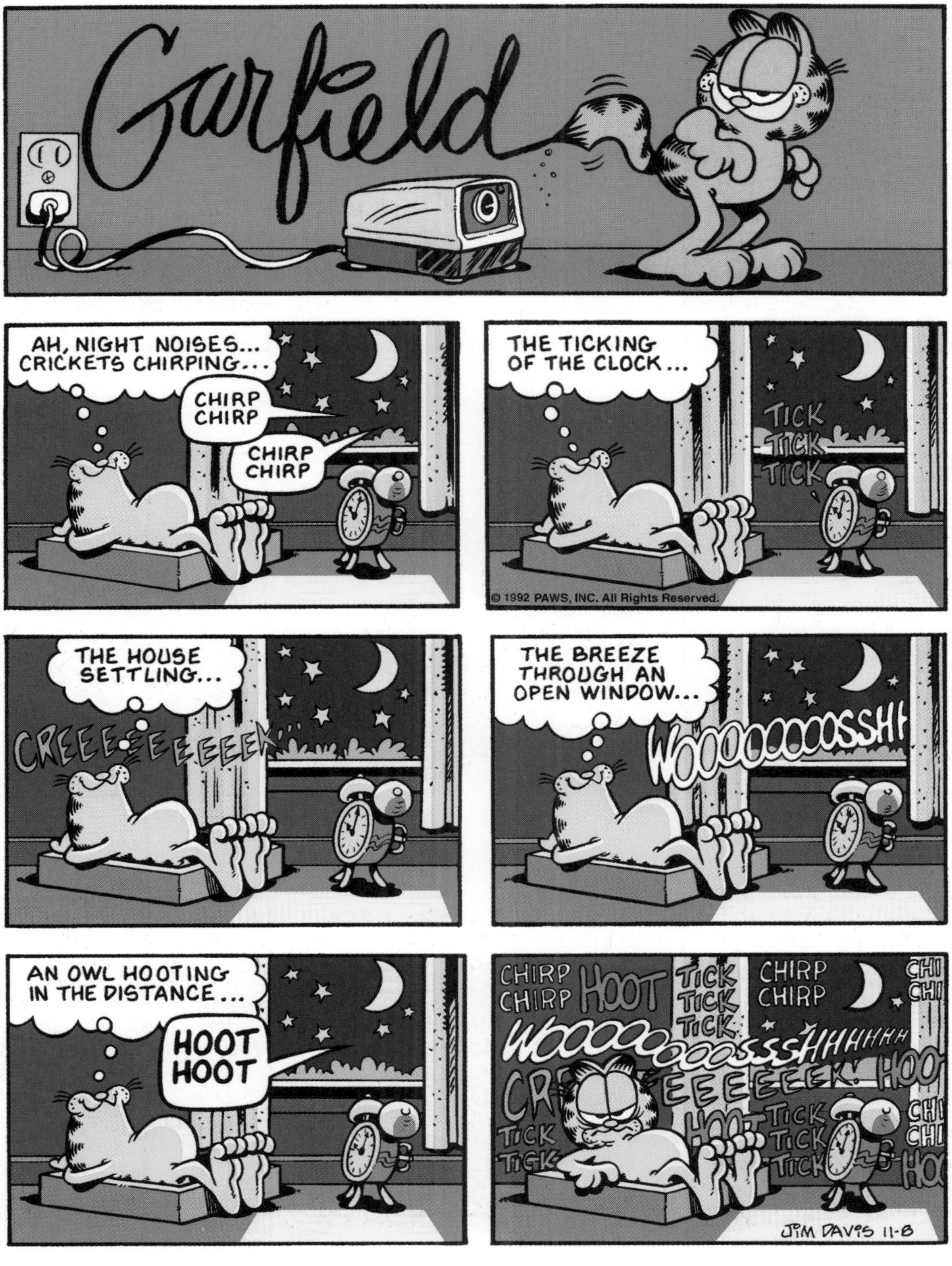
Garfield
AH, NIGHT NOISES... CRICKETS CHIRPING...
CHIRP CHIRP
CHIRP CHIRP
THE TICKING OF THE CLOCK...
TICK TICK TICK
© 1992 PAWS, INC. All Rights Reserved.
THE HOUSE SETTLING...
CREEEEEEEEEK...
THE BREEZE THROUGH AN OPEN WINDOW...
WOOOOOOOOOSSHH
AN OWL HOOTING IN THE DISTANCE...
HOOT HOOT
CHIRP CHIRP
HOOT
TICK TICK TICK
CHIRP CHIRP
WOOOOOOOOOSSSHHHHHH
EEEEEEEK!
JIM DAVIS 11-8

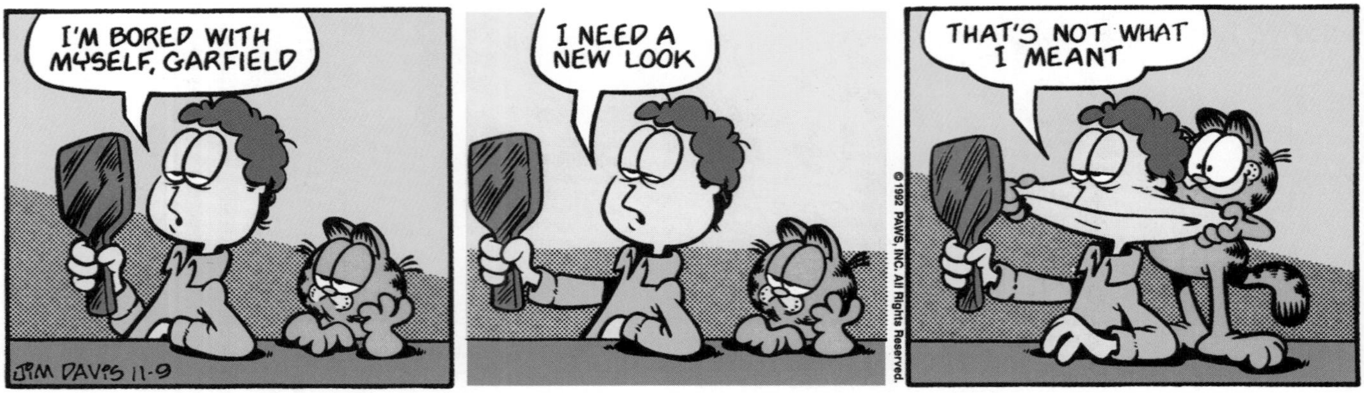
I'M BORED WITH MYSELF, GARFIELD
JIM DAVIS 11-9
I NEED A NEW LOOK
© 1992 PAWS, INC. All Rights Reserved.
THAT'S NOT WHAT I MEANT

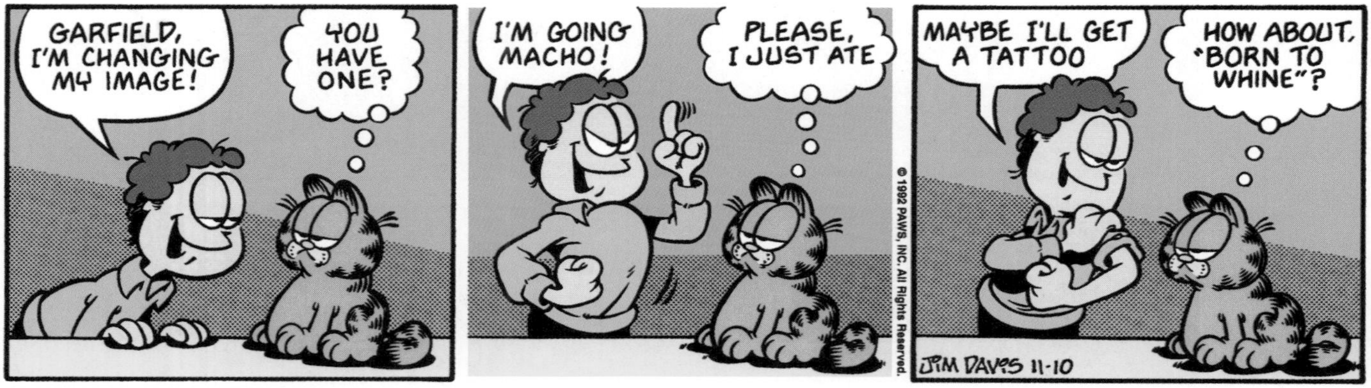
GARFIELD, I'M CHANGING MY IMAGE!
YOU HAVE ONE?
I'M GOING MACHO!
PLEASE, I JUST ATE
© 1992 PAWS, INC. All Rights Reserved.
MAYBE I'LL GET A TATTOO
HOW ABOUT, "BORN TO WHINE"?
JIM DAVIS 11-10

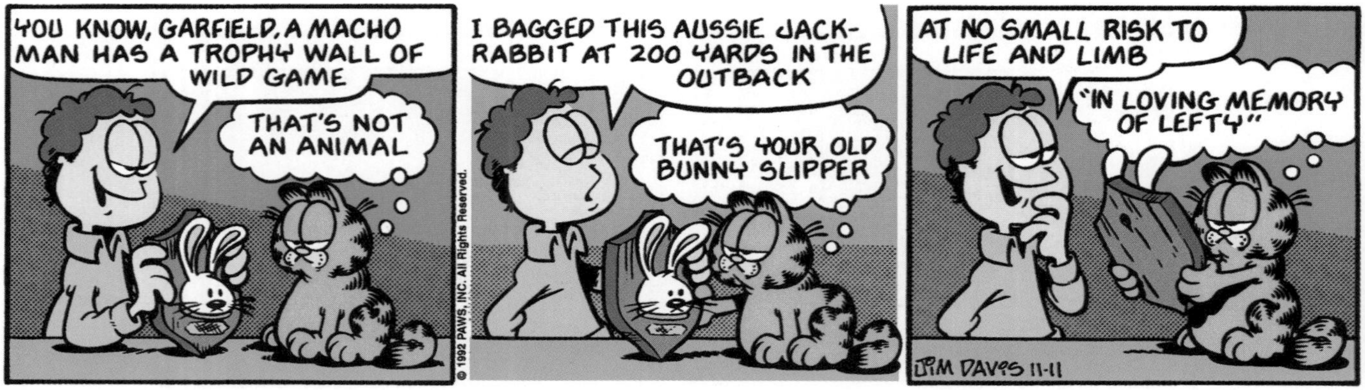
YOU KNOW, GARFIELD, A MACHO MAN HAS A TROPHY WALL OF WILD GAME
THAT'S NOT AN ANIMAL
© 1992 PAWS, INC. All Rights Reserved.
I BAGGED THIS AUSSIE JACK-RABBIT AT 200 YARDS IN THE OUTBACK
THAT'S YOUR OLD BUNNY SLIPPER
AT NO SMALL RISK TO LIFE AND LIMB
"IN LOVING MEMORY OF LEFTY"
JIM DAVIS 11-11

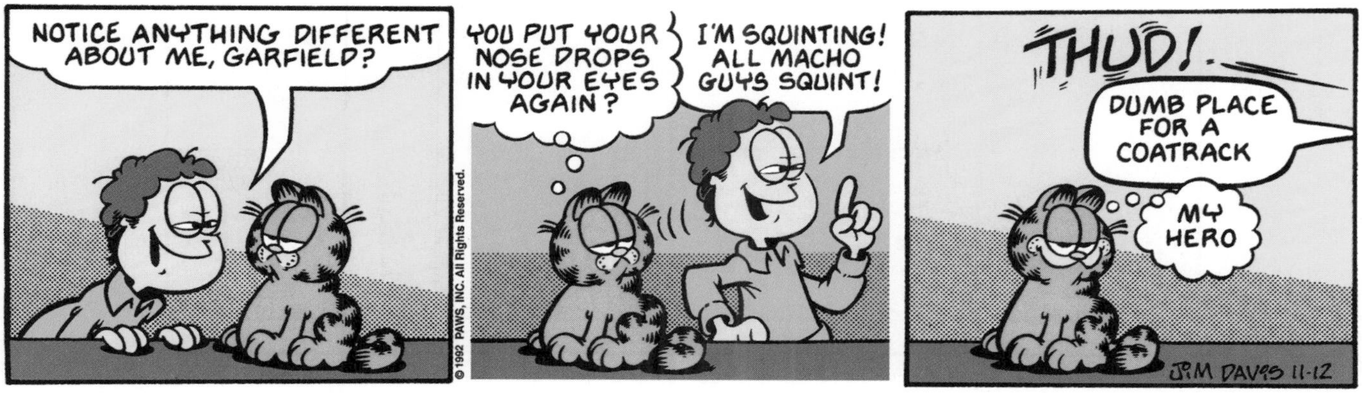
NOTICE ANYTHING DIFFERENT ABOUT ME, GARFIELD?
YOU PUT YOUR NOSE DROPS IN YOUR EYES AGAIN?
I'M SQUINTING! ALL MACHO GUYS SQUINT!
© 1992 PAWS, INC. All Rights Reserved.
THUD!
DUMB PLACE FOR A COATRACK
MY HERO
JIM DAVIS 11-12

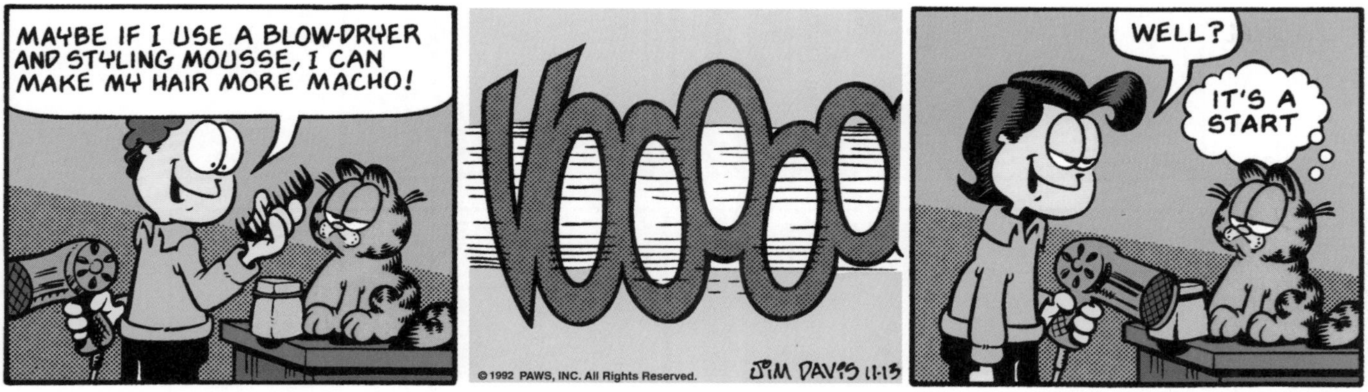
MAYBE IF I USE A BLOW-DRYER AND STYLING MOUSSE, I CAN MAKE MY HAIR MORE MACHO!
VOOOOO
© 1992 PAWS, INC. All Rights Reserved.
JIM DAVIS 11-13
WELL?
IT'S A START

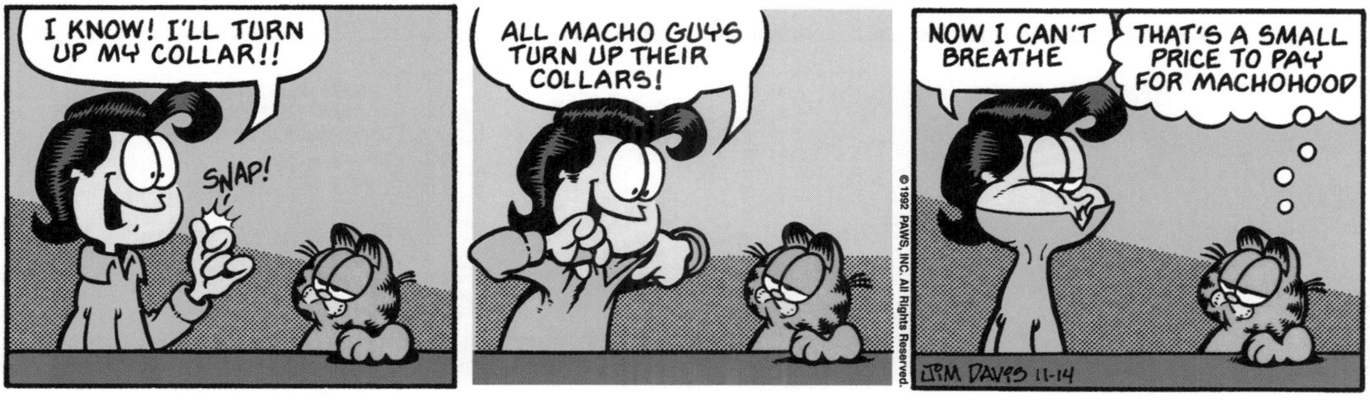
I KNOW! I'LL TURN UP MY COLLAR!!
SNAP!
ALL MACHO GUYS TURN UP THEIR COLLARS!
© 1992 PAWS, INC. All Rights Reserved.
NOW I CAN'T BREATHE
THAT'S A SMALL PRICE TO PAY FOR MACHOHOOD
JIM DAVIS 11-14

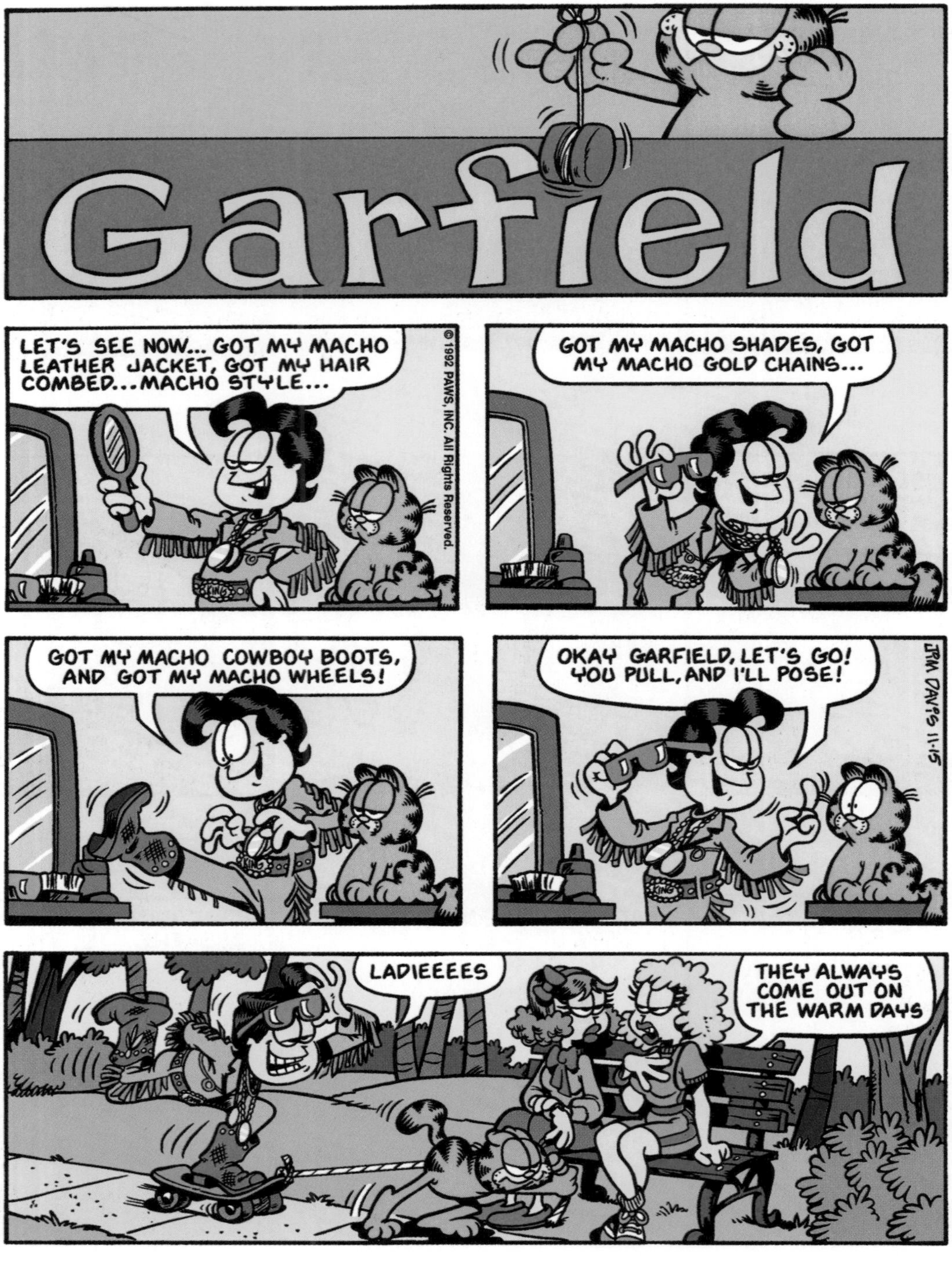
Garfield
LET'S SEE NOW... GOT MY MACHO LEATHER JACKET, GOT MY HAIR COMBED...MACHO STYLE...
© 1992 PAWS, INC. All Rights Reserved.
GOT MY MACHO SHADES, GOT MY MACHO GOLD CHAINS...
GOT MY MACHO COWBOY BOOTS, AND GOT MY MACHO WHEELS!
OKAY GARFIELD, LET'S GO! YOU PULL, AND I'LL POSE!
JIM DAVIS 11-15
LADIEEEES
THEY ALWAYS COME OUT ON THE WARM DAYS

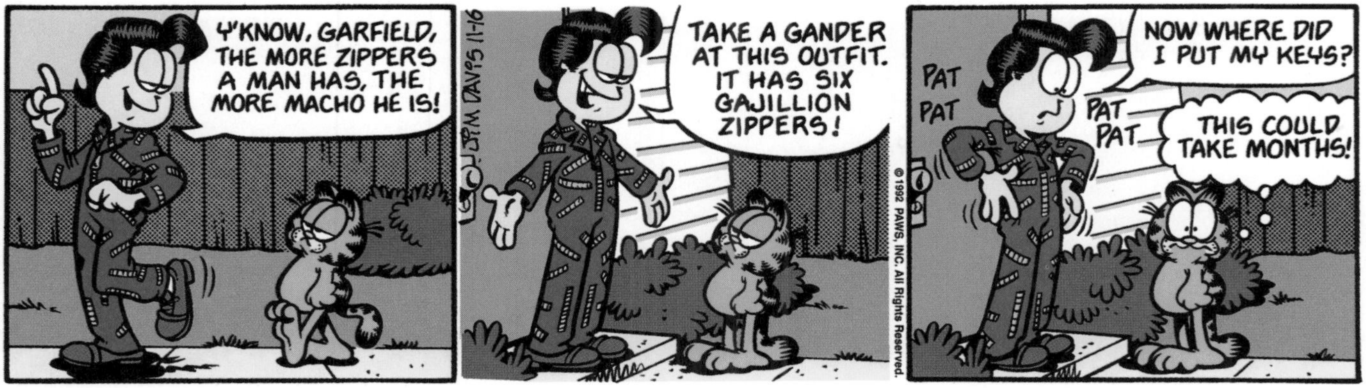
Y'KNOW, GARFIELD, THE MORE ZIPPERS A MAN HAS, THE MORE MACHO HE IS!
JIM DAVIS 11-16
TAKE A GANDER AT THIS OUTFIT. IT HAS SIX GAJILLION ZIPPERS!
© 1992 PAWS, INC. All Rights Reserved.
PAT PAT
NOW WHERE DID I PUT MY KEYS?
PAT PAT
THIS COULD TAKE MONTHS!

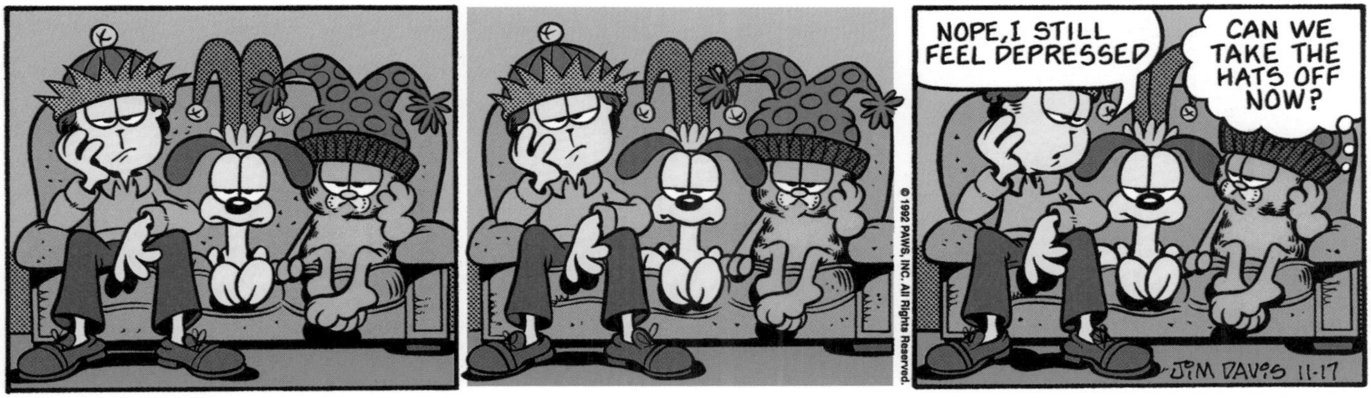
© 1992 PAWS, INC. All Rights Reserved.
NOPE, I STILL FEEL DEPRESSED
CAN WE TAKE THE HATS OFF NOW?
JIM DAVIS 11-17

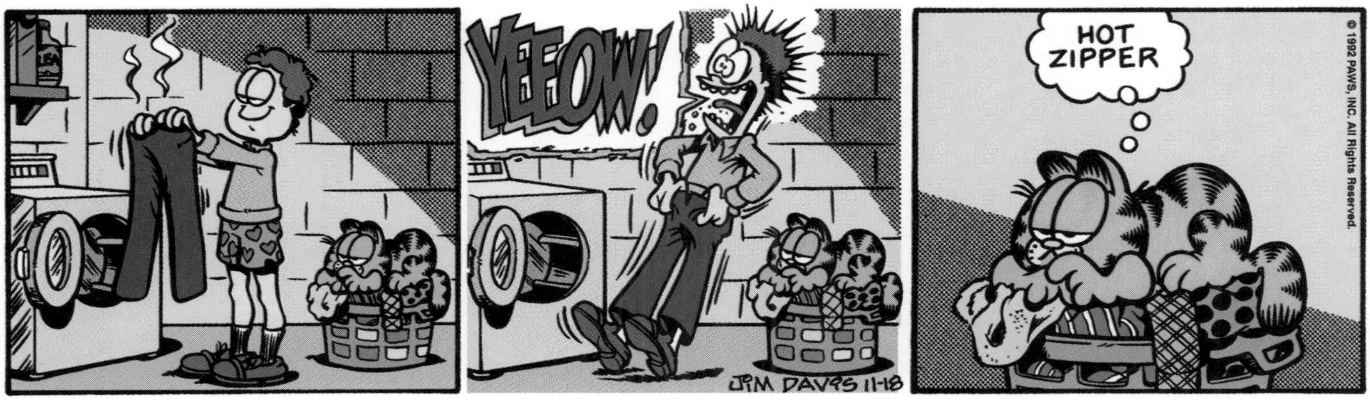
YEEOW!
JIM DAVIS 11-18
HOT ZIPPER
© 1992 PAWS, INC. All Rights Reserved.

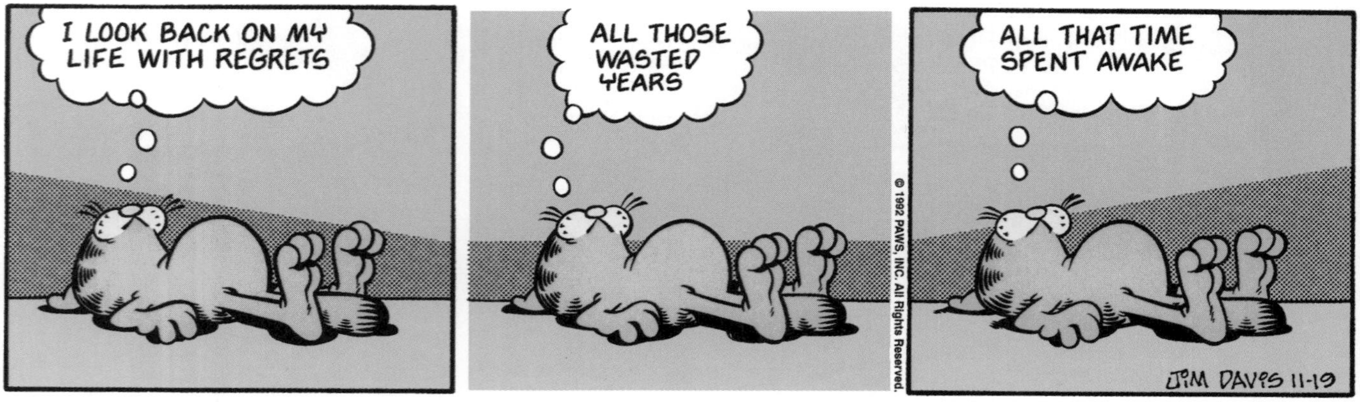
I LOOK BACK ON MY LIFE WITH REGRETS
ALL THOSE WASTED YEARS
© 1992 PAWS, INC. All Rights Reserved.
ALL THAT TIME SPENT AWAKE
JIM DAVIS 11-19

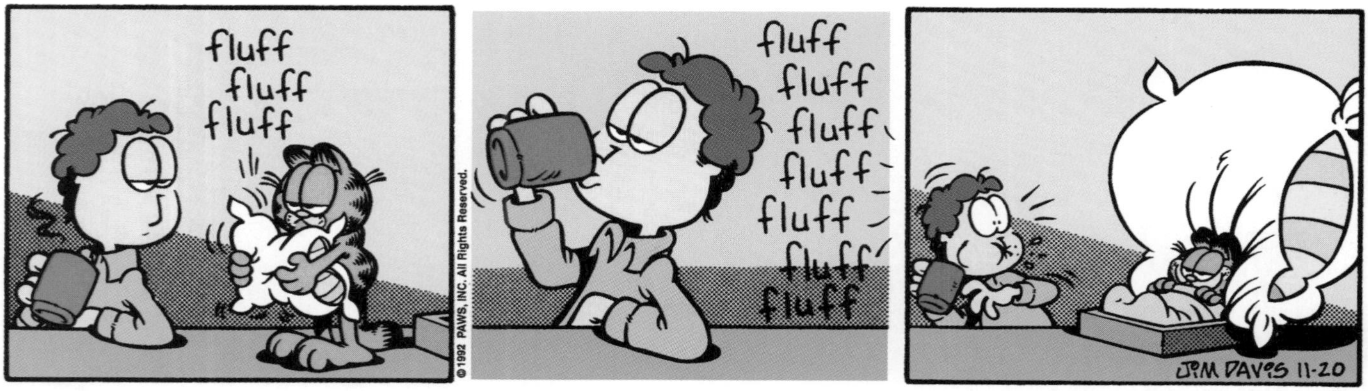
fluff fluff fluff
© 1992 PAWS, INC. All Rights Reserved.
fluff fluff fluff fluff fluff fluff fluff
JIM DAVIS 11-20

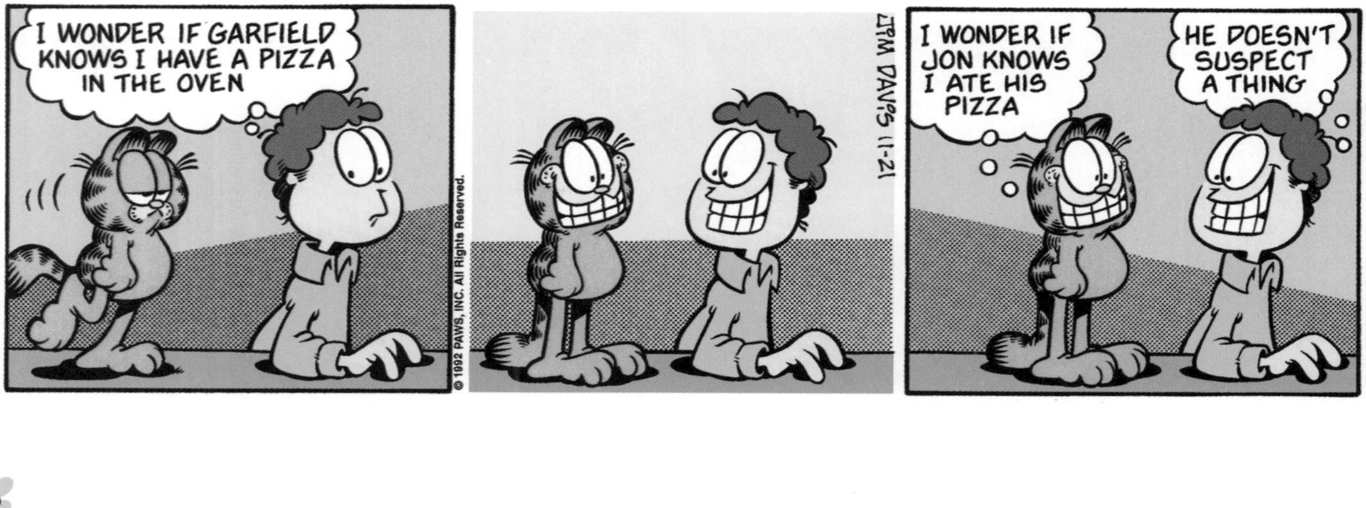
I WONDER IF GARFIELD KNOWS I HAVE A PIZZA IN THE OVEN
© 1992 PAWS, INC. All Rights Reserved.
JIM DAVIS 11-21
I WONDER IF JON KNOWS I ATE HIS PIZZA
HE DOESN'T SUSPECT A THING

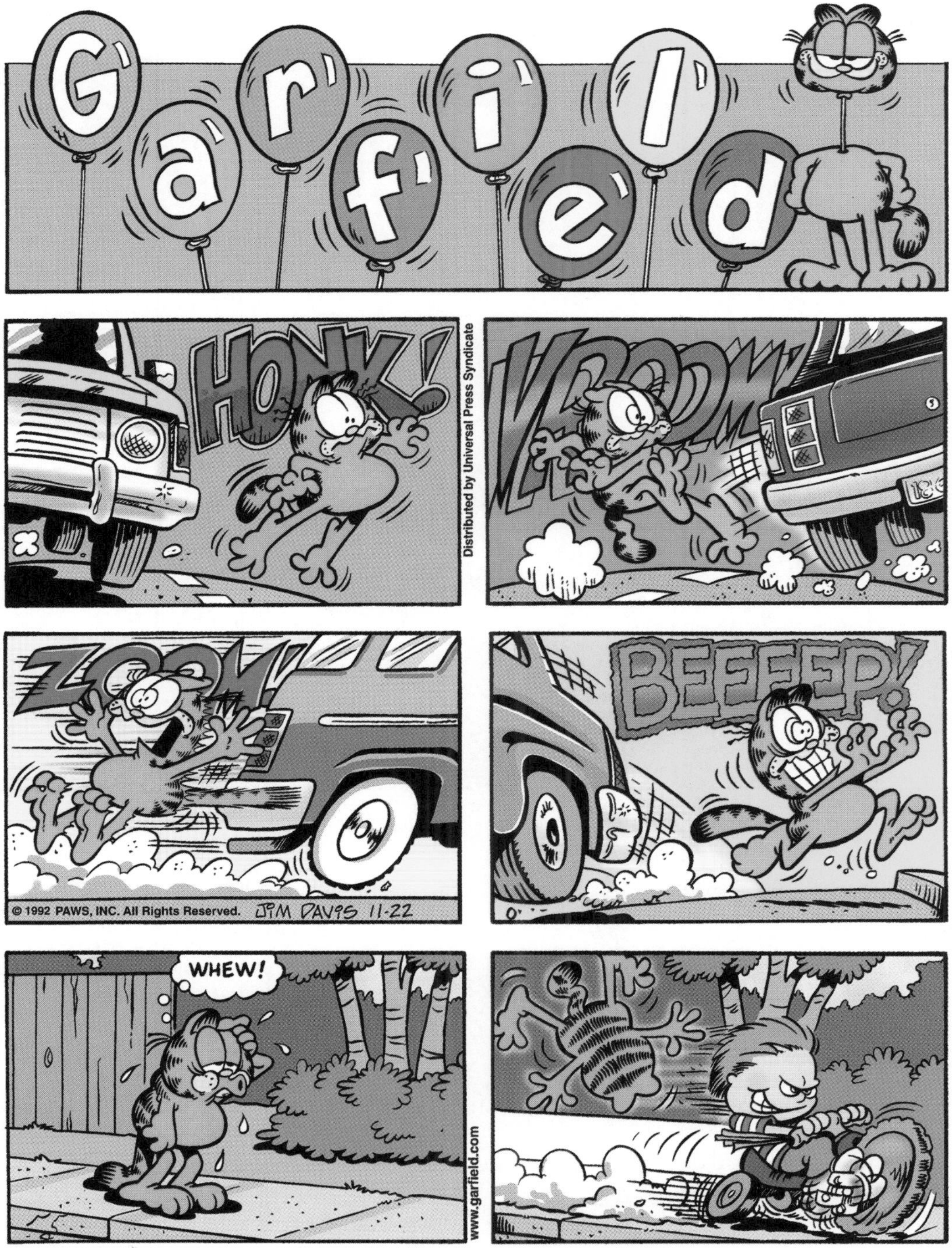
Garfield
HONK!
VROOOM!
ZOOM!
BEEEEEP!
WHEW!
Distributed by Universal Press Syndicate
© 1992 PAWS, INC. All Rights Reserved.
JIM DAVIS 11-22
www.garfield.com

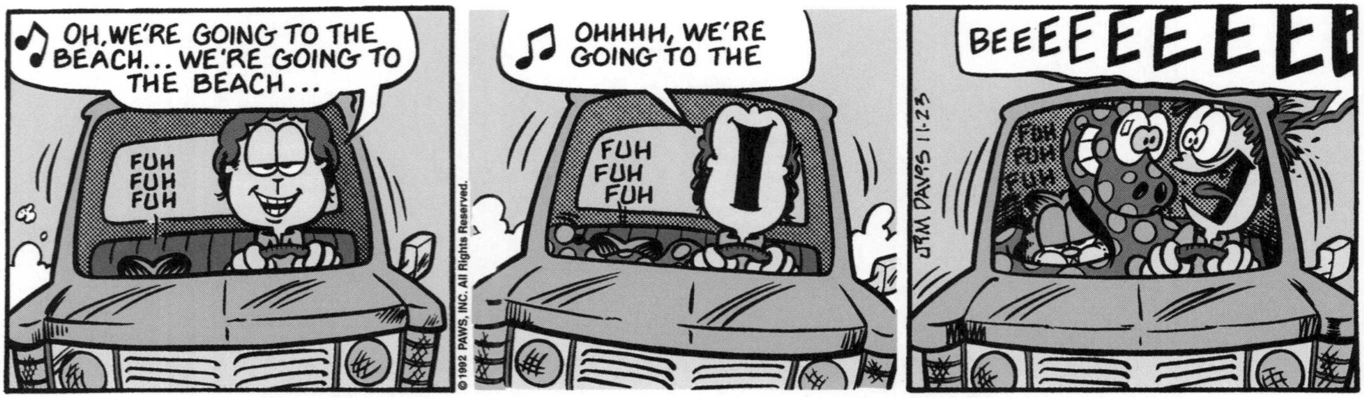
♪ OH, WE'RE GOING TO THE BEACH... WE'RE GOING TO THE BEACH...
FUH FUH FUH
© 1992 PAWS, INC. All Rights Reserved.
♫ OHHHH, WE'RE GOING TO THE
FUH FUH FUH
BEEEEEEEEE
JIM DAVIS 11-23

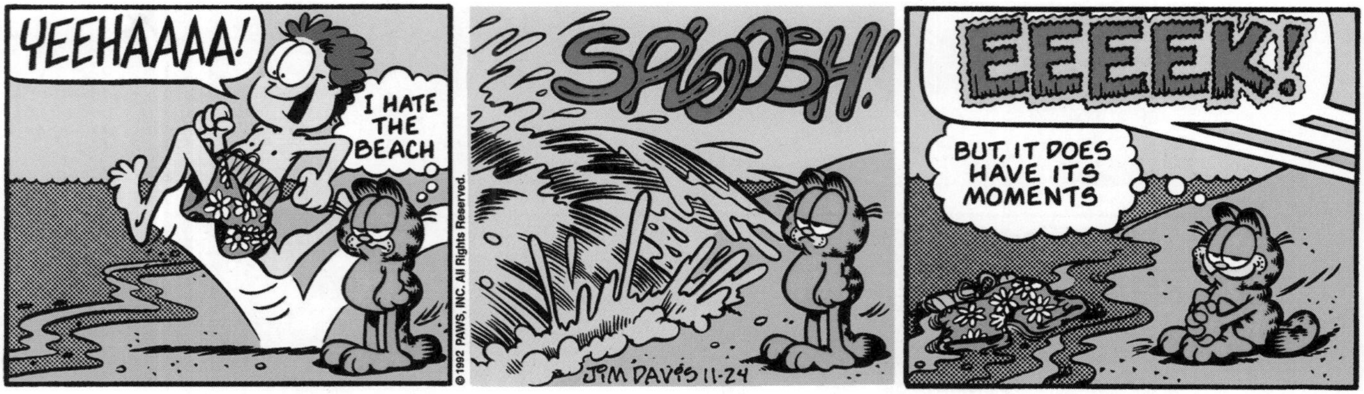
YEEHAAAA!
I HATE THE BEACH
© 1992 PAWS, INC. All Rights Reserved.
SPLOOSH!
JIM DAVIS 11-24
EEEEK!
BUT, IT DOES HAVE ITS MOMENTS

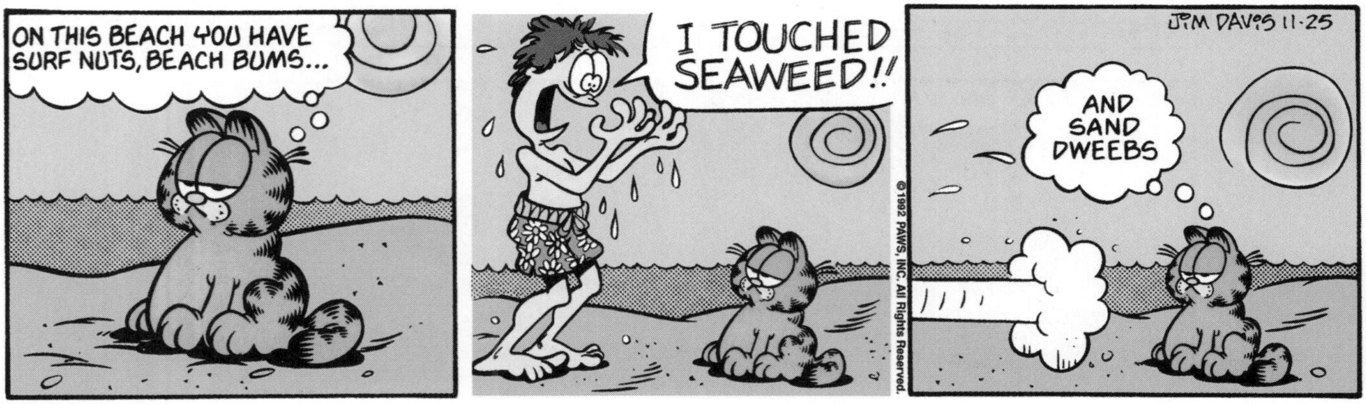
ON THIS BEACH YOU HAVE SURF NUTS, BEACH BUMS...
I TOUCHED SEAWEED!!
© 1992 PAWS, INC. All Rights Reserved.
JIM DAVIS 11-25
AND SAND DWEEBS

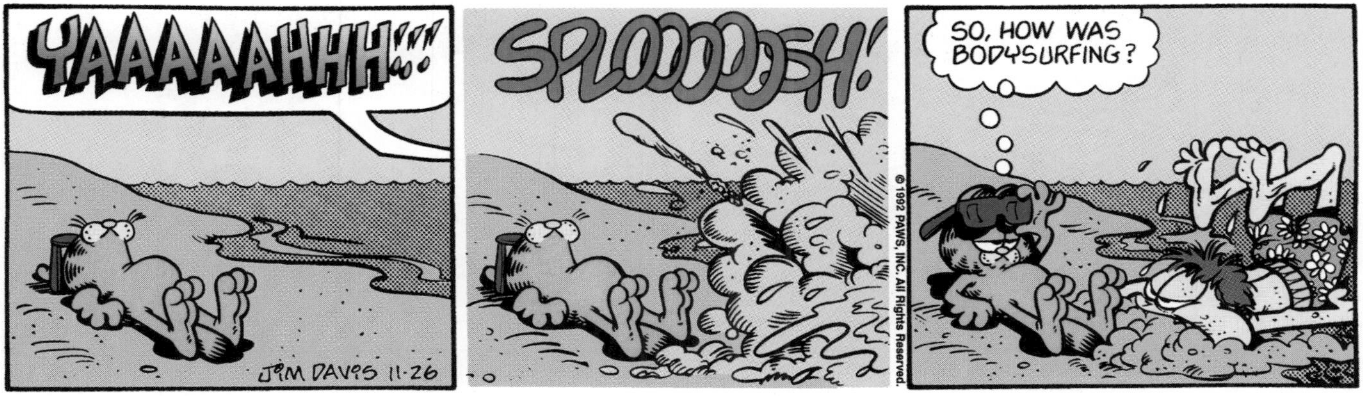
YAAAAAHHH!!!!
SPLOOOOOOSH!
SO, HOW WAS BODYSURFING?
JIM DAVIS 11-26
© 1992 PAWS, INC. All Rights Reserved.

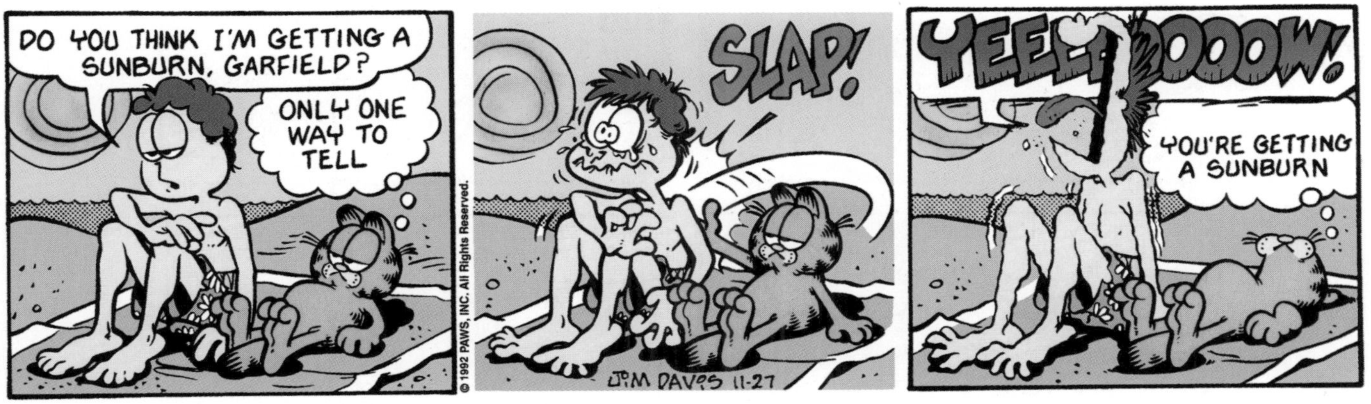
DO YOU THINK I'M GETTING A SUNBURN, GARFIELD?
ONLY ONE WAY TO TELL
SLAP!
YOU'RE GETTING A SUNBURN
JIM DAVIS 11-27
© 1992 PAWS, INC. All Rights Reserved.

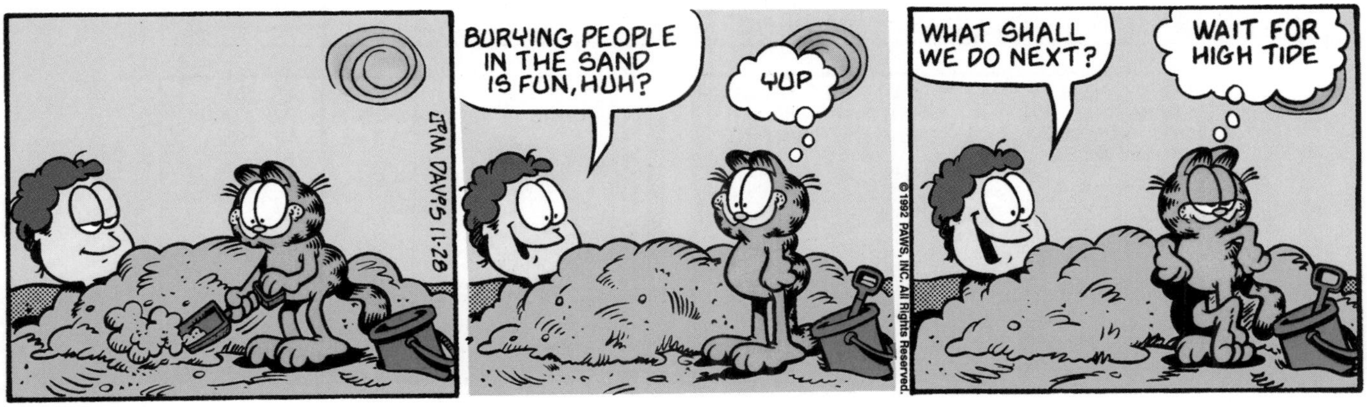
BURYING PEOPLE IN THE SAND IS FUN, HUH?
YUP
WHAT SHALL WE DO NEXT?
WAIT FOR HIGH TIDE
JIM DAVIS 11-28
© 1992 PAWS, INC. All Rights Reserved.

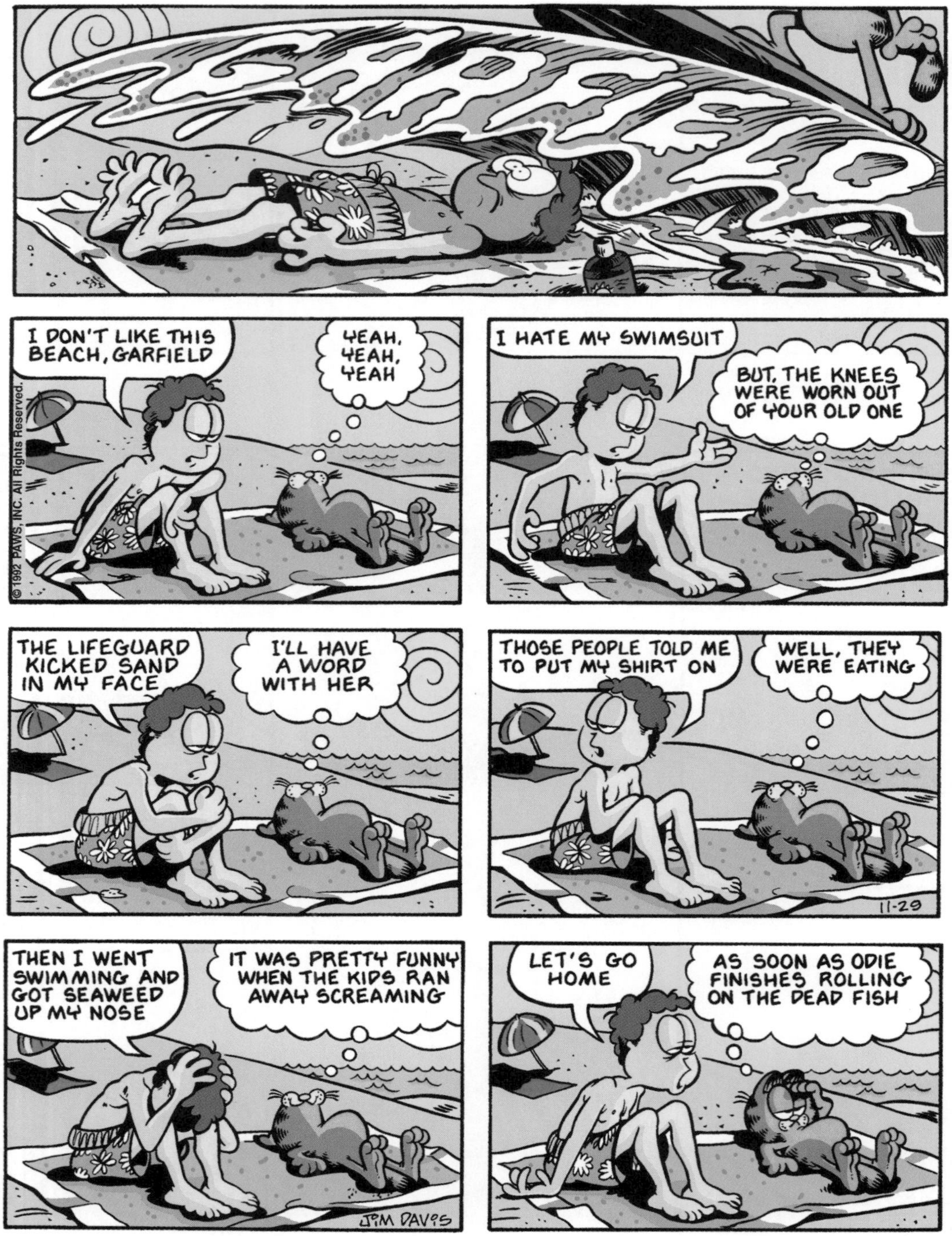
© 1992 PAWS, INC. All Rights Reserved.
I DON'T LIKE THIS BEACH, GARFIELD
YEAH, YEAH, YEAH
I HATE MY SWIMSUIT
BUT, THE KNEES WERE WORN OUT OF YOUR OLD ONE
THE LIFEGUARD KICKED SAND IN MY FACE
I'LL HAVE A WORD WITH HER
THOSE PEOPLE TOLD ME TO PUT MY SHIRT ON
WELL, THEY WERE EATING
11-29
THEN I WENT SWIMMING AND GOT SEAWEED UP MY NOSE
IT WAS PRETTY FUNNY WHEN THE KIDS RAN AWAY SCREAMING
JIM DAVIS
LET'S GO HOME
AS SOON AS ODIE FINISHES ROLLING ON THE DEAD FISH

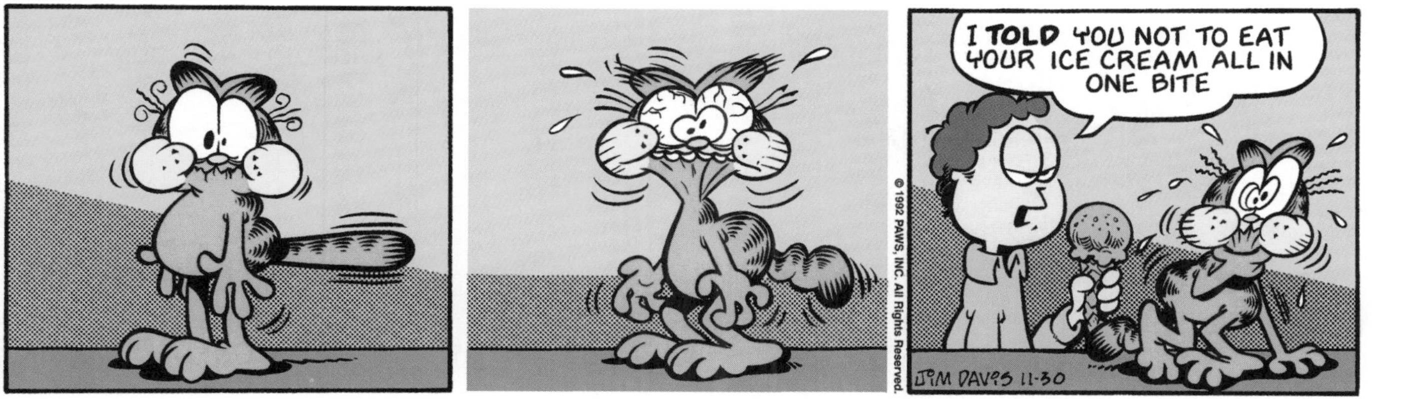
I **TOLD** YOU NOT TO EAT YOUR ICE CREAM ALL IN ONE BITE
© 1992 PAWS, INC. All Rights Reserved.
JIM DAVIS 11-30

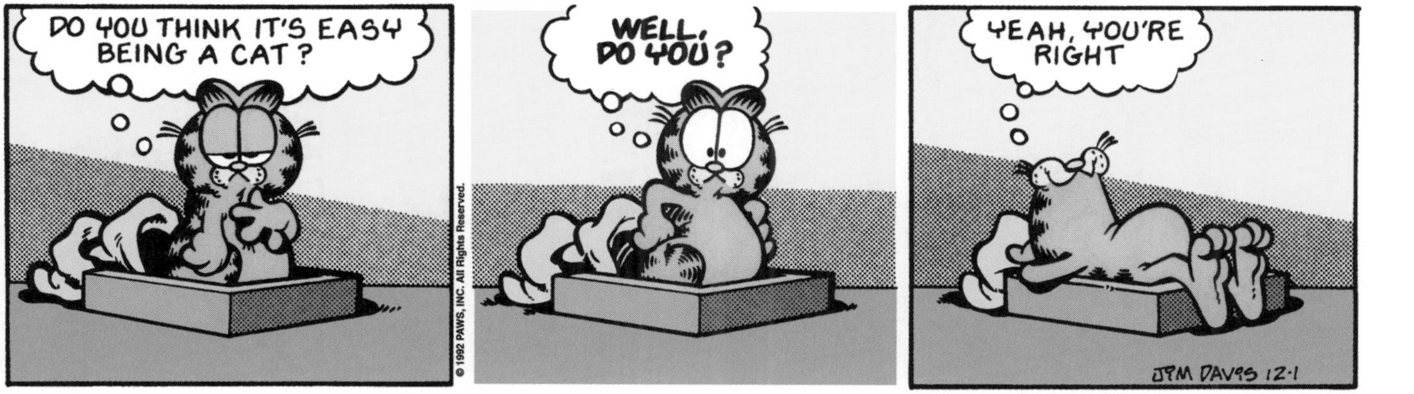
DO YOU THINK IT'S EASY BEING A CAT?
WELL, DO YOU?
YEAH, YOU'RE RIGHT
© 1992 PAWS, INC. All Rights Reserved.
JIM DAVIS 12-1

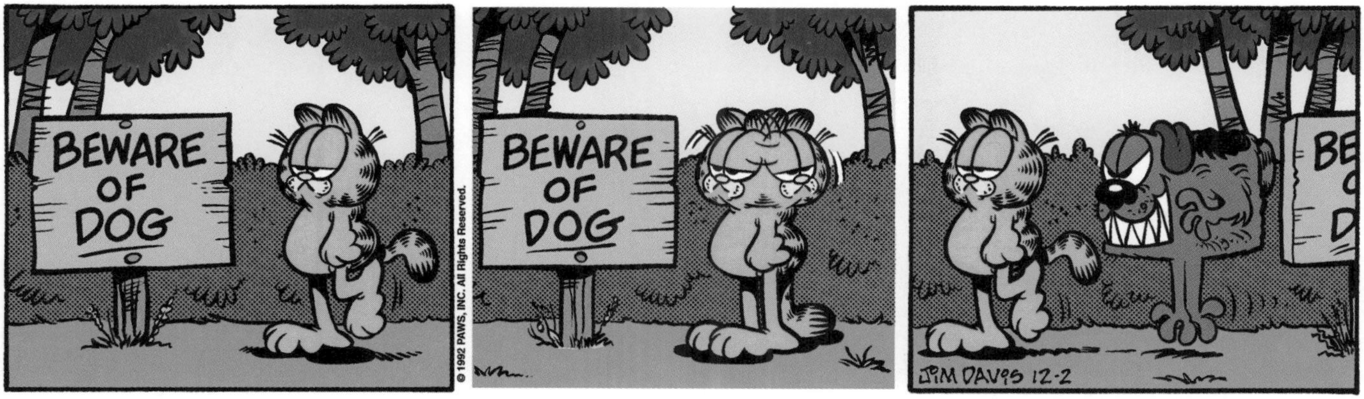
BEWARE OF DOG
BEWARE OF DOG
© 1992 PAWS, INC. All Rights Reserved.
JIM DAVIS 12-2

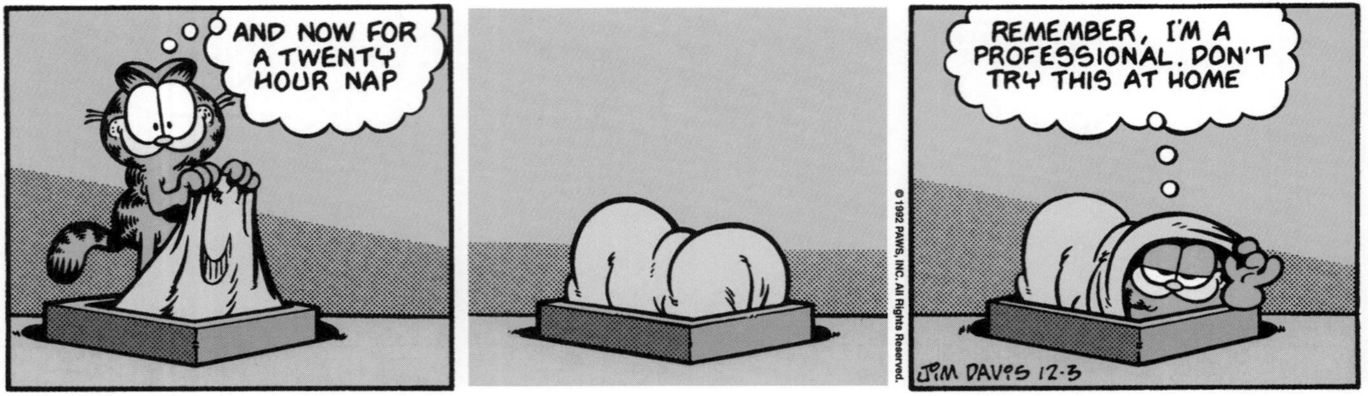
AND NOW FOR A TWENTY HOUR NAP
© 1992 PAWS, INC. All Rights Reserved.
REMEMBER, I'M A PROFESSIONAL. DON'T TRY THIS AT HOME
JIM DAVIS 12-3

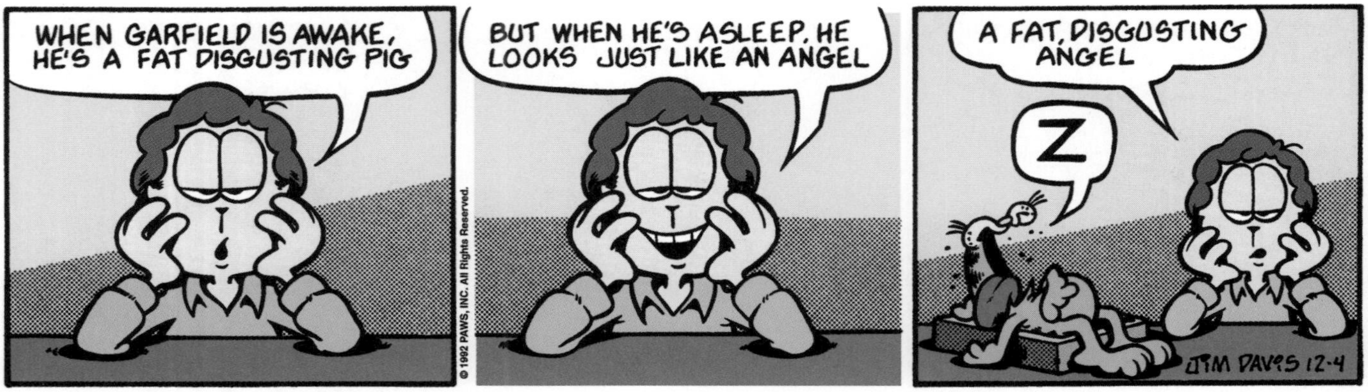
WHEN GARFIELD IS AWAKE, HE'S A FAT DISGUSTING PIG
© 1992 PAWS, INC. All Rights Reserved.
BUT WHEN HE'S ASLEEP, HE LOOKS JUST LIKE AN ANGEL
A FAT, DISGUSTING ANGEL
Z
JIM DAVIS 12-4

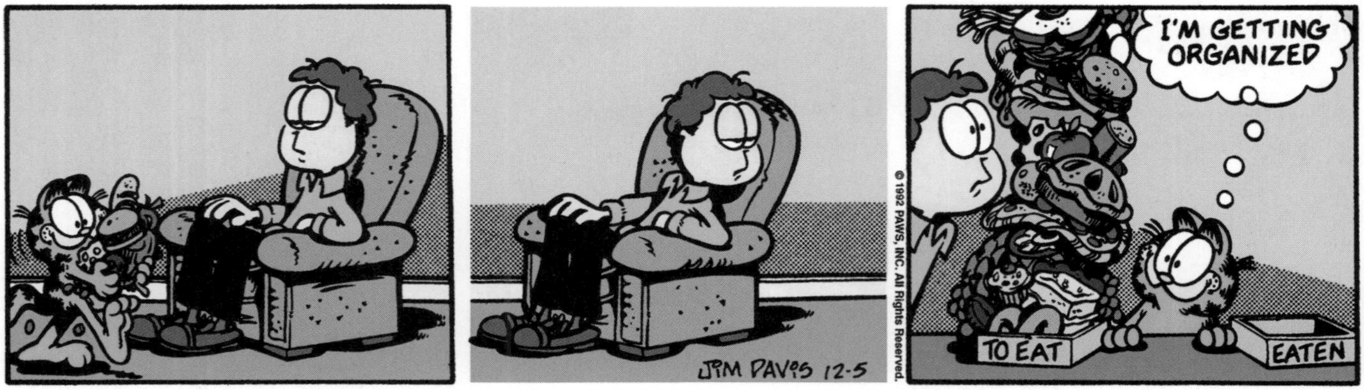
JIM DAVIS 12-5
© 1992 PAWS, INC. All Rights Reserved.
I'M GETTING ORGANIZED
TO EAT
EATEN

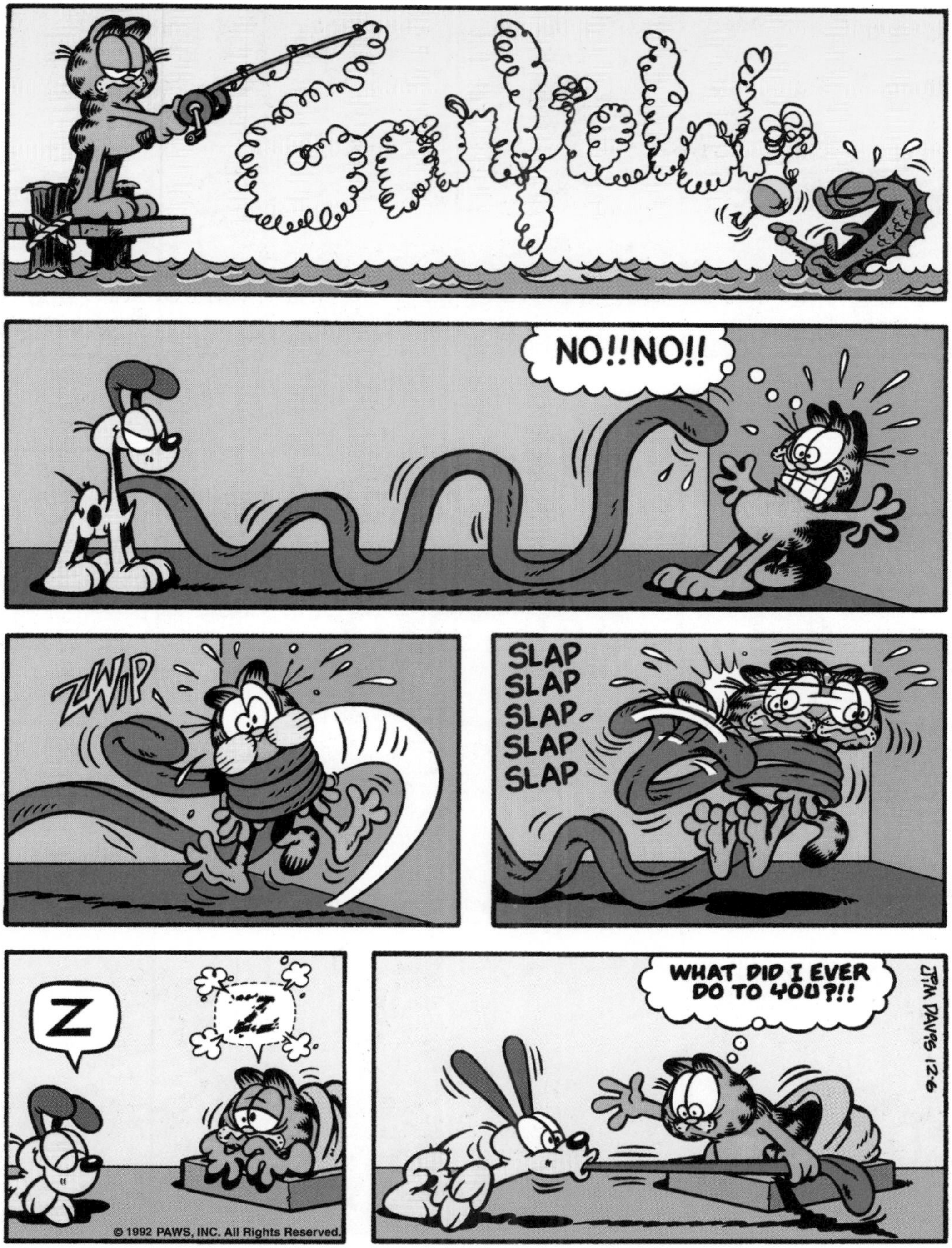
Garfield
NO!! NO!!
ZWIP
SLAP
SLAP
SLAP
SLAP
SLAP
SLAP
Z
Z
© 1992 PAWS, INC. All Rights Reserved.
WHAT DID I EVER DO TO YOU?!!
JIM DAVIS 12-6

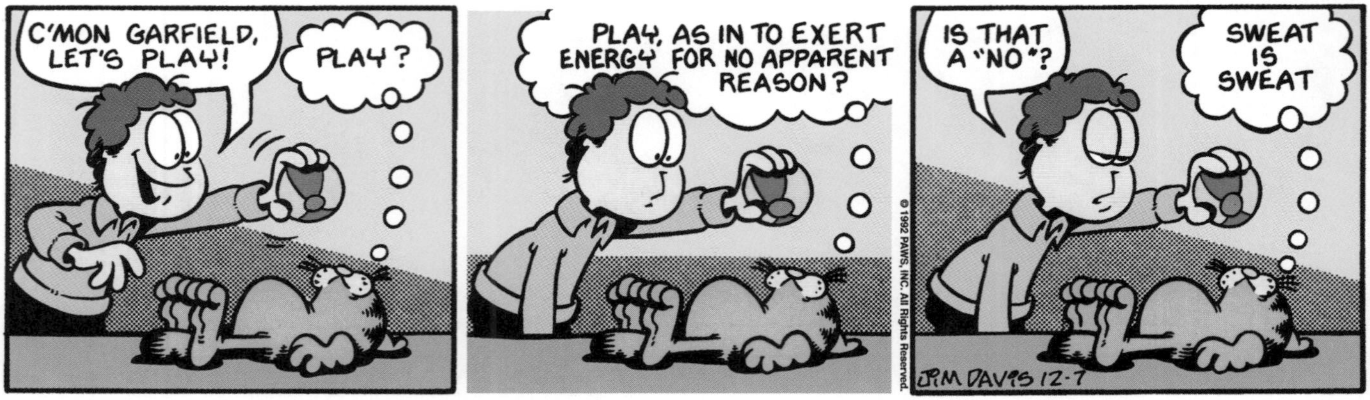
C'MON GARFIELD, LET'S PLAY!
PLAY?
PLAY, AS IN TO EXERT ENERGY FOR NO APPARENT REASON?
IS THAT A "NO"?
SWEAT IS SWEAT
© 1992 PAWS, INC. All Rights Reserved.
JIM DAVIS 12-7

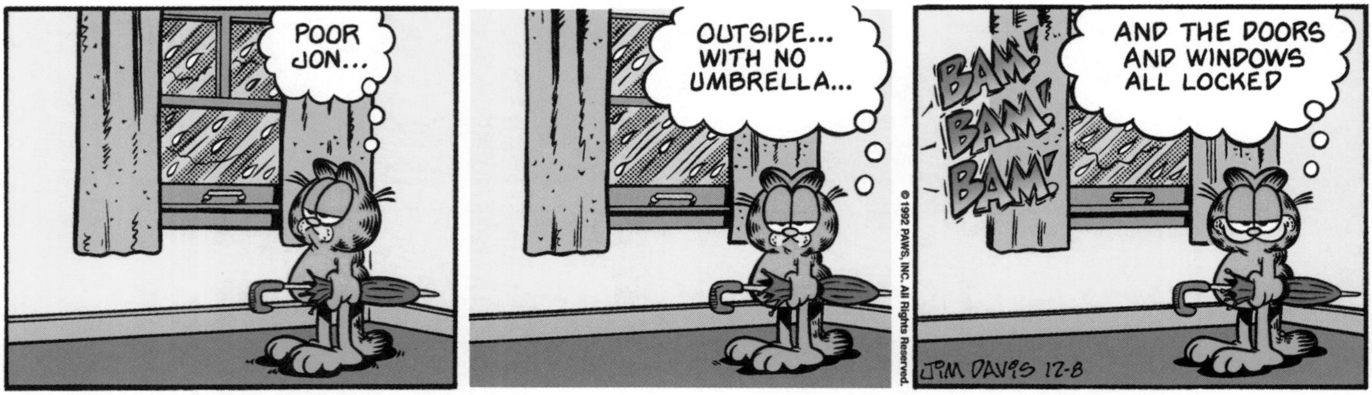
POOR JON...
OUTSIDE... WITH NO UMBRELLA...
BAM! BAM! BAM!
AND THE DOORS AND WINDOWS ALL LOCKED
© 1992 PAWS, INC. All Rights Reserved.
JIM DAVIS 12-8

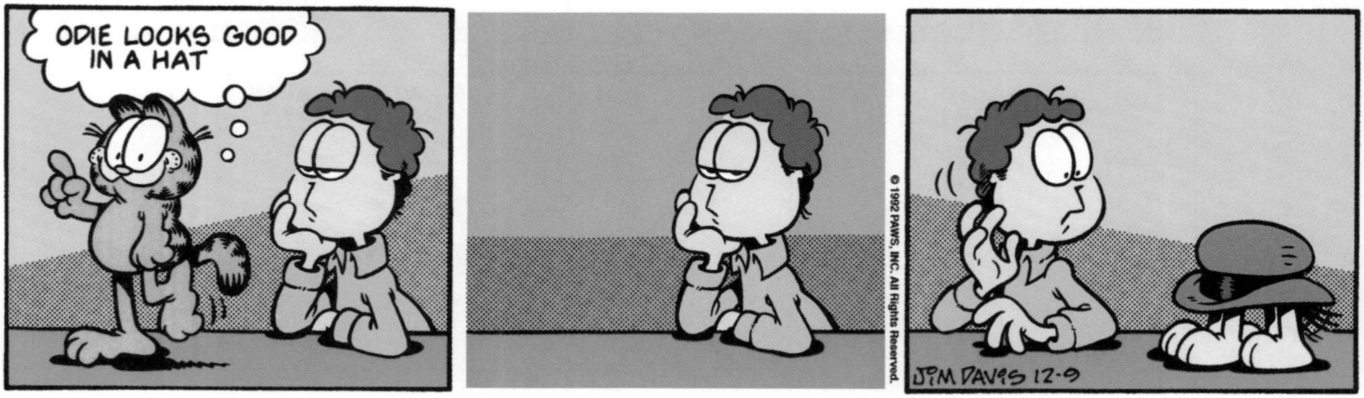
ODIE LOOKS GOOD IN A HAT
© 1992 PAWS, INC. All Rights Reserved.
JIM DAVIS 12-9

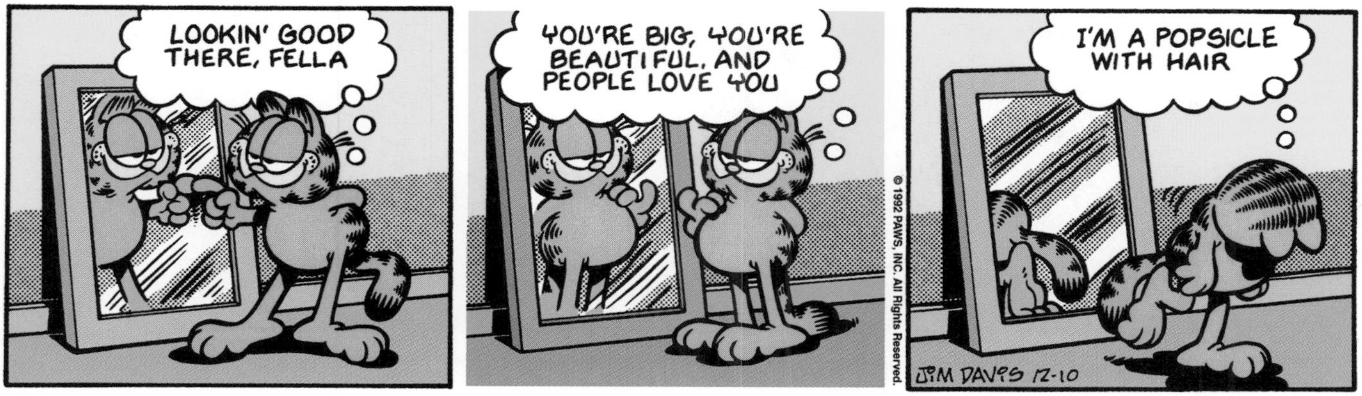
LOOKIN' GOOD THERE, FELLA
YOU'RE BIG, YOU'RE BEAUTIFUL, AND PEOPLE LOVE YOU
© 1992 PAWS, INC. All Rights Reserved.
I'M A POPSICLE WITH HAIR
JIM DAVIS 12-10

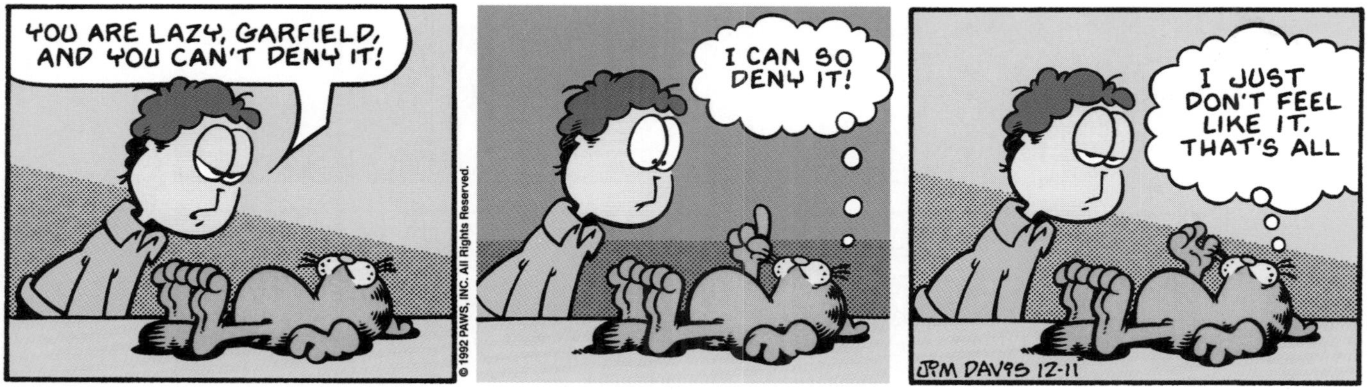
YOU ARE LAZY, GARFIELD, AND YOU CAN'T DENY IT!
© 1992 PAWS, INC. All Rights Reserved.
I CAN SO DENY IT!
I JUST DON'T FEEL LIKE IT, THAT'S ALL
JIM DAVIS 12-11

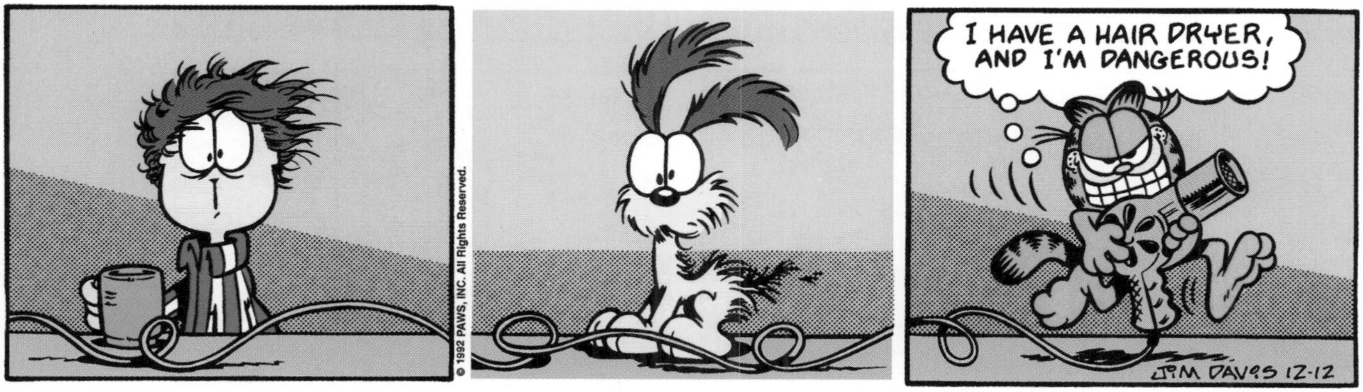
© 1992 PAWS, INC. All Rights Reserved.
I HAVE A HAIR DRYER, AND I'M DANGEROUS!
JIM DAVIS 12-12

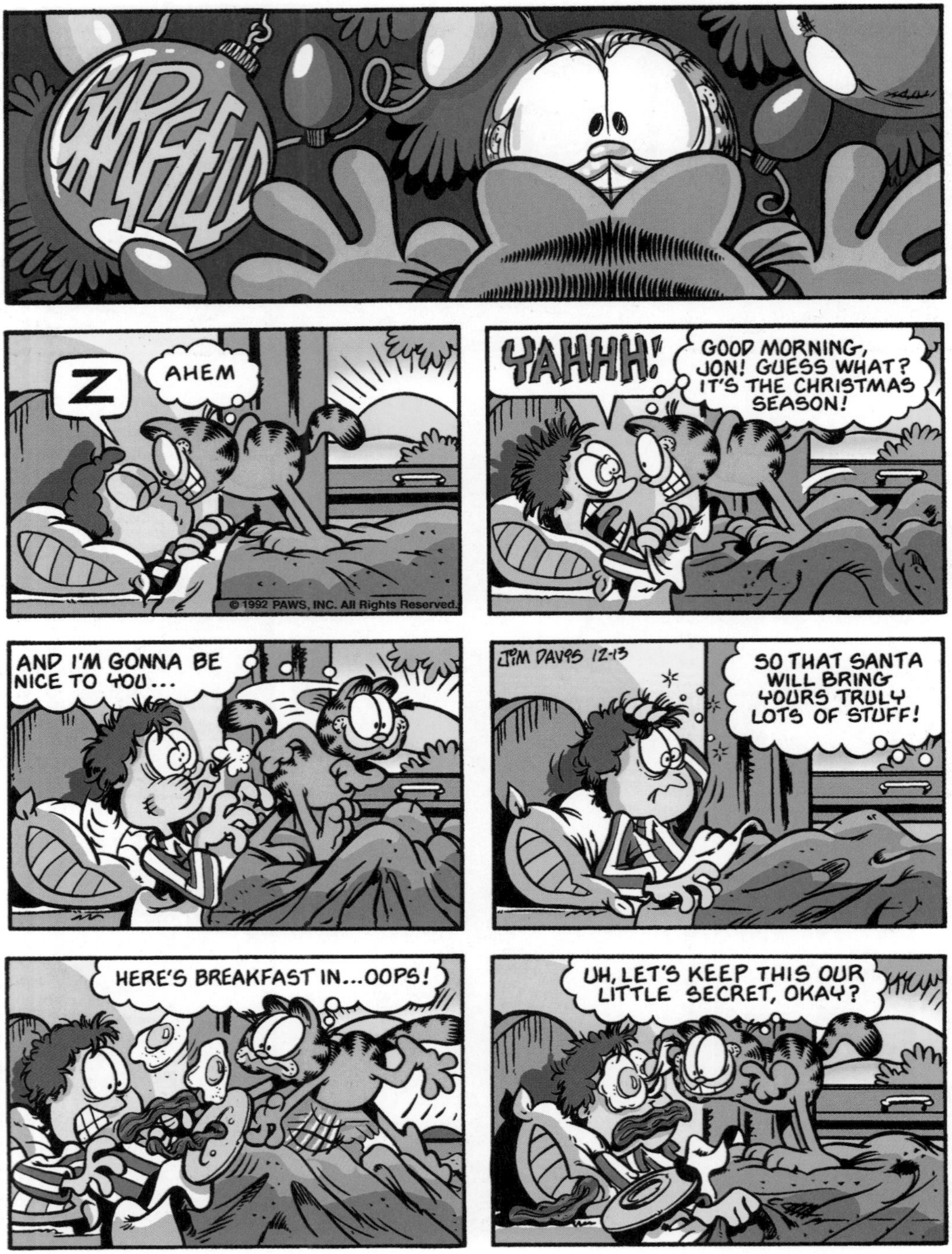
GARFIELD
Z
AHEM
© 1992 PAWS, INC. All Rights Reserved.
YAHHH!
GOOD MORNING, JON! GUESS WHAT? IT'S THE CHRISTMAS SEASON!
AND I'M GONNA BE NICE TO YOU...
JIM DAVIS 12-13
SO THAT SANTA WILL BRING YOURS TRULY LOTS OF STUFF!
HERE'S BREAKFAST IN...OOPS!
UH, LET'S KEEP THIS OUR LITTLE SECRET, OKAY?

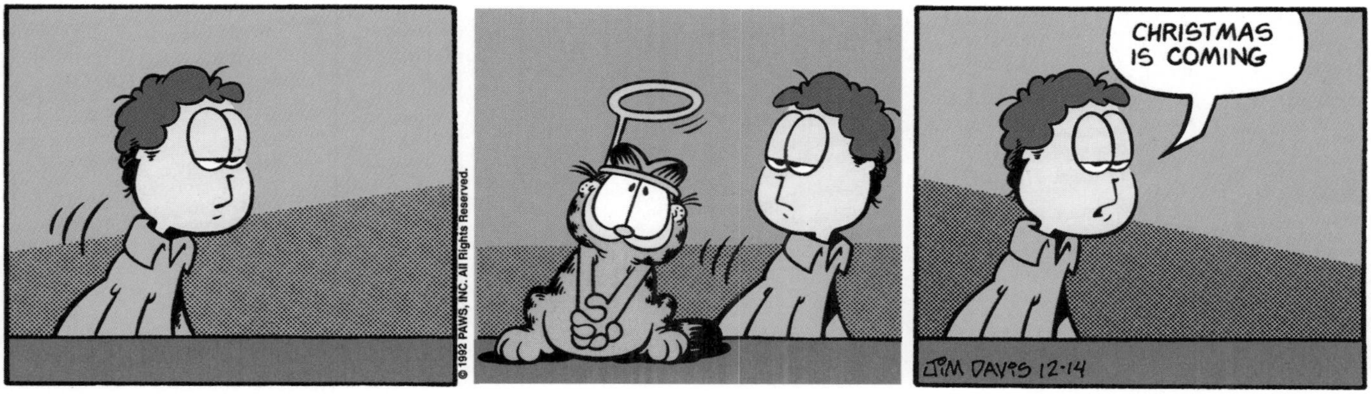
© 1992 PAWS, INC. All Rights Reserved.
CHRISTMAS IS COMING
JIM DAVIS 12-14

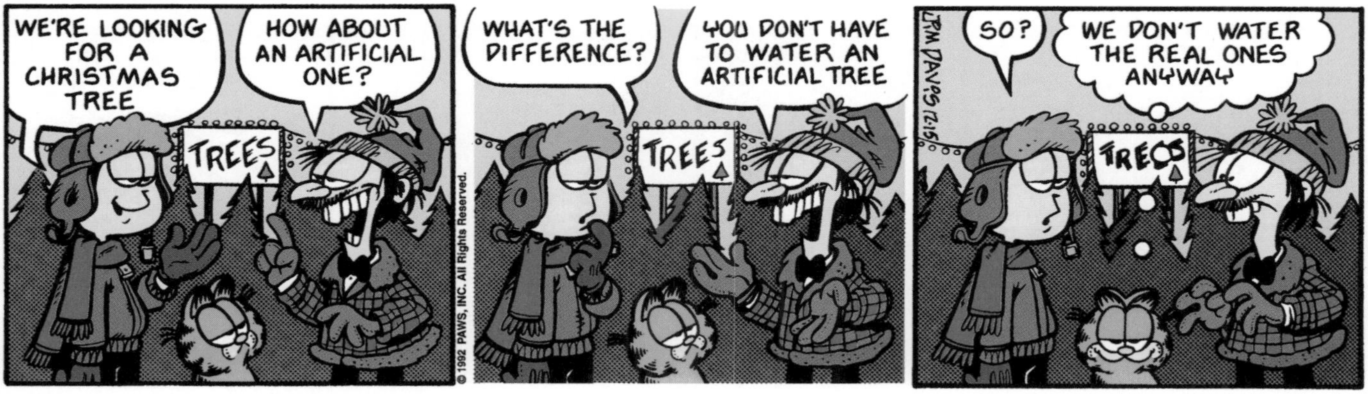
WE'RE LOOKING FOR A CHRISTMAS TREE
HOW ABOUT AN ARTIFICIAL ONE?
TREES
© 1992 PAWS, INC. All Rights Reserved.
WHAT'S THE DIFFERENCE?
YOU DON'T HAVE TO WATER AN ARTIFICIAL TREE
JIM DAVIS 12-15
SO?
WE DON'T WATER THE REAL ONES ANYWAY

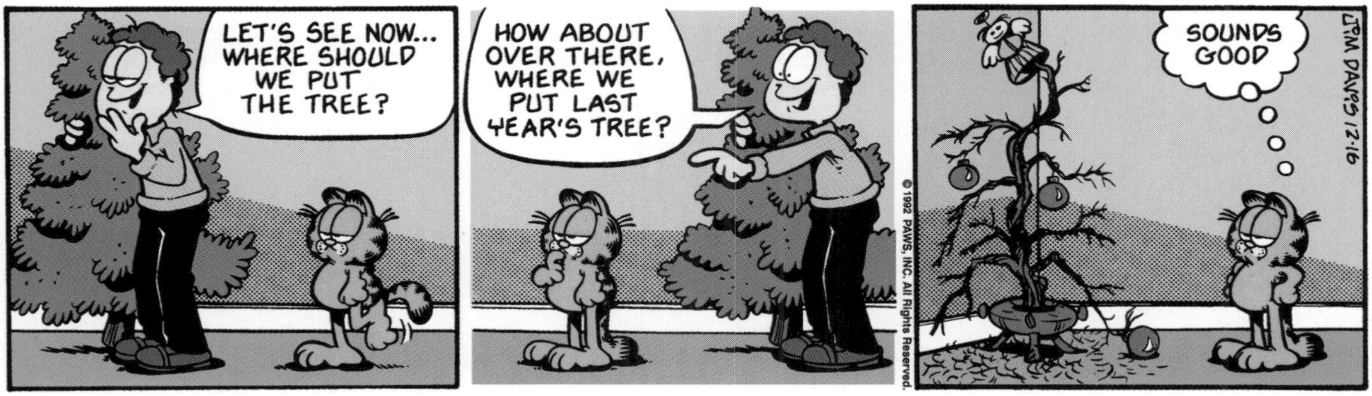
LET'S SEE NOW... WHERE SHOULD WE PUT THE TREE?
HOW ABOUT OVER THERE, WHERE WE PUT LAST YEAR'S TREE?
© 1992 PAWS, INC. All Rights Reserved.
SOUNDS GOOD
JIM DAVIS 12-16

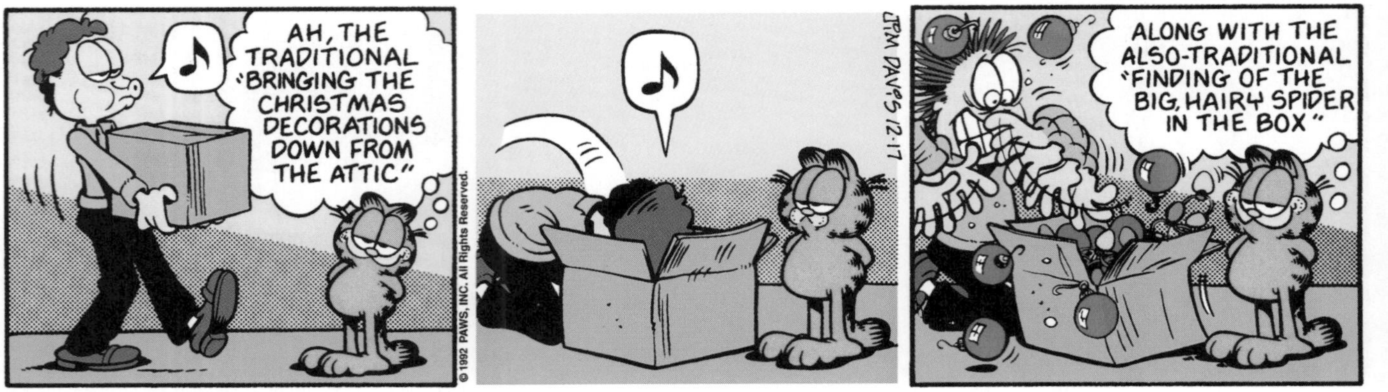
AH, THE TRADITIONAL "BRINGING THE CHRISTMAS DECORATIONS DOWN FROM THE ATTIC"
© 1992 PAWS, INC. All Rights Reserved.
JIM DAVIS 12-17
ALONG WITH THE ALSO-TRADITIONAL "FINDING OF THE BIG, HAIRY SPIDER IN THE BOX"

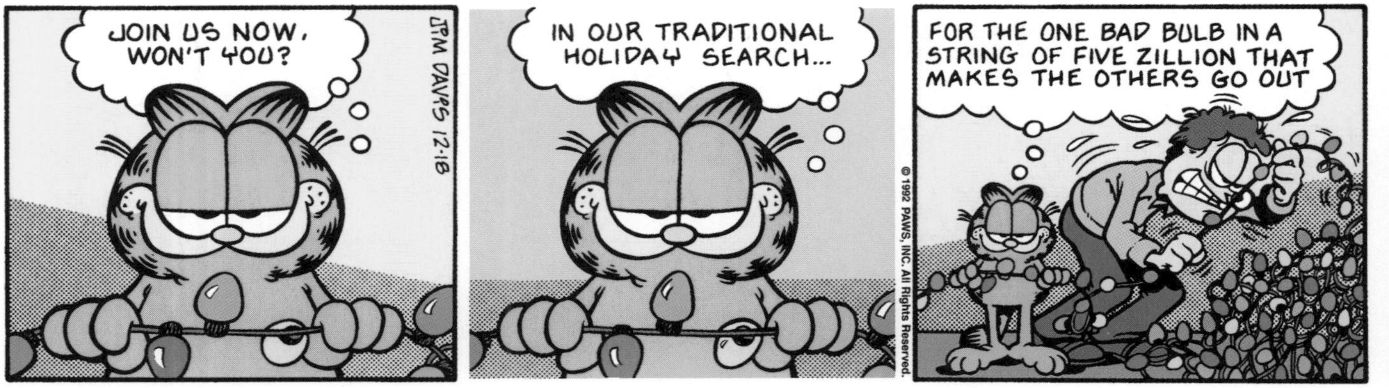
JOIN US NOW, WON'T YOU?
JIM DAVIS 12-18
IN OUR TRADITIONAL HOLIDAY SEARCH...
© 1992 PAWS, INC. All Rights Reserved.
FOR THE ONE BAD BULB IN A STRING OF FIVE ZILLION THAT MAKES THE OTHERS GO OUT

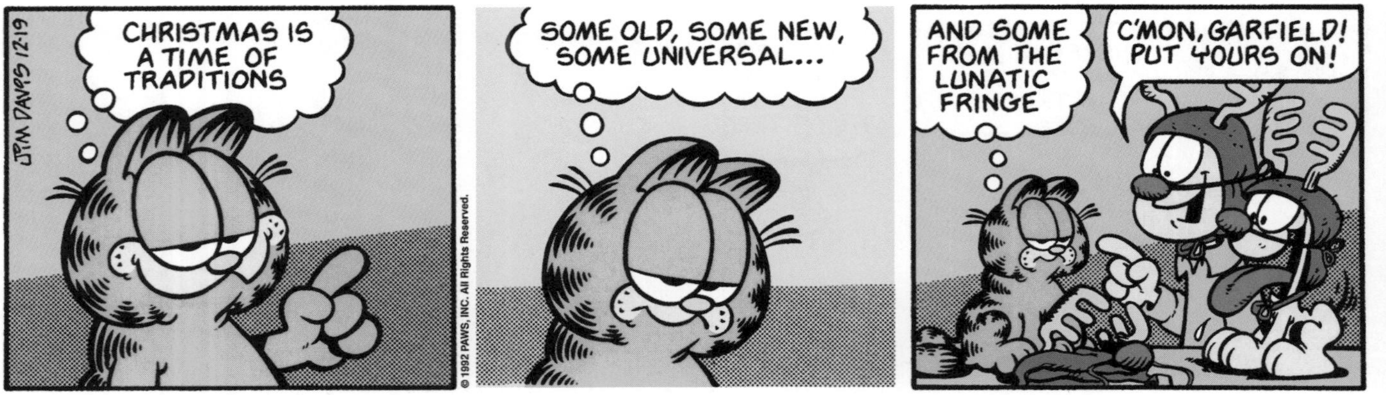
JIM DAVIS 12-19
CHRISTMAS IS A TIME OF TRADITIONS
© 1992 PAWS, INC. All Rights Reserved.
SOME OLD, SOME NEW, SOME UNIVERSAL...
AND SOME FROM THE LUNATIC FRINGE
C'MON, GARFIELD! PUT YOURS ON!

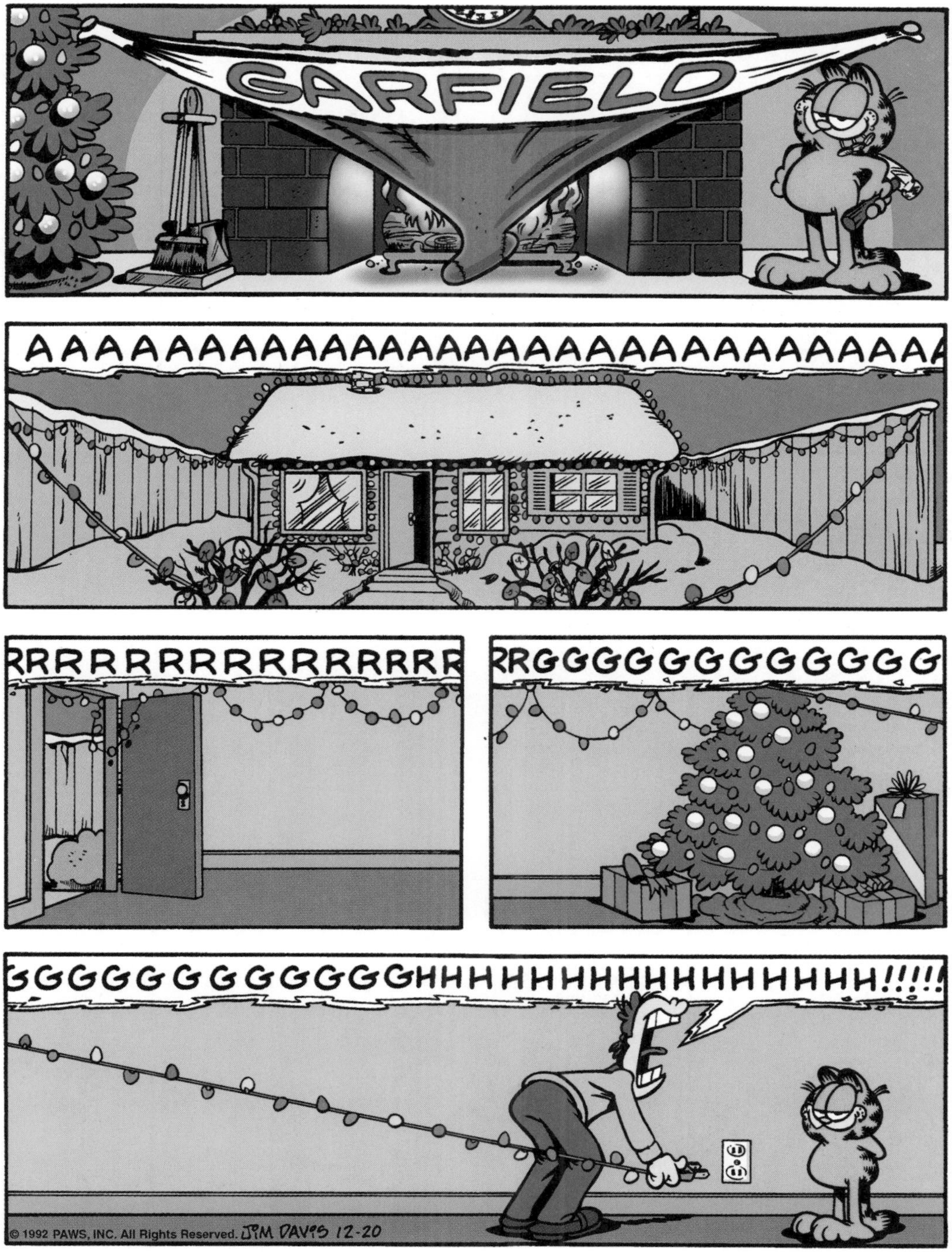
GARFIELD
AAAAAAAAAAAAAAAAAAAAAAAAAAAA
RRRRRRRRRRRRRR
RRGGGGGGGGGGGG
GGGGGGGGGGGGHHHHHHHHHHHHHHHH!!!!!
© 1992 PAWS, INC. All Rights Reserved. JIM DAVIS 12-20

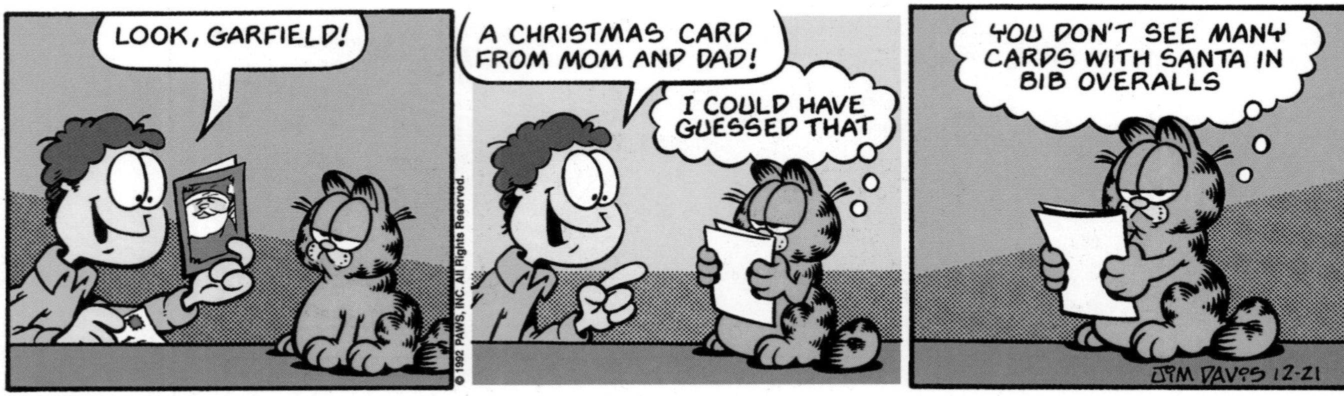
LOOK, GARFIELD!
A CHRISTMAS CARD FROM MOM AND DAD!
I COULD HAVE GUESSED THAT
YOU DON'T SEE MANY CARDS WITH SANTA IN BIB OVERALLS
© 1992 PAWS, INC. All Rights Reserved.
JIM DAVIS 12-21

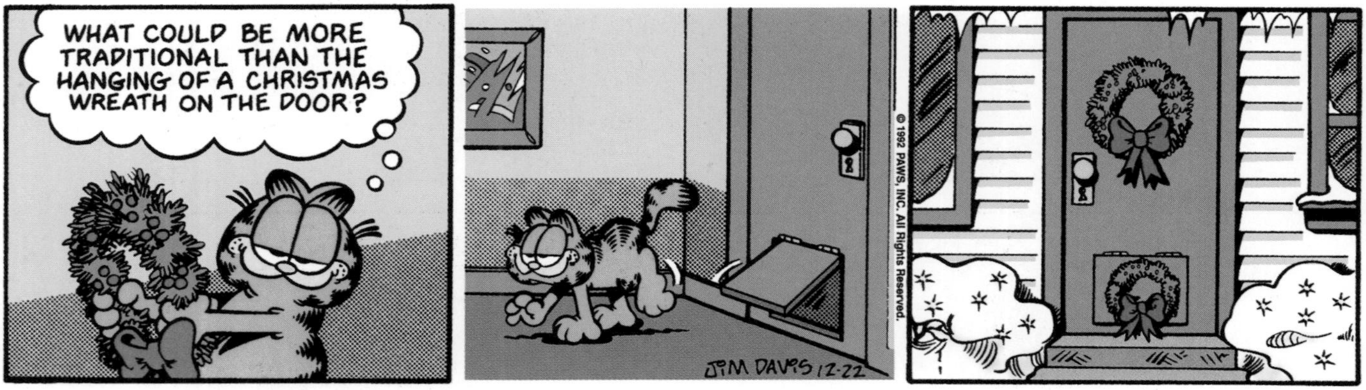
WHAT COULD BE MORE TRADITIONAL THAN THE HANGING OF A CHRISTMAS WREATH ON THE DOOR?
JIM DAVIS 12-22
© 1992 PAWS, INC. All Rights Reserved.

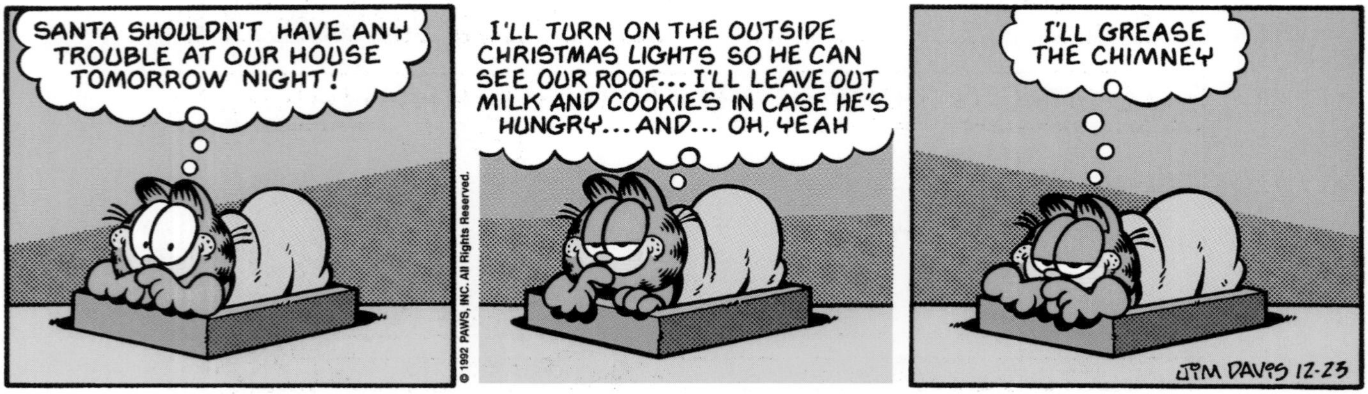
SANTA SHOULDN'T HAVE ANY TROUBLE AT OUR HOUSE TOMORROW NIGHT!
© 1992 PAWS, INC. All Rights Reserved.
I'LL TURN ON THE OUTSIDE CHRISTMAS LIGHTS SO HE CAN SEE OUR ROOF... I'LL LEAVE OUT MILK AND COOKIES IN CASE HE'S HUNGRY... AND... OH, YEAH
I'LL GREASE THE CHIMNEY
JIM DAVIS 12-23

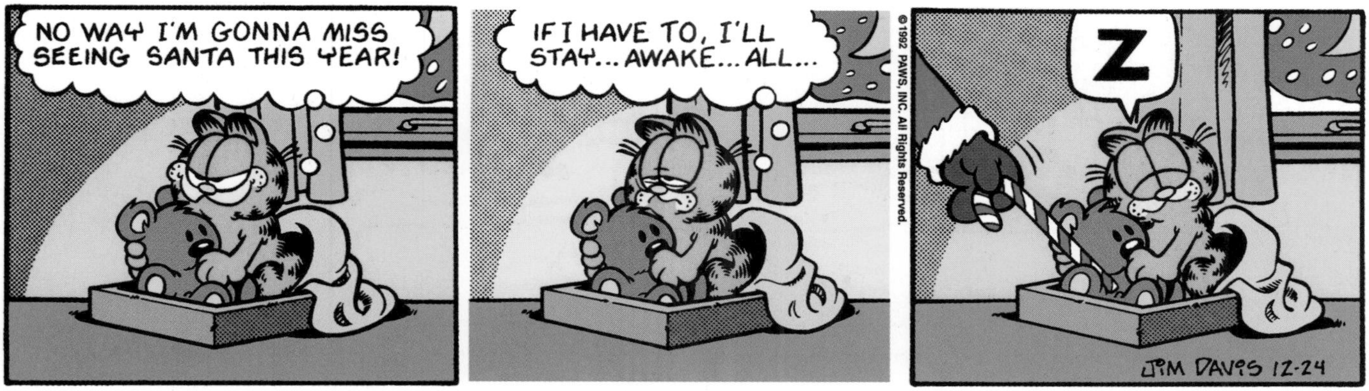
NO WAY I'M GONNA MISS SEEING SANTA THIS YEAR!
IF I HAVE TO, I'LL STAY... AWAKE... ALL...
© 1992 PAWS, INC. All Rights Reserved.
Z
JIM DAVIS 12-24

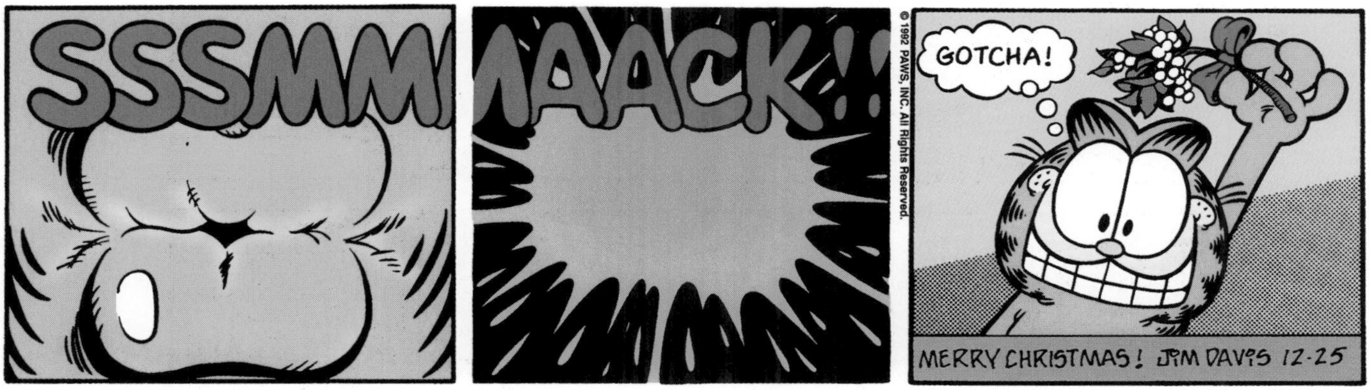
SSSMMMAACK!!
© 1992 PAWS, INC. All Rights Reserved.
GOTCHA!
MERRY CHRISTMAS! JIM DAVIS 12-25

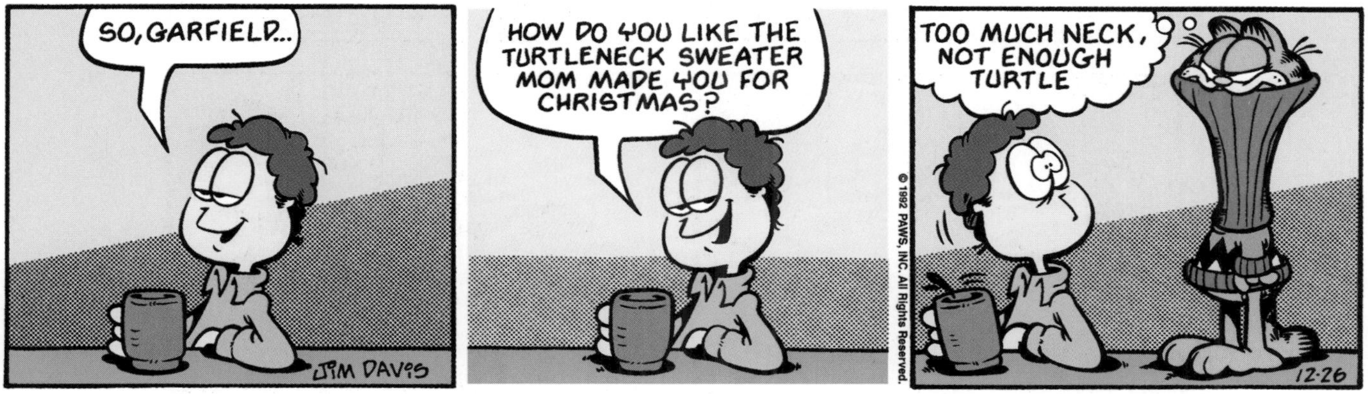
SO, GARFIELD...
JIM DAVIS
HOW DO YOU LIKE THE TURTLENECK SWEATER MOM MADE YOU FOR CHRISTMAS?
© 1992 PAWS, INC. All Rights Reserved.
TOO MUCH NECK, NOT ENOUGH TURTLE
12-26

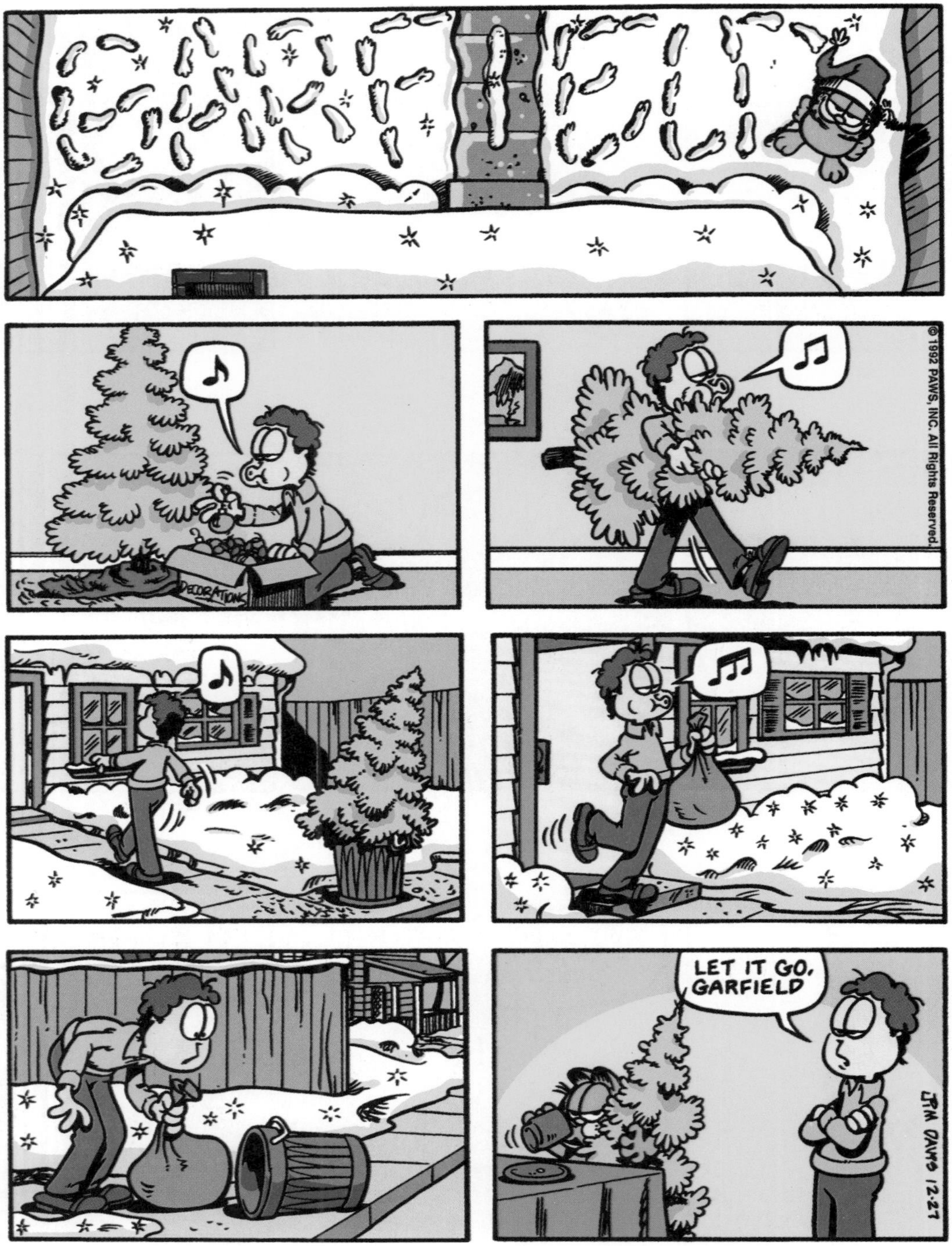

DECORATIONS
LET IT GO, GARFIELD
JIM DAVIS 12-27

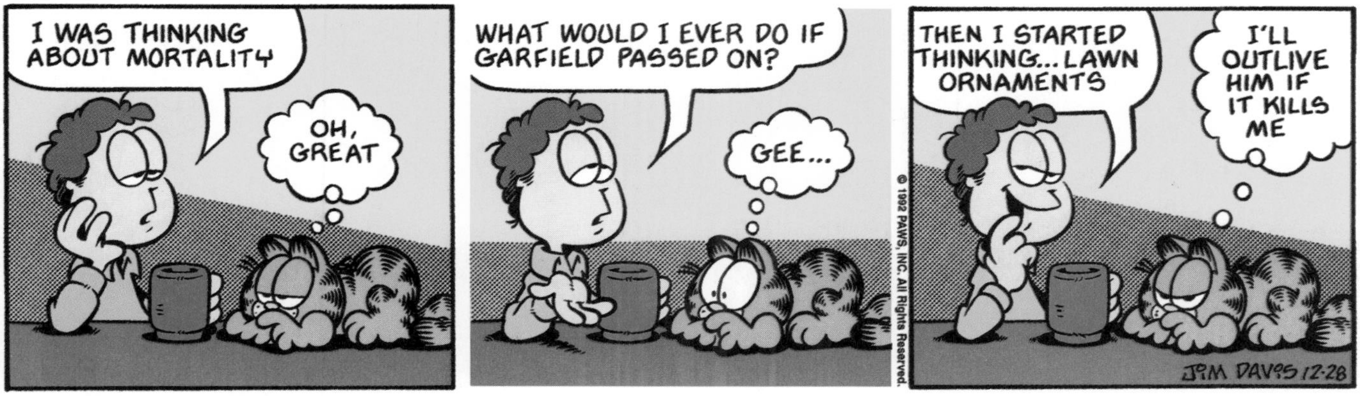
I WAS THINKING ABOUT MORTALITY
OH, GREAT
WHAT WOULD I EVER DO IF GARFIELD PASSED ON?
GEE...
© 1992 PAWS, INC. All Rights Reserved.
THEN I STARTED THINKING... LAWN ORNAMENTS
I'LL OUTLIVE HIM IF IT KILLS ME
JIM DAVIS 12-28

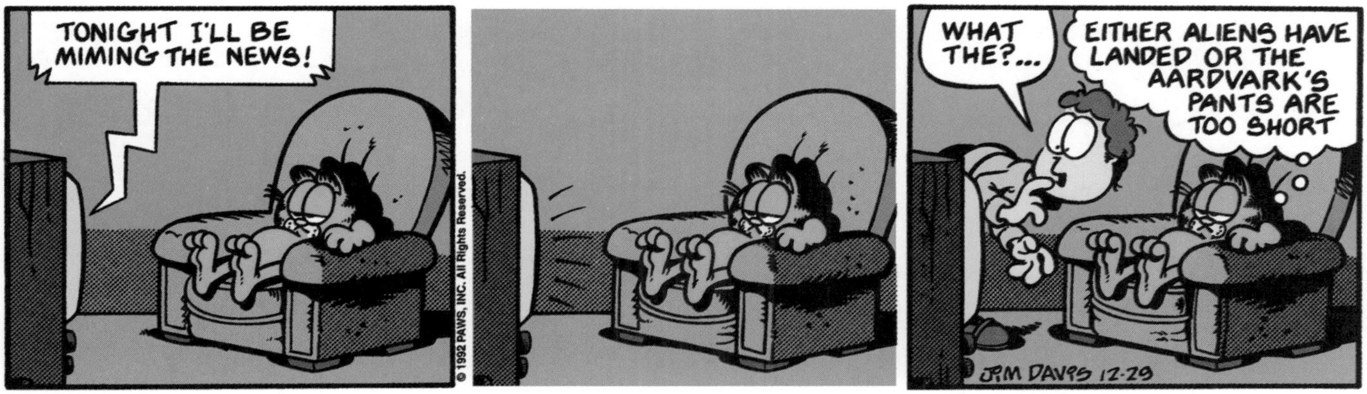
TONIGHT I'LL BE MIMING THE NEWS!
© 1992 PAWS, INC. All Rights Reserved.
WHAT THE?...
EITHER ALIENS HAVE LANDED OR THE AARDVARK'S PANTS ARE TOO SHORT
JIM DAVIS 12-29

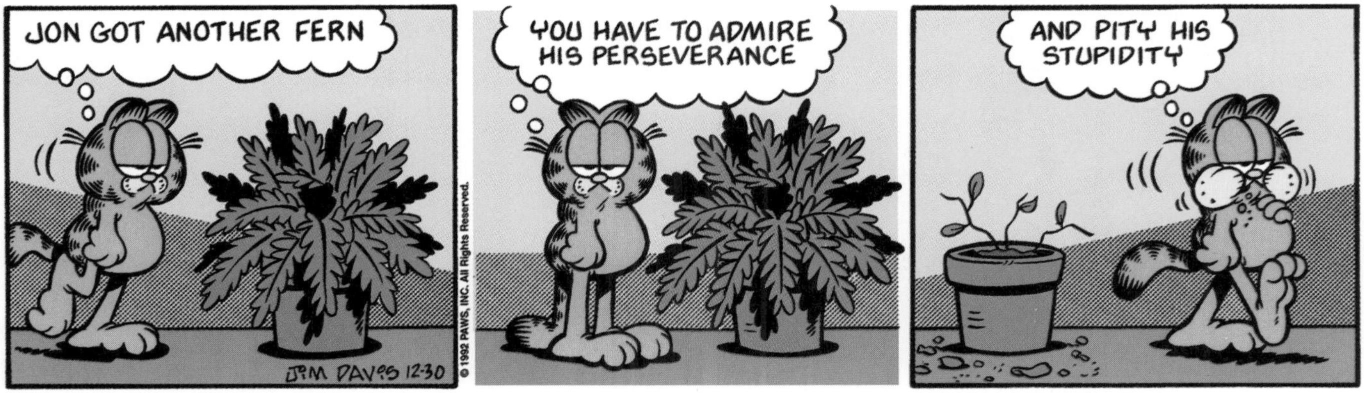
JON GOT ANOTHER FERN
JIM DAVIS 12-30
© 1992 PAWS, INC. All Rights Reserved.
YOU HAVE TO ADMIRE HIS PERSEVERANCE
AND PITY HIS STUPIDITY

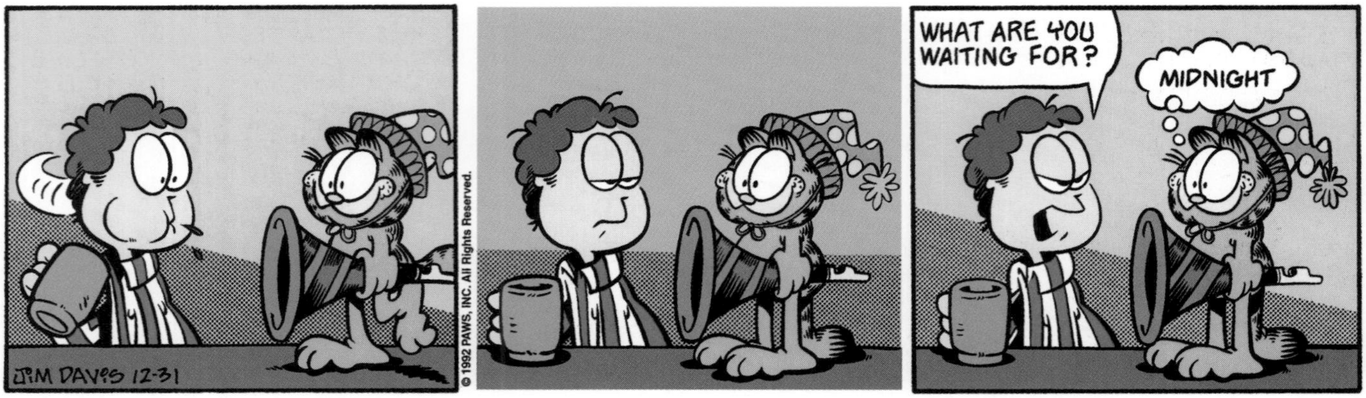
JIM DAVIS 12-31
© 1992 PAWS, INC. All Rights Reserved.
WHAT ARE YOU WAITING FOR?
MIDNIGHT

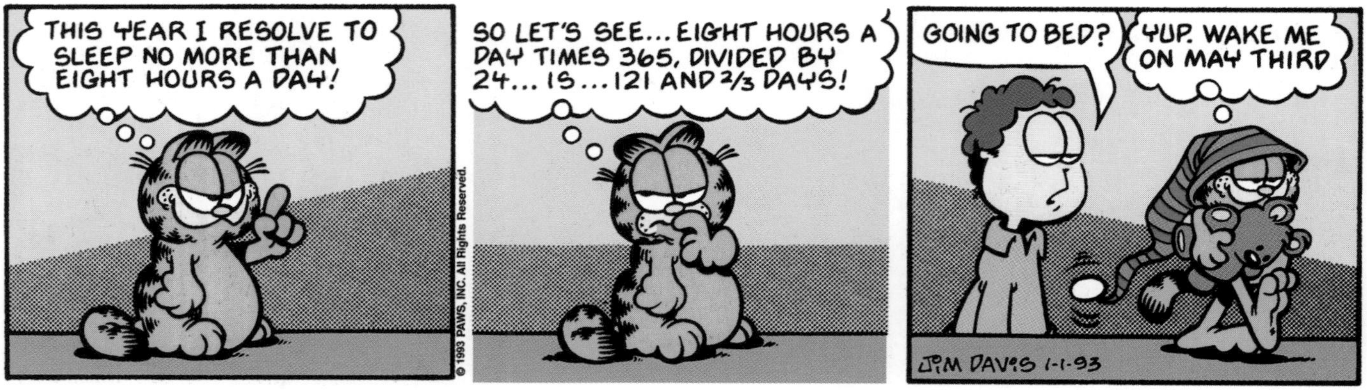
THIS YEAR I RESOLVE TO SLEEP NO MORE THAN EIGHT HOURS A DAY!
© 1993 PAWS, INC. All Rights Reserved.
SO LET'S SEE... EIGHT HOURS A DAY TIMES 365, DIVIDED BY 24... IS... 121 AND 2/3 DAYS!
GOING TO BED?
YUP. WAKE ME ON MAY THIRD
JIM DAVIS 1-1-93

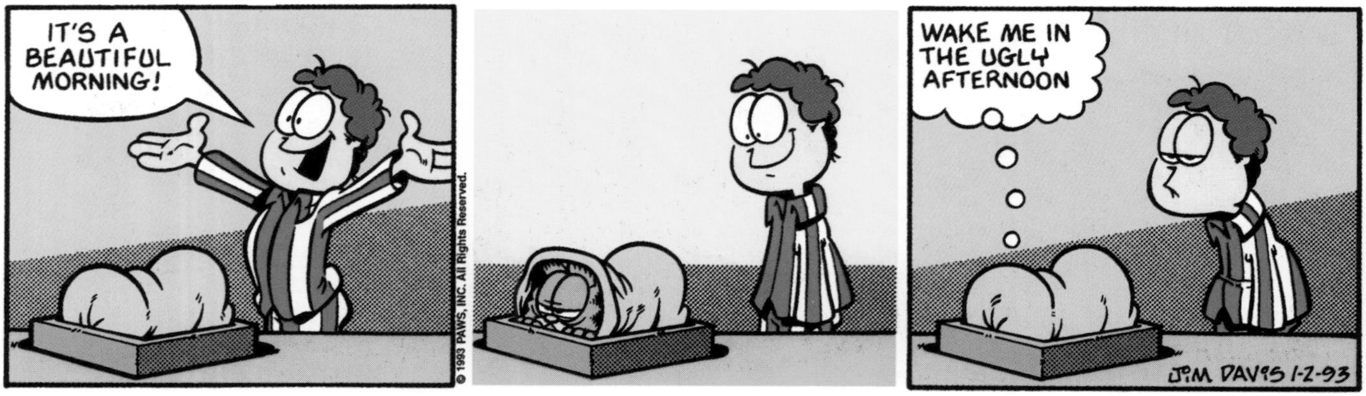
IT'S A BEAUTIFUL MORNING!
© 1993 PAWS, INC. All Rights Reserved.
WAKE ME IN THE UGLY AFTERNOON
JIM DAVIS 1-2-93

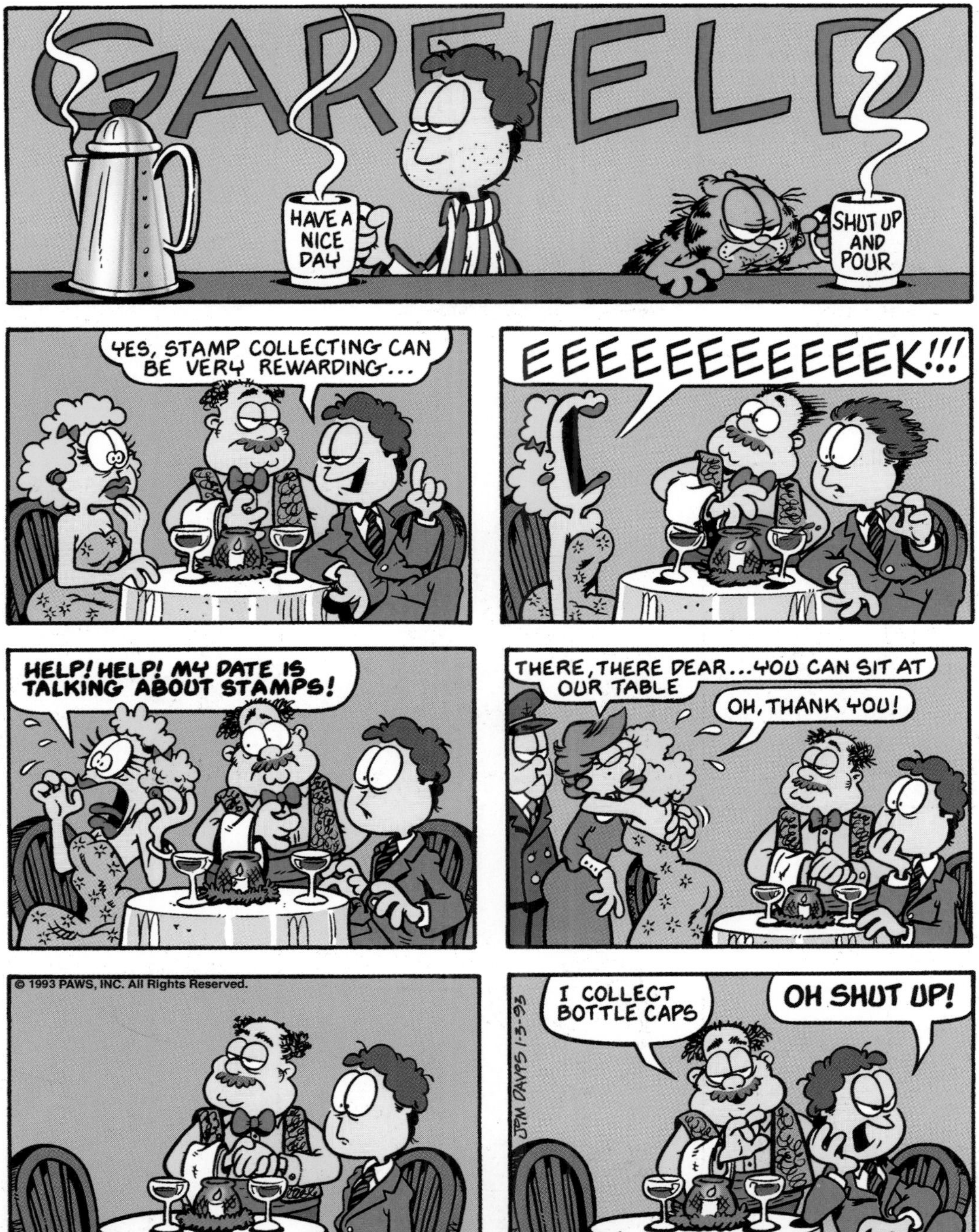
GARFIELD
HAVE A NICE DAY
SHUT UP AND POUR
YES, STAMP COLLECTING CAN BE VERY REWARDING...
EEEEEEEEEEEEK!!!
HELP! HELP! MY DATE IS TALKING ABOUT STAMPS!
THERE, THERE DEAR...YOU CAN SIT AT OUR TABLE
OH, THANK YOU!
© 1993 PAWS, INC. All Rights Reserved.
JIM DAVIS 1-3-93
I COLLECT BOTTLE CAPS
OH SHUT UP!

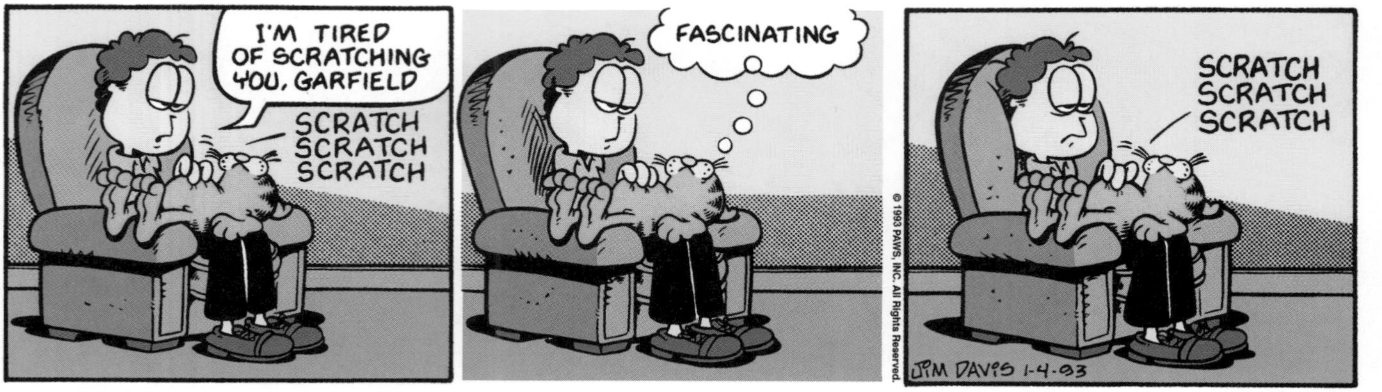
I'M TIRED OF SCRATCHING YOU, GARFIELD
SCRATCH SCRATCH SCRATCH
FASCINATING
SCRATCH SCRATCH SCRATCH
© 1993 PAWS, INC. All Rights Reserved.
JIM DAVIS 1-4-93

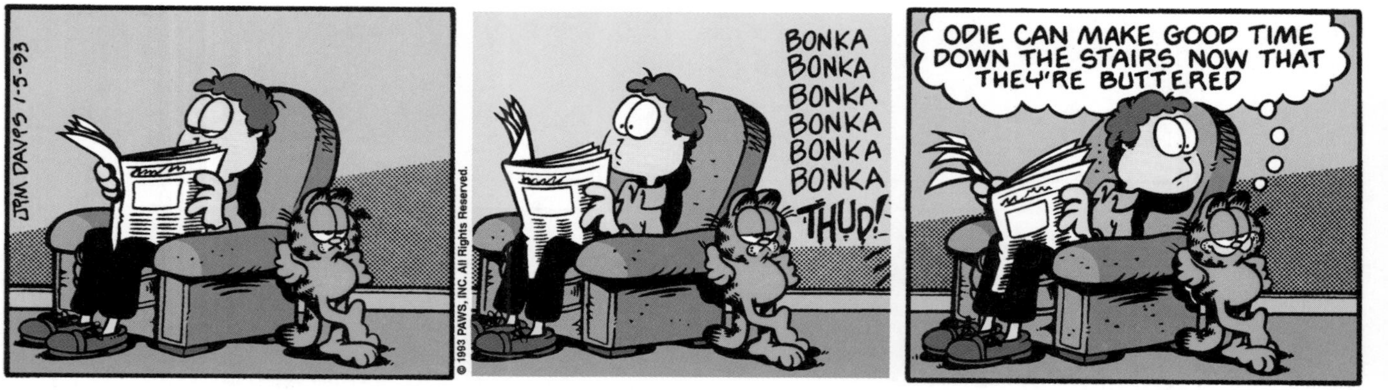
JIM DAVIS 1-5-93
© 1993 PAWS, INC. All Rights Reserved.
BONKA BONKA BONKA BONKA BONKA BONKA
THUD!
ODIE CAN MAKE GOOD TIME DOWN THE STAIRS NOW THAT THEY'RE BUTTERED

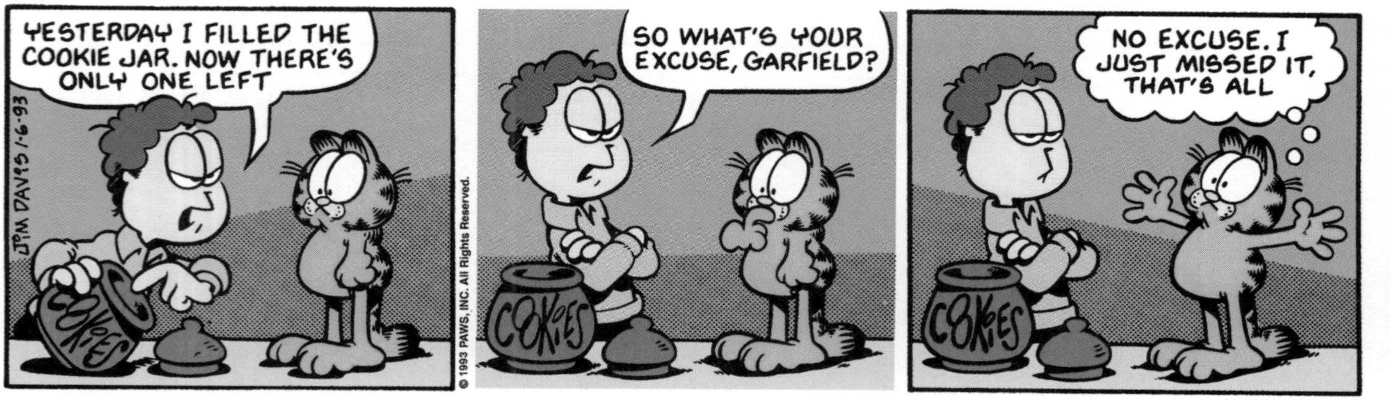
YESTERDAY I FILLED THE COOKIE JAR. NOW THERE'S ONLY ONE LEFT
JIM DAVIS 1-6-93
COOKIES
© 1993 PAWS, INC. All Rights Reserved.
SO WHAT'S YOUR EXCUSE, GARFIELD?
COOKIES
NO EXCUSE. I JUST MISSED IT, THAT'S ALL
COOKIES

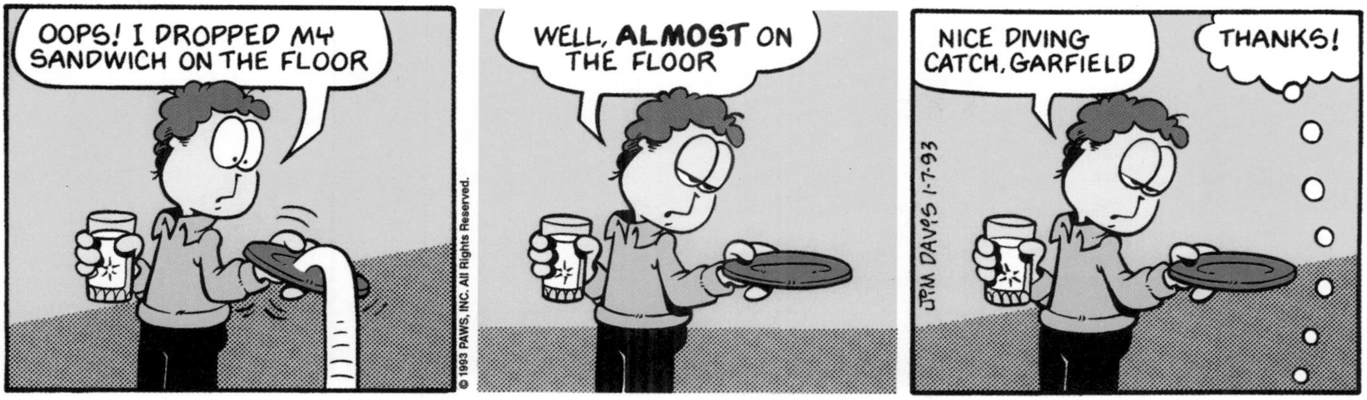
OOPS! I DROPPED MY SANDWICH ON THE FLOOR
© 1993 PAWS, INC. All Rights Reserved.
WELL, ALMOST ON THE FLOOR
NICE DIVING CATCH, GARFIELD
THANKS!
JIM DAVIS 1-7-93

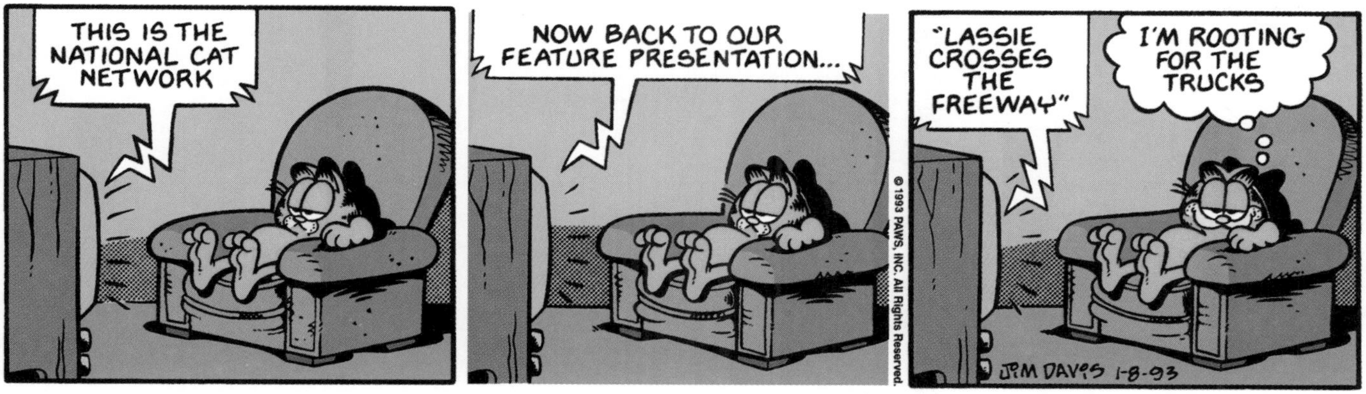
THIS IS THE NATIONAL CAT NETWORK
NOW BACK TO OUR FEATURE PRESENTATION...
© 1993 PAWS, INC. All Rights Reserved.
"LASSIE CROSSES THE FREEWAY"
I'M ROOTING FOR THE TRUCKS
JIM DAVIS 1-8-93

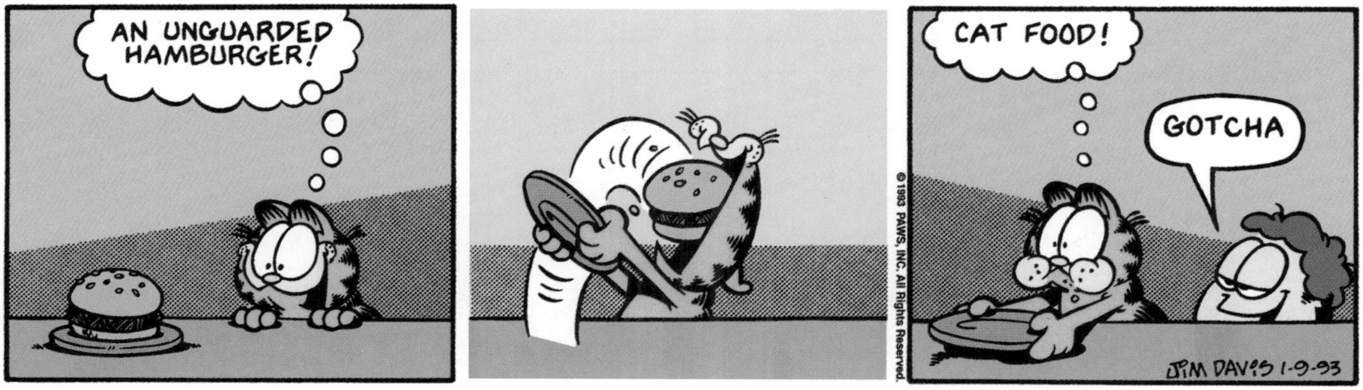
AN UNGUARDED HAMBURGER!
© 1993 PAWS, INC. All Rights Reserved.
CAT FOOD!
GOTCHA
JIM DAVIS 1-9-93

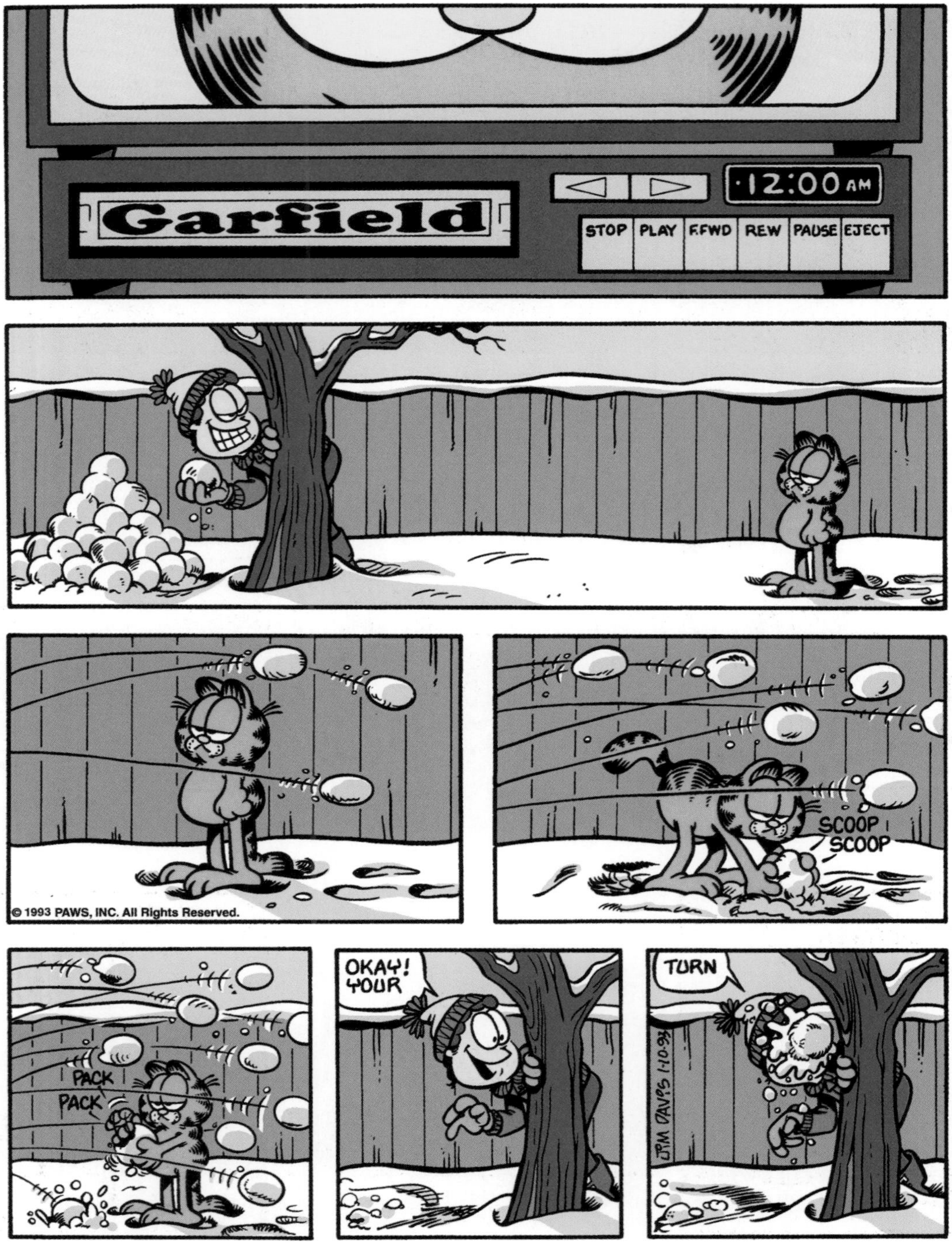
Garfield
STOP
PLAY
F.FWD
REW
PAUSE
EJECT
·12:00 AM
SCOOP
SCOOP
PACK
PACK
OKAY! YOUR
TURN

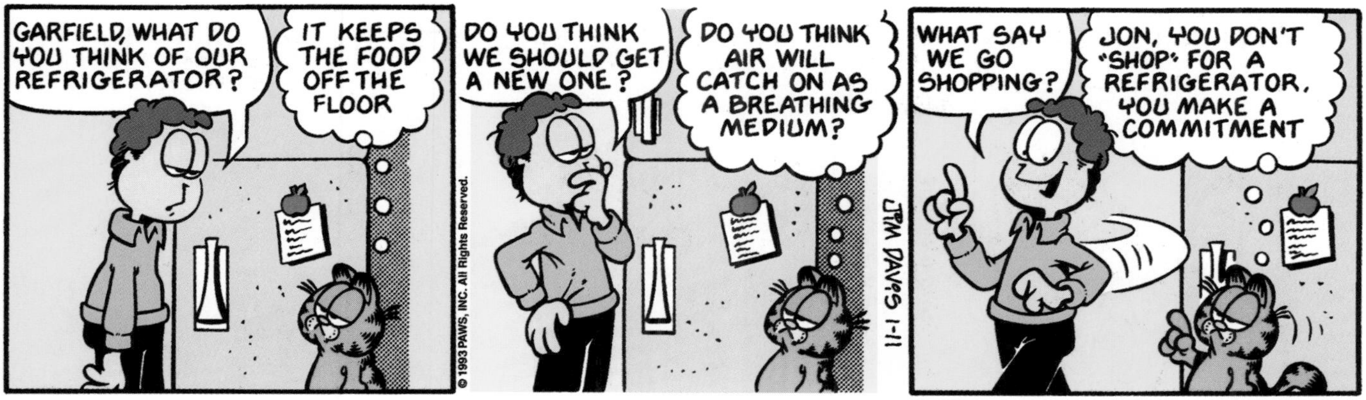
GARFIELD, WHAT DO YOU THINK OF OUR REFRIGERATOR?
IT KEEPS THE FOOD OFF THE FLOOR
DO YOU THINK WE SHOULD GET A NEW ONE?
DO YOU THINK AIR WILL CATCH ON AS A BREATHING MEDIUM?
WHAT SAY WE GO SHOPPING?
JON, YOU DON'T "SHOP" FOR A REFRIGERATOR, YOU MAKE A COMMITMENT
© 1993 PAWS, INC. All Rights Reserved.
JIM DAVIS 1-11

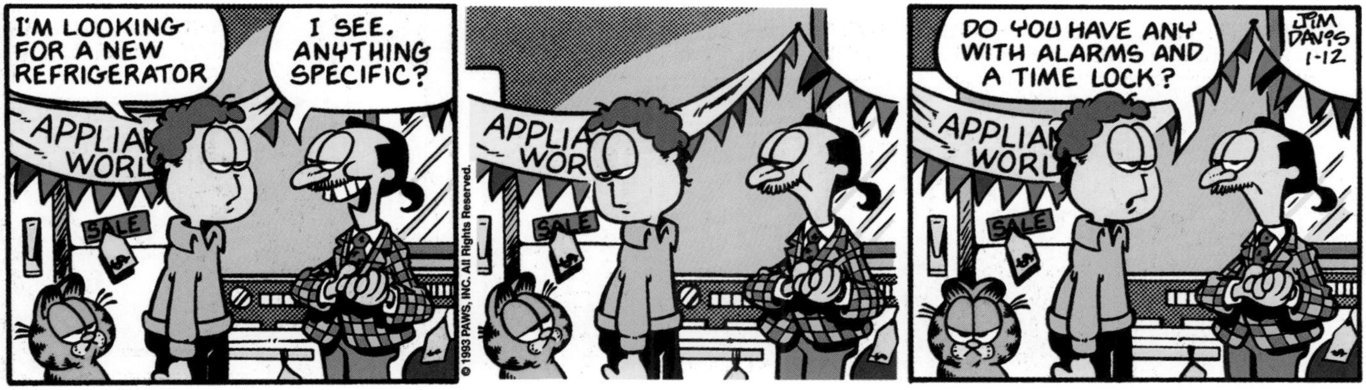
I'M LOOKING FOR A NEW REFRIGERATOR
I SEE. ANYTHING SPECIFIC?
DO YOU HAVE ANY WITH ALARMS AND A TIME LOCK?
© 1993 PAWS, INC. All Rights Reserved.
JIM DAVIS 1-12

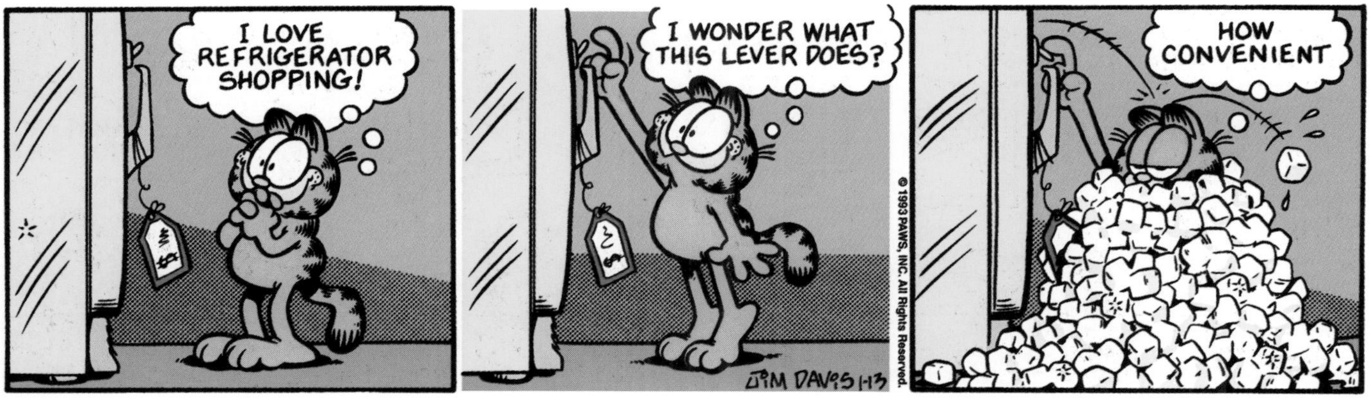
I LOVE REFRIGERATOR SHOPPING!
I WONDER WHAT THIS LEVER DOES?
HOW CONVENIENT
© 1993 PAWS, INC. All Rights Reserved.
JIM DAVIS 1-13

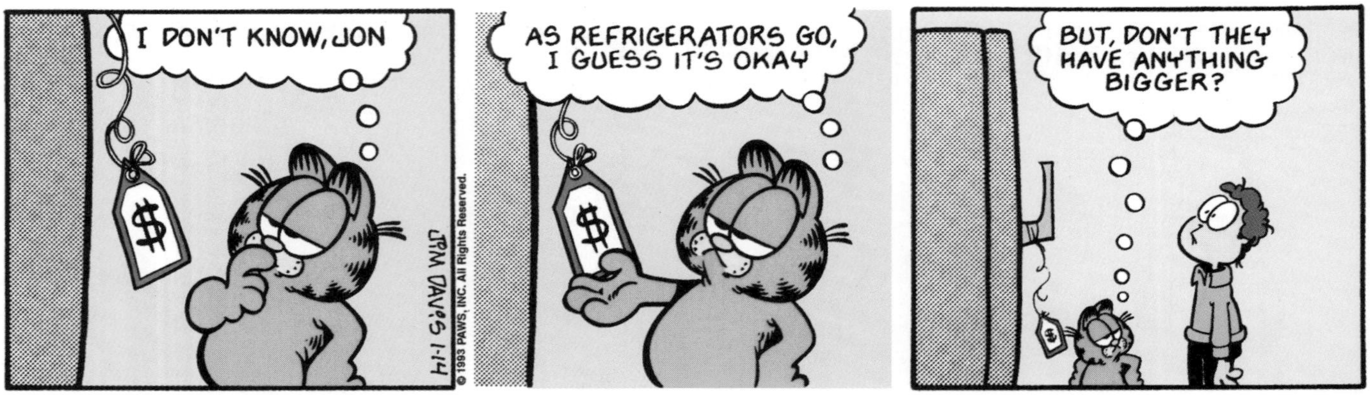
I DON'T KNOW, JON
JIM DAVIS 1-14
© 1993 PAWS, INC. All Rights Reserved.
AS REFRIGERATORS GO, I GUESS IT'S OKAY
BUT, DON'T THEY HAVE ANYTHING BIGGER?

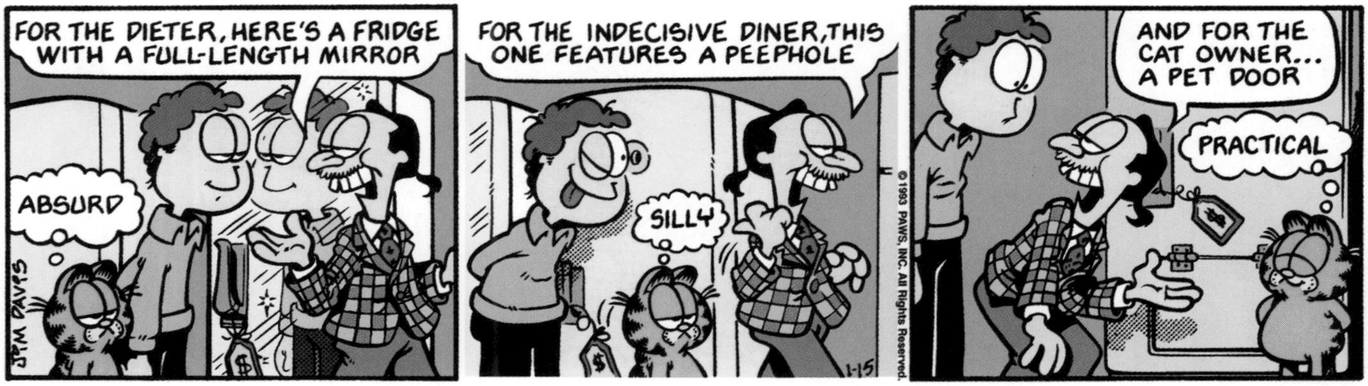
FOR THE DIETER, HERE'S A FRIDGE WITH A FULL-LENGTH MIRROR
ABSURD
JIM DAVIS
FOR THE INDECISIVE DINER, THIS ONE FEATURES A PEEPHOLE
SILLY
1-15
© 1993 PAWS, INC. All Rights Reserved.
AND FOR THE CAT OWNER... A PET DOOR
PRACTICAL

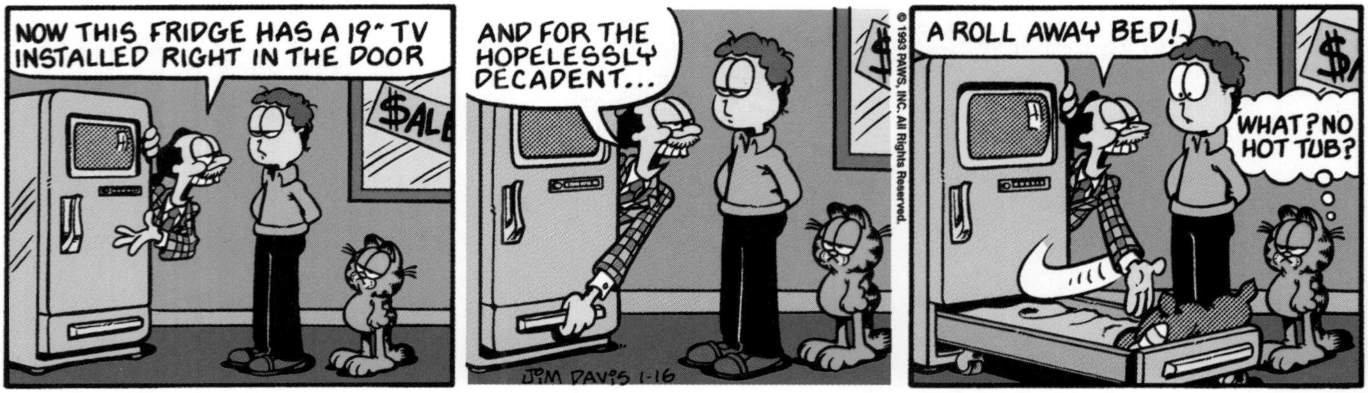
NOW THIS FRIDGE HAS A 19" TV INSTALLED RIGHT IN THE DOOR
AND FOR THE HOPELESSLY DECADENT...
JIM DAVIS 1-16
© 1993 PAWS, INC. All Rights Reserved.
A ROLL AWAY BED!
WHAT? NO HOT TUB?

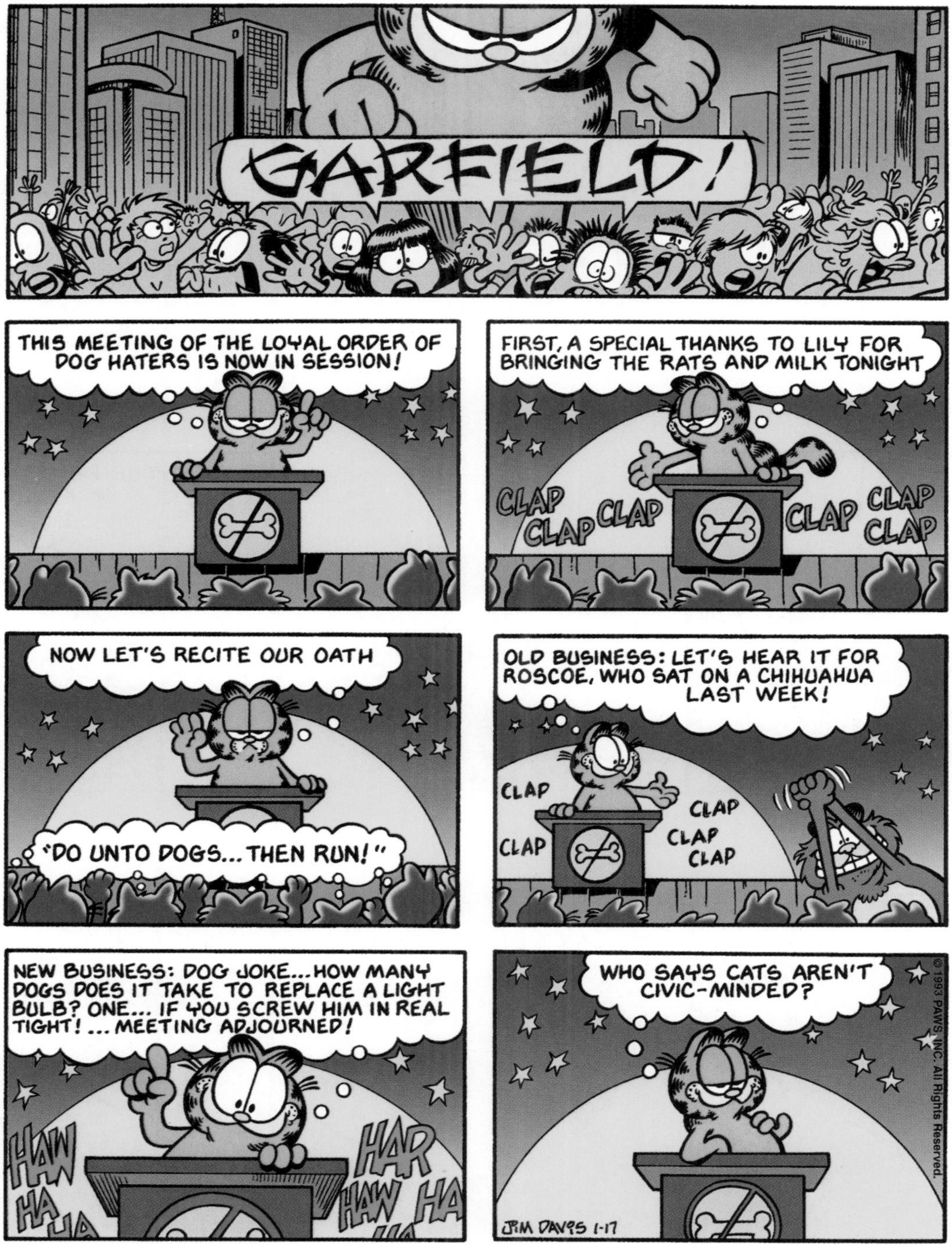
GARFIELD!
THIS MEETING OF THE LOYAL ORDER OF DOG HATERS IS NOW IN SESSION!
FIRST, A SPECIAL THANKS TO LILY FOR BRINGING THE RATS AND MILK TONIGHT
CLAP CLAP CLAP CLAP CLAP CLAP
NOW LET'S RECITE OUR OATH
"DO UNTO DOGS... THEN RUN!"
OLD BUSINESS: LET'S HEAR IT FOR ROSCOE, WHO SAT ON A CHIHUAHUA LAST WEEK!
CLAP CLAP CLAP CLAP CLAP
NEW BUSINESS: DOG JOKE... HOW MANY DOGS DOES IT TAKE TO REPLACE A LIGHT BULB? ONE... IF YOU SCREW HIM IN REAL TIGHT! ... MEETING ADJOURNED!
HAW HA HAR HAW HA
WHO SAYS CATS AREN'T CIVIC-MINDED?
JIM DAVIS 1-17
© 1993 PAWS, INC. All Rights Reserved.

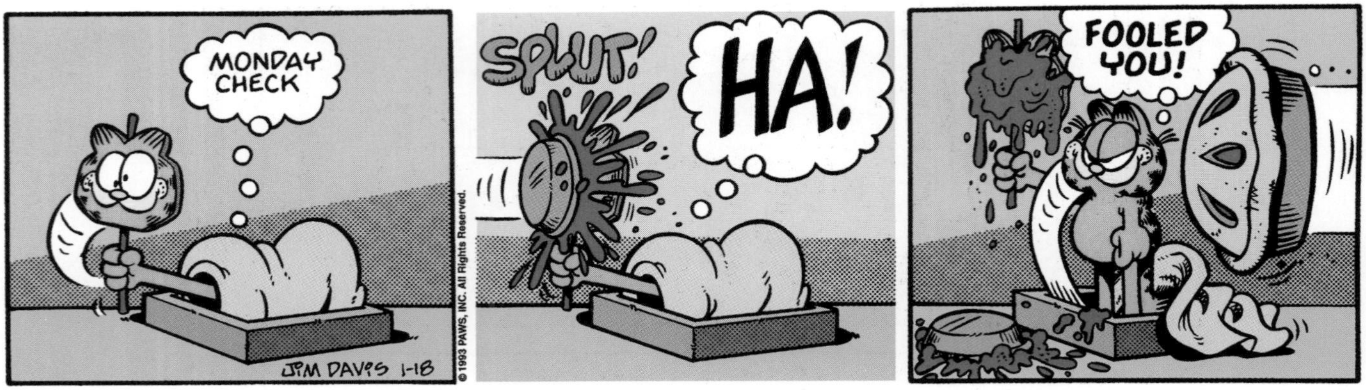
MONDAY CHECK
JIM DAVIS 1-18
© 1993 PAWS, INC. All Rights Reserved.
SPLUT!
HA!
FOOLED YOU!
...

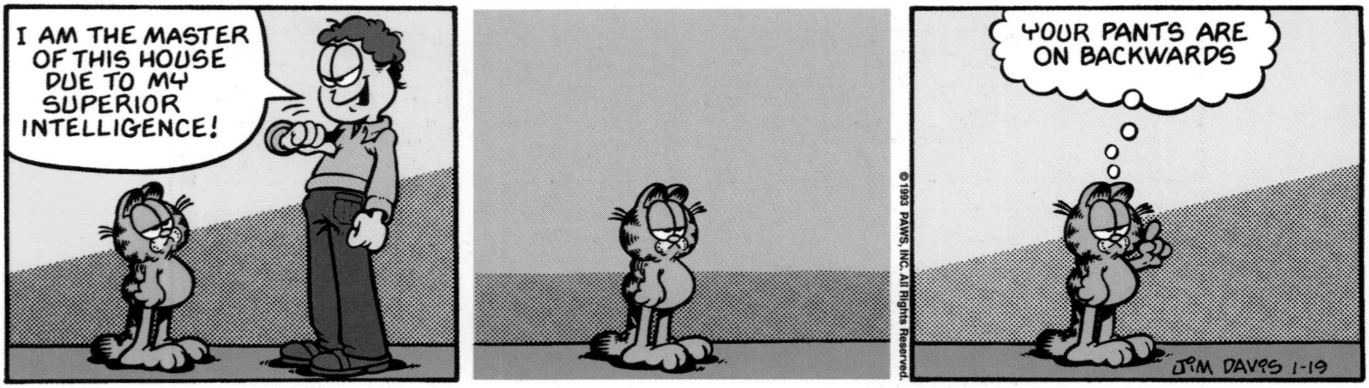
I AM THE MASTER OF THIS HOUSE DUE TO MY SUPERIOR INTELLIGENCE!
© 1993 PAWS, INC. All Rights Reserved.
YOUR PANTS ARE ON BACKWARDS
JIM DAVIS 1-19

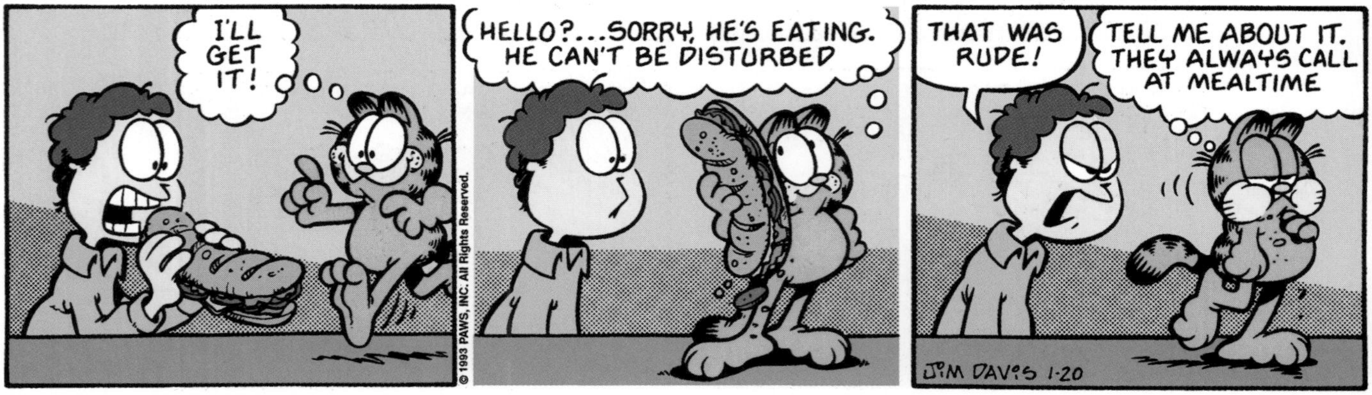
I'LL GET IT!
© 1993 PAWS, INC. All Rights Reserved.
HELLO?...SORRY, HE'S EATING. HE CAN'T BE DISTURBED
THAT WAS RUDE!
TELL ME ABOUT IT. THEY ALWAYS CALL AT MEALTIME
JIM DAVIS 1-20

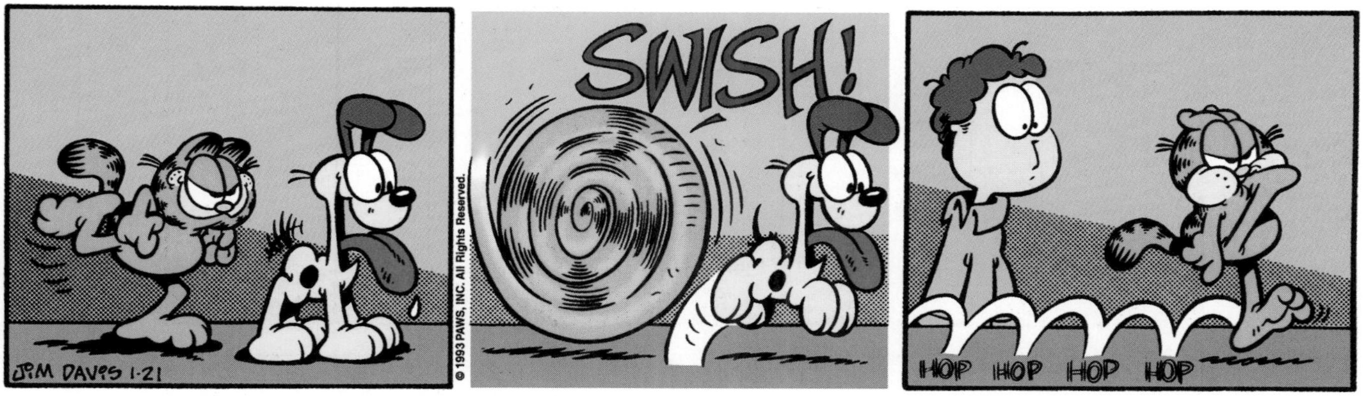
JIM DAVIS 1-21
© 1993 PAWS, INC. All Rights Reserved.
SWISH!
HOP HOP HOP HOP

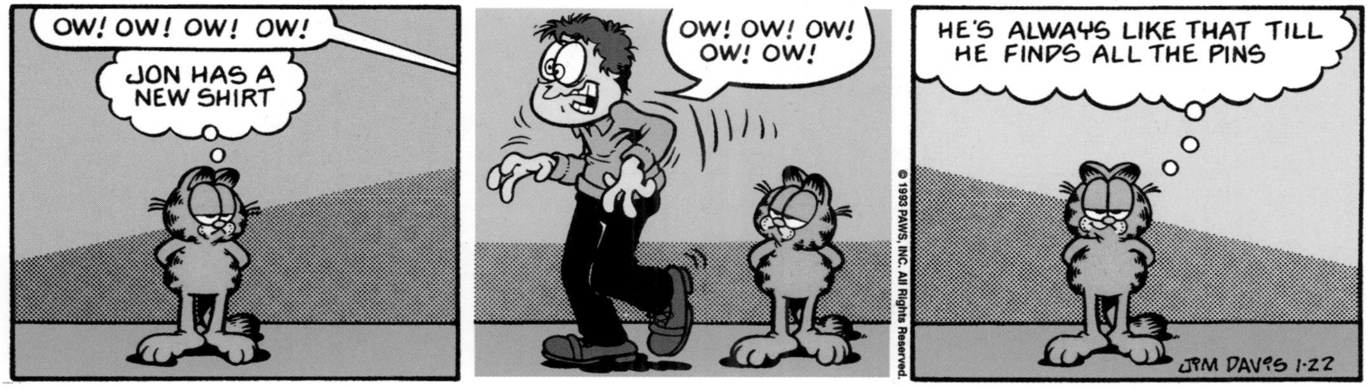
OW! OW! OW! OW!
JON HAS A NEW SHIRT
OW! OW! OW! OW! OW!
© 1993 PAWS, INC. All Rights Reserved.
HE'S ALWAYS LIKE THAT TILL HE FINDS ALL THE PINS
JIM DAVIS 1-22

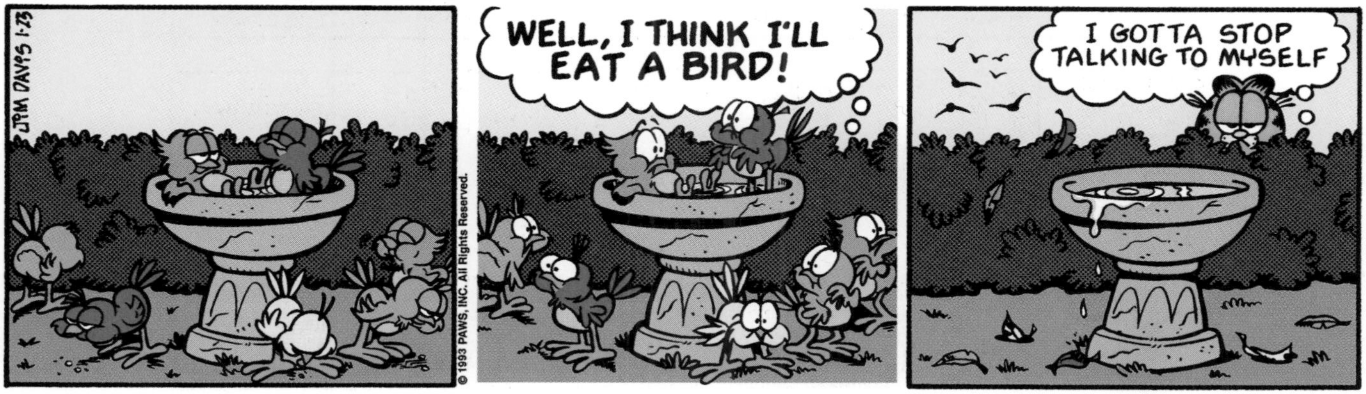
JIM DAVIS 1-23
© 1993 PAWS, INC. All Rights Reserved.
WELL, I THINK I'LL EAT A BIRD!
I GOTTA STOP TALKING TO MYSELF

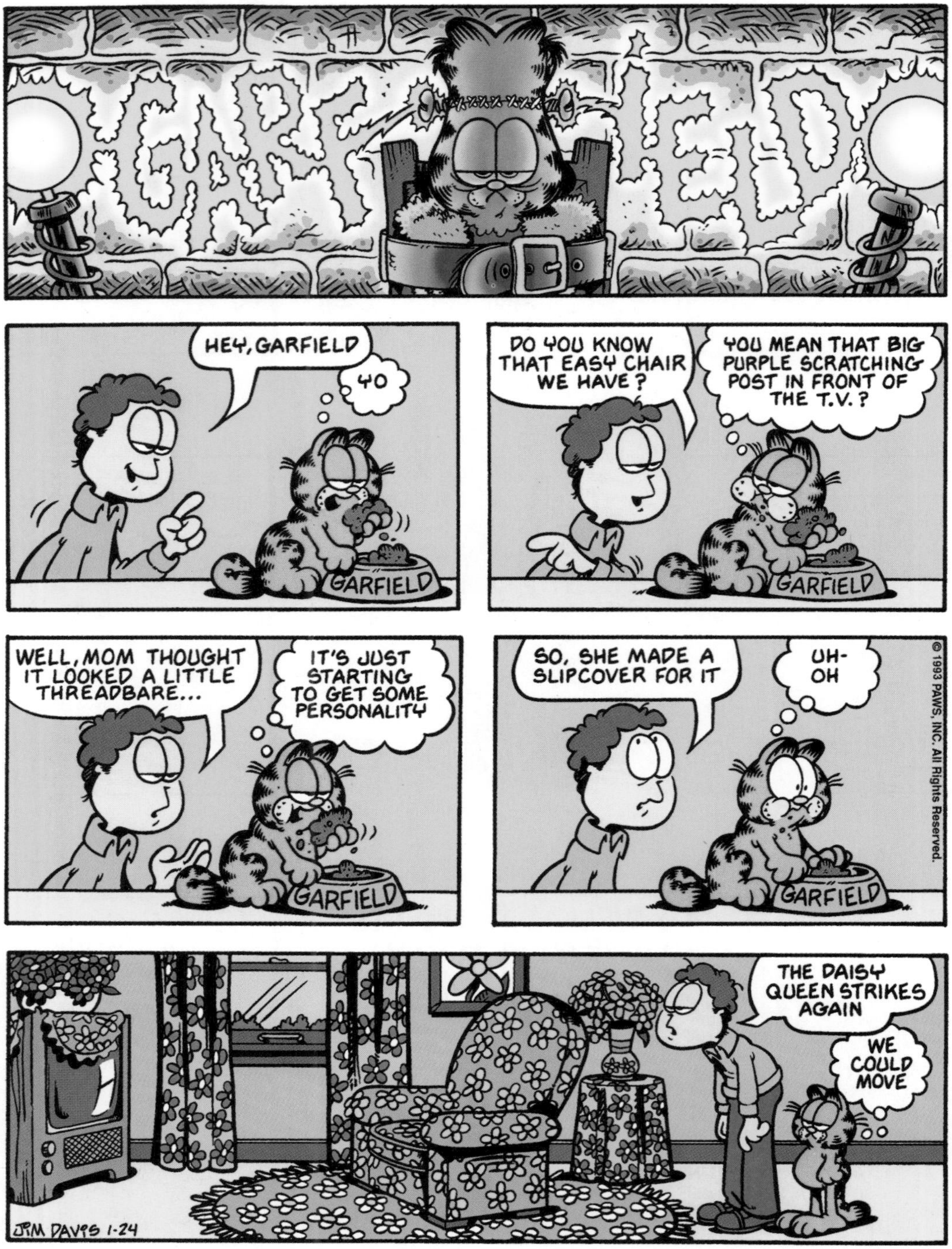
GARFIELD
HEY, GARFIELD
YO
GARFIELD
DO YOU KNOW THAT EASY CHAIR WE HAVE?
YOU MEAN THAT BIG PURPLE SCRATCHING POST IN FRONT OF THE T.V.?
GARFIELD
WELL, MOM THOUGHT IT LOOKED A LITTLE THREADBARE...
IT'S JUST STARTING TO GET SOME PERSONALITY
GARFIELD
SO, SHE MADE A SLIPCOVER FOR IT
UH-OH
GARFIELD
THE DAISY QUEEN STRIKES AGAIN
WE COULD MOVE
JIM DAVIS 1-24

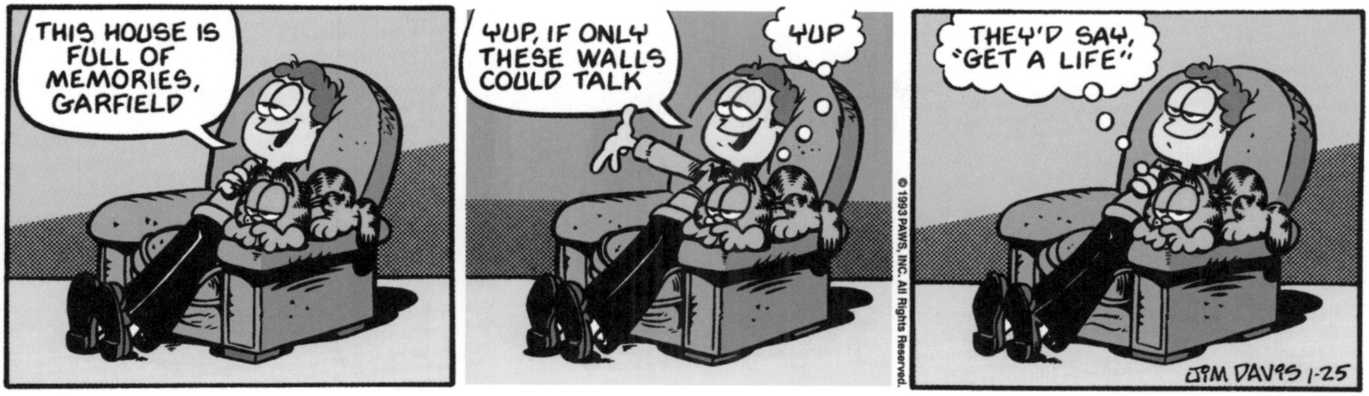
THIS HOUSE IS FULL OF MEMORIES, GARFIELD
YUP, IF ONLY THESE WALLS COULD TALK
YUP
THEY'D SAY, "GET A LIFE"
© 1993 PAWS, INC. All Rights Reserved.
JIM DAVIS 1-25

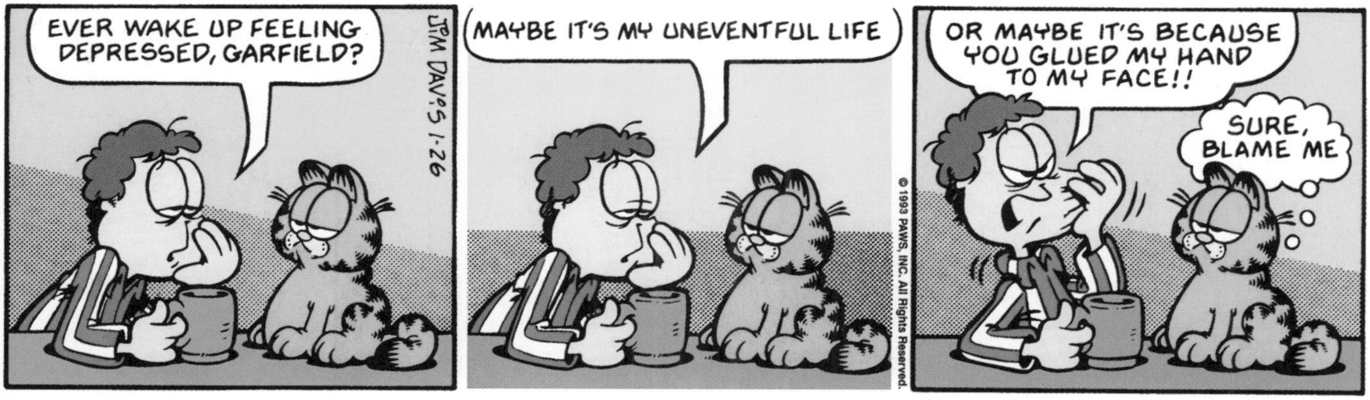
EVER WAKE UP FEELING DEPRESSED, GARFIELD?
JIM DAVIS 1-26
MAYBE IT'S MY UNEVENTFUL LIFE
OR MAYBE IT'S BECAUSE YOU GLUED MY HAND TO MY FACE!!
SURE, BLAME ME
© 1993 PAWS, INC. All Rights Reserved.

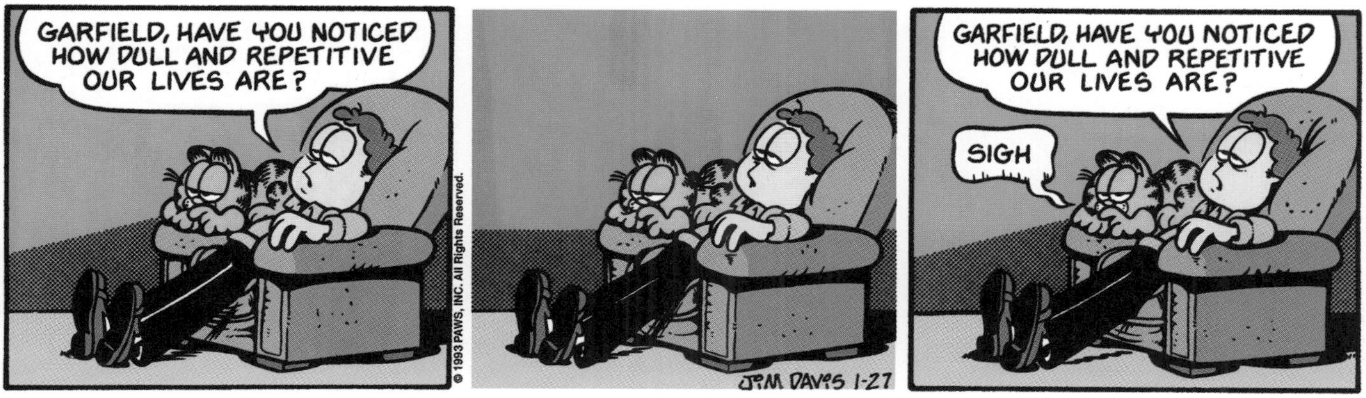
GARFIELD, HAVE YOU NOTICED HOW DULL AND REPETITIVE OUR LIVES ARE?
© 1993 PAWS, INC. All Rights Reserved.
JIM DAVIS 1-27
GARFIELD, HAVE YOU NOTICED HOW DULL AND REPETITIVE OUR LIVES ARE?
SIGH

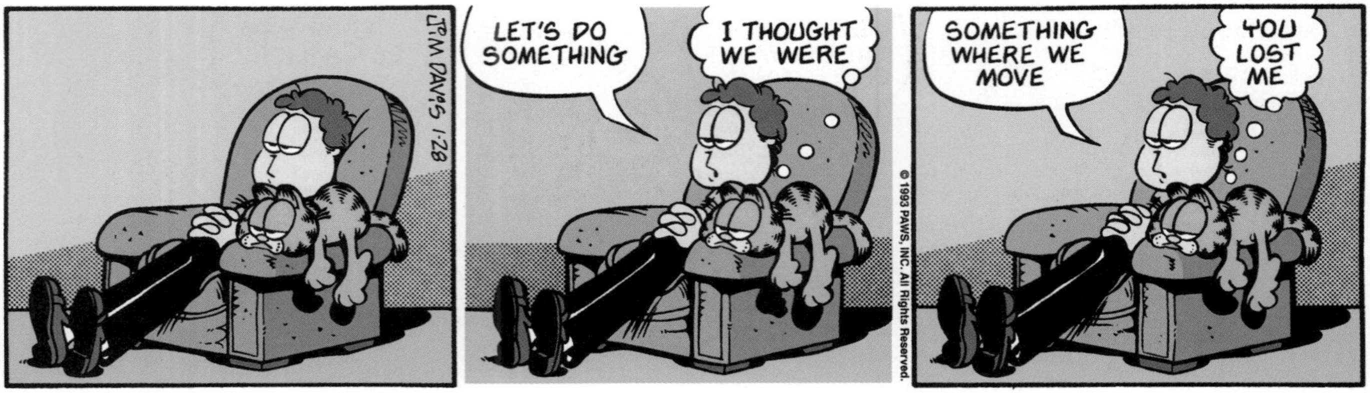
JIM DAVIS 1-28
LET'S DO SOMETHING
I THOUGHT WE WERE
SOMETHING WHERE WE MOVE
YOU LOST ME
© 1993 PAWS, INC. All Rights Reserved.

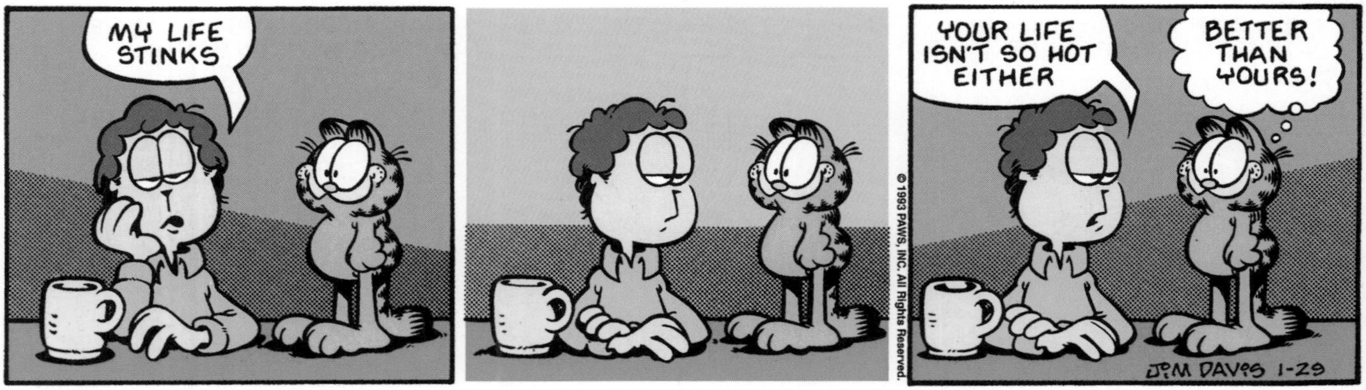
MY LIFE STINKS
YOUR LIFE ISN'T SO HOT EITHER
BETTER THAN YOURS!
© 1993 PAWS, INC. All Rights Reserved.
JIM DAVIS 1-29

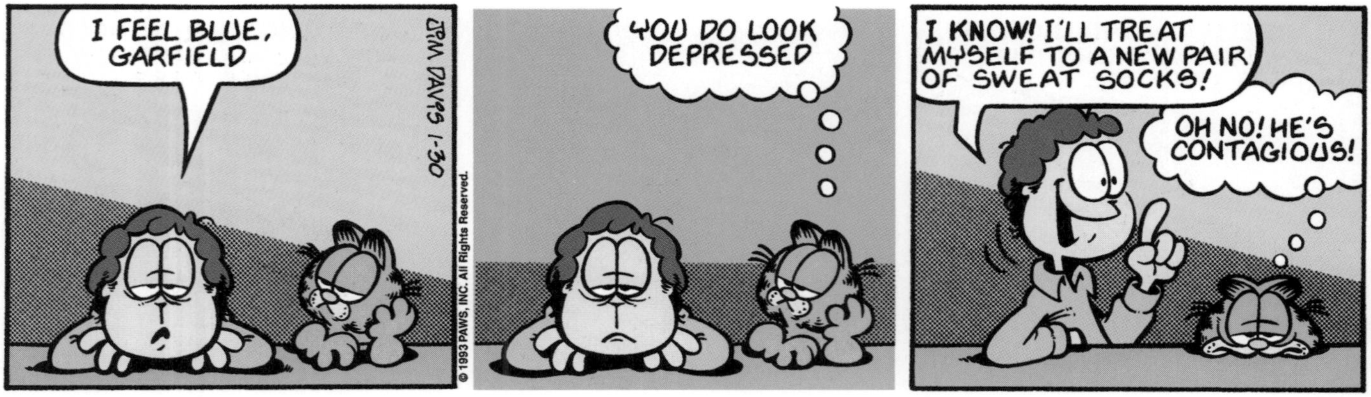
JIM DAVIS 1-30
I FEEL BLUE, GARFIELD
© 1993 PAWS, INC. All Rights Reserved.
YOU DO LOOK DEPRESSED
I KNOW! I'LL TREAT MYSELF TO A NEW PAIR OF SWEAT SOCKS!
OH NO! HE'S CONTAGIOUS!

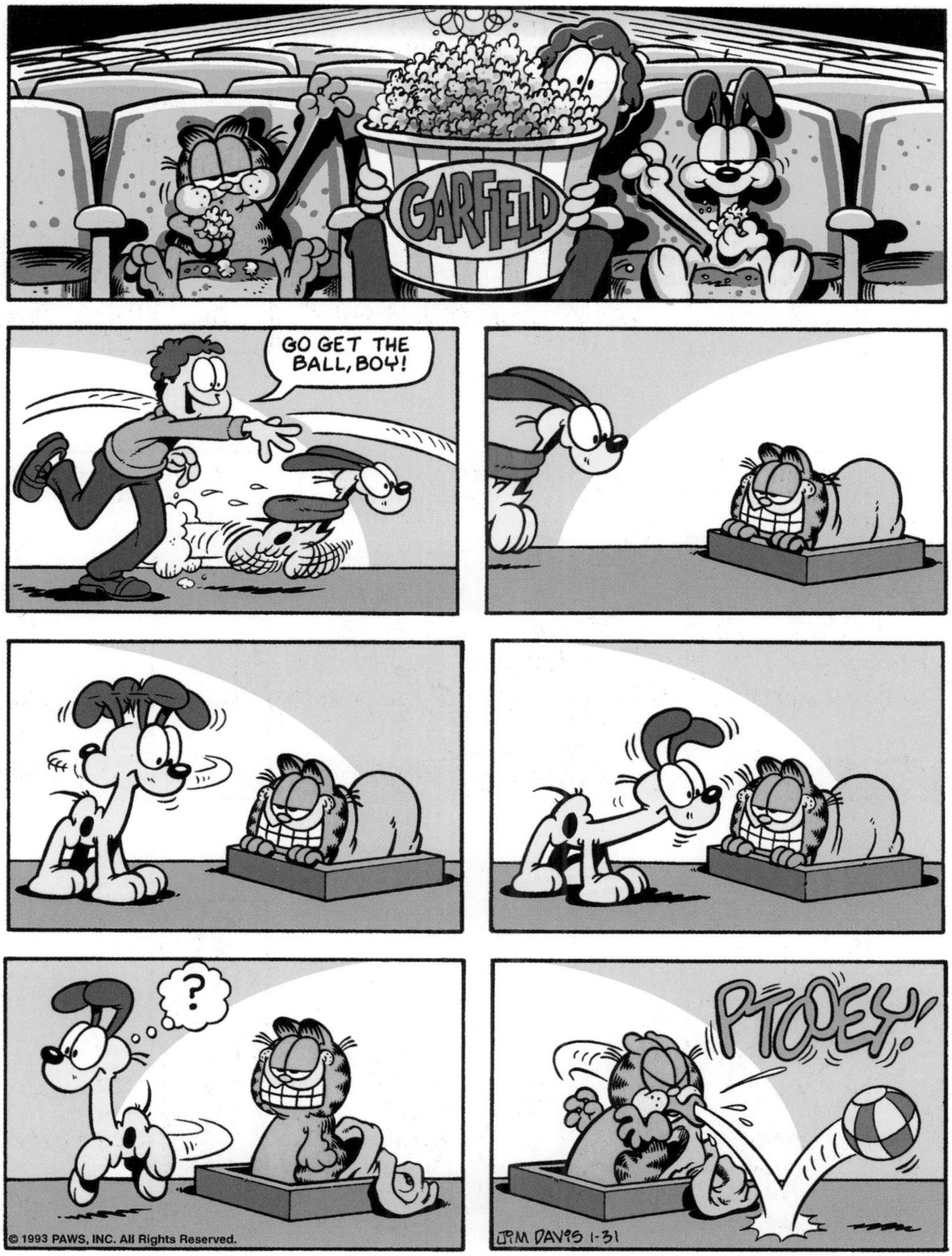
GARFIELD
GO GET THE BALL, BOY!
?
PTOOEY!
JIM DAVIS 1-31

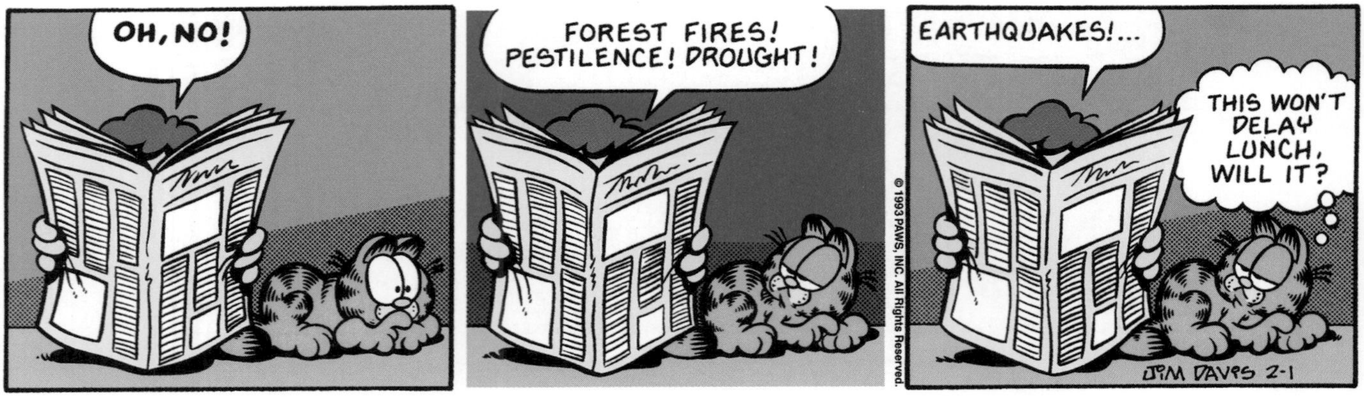
OH, NO!
FOREST FIRES! PESTILENCE! DROUGHT!
EARTHQUAKES!...
THIS WON'T DELAY LUNCH, WILL IT?
JIM DAVIS 2-1
© 1993 PAWS, INC. All Rights Reserved.

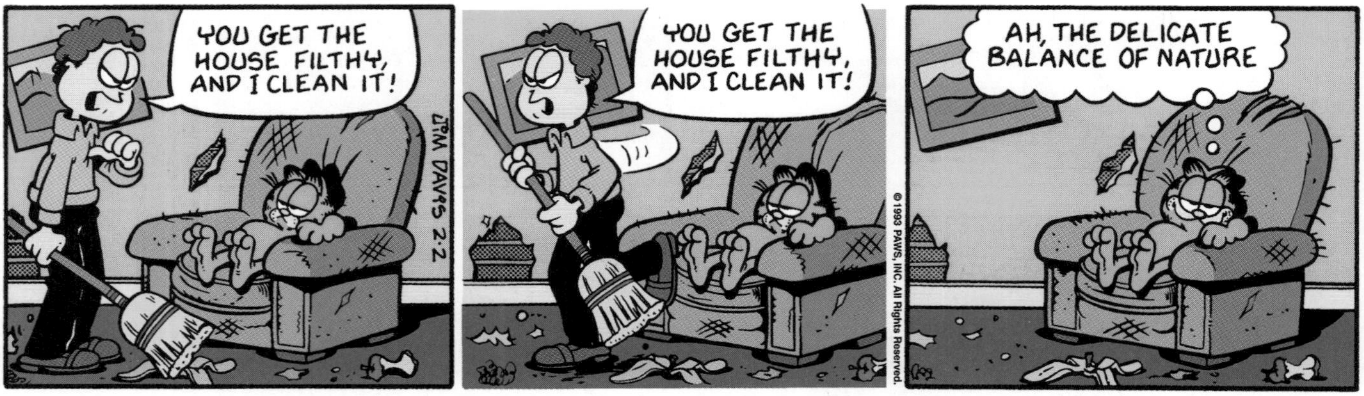
YOU GET THE HOUSE FILTHY, AND I CLEAN IT!
JIM DAVIS 2-2
YOU GET THE HOUSE FILTHY, AND I CLEAN IT!
AH, THE DELICATE BALANCE OF NATURE
© 1993 PAWS, INC. All Rights Reserved.

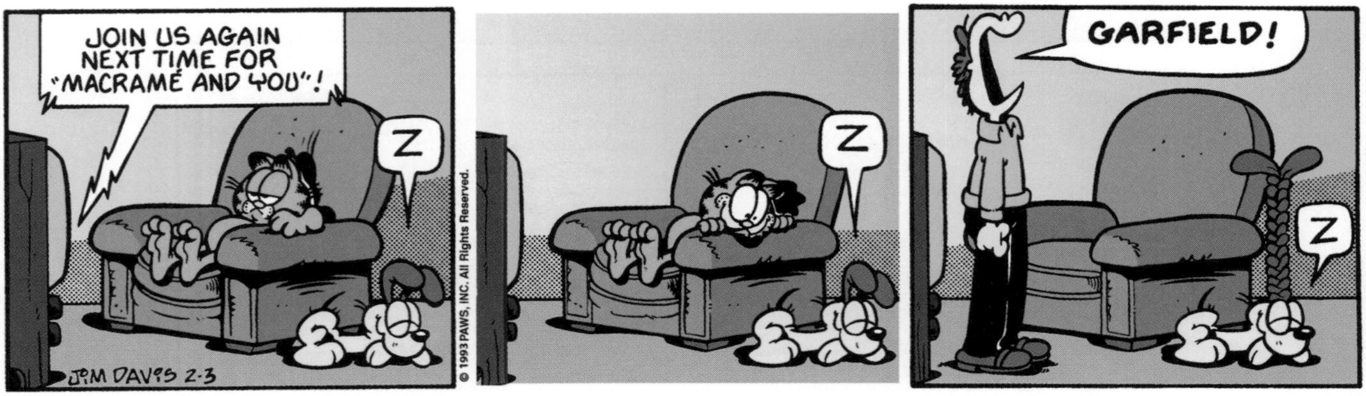
JOIN US AGAIN NEXT TIME FOR "MACRAMÉ AND YOU"!
Z
JIM DAVIS 2-3
© 1993 PAWS, INC. All Rights Reserved.
Z
GARFIELD!
Z

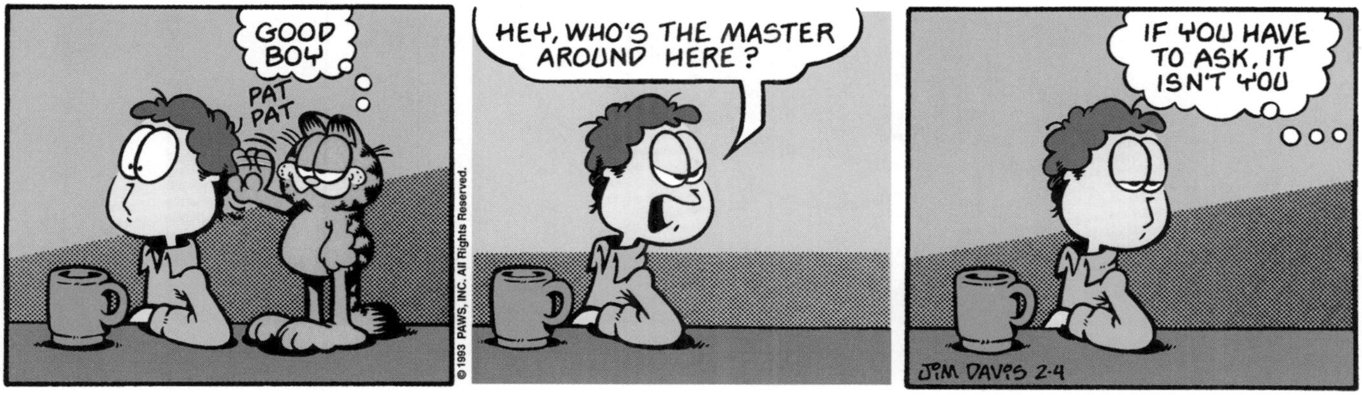
GOOD BOY
PAT PAT
© 1993 PAWS, INC. All Rights Reserved.
HEY, WHO'S THE MASTER AROUND HERE?
IF YOU HAVE TO ASK, IT ISN'T YOU
JIM DAVIS 2-4

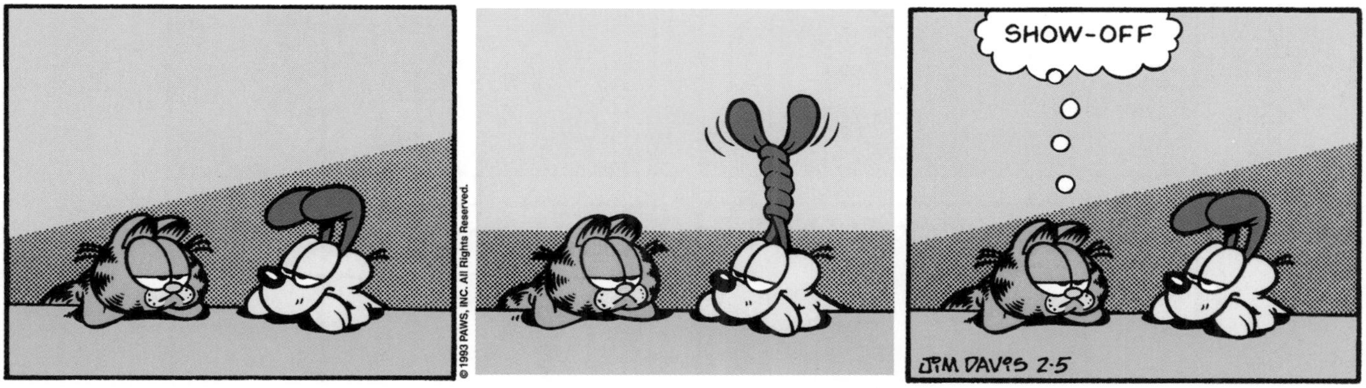
© 1993 PAWS, INC. All Rights Reserved.
SHOW-OFF
JIM DAVIS 2-5

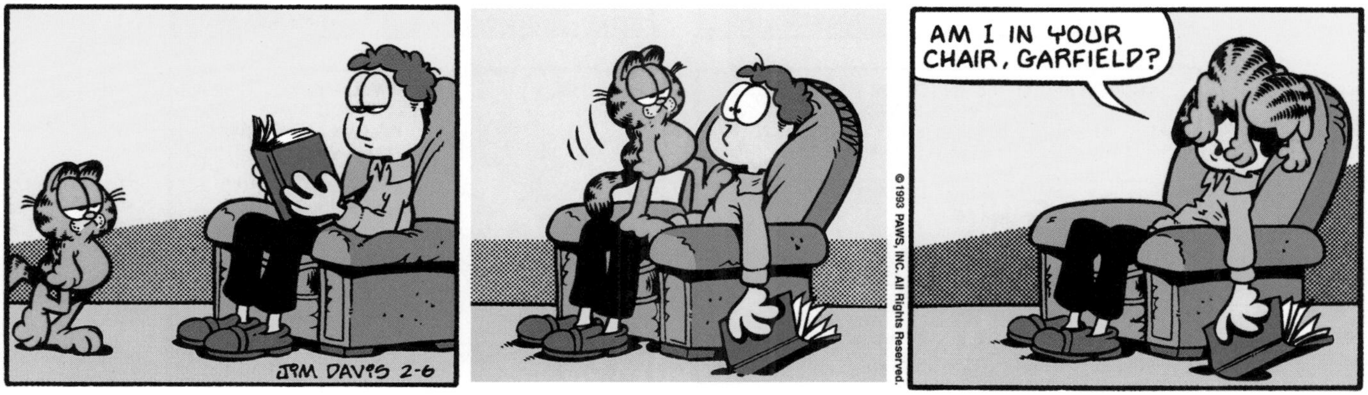
JIM DAVIS 2-6
© 1993 PAWS, INC. All Rights Reserved.
AM I IN YOUR CHAIR, GARFIELD?

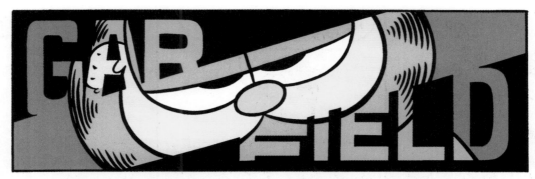

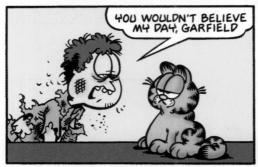

GARFIELD
YOU WOULDN'T BELIEVE MY DAY, GARFIELD
FIRST, I TRIPPED AND FELL DOWN SIX FLIGHTS OF STAIRS
© 1993 PAWS, INC. All Rights Reserved.
WHEN I LANDED, I GOT MY HEAD STUCK IN A BUCKET OF PORK CHOPS
THEN, A ROAMING PACK OF HUNGRY WOLVES MISTOOK ME FOR LUNCH...
...AND CHASED ME INTO AN OPEN ELEVATOR SHAFT, WHICH WOULDN'T HAVE BEEN SO BAD HAD IT NOT BEEN FOR THE RABID SHAFT BADGERS
AND THEN I...
HEY, MR. MOTOR MOUTH, DON'T YOU WANT TO KNOW HOW **MY** DAY WENT?
JIM DAVIS 2-7

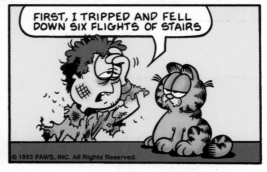

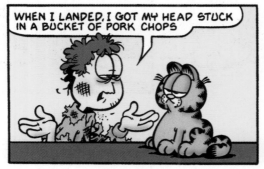

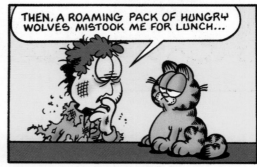

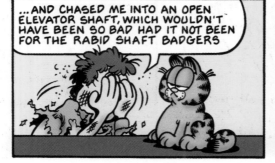

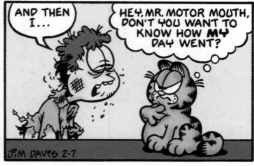

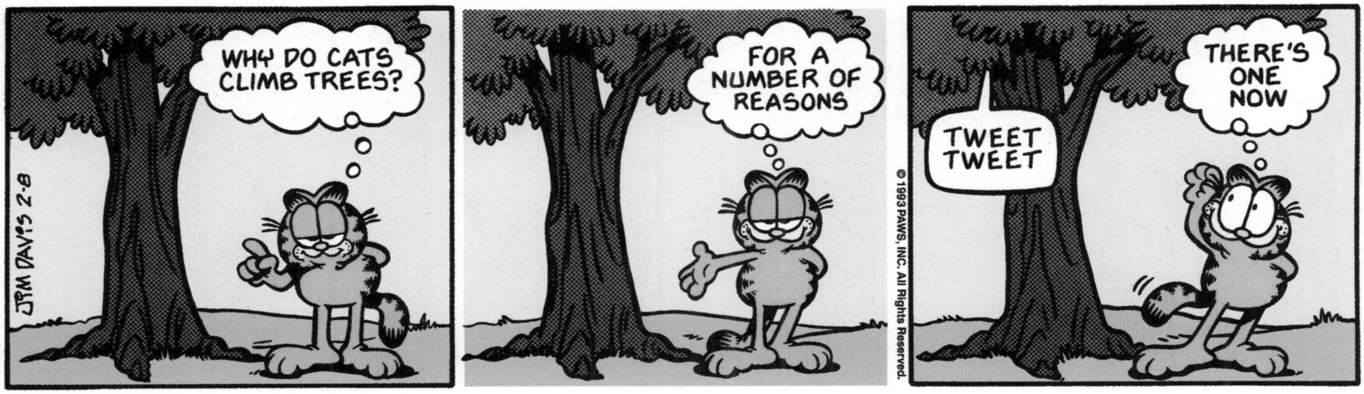
JIM DAVIS 2-8
WHY DO CATS CLIMB TREES?
FOR A NUMBER OF REASONS
© 1993 PAWS, INC. All Rights Reserved.
TWEET TWEET
THERE'S ONE NOW

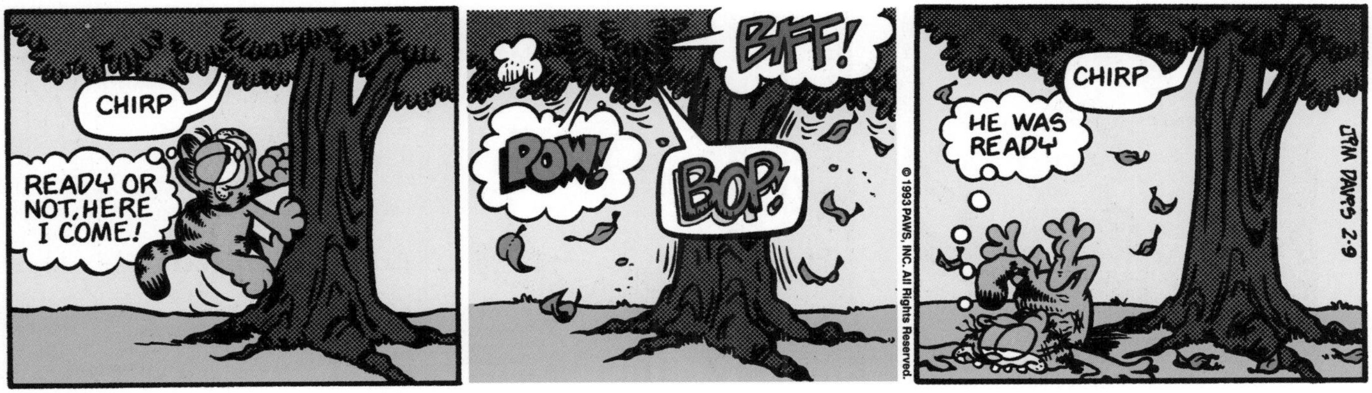
CHIRP
READY OR NOT, HERE I COME!
POW!
BOP!
BIFF!
© 1993 PAWS, INC. All Rights Reserved.
CHIRP
HE WAS READY
JIM DAVIS 2-9

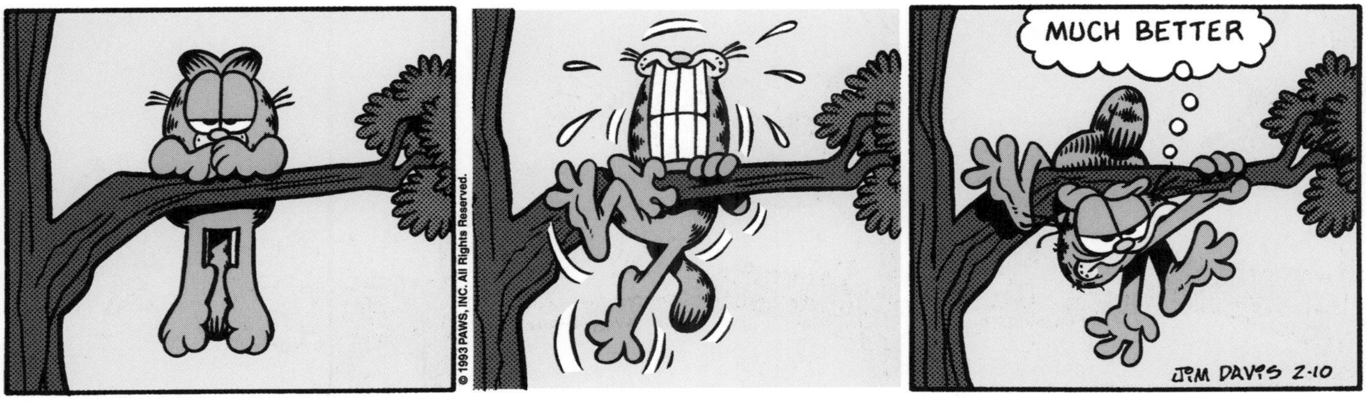
© 1993 PAWS, INC. All Rights Reserved.
MUCH BETTER
JIM DAVIS 2-10

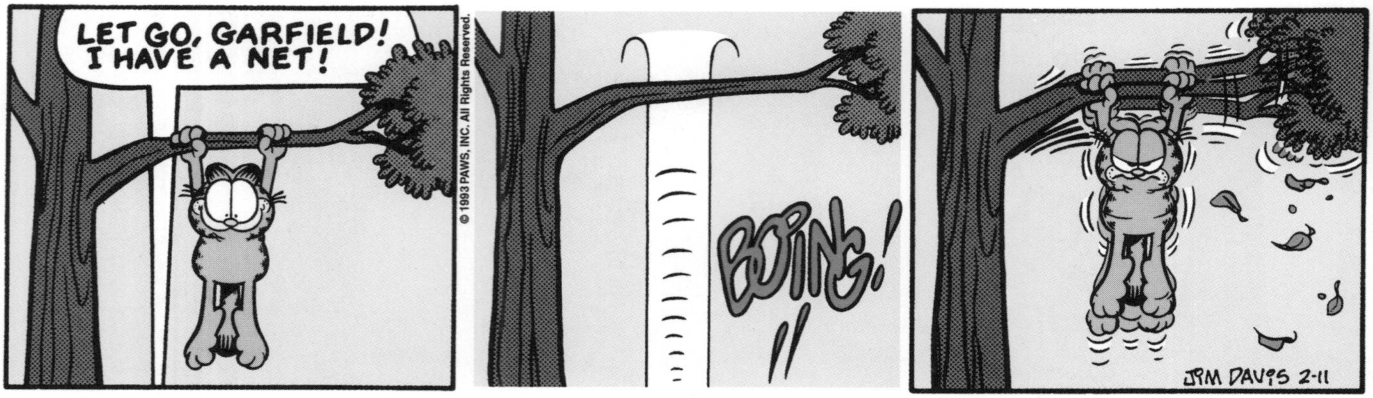
LET GO, GARFIELD! I HAVE A NET!
© 1993 PAWS, INC. All Rights Reserved.
BOING!
JIM DAVIS 2-11

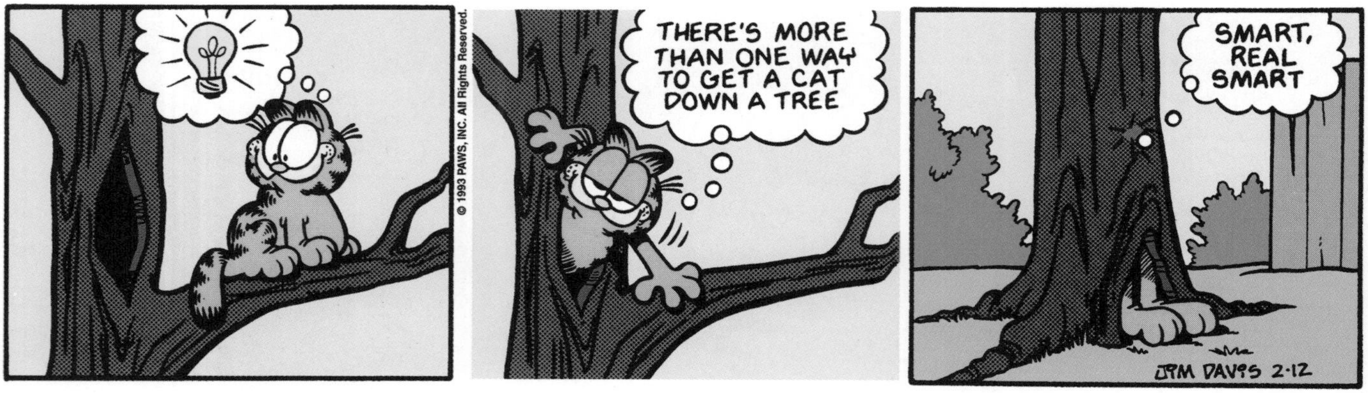
© 1993 PAWS, INC. All Rights Reserved.
THERE'S MORE THAN ONE WAY TO GET A CAT DOWN A TREE
SMART, REAL SMART
JIM DAVIS 2-12

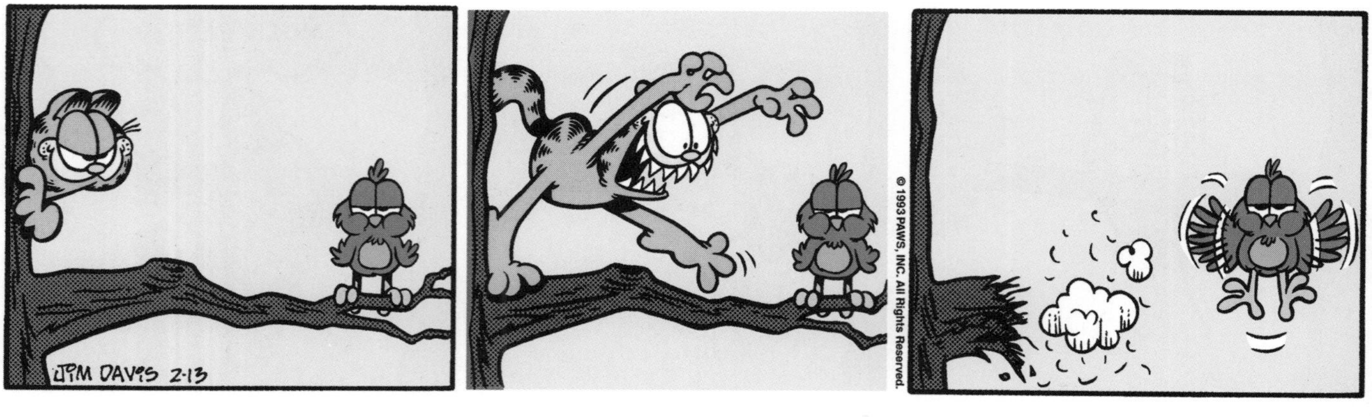
JIM DAVIS 2-13
© 1993 PAWS, INC. All Rights Reserved.

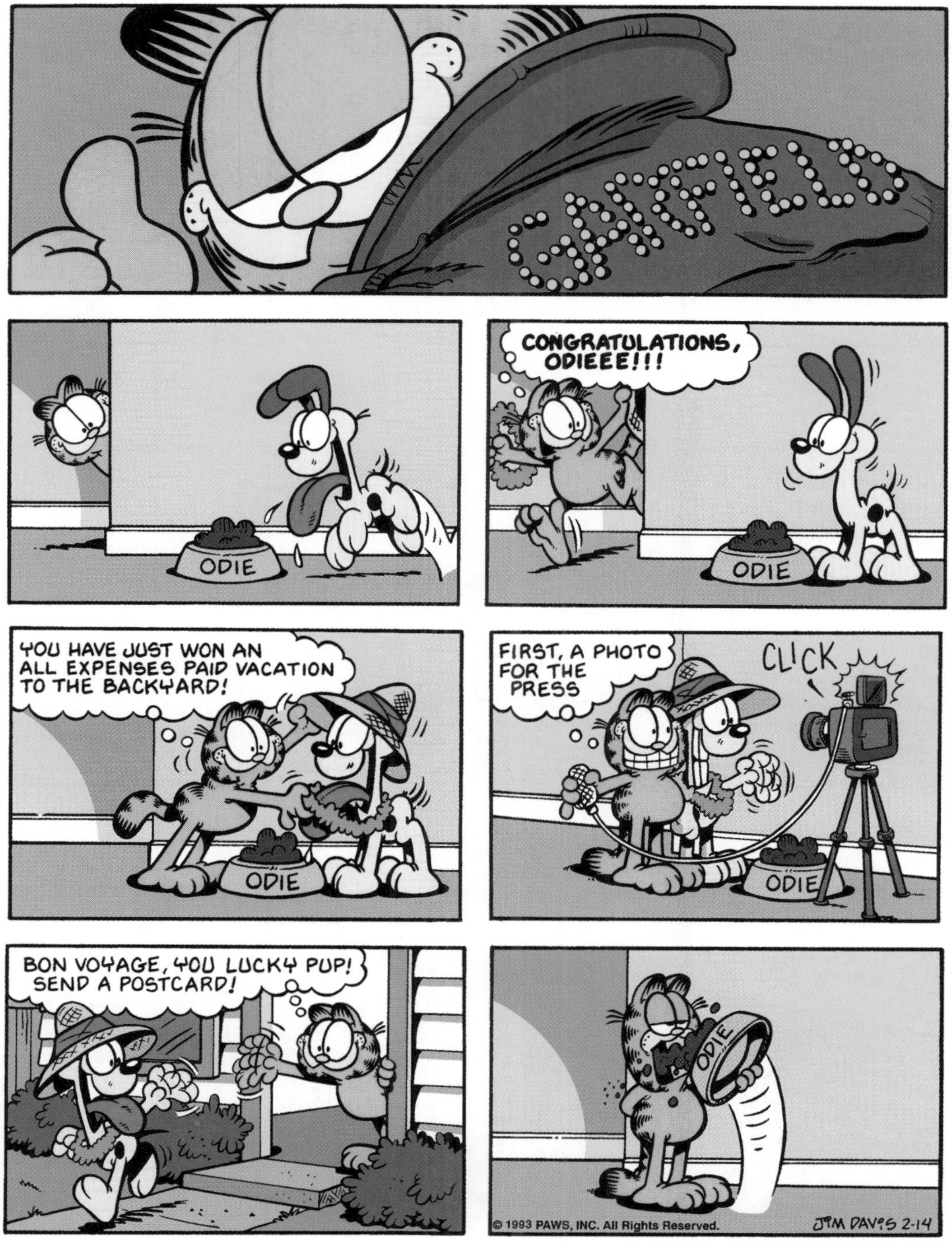
GARFIELD
ODIE
CONGRATULATIONS, ODIEEE!!!
ODIE
YOU HAVE JUST WON AN ALL EXPENSES PAID VACATION TO THE BACKYARD!
ODIE
FIRST, A PHOTO FOR THE PRESS
CLICK
ODIE
BON VOYAGE, YOU LUCKY PUP! SEND A POSTCARD!
ODIE
JIM DAVIS 2-14

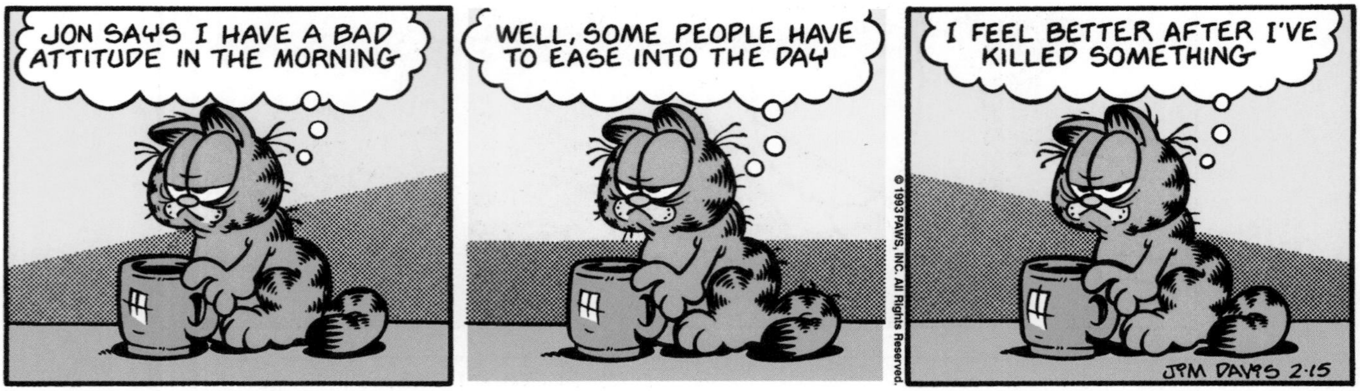
JON SAYS I HAVE A BAD ATTITUDE IN THE MORNING
WELL, SOME PEOPLE HAVE TO EASE INTO THE DAY
I FEEL BETTER AFTER I'VE KILLED SOMETHING
© 1993 PAWS, INC. All Rights Reserved.
JIM DAVIS 2-15

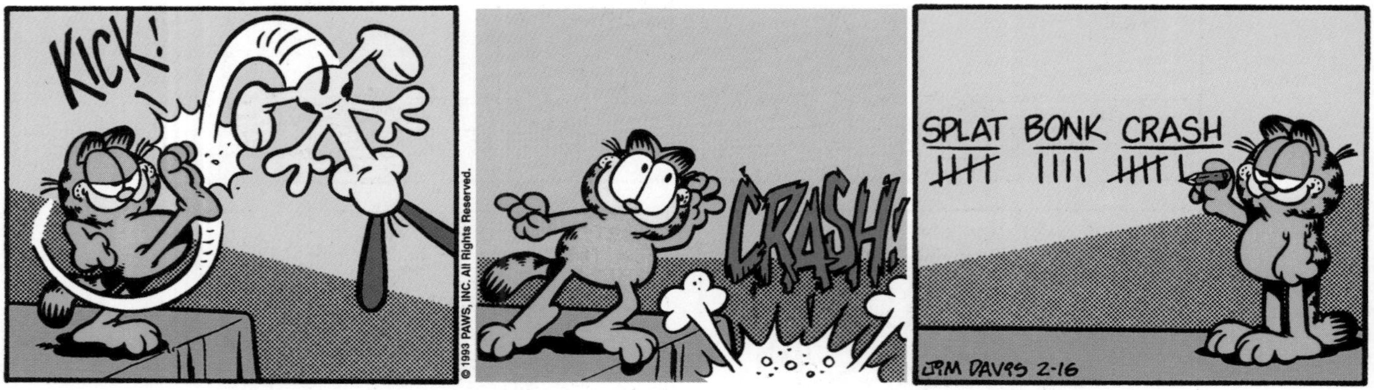
KICK!
© 1993 PAWS, INC. All Rights Reserved.
CRASH!
SPLAT BONK CRASH
JIM DAVIS 2-16

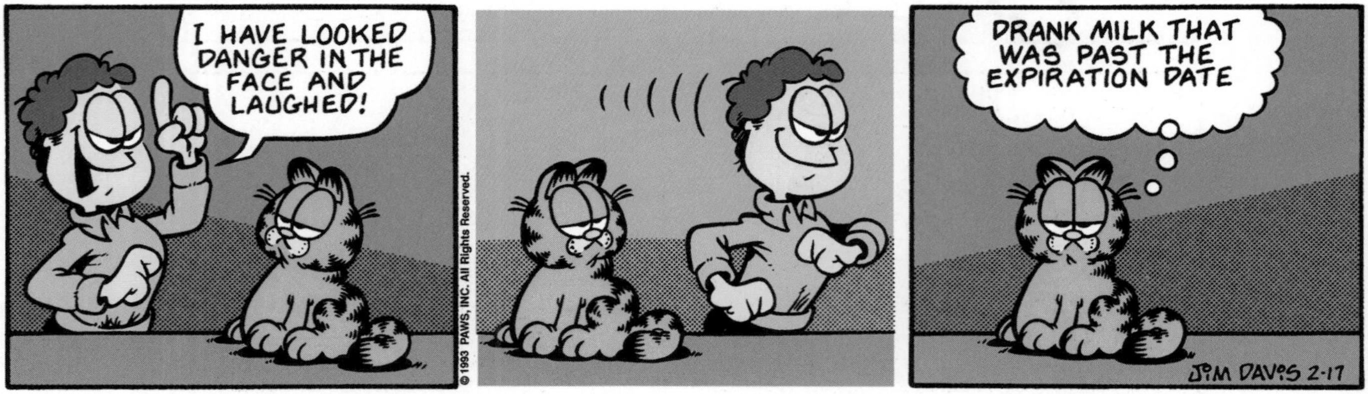
I HAVE LOOKED DANGER IN THE FACE AND LAUGHED!
© 1993 PAWS, INC. All Rights Reserved.
DRANK MILK THAT WAS PAST THE EXPIRATION DATE
JIM DAVIS 2-17

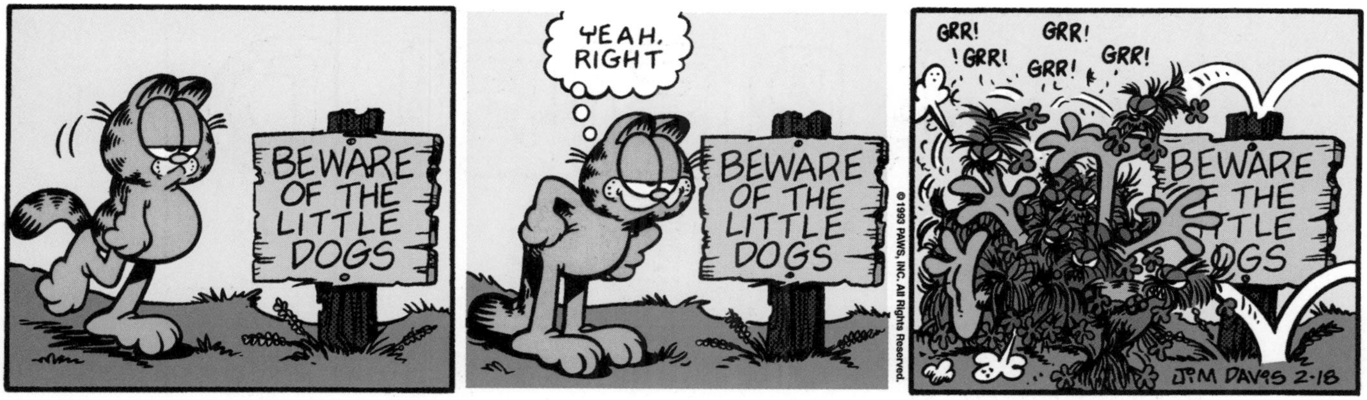
BEWARE OF THE LITTLE DOGS
YEAH, RIGHT
GRR! GRR! GRR! GRR! GRR!
JIM DAVIS 2-18

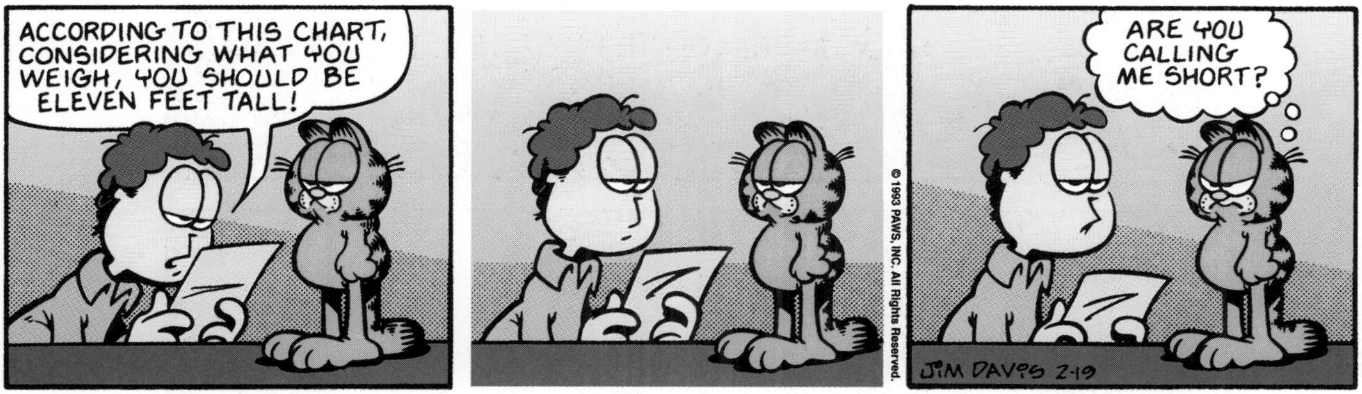
ACCORDING TO THIS CHART, CONSIDERING WHAT YOU WEIGH, YOU SHOULD BE ELEVEN FEET TALL!
ARE YOU CALLING ME SHORT?
JIM DAVIS 2-19

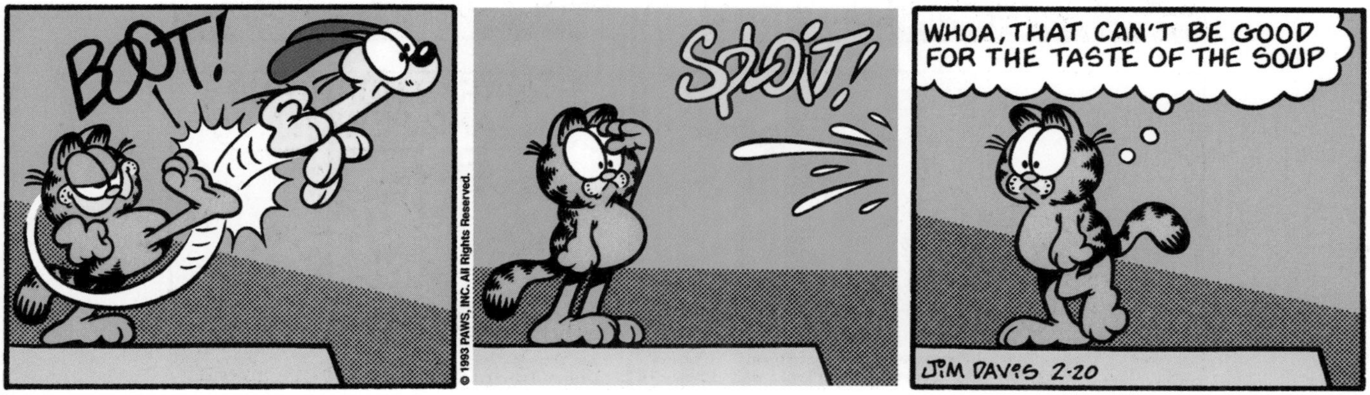
BOOT!
SPLOIT!
WHOA, THAT CAN'T BE GOOD FOR THE TASTE OF THE SOUP
JIM DAVIS 2-20

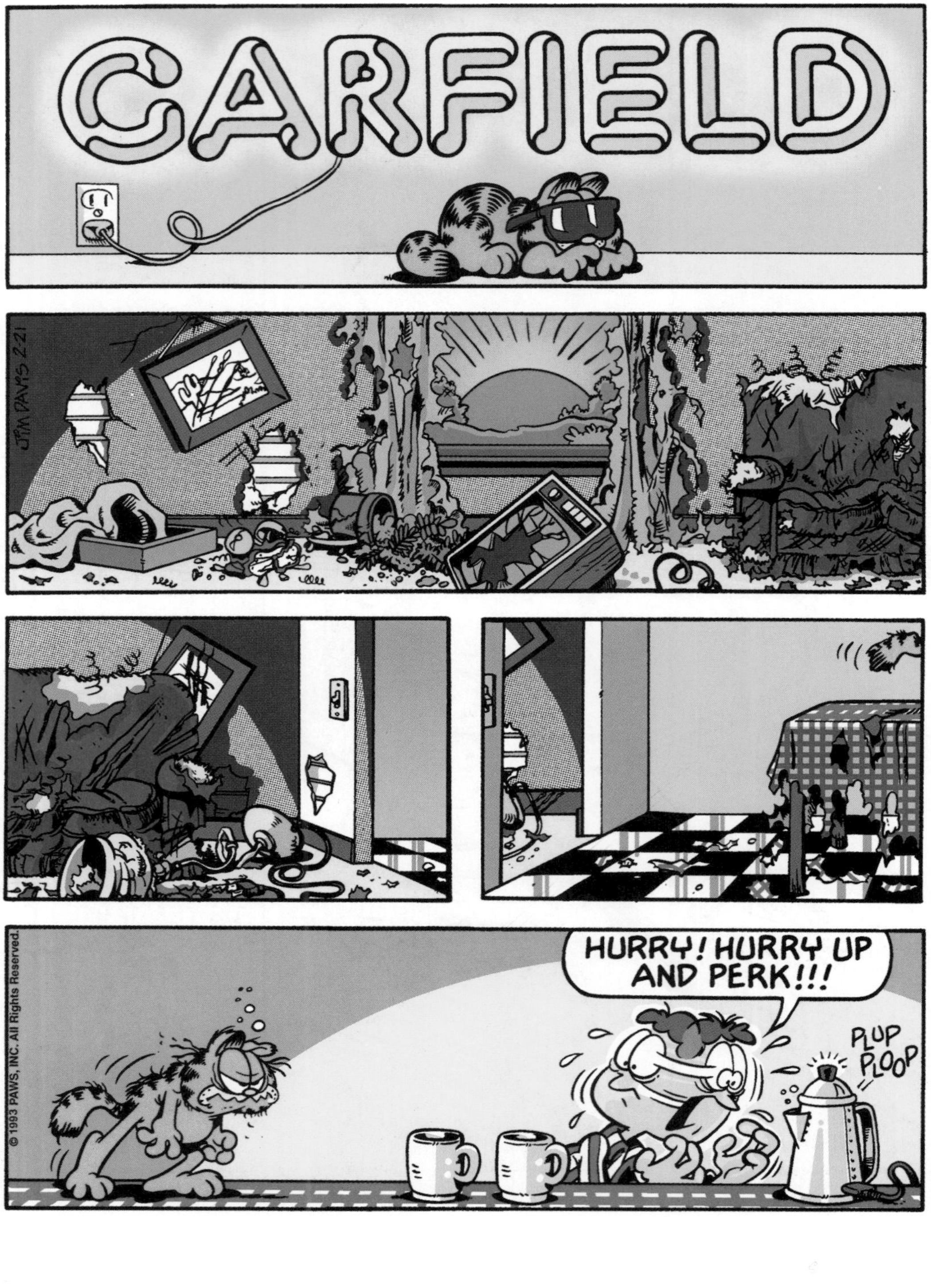
GARFIELD
JIM DAVIS 2-21
© 1993 PAWS, INC. All Rights Reserved.
HURRY! HURRY UP AND PERK!!!
PLUP PLOOP

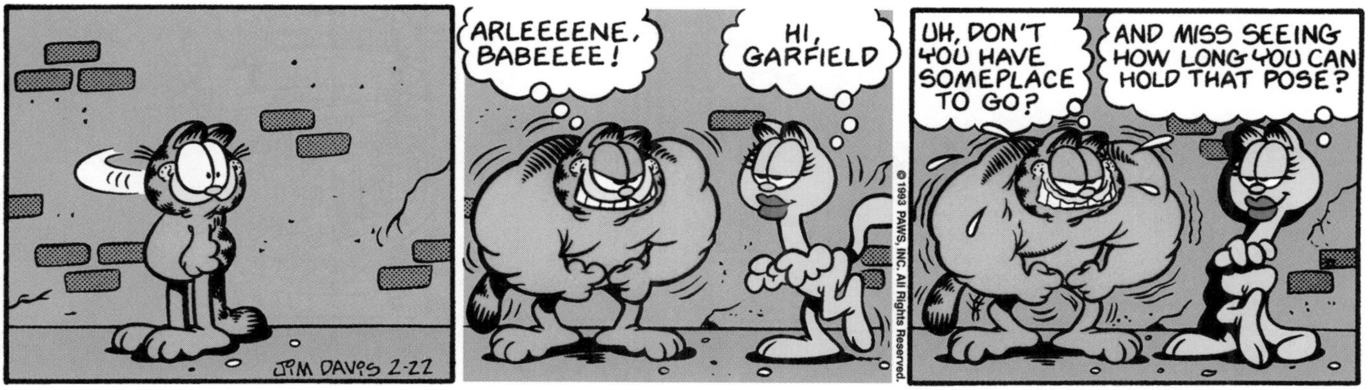
ARLEEEENE, BABEEEE!
HI, GARFIELD
UH, DON'T YOU HAVE SOMEPLACE TO GO?
AND MISS SEEING HOW LONG YOU CAN HOLD THAT POSE?
JIM DAVIS 2-22

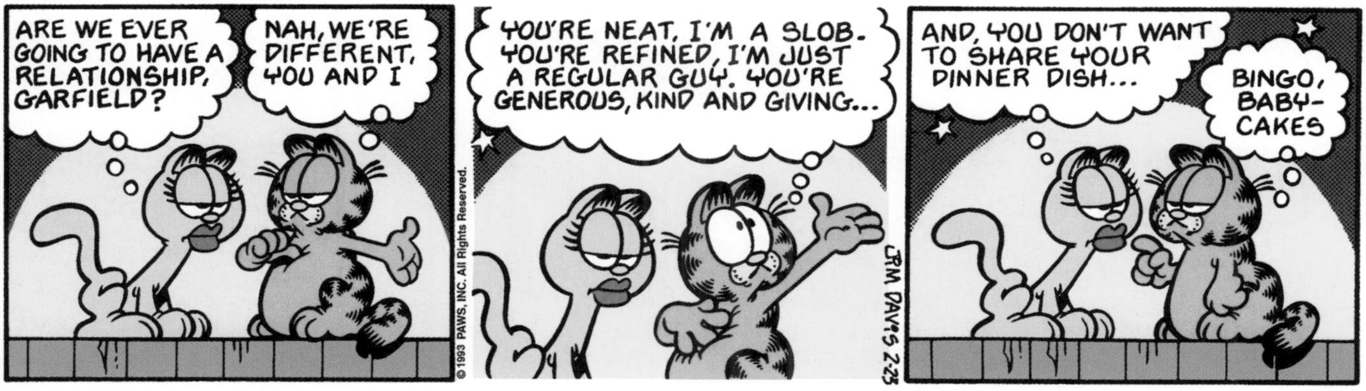
ARE WE EVER GOING TO HAVE A RELATIONSHIP, GARFIELD?
NAH, WE'RE DIFFERENT, YOU AND I
YOU'RE NEAT, I'M A SLOB. YOU'RE REFINED, I'M JUST A REGULAR GUY. YOU'RE GENEROUS, KIND AND GIVING...
AND, YOU DON'T WANT TO SHARE YOUR DINNER DISH...
BINGO, BABY-CAKES
JIM DAVIS 2-23

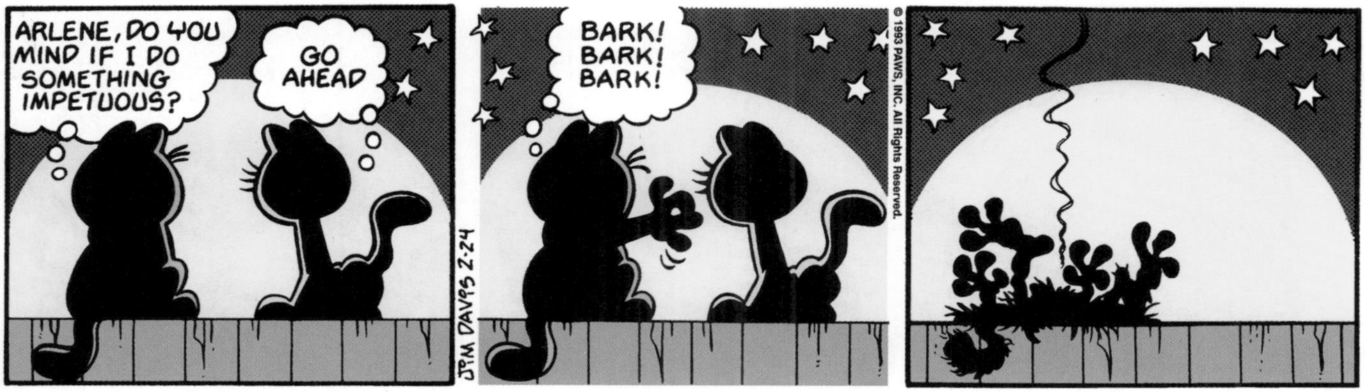
ARLENE, DO YOU MIND IF I DO SOMETHING IMPETUOUS?
GO AHEAD
BARK! BARK! BARK!
JIM DAVIS 2-24

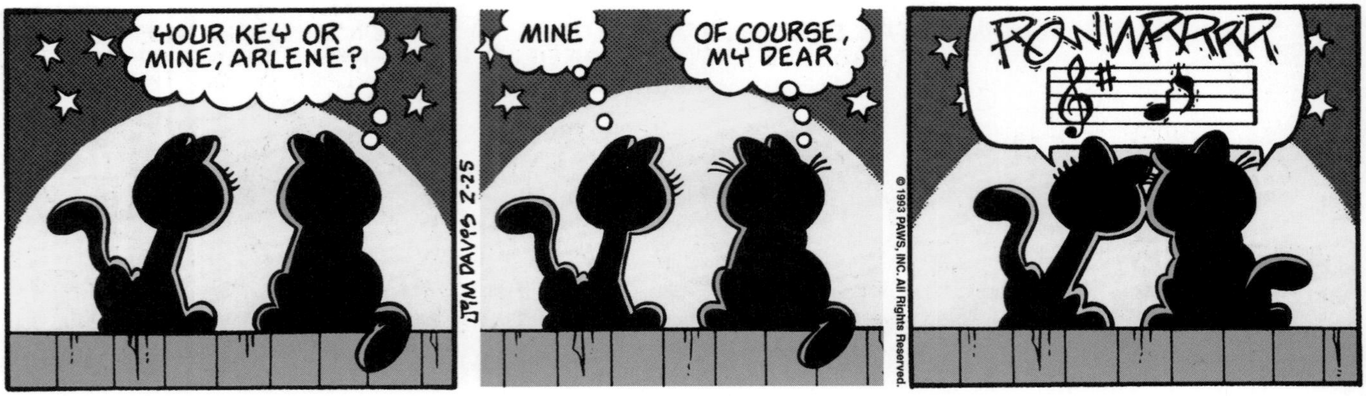
YOUR KEY OR MINE, ARLENE?
JIM DAVIS 2-25
MINE
OF COURSE, MY DEAR
© 1993 PAWS, INC. All Rights Reserved.
RONWRRRR

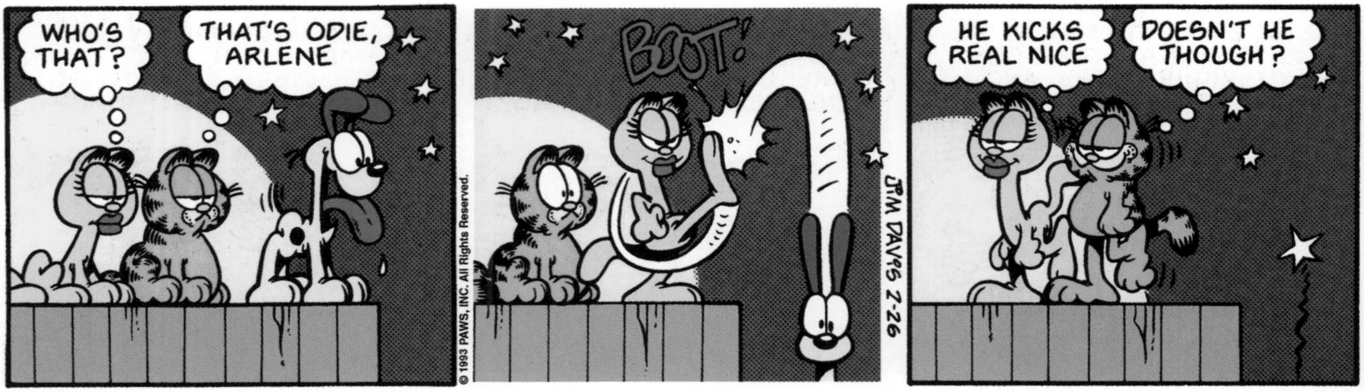
WHO'S THAT?
THAT'S ODIE, ARLENE
© 1993 PAWS, INC. All Rights Reserved.
BOOT!
JIM DAVIS 2-26
HE KICKS REAL NICE
DOESN'T HE THOUGH?

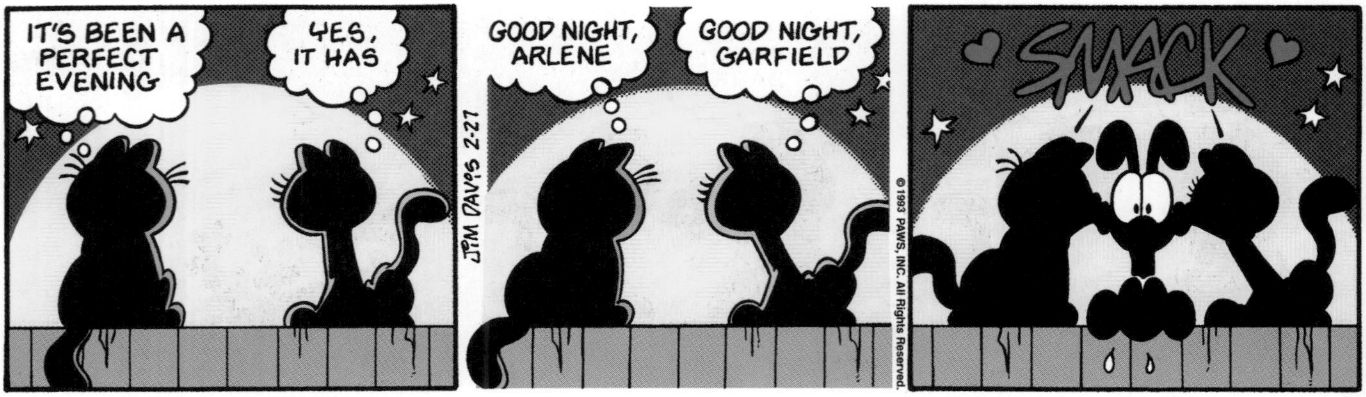
IT'S BEEN A PERFECT EVENING
YES, IT HAS
JIM DAVIS 2-27
GOOD NIGHT, ARLENE
GOOD NIGHT, GARFIELD
© 1993 PAWS, INC. All Rights Reserved.
SMACK

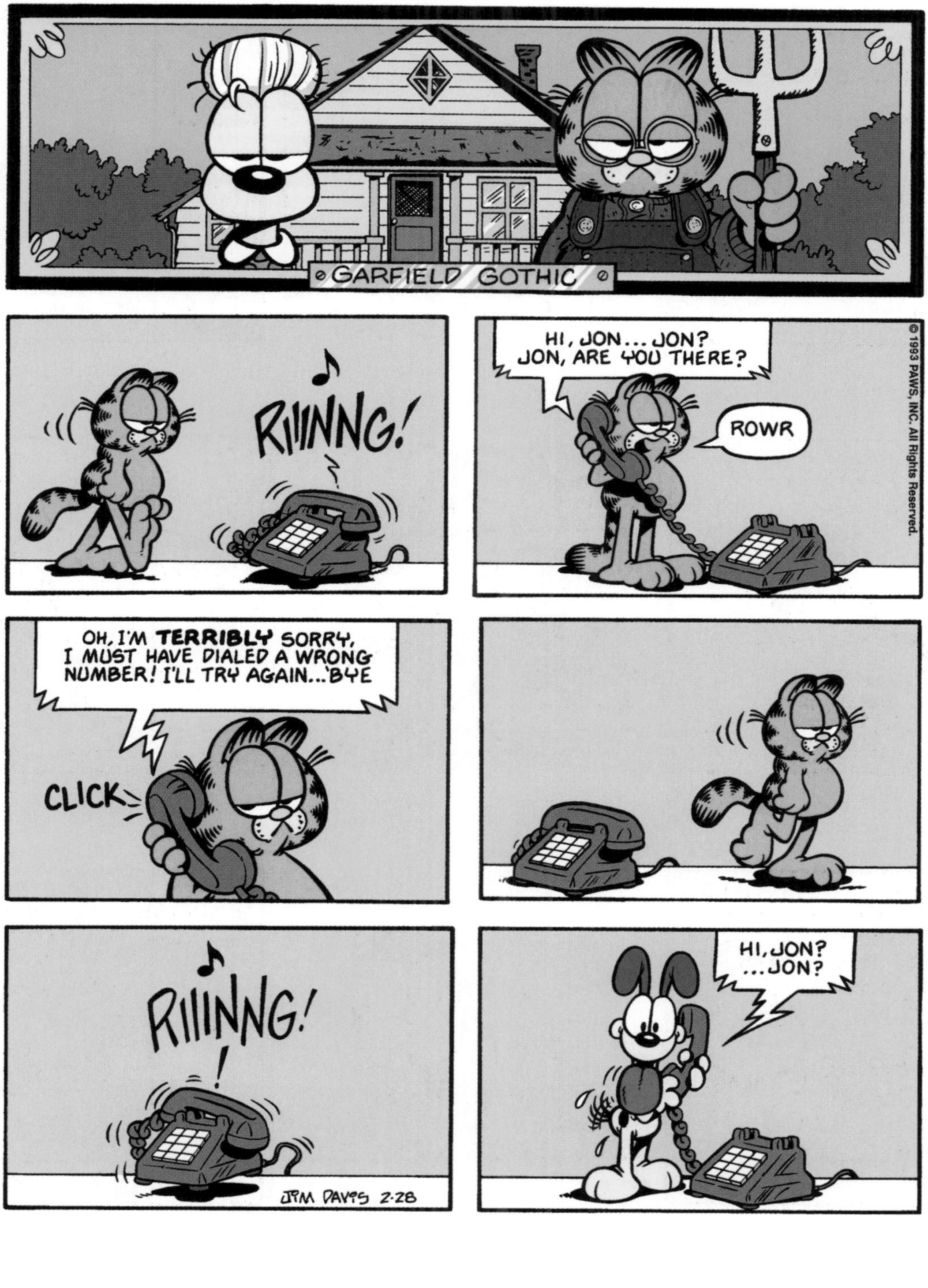
GARFIELD GOTHIC
RIIINNG!
HI, JON... JON?
JON, ARE YOU THERE?
ROWR
OH, I'M TERRIBLY SORRY, I MUST HAVE DIALED A WRONG NUMBER! I'LL TRY AGAIN...'BYE
CLICK
RIIINNG!
JIM DAVIS 2-28
HI, JON?
...JON?
© 1993 PAWS, INC. All Rights Reserved.

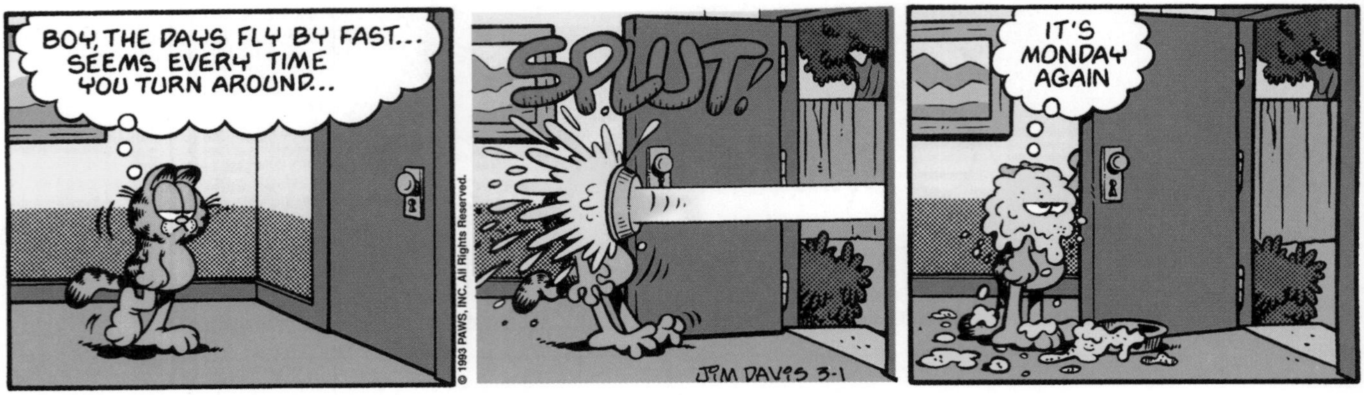
BOY, THE DAYS FLY BY FAST... SEEMS EVERY TIME YOU TURN AROUND...
SPLUT!
IT'S MONDAY AGAIN
© 1993 PAWS, INC. All Rights Reserved.
JIM DAVIS 3-1

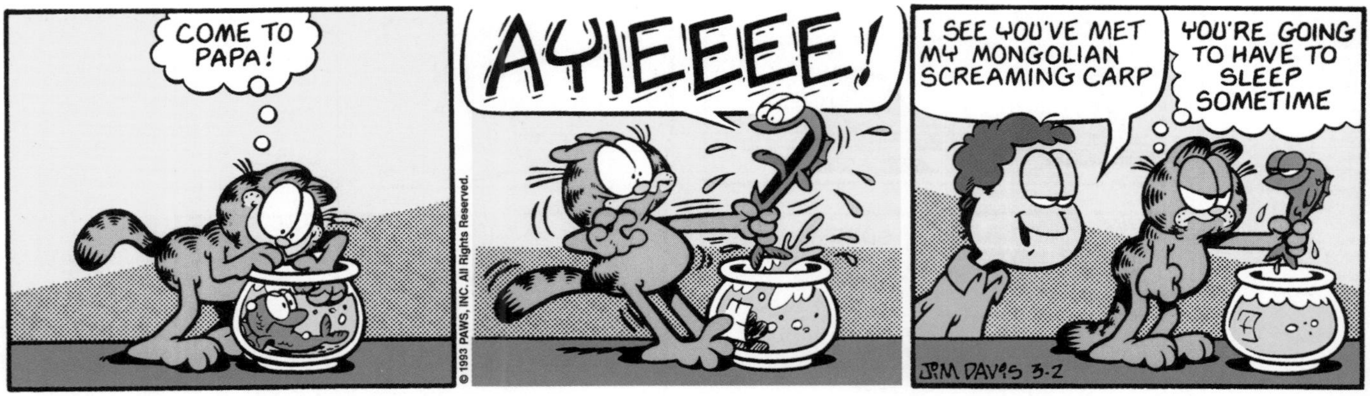
COME TO PAPA!
AYIEEEEE!
I SEE YOU'VE MET MY MONGOLIAN SCREAMING CARP
YOU'RE GOING TO HAVE TO SLEEP SOMETIME
© 1993 PAWS, INC. All Rights Reserved.
JIM DAVIS 3-2

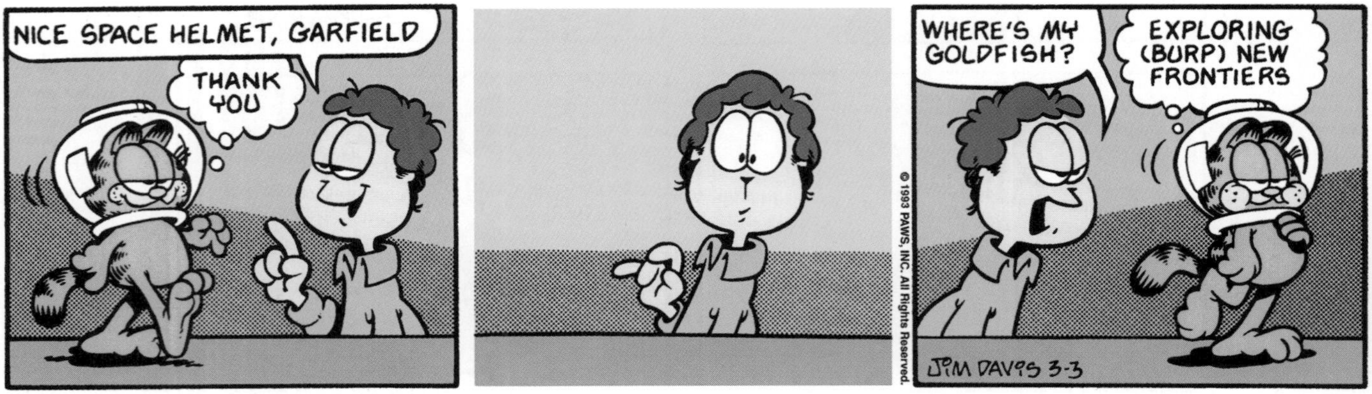
NICE SPACE HELMET, GARFIELD
THANK YOU
WHERE'S MY GOLDFISH?
EXPLORING (BURP) NEW FRONTIERS
© 1993 PAWS, INC. All Rights Reserved.
JIM DAVIS 3-3

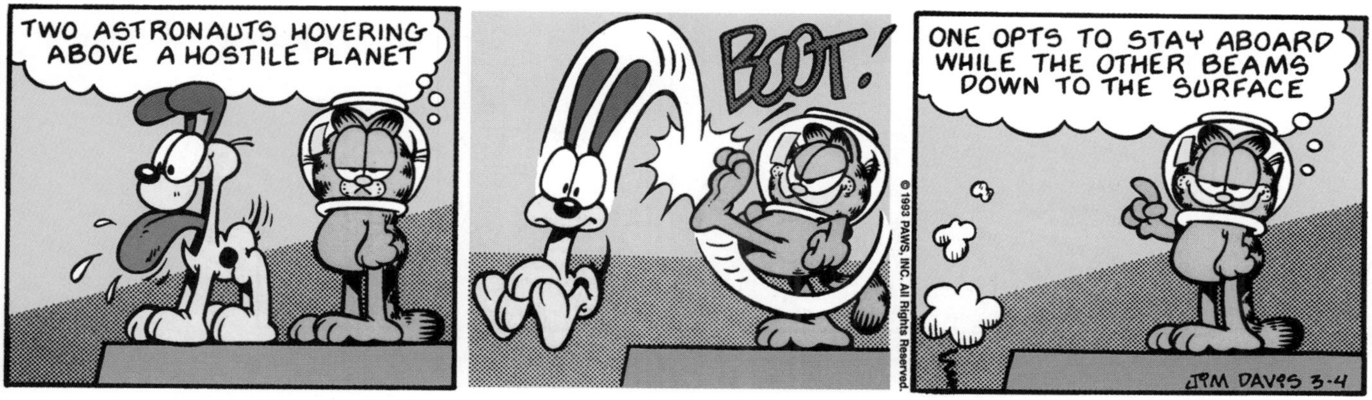
TWO ASTRONAUTS HOVERING ABOVE A HOSTILE PLANET
BOOT!
ONE OPTS TO STAY ABOARD WHILE THE OTHER BEAMS DOWN TO THE SURFACE
JIM DAVIS 3-4
© 1993 PAWS, INC. All Rights Reserved.

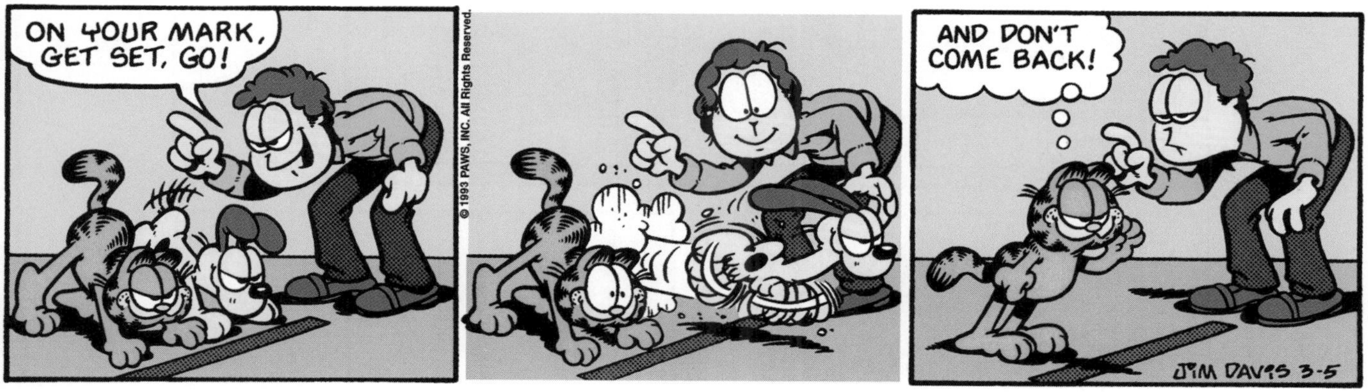
ON YOUR MARK, GET SET, GO!
AND DON'T COME BACK!
JIM DAVIS 3-5
© 1993 PAWS, INC. All Rights Reserved.

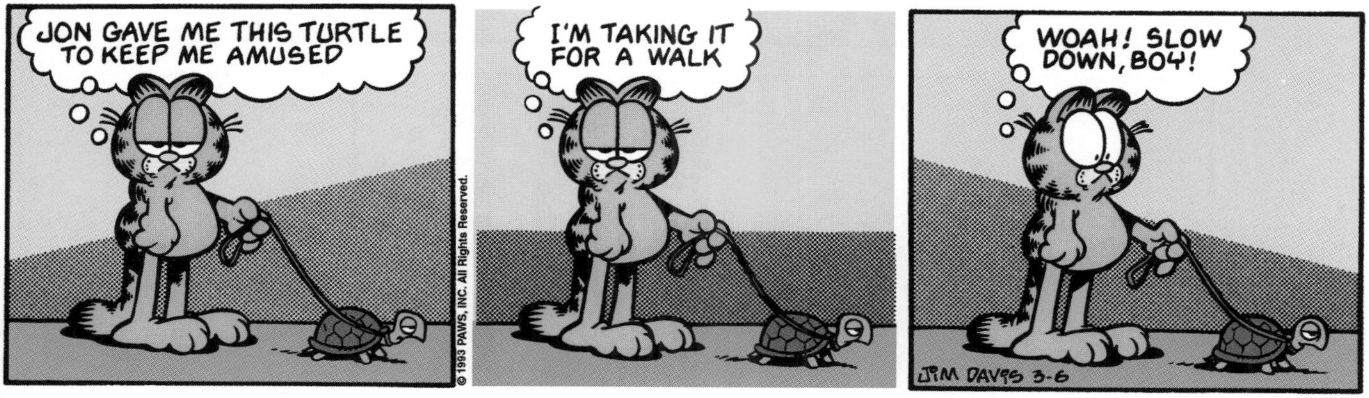
JON GAVE ME THIS TURTLE TO KEEP ME AMUSED
I'M TAKING IT FOR A WALK
WOAH! SLOW DOWN, BOY!
JIM DAVIS 3-6
© 1993 PAWS, INC. All Rights Reserved.

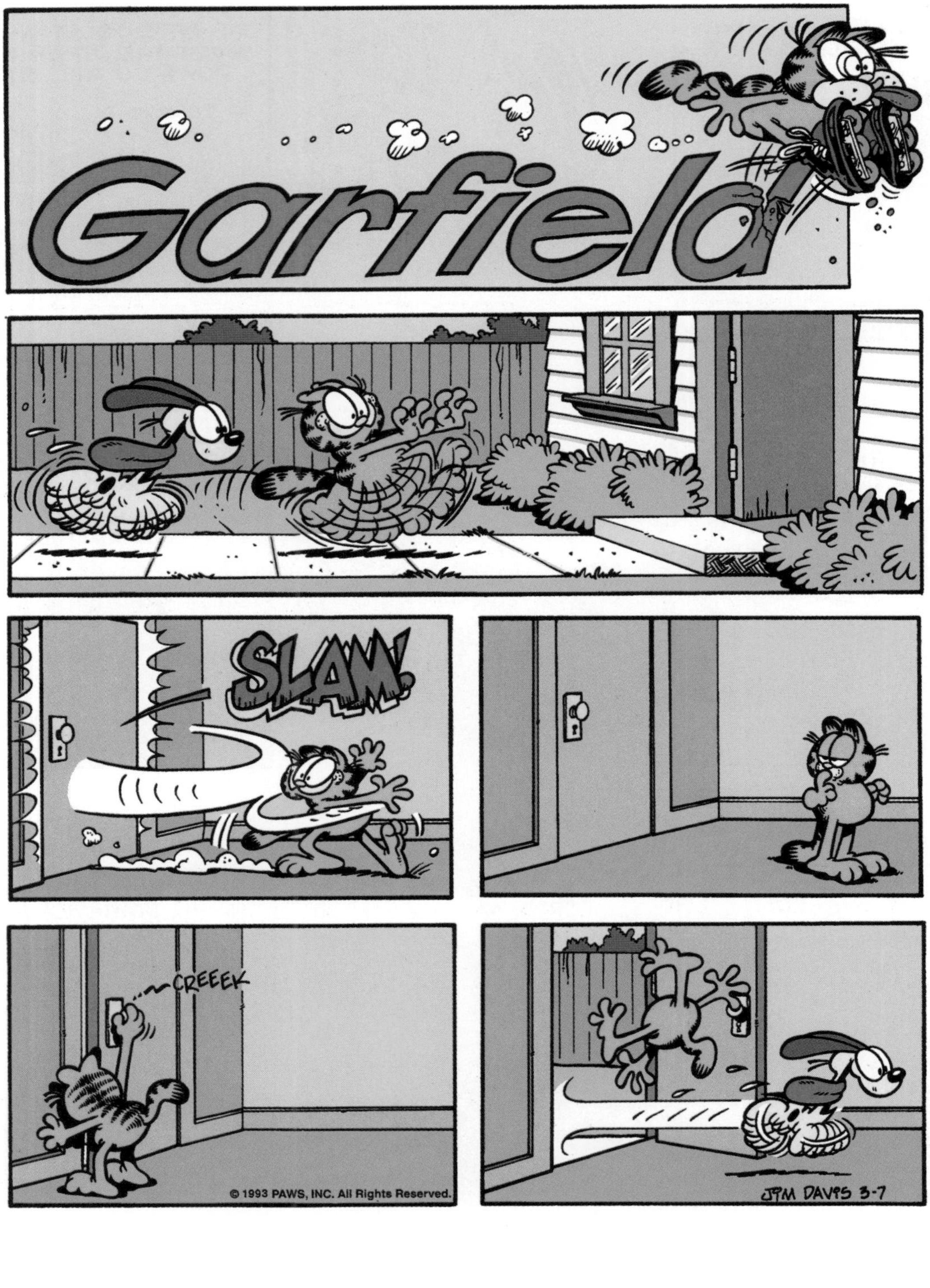
Garfield
SLAM!
CREEEK
© 1993 PAWS, INC. All Rights Reserved.
JIM DAVIS 3-7

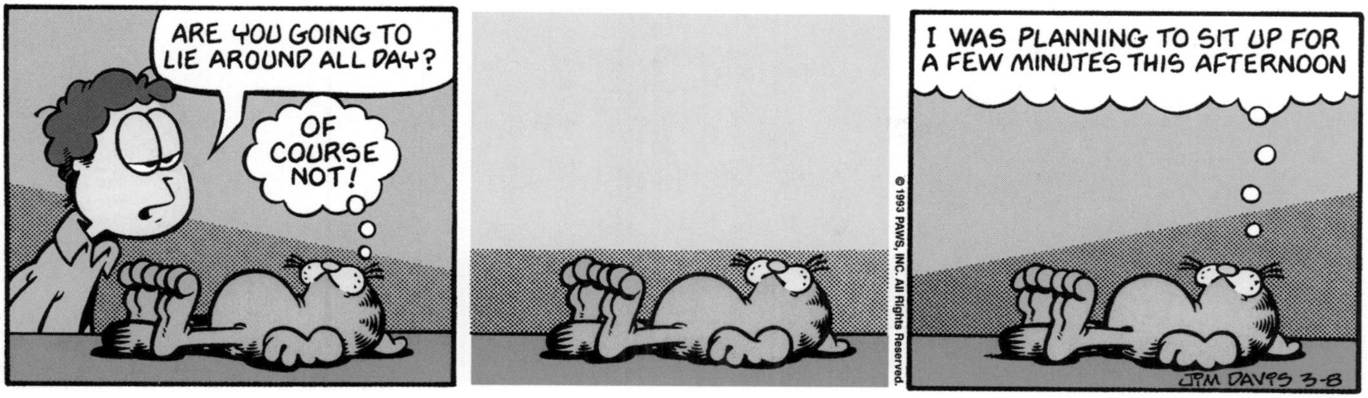
ARE YOU GOING TO LIE AROUND ALL DAY?
OF COURSE NOT!
I WAS PLANNING TO SIT UP FOR A FEW MINUTES THIS AFTERNOON
JIM DAVIS 3-8

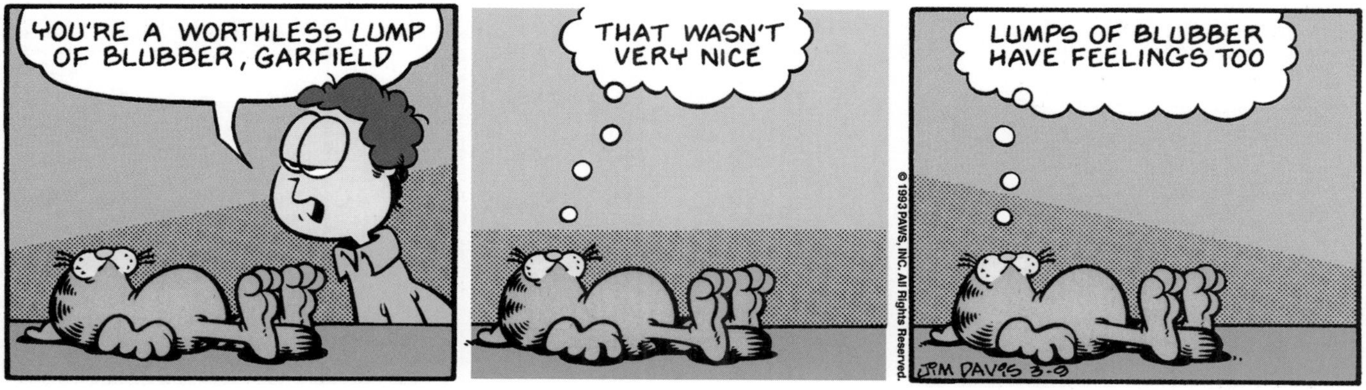
YOU'RE A WORTHLESS LUMP OF BLUBBER, GARFIELD
THAT WASN'T VERY NICE
LUMPS OF BLUBBER HAVE FEELINGS TOO
JIM DAVIS 3-9

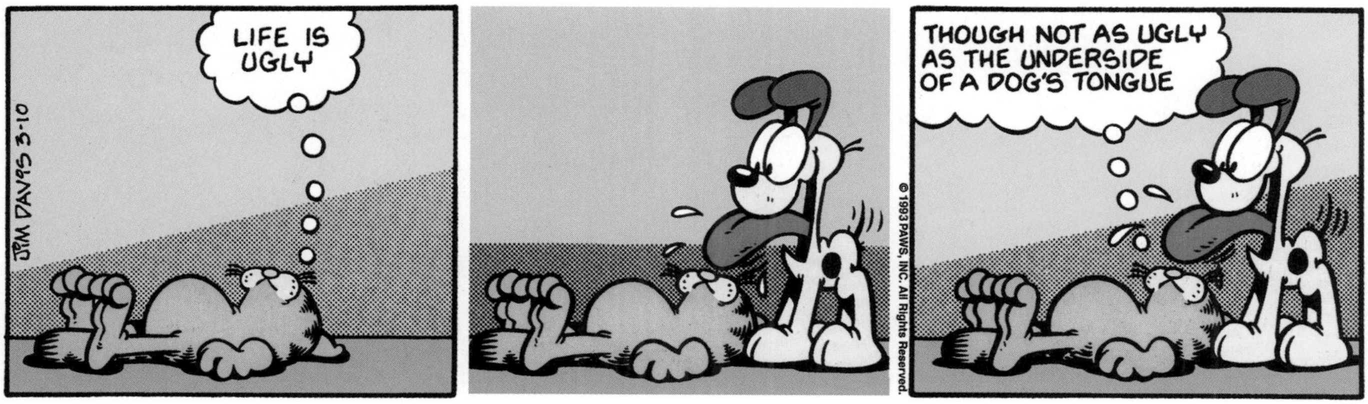
JIM DAVIS 3-10
LIFE IS UGLY
THOUGH NOT AS UGLY AS THE UNDERSIDE OF A DOG'S TONGUE

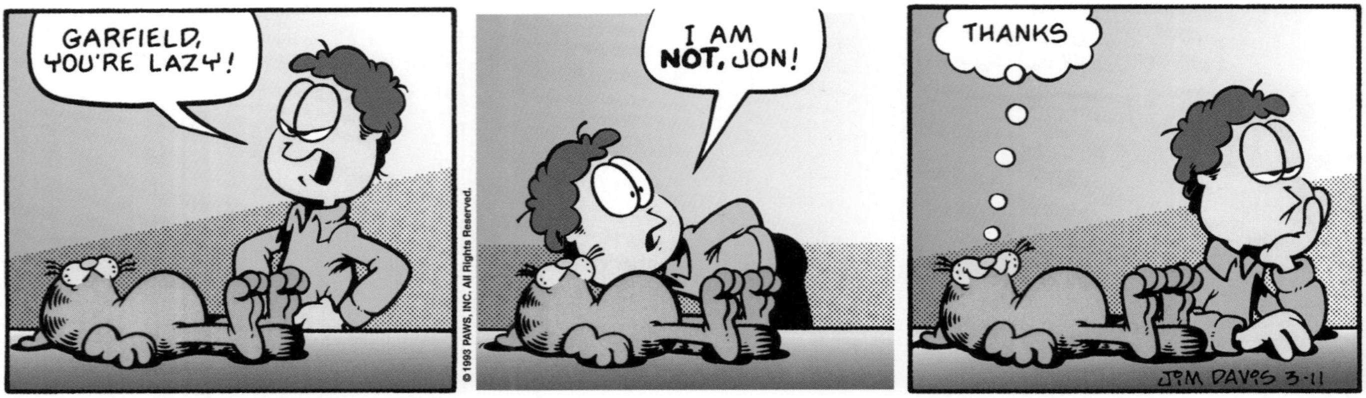
GARFIELD, YOU'RE LAZY!
I AM NOT, JON!
THANKS
JIM DAVIS 3-11
© 1993 PAWS, INC. All Rights Reserved.

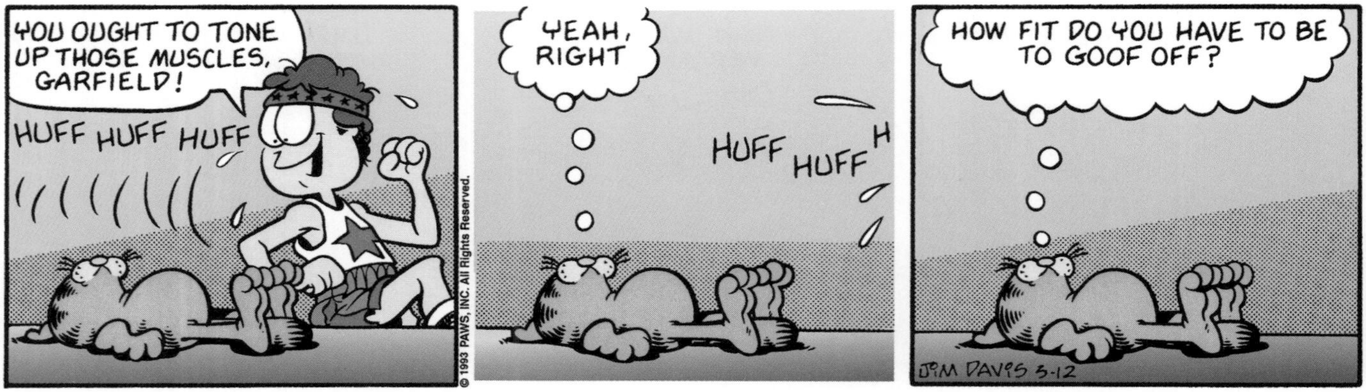
YOU OUGHT TO TONE UP THOSE MUSCLES, GARFIELD!
HUFF HUFF HUFF
YEAH, RIGHT
HUFF HUFF H
HOW FIT DO YOU HAVE TO BE TO GOOF OFF?
JIM DAVIS 3-12
© 1993 PAWS, INC. All Rights Reserved.

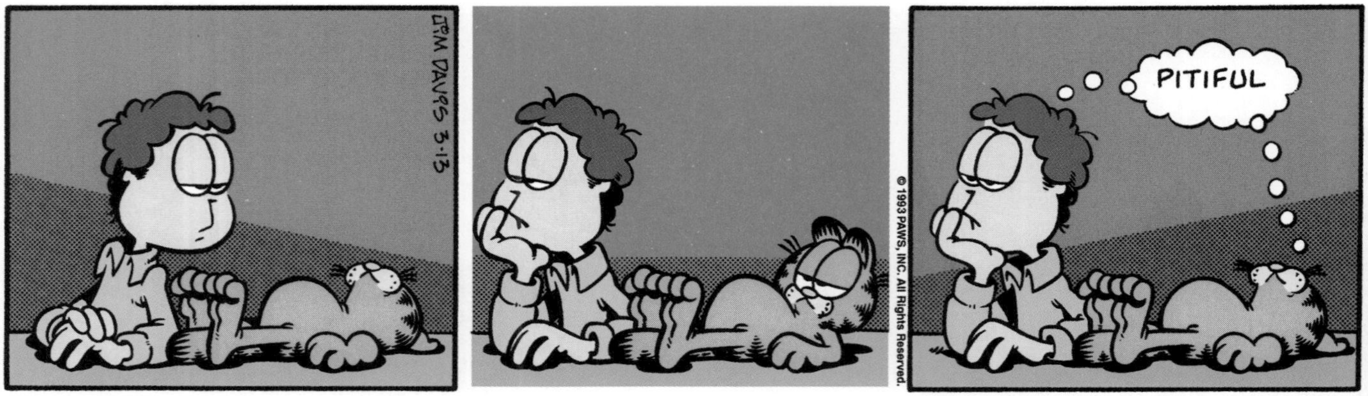
JIM DAVIS 3-13
PITIFUL
© 1993 PAWS, INC. All Rights Reserved.

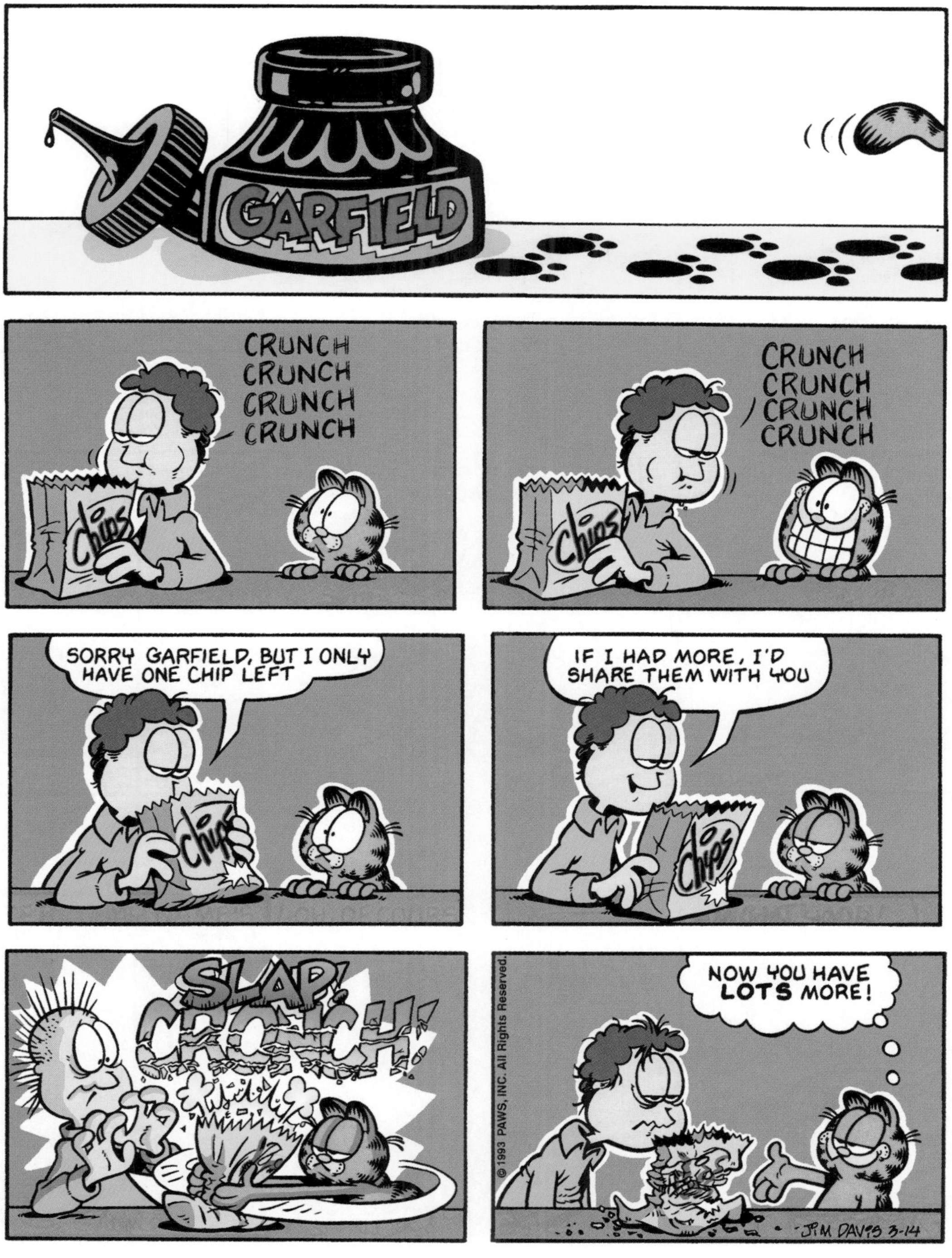
GARFIELD
CRUNCH CRUNCH CRUNCH CRUNCH
CHIPS
CRUNCH CRUNCH CRUNCH CRUNCH
CHIPS
SORRY GARFIELD, BUT I ONLY HAVE ONE CHIP LEFT
CHIPS
IF I HAD MORE, I'D SHARE THEM WITH YOU
CHIPS
SLAP! CRUNCH!
NOW YOU HAVE LOTS MORE!
JIM DAVIS 3-14

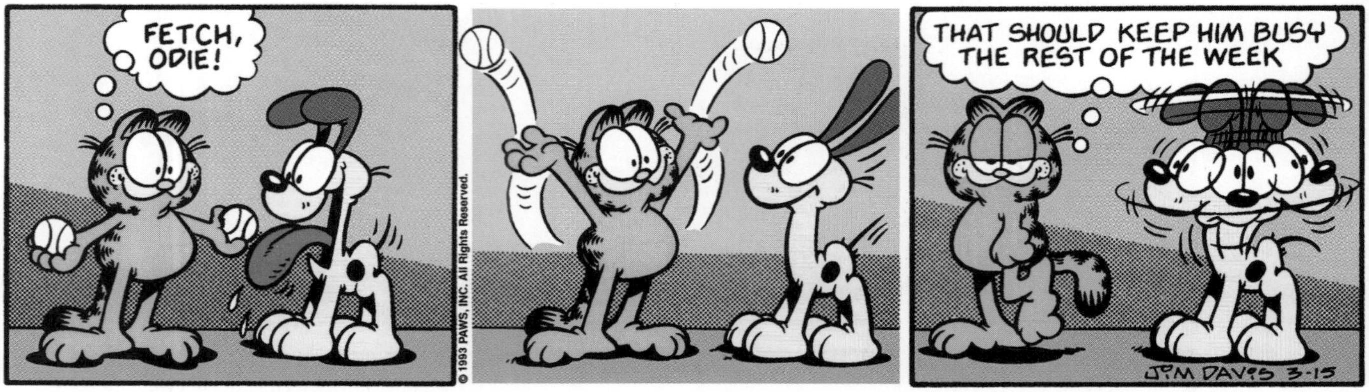
FETCH, ODIE!
THAT SHOULD KEEP HIM BUSY THE REST OF THE WEEK
JIM DAVIS 3-15

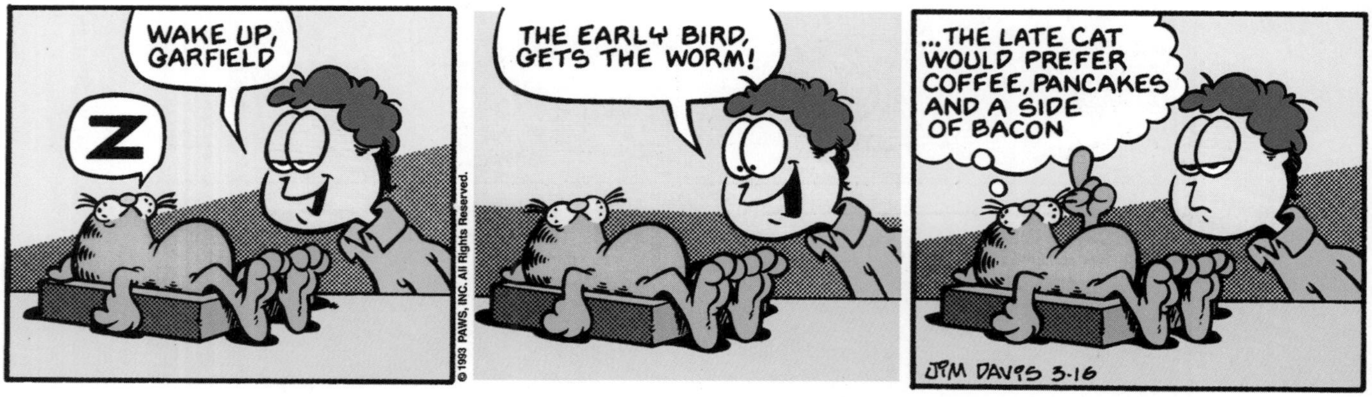
WAKE UP, GARFIELD
Z
THE EARLY BIRD GETS THE WORM!
...THE LATE CAT WOULD PREFER COFFEE, PANCAKES AND A SIDE OF BACON
JIM DAVIS 3-16

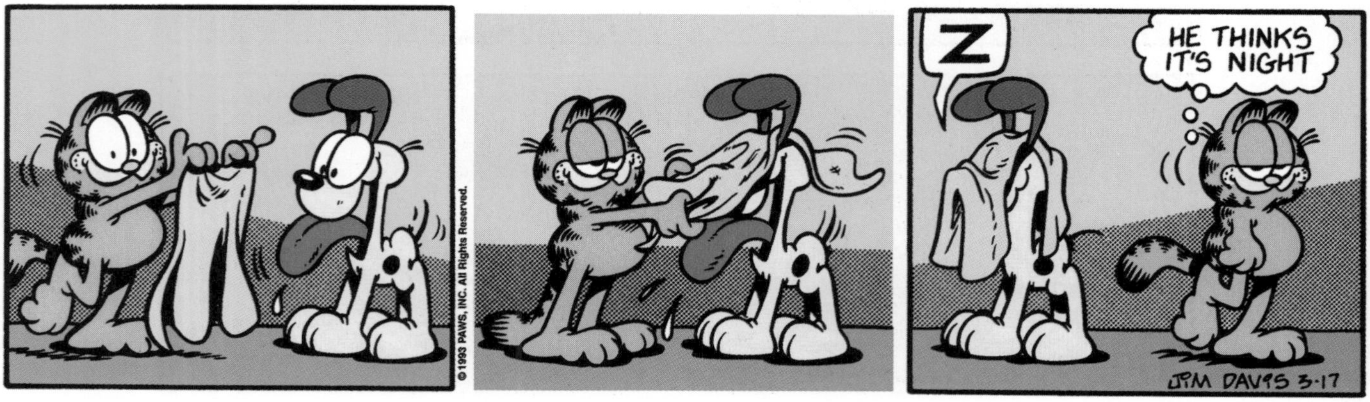
Z
HE THINKS IT'S NIGHT
JIM DAVIS 3-17

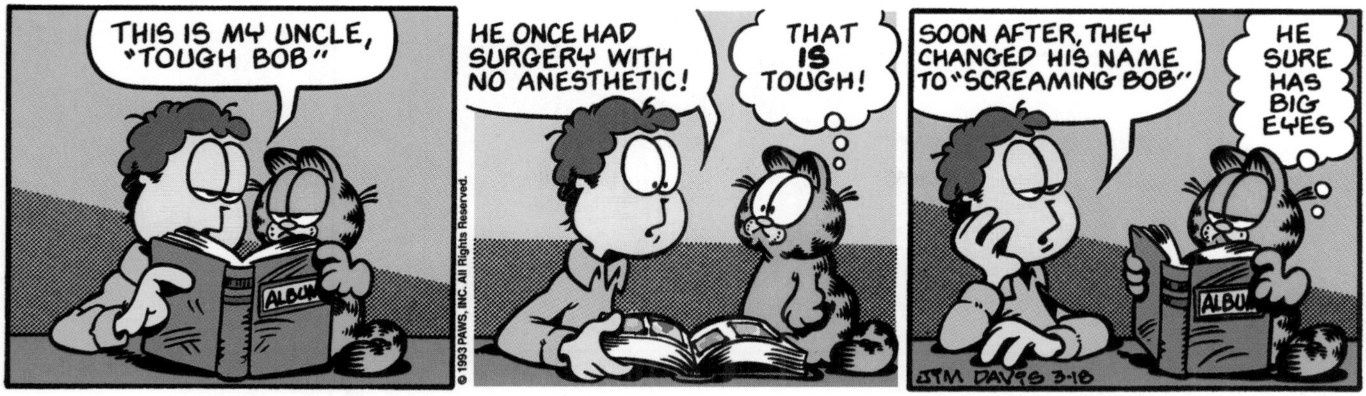
THIS IS MY UNCLE, "TOUGH BOB"
HE ONCE HAD SURGERY WITH NO ANESTHETIC!
THAT IS TOUGH!
SOON AFTER, THEY CHANGED HIS NAME TO "SCREAMING BOB"
HE SURE HAS BIG EYES
ALBUM
© 1993 PAWS, INC. All Rights Reserved.
JIM DAVIS 3-18

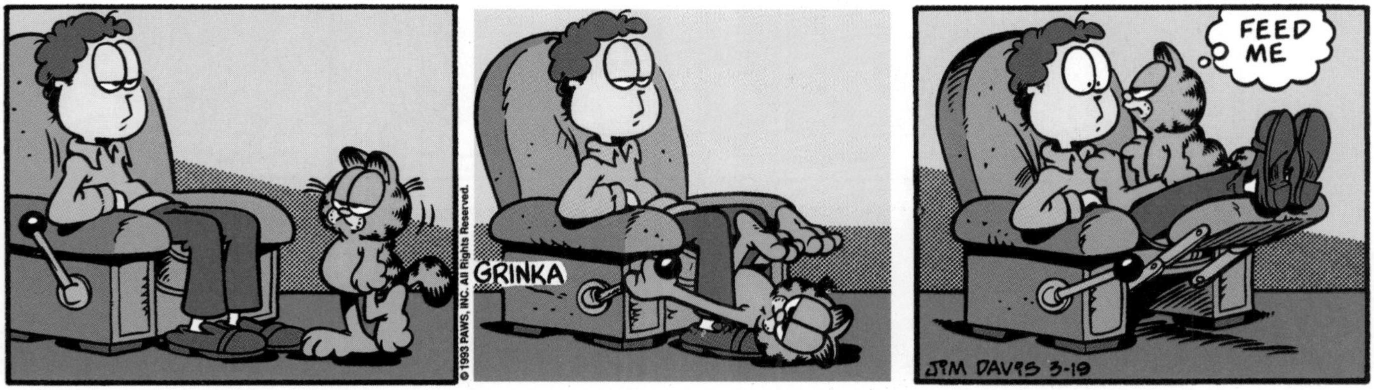
GRINKA
FEED ME
© 1993 PAWS, INC. All Rights Reserved.
JIM DAVIS 3-19

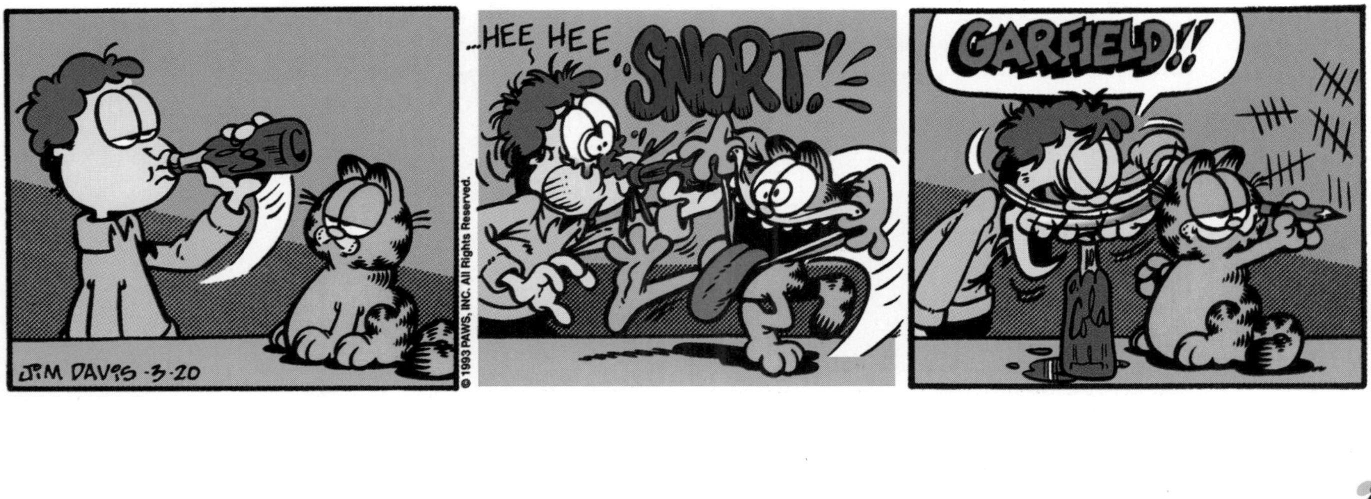
JIM DAVIS 3-20
...HEE HEE
SNORT!
GARFIELD!!
© 1993 PAWS, INC. All Rights Reserved.

GARFIELD
SLURRP!
© 1993 PAWS, INC. All Rights Reserved.
SLURRP!
LOOK OUT!
JIM DAVIS 3-21

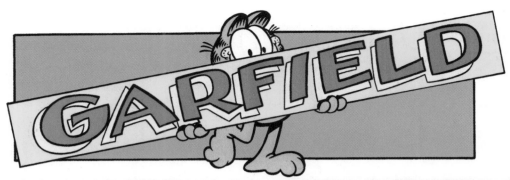

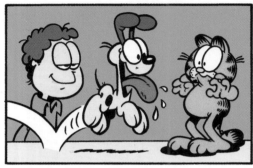

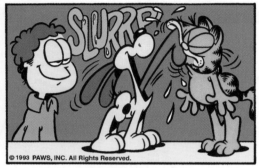

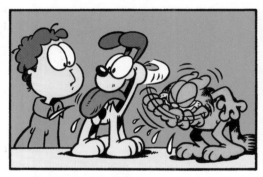

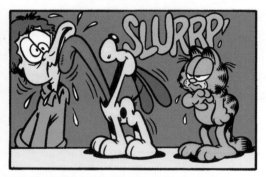

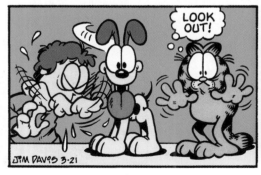

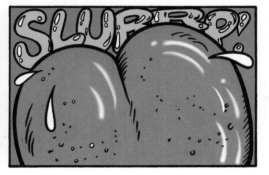

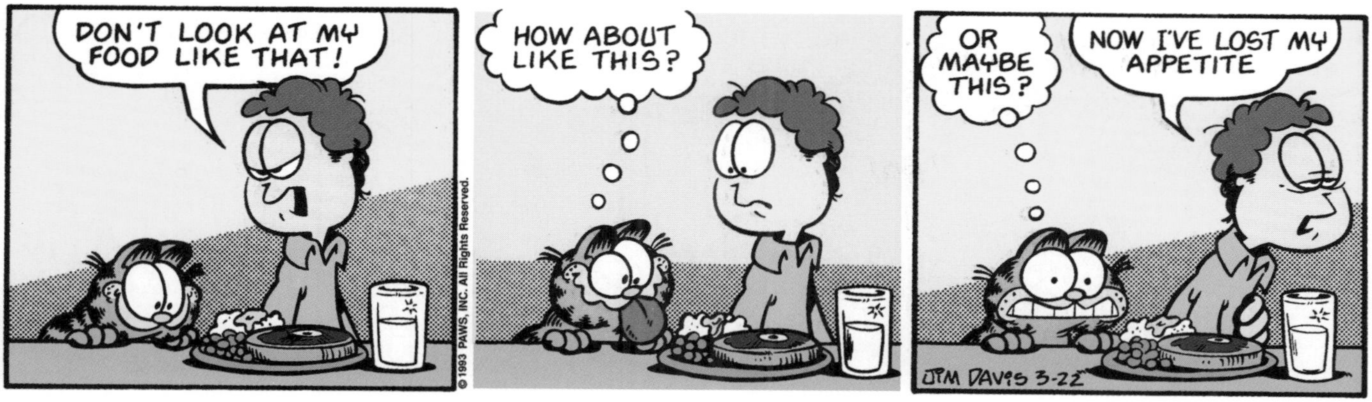
DON'T LOOK AT MY FOOD LIKE THAT!
© 1993 PAWS, INC. All Rights Reserved.
HOW ABOUT LIKE THIS?
OR MAYBE THIS?
NOW I'VE LOST MY APPETITE
JIM DAVIS 3-22

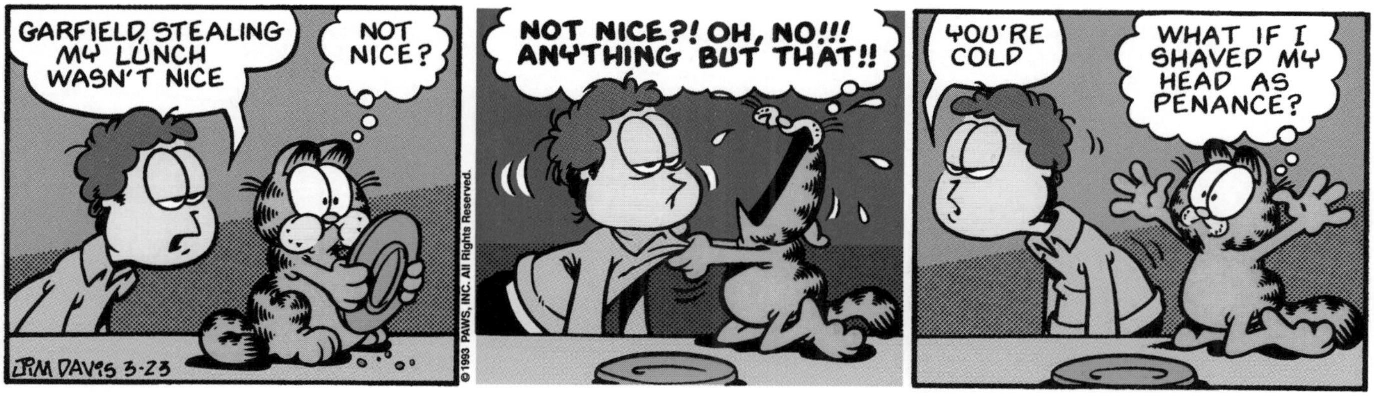
GARFIELD, STEALING MY LUNCH WASN'T NICE
NOT NICE?
JIM DAVIS 3-23
© 1993 PAWS, INC. All Rights Reserved.
NOT NICE?! OH, NO!!! ANYTHING BUT THAT!!
YOU'RE COLD
WHAT IF I SHAVED MY HEAD AS PENANCE?

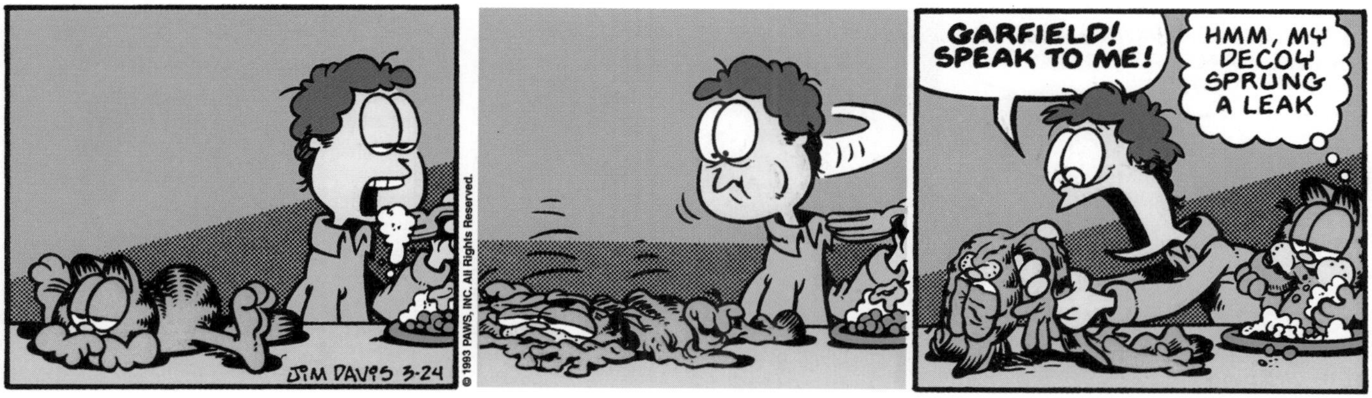
JIM DAVIS 3-24
© 1993 PAWS, INC. All Rights Reserved.
GARFIELD! SPEAK TO ME!
HMM, MY DECOY SPRUNG A LEAK

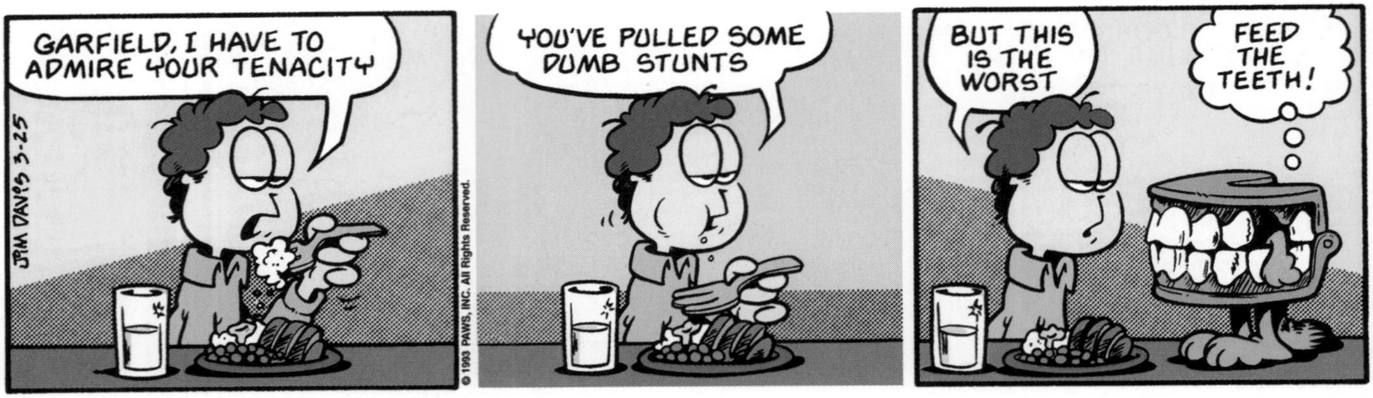
GARFIELD, I HAVE TO ADMIRE YOUR TENACITY
JIM DAVIS 3-25
YOU'VE PULLED SOME DUMB STUNTS
© 1993 PAWS, INC. All Rights Reserved.
BUT THIS IS THE WORST
FEED THE TEETH!

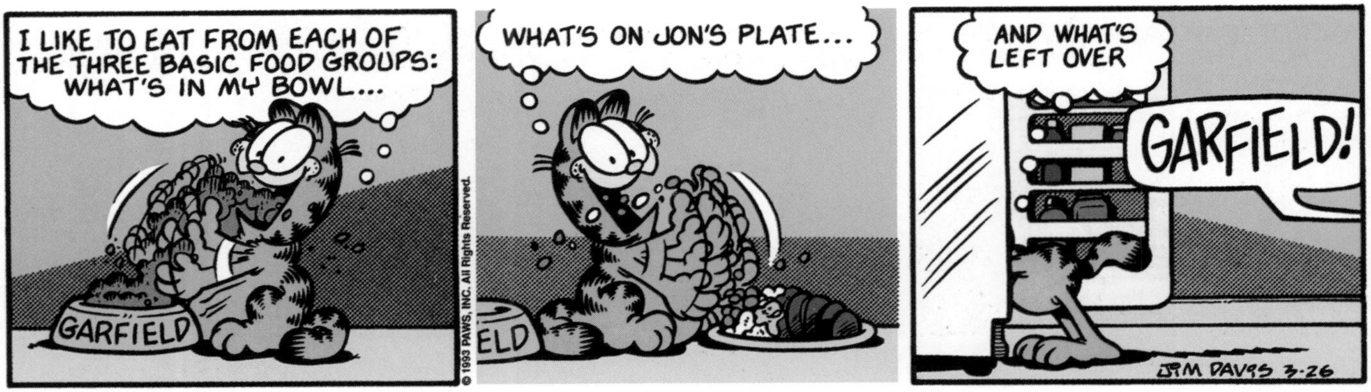
I LIKE TO EAT FROM EACH OF THE THREE BASIC FOOD GROUPS: WHAT'S IN MY BOWL...
GARFIELD
© 1993 PAWS, INC. All Rights Reserved.
WHAT'S ON JON'S PLATE...
ELD
AND WHAT'S LEFT OVER
GARFIELD!
JIM DAVIS 3-26

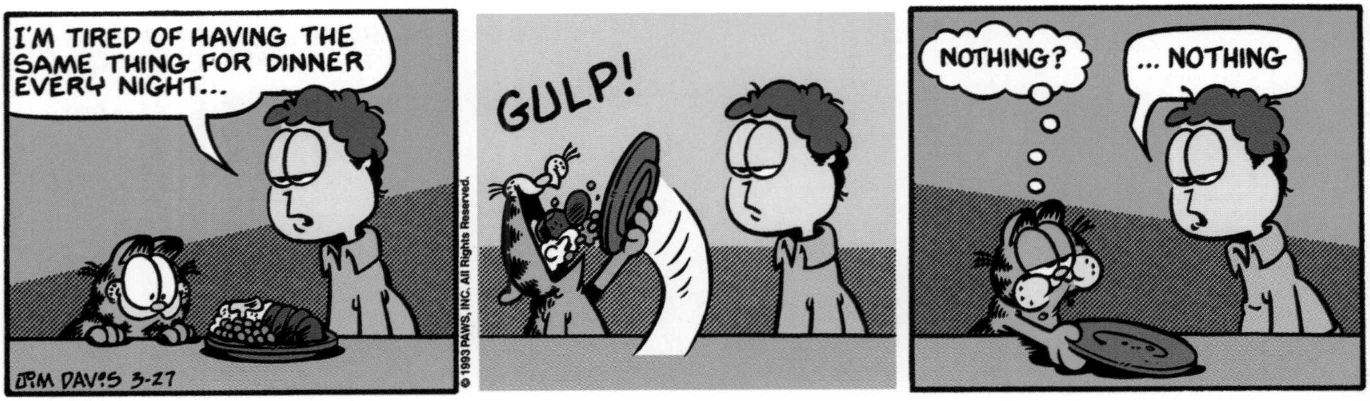
I'M TIRED OF HAVING THE SAME THING FOR DINNER EVERY NIGHT...
JIM DAVIS 3-27
© 1993 PAWS, INC. All Rights Reserved.
GULP!
NOTHING?
... NOTHING

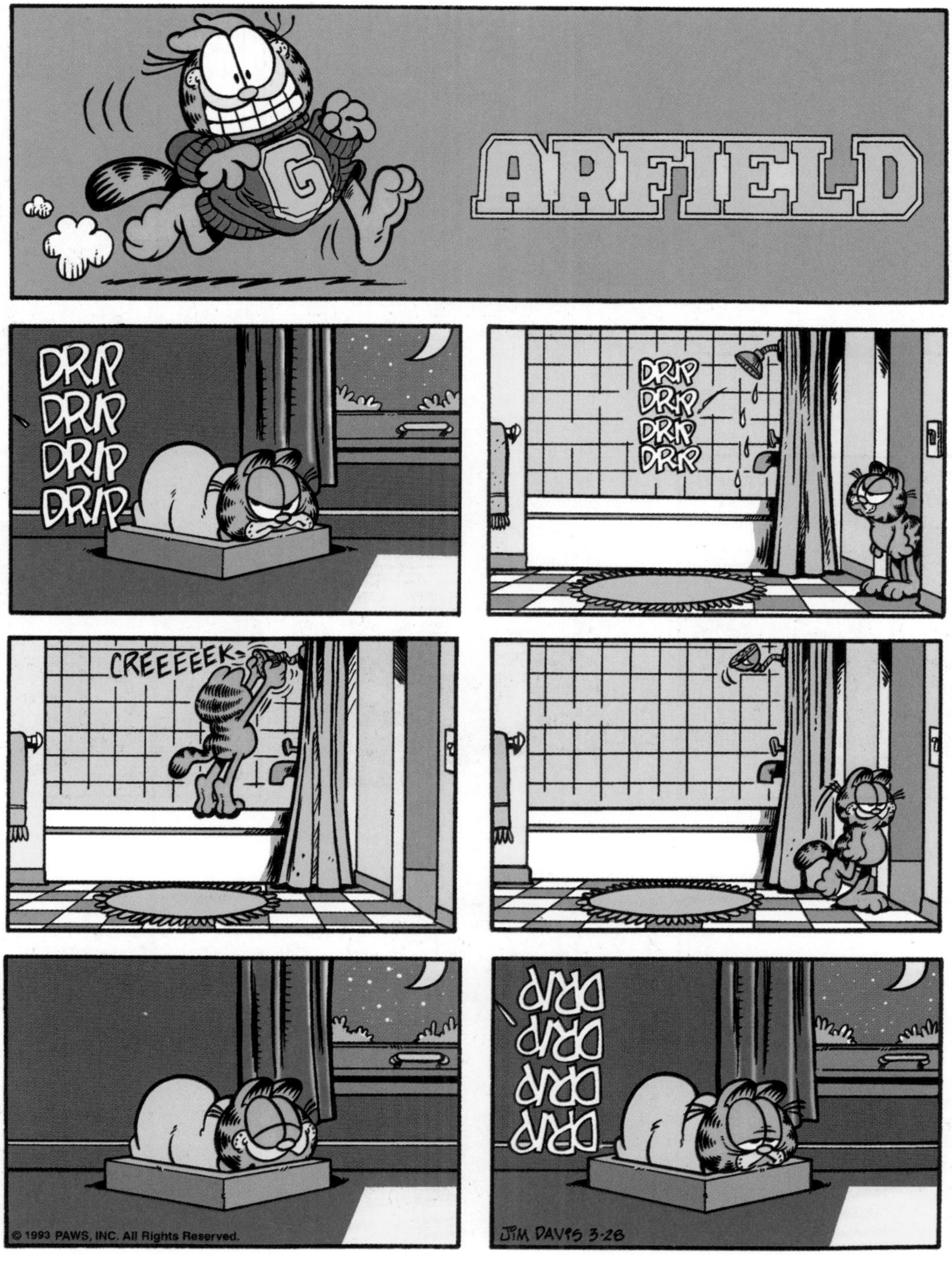
ARFIELD
DRIP
DRIP
DRIP
DRIP
DRIP
DRIP
DRIP
DRIP
CREEEEEEK
DRIP
DRIP
DRIP
DRIP
© 1993 PAWS, INC. All Rights Reserved.
JIM DAVIS 3-28

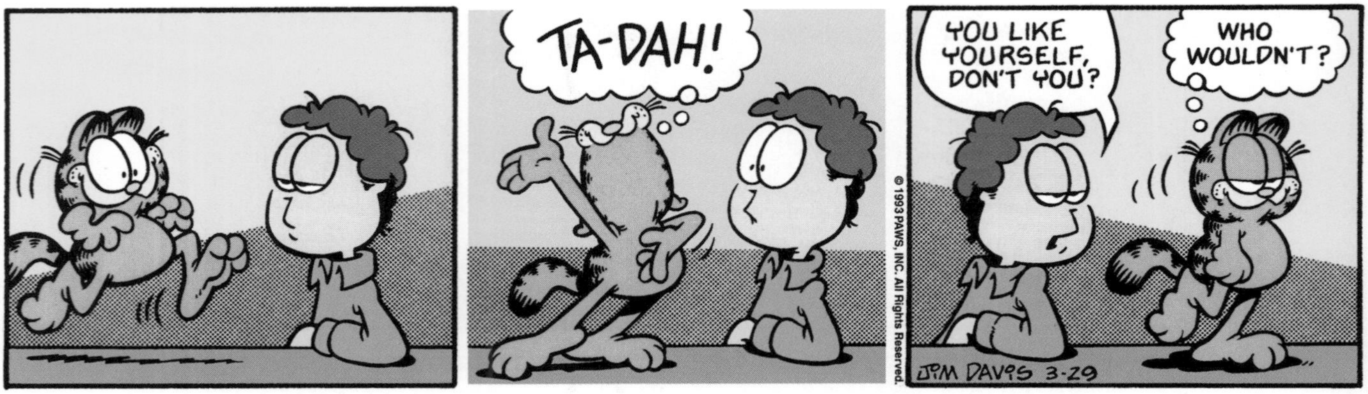
TA-DAH!
YOU LIKE YOURSELF, DON'T YOU?
WHO WOULDN'T?
© 1993 PAWS, INC. All Rights Reserved.
JIM DAVIS 3-29

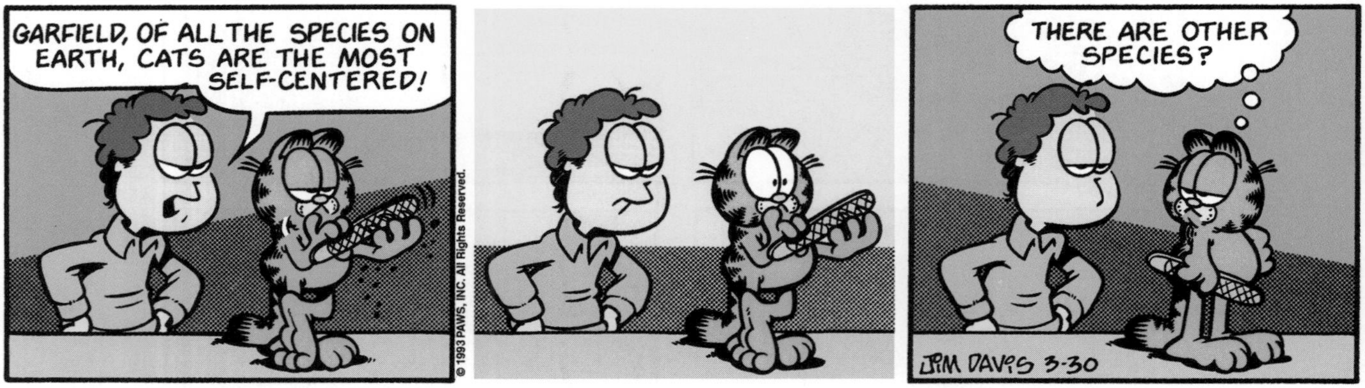
GARFIELD, OF ALL THE SPECIES ON EARTH, CATS ARE THE MOST SELF-CENTERED!
© 1993 PAWS, INC. All Rights Reserved.
THERE ARE OTHER SPECIES?
JIM DAVIS 3-30

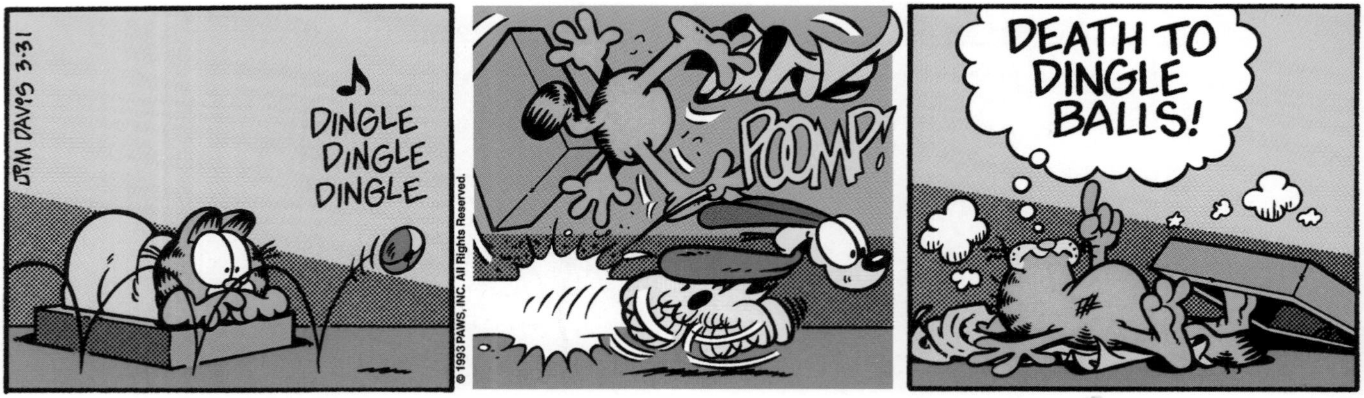
JIM DAVIS 3-31
DINGLE DINGLE DINGLE
© 1993 PAWS, INC. All Rights Reserved.
POOMP!
DEATH TO DINGLE BALLS!

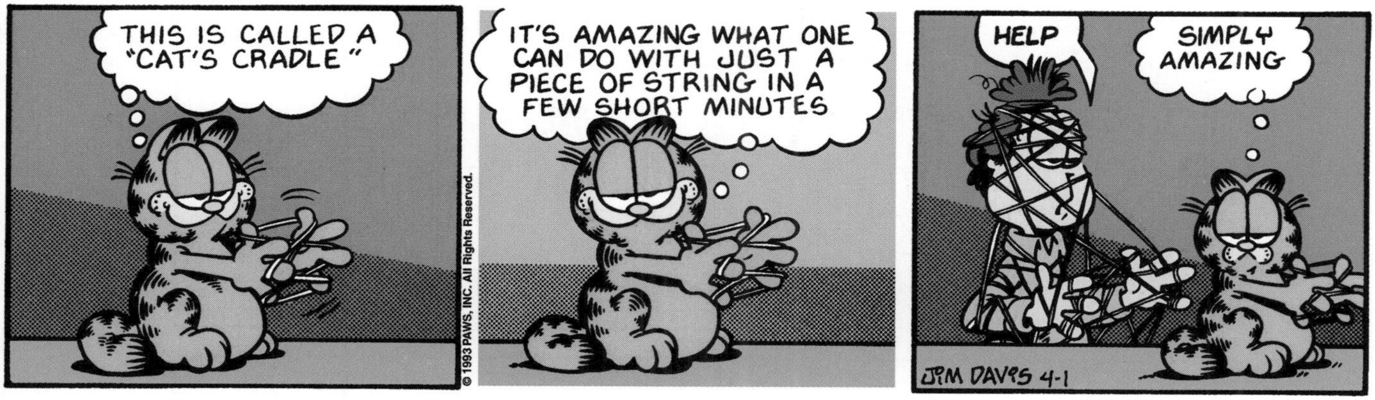
THIS IS CALLED A "CAT'S CRADLE"
IT'S AMAZING WHAT ONE CAN DO WITH JUST A PIECE OF STRING IN A FEW SHORT MINUTES
HELP
SIMPLY AMAZING
JIM DAVIS 4-1

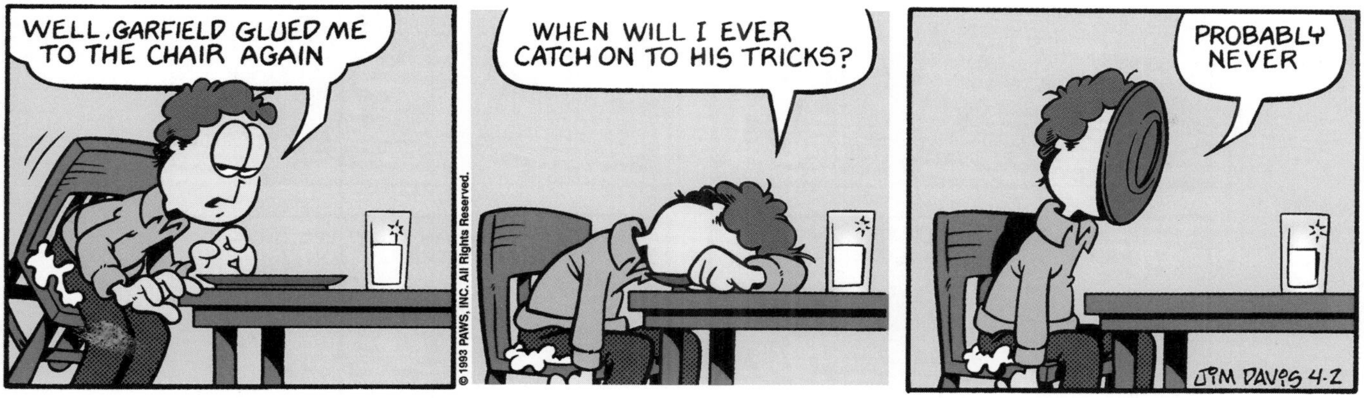
WELL, GARFIELD GLUED ME TO THE CHAIR AGAIN
WHEN WILL I EVER CATCH ON TO HIS TRICKS?
PROBABLY NEVER
JIM DAVIS 4-2

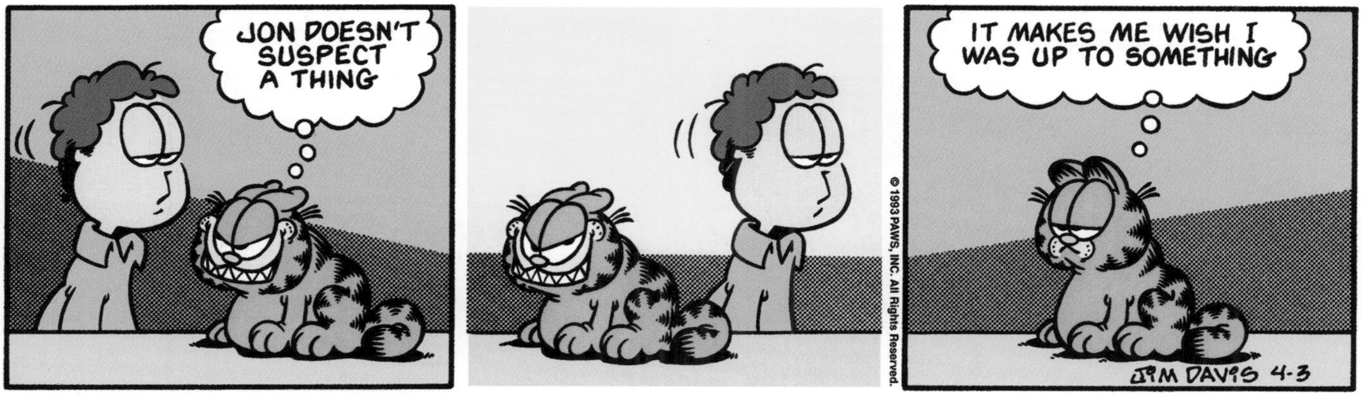
JON DOESN'T SUSPECT A THING
IT MAKES ME WISH I WAS UP TO SOMETHING
JIM DAVIS 4-3

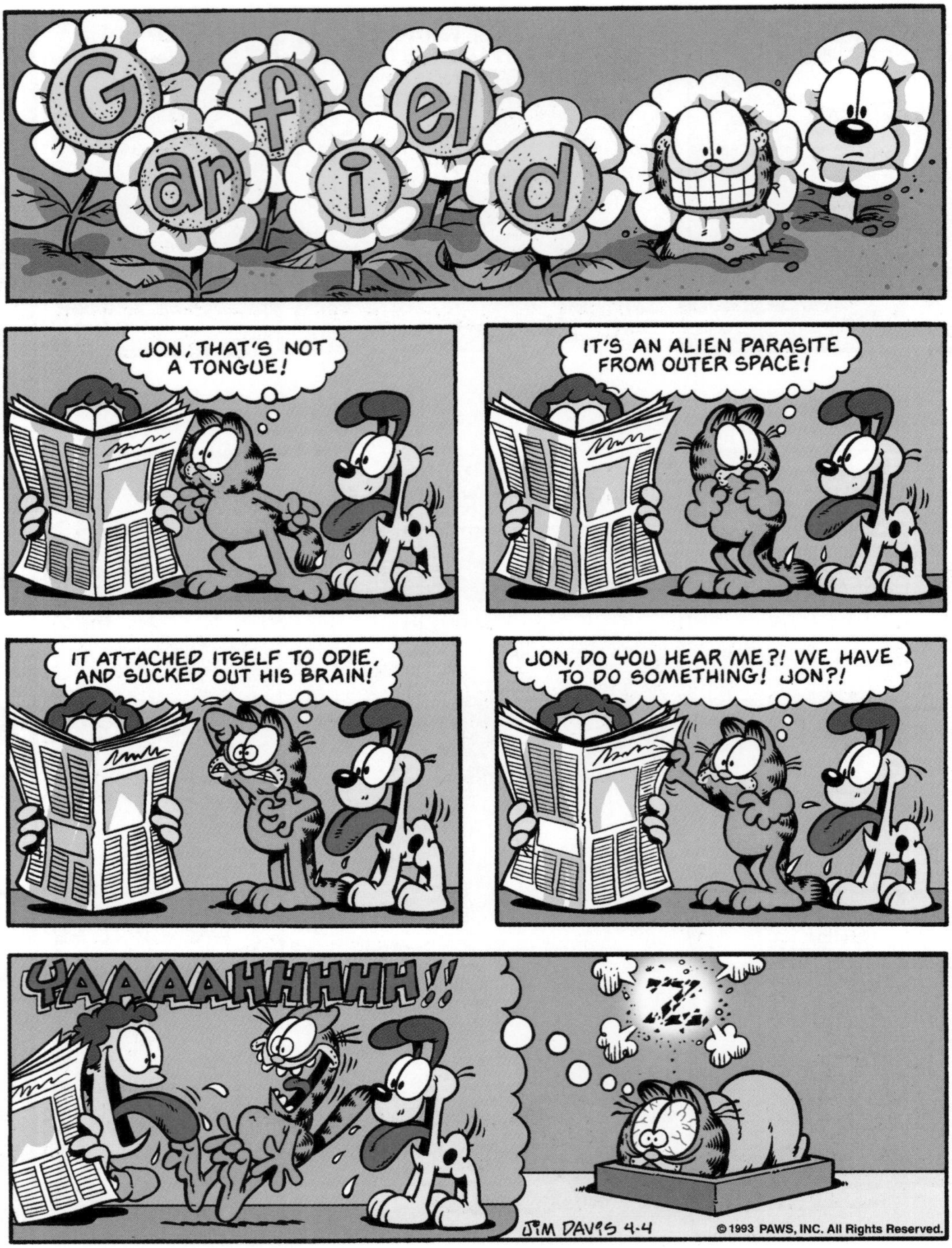
Garfield
JON, THAT'S NOT A TONGUE!
IT'S AN ALIEN PARASITE FROM OUTER SPACE!
IT ATTACHED ITSELF TO ODIE, AND SUCKED OUT HIS BRAIN!
JON, DO YOU HEAR ME?! WE HAVE TO DO SOMETHING! JON?!
YAAAAAHHHHH!!
JIM DAVIS 4-4
© 1993 PAWS, INC. All Rights Reserved.

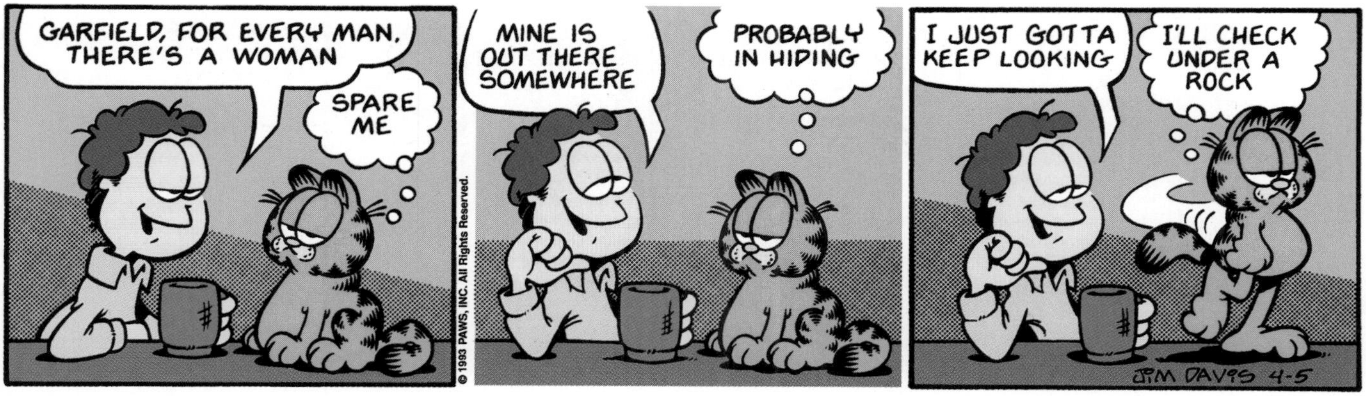
GARFIELD, FOR EVERY MAN, THERE'S A WOMAN
SPARE ME
MINE IS OUT THERE SOMEWHERE
PROBABLY IN HIDING
I JUST GOTTA KEEP LOOKING
I'LL CHECK UNDER A ROCK
© 1993 PAWS, INC. All Rights Reserved.
JIM DAVIS 4-5

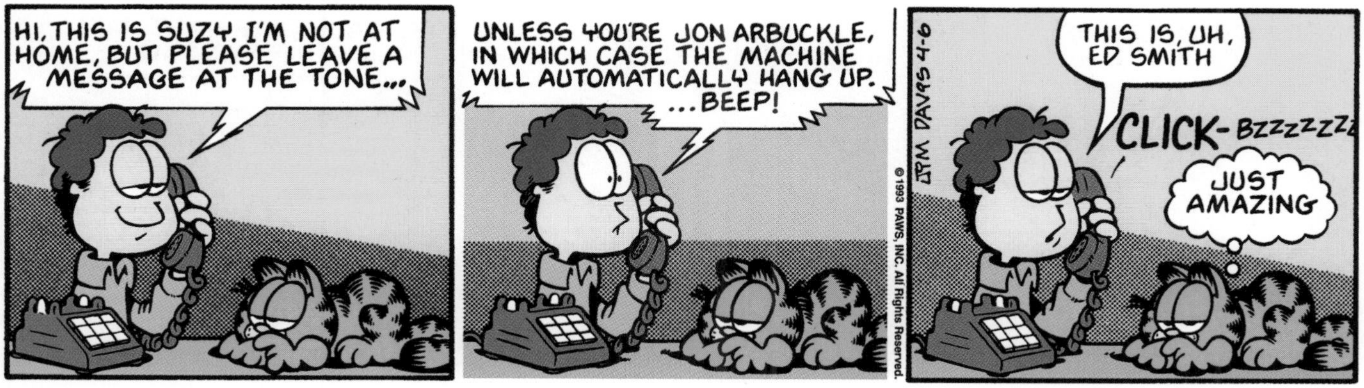
HI, THIS IS SUZY. I'M NOT AT HOME, BUT PLEASE LEAVE A MESSAGE AT THE TONE...
UNLESS YOU'RE JON ARBUCKLE, IN WHICH CASE THE MACHINE WILL AUTOMATICALLY HANG UP. ...BEEP!
JIM DAVIS 4-6
© 1993 PAWS, INC. All Rights Reserved.
THIS IS, UH, ED SMITH
CLICK-BZZZZZZZ
JUST AMAZING

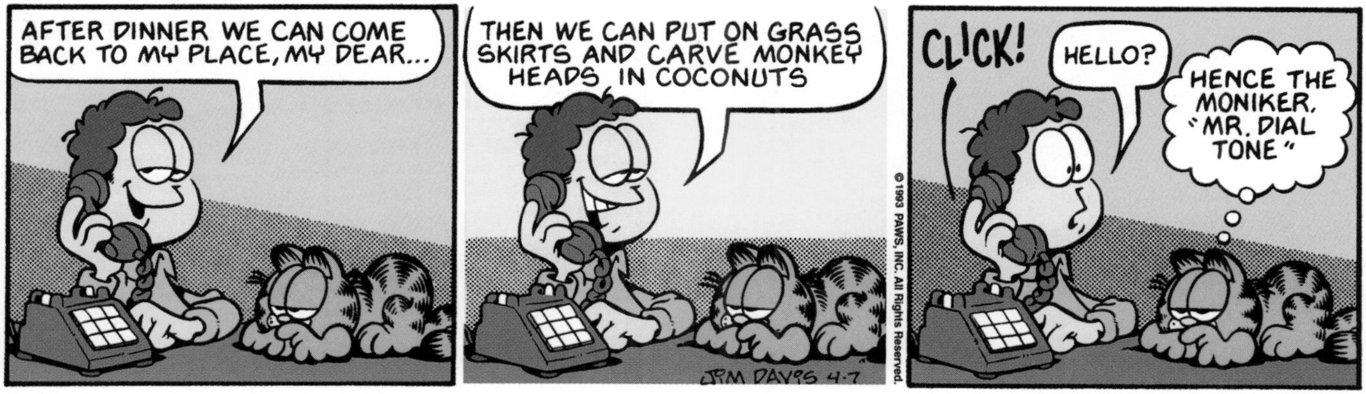
AFTER DINNER WE CAN COME BACK TO MY PLACE, MY DEAR...
THEN WE CAN PUT ON GRASS SKIRTS AND CARVE MONKEY HEADS IN COCONUTS
JIM DAVIS 4-7
© 1993 PAWS, INC. All Rights Reserved.
CLICK!
HELLO?
HENCE THE MONIKER, "MR. DIAL TONE"

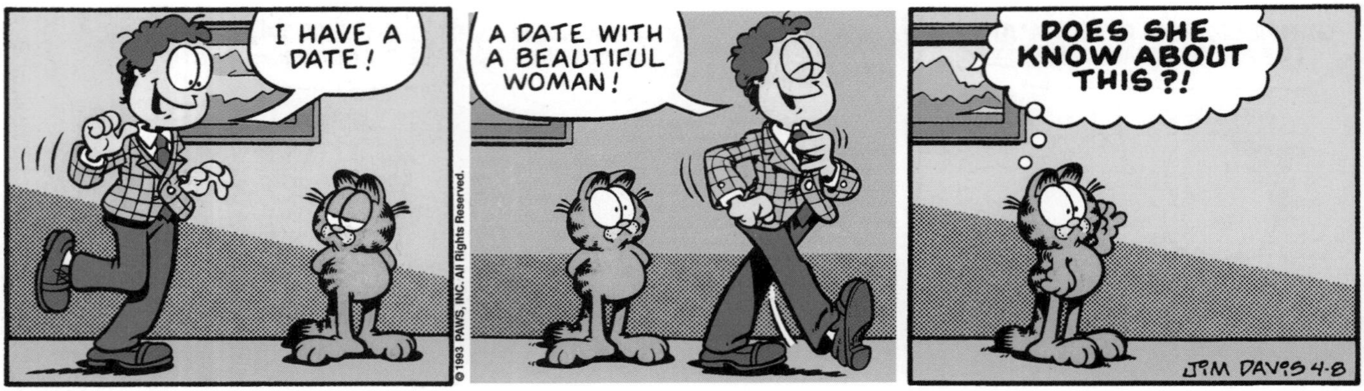
I HAVE A DATE!
A DATE WITH A BEAUTIFUL WOMAN!
DOES SHE KNOW ABOUT THIS?!
© 1993 PAWS, INC. All Rights Reserved.
JIM DAVIS 4-8

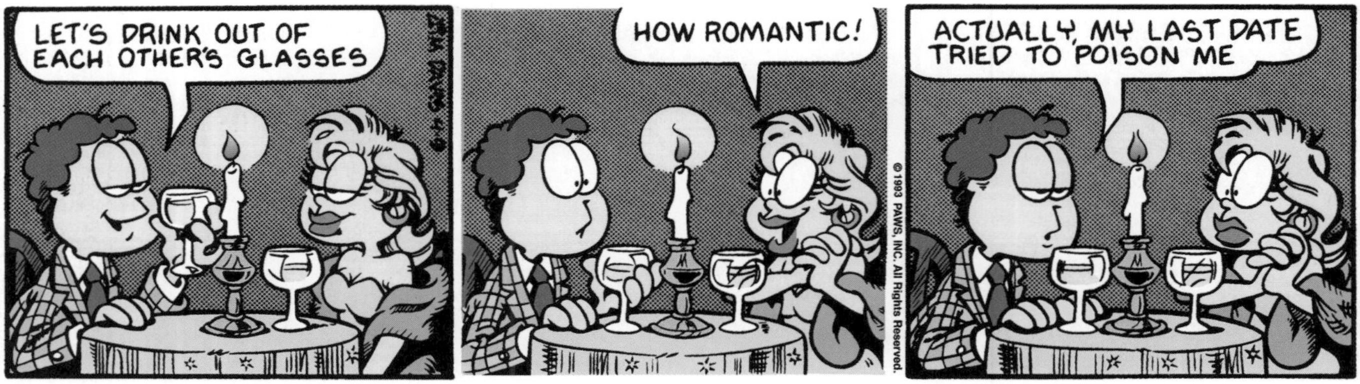
LET'S DRINK OUT OF EACH OTHER'S GLASSES
HOW ROMANTIC!
ACTUALLY, MY LAST DATE TRIED TO POISON ME
© 1993 PAWS, INC. All Rights Reserved.

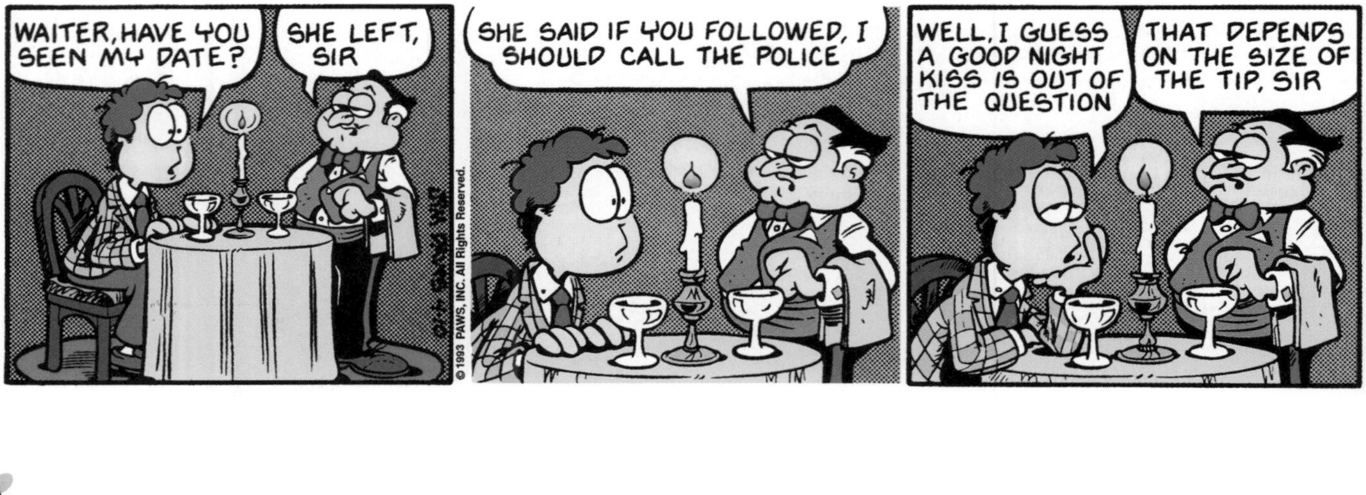
WAITER, HAVE YOU SEEN MY DATE?
SHE LEFT, SIR
SHE SAID IF YOU FOLLOWED, I SHOULD CALL THE POLICE
WELL, I GUESS A GOOD NIGHT KISS IS OUT OF THE QUESTION
THAT DEPENDS ON THE SIZE OF THE TIP, SIR
© 1993 PAWS, INC. All Rights Reserved.

The Garfield Birthday Gallery

1978

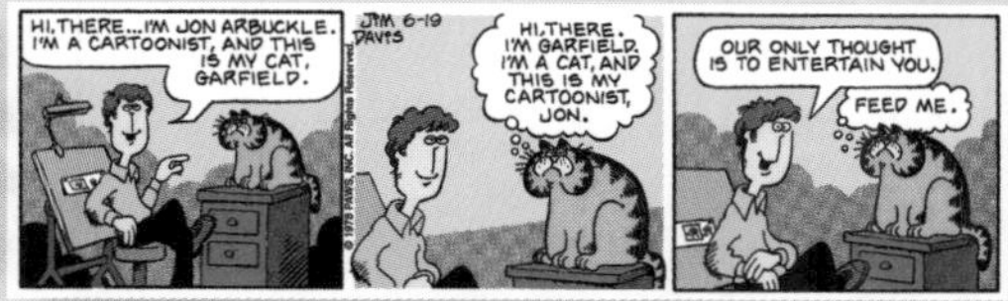

HI, THERE... I'M JON ARBUCKLE. I'M A CARTOONIST, AND THIS IS MY CAT, GARFIELD.
JIM DAVIS 6-19
HI, THERE. I'M GARFIELD. I'M A CAT, AND THIS IS MY CARTOONIST, JON.
OUR ONLY THOUGHT IS TO ENTERTAIN YOU.
FEED ME.

1979

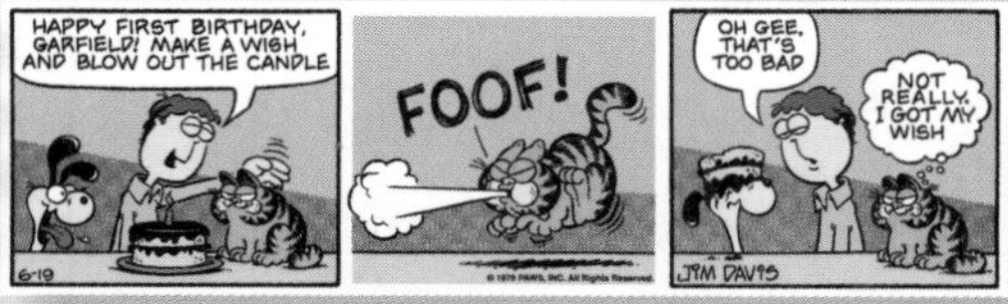

HAPPY FIRST BIRTHDAY, GARFIELD! MAKE A WISH AND BLOW OUT THE CANDLE
FOOF!
OH GEE. THAT'S TOO BAD
NOT REALLY. I GOT MY WISH
JIM DAVIS

1980

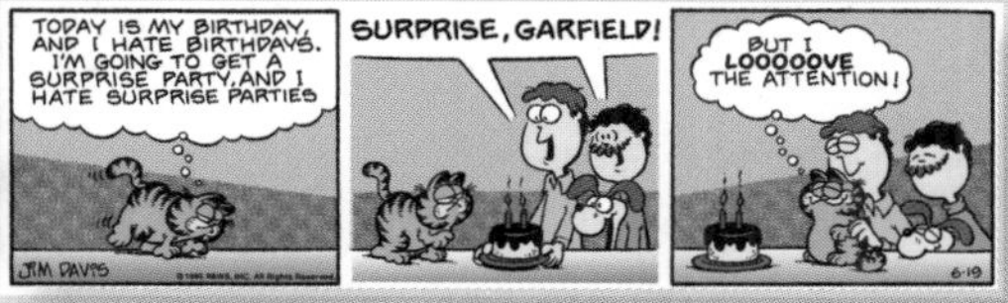

TODAY IS MY BIRTHDAY, AND I HATE BIRTHDAYS. I'M GOING TO GET A SURPRISE PARTY, AND I HATE SURPRISE PARTIES
SURPRISE, GARFIELD!
BUT I LOOOOOVE THE ATTENTION!
JIM DAVIS

1981

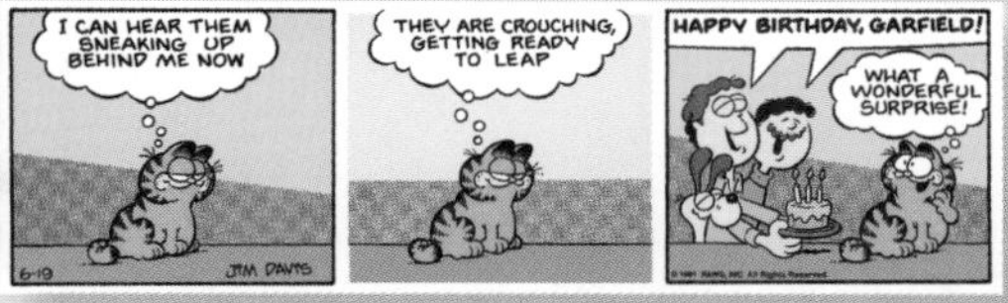

I CAN HEAR THEM SNEAKING UP BEHIND ME NOW
THEY ARE CROUCHING, GETTING READY TO LEAP
HAPPY BIRTHDAY, GARFIELD!
WHAT A WONDERFUL SURPRISE!
JIM DAVIS

1982

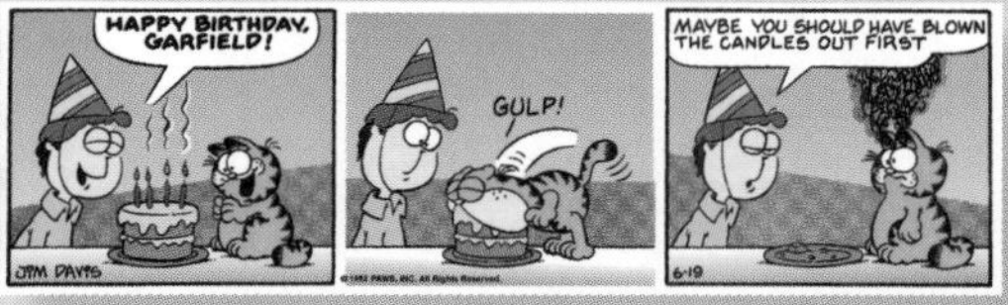

HAPPY BIRTHDAY, GARFIELD!
GULP!
MAYBE YOU SHOULD HAVE BLOWN THE CANDLES OUT FIRST
JIM DAVIS

1983

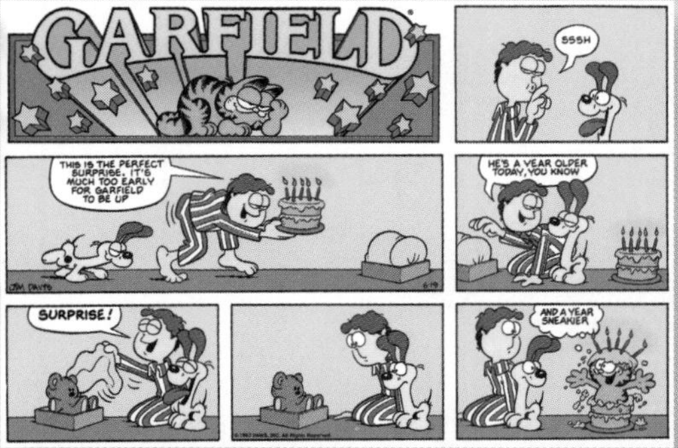

GARFIELD
SSSH
THIS IS THE PERFECT SURPRISE. IT'S MUCH TOO EARLY FOR GARFIELD TO BE UP
HE'S A YEAR OLDER TODAY, YOU KNOW
SURPRISE!
AND A YEAR SNEAKIER

1984

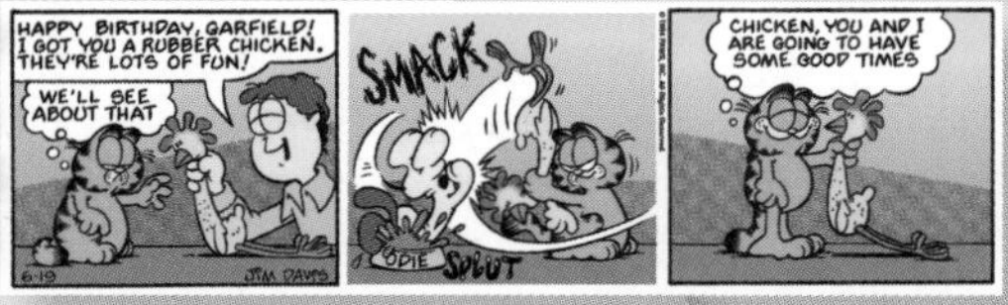

HAPPY BIRTHDAY, GARFIELD! I GOT YOU A RUBBER CHICKEN. THEY'RE LOTS OF FUN!
WE'LL SEE ABOUT THAT
SMACK
SPLUT
CHICKEN, YOU AND I ARE GOING TO HAVE SOME GOOD TIMES
JIM DAVIS

1985

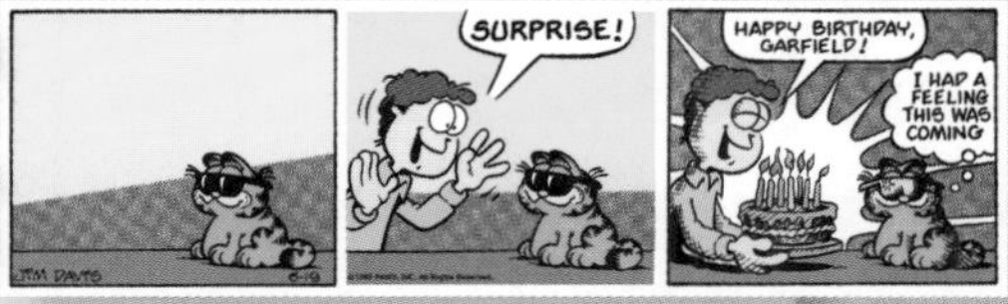

SURPRISE!
HAPPY BIRTHDAY, GARFIELD!
I HAD A FEELING THIS WAS COMING
JIM DAVIS

1986

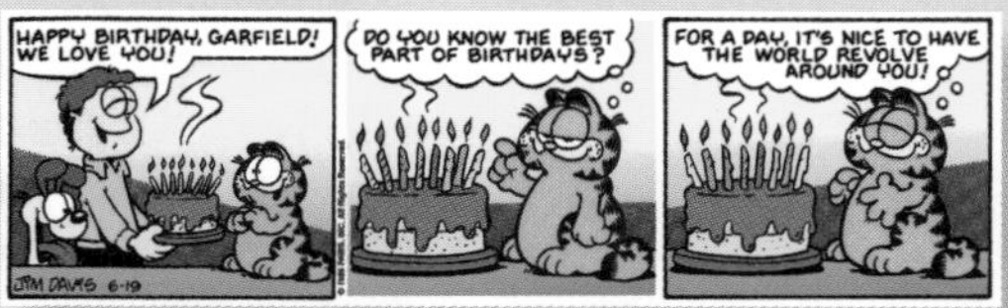

HAPPY BIRTHDAY, GARFIELD! WE LOVE YOU!
DO YOU KNOW THE BEST PART OF BIRTHDAYS?
FOR A DAY, IT'S NICE TO HAVE THE WORLD REVOLVE AROUND YOU!
JIM DAVIS 6-19

1987

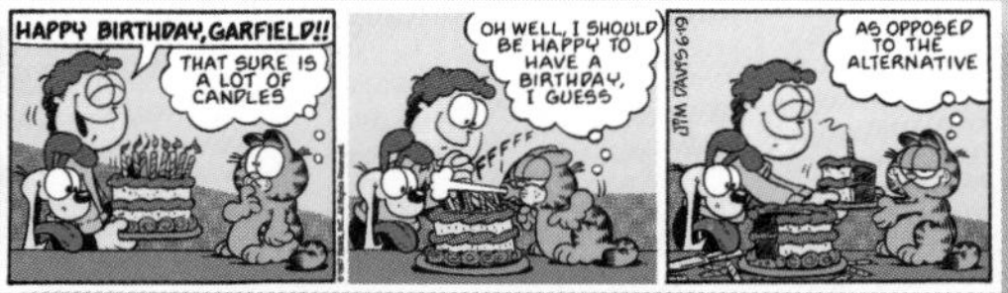

HAPPY BIRTHDAY, GARFIELD!!
THAT SURE IS A LOT OF CANDLES
OH WELL, I SHOULD BE HAPPY TO HAVE A BIRTHDAY, I GUESS
AS OPPOSED TO THE ALTERNATIVE

1988

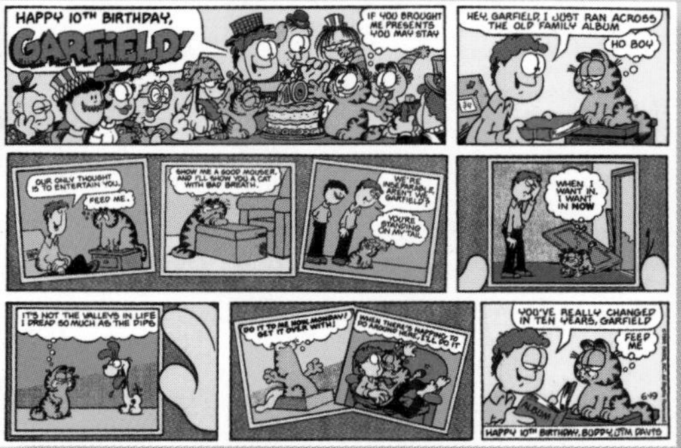

HAPPY 10TH BIRTHDAY, GARFIELD
IF YOU BROUGHT ME PRESENTS YOU MAY STAY
HEY, GARFIELD! I JUST RAN ACROSS THE OLD FAMILY ALBUM
HO BOY
OUR ONLY THOUGHT IS TO ENTERTAIN YOU.
FEED ME.
WHEN I WANT IN, I WANT IN NOW
IT'S NOT THE VALLEYS IN LIFE I DREAD SO MUCH AS THE DIPS
YOU'VE REALLY CHANGED IN TEN YEARS, GARFIELD
FEED ME.
HAPPY 10TH BIRTHDAY, BUDDY, JIM DAVIS

1989

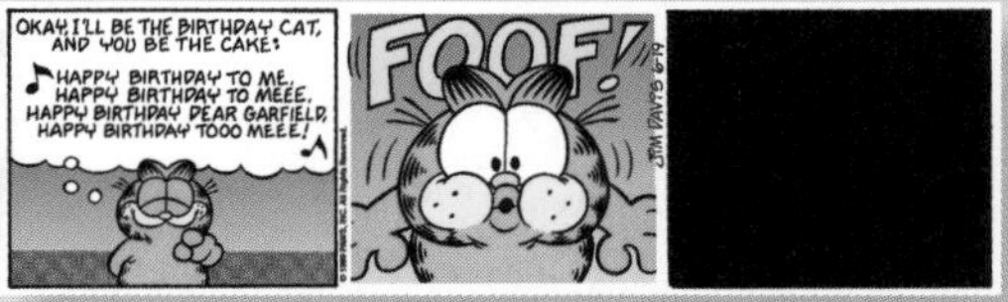

OKAY, I'LL BE THE BIRTHDAY CAT, AND YOU BE THE CAKE:
HAPPY BIRTHDAY TO ME, HAPPY BIRTHDAY TO MEEE. HAPPY BIRTHDAY DEAR GARFIELD, HAPPY BIRTHDAY TOOO MEEE!
FOOF!
JIM DAVIS 6-19

1990

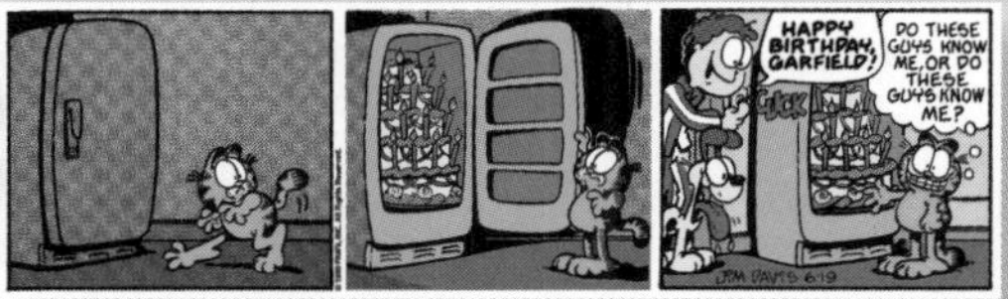

HAPPY BIRTHDAY, GARFIELD!
DO THESE GUYS KNOW ME, OR DO THESE GUYS KNOW ME?
JIM DAVIS 6-19

1991

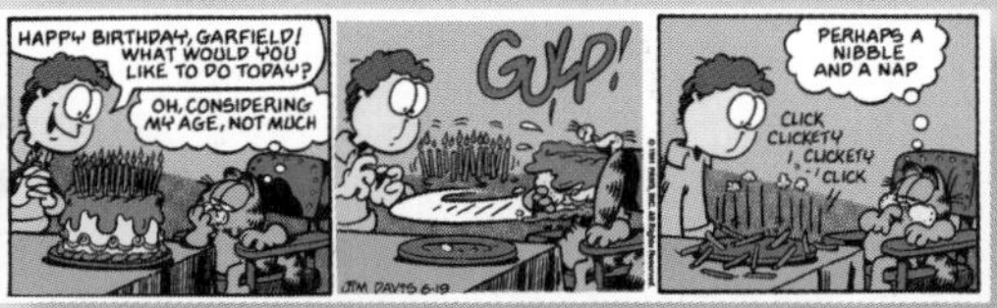

HAPPY BIRTHDAY, GARFIELD! WHAT WOULD YOU LIKE TO DO TODAY?
OH, CONSIDERING MY AGE, NOT MUCH
GULP!
PERHAPS A NIBBLE AND A NAP
CLICK CLICKETY CLICKETY CLICK
JIM DAVIS 6-19

1992

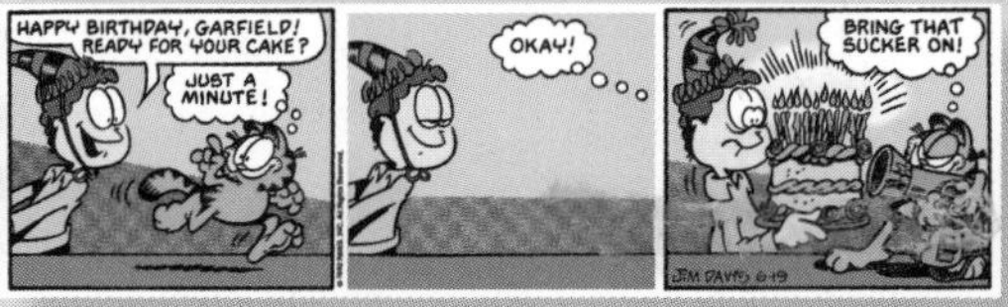

HAPPY BIRTHDAY, GARFIELD! READY FOR YOUR CAKE?
JUST A MINUTE!
OKAY!
BRING THAT SUCKER ON!
JIM DAVIS 6-19

1993

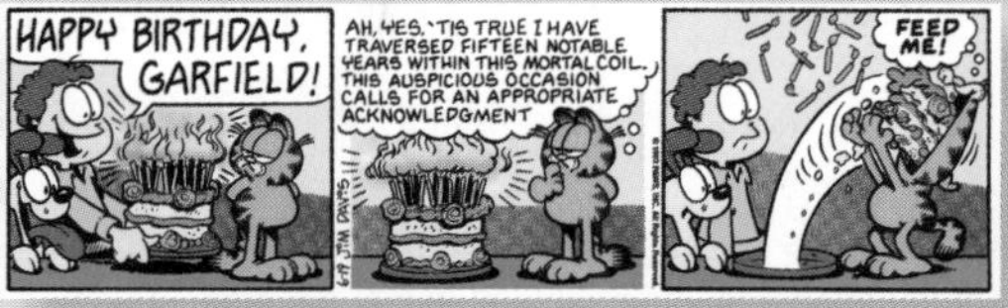

HAPPY BIRTHDAY, GARFIELD!
AH, YES. 'TIS TRUE I HAVE TRAVERSED FIFTEEN NOTABLE YEARS WITHIN THIS MORTAL COIL. THIS AUSPICIOUS OCCASION CALLS FOR AN APPROPRIATE ACKNOWLEDGMENT
FEED ME!

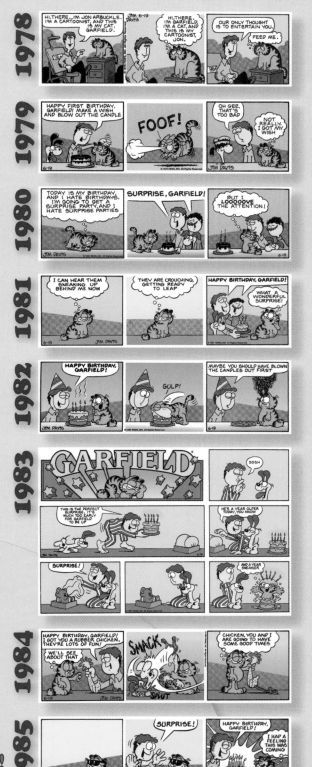

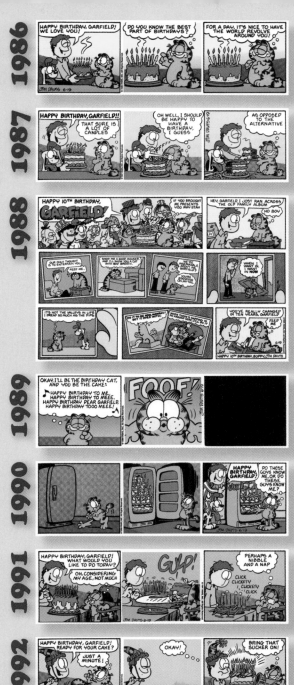

Feast your eyes on the Garfield Birthday Gallery. The famished feline has been perfecting the art of eating for fifteen years now. That's a bellyful of laughs and lasagna. And rest assured that the Picasso of cats will continue to color your world with fun for many years to come.

CELEBRATING 15 Fabulous Years! 1978·1993

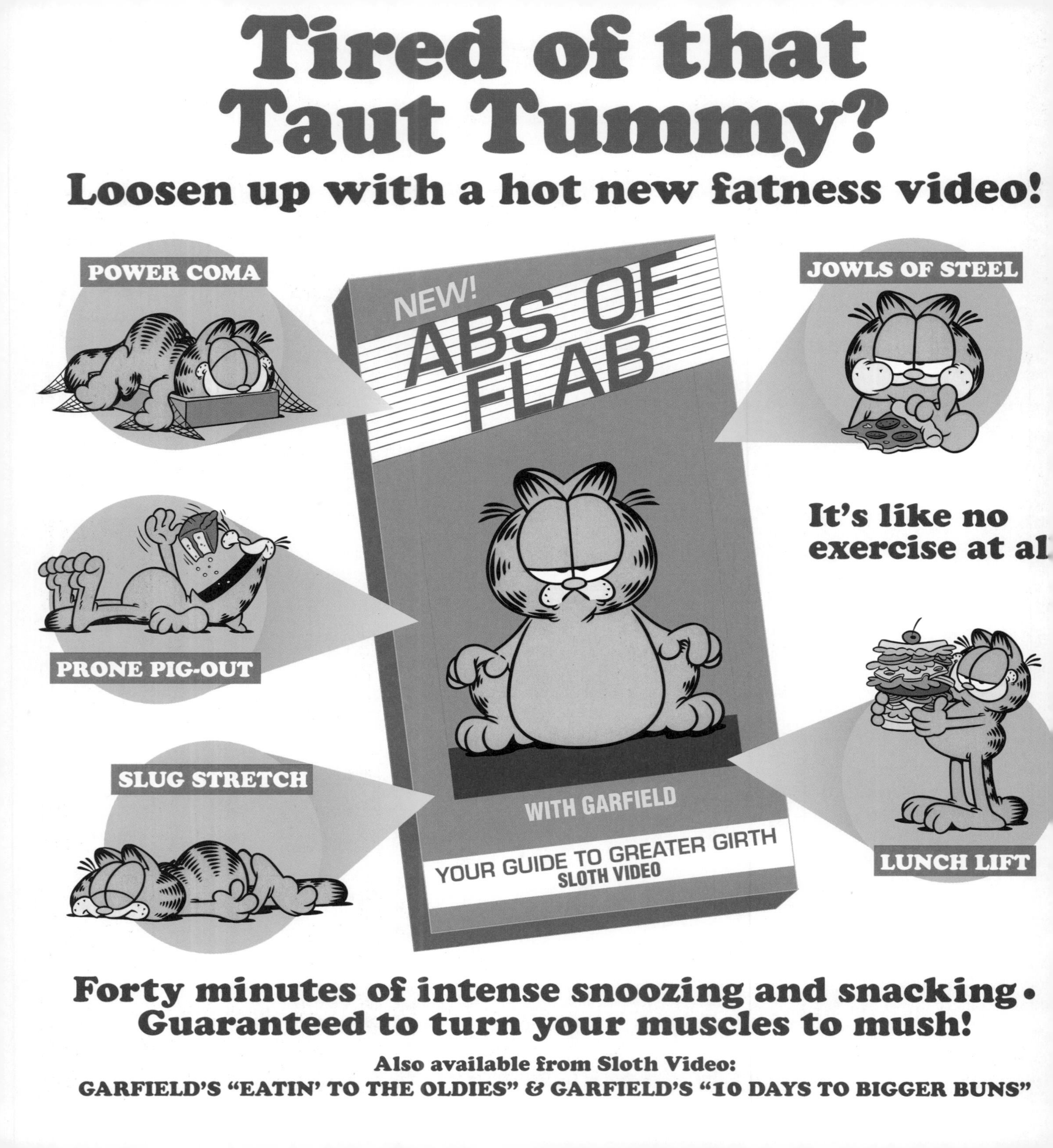

Tired of that Taut Tummy?
Loosen up with a hot new fatness video!
POWER COMA
JOWLS OF STEEL
NEW!
ABS OF FLAB
It's like no exercise at al
PRONE PIG-OUT
SLUG STRETCH
WITH GARFIELD
YOUR GUIDE TO GREATER GIRTH
SLOTH VIDEO
LUNCH LIFT
Forty minutes of intense snoozing and snacking •
Guaranteed to turn your muscles to mush!
Also available from Sloth Video:
GARFIELD'S "EATIN' TO THE OLDIES" & GARFIELD'S "10 DAYS TO BIGGER BUNS"

Garfield
pulls his
weight

BY JIM DAVIS

Ballantine Books • New York

Z
GARFIELD
CLOUDY DAYS ARE SO DEPRESSING
AH, THERE'S THE SUN
THERE IT GOES AGAIN
JIM DAVIS 4-11

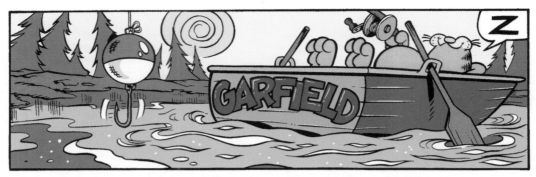

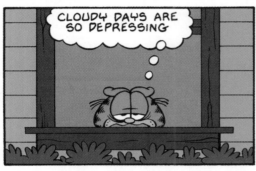

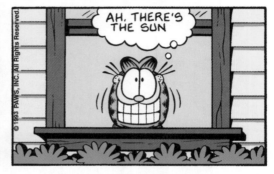

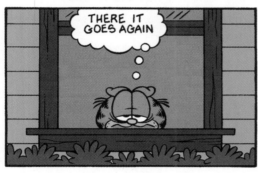

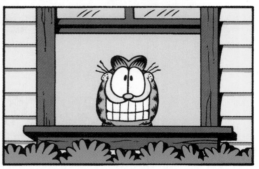

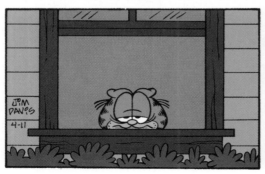

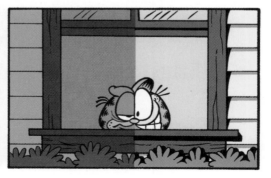

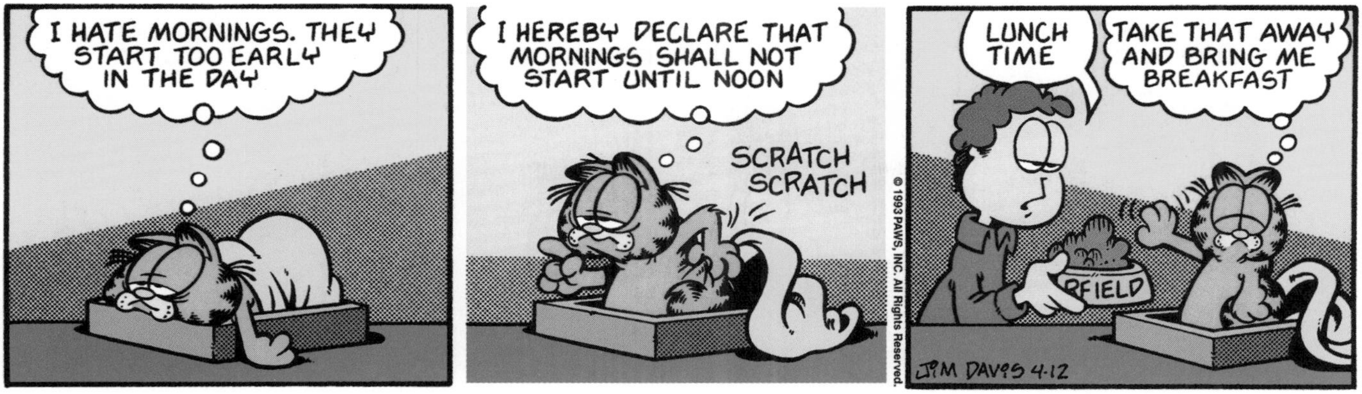
I HATE MORNINGS. THEY START TOO EARLY IN THE DAY
I HEREBY DECLARE THAT MORNINGS SHALL NOT START UNTIL NOON
SCRATCH SCRATCH
© 1993 PAWS, INC. All Rights Reserved.
LUNCH TIME
TAKE THAT AWAY AND BRING ME BREAKFAST
RFIELD
JIM DAVIS 4-12

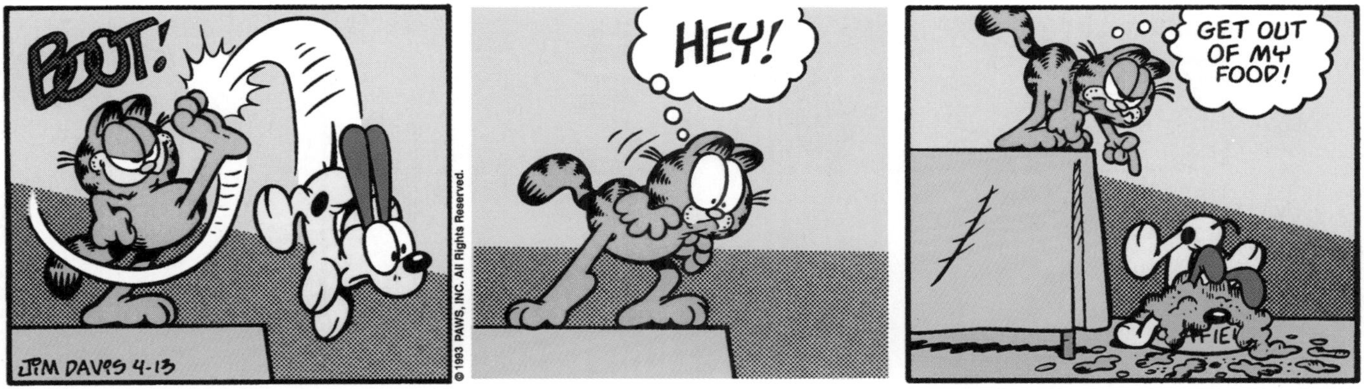
BOOT!
JIM DAVIS 4-13
© 1993 PAWS, INC. All Rights Reserved.
HEY!
GET OUT OF MY FOOD!

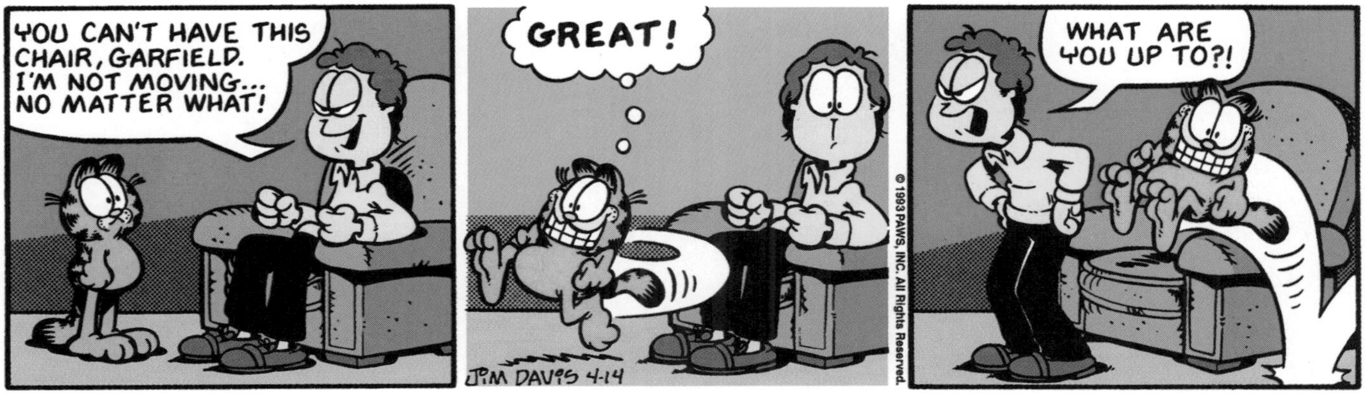
YOU CAN'T HAVE THIS CHAIR, GARFIELD. I'M NOT MOVING... NO MATTER WHAT!
GREAT!
JIM DAVIS 4-14
© 1993 PAWS, INC. All Rights Reserved.
WHAT ARE YOU UP TO?!

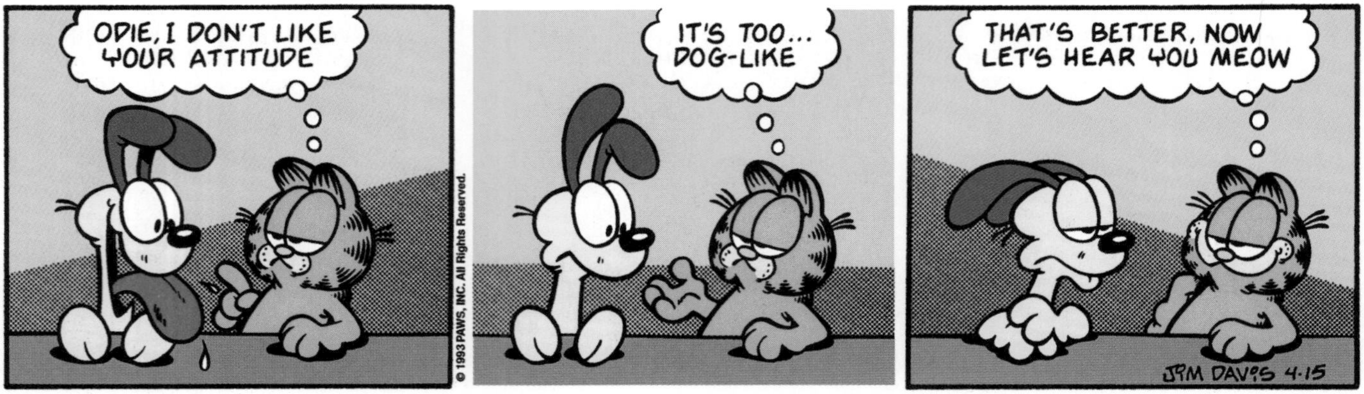
ODIE, I DON'T LIKE YOUR ATTITUDE
IT'S TOO... DOG-LIKE
THAT'S BETTER, NOW LET'S HEAR YOU MEOW
JIM DAVIS 4-15
© 1993 PAWS, INC. All Rights Reserved.

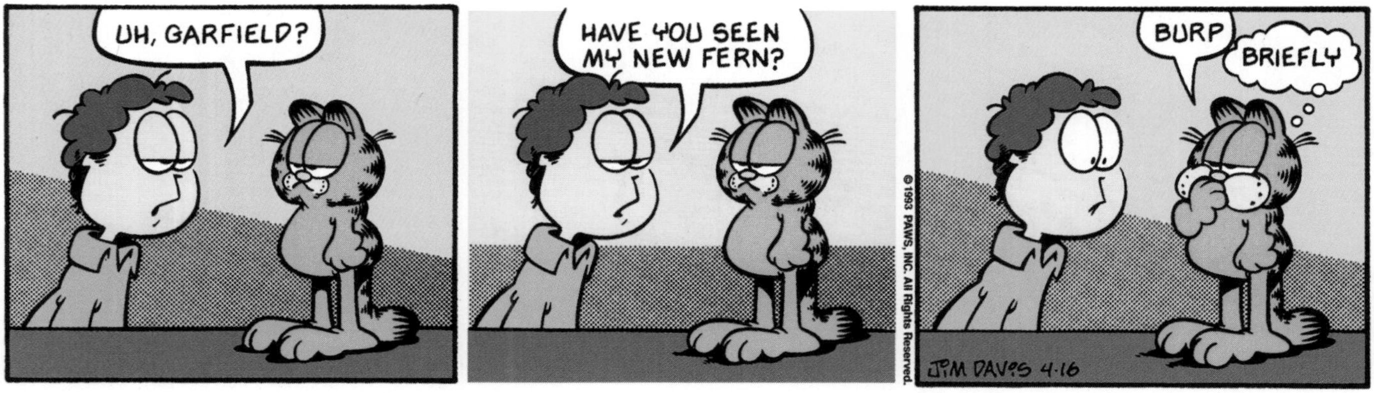
UH, GARFIELD?
HAVE YOU SEEN MY NEW FERN?
BURP
BRIEFLY
JIM DAVIS 4-16
© 1993 PAWS, INC. All Rights Reserved.

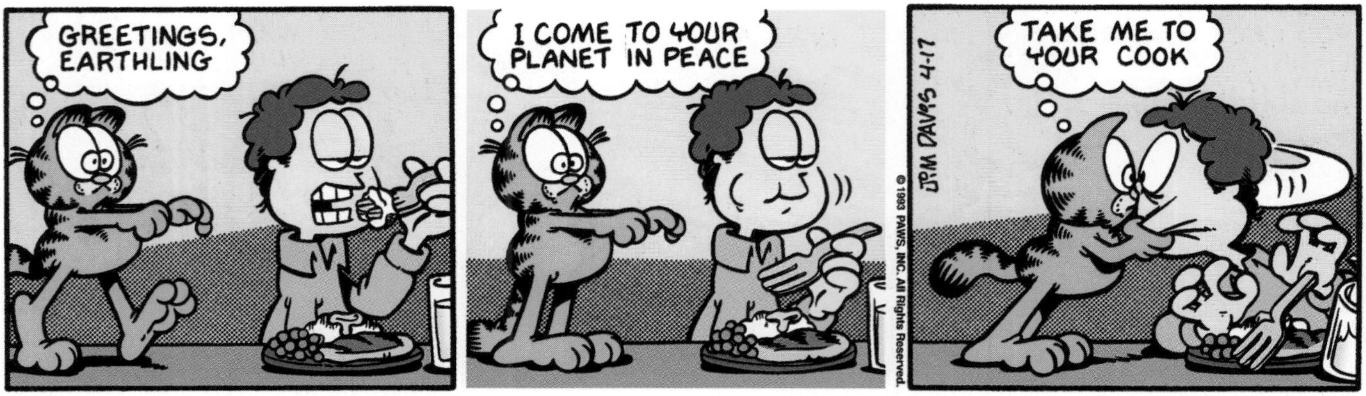
GREETINGS, EARTHLING
I COME TO YOUR PLANET IN PEACE
TAKE ME TO YOUR COOK
JIM DAVIS 4-17
© 1993 PAWS, INC. All Rights Reserved.

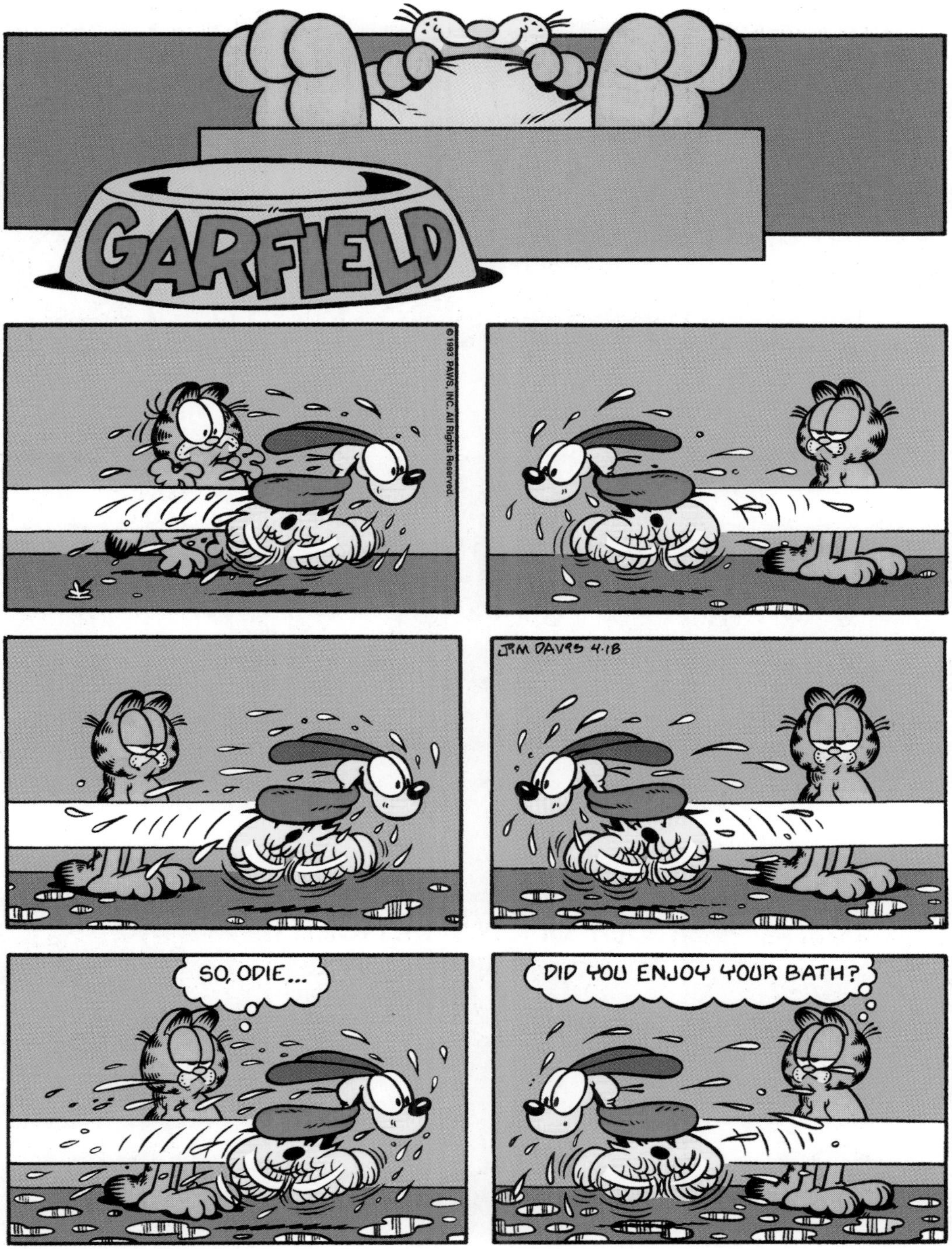
GARFIELD
© 1993 PAWS, INC. All Rights Reserved.
JIM DAVIS 4·18
SO, ODIE...
DID YOU ENJOY YOUR BATH?

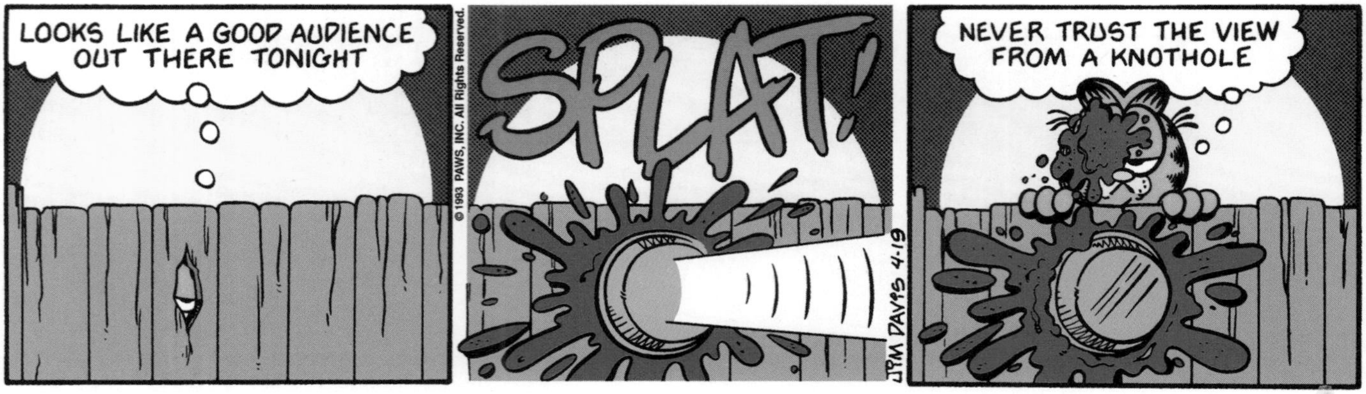
LOOKS LIKE A GOOD AUDIENCE OUT THERE TONIGHT
SPLAT!
© 1993 PAWS, INC. All Rights Reserved.
JIM DAVIS 4-19
NEVER TRUST THE VIEW FROM A KNOTHOLE

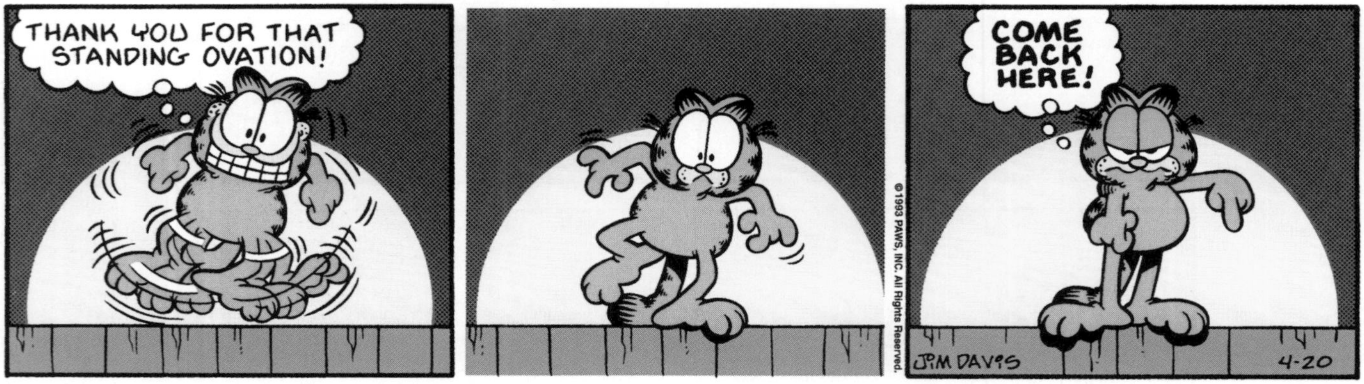
THANK YOU FOR THAT STANDING OVATION!
© 1993 PAWS, INC. All Rights Reserved.
COME BACK HERE!
JIM DAVIS
4-20

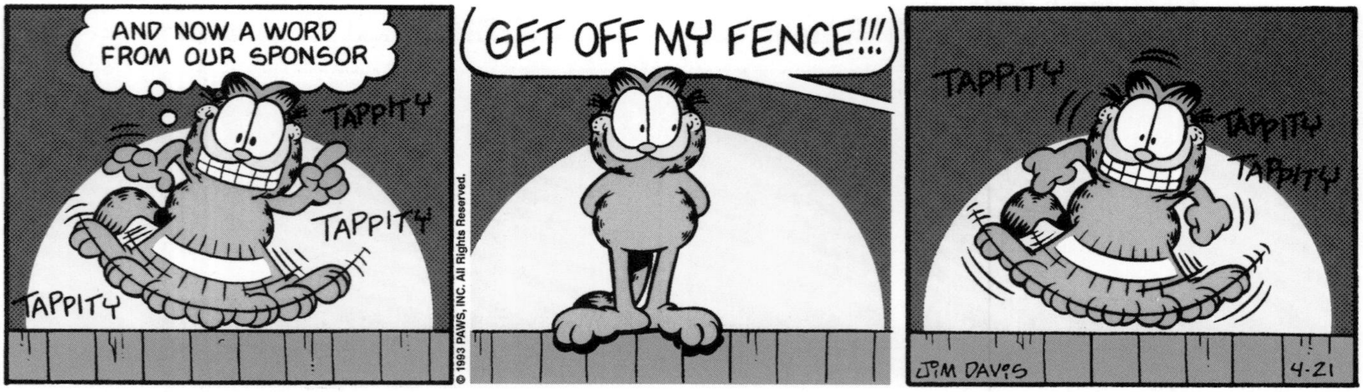
AND NOW A WORD FROM OUR SPONSOR
TAPPITY
TAPPITY
TAPPITY
© 1993 PAWS, INC. All Rights Reserved.
GET OFF MY FENCE!!!
TAPPITY
TAPPITY
TAPPITY
JIM DAVIS
4-21

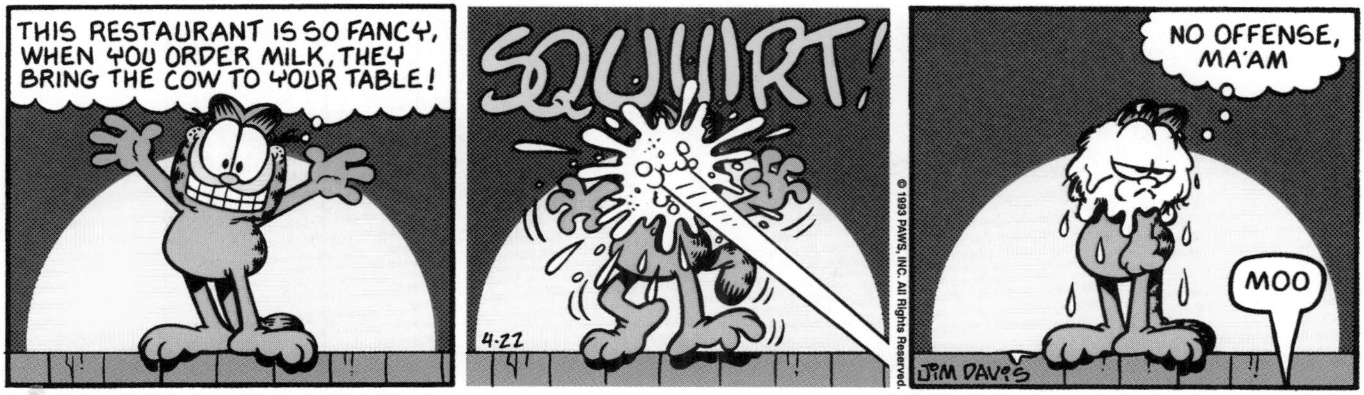
THIS RESTAURANT IS SO FANCY, WHEN YOU ORDER MILK, THEY BRING THE COW TO YOUR TABLE!
SQUIIIRT!
4-22
© 1993 PAWS, INC. All Rights Reserved.
NO OFFENSE, MA'AM
MOO
JIM DAVIS

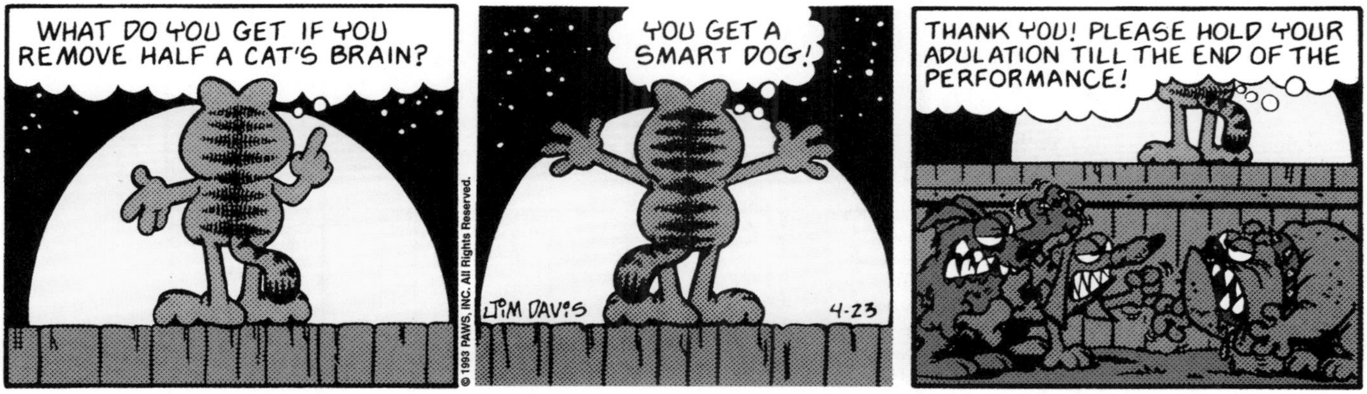
WHAT DO YOU GET IF YOU REMOVE HALF A CAT'S BRAIN?
© 1993 PAWS, INC. All Rights Reserved.
YOU GET A SMART DOG!
JIM DAVIS
4-23
THANK YOU! PLEASE HOLD YOUR ADULATION TILL THE END OF THE PERFORMANCE!

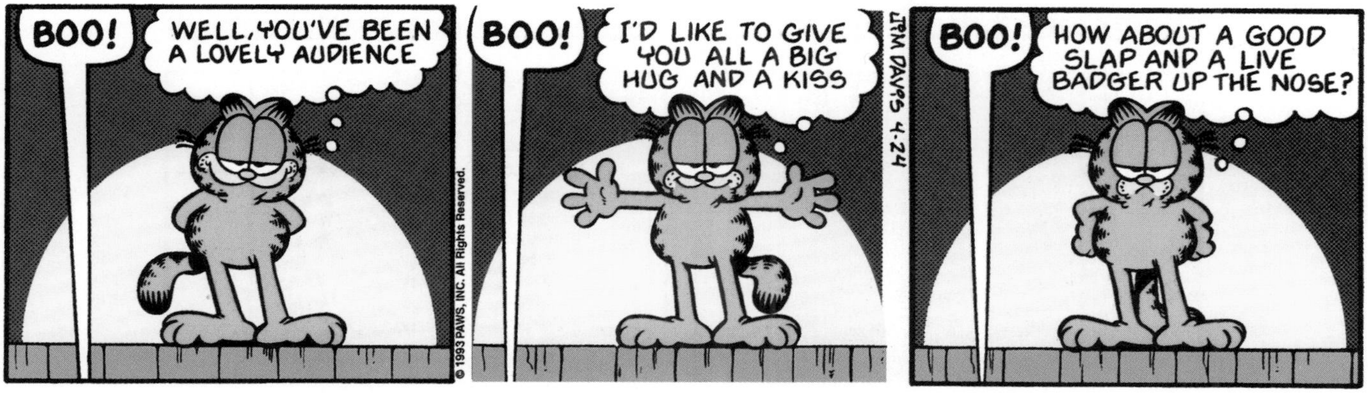
BOO!
WELL, YOU'VE BEEN A LOVELY AUDIENCE
© 1993 PAWS, INC. All Rights Reserved.
BOO!
I'D LIKE TO GIVE YOU ALL A BIG HUG AND A KISS
JIM DAVIS 4-24
BOO!
HOW ABOUT A GOOD SLAP AND A LIVE BADGER UP THE NOSE?

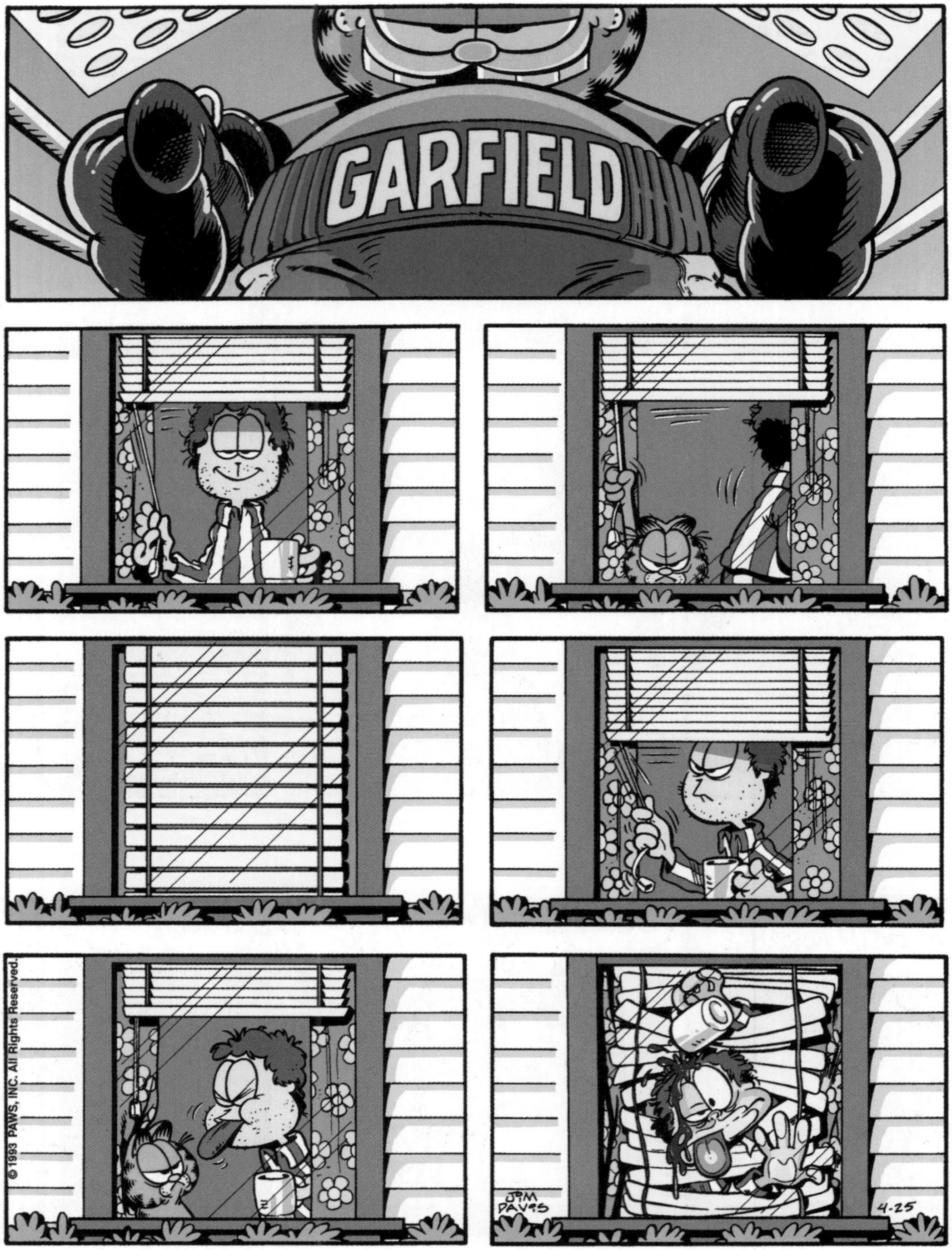
GARFIELD
© 1993 PAWS, INC. All Rights Reserved.
JIM DAVIS
4-25

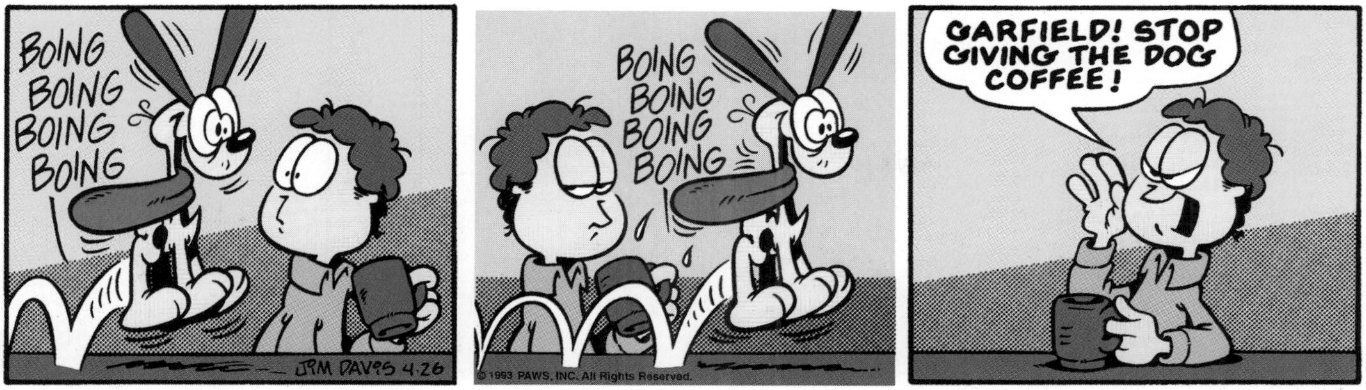
BOING BOING BOING BOING
JIM DAVIS 4.26
BOING BOING BOING BOING
© 1993 PAWS, INC. All Rights Reserved.
GARFIELD! STOP GIVING THE DOG COFFEE!

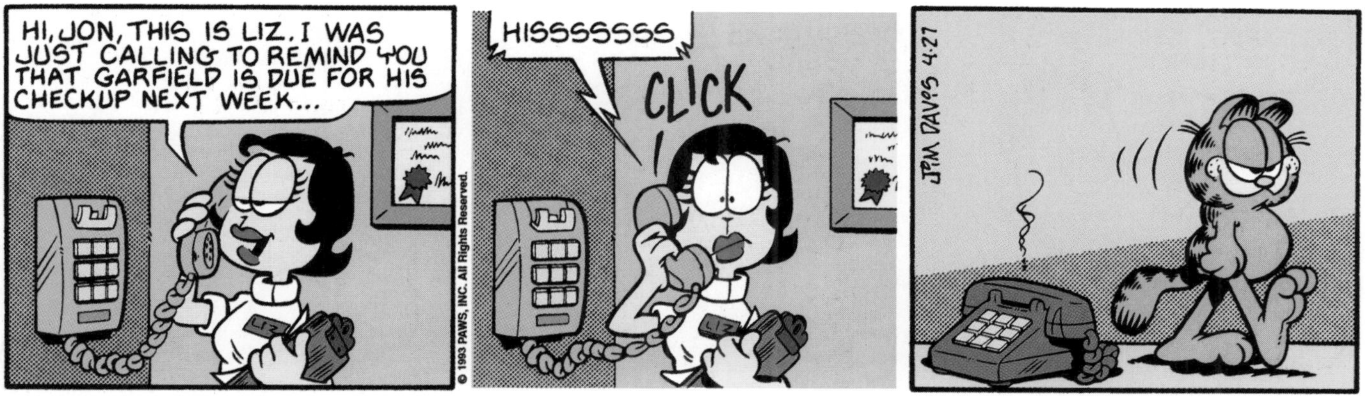
HI, JON, THIS IS LIZ. I WAS JUST CALLING TO REMIND YOU THAT GARFIELD IS DUE FOR HIS CHECKUP NEXT WEEK...
© 1993 PAWS, INC. All Rights Reserved.
HISSSSSSS
CLICK
JIM DAVIS 4.27

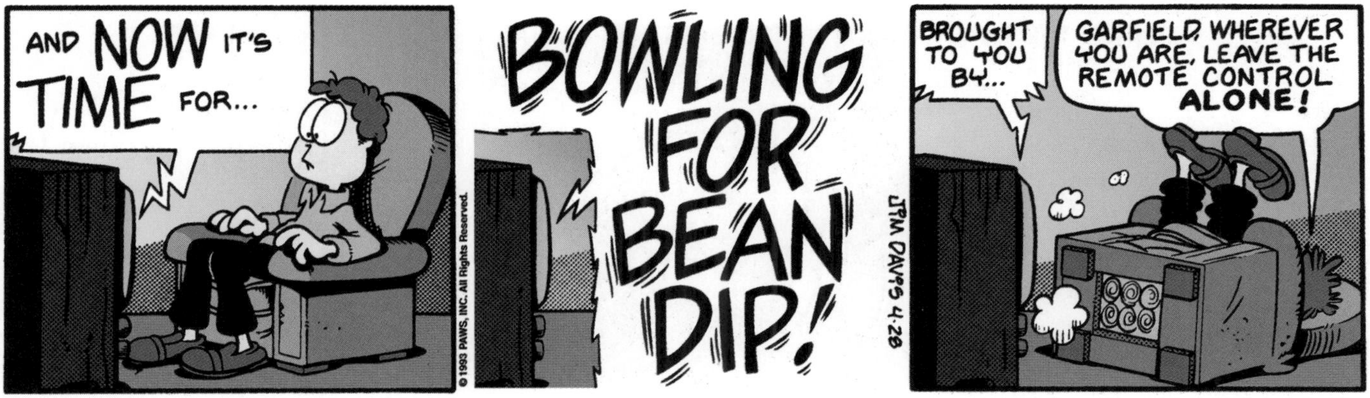
AND NOW IT'S TIME FOR...
© 1993 PAWS, INC. All Rights Reserved.
BOWLING FOR BEAN DIP!
JIM DAVIS 4.28
BROUGHT TO YOU BY...
GARFIELD, WHEREVER YOU ARE, LEAVE THE REMOTE CONTROL ALONE!

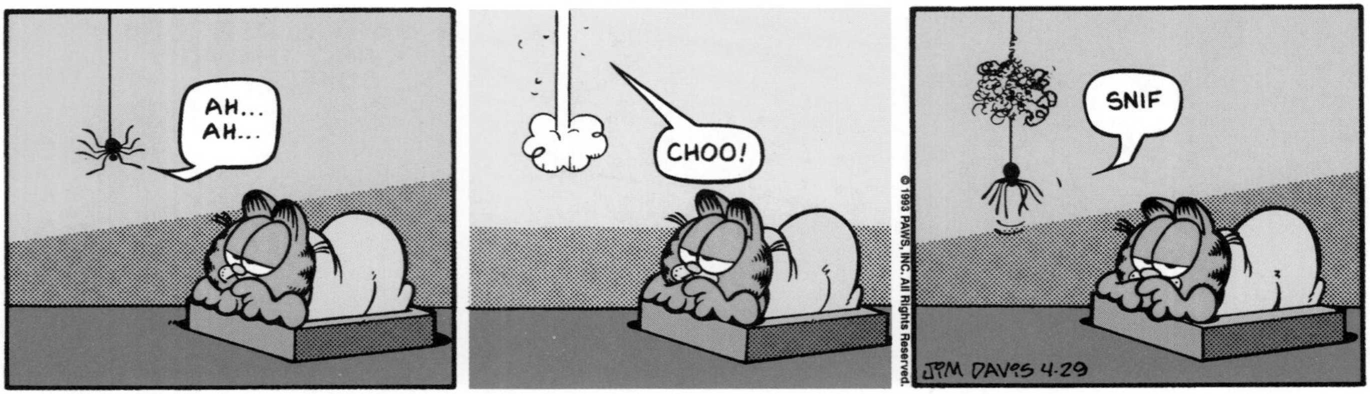
AH...
AH...
CHOO!
SNIF
© 1993 PAWS, INC. All Rights Reserved.
JIM DAVIS 4-29

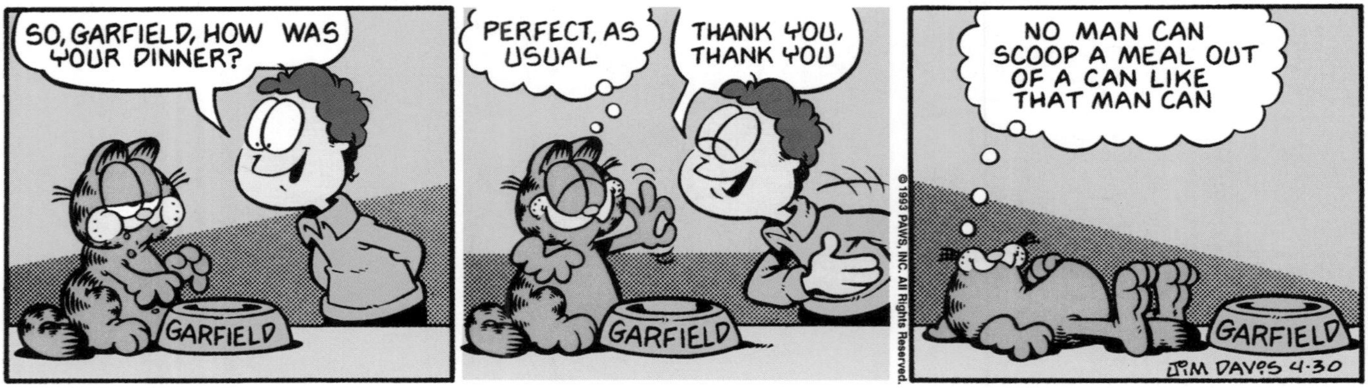
SO, GARFIELD, HOW WAS YOUR DINNER?
GARFIELD
PERFECT, AS USUAL
THANK YOU, THANK YOU
GARFIELD
NO MAN CAN SCOOP A MEAL OUT OF A CAN LIKE THAT MAN CAN
GARFIELD
© 1993 PAWS, INC. All Rights Reserved.
JIM DAVIS 4-30

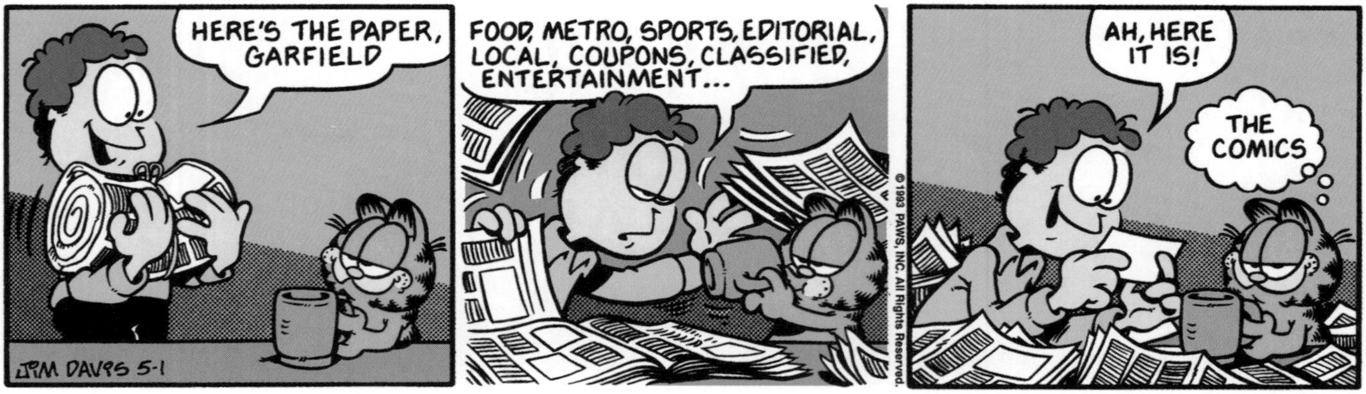
HERE'S THE PAPER, GARFIELD
FOOD, METRO, SPORTS, EDITORIAL, LOCAL, COUPONS, CLASSIFIED, ENTERTAINMENT...
AH, HERE IT IS!
THE COMICS
© 1993 PAWS, INC. All Rights Reserved.
JIM DAVIS 5-1

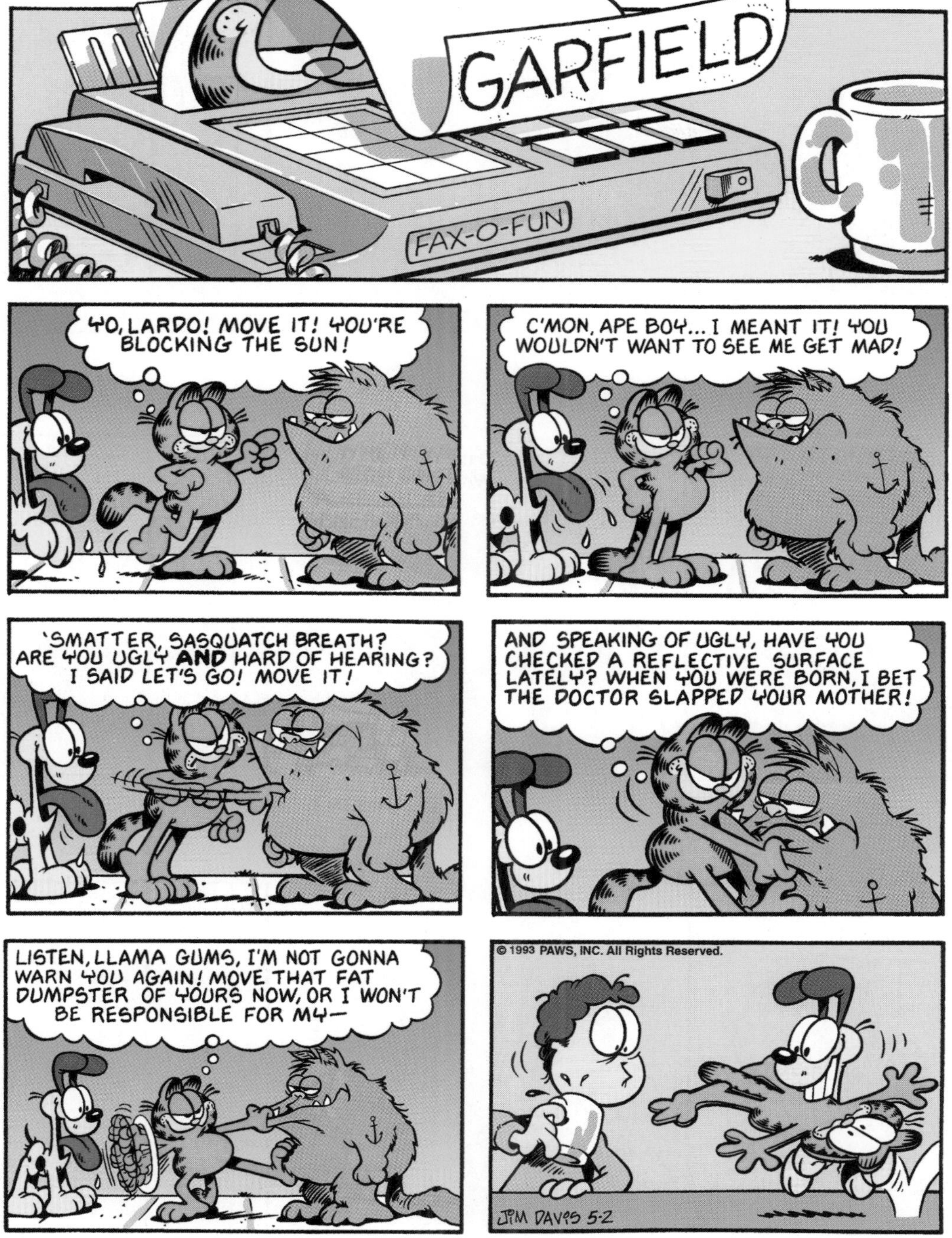
GARFIELD
FAX-O-FUN
YO, LARDO! MOVE IT! YOU'RE BLOCKING THE SUN!
C'MON, APE BOY... I MEANT IT! YOU WOULDN'T WANT TO SEE ME GET MAD!
'SMATTER, SASQUATCH BREATH? ARE YOU UGLY **AND** HARD OF HEARING? I SAID LET'S GO! MOVE IT!
AND SPEAKING OF UGLY, HAVE YOU CHECKED A REFLECTIVE SURFACE LATELY? WHEN YOU WERE BORN, I BET THE DOCTOR SLAPPED YOUR MOTHER!
LISTEN, LLAMA GUMS, I'M NOT GONNA WARN YOU AGAIN! MOVE THAT FAT DUMPSTER OF YOURS NOW, OR I WON'T BE RESPONSIBLE FOR MY—
© 1993 PAWS, INC. All Rights Reserved.
JIM DAVIS 5-2

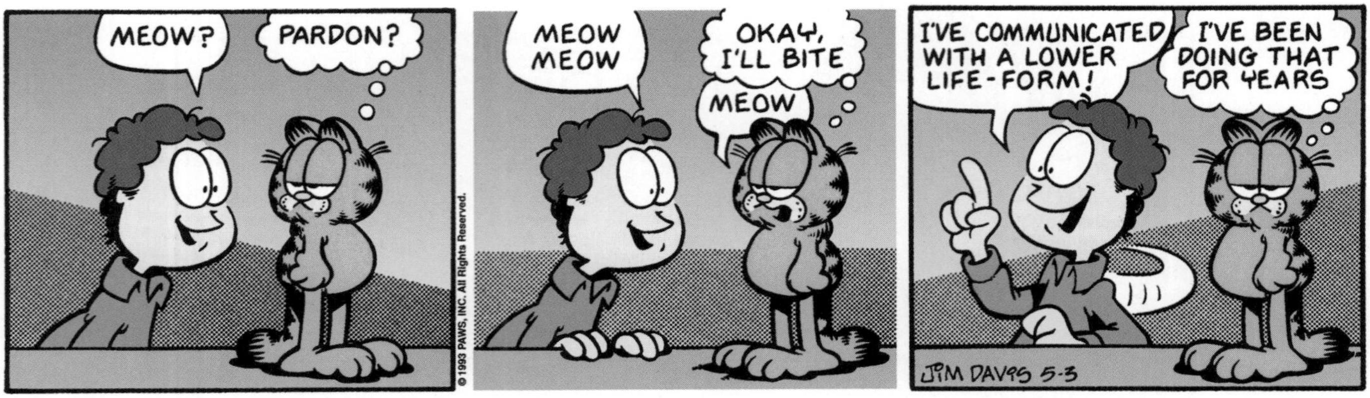
MEOW?
PARDON?
© 1993 PAWS, INC. All Rights Reserved.
MEOW MEOW
OKAY, I'LL BITE
MEOW
I'VE COMMUNICATED WITH A LOWER LIFE-FORM!
I'VE BEEN DOING THAT FOR YEARS
JIM DAVIS 5-3

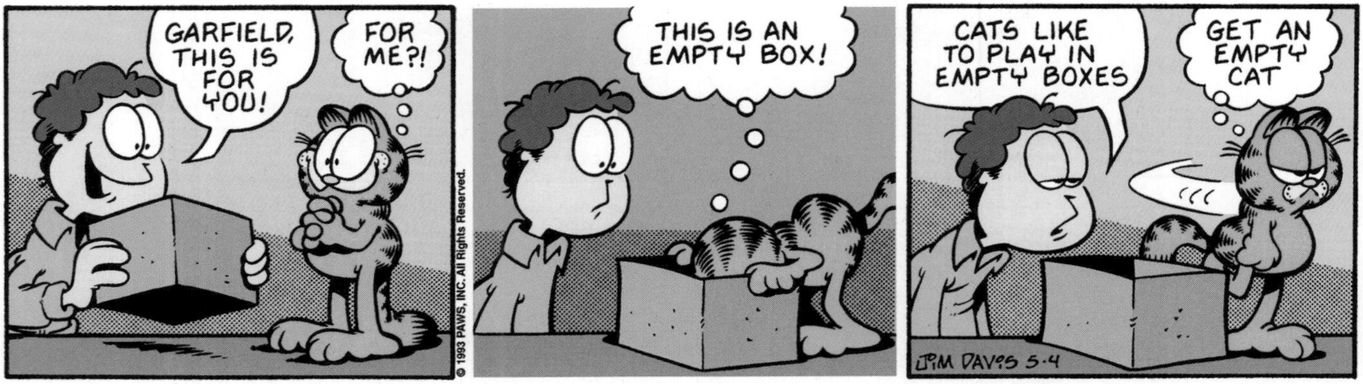
GARFIELD, THIS IS FOR YOU!
FOR ME?!
© 1993 PAWS, INC. All Rights Reserved.
THIS IS AN EMPTY BOX!
CATS LIKE TO PLAY IN EMPTY BOXES
GET AN EMPTY CAT
JIM DAVIS 5-4

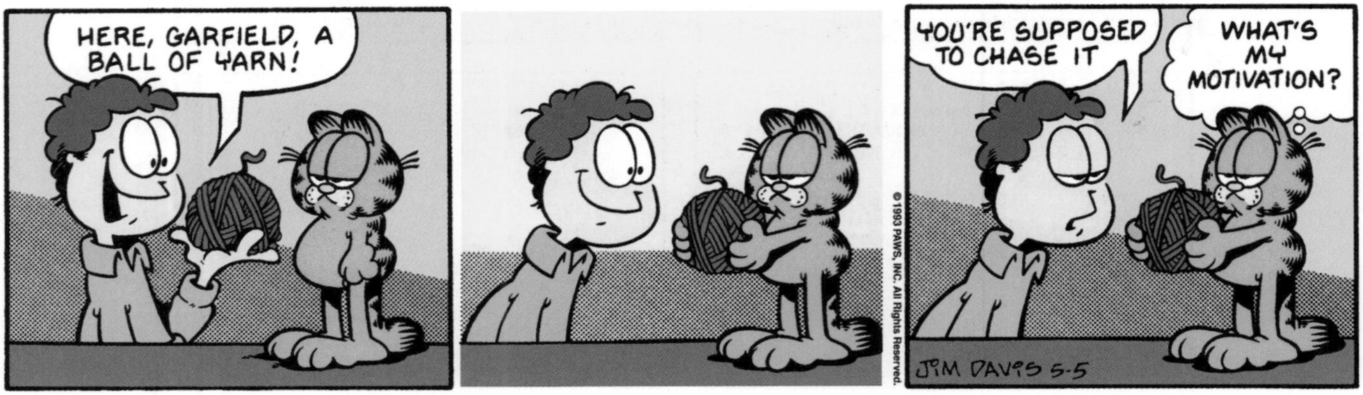
HERE, GARFIELD, A BALL OF YARN!
© 1993 PAWS, INC. All Rights Reserved.
YOU'RE SUPPOSED TO CHASE IT
WHAT'S MY MOTIVATION?
JIM DAVIS 5-5

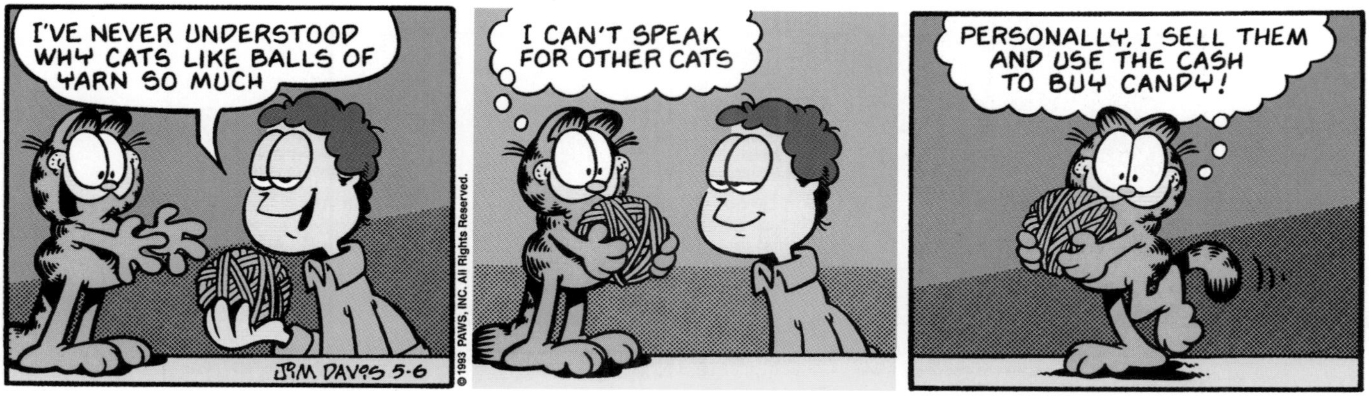
I'VE NEVER UNDERSTOOD WHY CATS LIKE BALLS OF YARN SO MUCH
I CAN'T SPEAK FOR OTHER CATS
PERSONALLY, I SELL THEM AND USE THE CASH TO BUY CANDY!
JIM DAVIS 5-6
© 1993 PAWS, INC. All Rights Reserved.

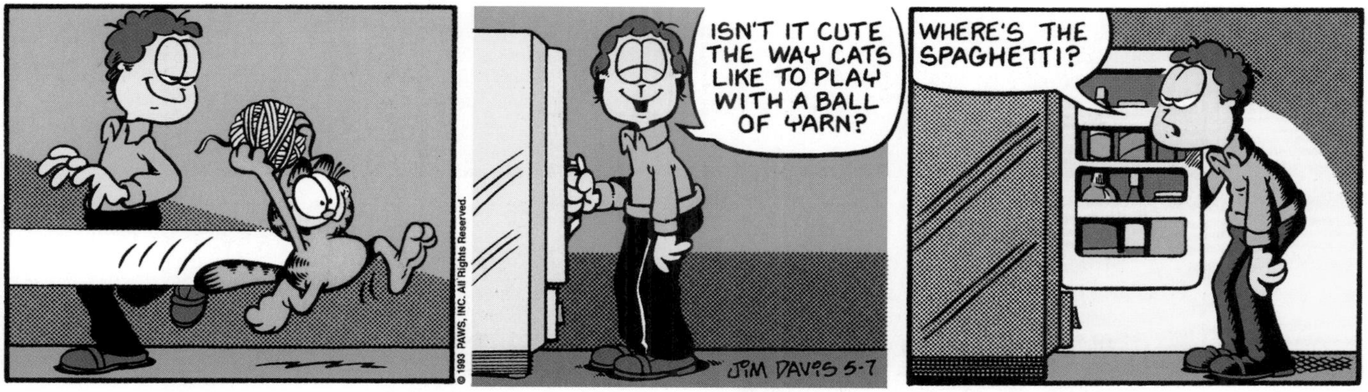
ISN'T IT CUTE THE WAY CATS LIKE TO PLAY WITH A BALL OF YARN?
WHERE'S THE SPAGHETTI?
JIM DAVIS 5-7
© 1993 PAWS, INC. All Rights Reserved.

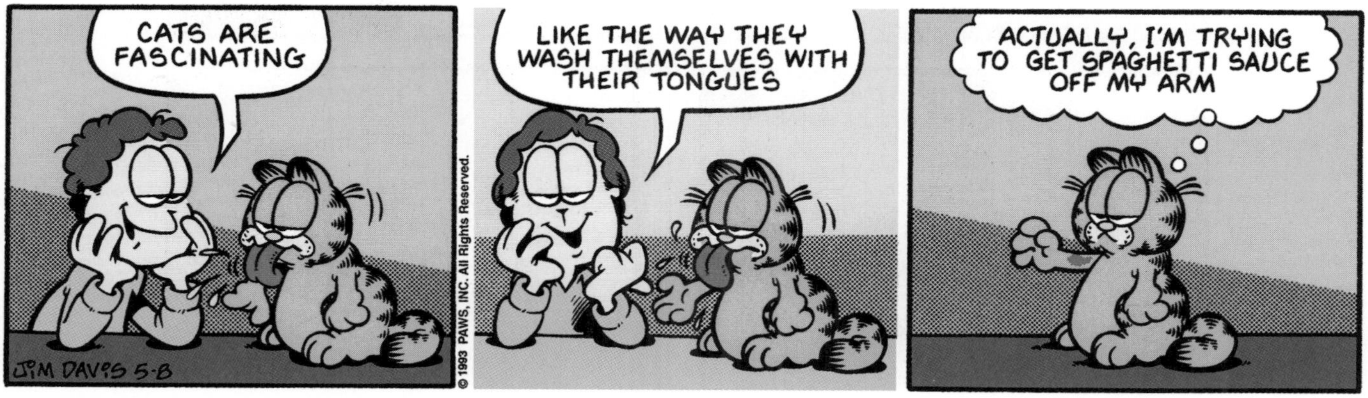
CATS ARE FASCINATING
LIKE THE WAY THEY WASH THEMSELVES WITH THEIR TONGUES
ACTUALLY, I'M TRYING TO GET SPAGHETTI SAUCE OFF MY ARM
JIM DAVIS 5-8
© 1993 PAWS, INC. All Rights Reserved.

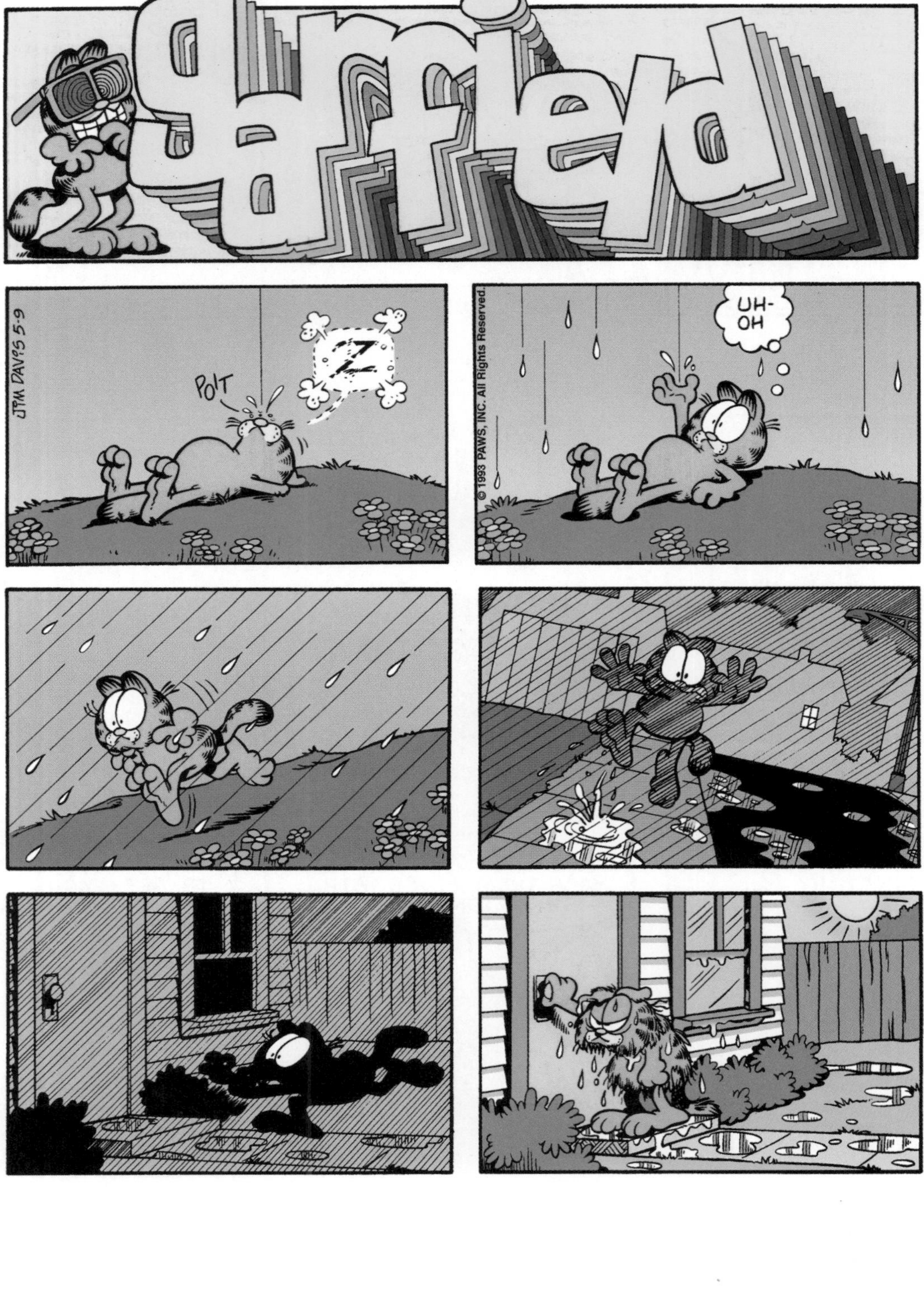
garfield
JIM DAVIS 5-9
POIT
Z
© 1993 PAWS, INC. All Rights Reserved.
UH-OH

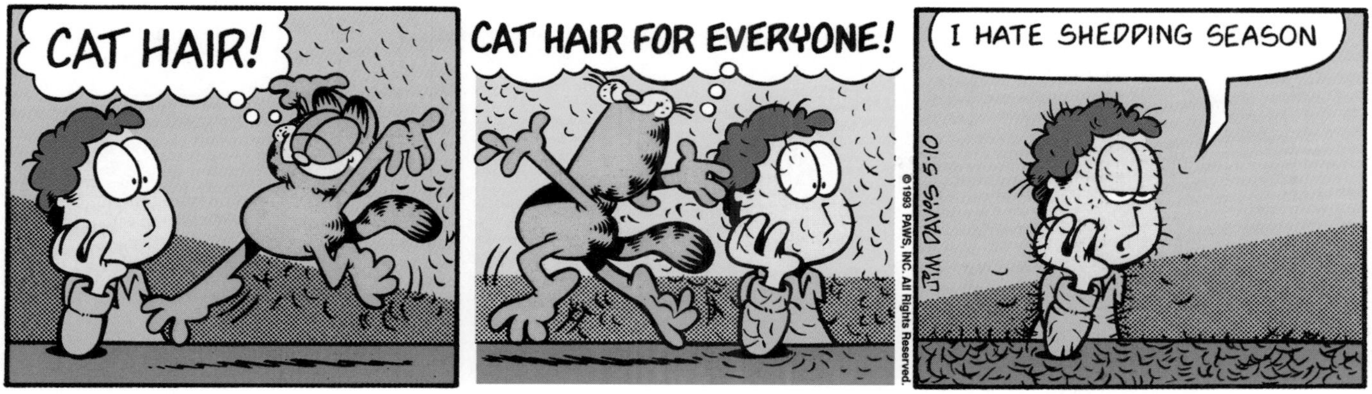
CAT HAIR!
CAT HAIR FOR EVERYONE!
© 1993 PAWS, INC. All Rights Reserved.
JIM DAVIS 5-10
I HATE SHEDDING SEASON

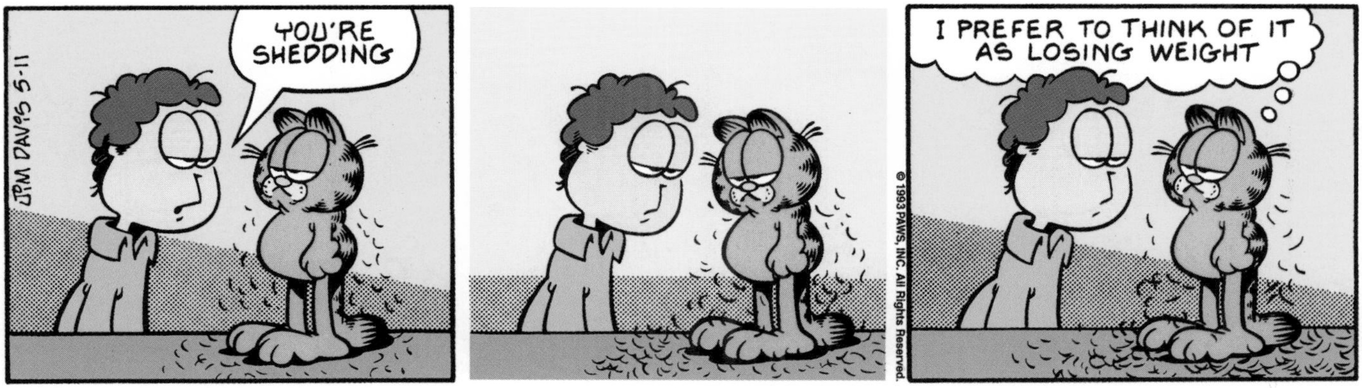
JIM DAVIS 5-11
YOU'RE SHEDDING
© 1993 PAWS, INC. All Rights Reserved.
I PREFER TO THINK OF IT AS LOSING WEIGHT

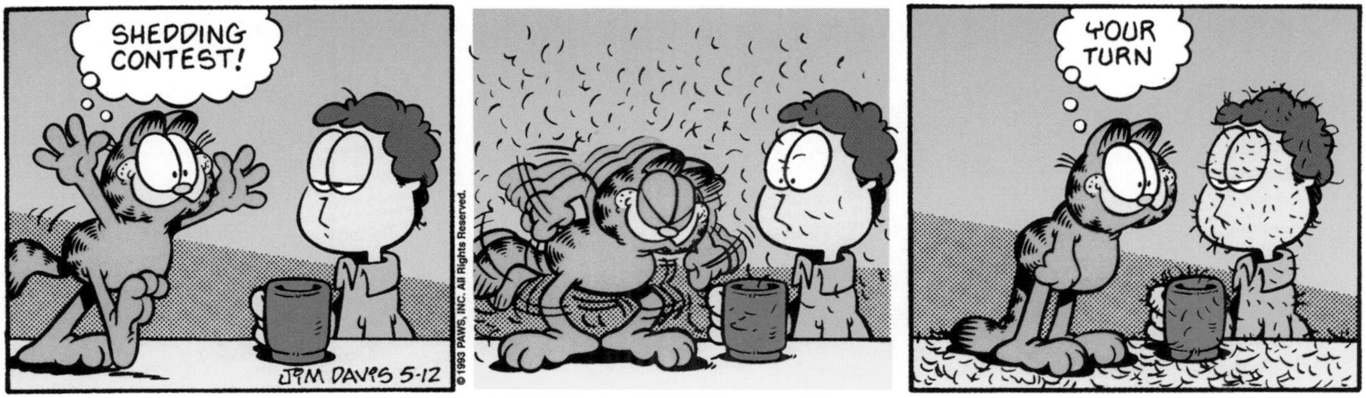
SHEDDING CONTEST!
JIM DAVIS 5-12
© 1993 PAWS, INC. All Rights Reserved.
YOUR TURN

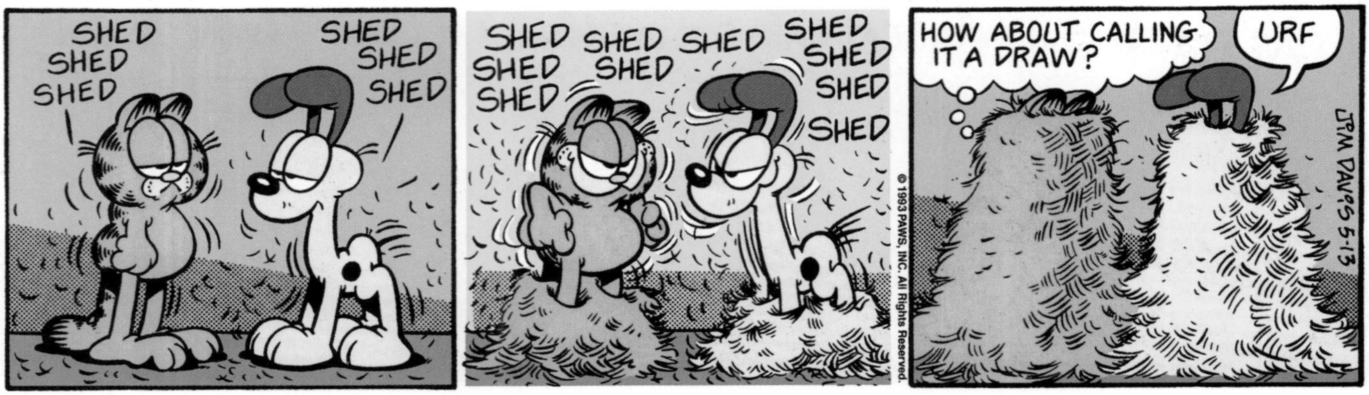
SHED
SHED
SHED
SHED
SHED
SHED
SHED
SHED
SHED
SHED
SHED
SHED
SHED
SHED
SHED
SHED
© 1993 PAWS, INC. All Rights Reserved.
HOW ABOUT CALLING IT A DRAW?
URF
JIM DAVIS 5-13

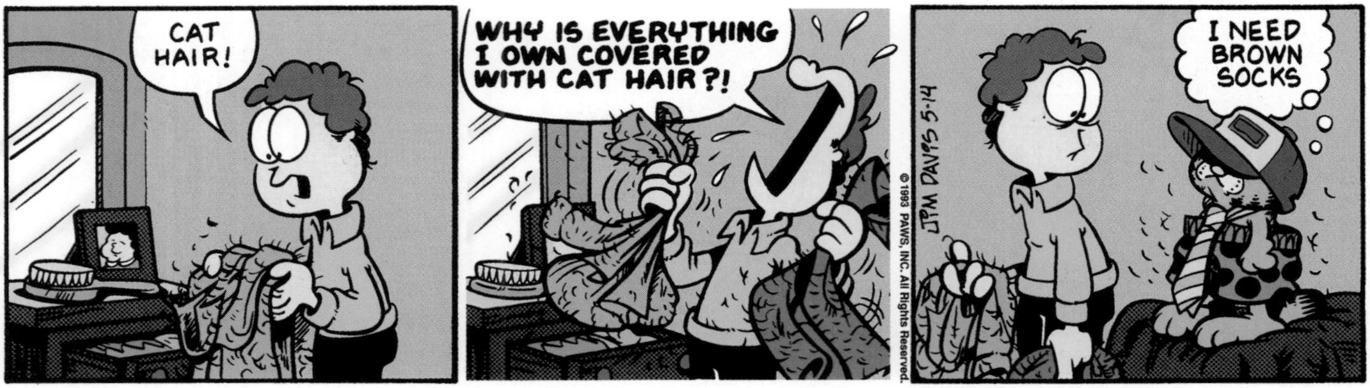
CAT HAIR!
WHY IS EVERYTHING I OWN COVERED WITH CAT HAIR?!
© 1993 PAWS, INC. All Rights Reserved.
JIM DAVIS 5-14
I NEED BROWN SOCKS

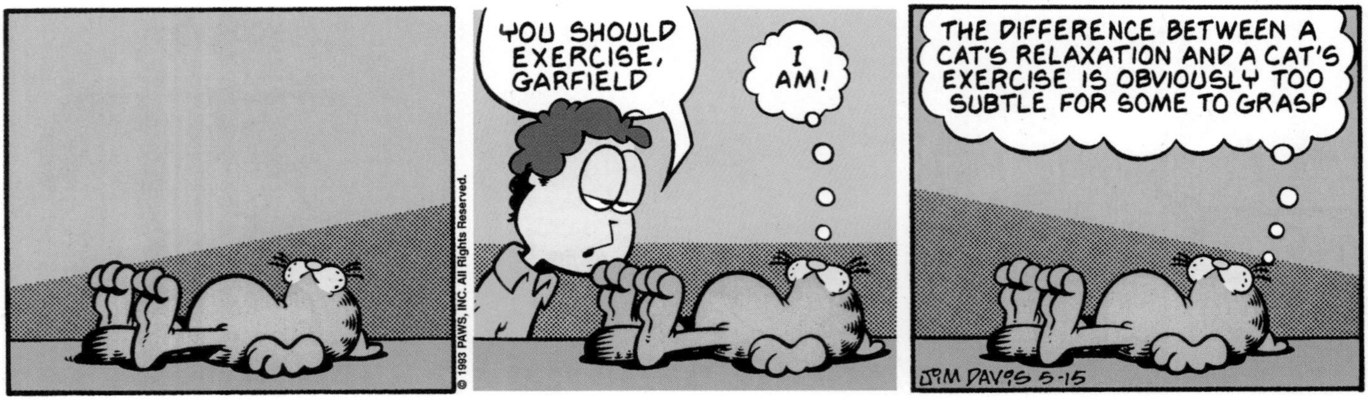
© 1993 PAWS, INC. All Rights Reserved.
YOU SHOULD EXERCISE, GARFIELD
I AM!
THE DIFFERENCE BETWEEN A CAT'S RELAXATION AND A CAT'S EXERCISE IS OBVIOUSLY TOO SUBTLE FOR SOME TO GRASP
JIM DAVIS 5-15

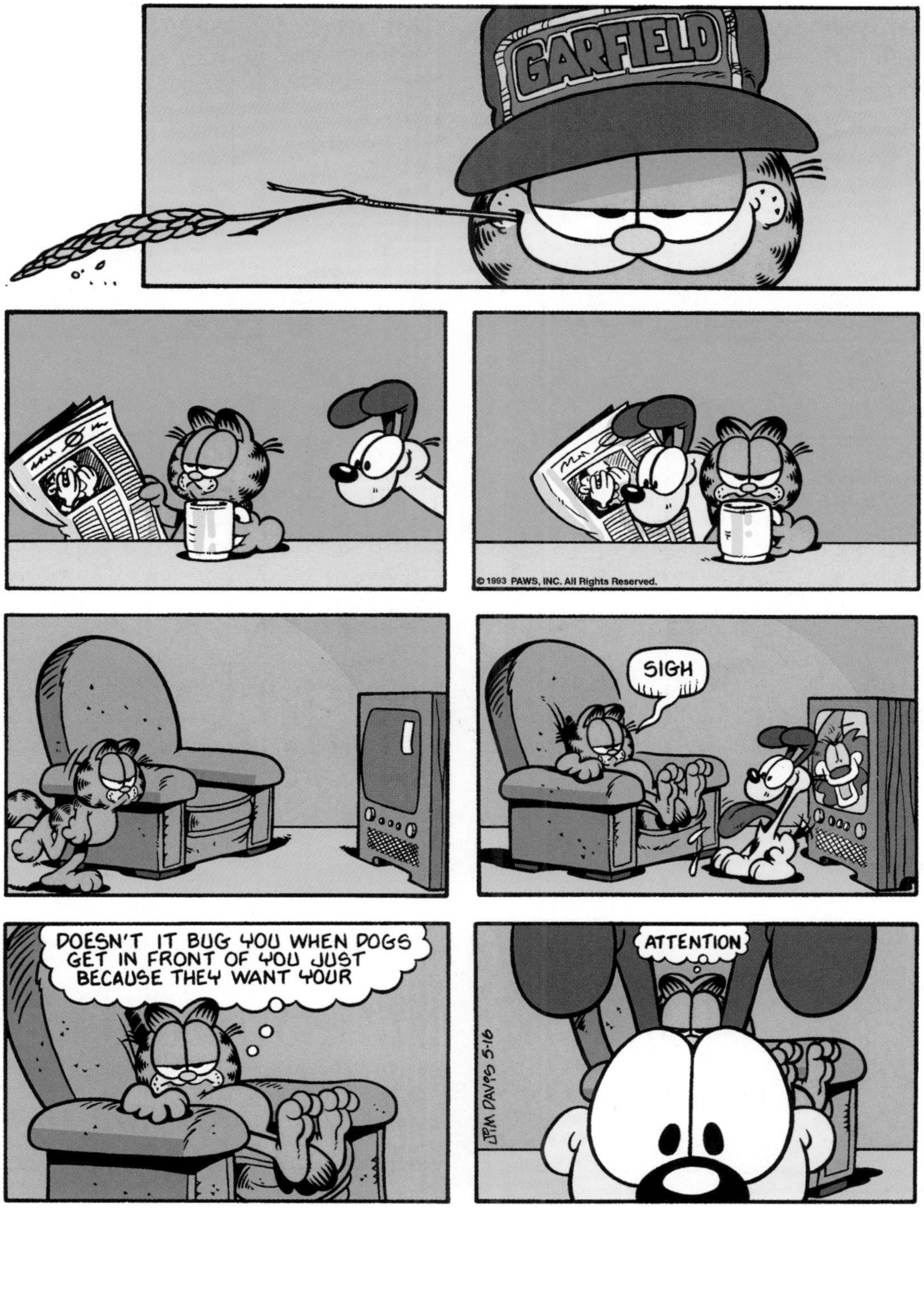
GARFIELD
SIGH
DOESN'T IT BUG YOU WHEN DOGS GET IN FRONT OF YOU JUST BECAUSE THEY WANT YOUR
ATTENTION
JPM DAVPS 5-16

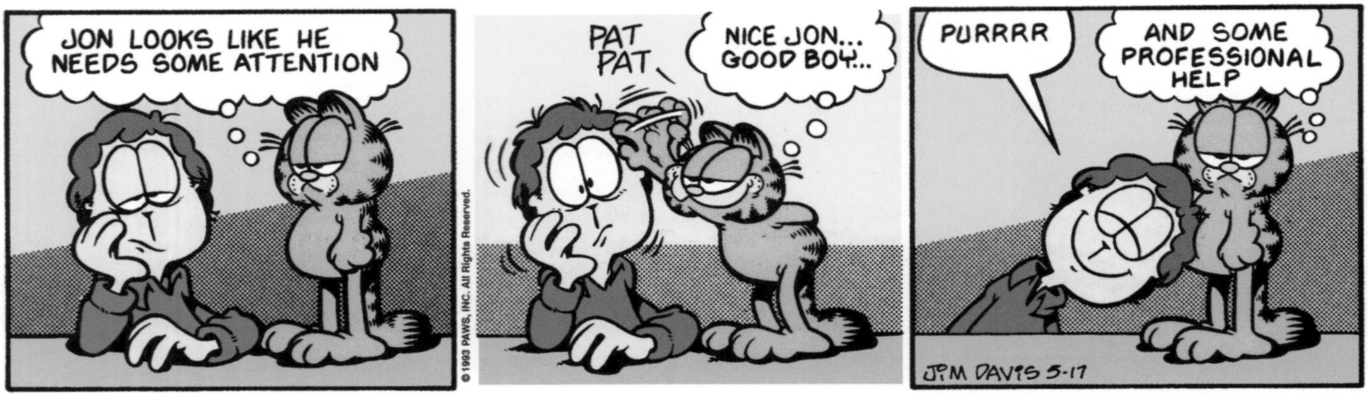
JON LOOKS LIKE HE NEEDS SOME ATTENTION
© 1993 PAWS, INC. All Rights Reserved.
PAT PAT
NICE JON... GOOD BOY...
PURRRR
AND SOME PROFESSIONAL HELP
JIM DAVIS 5-17

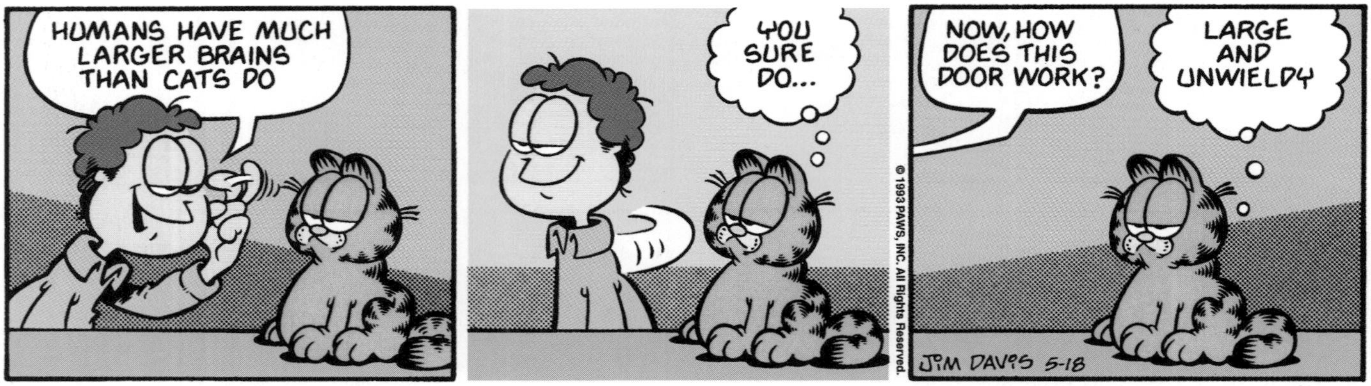
HUMANS HAVE MUCH LARGER BRAINS THAN CATS DO
YOU SURE DO...
© 1993 PAWS, INC. All Rights Reserved.
NOW, HOW DOES THIS DOOR WORK?
LARGE AND UNWIELDY
JIM DAVIS 5-18

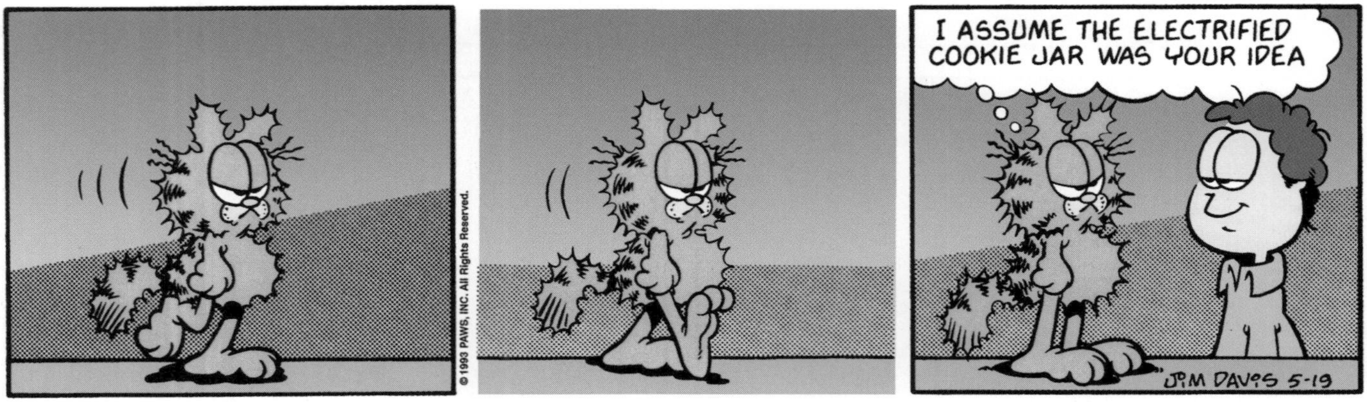
© 1993 PAWS, INC. All Rights Reserved.
I ASSUME THE ELECTRIFIED COOKIE JAR WAS YOUR IDEA
JIM DAVIS 5-19

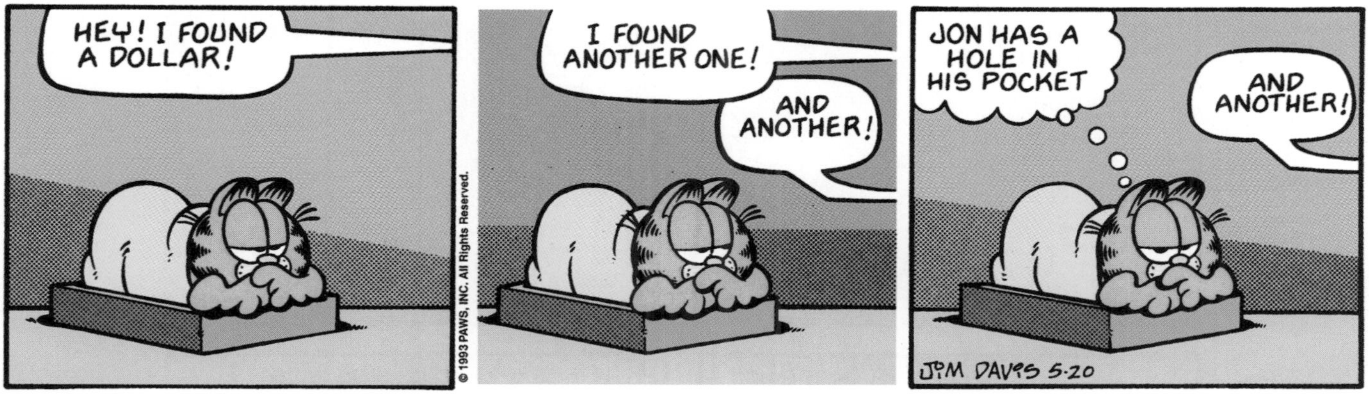
HEY! I FOUND A DOLLAR!
© 1993 PAWS, INC. All Rights Reserved.
I FOUND ANOTHER ONE!
AND ANOTHER!
JON HAS A HOLE IN HIS POCKET
AND ANOTHER!
JIM DAVIS 5-20

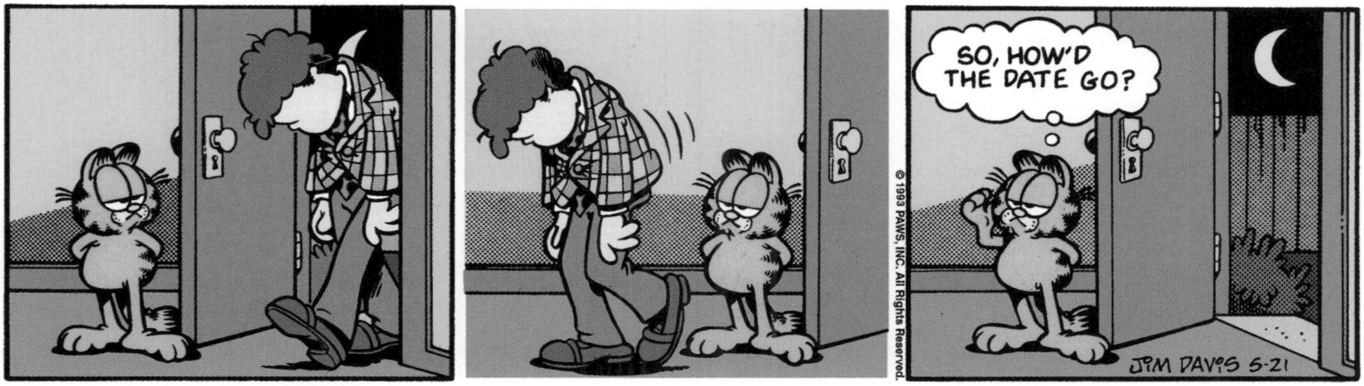
© 1993 PAWS, INC. All Rights Reserved.
SO, HOW'D THE DATE GO?
JIM DAVIS 5-21

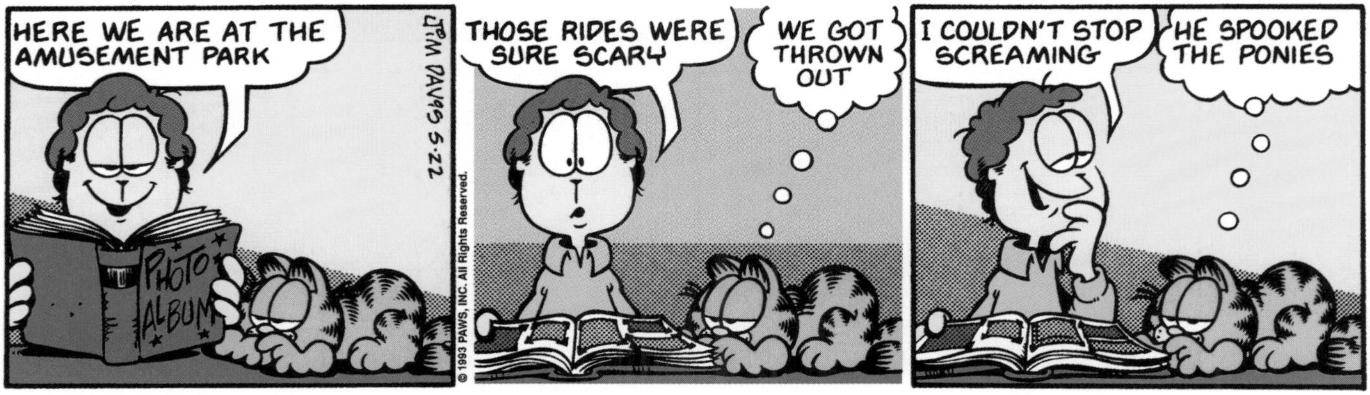
HERE WE ARE AT THE AMUSEMENT PARK
PHOTO ALBUM
JIM DAVIS 5-22
© 1993 PAWS, INC. All Rights Reserved.
THOSE RIDES WERE SURE SCARY
WE GOT THROWN OUT
I COULDN'T STOP SCREAMING
HE SPOOKED THE PONIES

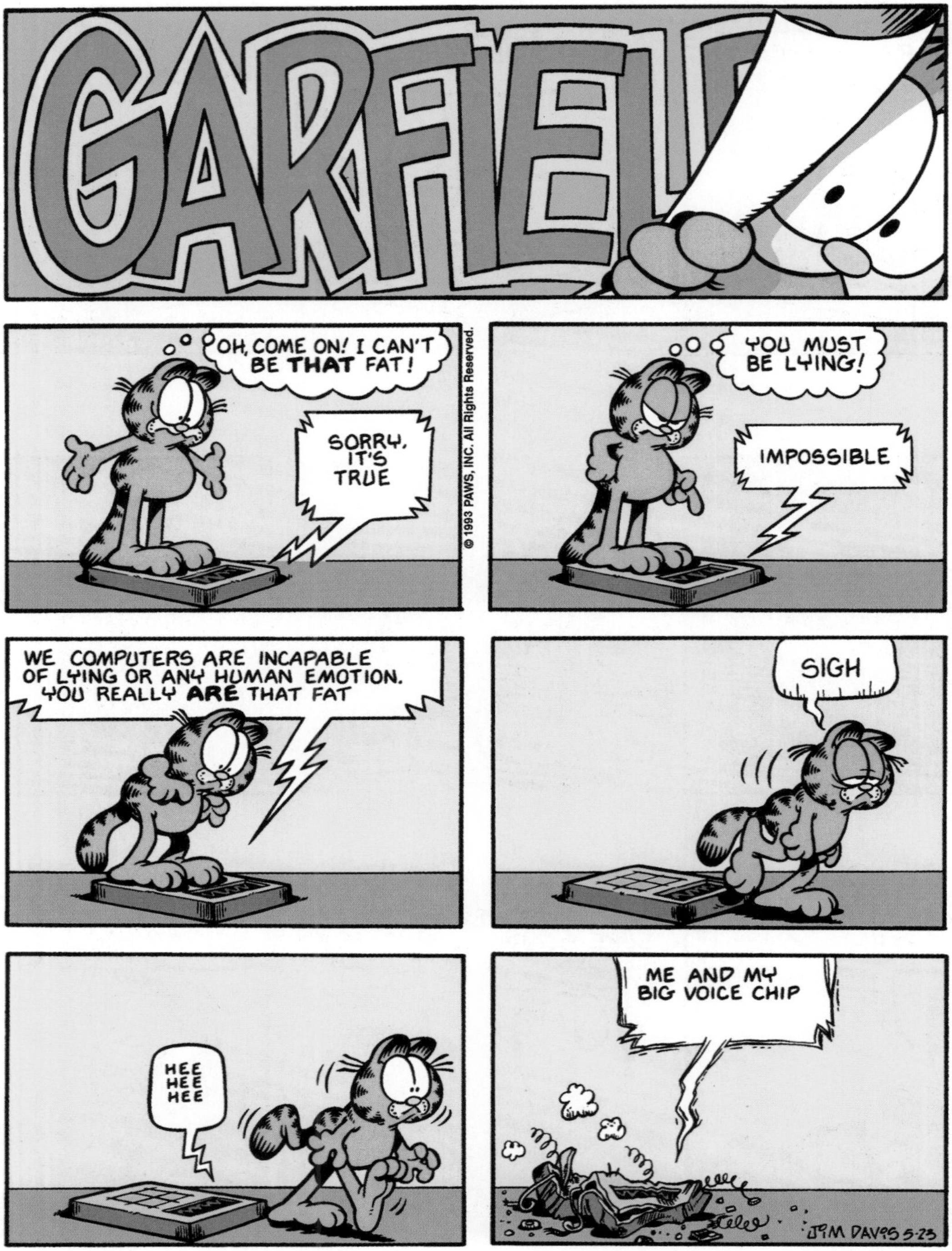
GARFIELD
OH, COME ON! I CAN'T BE THAT FAT!
SORRY, IT'S TRUE
© 1993 PAWS, INC. All Rights Reserved.
YOU MUST BE LYING!
IMPOSSIBLE
WE COMPUTERS ARE INCAPABLE OF LYING OR ANY HUMAN EMOTION. YOU REALLY ARE THAT FAT
SIGH
HEE HEE HEE
ME AND MY BIG VOICE CHIP
JIM DAVIS 5-23

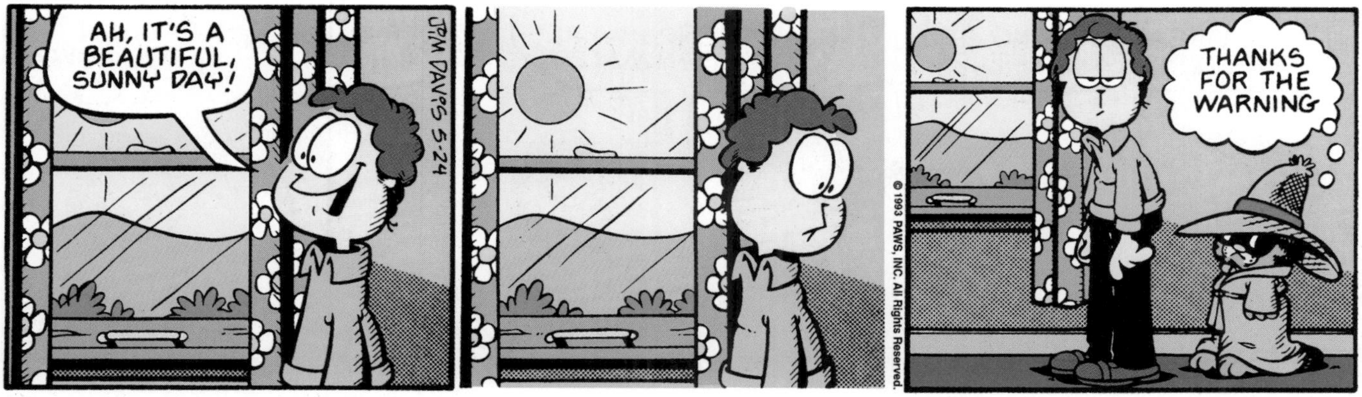
JIM DAVIS 5-24
AH, IT'S A BEAUTIFUL, SUNNY DAY!
© 1993 PAWS, INC. All Rights Reserved.
THANKS FOR THE WARNING

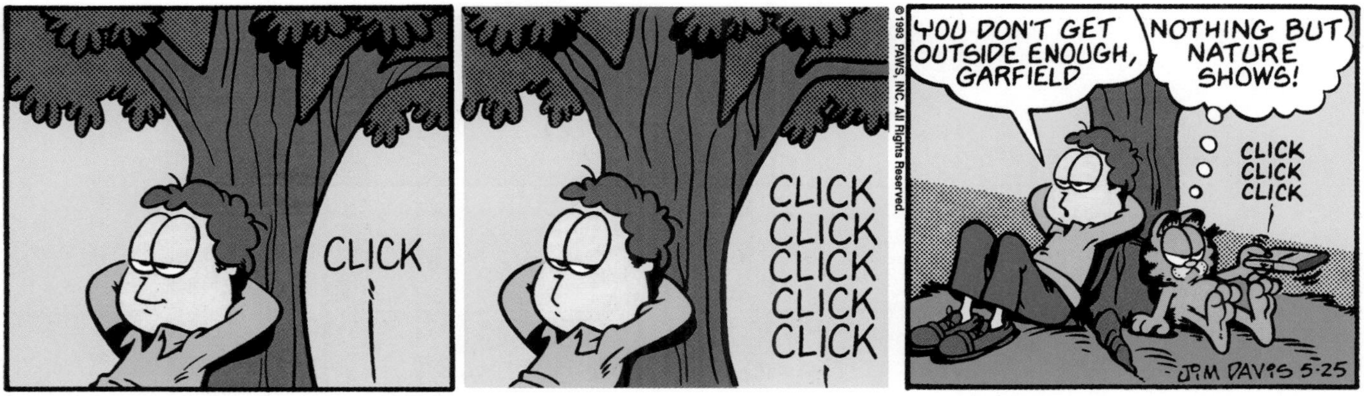
CLICK
CLICK CLICK CLICK CLICK CLICK
© 1993 PAWS, INC. All Rights Reserved.
YOU DON'T GET OUTSIDE ENOUGH, GARFIELD
NOTHING BUT NATURE SHOWS!
CLICK CLICK CLICK
JIM DAVIS 5-25

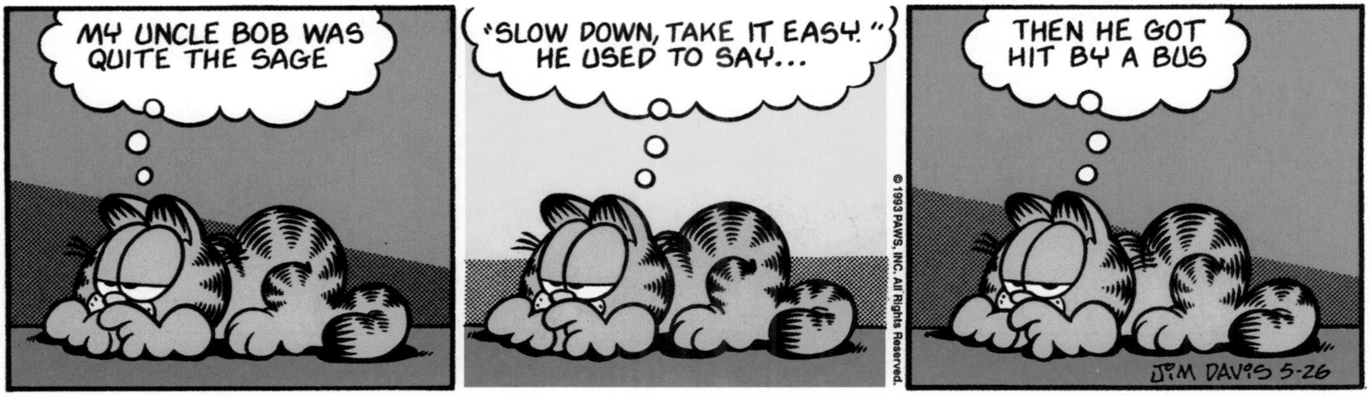
MY UNCLE BOB WAS QUITE THE SAGE
"SLOW DOWN, TAKE IT EASY." HE USED TO SAY...
© 1993 PAWS, INC. All Rights Reserved.
THEN HE GOT HIT BY A BUS
JIM DAVIS 5-26

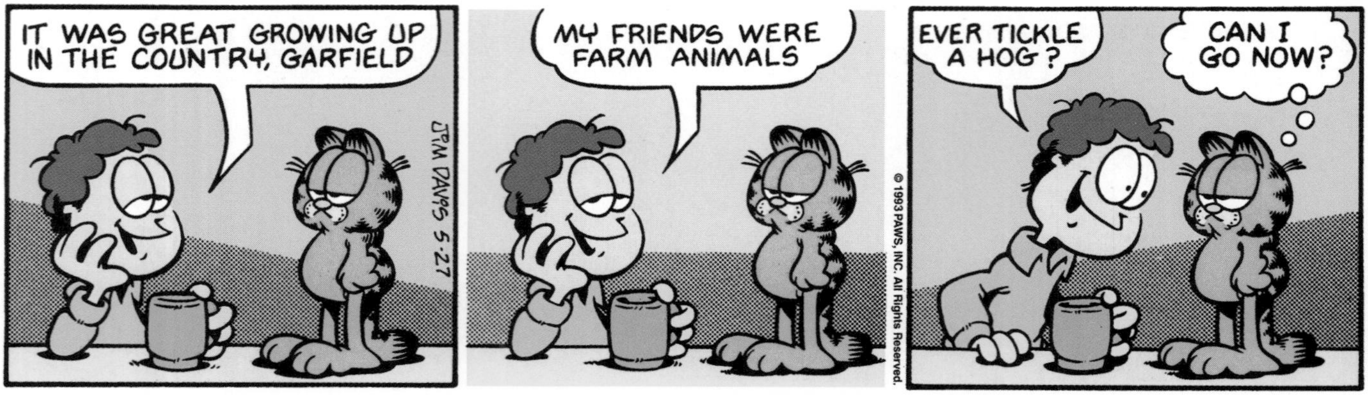
IT WAS GREAT GROWING UP IN THE COUNTRY, GARFIELD
JIM DAVIS 5-27
MY FRIENDS WERE FARM ANIMALS
© 1993 PAWS, INC. All Rights Reserved.
EVER TICKLE A HOG?
CAN I GO NOW?

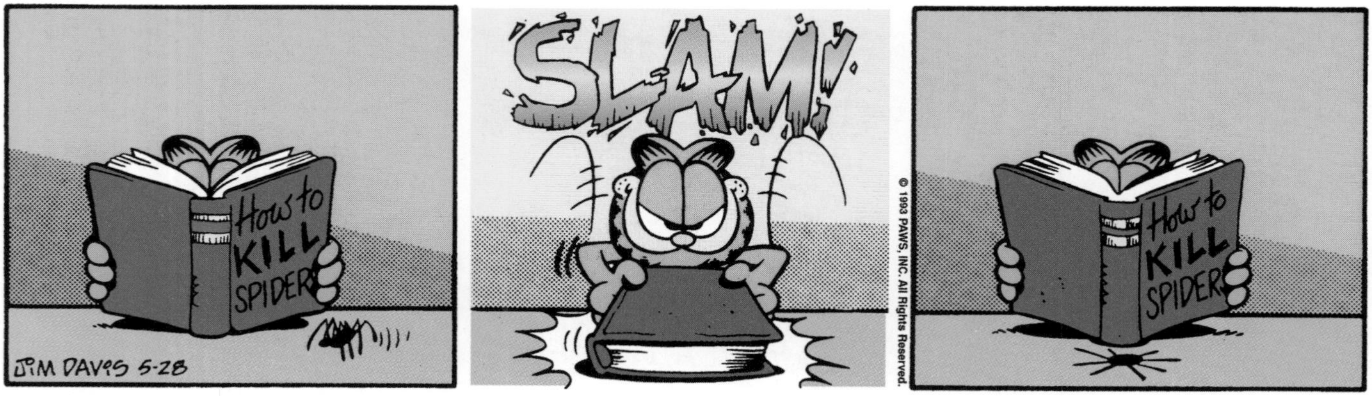
How to KILL SPIDERS
JIM DAVIS 5-28
SLAM!
© 1993 PAWS, INC. All Rights Reserved.
How to KILL SPIDERS

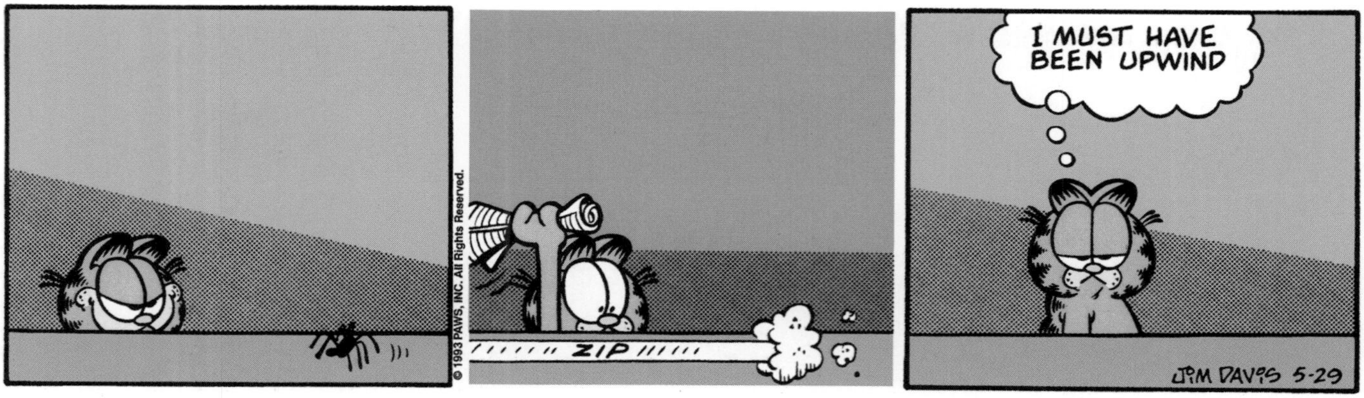
© 1993 PAWS, INC. All Rights Reserved.
ZIP
I MUST HAVE BEEN UPWIND
JIM DAVIS 5-29

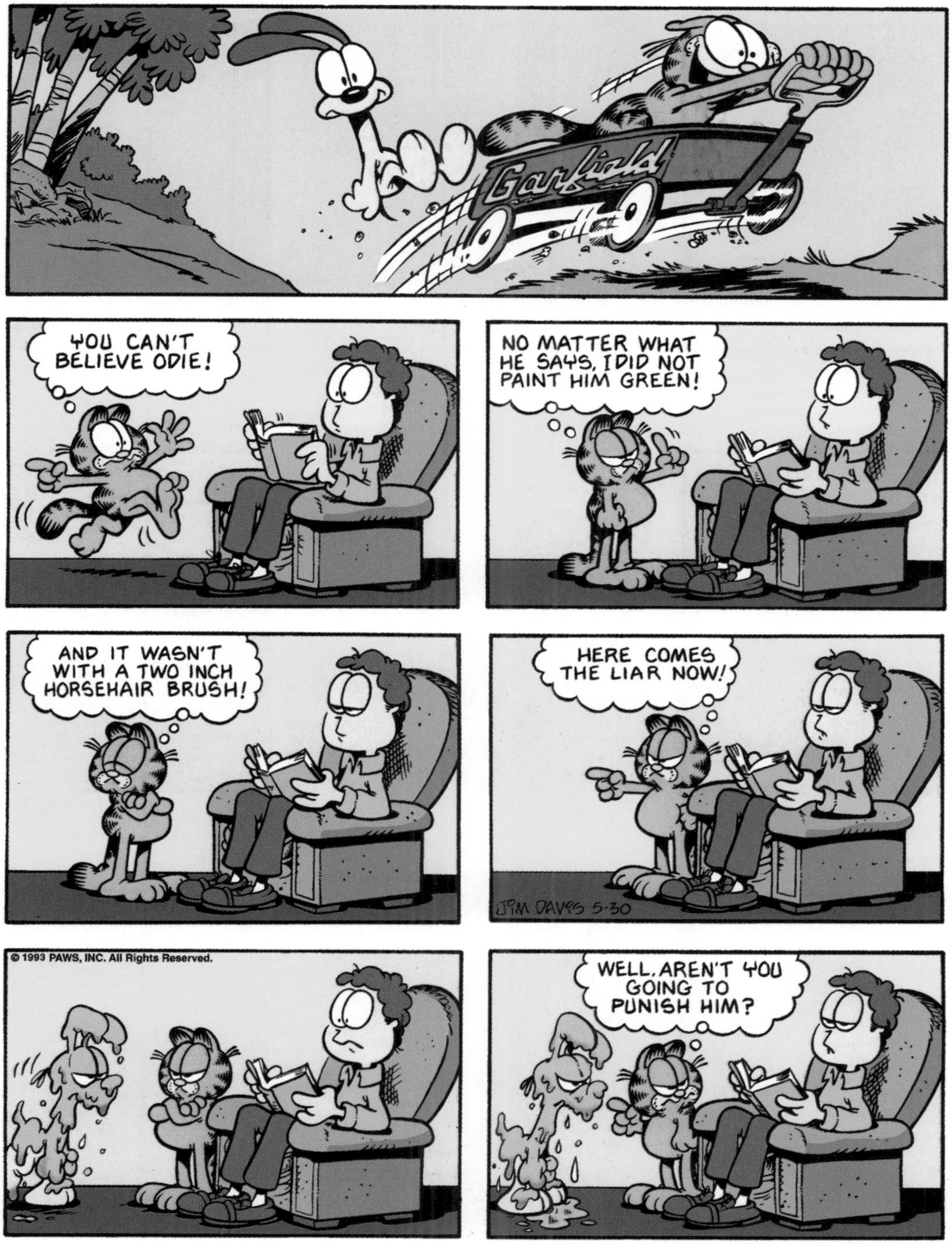
Garfield
YOU CAN'T BELIEVE ODIE!
NO MATTER WHAT HE SAYS, I DID NOT PAINT HIM GREEN!
AND IT WASN'T WITH A TWO INCH HORSEHAIR BRUSH!
HERE COMES THE LIAR NOW!
JIM DAVIS 5-30
© 1993 PAWS, INC. All Rights Reserved.
WELL, AREN'T YOU GOING TO PUNISH HIM?

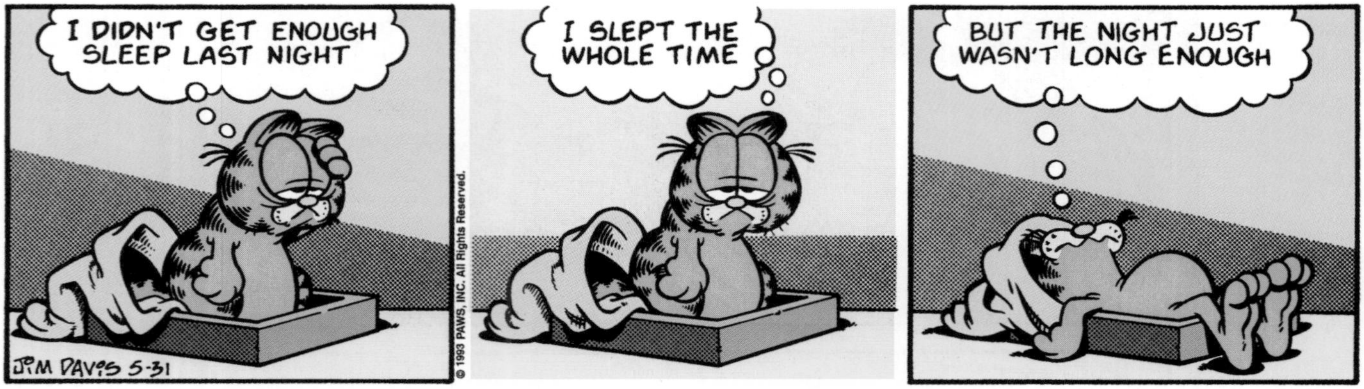
I DIDN'T GET ENOUGH SLEEP LAST NIGHT
JIM DAVIS 5-31
© 1993 PAWS, INC. All Rights Reserved.
I SLEPT THE WHOLE TIME
BUT THE NIGHT JUST WASN'T LONG ENOUGH

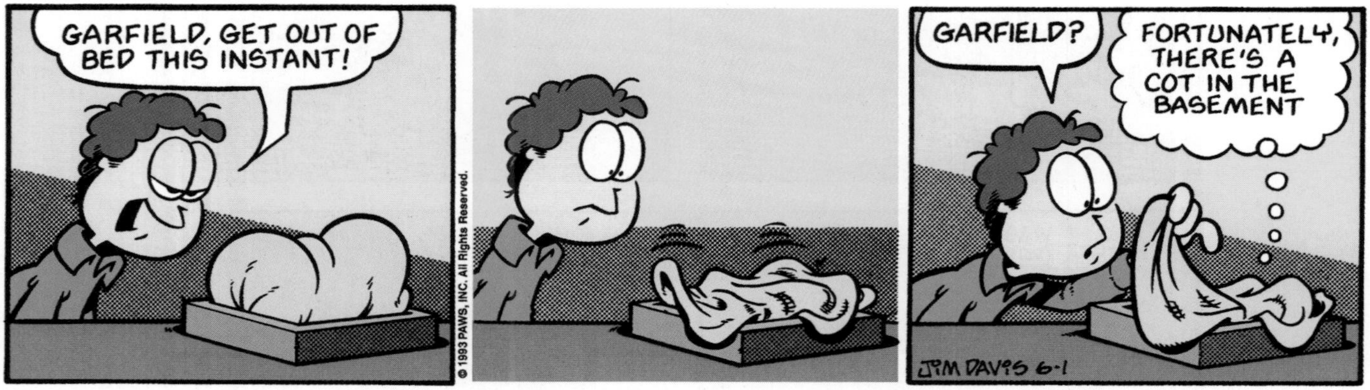
GARFIELD, GET OUT OF BED THIS INSTANT!
© 1993 PAWS, INC. All Rights Reserved.
GARFIELD?
FORTUNATELY, THERE'S A COT IN THE BASEMENT
JIM DAVIS 6-1

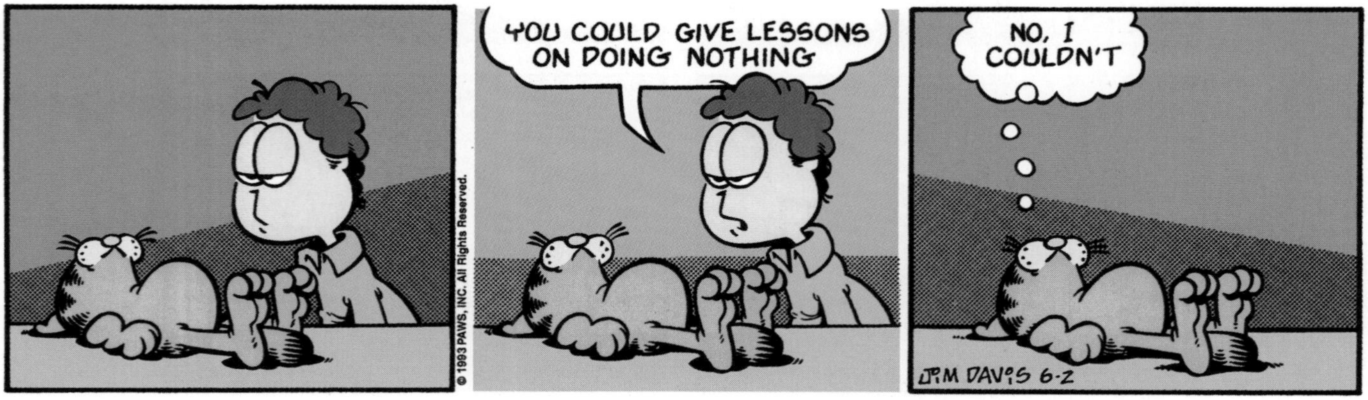
© 1993 PAWS, INC. All Rights Reserved.
YOU COULD GIVE LESSONS ON DOING NOTHING
NO, I COULDN'T
JIM DAVIS 6-2

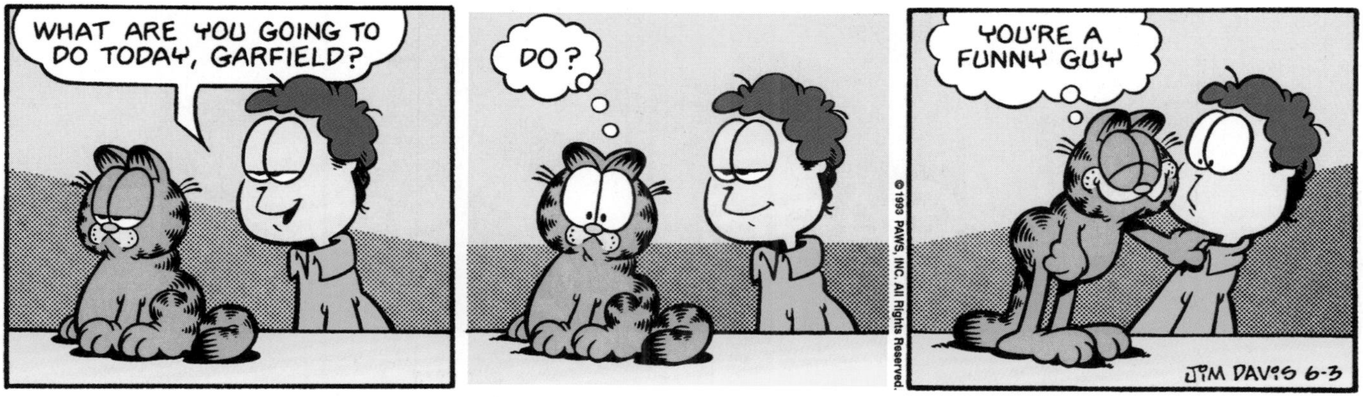
WHAT ARE YOU GOING TO DO TODAY, GARFIELD?
DO?
© 1993 PAWS, INC. All Rights Reserved.
YOU'RE A FUNNY GUY
JIM DAVIS 6-3

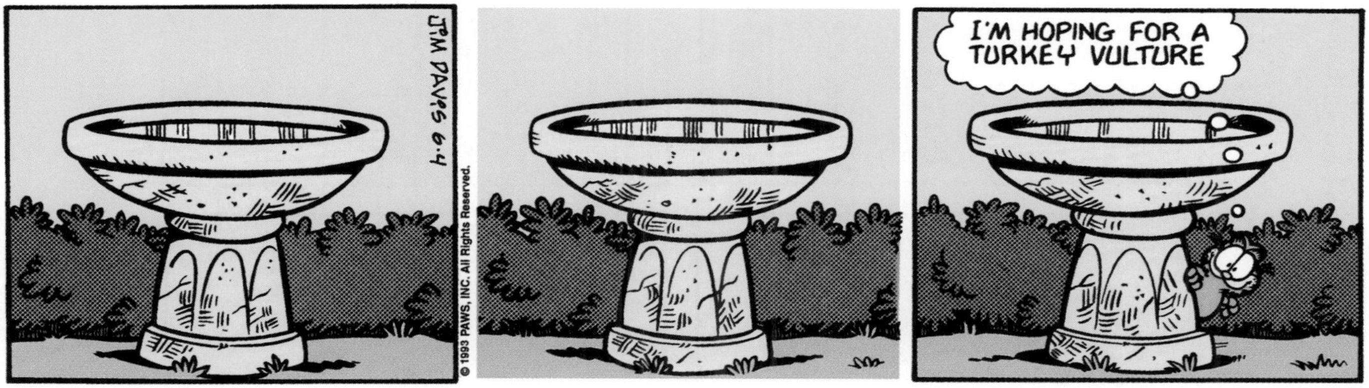
JIM DAVIS 6-4
© 1993 PAWS, INC. All Rights Reserved.
I'M HOPING FOR A TURKEY VULTURE

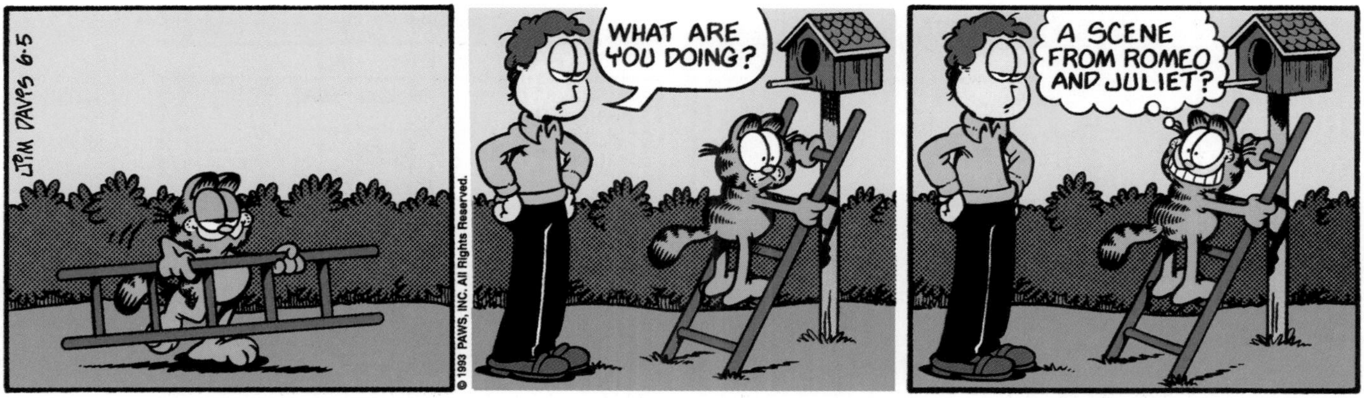
JIM DAVIS 6-5
© 1993 PAWS, INC. All Rights Reserved.
WHAT ARE YOU DOING?
A SCENE FROM ROMEO AND JULIET?

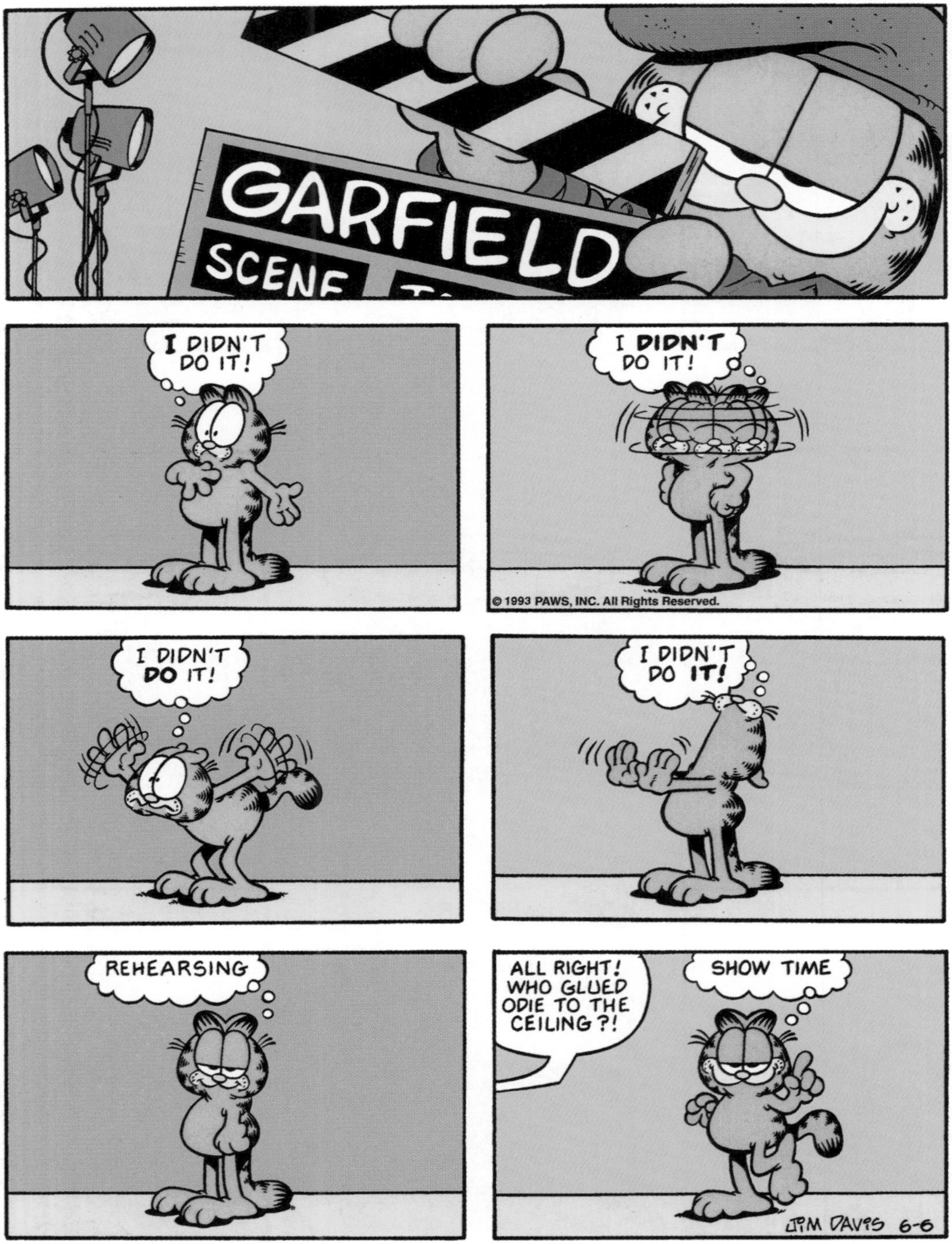
GARFIELD
SCENE
I DIDN'T DO IT!
I DIDN'T DO IT!
© 1993 PAWS, INC. All Rights Reserved.
I DIDN'T DO IT!
I DIDN'T DO IT!
REHEARSING
ALL RIGHT! WHO GLUED ODIE TO THE CEILING?!
SHOW TIME
JIM DAVIS 6-6

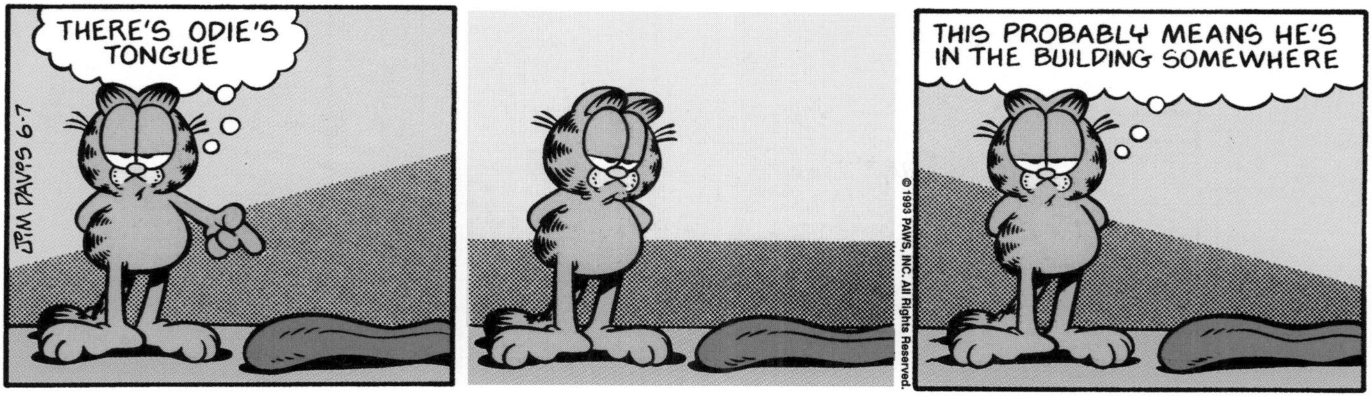
THERE'S ODIE'S TONGUE
JIM DAVIS 6-7
© 1993 PAWS, INC. All Rights Reserved.
THIS PROBABLY MEANS HE'S IN THE BUILDING SOMEWHERE

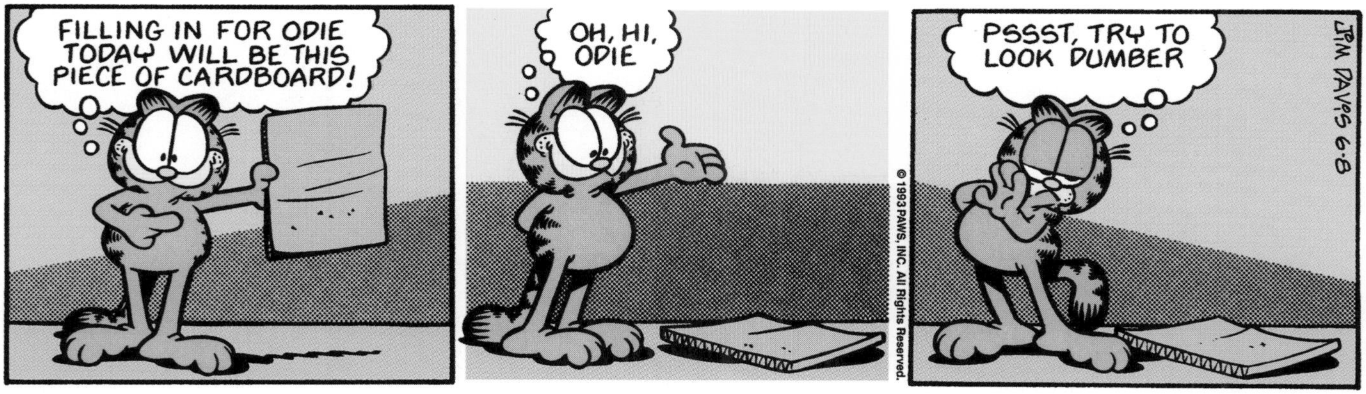
FILLING IN FOR ODIE TODAY WILL BE THIS PIECE OF CARDBOARD!
OH, HI, ODIE
© 1993 PAWS, INC. All Rights Reserved.
PSSST, TRY TO LOOK DUMBER
JIM DAVIS 6-8

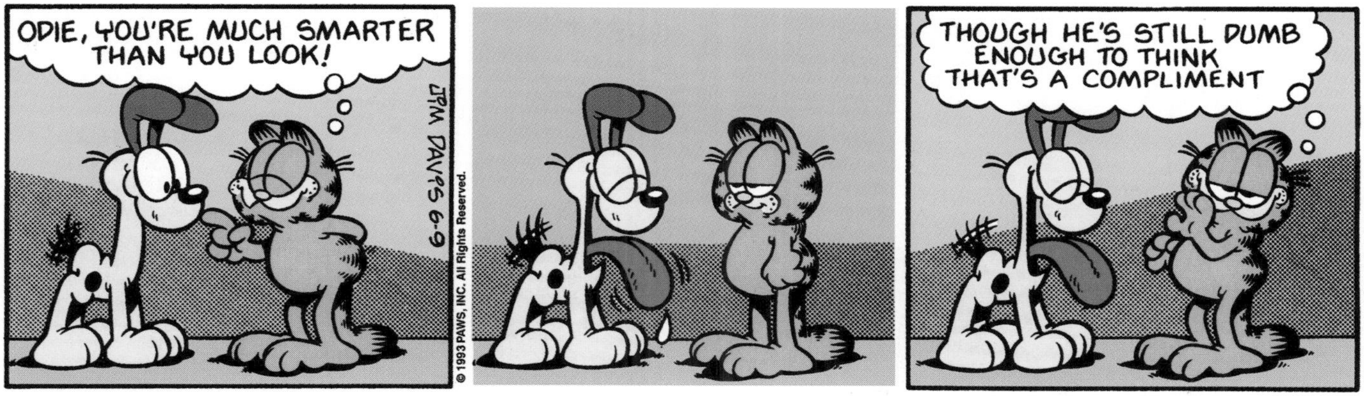
ODIE, YOU'RE MUCH SMARTER THAN YOU LOOK!
JIM DAVIS 6-9
© 1993 PAWS, INC. All Rights Reserved.
THOUGH HE'S STILL DUMB ENOUGH TO THINK THAT'S A COMPLIMENT

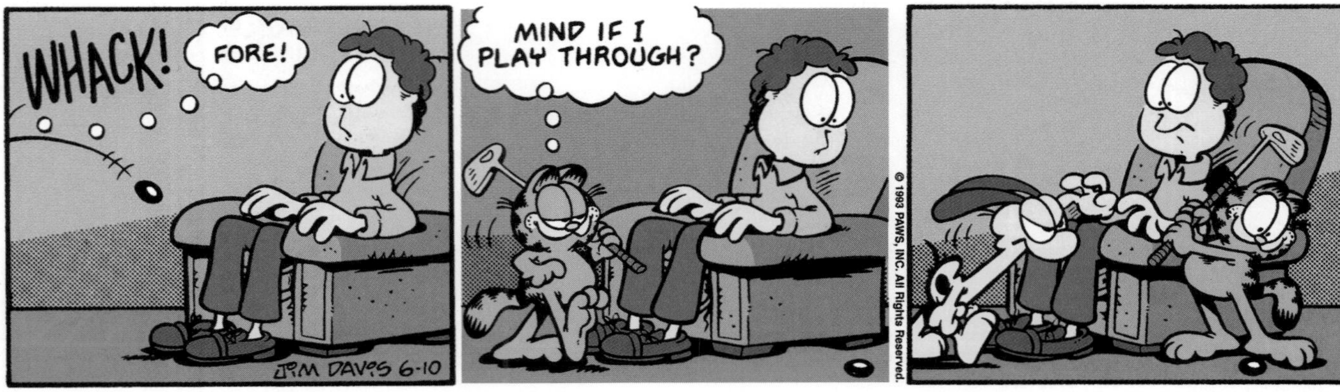
WHACK!
FORE!
JIM DAVIS 6-10
MIND IF I PLAY THROUGH?
© 1983 PAWS, INC. All Rights Reserved.

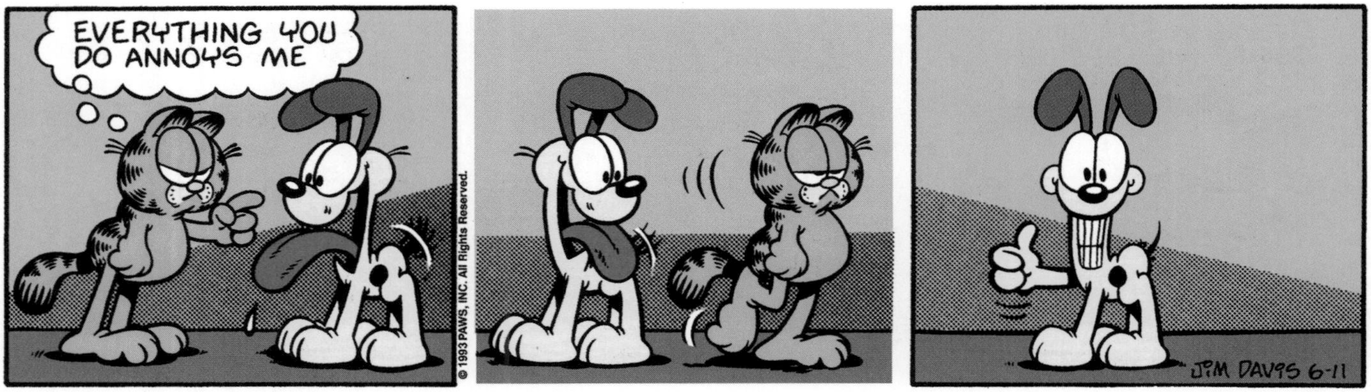
EVERYTHING YOU DO ANNOYS ME
© 1993 PAWS, INC. All Rights Reserved.
JIM DAVIS 6-11

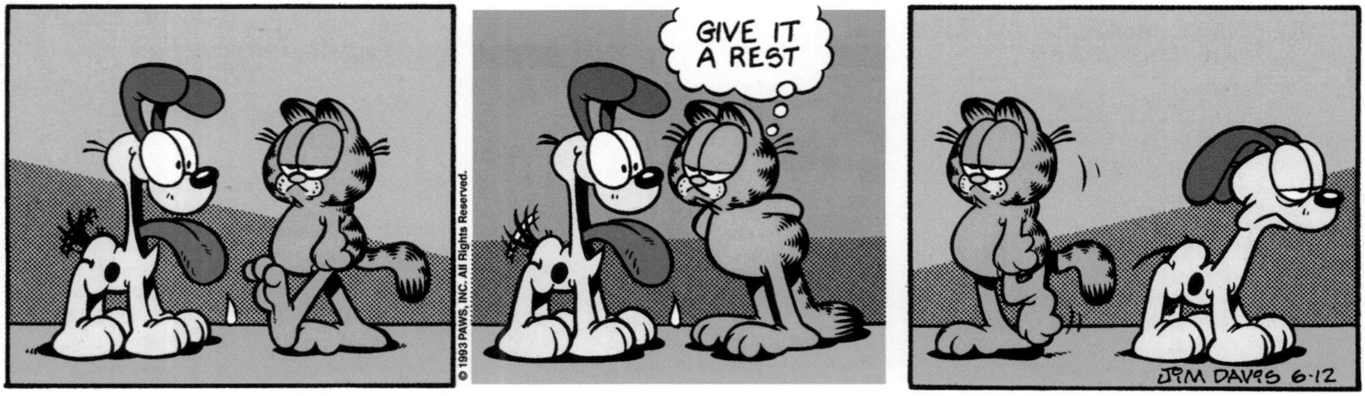
© 1993 PAWS, INC. All Rights Reserved.
GIVE IT A REST
JIM DAVIS 6-12

GARFIELD
SNORE
BOING
♪
Z
YAY!
YAH-HOO!
SNORE
♪
JPM DAVPS
THRILL SEEKERS
WHEE!
YEE-HA!
6-13

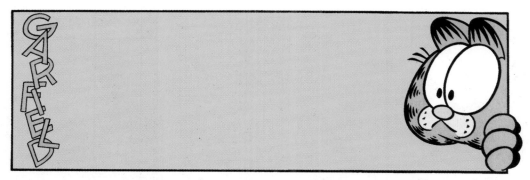

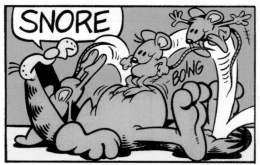

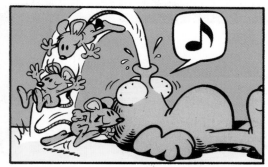

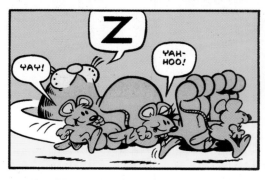

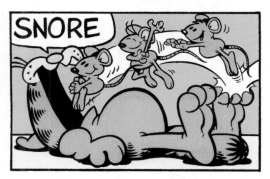

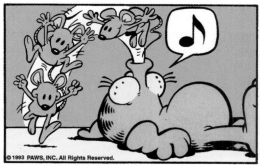

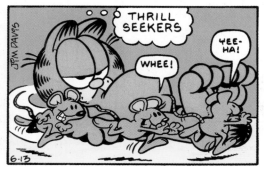

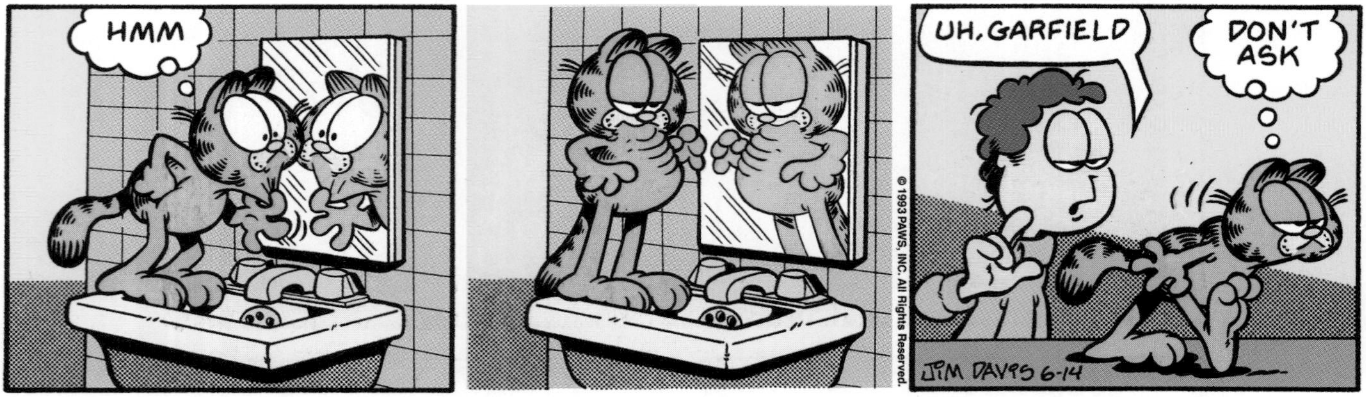
HMM
UH, GARFIELD
DON'T ASK
© 1993 PAWS, INC. All Rights Reserved.
JIM DAVIS 6-14

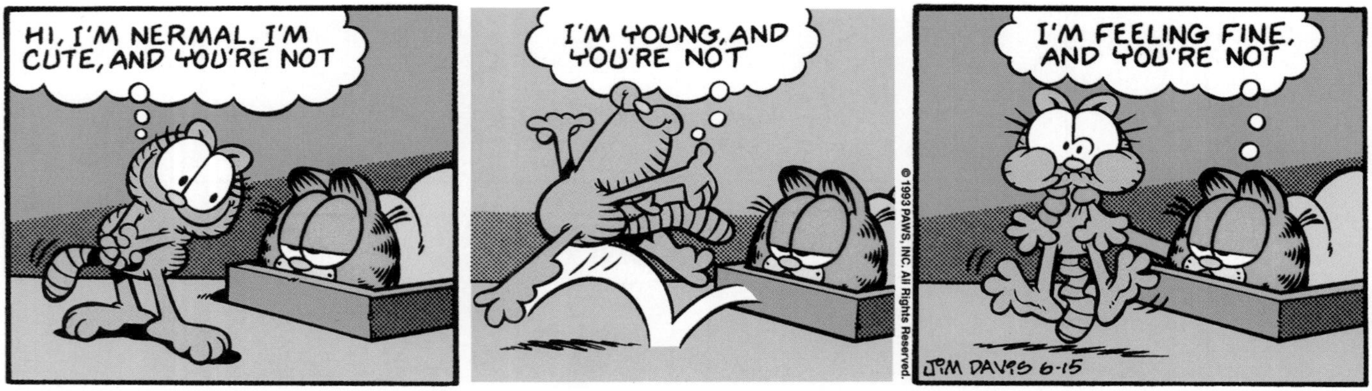
HI, I'M NERMAL. I'M CUTE, AND YOU'RE NOT
I'M YOUNG, AND YOU'RE NOT
I'M FEELING FINE, AND YOU'RE NOT
© 1993 PAWS, INC. All Rights Reserved.
JIM DAVIS 6-15

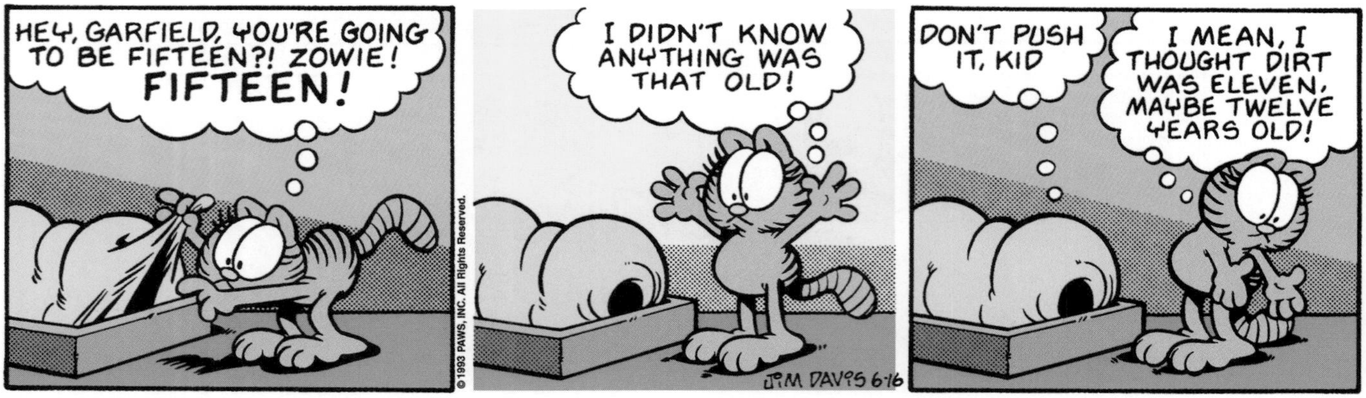
HEY, GARFIELD, YOU'RE GOING TO BE FIFTEEN?! ZOWIE! FIFTEEN!
I DIDN'T KNOW ANYTHING WAS THAT OLD!
DON'T PUSH IT, KID
I MEAN, I THOUGHT DIRT WAS ELEVEN, MAYBE TWELVE YEARS OLD!
© 1993 PAWS, INC. All Rights Reserved.
JIM DAVIS 6-16

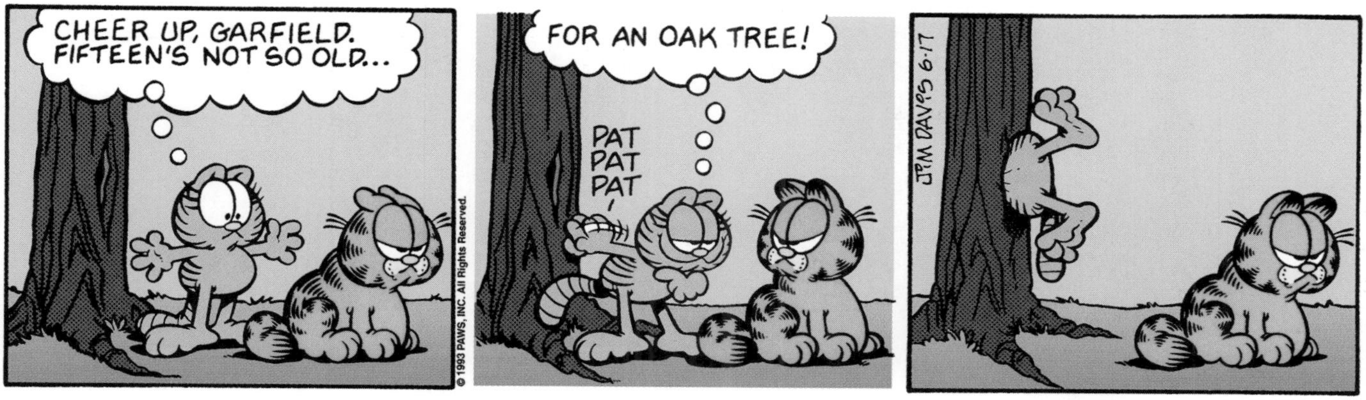
CHEER UP, GARFIELD. FIFTEEN'S NOT SO OLD...
© 1993 PAWS, INC. All Rights Reserved.
FOR AN OAK TREE!
PAT PAT PAT
JIM DAVIS 6-17

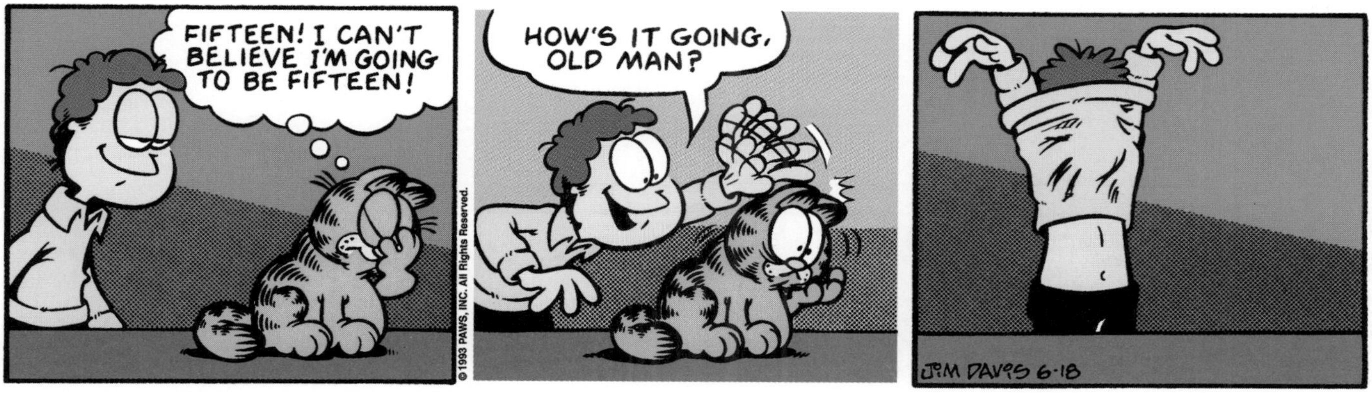
FIFTEEN! I CAN'T BELIEVE I'M GOING TO BE FIFTEEN!
© 1993 PAWS, INC. All Rights Reserved.
HOW'S IT GOING, OLD MAN?
JIM DAVIS 6-18

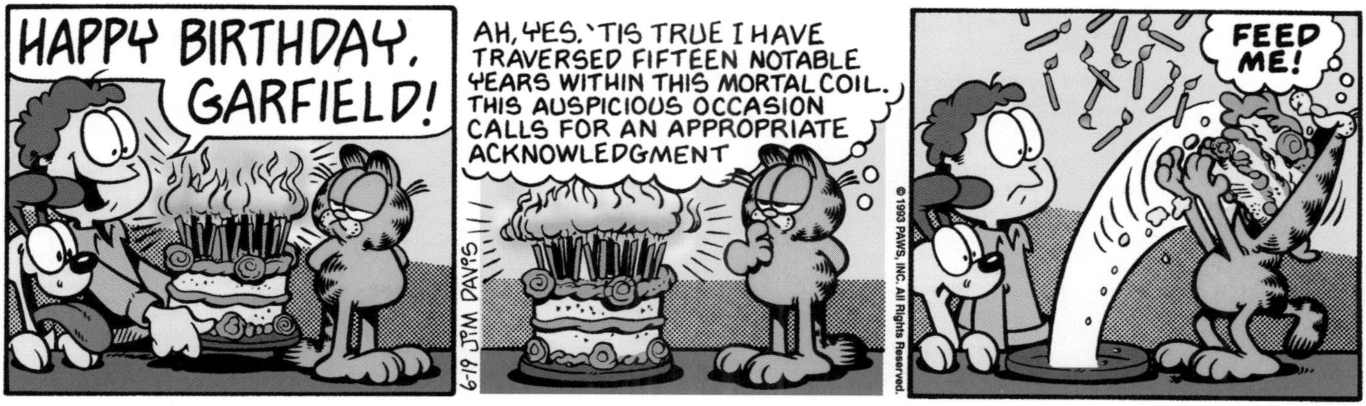
HAPPY BIRTHDAY, GARFIELD!
JIM DAVIS 6-19
AH, YES. 'TIS TRUE I HAVE TRAVERSED FIFTEEN NOTABLE YEARS WITHIN THIS MORTAL COIL. THIS AUSPICIOUS OCCASION CALLS FOR AN APPROPRIATE ACKNOWLEDGMENT
© 1993 PAWS, INC. All Rights Reserved.
FEED ME!

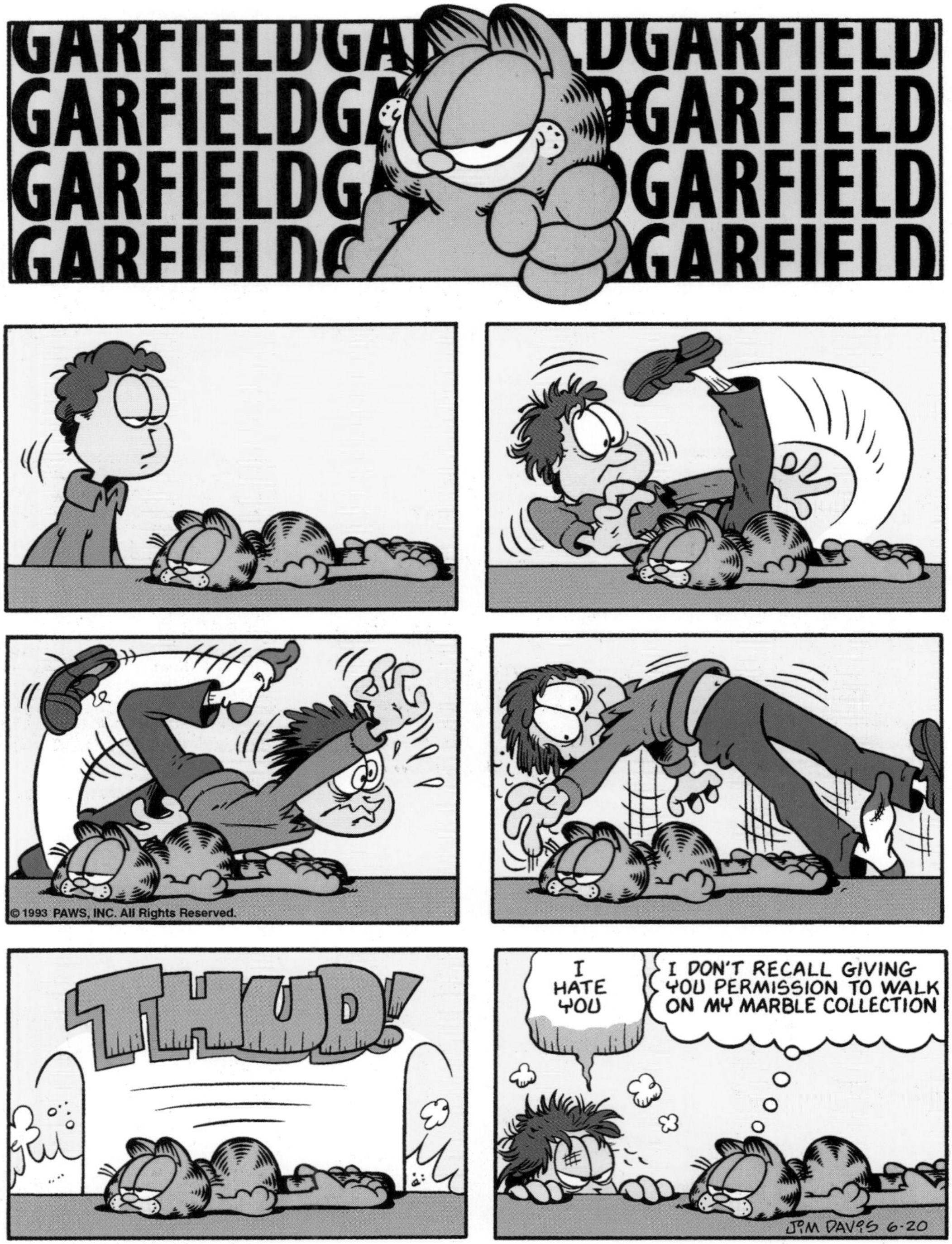
GARFIELD
© 1993 PAWS, INC. All Rights Reserved.
THUD!
I HATE YOU
I DON'T RECALL GIVING YOU PERMISSION TO WALK ON MY MARBLE COLLECTION
JIM DAVIS 6-20

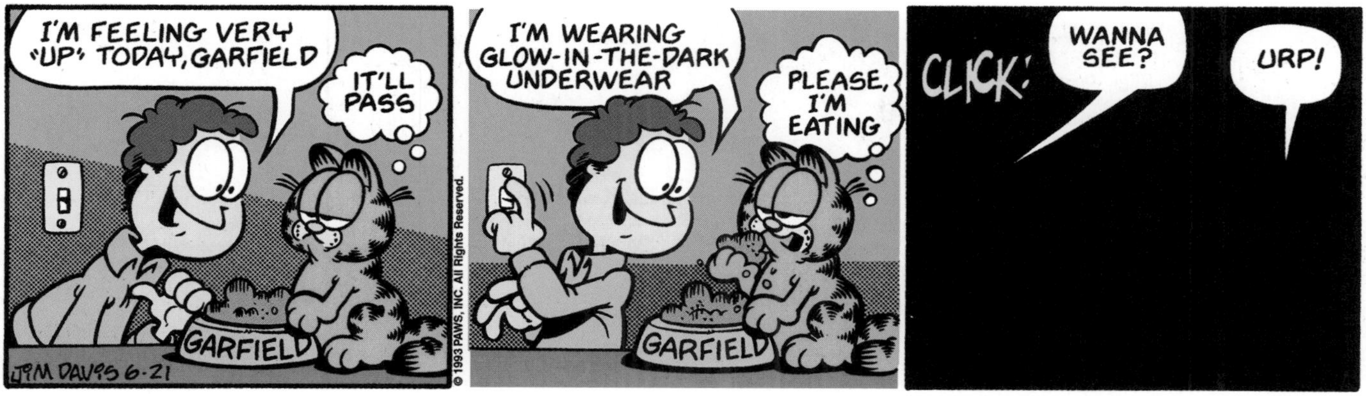
I'M FEELING VERY "UP" TODAY, GARFIELD
IT'LL PASS
GARFIELD
JIM DAVIS 6-21
© 1993 PAWS, INC. All Rights Reserved.
I'M WEARING GLOW-IN-THE-DARK UNDERWEAR
PLEASE, I'M EATING
GARFIELD
CLICK!
WANNA SEE?
URP!

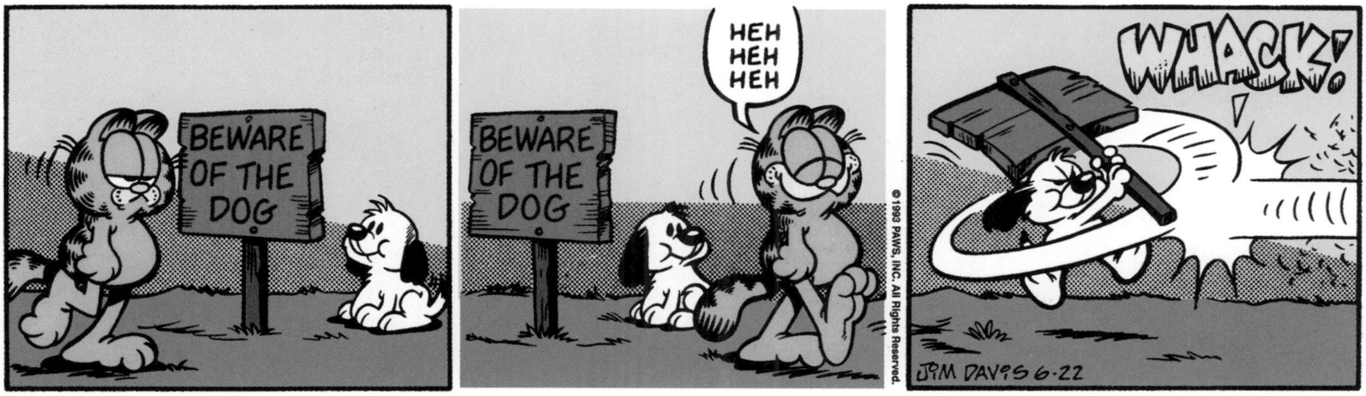
BEWARE OF THE DOG
BEWARE OF THE DOG
HEH HEH HEH
© 1993 PAWS, INC. All Rights Reserved.
WHACK!
JIM DAVIS 6-22

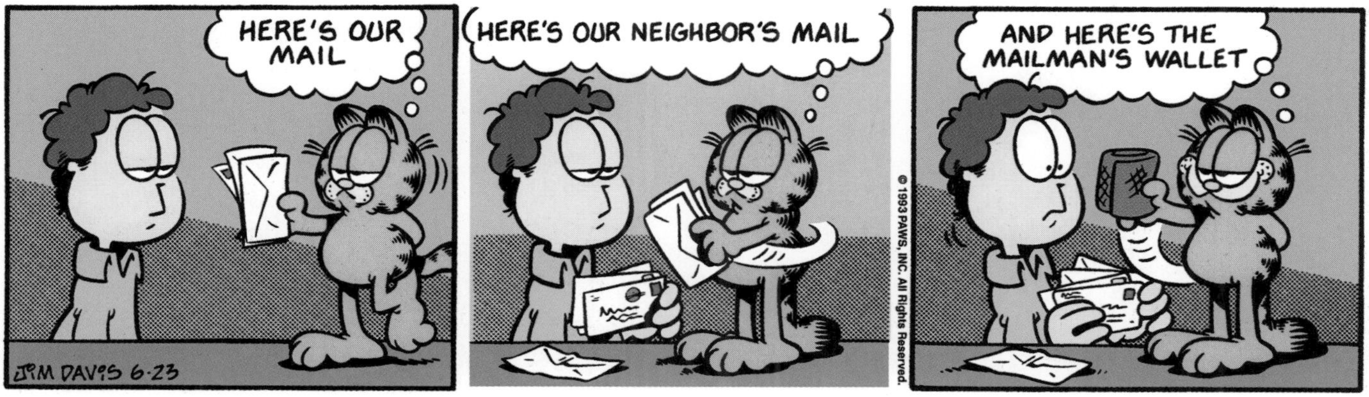
HERE'S OUR MAIL
JIM DAVIS 6-23
HERE'S OUR NEIGHBOR'S MAIL
© 1993 PAWS, INC. All Rights Reserved.
AND HERE'S THE MAILMAN'S WALLET

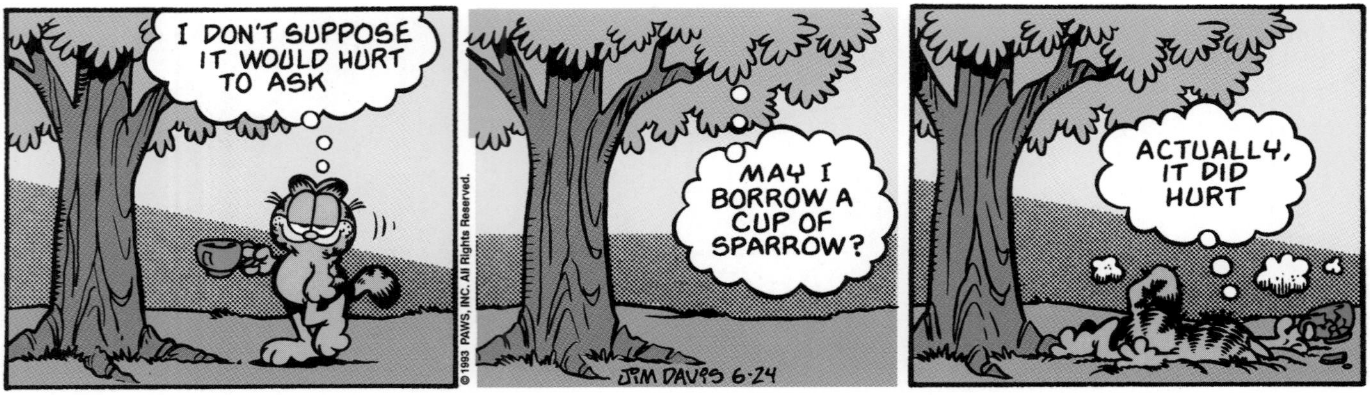
I DON'T SUPPOSE IT WOULD HURT TO ASK
© 1993 PAWS, INC. All Rights Reserved.
MAY I BORROW A CUP OF SPARROW?
JIM DAVIS 6-24
ACTUALLY, IT DID HURT

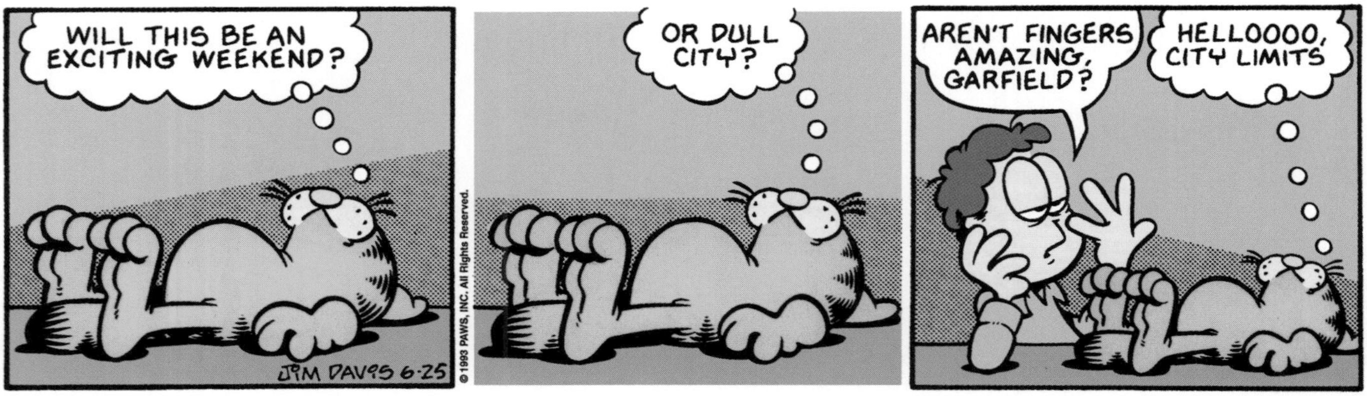
WILL THIS BE AN EXCITING WEEKEND?
JIM DAVIS 6-25
© 1993 PAWS, INC. All Rights Reserved.
OR DULL CITY?
AREN'T FINGERS AMAZING, GARFIELD?
HELLOOOO, CITY LIMITS

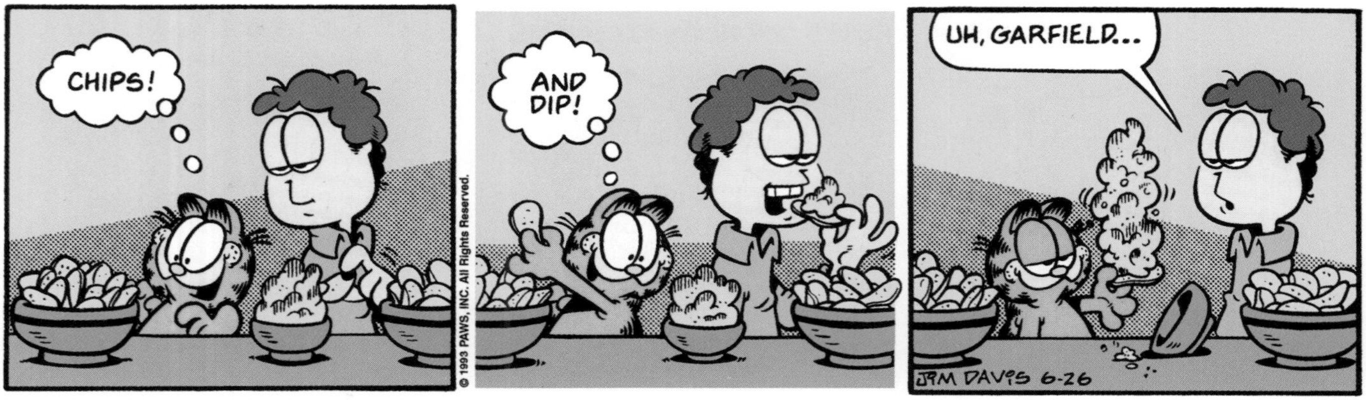
CHIPS!
© 1993 PAWS, INC. All Rights Reserved.
AND DIP!
UH, GARFIELD...
JIM DAVIS 6-26

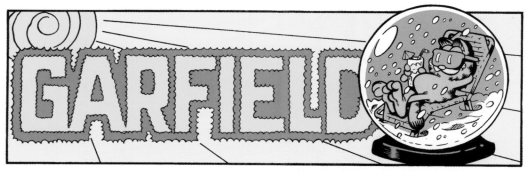

THIS IS IT, GARFIELD! IT'S A NEW DAY. I HAVE A NEW HAIRDO AND THE CHICKS ARE OUT!

© 1993 PAWS, INC. All Rights Reserved.

OOOOWEEE! WHAT A BABE!

I JUST PUT MY HEAD IN A BIRDBATH, DIDN'T I?

UH-HUH

EXCUSE ME. WHAT ARE YOU LOOKING AT?

CLOUDS! GO AWAY!

I'LL BET YOU SAY THAT TO ALL THE GIRLS

IS SHE GONE YET?

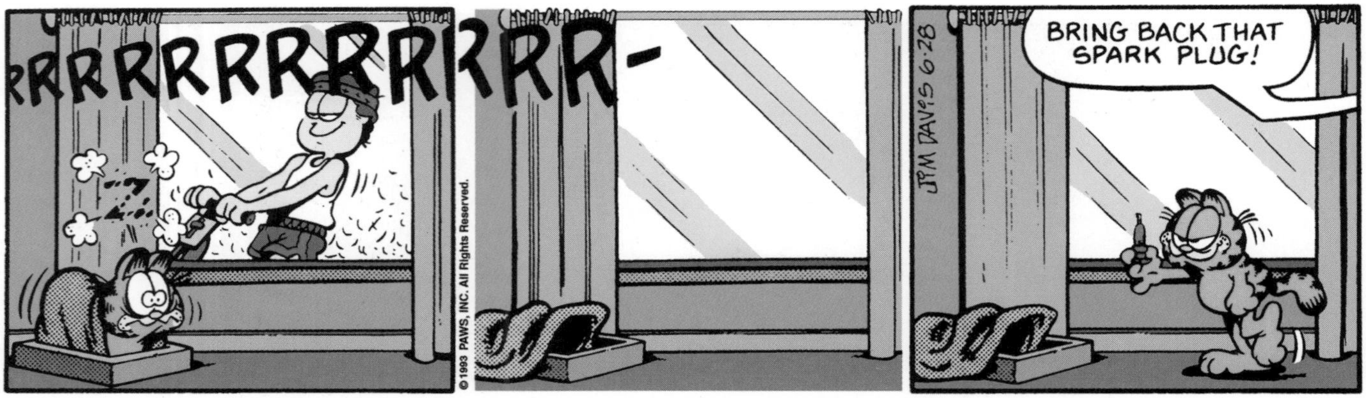
RRRRRRRRRRRR-
© 1993 PAWS, INC. All Rights Reserved.
JIM DAVIS 6-28
BRING BACK THAT SPARK PLUG!

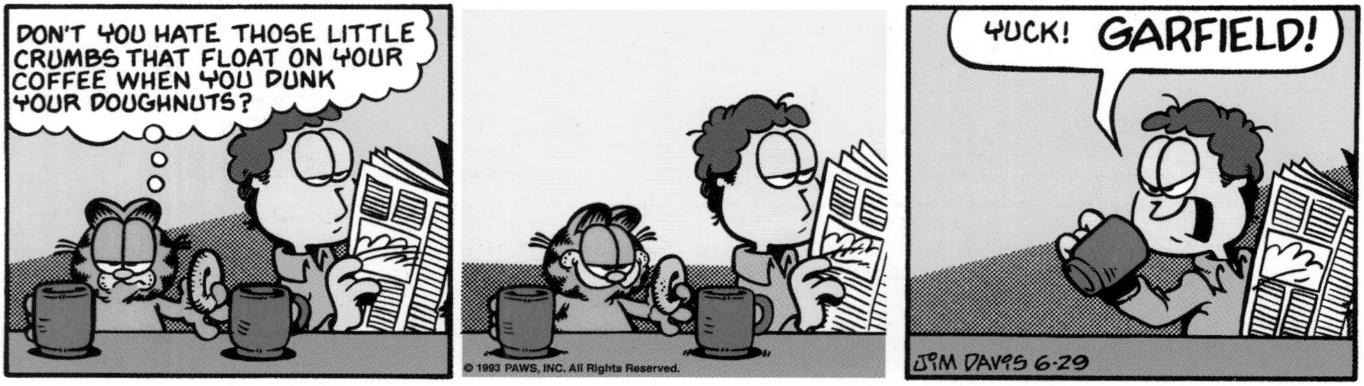
DON'T YOU HATE THOSE LITTLE CRUMBS THAT FLOAT ON YOUR COFFEE WHEN YOU DUNK YOUR DOUGHNUTS?
© 1993 PAWS, INC. All Rights Reserved.
YUCK! GARFIELD!
JIM DAVIS 6-29

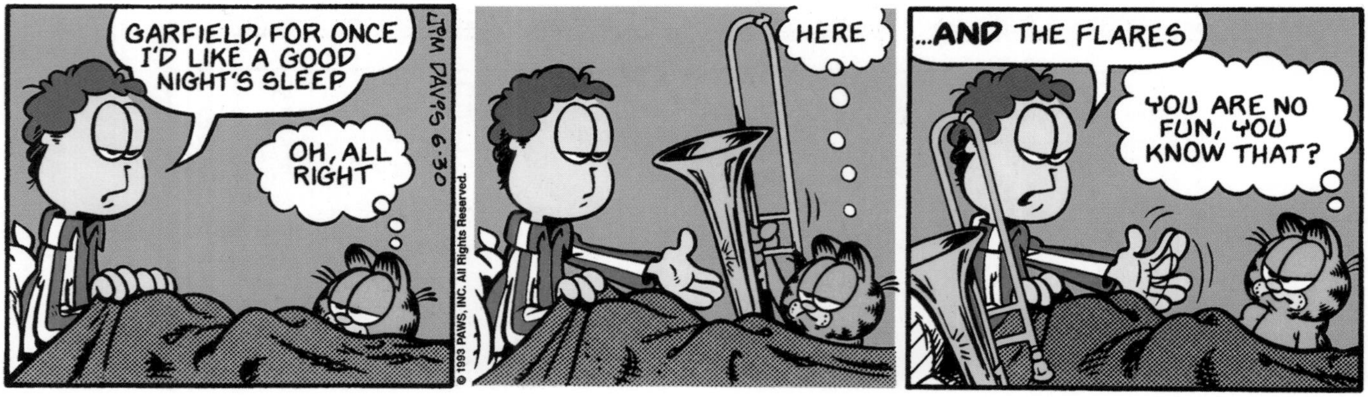
GARFIELD, FOR ONCE I'D LIKE A GOOD NIGHT'S SLEEP
JIM DAVIS 6-30
OH, ALL RIGHT
© 1993 PAWS, INC. All Rights Reserved.
HERE
...AND THE FLARES
YOU ARE NO FUN, YOU KNOW THAT?

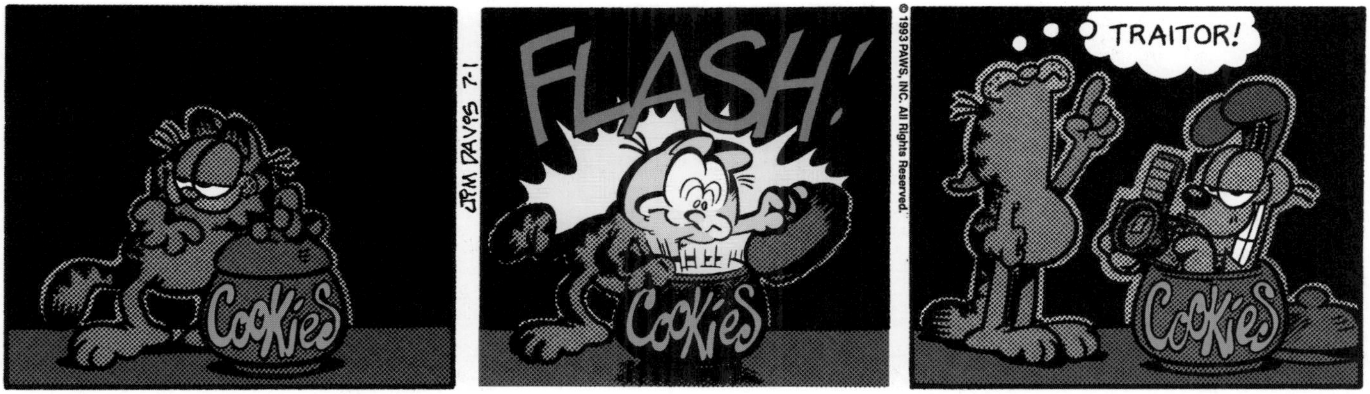
JIM DAVIS 7-1
FLASH!
© 1993 PAWS, INC. All Rights Reserved.
TRAITOR!

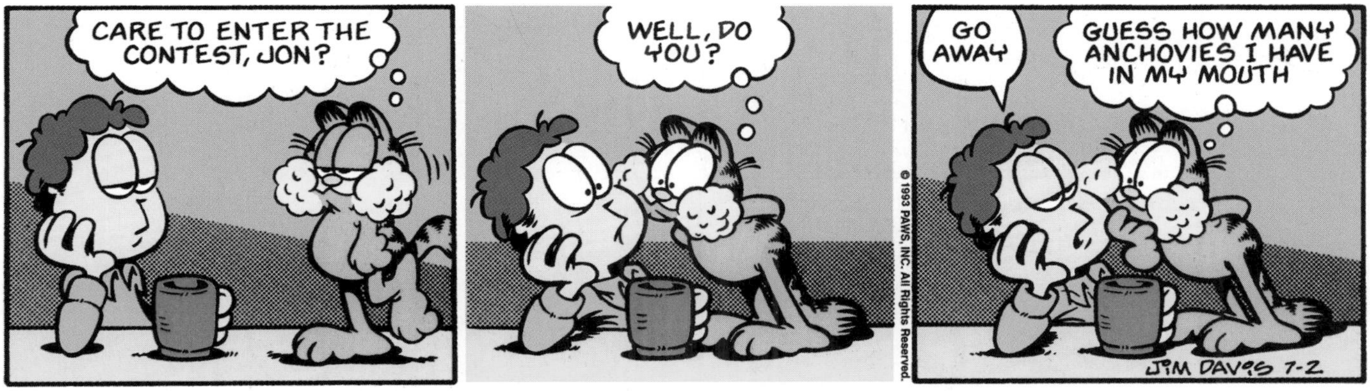
CARE TO ENTER THE CONTEST, JON?
WELL, DO YOU?
© 1993 PAWS, INC. All Rights Reserved.
GO AWAY
GUESS HOW MANY ANCHOVIES I HAVE IN MY MOUTH
JIM DAVIS 7-2

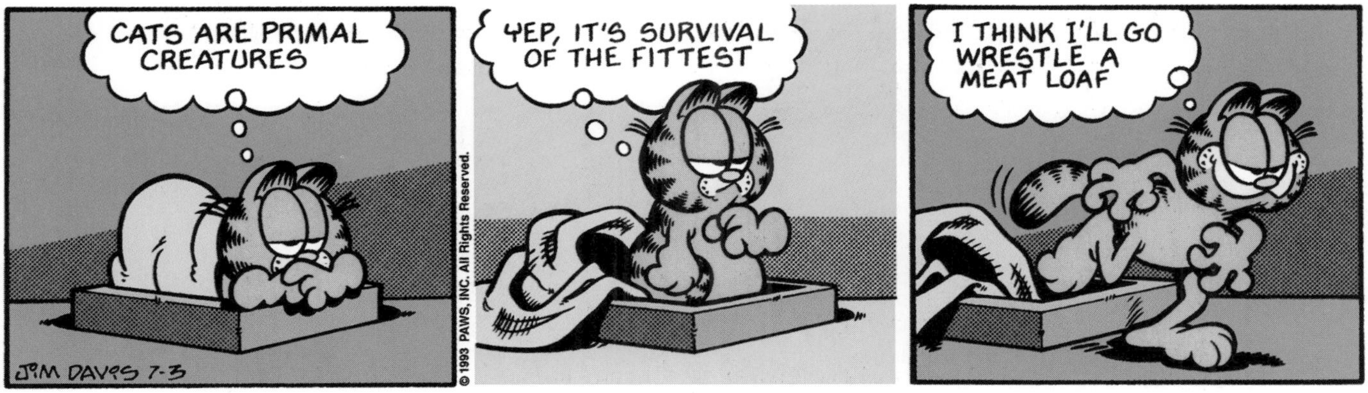
CATS ARE PRIMAL CREATURES
JIM DAVIS 7-3
© 1993 PAWS, INC. All Rights Reserved.
YEP, IT'S SURVIVAL OF THE FITTEST
I THINK I'LL GO WRESTLE A MEAT LOAF

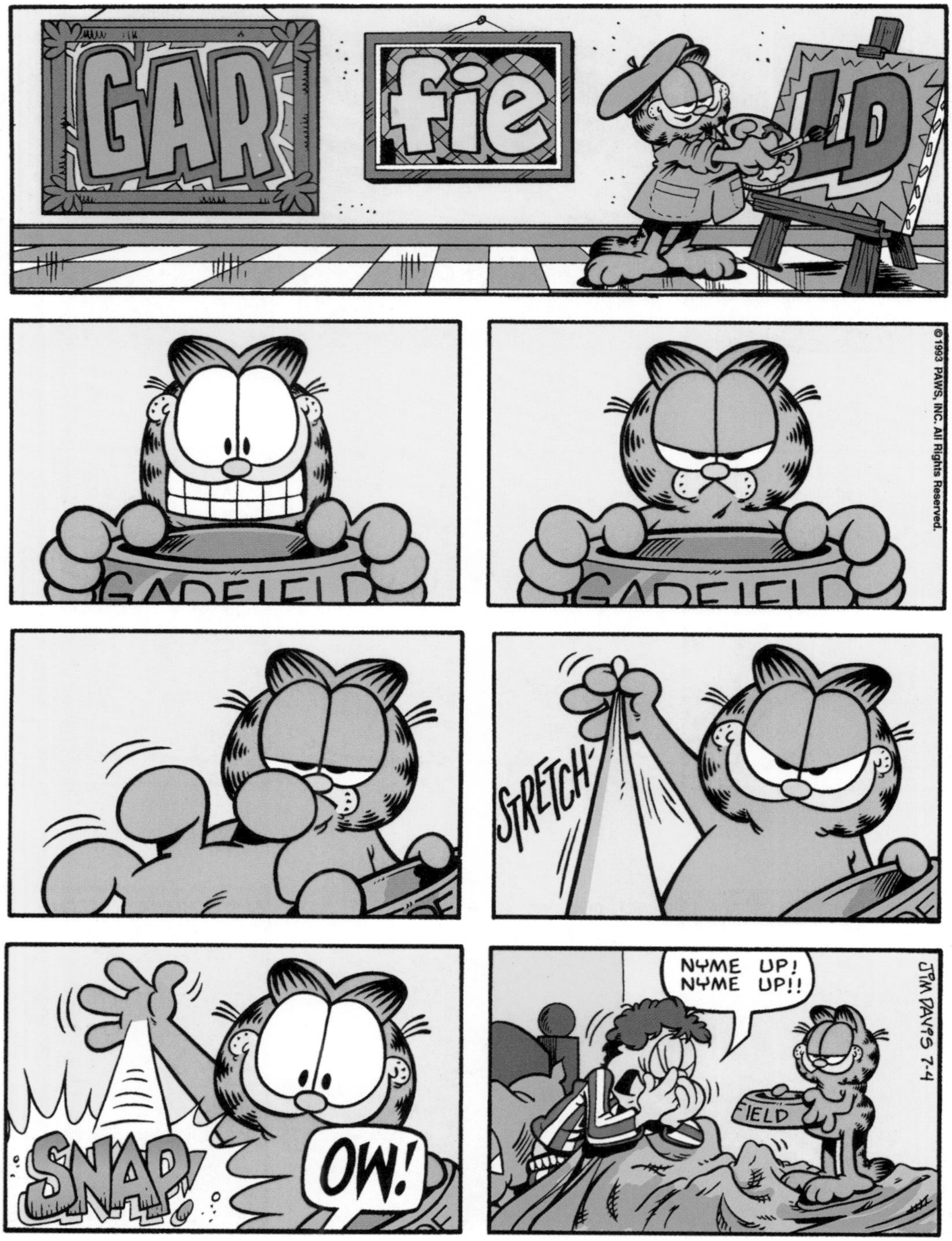
GAR
fie
LD
© 1993 PAWS, INC. All Rights Reserved.
STRETCH
SNAP
OW!
NYME UP!
NYME UP!!
JIM DAVIS 7-4

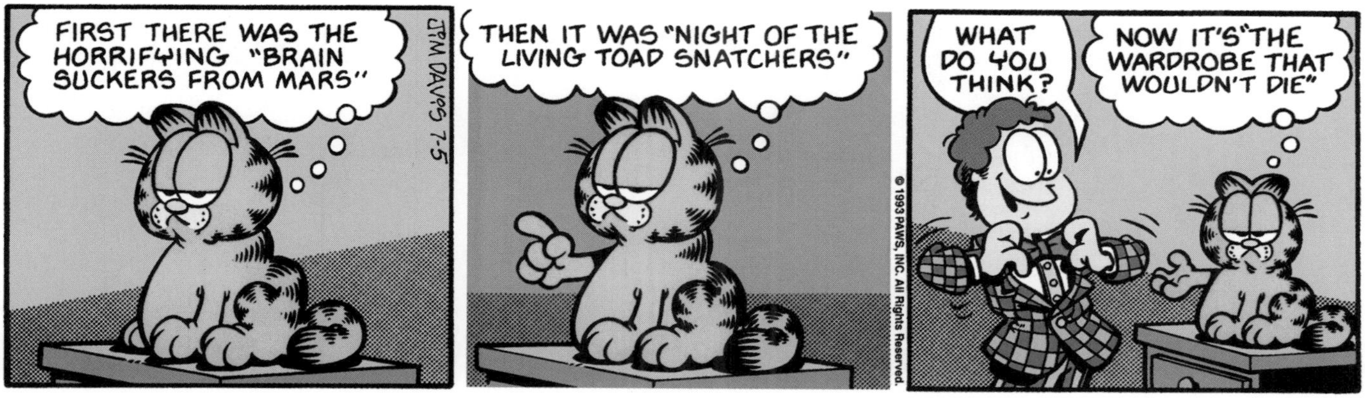
FIRST THERE WAS THE HORRIFYING "BRAIN SUCKERS FROM MARS"
JIM DAVIS 7-5
THEN IT WAS "NIGHT OF THE LIVING TOAD SNATCHERS"
© 1993 PAWS, INC. All Rights Reserved.
WHAT DO YOU THINK?
NOW IT'S "THE WARDROBE THAT WOULDN'T DIE"

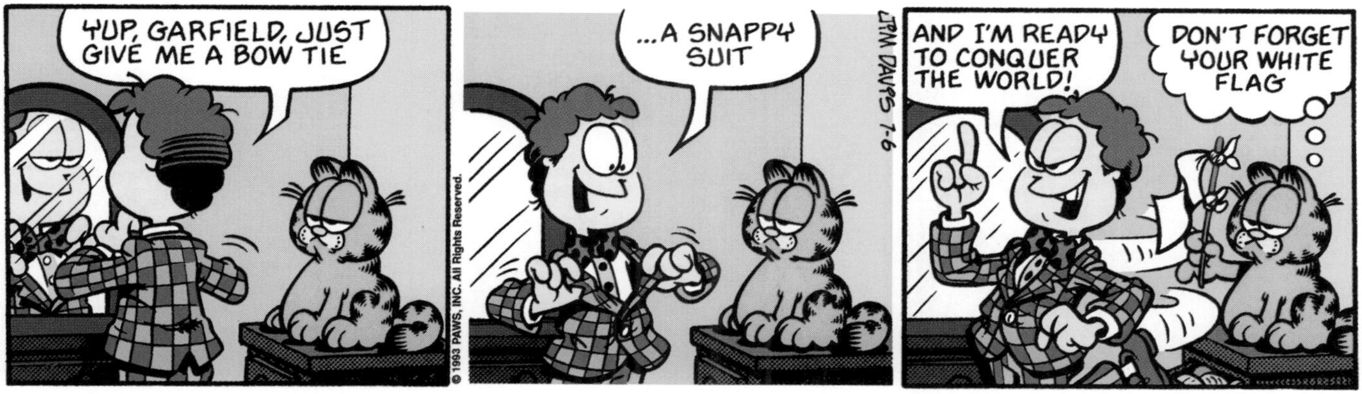
YUP, GARFIELD, JUST GIVE ME A BOW TIE
© 1993 PAWS, INC. All Rights Reserved.
...A SNAPPY SUIT
JIM DAVIS 7-6
AND I'M READY TO CONQUER THE WORLD!
DON'T FORGET YOUR WHITE FLAG

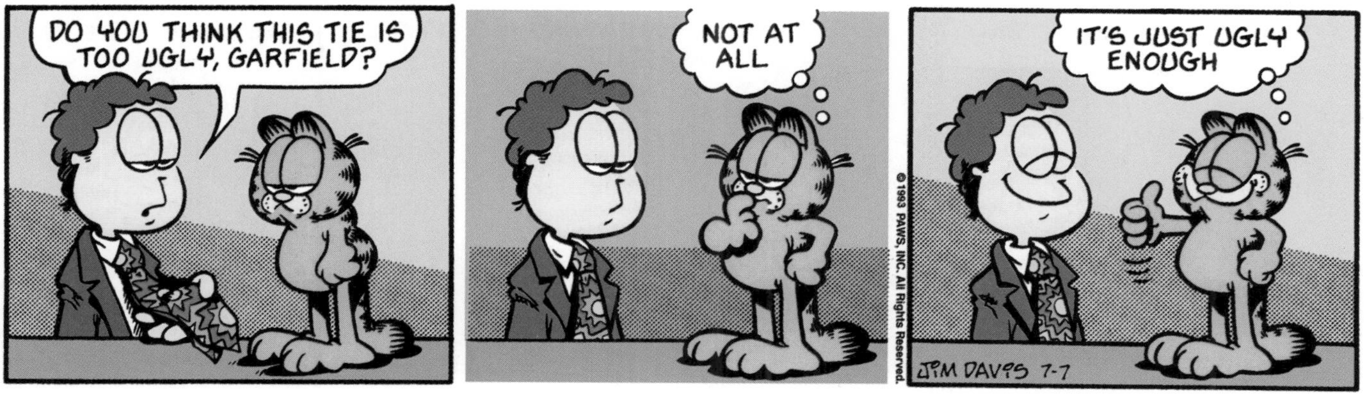
DO YOU THINK THIS TIE IS TOO UGLY, GARFIELD?
NOT AT ALL
© 1993 PAWS, INC. All Rights Reserved.
IT'S JUST UGLY ENOUGH
JIM DAVIS 7-7

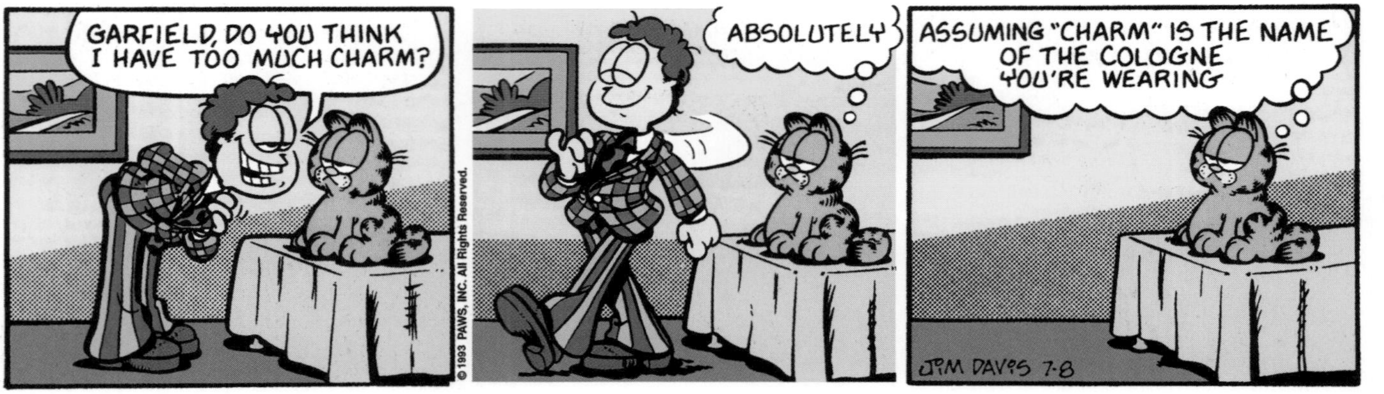
GARFIELD, DO YOU THINK I HAVE TOO MUCH CHARM?
© 1993 PAWS, INC. All Rights Reserved.
ABSOLUTELY
ASSUMING "CHARM" IS THE NAME OF THE COLOGNE YOU'RE WEARING
JIM DAVIS 7-8

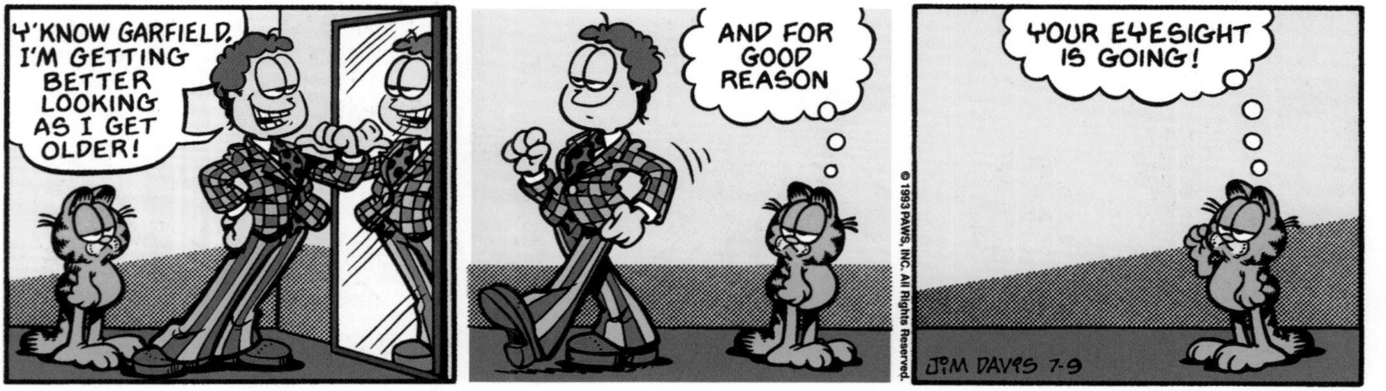
Y'KNOW GARFIELD, I'M GETTING BETTER LOOKING AS I GET OLDER!
AND FOR GOOD REASON
© 1993 PAWS, INC. All Rights Reserved.
YOUR EYESIGHT IS GOING!
JIM DAVIS 7-9

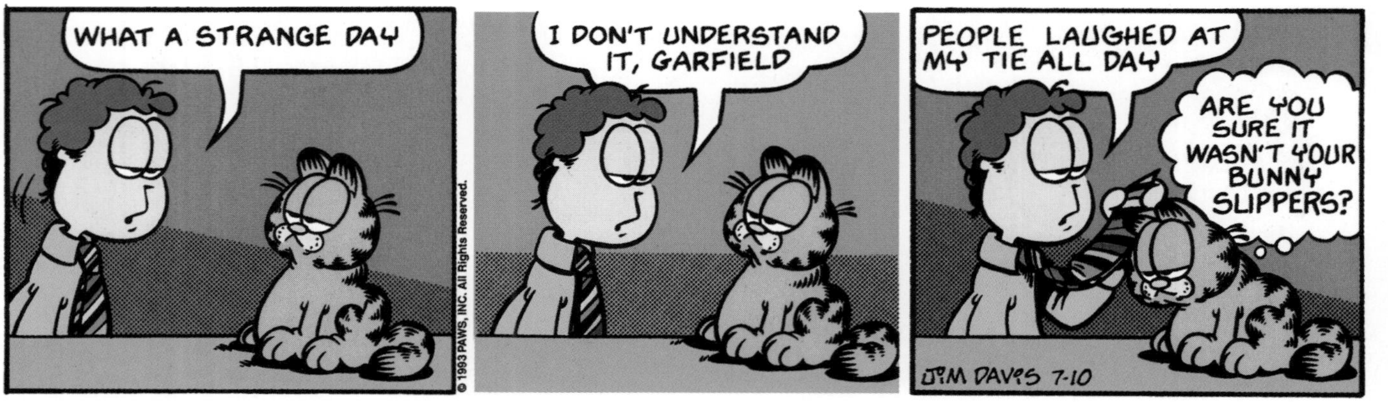
WHAT A STRANGE DAY
© 1993 PAWS, INC. All Rights Reserved.
I DON'T UNDERSTAND IT, GARFIELD
PEOPLE LAUGHED AT MY TIE ALL DAY
ARE YOU SURE IT WASN'T YOUR BUNNY SLIPPERS?
JIM DAVIS 7-10

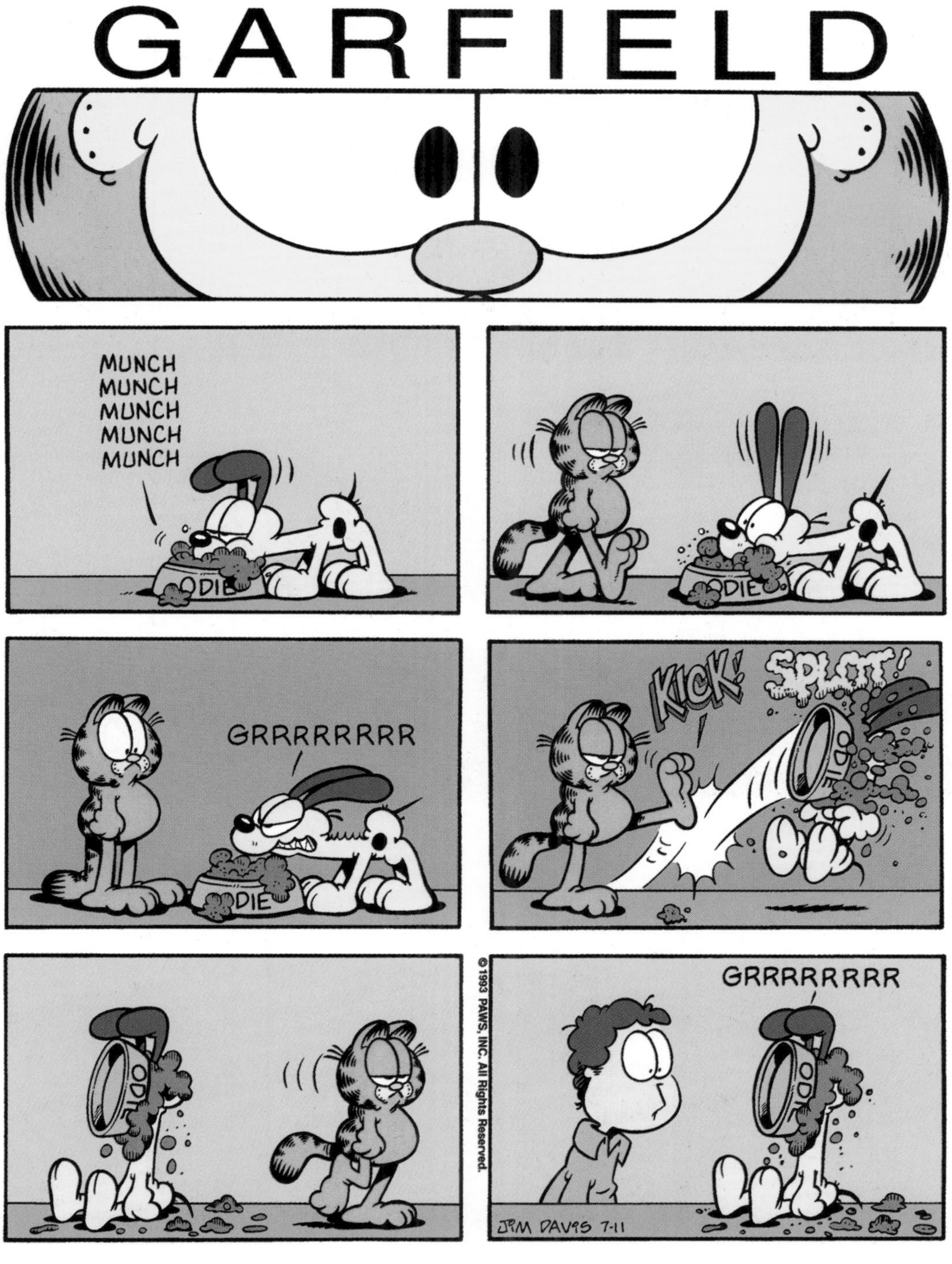
GARFIELD
MUNCH
MUNCH
MUNCH
MUNCH
MUNCH
ODIE
ODIE
GRRRRRRRR
ODIE
KICK!
SPLOT!
ODIE
ODIE
© 1993 PAWS, INC. All Rights Reserved.
GRRRRRRRR
ODIE
JIM DAVIS 7-11

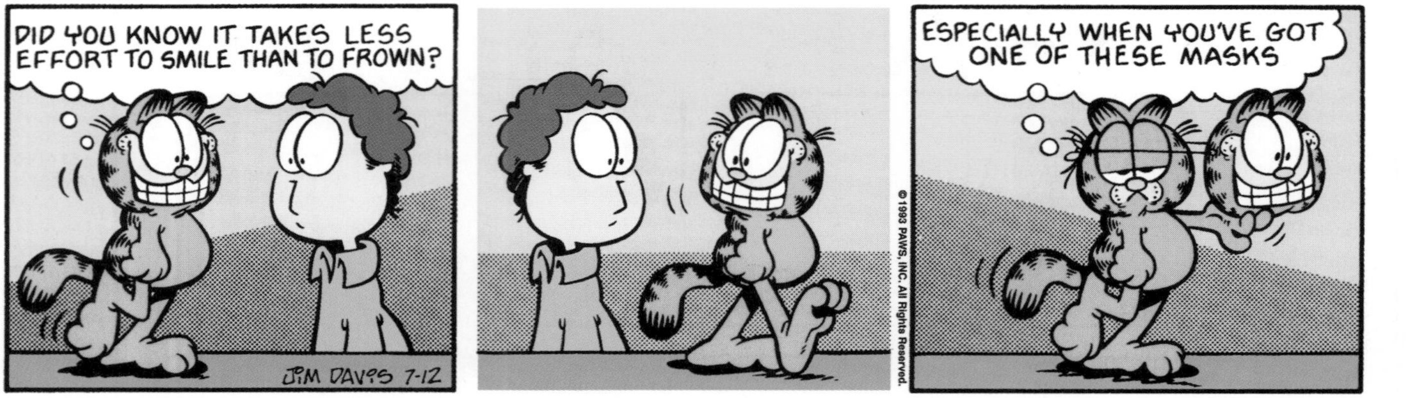
DID YOU KNOW IT TAKES LESS EFFORT TO SMILE THAN TO FROWN?
JIM DAVIS 7-12
© 1993 PAWS, INC. All Rights Reserved.
ESPECIALLY WHEN YOU'VE GOT ONE OF THESE MASKS

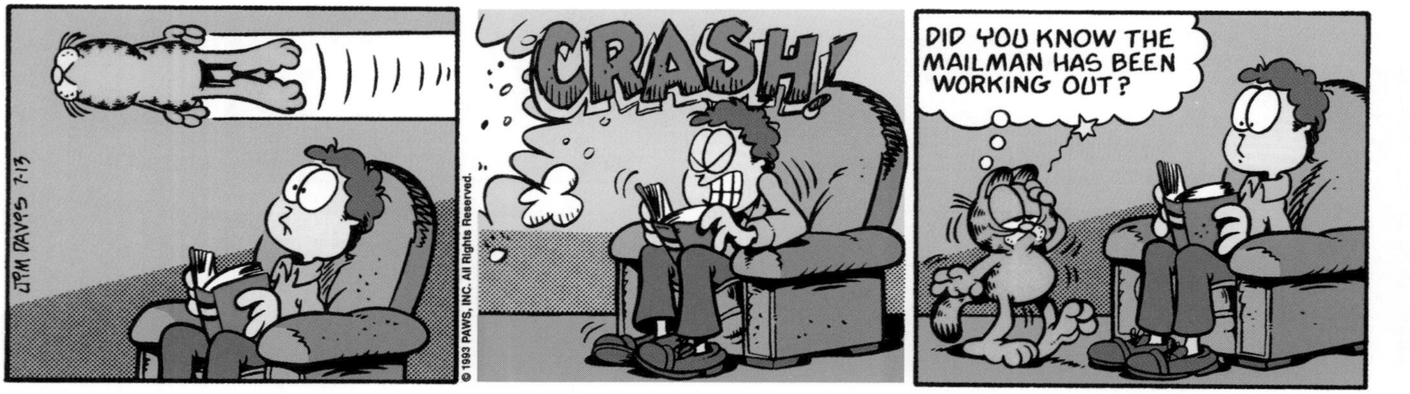
JIM DAVIS 7-13
© 1993 PAWS, INC. All Rights Reserved.
CRASH!
DID YOU KNOW THE MAILMAN HAS BEEN WORKING OUT?

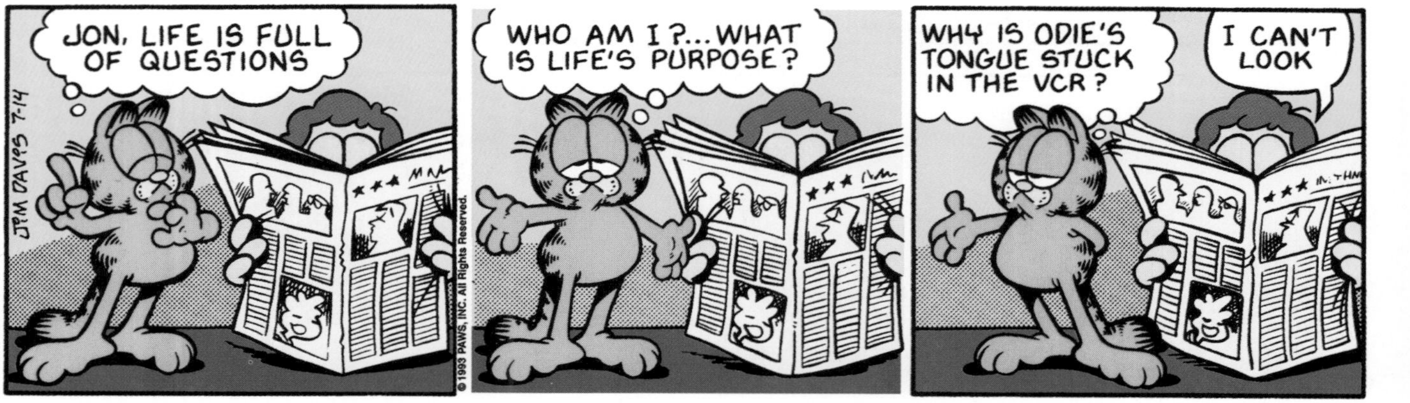
JON, LIFE IS FULL OF QUESTIONS
JIM DAVIS 7-14
© 1993 PAWS, INC. All Rights Reserved.
WHO AM I?... WHAT IS LIFE'S PURPOSE?
WHY IS ODIE'S TONGUE STUCK IN THE VCR?
I CAN'T LOOK

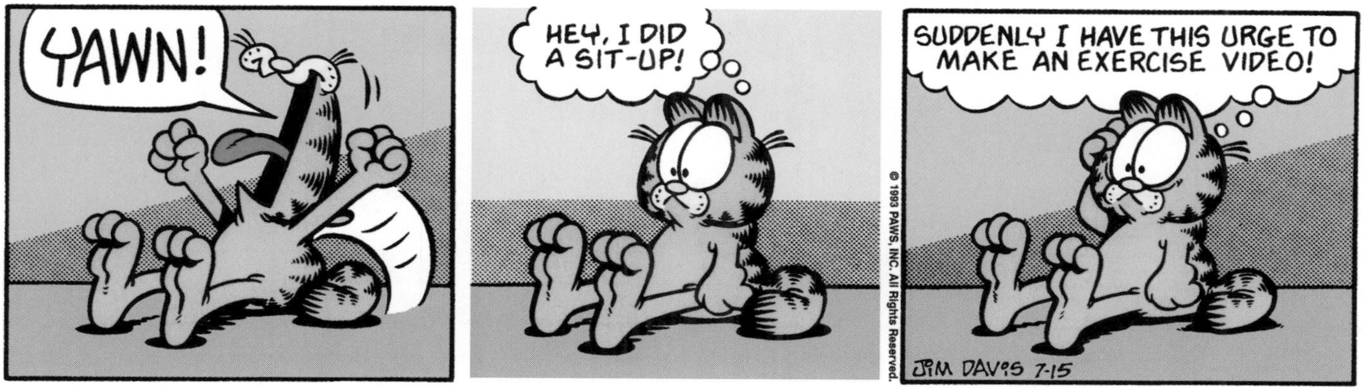
YAWN!
HEY, I DID A SIT-UP!
SUDDENLY I HAVE THIS URGE TO MAKE AN EXERCISE VIDEO!
© 1993 PAWS, INC. All Rights Reserved.
JIM DAVIS 7-15

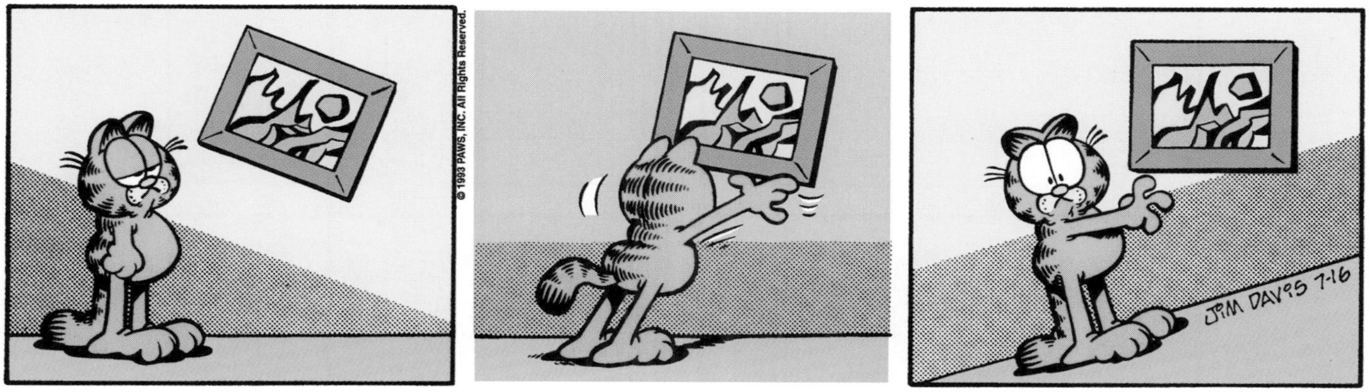
© 1993 PAWS, INC. All Rights Reserved.
JIM DAVIS 7-16

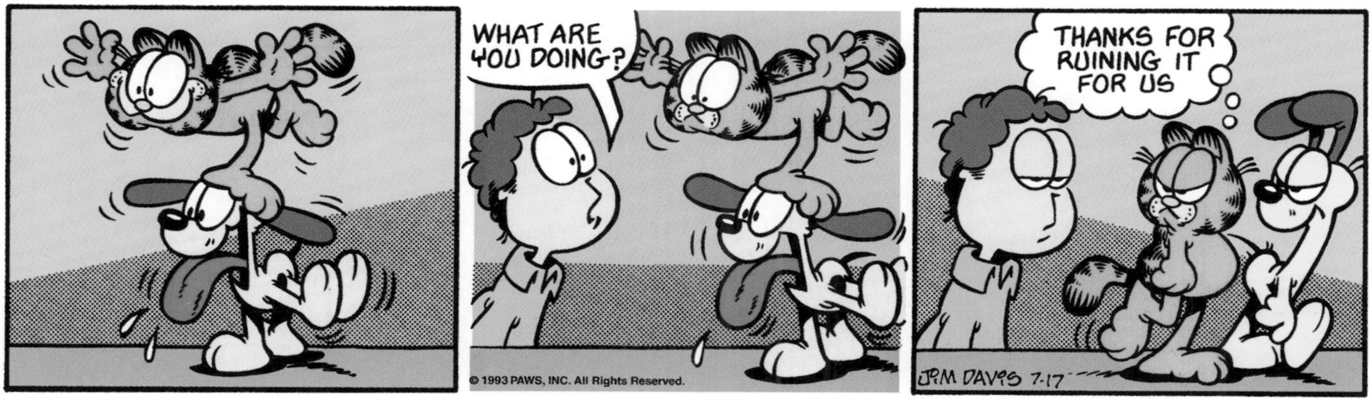
WHAT ARE YOU DOING?
THANKS FOR RUINING IT FOR US
© 1993 PAWS, INC. All Rights Reserved.
JIM DAVIS 7-17

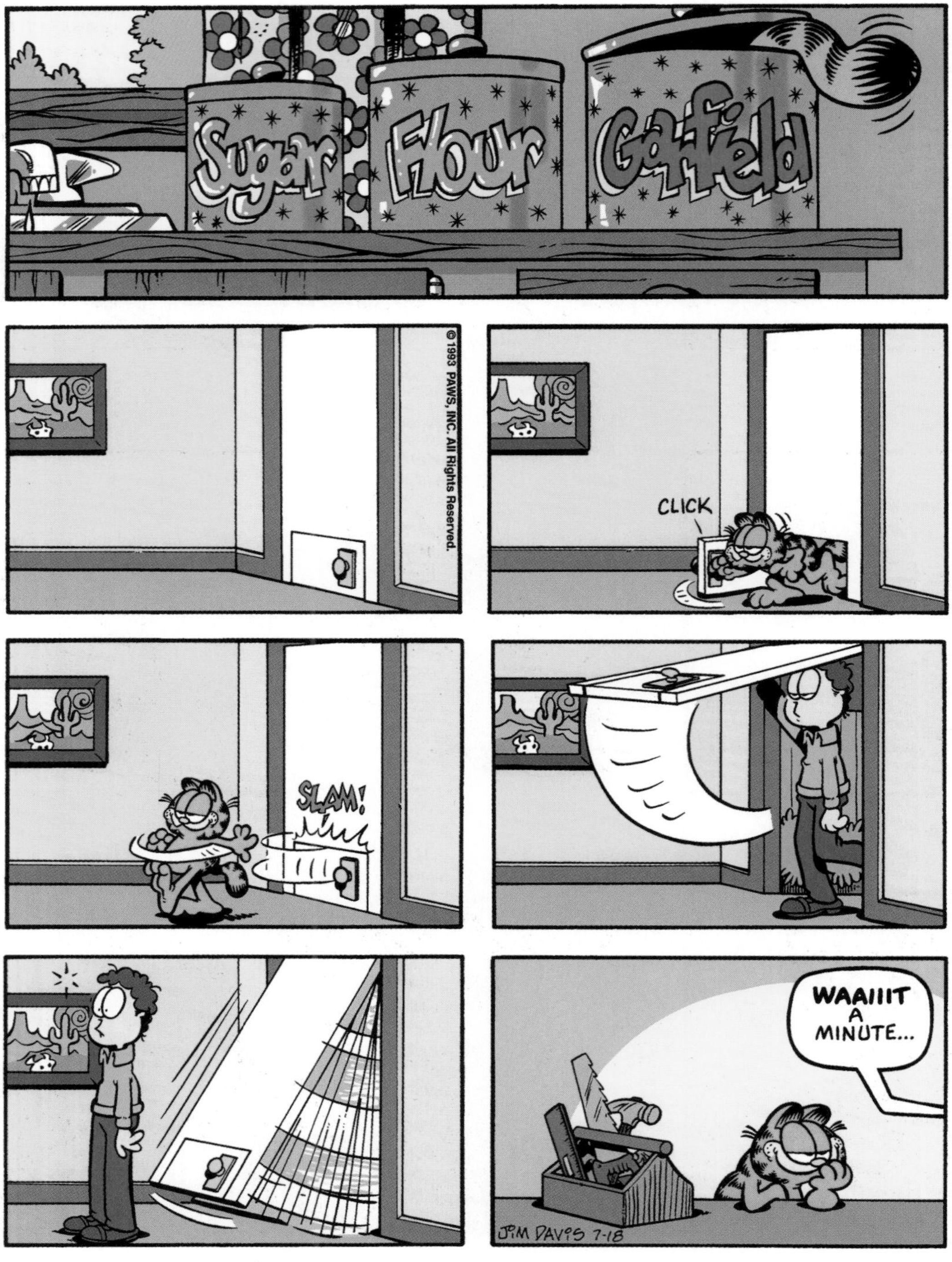
Sugar
Flour
Garfield
© 1993 PAWS, INC. All Rights Reserved.
CLICK
SLAM!
WAAIIIT A MINUTE...
JIM DAVIS 7-18

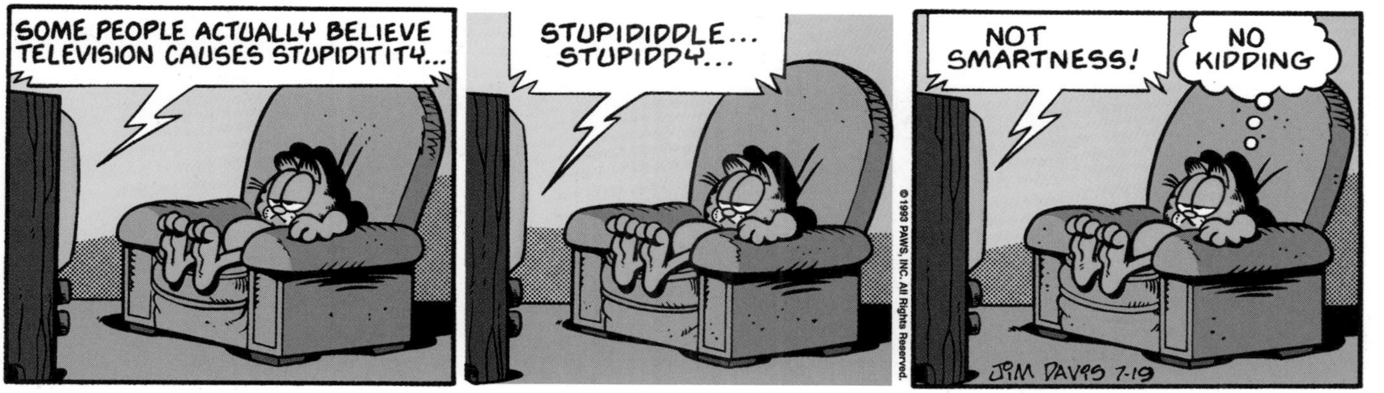
SOME PEOPLE ACTUALLY BELIEVE TELEVISION CAUSES STUPIDITITY...
STUPIDIDDLE... STUPIDDY...
NOT SMARTNESS!
NO KIDDING
© 1993 PAWS, INC. All Rights Reserved.
JIM DAVIS 7-19

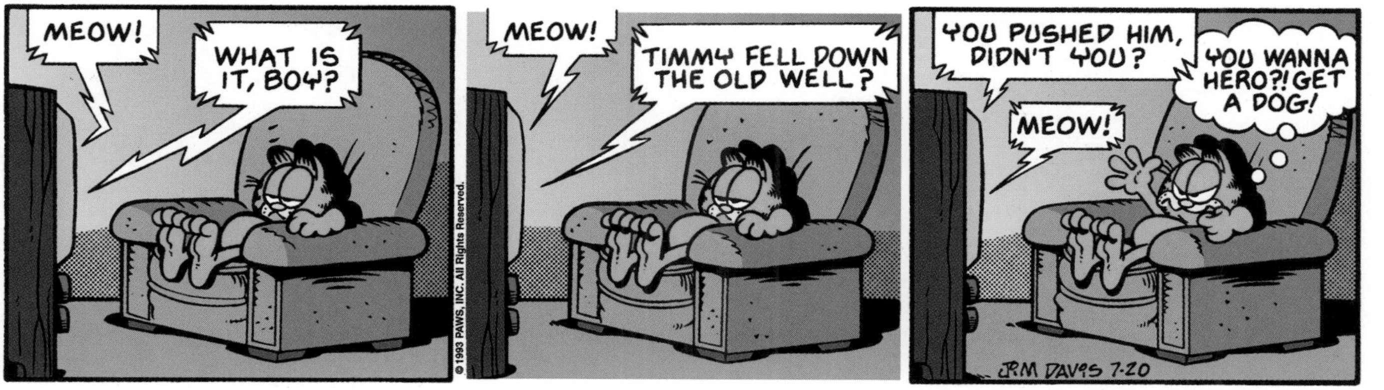
MEOW!
WHAT IS IT, BOY?
MEOW!
TIMMY FELL DOWN THE OLD WELL?
YOU PUSHED HIM, DIDN'T YOU?
MEOW!
YOU WANNA HERO?! GET A DOG!
© 1993 PAWS, INC. All Rights Reserved.
JIM DAVIS 7-20

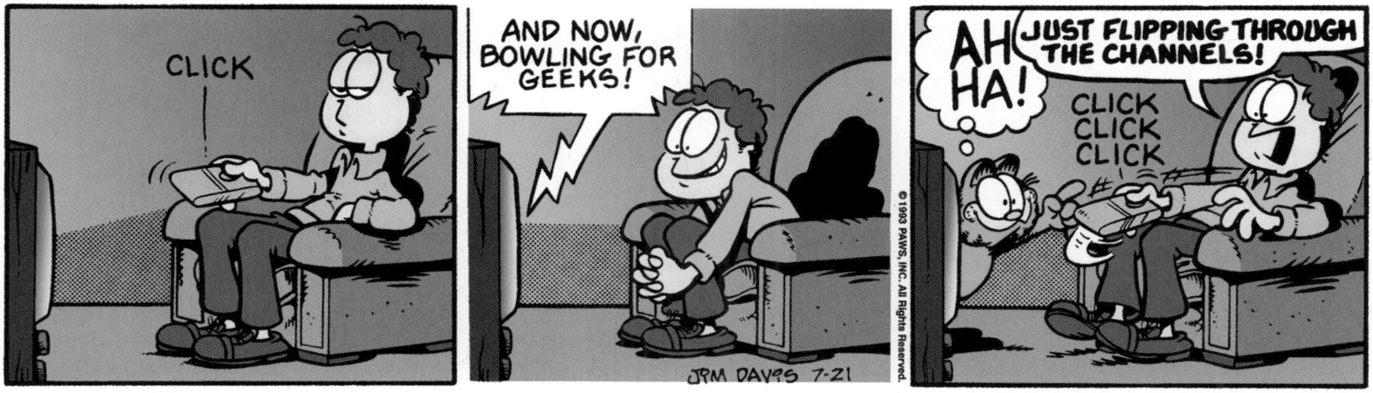
CLICK
AND NOW, BOWLING FOR GEEKS!
AH HA!
JUST FLIPPING THROUGH THE CHANNELS!
CLICK CLICK CLICK
© 1993 PAWS, INC. All Rights Reserved.
JIM DAVIS 7-21

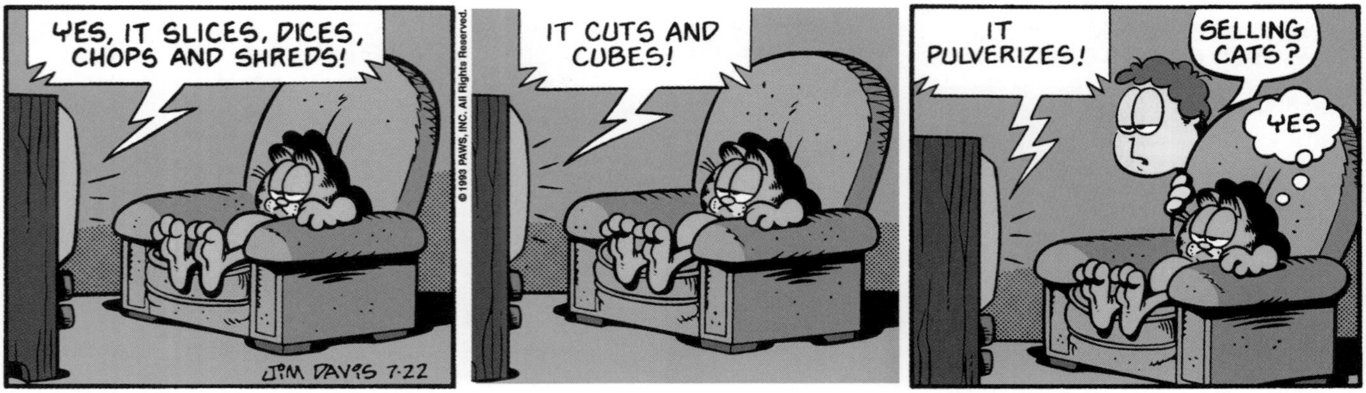
YES, IT SLICES, DICES, CHOPS AND SHREDS!
JIM DAVIS 7-22
© 1993 PAWS, INC. All Rights Reserved.
IT CUTS AND CUBES!
IT PULVERIZES!
SELLING CATS?
YES

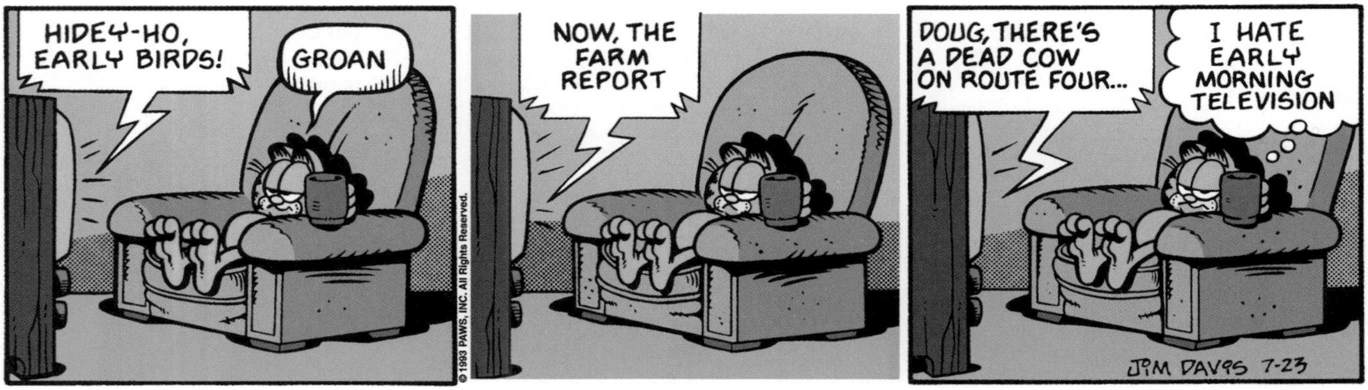
HIDEY-HO, EARLY BIRDS!
GROAN
© 1993 PAWS, INC. All Rights Reserved.
NOW, THE FARM REPORT
DOUG, THERE'S A DEAD COW ON ROUTE FOUR...
I HATE EARLY MORNING TELEVISION
JIM DAVIS 7-23

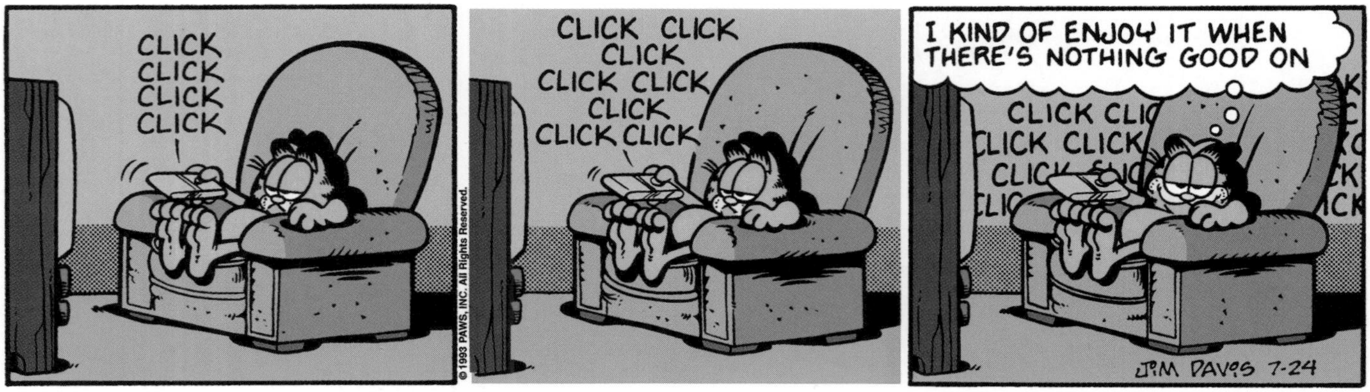
CLICK
CLICK
CLICK
CLICK
© 1993 PAWS, INC. All Rights Reserved.
CLICK CLICK
CLICK
CLICK CLICK
CLICK
CLICK CLICK
I KIND OF ENJOY IT WHEN THERE'S NOTHING GOOD ON
JIM DAVIS 7-24

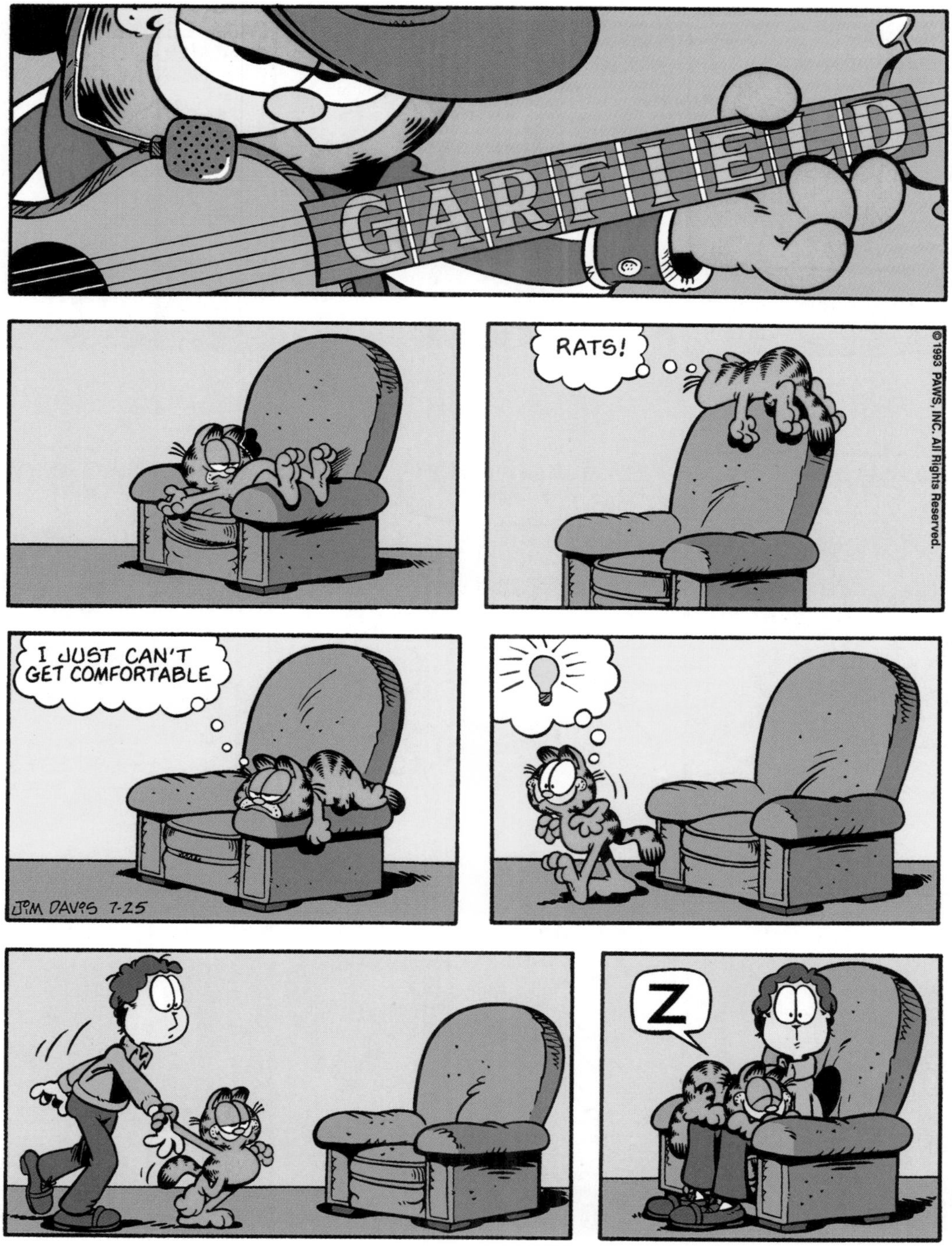
GARFIELD
RATS!
© 1993 PAWS, INC. All Rights Reserved.
I JUST CAN'T GET COMFORTABLE
JIM DAVIS 7-25
Z

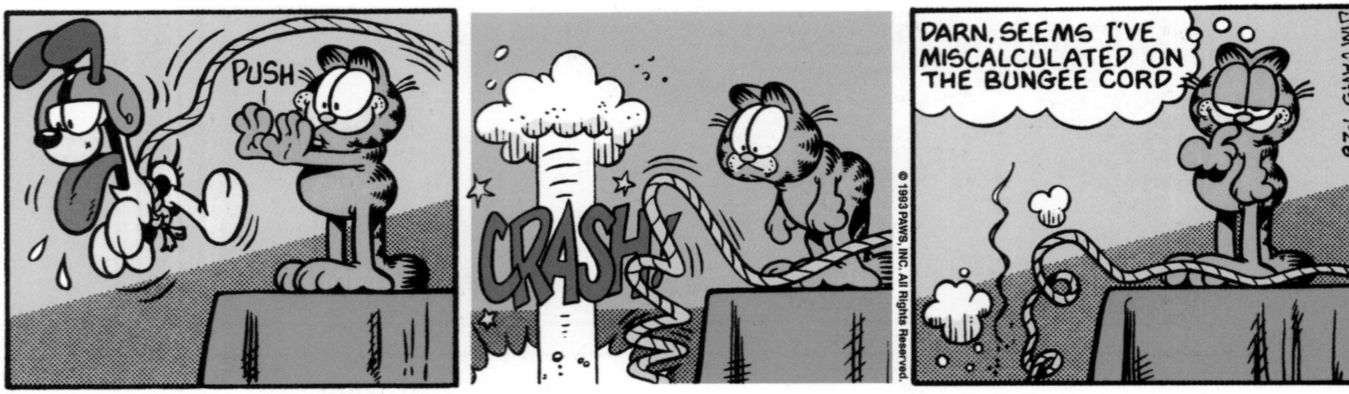
PUSH
CRASH
DARN, SEEMS I'VE MISCALCULATED ON THE BUNGEE CORD
JIM DAVIS 7-26
© 1993 PAWS, INC. All Rights Reserved.

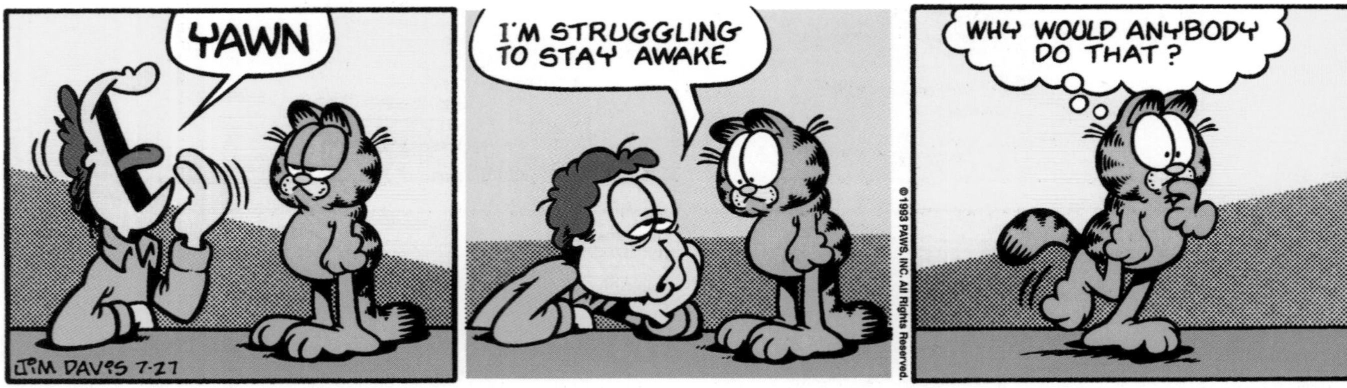
YAWN
JIM DAVIS 7-27
I'M STRUGGLING TO STAY AWAKE
WHY WOULD ANYBODY DO THAT?
© 1993 PAWS, INC. All Rights Reserved.

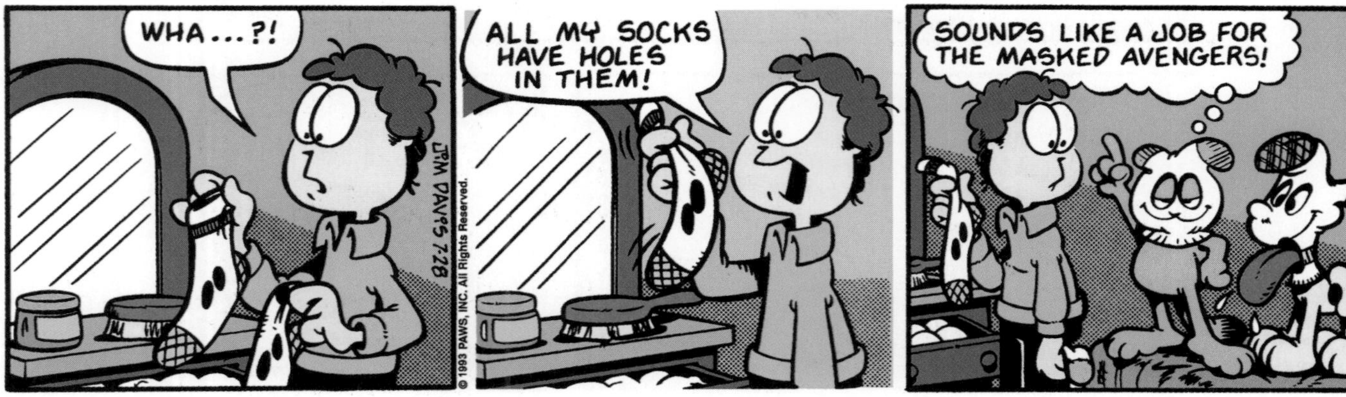
WHA...?!
JIM DAVIS 7-28
© 1993 PAWS, INC. All Rights Reserved.
ALL MY SOCKS HAVE HOLES IN THEM!
SOUNDS LIKE A JOB FOR THE MASKED AVENGERS!

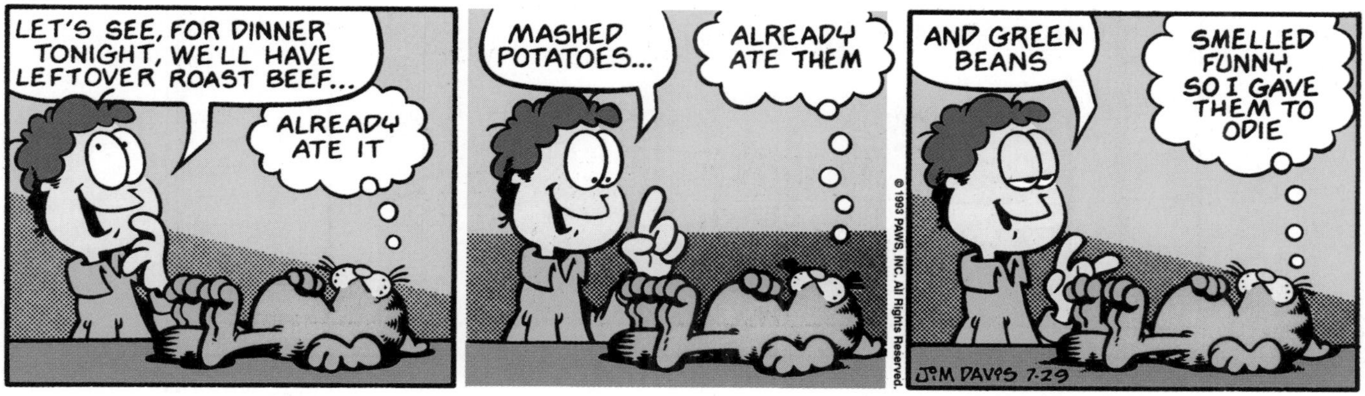
LET'S SEE, FOR DINNER TONIGHT, WE'LL HAVE LEFTOVER ROAST BEEF...
ALREADY ATE IT
MASHED POTATOES...
ALREADY ATE THEM
AND GREEN BEANS
SMELLED FUNNY, SO I GAVE THEM TO ODIE
JIM DAVIS 7-29

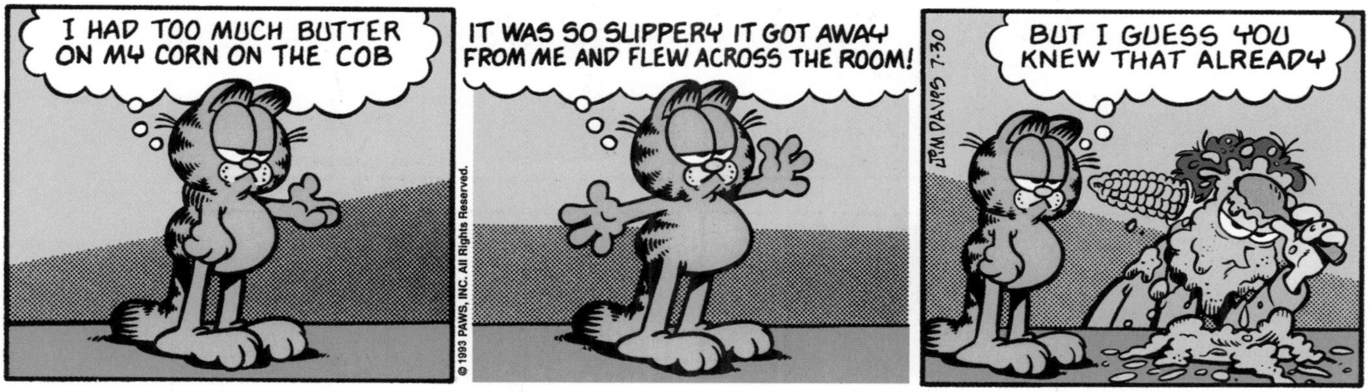
I HAD TOO MUCH BUTTER ON MY CORN ON THE COB
IT WAS SO SLIPPERY IT GOT AWAY FROM ME AND FLEW ACROSS THE ROOM!
BUT I GUESS YOU KNEW THAT ALREADY
JIM DAVIS 7-30

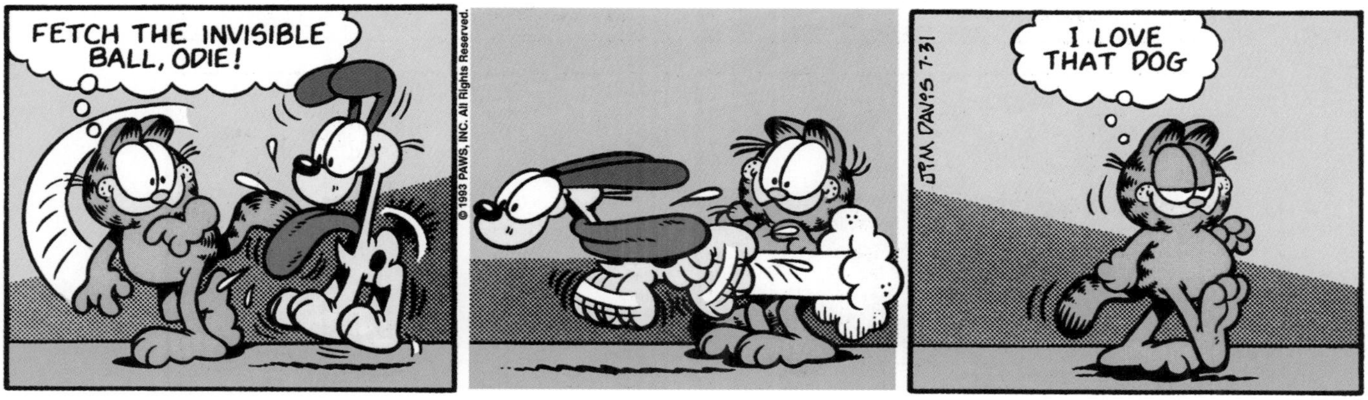
FETCH THE INVISIBLE BALL, ODIE!
I LOVE THAT DOG
JIM DAVIS 7-31

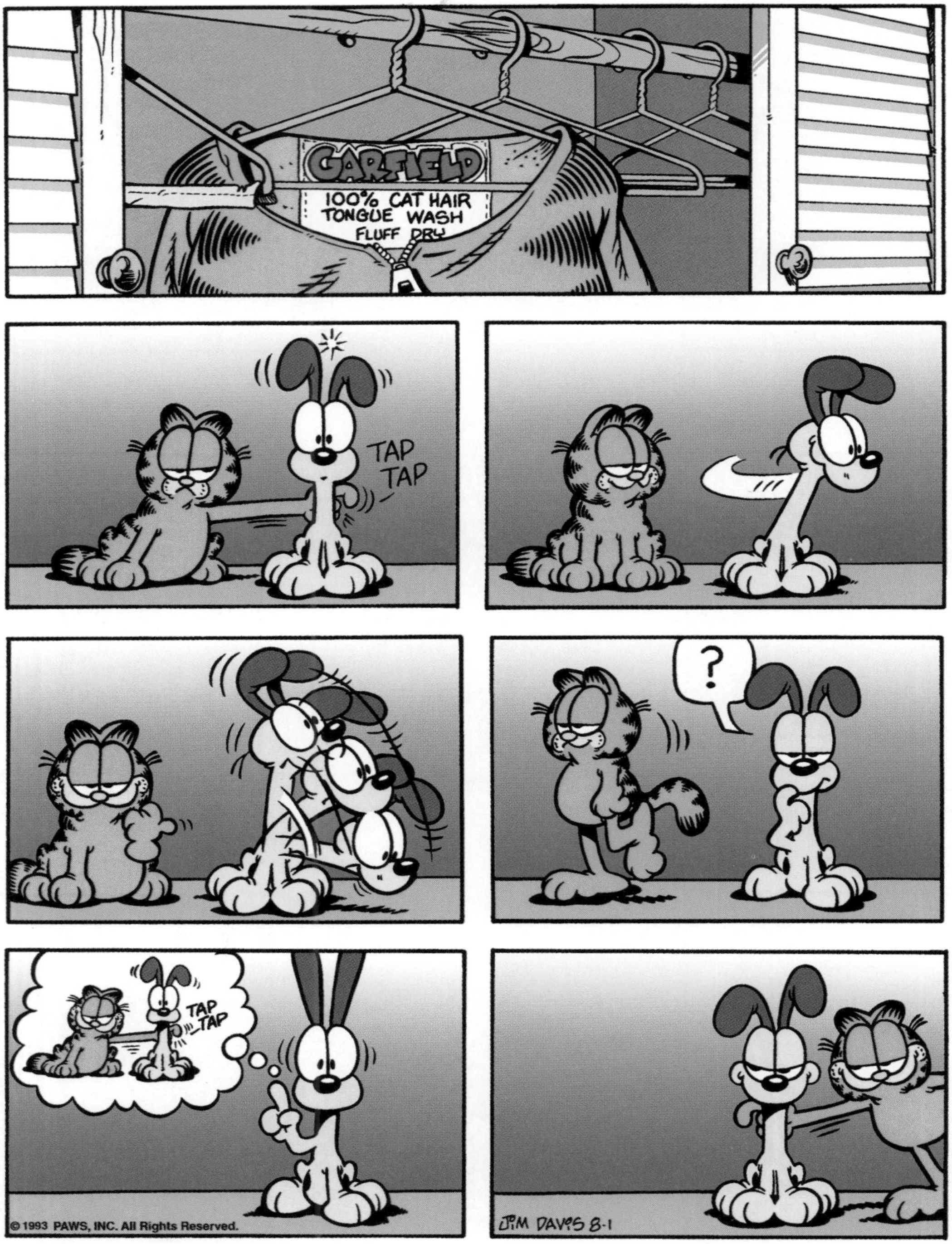
GARFIELD
100% CAT HAIR
TONGUE WASH
FLUFF DRY
TAP
TAP
?
TAP
TAP
© 1993 PAWS, INC. All Rights Reserved.
JIM DAVIS 8-1

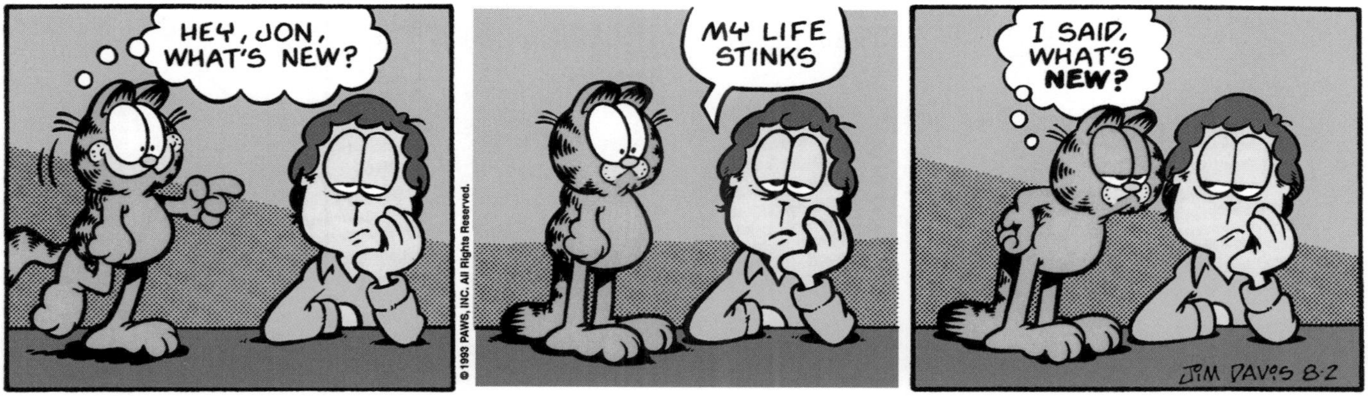
HEY, JON, WHAT'S NEW?
© 1993 PAWS, INC. All Rights Reserved.
MY LIFE STINKS
I SAID, WHAT'S **NEW?**
JIM DAVIS 8-2

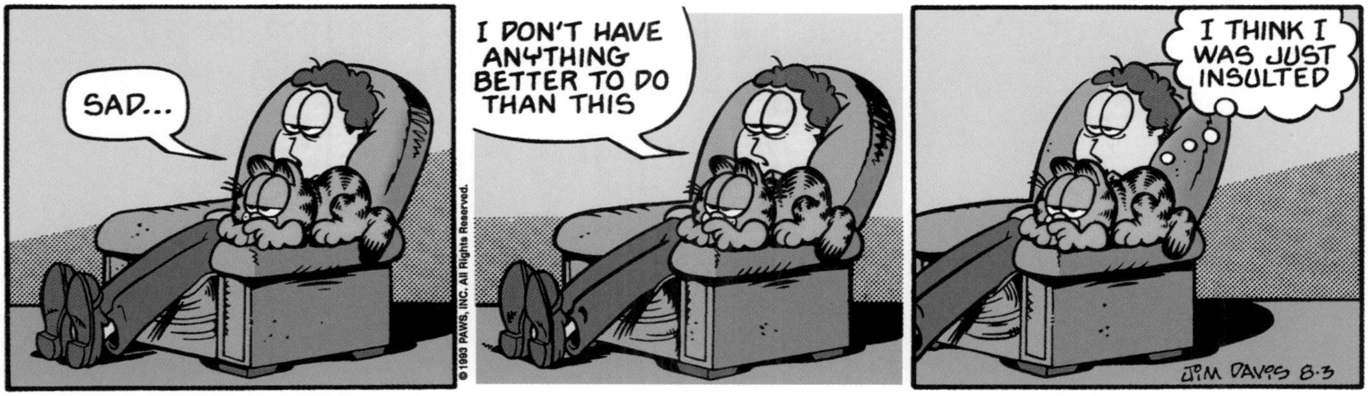
SAD...
© 1993 PAWS, INC. All Rights Reserved.
I DON'T HAVE ANYTHING BETTER TO DO THAN THIS
I THINK I WAS JUST INSULTED
JIM DAVIS 8-3

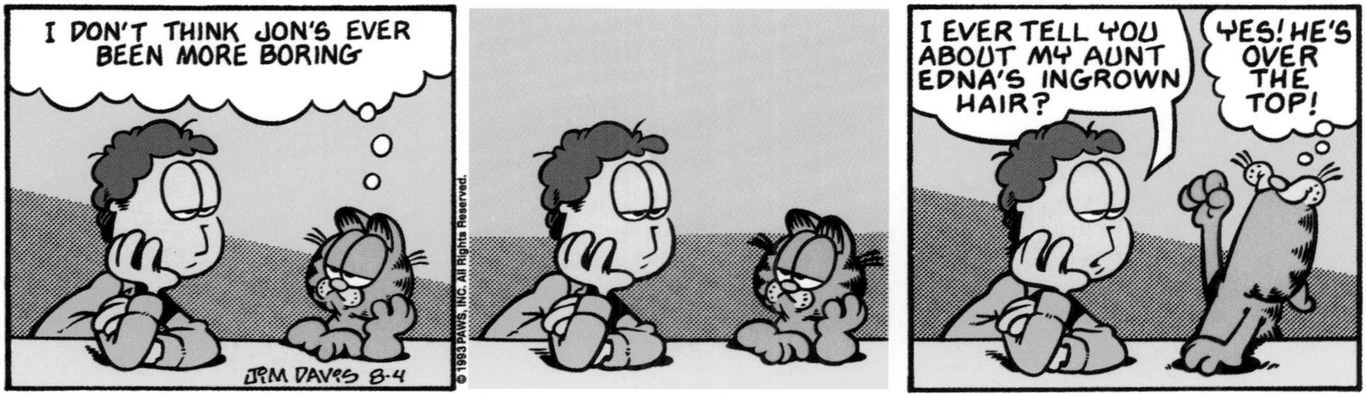
I DON'T THINK JON'S EVER BEEN MORE BORING
JIM DAVIS 8-4
© 1993 PAWS, INC. All Rights Reserved.
I EVER TELL YOU ABOUT MY AUNT EDNA'S INGROWN HAIR?
YES! HE'S OVER THE TOP!

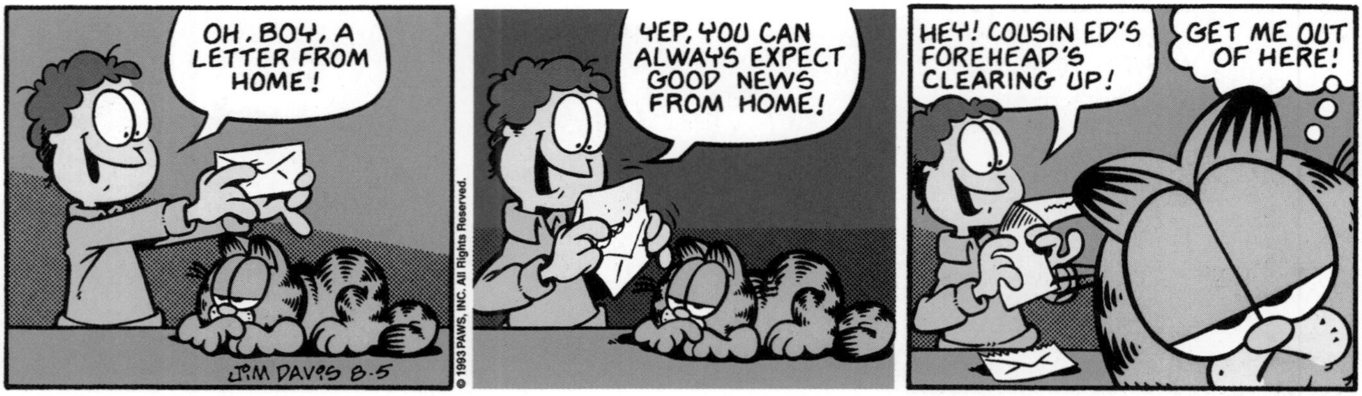
OH, BOY, A LETTER FROM HOME!
YEP, YOU CAN ALWAYS EXPECT GOOD NEWS FROM HOME!
HEY! COUSIN ED'S FOREHEAD'S CLEARING UP!
GET ME OUT OF HERE!
JIM DAVIS 8-5

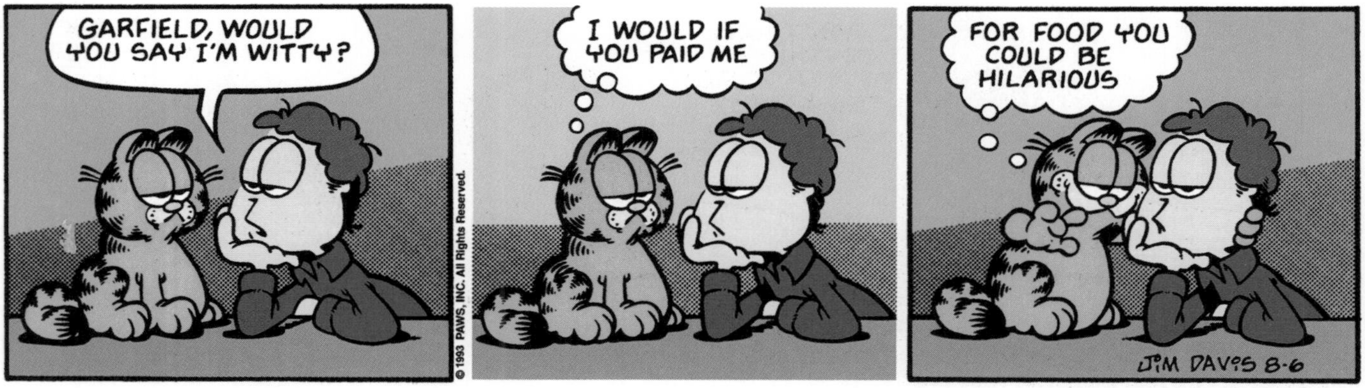
GARFIELD, WOULD YOU SAY I'M WITTY?
I WOULD IF YOU PAID ME
FOR FOOD YOU COULD BE HILARIOUS
JIM DAVIS 8-6

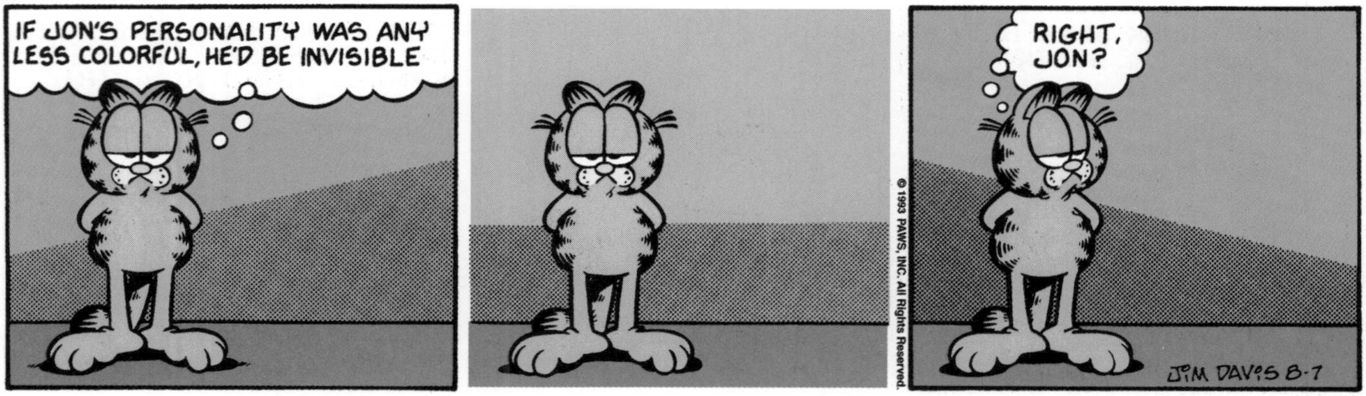
IF JON'S PERSONALITY WAS ANY LESS COLORFUL, HE'D BE INVISIBLE
RIGHT, JON?
JIM DAVIS 8-7

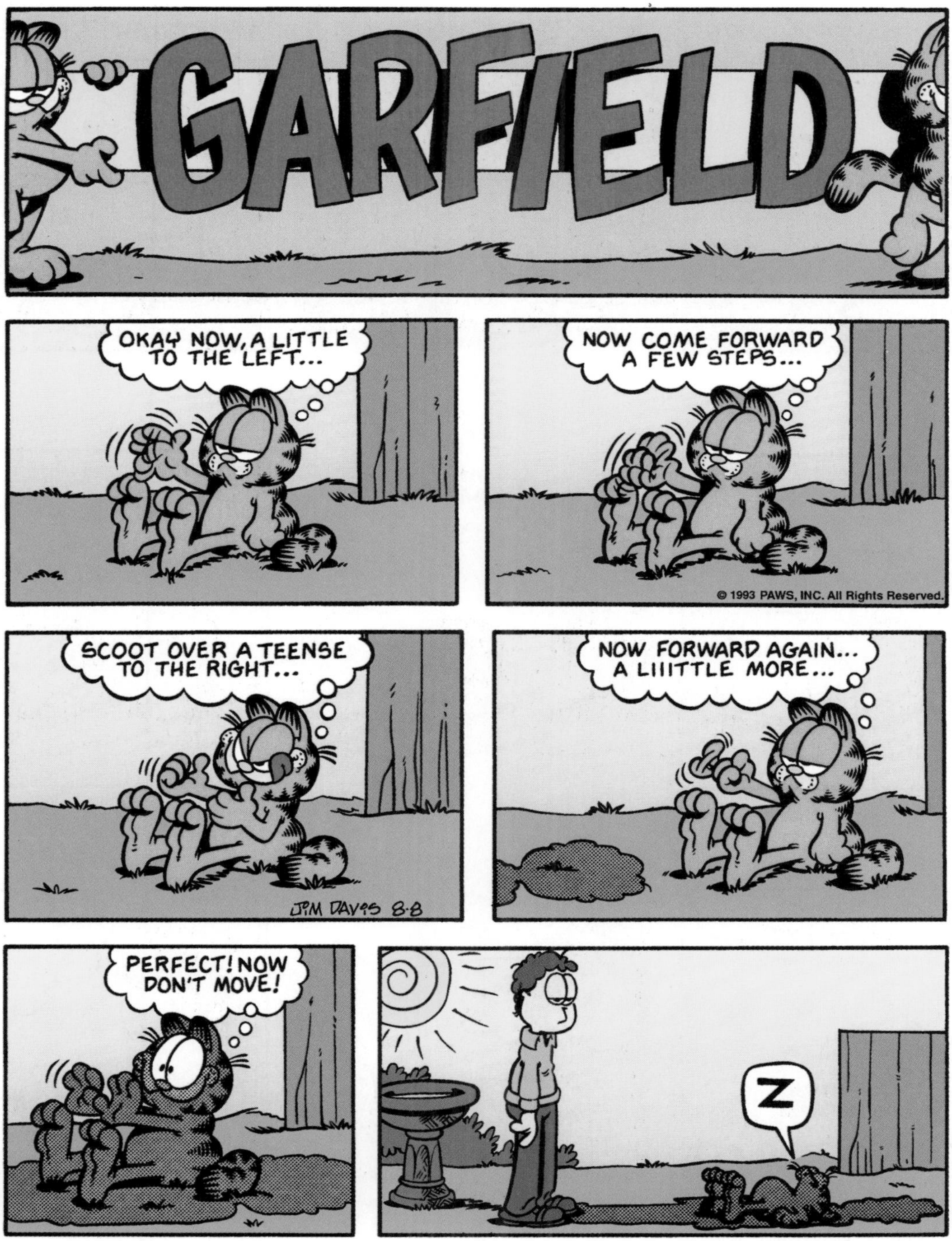
GARFIELD
OKAY NOW, A LITTLE TO THE LEFT...
NOW COME FORWARD A FEW STEPS...
© 1993 PAWS, INC. All Rights Reserved.
SCOOT OVER A TEENSE TO THE RIGHT...
JIM DAVIS 8-8
NOW FORWARD AGAIN... A LIIITTLE MORE...
PERFECT! NOW DON'T MOVE!
Z

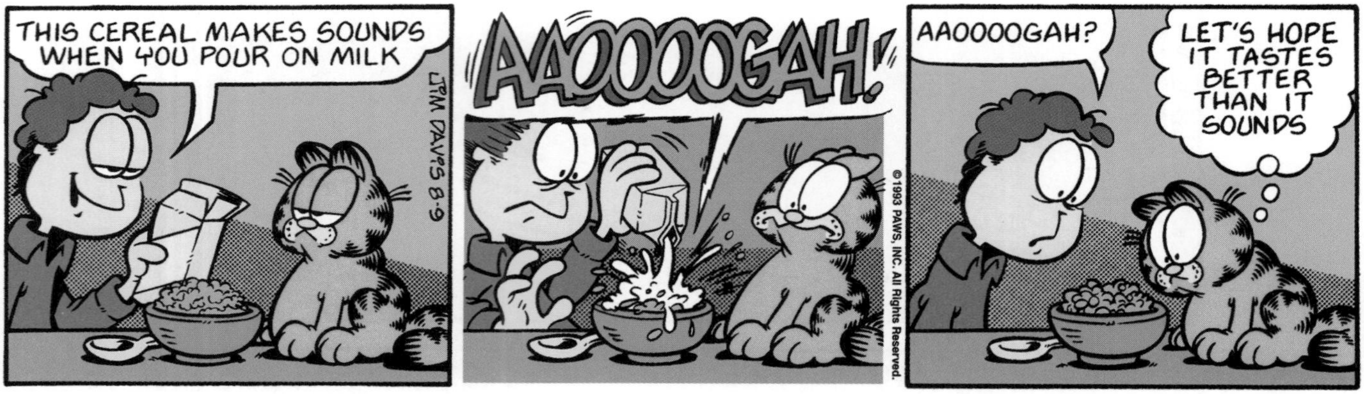
THIS CEREAL MAKES SOUNDS WHEN YOU POUR ON MILK
JIM DAVIS 8-9
AAOOOOGAH!
© 1993 PAWS, INC. All Rights Reserved.
AAOOOOGAH?
LET'S HOPE IT TASTES BETTER THAN IT SOUNDS

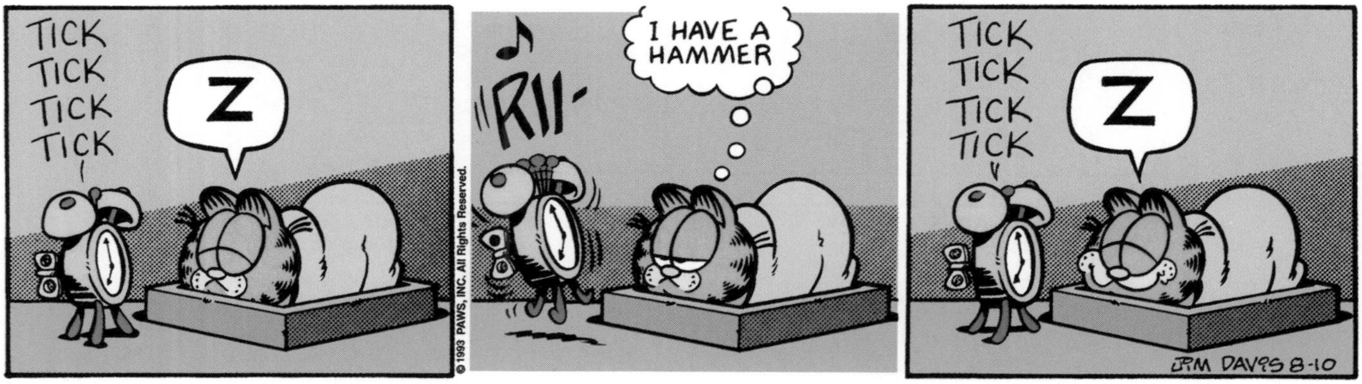
TICK
TICK
TICK
TICK
Z
© 1993 PAWS, INC. All Rights Reserved.
I HAVE A HAMMER
TICK
TICK
TICK
TICK
Z
JIM DAVIS 8-10

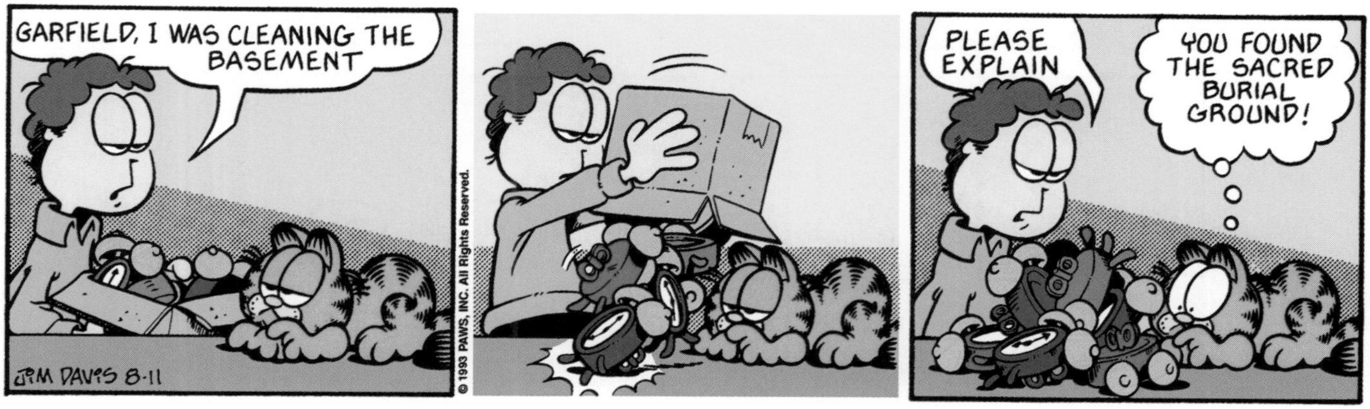
GARFIELD, I WAS CLEANING THE BASEMENT
JIM DAVIS 8-11
© 1993 PAWS, INC. All Rights Reserved.
PLEASE EXPLAIN
YOU FOUND THE SACRED BURIAL GROUND!

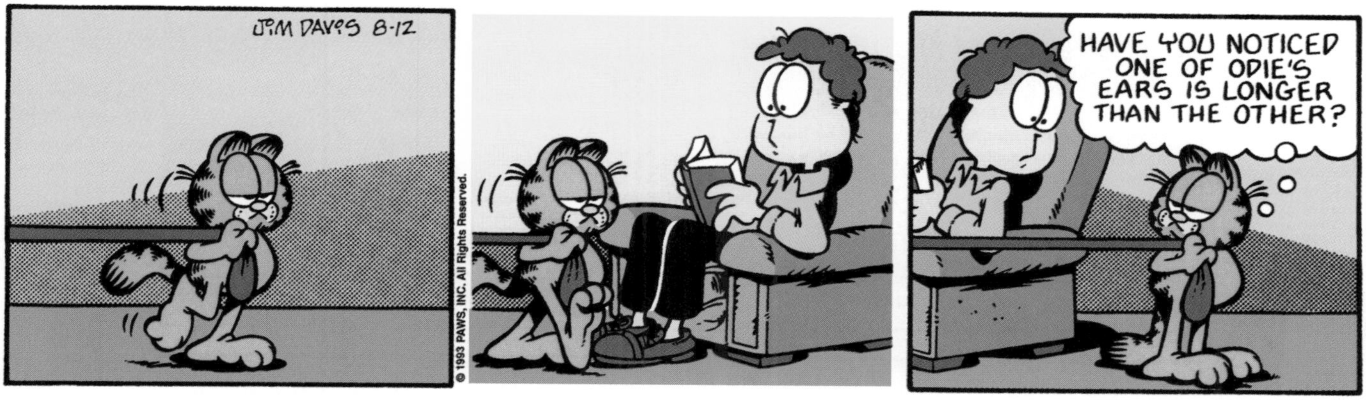
JIM DAVIS 8-12
© 1993 PAWS, INC. All Rights Reserved.
HAVE YOU NOTICED ONE OF ODIE'S EARS IS LONGER THAN THE OTHER?

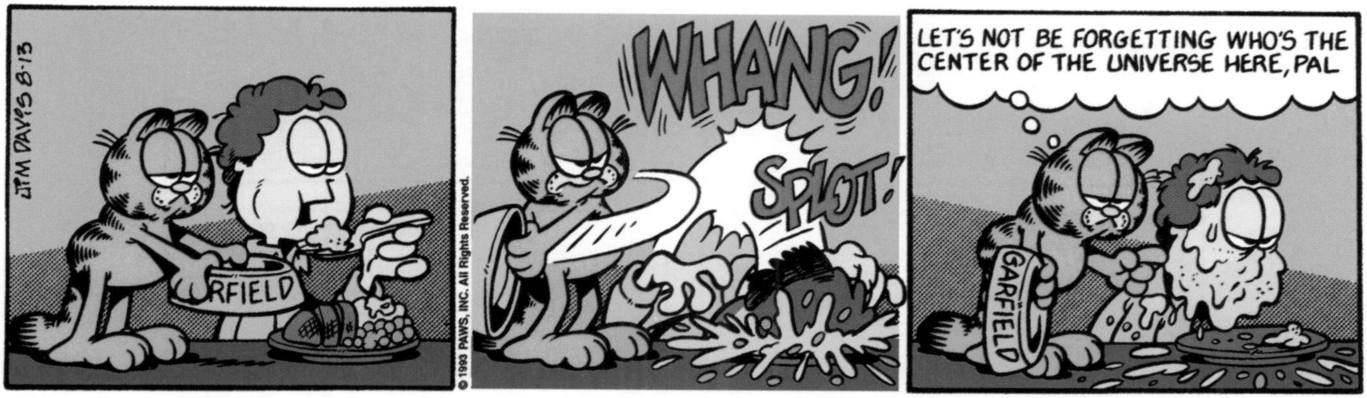
JIM DAVIS 8-13
RFIELD
© 1993 PAWS, INC. All Rights Reserved.
WHANG!
SPLOT!
LET'S NOT BE FORGETTING WHO'S THE CENTER OF THE UNIVERSE HERE, PAL
GARFIELD

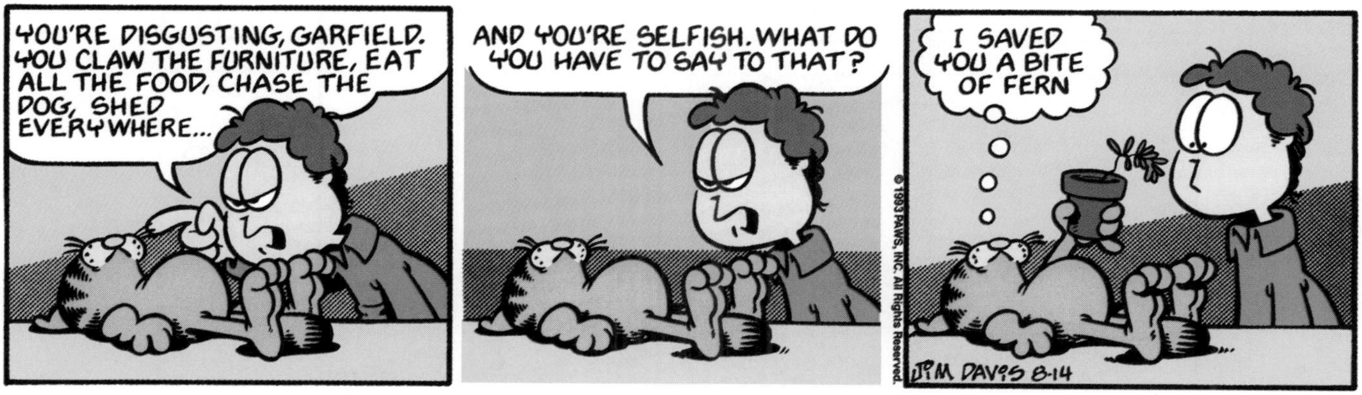
YOU'RE DISGUSTING, GARFIELD. YOU CLAW THE FURNITURE, EAT ALL THE FOOD, CHASE THE DOG, SHED EVERYWHERE...
AND YOU'RE SELFISH. WHAT DO YOU HAVE TO SAY TO THAT?
© 1993 PAWS, INC. All Rights Reserved.
I SAVED YOU A BITE OF FERN
JIM DAVIS 8-14

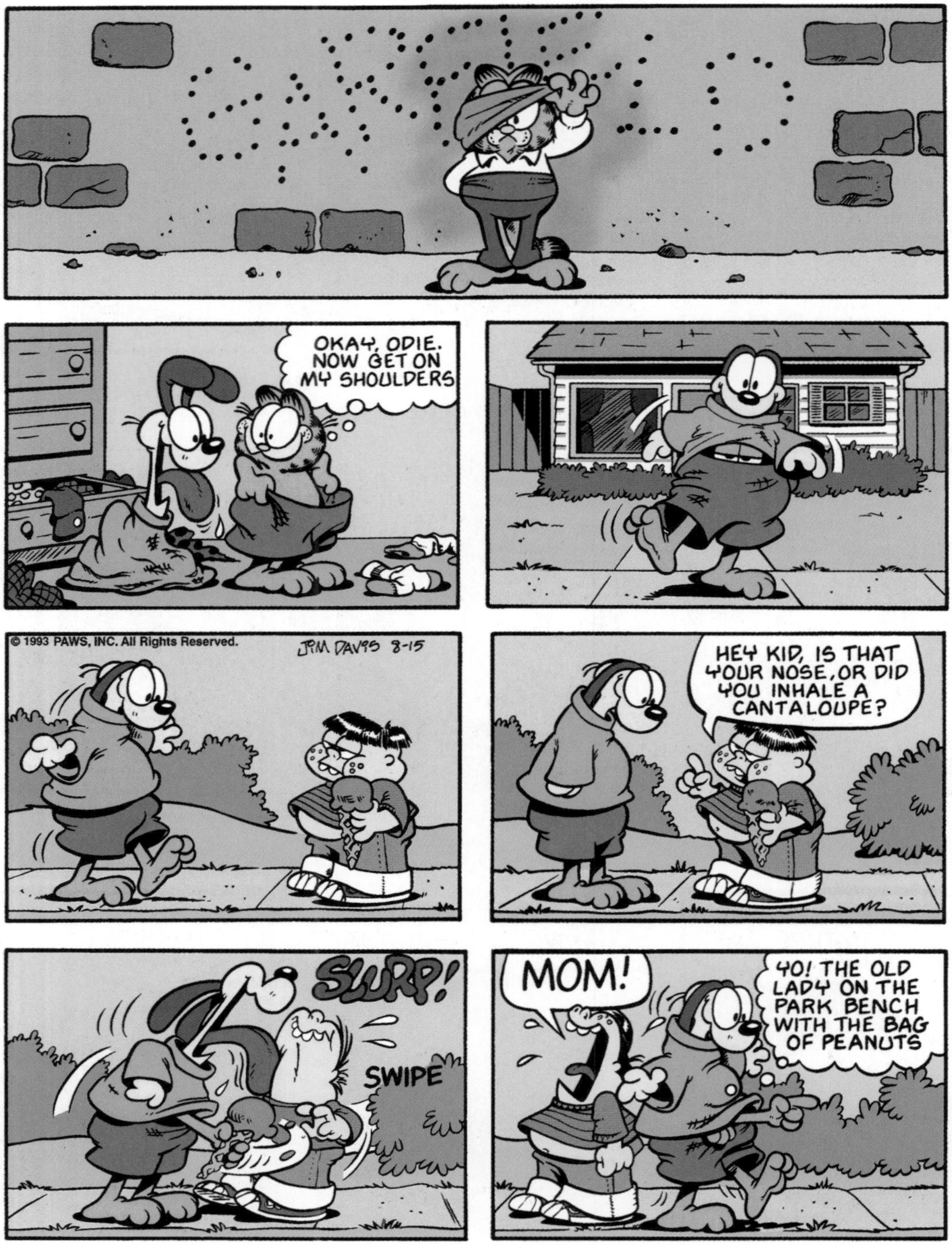
GARFIELD
OKAY, ODIE. NOW GET ON MY SHOULDERS
© 1993 PAWS, INC. All Rights Reserved.
JIM DAVIS 8-15
HEY KID, IS THAT YOUR NOSE, OR DID YOU INHALE A CANTALOUPE?
SLURP!
SWIPE
MOM!
YO! THE OLD LADY ON THE PARK BENCH WITH THE BAG OF PEANUTS

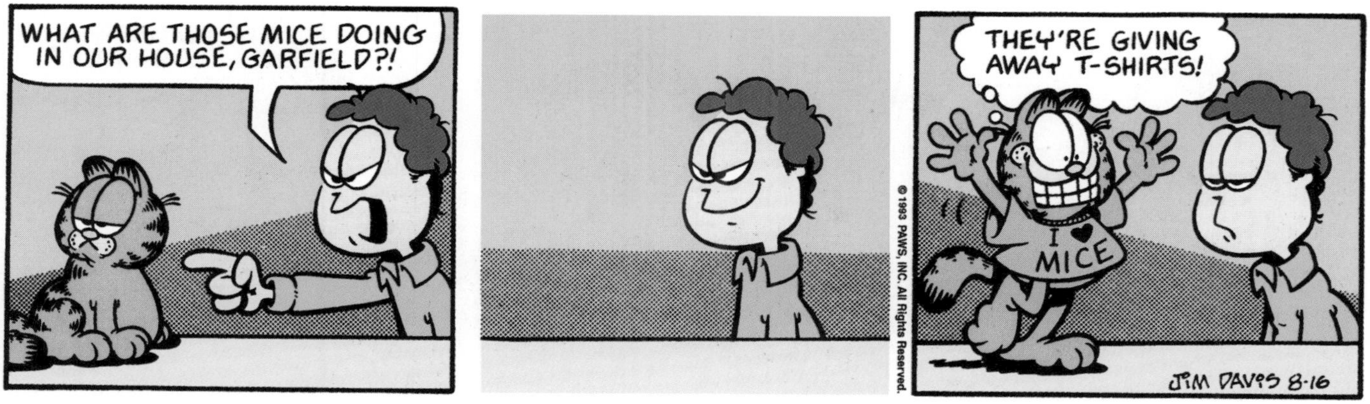
WHAT ARE THOSE MICE DOING IN OUR HOUSE, GARFIELD?!
THEY'RE GIVING AWAY T-SHIRTS!
I ♥ MICE
© 1993 PAWS, INC. All Rights Reserved.
JIM DAVIS 8-16

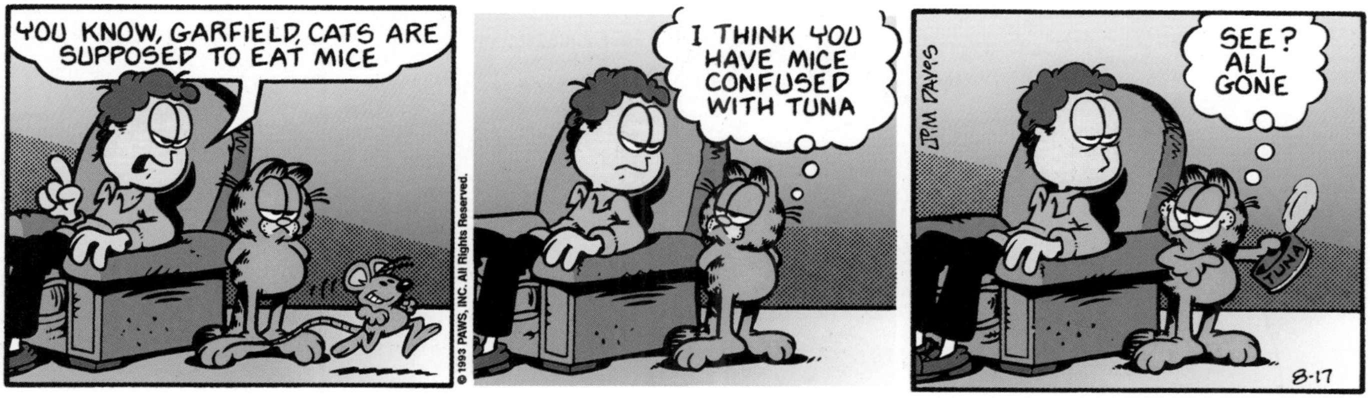
YOU KNOW, GARFIELD, CATS ARE SUPPOSED TO EAT MICE
I THINK YOU HAVE MICE CONFUSED WITH TUNA
SEE? ALL GONE
TUNA
© 1993 PAWS, INC. All Rights Reserved.
JIM DAVIS
8-17

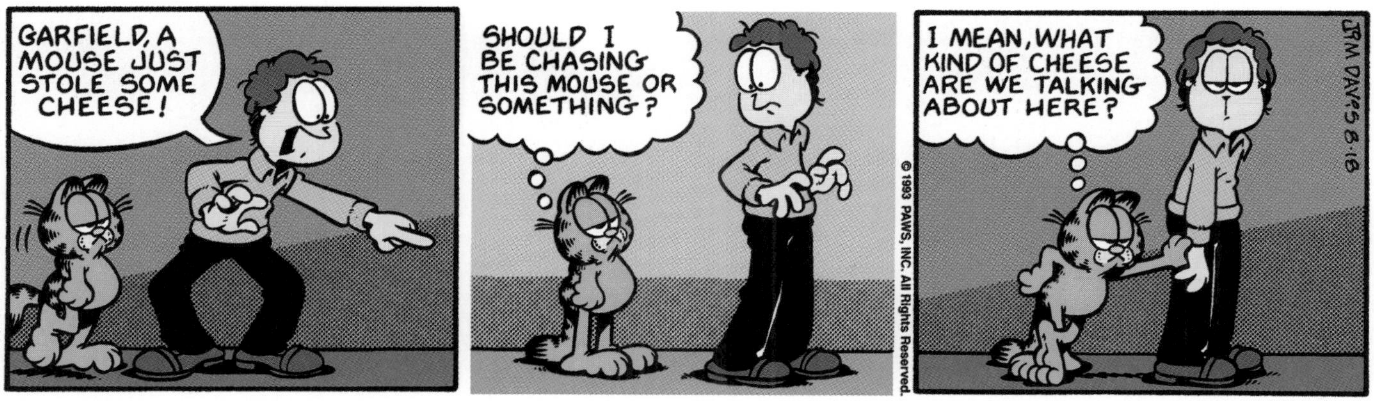
GARFIELD, A MOUSE JUST STOLE SOME CHEESE!
SHOULD I BE CHASING THIS MOUSE OR SOMETHING?
I MEAN, WHAT KIND OF CHEESE ARE WE TALKING ABOUT HERE?
© 1993 PAWS, INC. All Rights Reserved.
JIM DAVIS 8-18

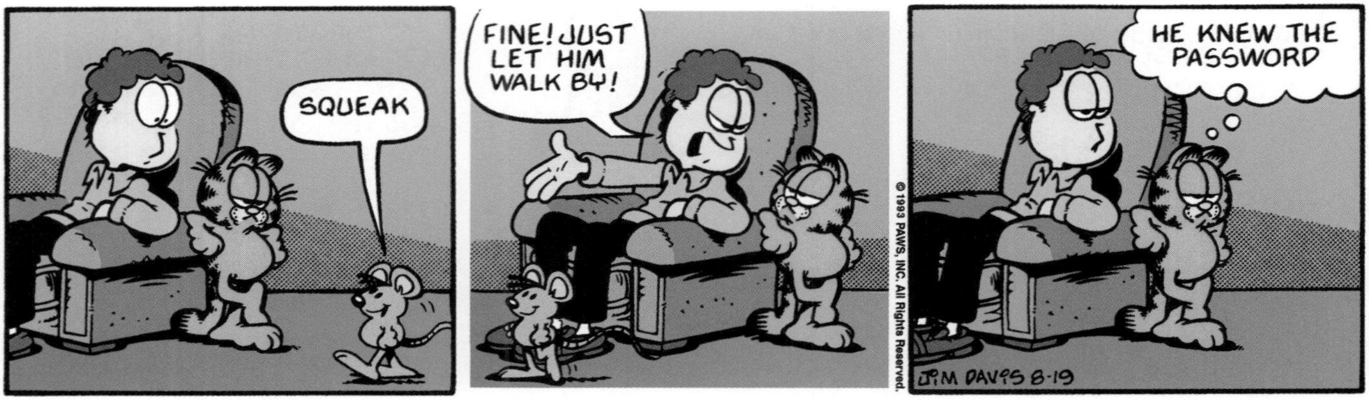
SQUEAK
FINE! JUST LET HIM WALK BY!
HE KNEW THE PASSWORD
© 1993 PAWS, INC. All Rights Reserved.
JIM DAVIS 8-19

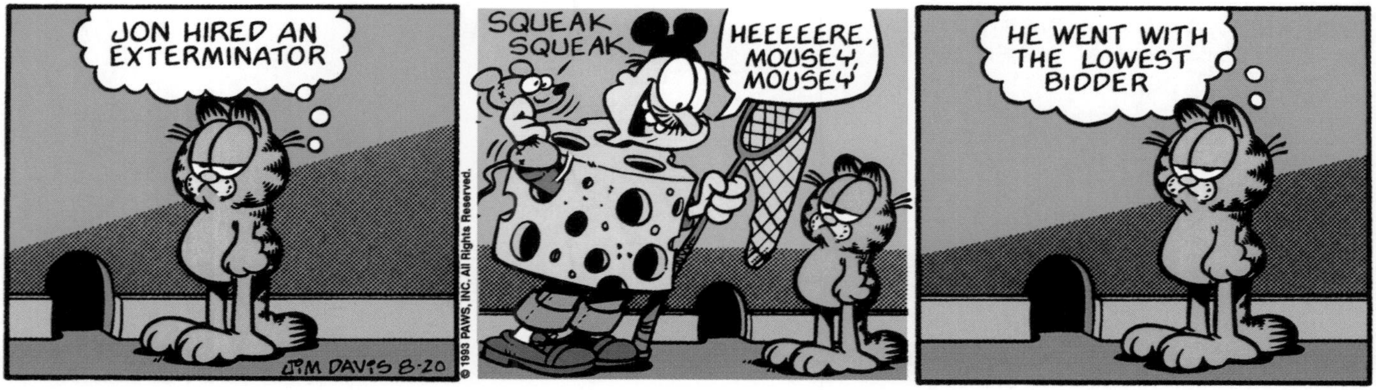
JON HIRED AN EXTERMINATOR
JIM DAVIS 8-20
SQUEAK SQUEAK
HEEEEERE, MOUSEY, MOUSEY
© 1993 PAWS, INC. All Rights Reserved.
HE WENT WITH THE LOWEST BIDDER

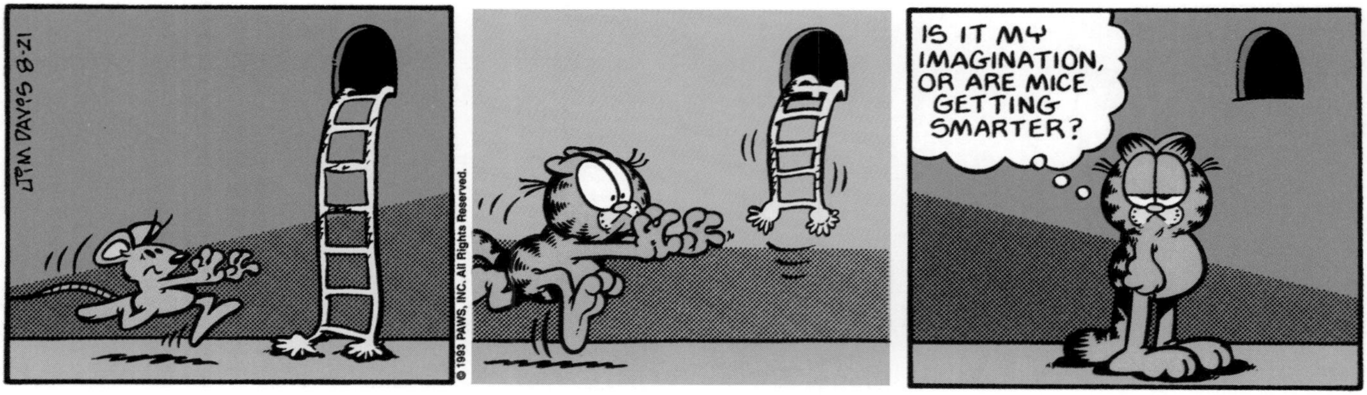
JIM DAVIS 8-21
© 1993 PAWS, INC. All Rights Reserved.
IS IT MY IMAGINATION, OR ARE MICE GETTING SMARTER?

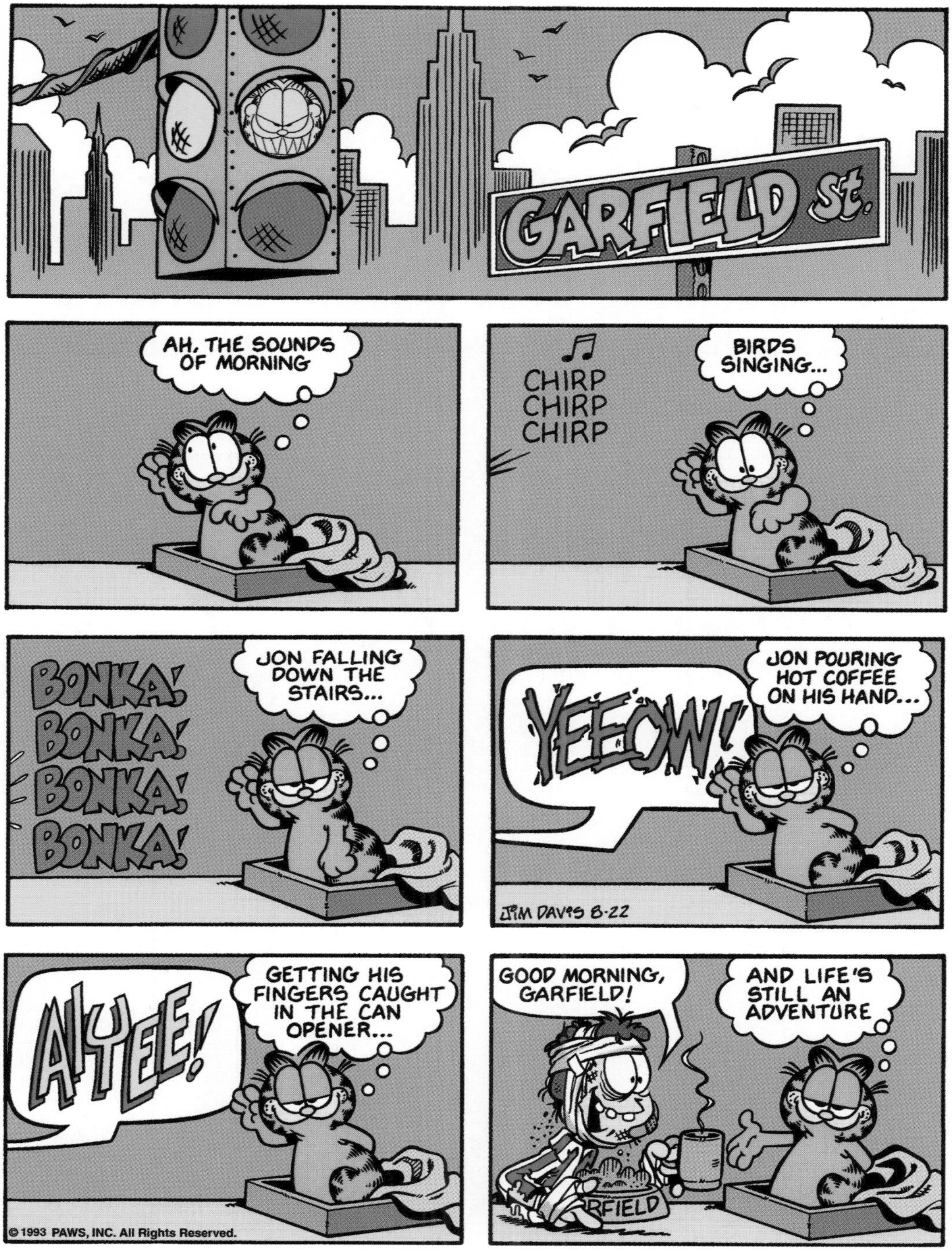

GARFIELD St.
AH, THE SOUNDS OF MORNING
CHIRP CHIRP CHIRP
BIRDS SINGING...
BONKA! BONKA! BONKA! BONKA!
JON FALLING DOWN THE STAIRS...
YEEOW!
JON POURING HOT COFFEE ON HIS HAND...
JIM DAVIS 8-22
AIYEE!
GETTING HIS FINGERS CAUGHT IN THE CAN OPENER...
GOOD MORNING, GARFIELD!
AND LIFE'S STILL AN ADVENTURE
RFIELD

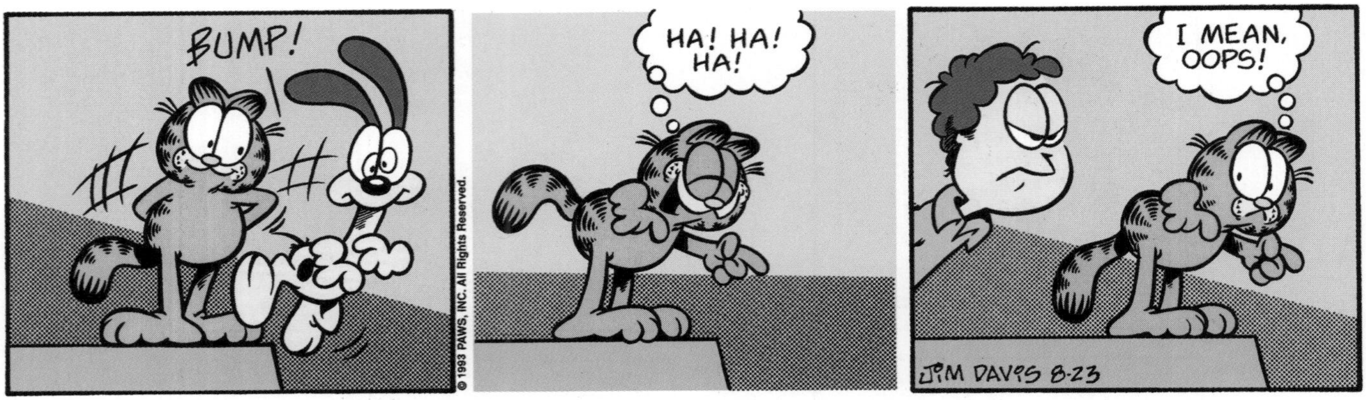
BUMP!
© 1993 PAWS, INC. All Rights Reserved.
HA! HA! HA!
I MEAN, OOPS!
JIM DAVIS 8-23

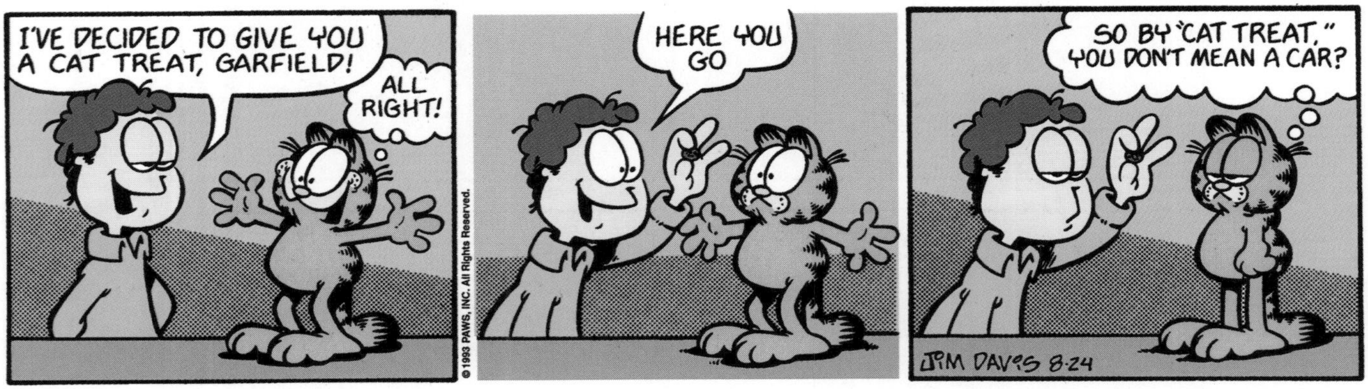
I'VE DECIDED TO GIVE YOU A CAT TREAT, GARFIELD!
ALL RIGHT!
© 1993 PAWS, INC. All Rights Reserved.
HERE YOU GO
SO BY "CAT TREAT," YOU DON'T MEAN A CAR?
JIM DAVIS 8-24

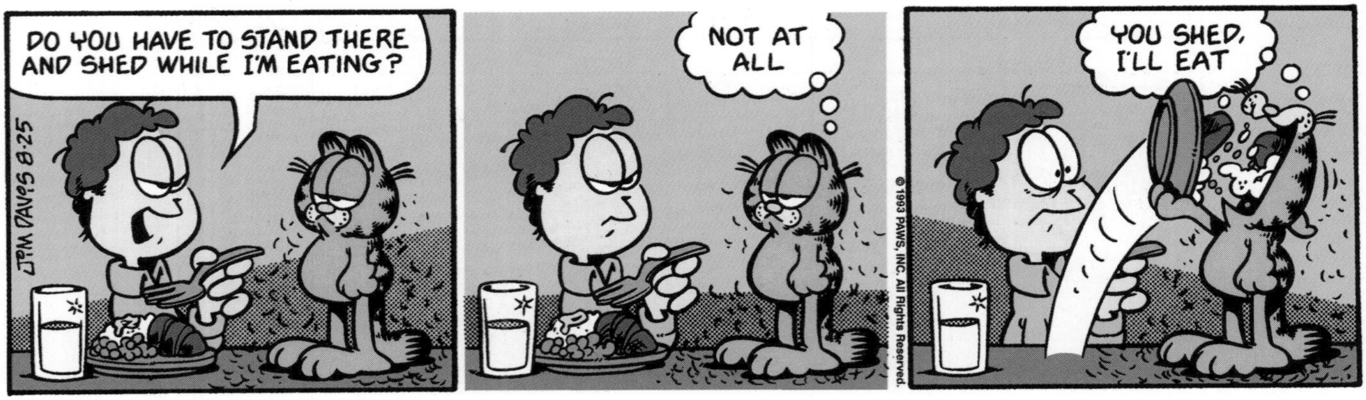
DO YOU HAVE TO STAND THERE AND SHED WHILE I'M EATING?
JIM DAVIS 8-25
NOT AT ALL
© 1993 PAWS, INC. All Rights Reserved.
YOU SHED, I'LL EAT

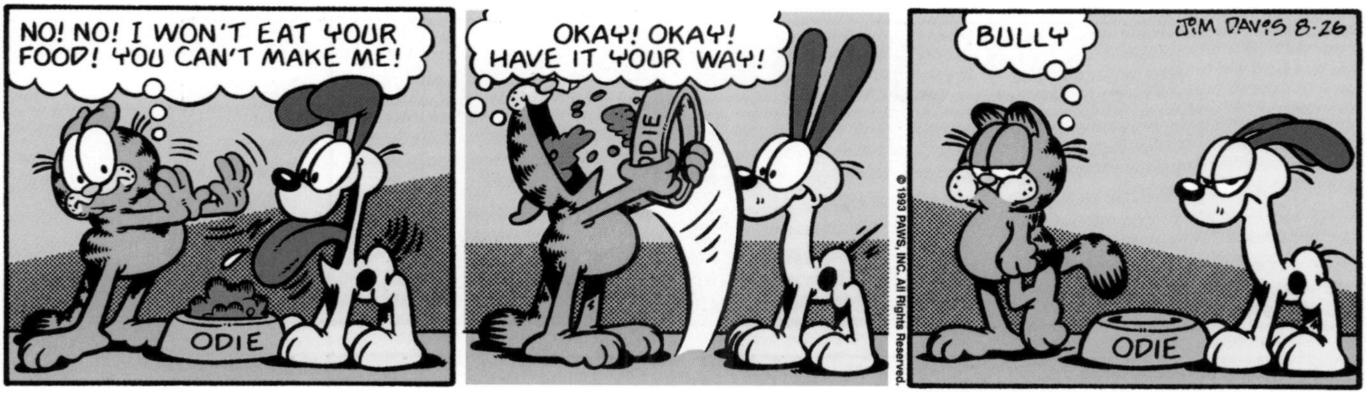
NO! NO! I WON'T EAT YOUR FOOD! YOU CAN'T MAKE ME!
ODIE
OKAY! OKAY! HAVE IT YOUR WAY!
ODIE
BULLY
JIM DAVIS 8-26
ODIE

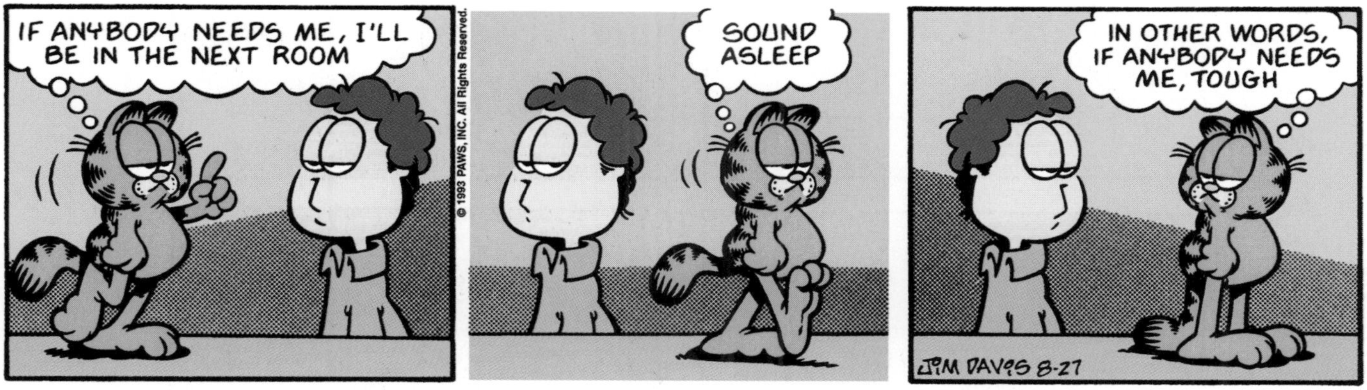
IF ANYBODY NEEDS ME, I'LL BE IN THE NEXT ROOM
SOUND ASLEEP
IN OTHER WORDS, IF ANYBODY NEEDS ME, TOUGH
JIM DAVIS 8-27

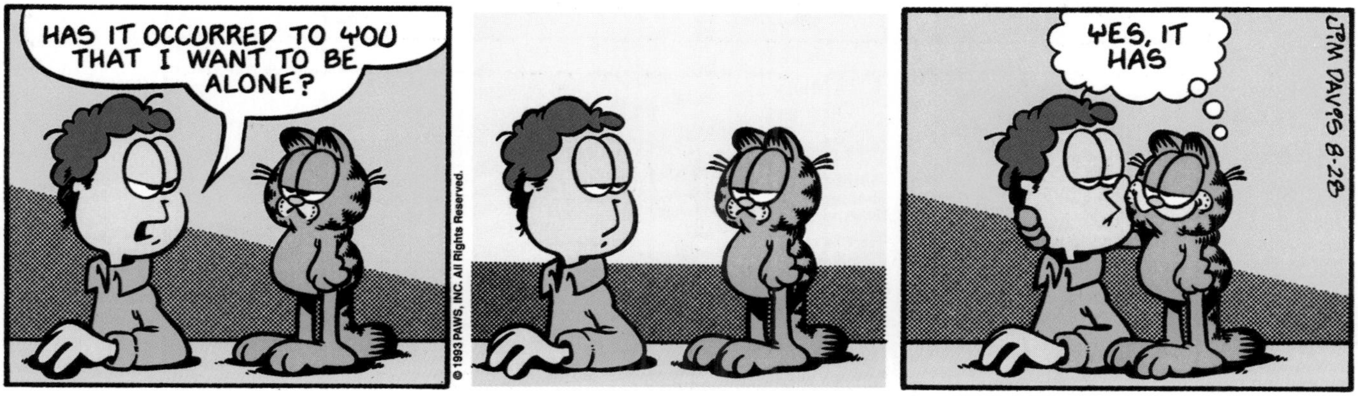
HAS IT OCCURRED TO YOU THAT I WANT TO BE ALONE?
YES, IT HAS
JIM DAVIS 8-28

© 1993 PAWS, INC. All Rights Reserved.
TRIP
DINGLE
SPLAT!
Grrrrrrrrr
BARK ARF BARK
BARK ARF
ARF
ARF ARF
ARF
JIM DAVIS 8-29
THUD!
SIGH

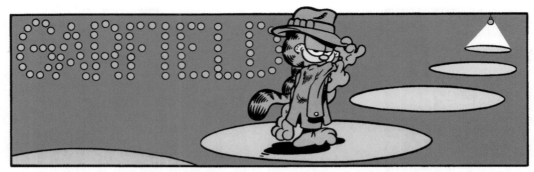

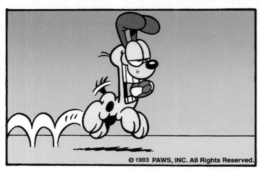

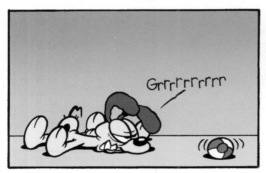

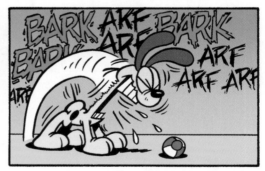

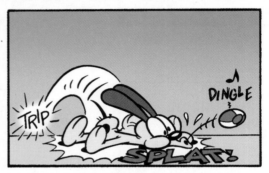

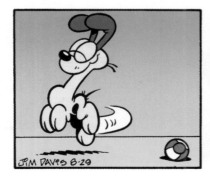

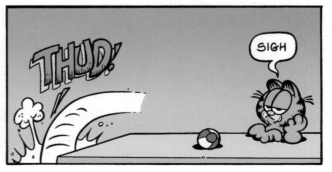

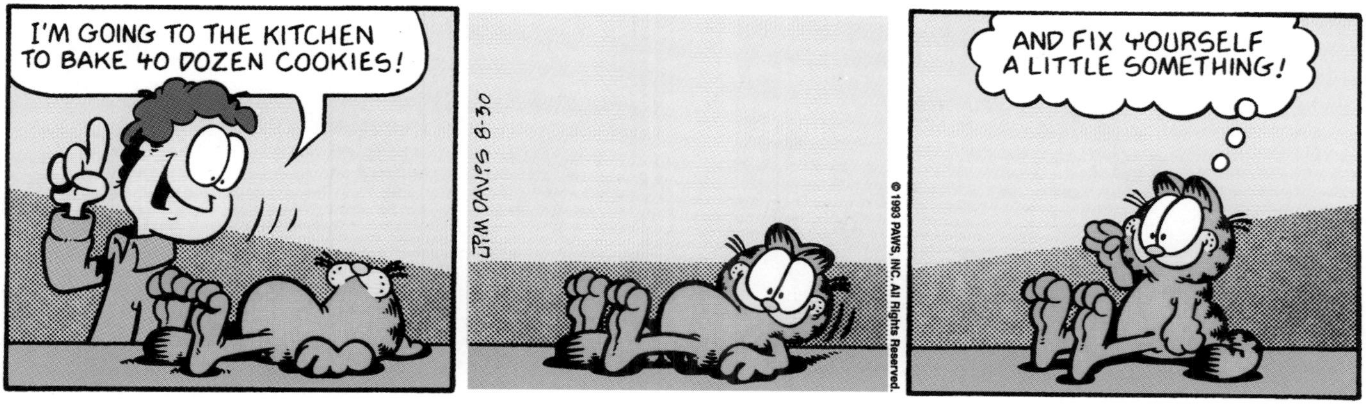
I'M GOING TO THE KITCHEN TO BAKE 40 DOZEN COOKIES!
JIM DAVIS 8-30
© 1993 PAWS, INC. All Rights Reserved.
AND FIX YOURSELF A LITTLE SOMETHING!

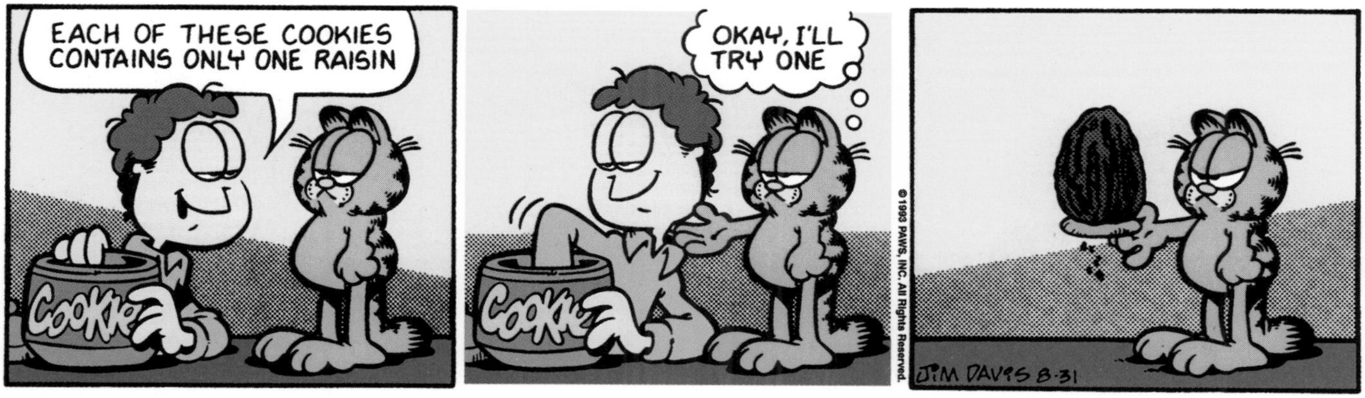
EACH OF THESE COOKIES CONTAINS ONLY ONE RAISIN
COOKIES
OKAY, I'LL TRY ONE
© 1993 PAWS, INC. All Rights Reserved.
JIM DAVIS 8-31

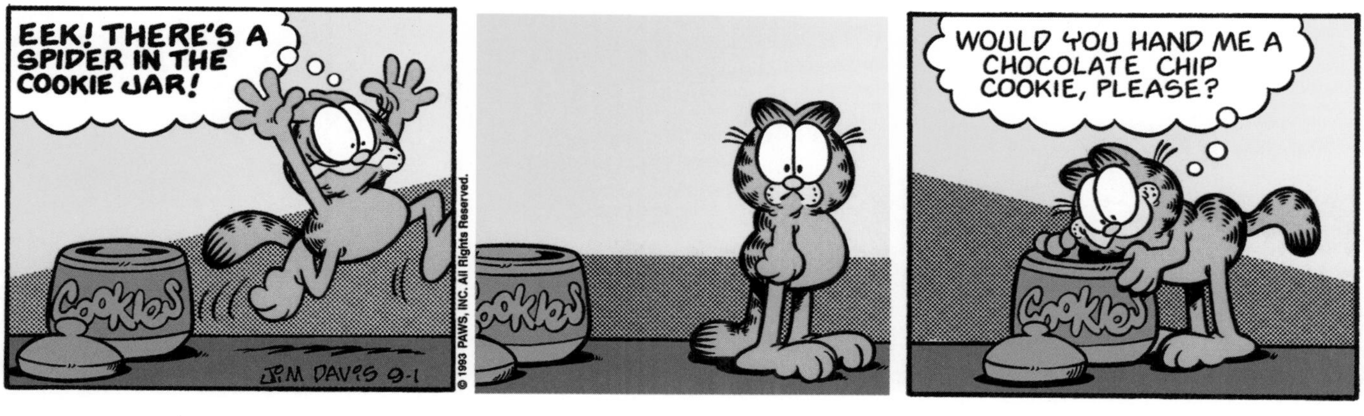
EEK! THERE'S A SPIDER IN THE COOKIE JAR!
COOKIES
JIM DAVIS 9-1
© 1993 PAWS, INC. All Rights Reserved.
WOULD YOU HAND ME A CHOCOLATE CHIP COOKIE, PLEASE?

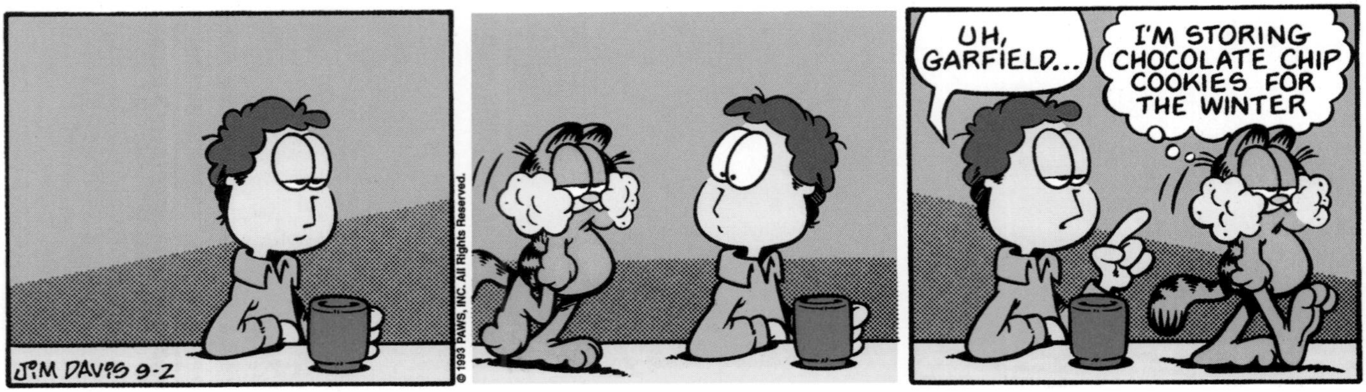
JIM DAVIS 9-2
© 1993 PAWS, INC. All Rights Reserved.
UH, GARFIELD...
I'M STORING CHOCOLATE CHIP COOKIES FOR THE WINTER

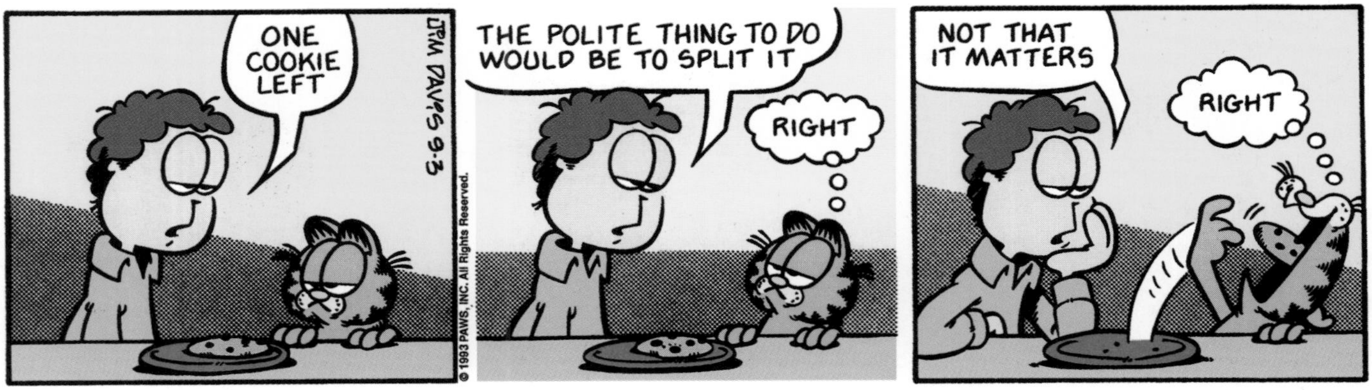
ONE COOKIE LEFT
JIM DAVIS 9-3
© 1993 PAWS, INC. All Rights Reserved.
THE POLITE THING TO DO WOULD BE TO SPLIT IT
RIGHT
NOT THAT IT MATTERS
RIGHT

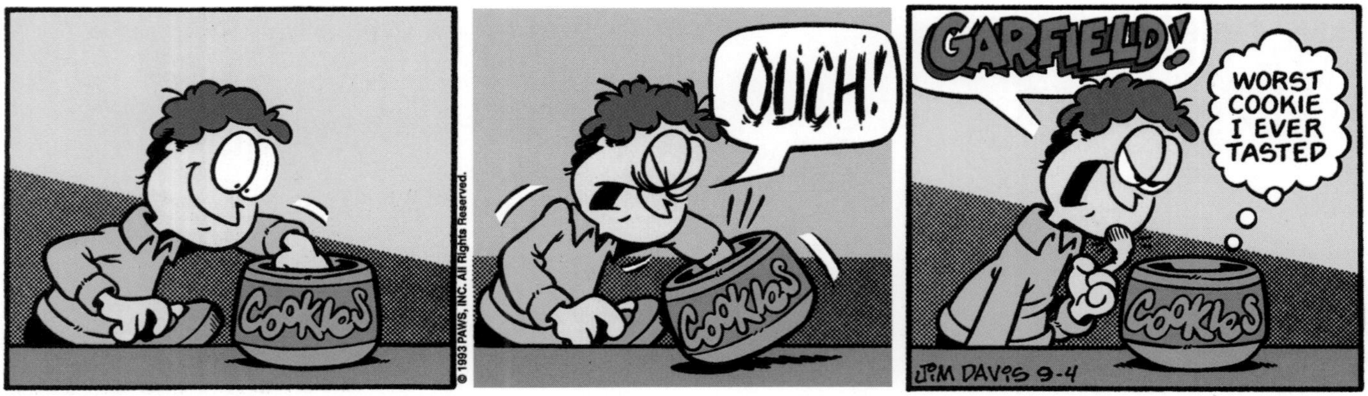
COOKIES
© 1993 PAWS, INC. All Rights Reserved.
OUCH!
COOKIES
GARFIELD!
WORST COOKIE I EVER TASTED
COOKIES
JIM DAVIS 9-4

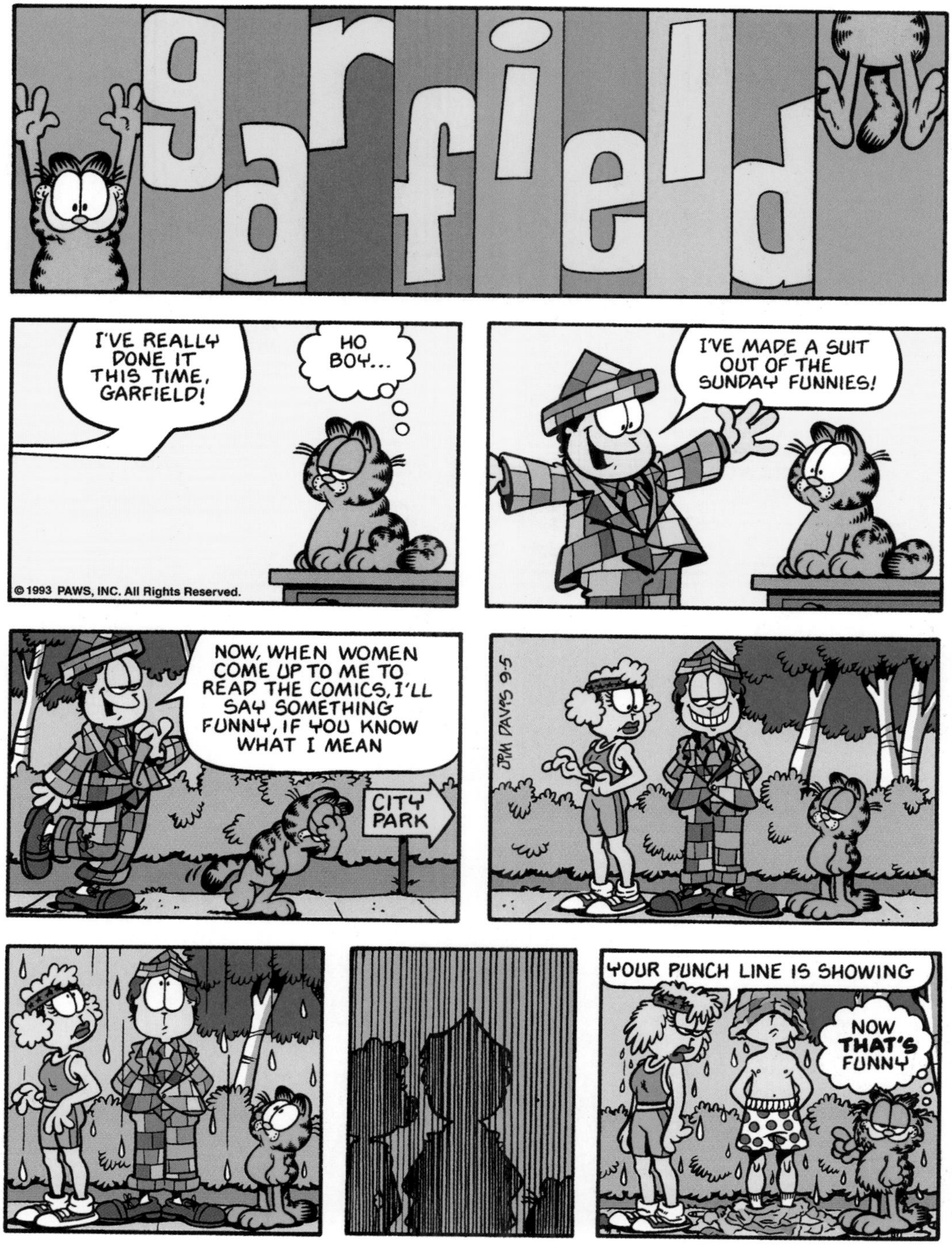
garfield
I'VE REALLY DONE IT THIS TIME, GARFIELD!
HO BOY...
I'VE MADE A SUIT OUT OF THE SUNDAY FUNNIES!
NOW, WHEN WOMEN COME UP TO ME TO READ THE COMICS, I'LL SAY SOMETHING FUNNY, IF YOU KNOW WHAT I MEAN
CITY PARK
JPM DAVIS 9-5
YOUR PUNCH LINE IS SHOWING
NOW THAT'S FUNNY

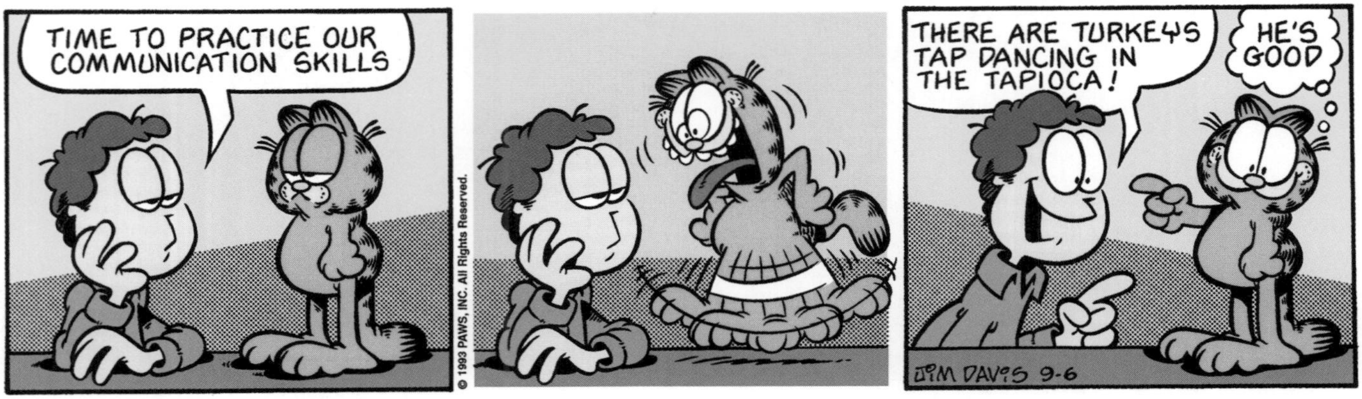
TIME TO PRACTICE OUR COMMUNICATION SKILLS
© 1993 PAWS, INC. All Rights Reserved.
THERE ARE TURKEYS TAP DANCING IN THE TAPIOCA!
HE'S GOOD
JIM DAVIS 9-6

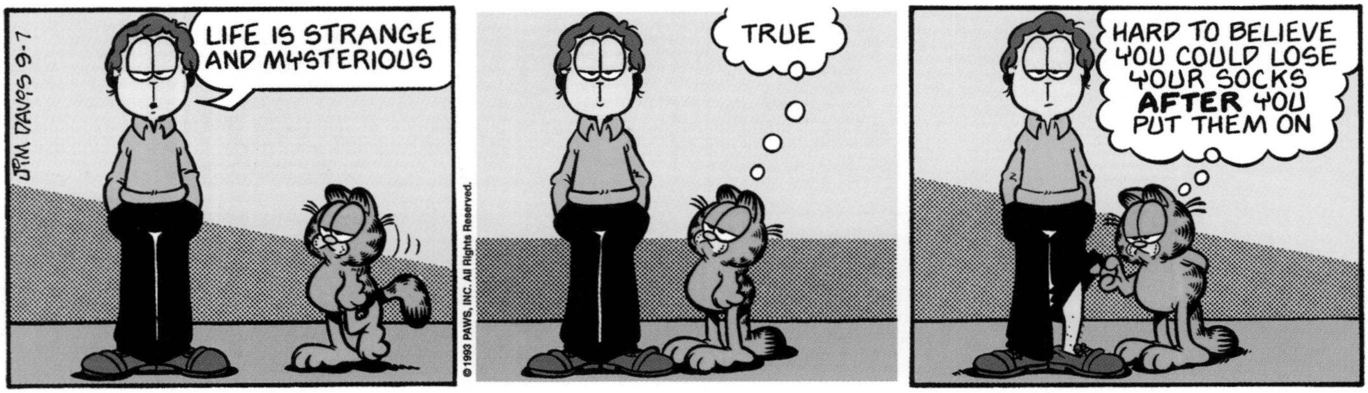
JIM DAVIS 9-7
LIFE IS STRANGE AND MYSTERIOUS
© 1993 PAWS, INC. All Rights Reserved.
TRUE
HARD TO BELIEVE YOU COULD LOSE YOUR SOCKS **AFTER** YOU PUT THEM ON

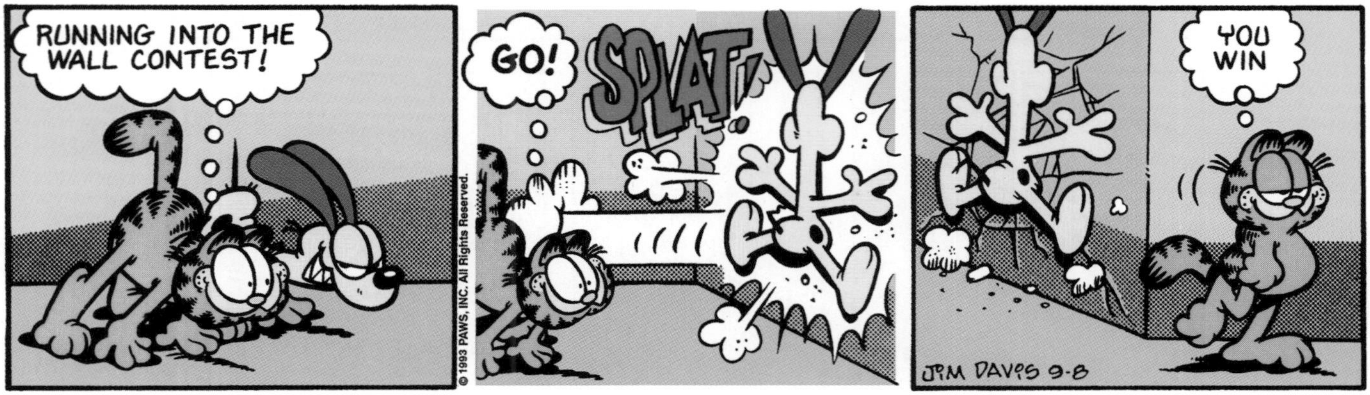
RUNNING INTO THE WALL CONTEST!
© 1993 PAWS, INC. All Rights Reserved.
GO!
SPLAT!
YOU WIN
JIM DAVIS 9-8

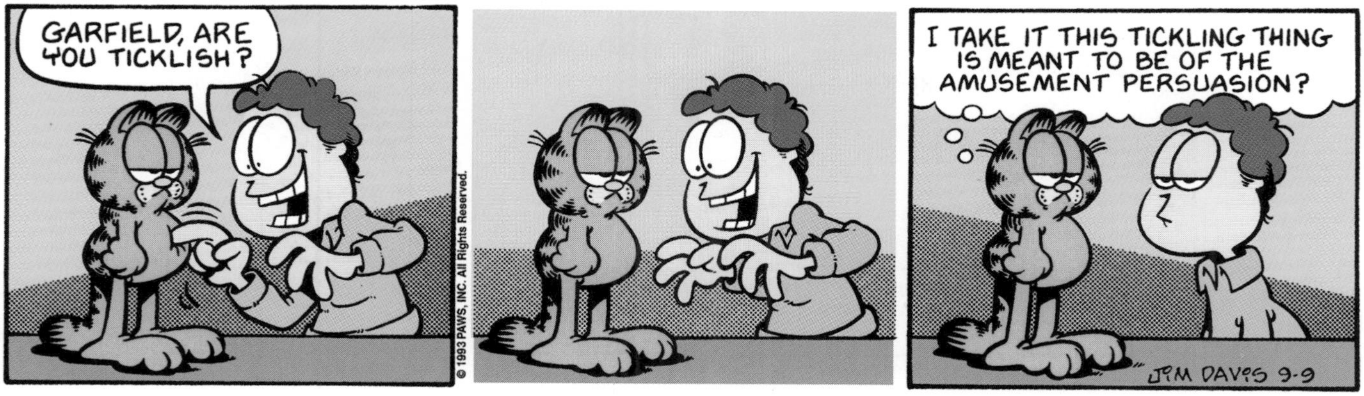
GARFIELD, ARE YOU TICKLISH?
© 1993 PAWS, INC. All Rights Reserved.
I TAKE IT THIS TICKLING THING IS MEANT TO BE OF THE AMUSEMENT PERSUASION?
JIM DAVIS 9-9

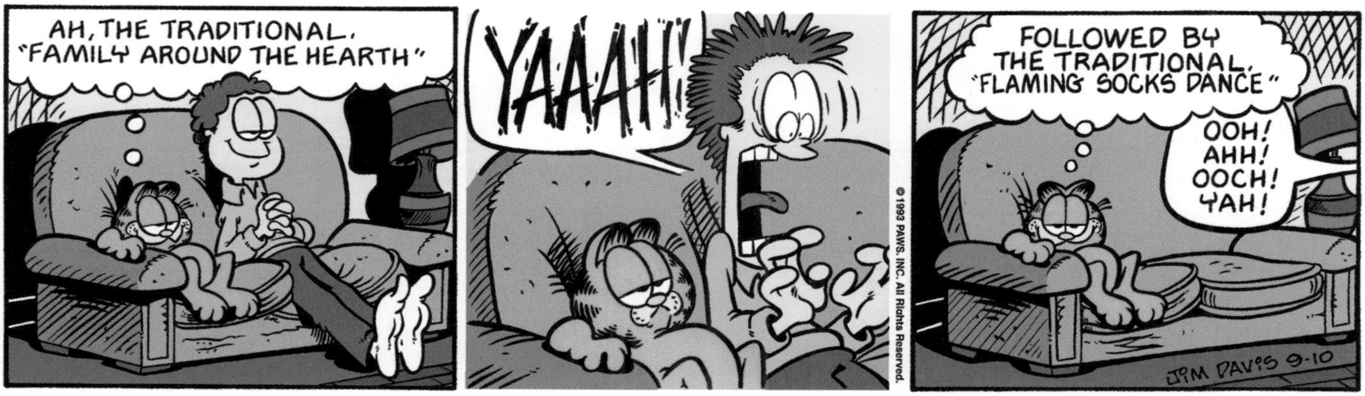
AH, THE TRADITIONAL "FAMILY AROUND THE HEARTH"
YAAAH!
© 1993 PAWS, INC. All Rights Reserved.
FOLLOWED BY THE TRADITIONAL "FLAMING SOCKS DANCE"
OOH! AHH! OOCH! YAH!
JIM DAVIS 9-10

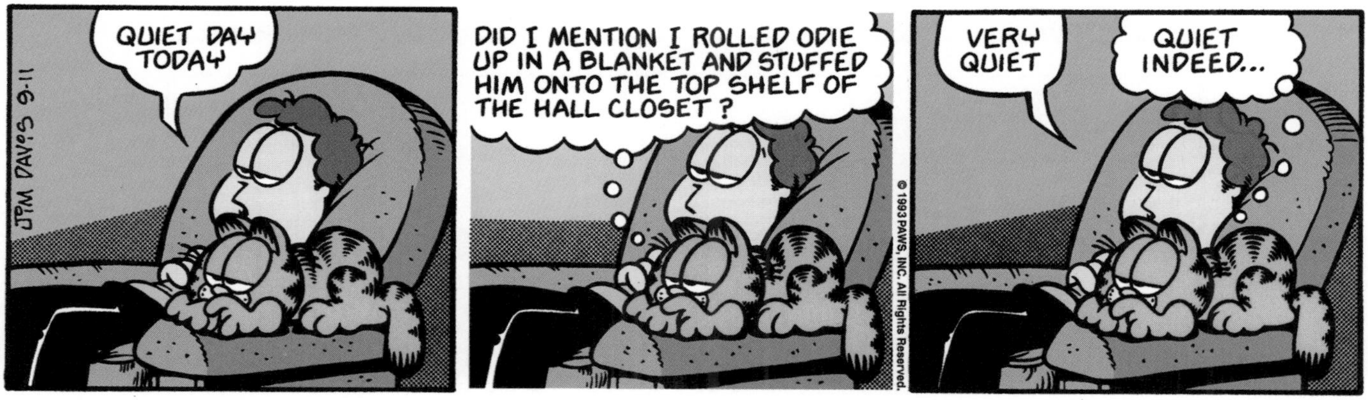
JIM DAVIS 9-11
QUIET DAY TODAY
DID I MENTION I ROLLED ODIE UP IN A BLANKET AND STUFFED HIM ONTO THE TOP SHELF OF THE HALL CLOSET?
© 1993 PAWS, INC. All Rights Reserved.
VERY QUIET
QUIET INDEED...

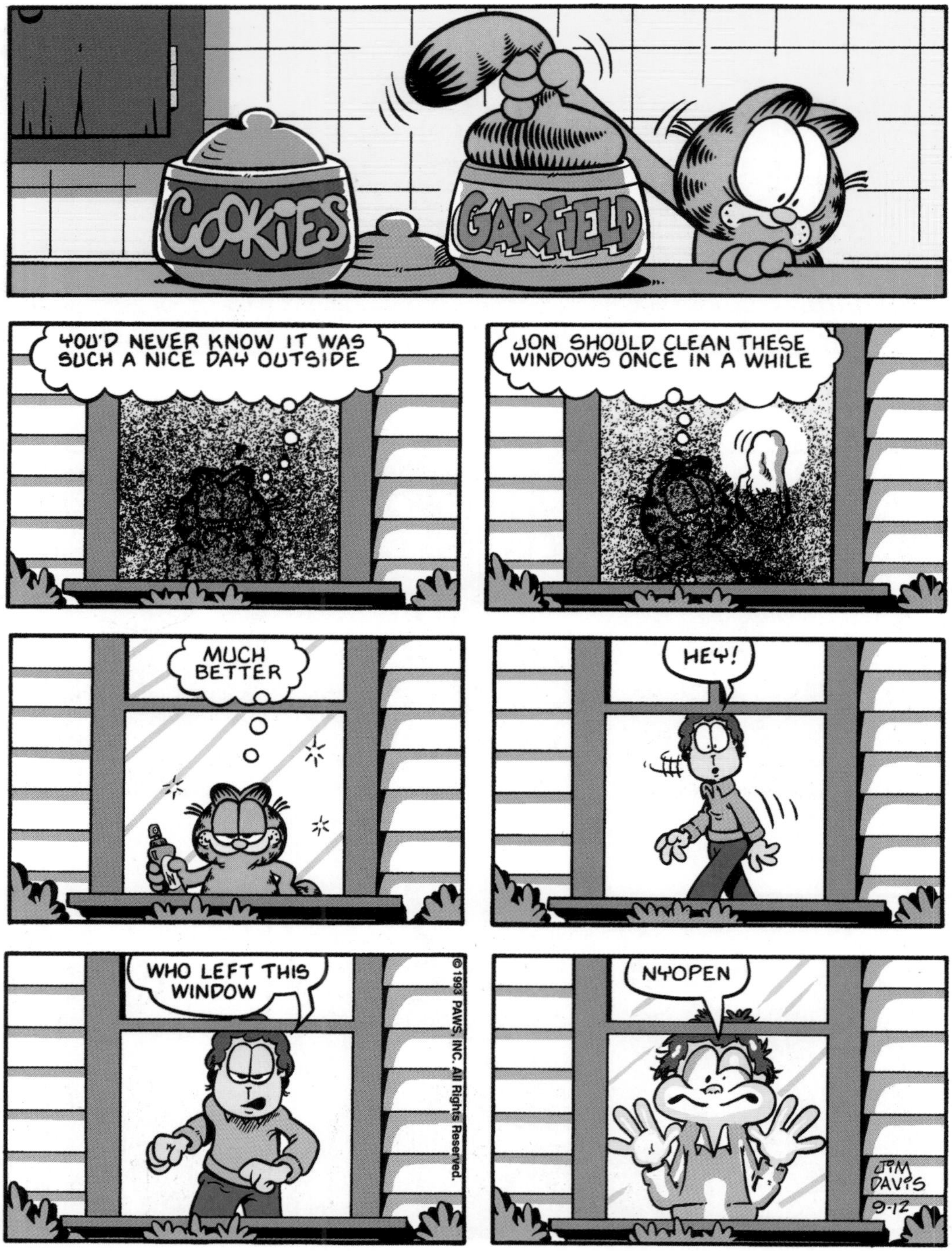
COOKIES
GARFIELD
YOU'D NEVER KNOW IT WAS SUCH A NICE DAY OUTSIDE
JON SHOULD CLEAN THESE WINDOWS ONCE IN A WHILE
MUCH BETTER
HEY!
WHO LEFT THIS WINDOW
NYOPEN
© 1993 PAWS, INC. All Rights Reserved.
JIM DAVIS
9-12

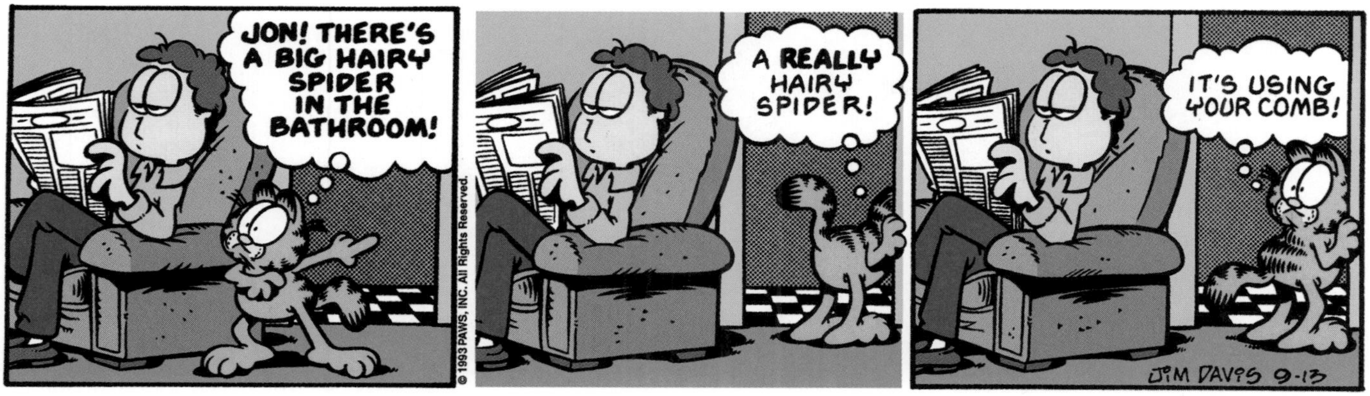
JON! THERE'S A BIG HAIRY SPIDER IN THE BATHROOM!
© 1993 PAWS, INC. All Rights Reserved.
A REALLY HAIRY SPIDER!
IT'S USING YOUR COMB!
JIM DAVIS 9-13

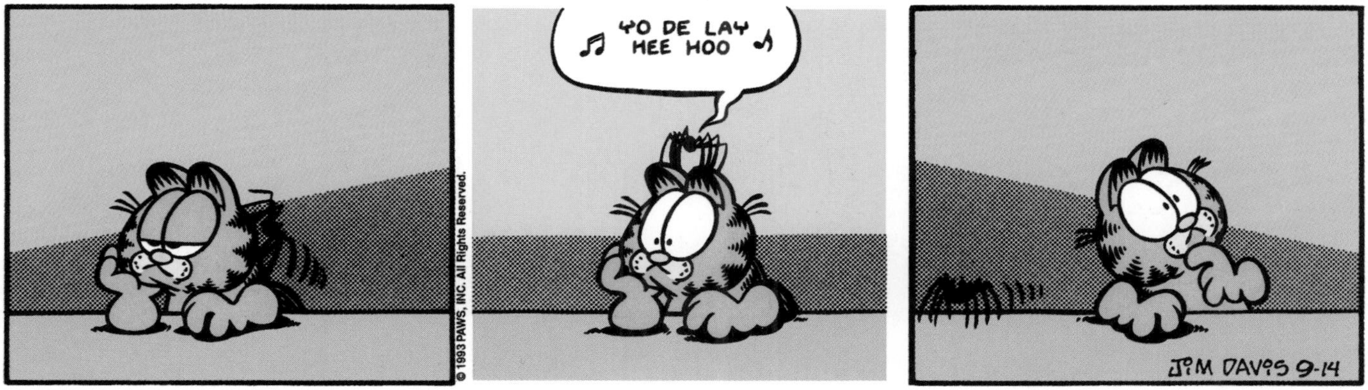
© 1993 PAWS, INC. All Rights Reserved.
YO DE LAY HEE HOO
JIM DAVIS 9-14

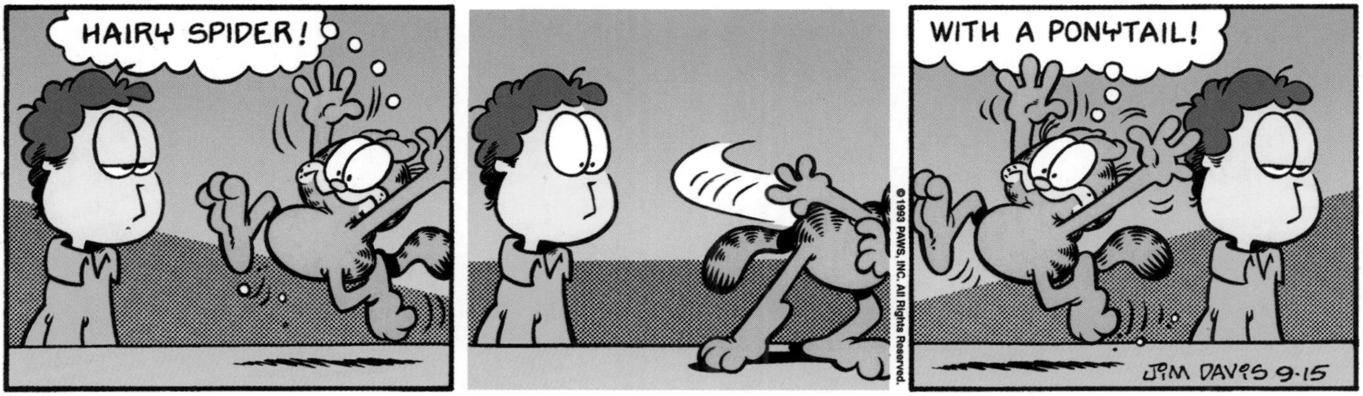
HAIRY SPIDER!
© 1993 PAWS, INC. All Rights Reserved.
WITH A PONYTAIL!
JIM DAVIS 9-15

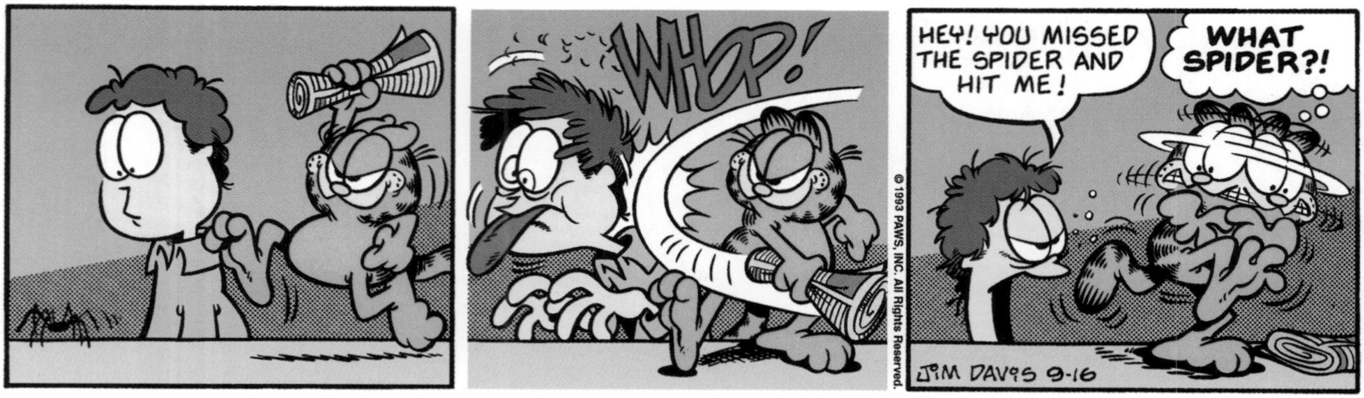
WHOP!
HEY! YOU MISSED THE SPIDER AND HIT ME!
WHAT SPIDER?!
© 1993 PAWS, INC. All Rights Reserved.
JIM DAVIS 9-16

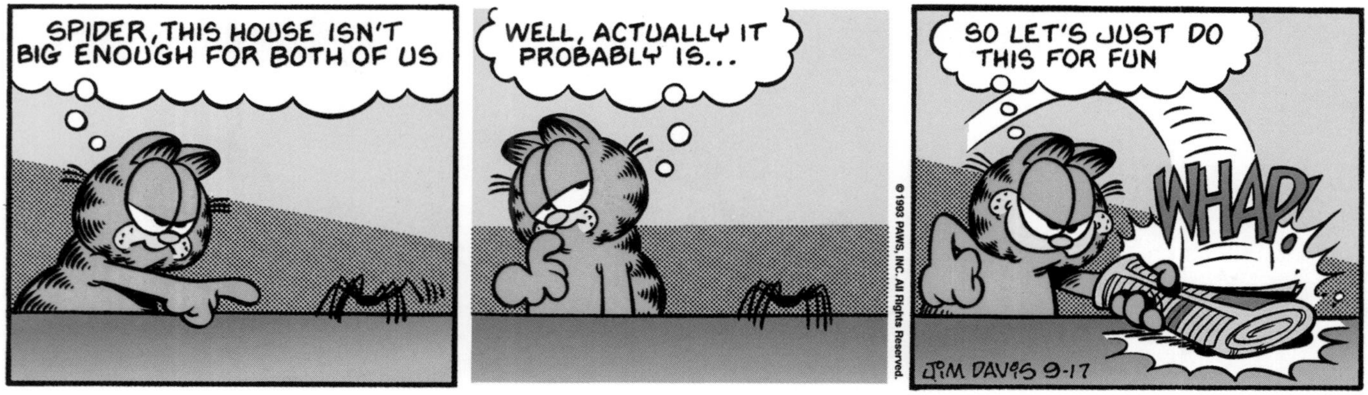
SPIDER, THIS HOUSE ISN'T BIG ENOUGH FOR BOTH OF US
WELL, ACTUALLY IT PROBABLY IS...
SO LET'S JUST DO THIS FOR FUN
WHAP!
© 1993 PAWS, INC. All Rights Reserved.
JIM DAVIS 9-17

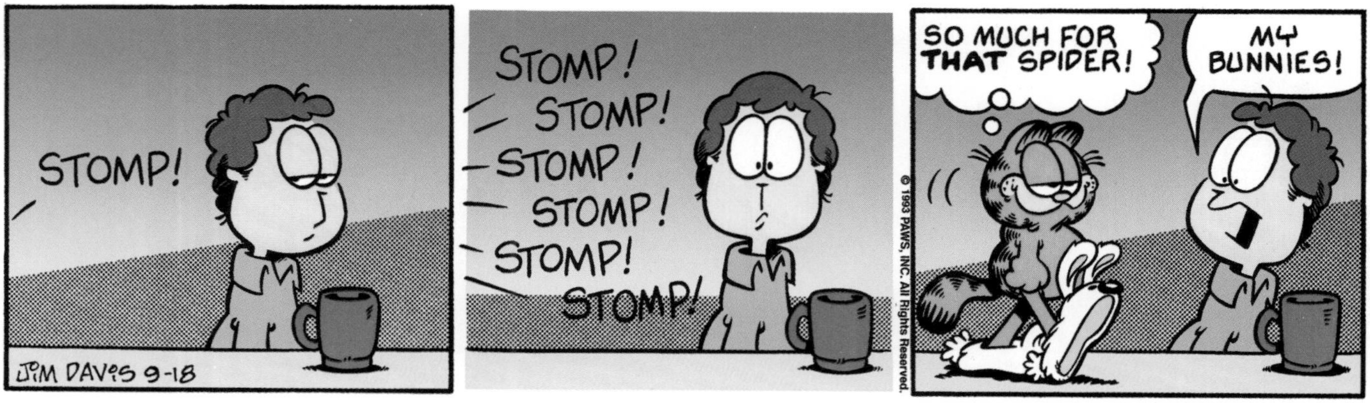
STOMP!
JIM DAVIS 9-18
STOMP!
STOMP!
STOMP!
STOMP!
STOMP!
STOMP!
SO MUCH FOR THAT SPIDER!
MY BUNNIES!
© 1993 PAWS, INC. All Rights Reserved.

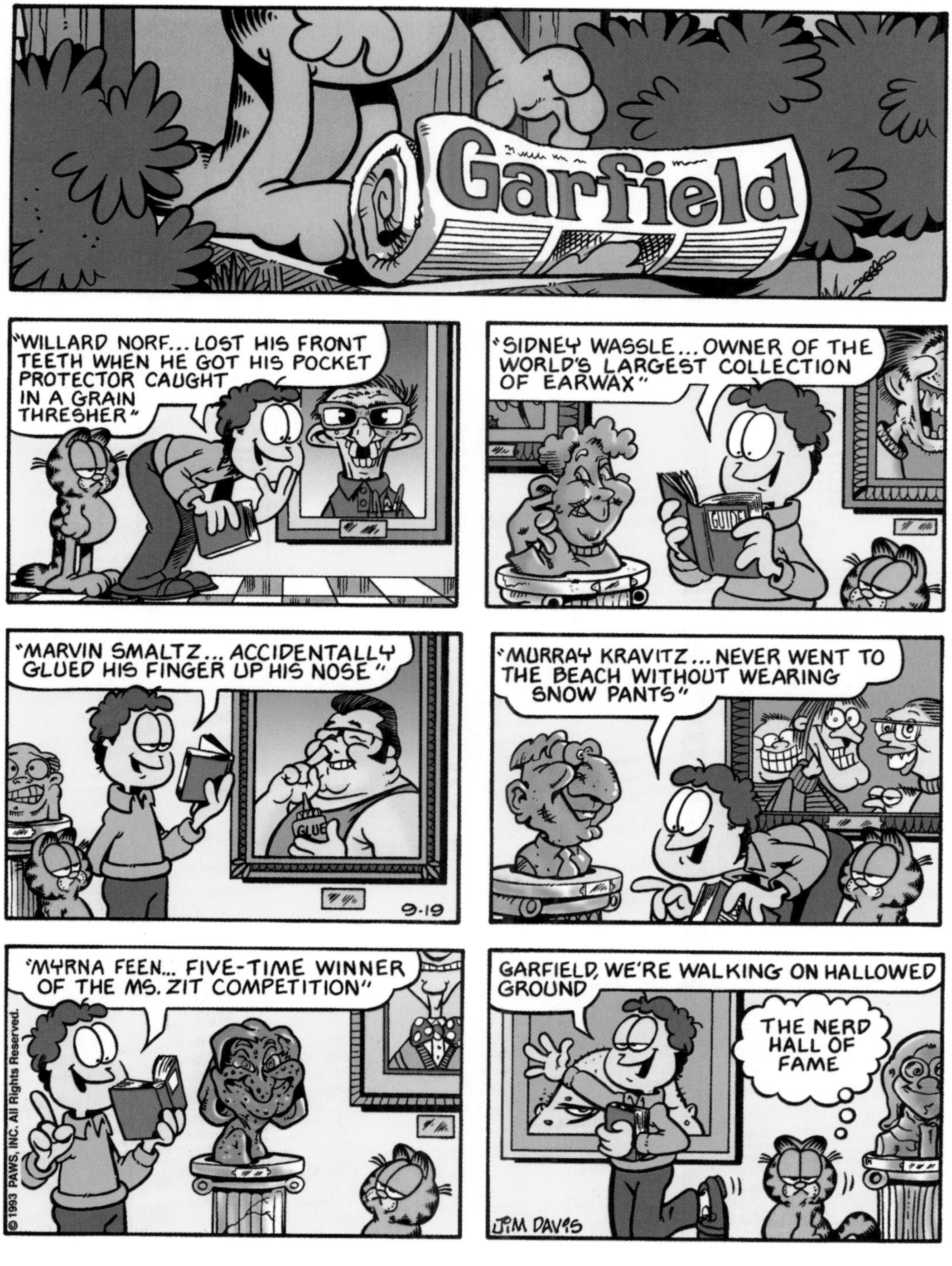
Garfield
"WILLARD NORF... LOST HIS FRONT TEETH WHEN HE GOT HIS POCKET PROTECTOR CAUGHT IN A GRAIN THRESHER"
"SIDNEY WASSLE... OWNER OF THE WORLD'S LARGEST COLLECTION OF EARWAX"
GUIDE
"MARVIN SMALTZ... ACCIDENTALLY GLUED HIS FINGER UP HIS NOSE"
GLUE
9-19
"MURRAY KRAVITZ... NEVER WENT TO THE BEACH WITHOUT WEARING SNOW PANTS"
"MYRNA FEEN... FIVE-TIME WINNER OF THE MS. ZIT COMPETITION"
GARFIELD, WE'RE WALKING ON HALLOWED GROUND
THE NERD HALL OF FAME
JIM DAVIS

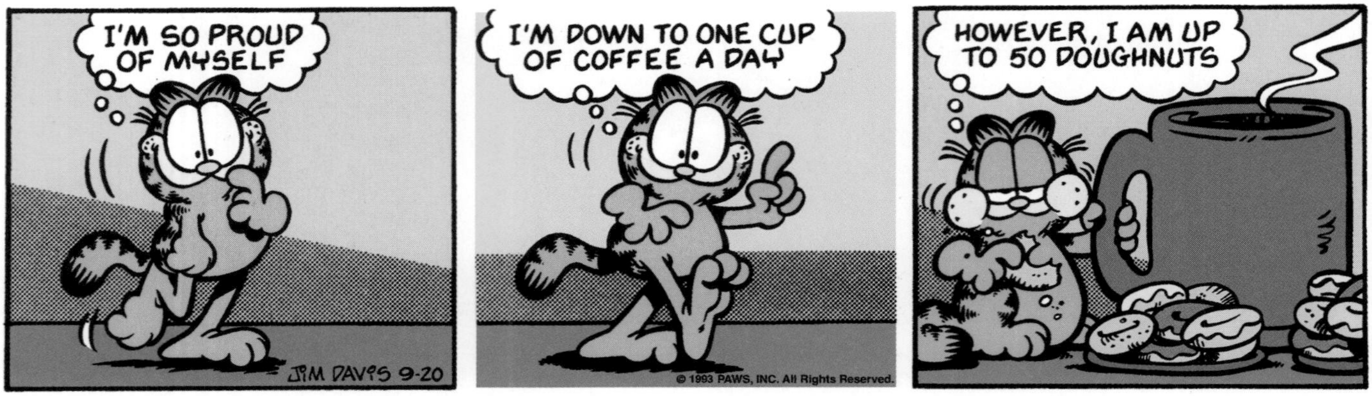
I'M SO PROUD OF MYSELF
JIM DAVIS 9-20
I'M DOWN TO ONE CUP OF COFFEE A DAY
© 1993 PAWS, INC. All Rights Reserved.
HOWEVER, I AM UP TO 50 DOUGHNUTS

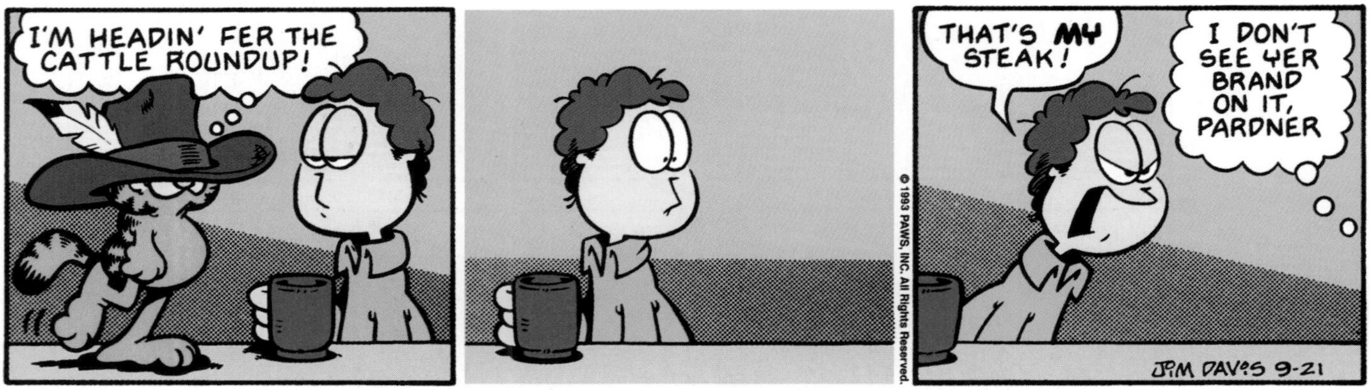
I'M HEADIN' FER THE CATTLE ROUNDUP!
© 1993 PAWS, INC. All Rights Reserved.
THAT'S MY STEAK!
I DON'T SEE YER BRAND ON IT, PARDNER
JIM DAVIS 9-21

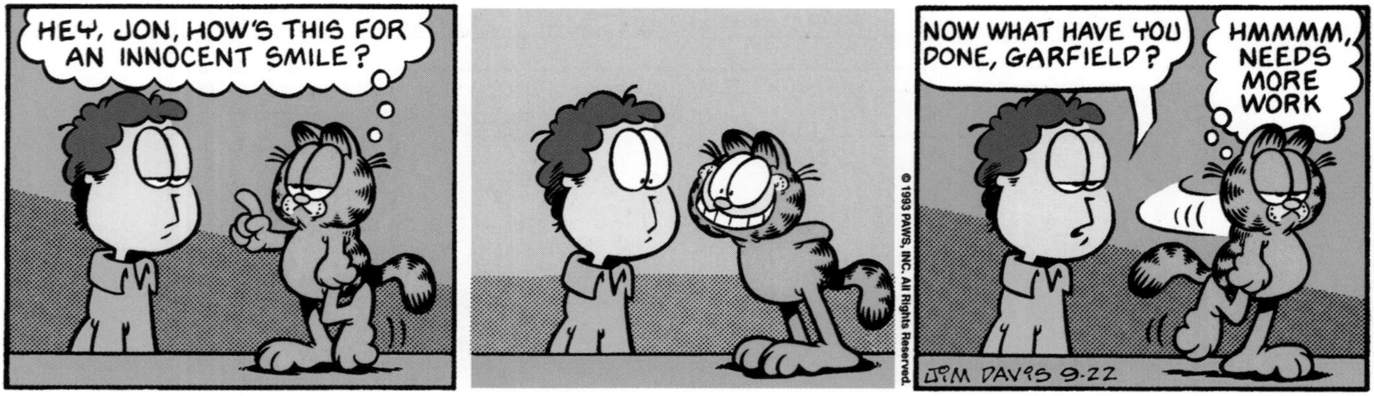
HEY, JON, HOW'S THIS FOR AN INNOCENT SMILE?
© 1993 PAWS, INC. All Rights Reserved.
NOW WHAT HAVE YOU DONE, GARFIELD?
HMMMM, NEEDS MORE WORK
JIM DAVIS 9-22

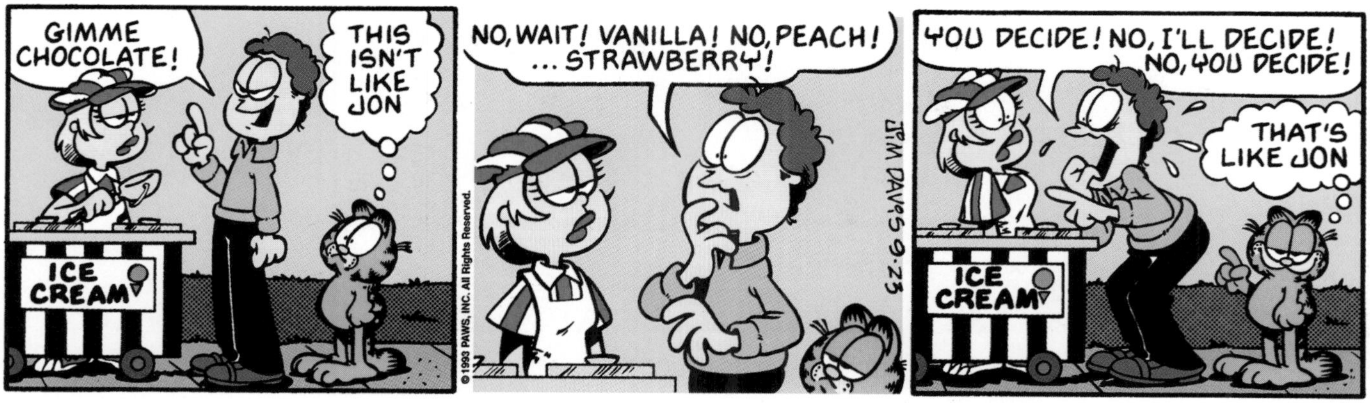
GIMME CHOCOLATE!
THIS ISN'T LIKE JON
ICE CREAM
NO, WAIT! VANILLA! NO, PEACH! ... STRAWBERRY!
© 1993 PAWS, INC. All Rights Reserved.
JIM DAVIS 9-23
YOU DECIDE! NO, I'LL DECIDE! NO, YOU DECIDE!
THAT'S LIKE JON
ICE CREAM

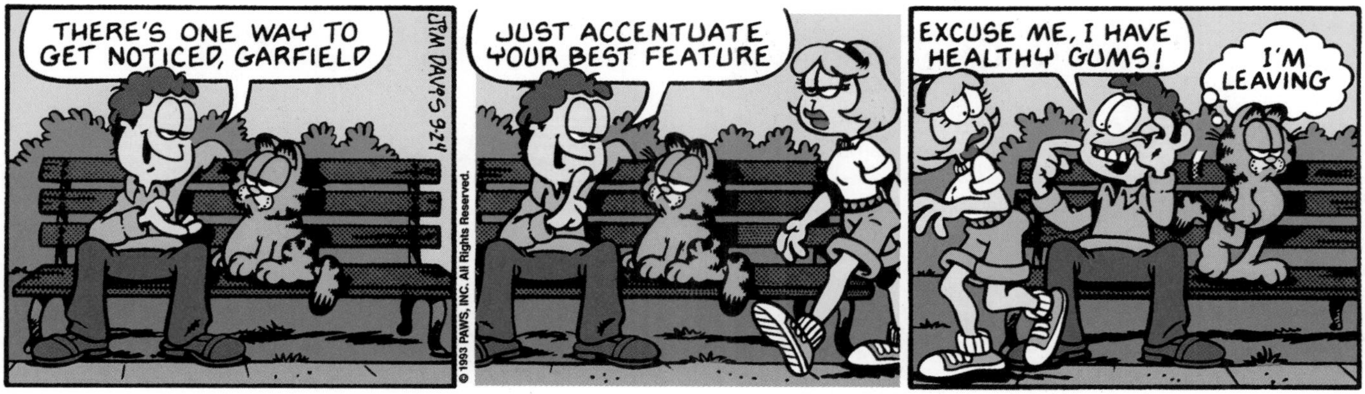
THERE'S ONE WAY TO GET NOTICED, GARFIELD
JIM DAVIS 9-24
© 1993 PAWS, INC. All Rights Reserved.
JUST ACCENTUATE YOUR BEST FEATURE
EXCUSE ME, I HAVE HEALTHY GUMS!
I'M LEAVING

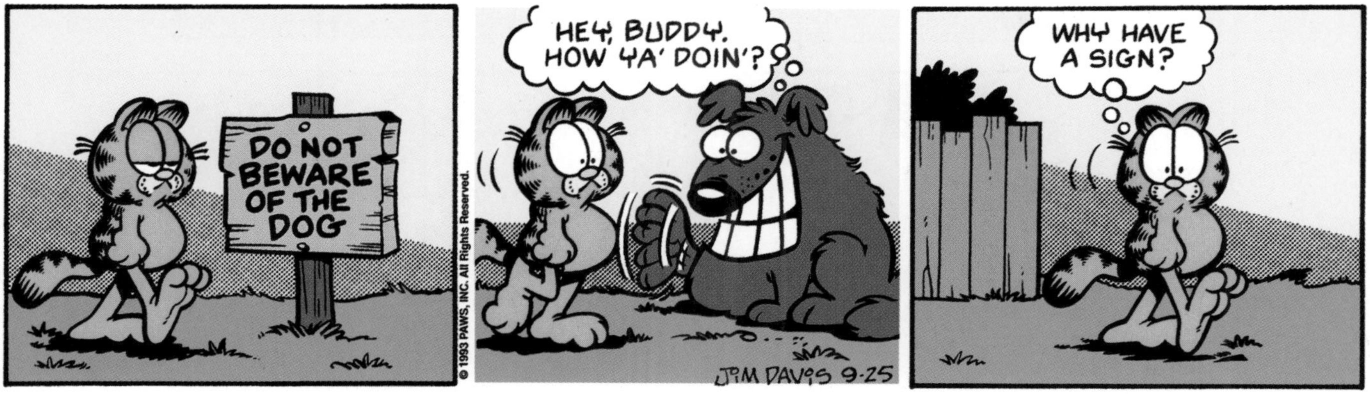
DO NOT BEWARE OF THE DOG
© 1993 PAWS, INC. All Rights Reserved.
HEY, BUDDY. HOW YA' DOIN'?
JIM DAVIS 9-25
WHY HAVE A SIGN?

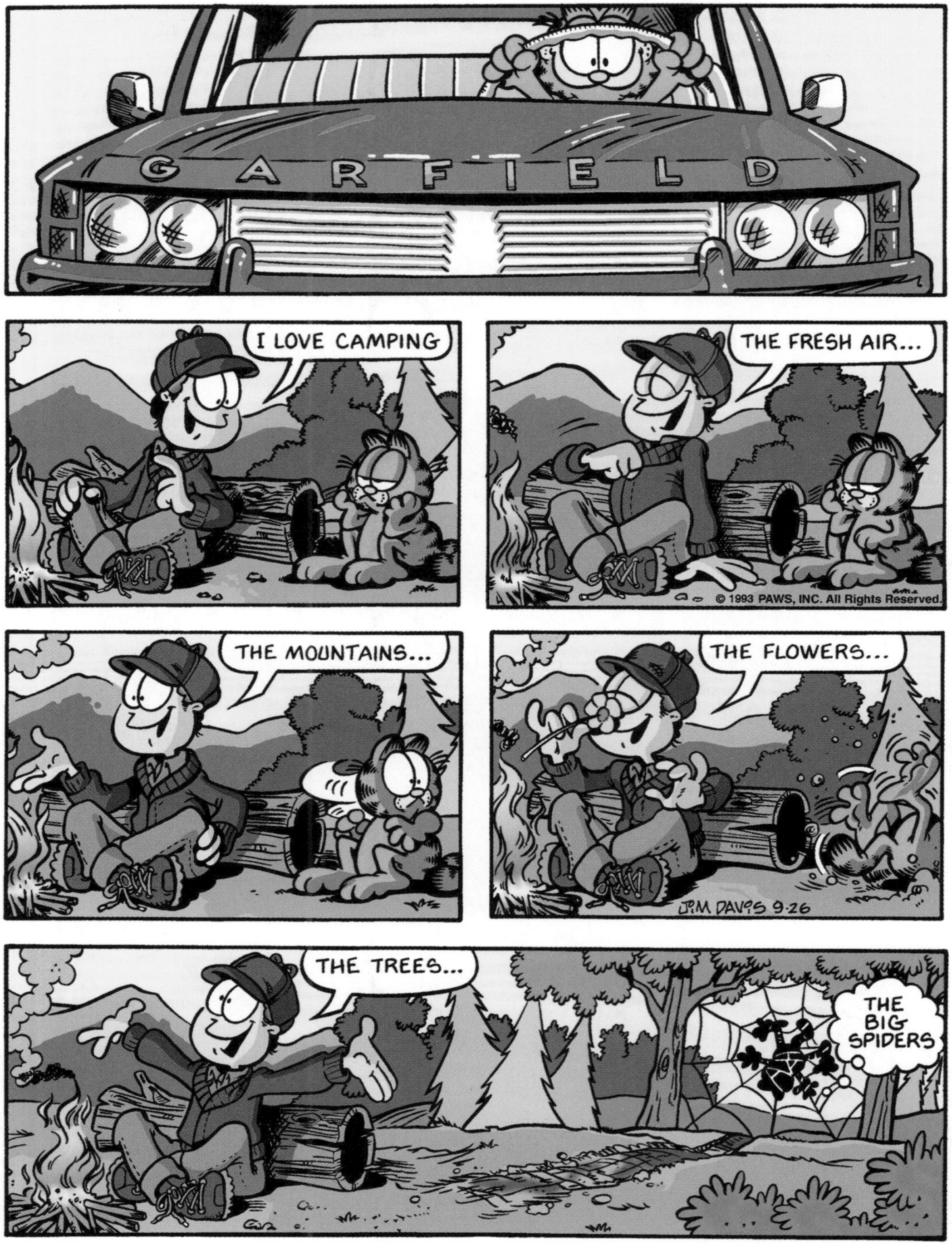
GARFIELD
I LOVE CAMPING
THE FRESH AIR...
© 1993 PAWS, INC. All Rights Reserved.
THE MOUNTAINS...
THE FLOWERS...
JIM DAVIS 9-26
THE TREES...
THE BIG SPIDERS

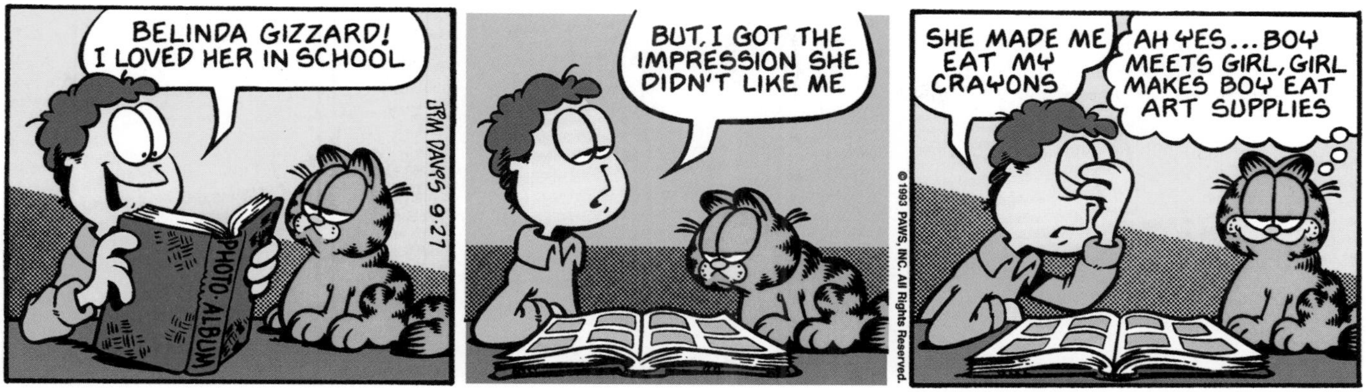
BELINDA GIZZARD! I LOVED HER IN SCHOOL
PHOTO ALBUM
JIM DAVIS 9-27
BUT, I GOT THE IMPRESSION SHE DIDN'T LIKE ME
© 1993 PAWS, INC. All Rights Reserved.
SHE MADE ME EAT MY CRAYONS
AH YES... BOY MEETS GIRL, GIRL MAKES BOY EAT ART SUPPLIES

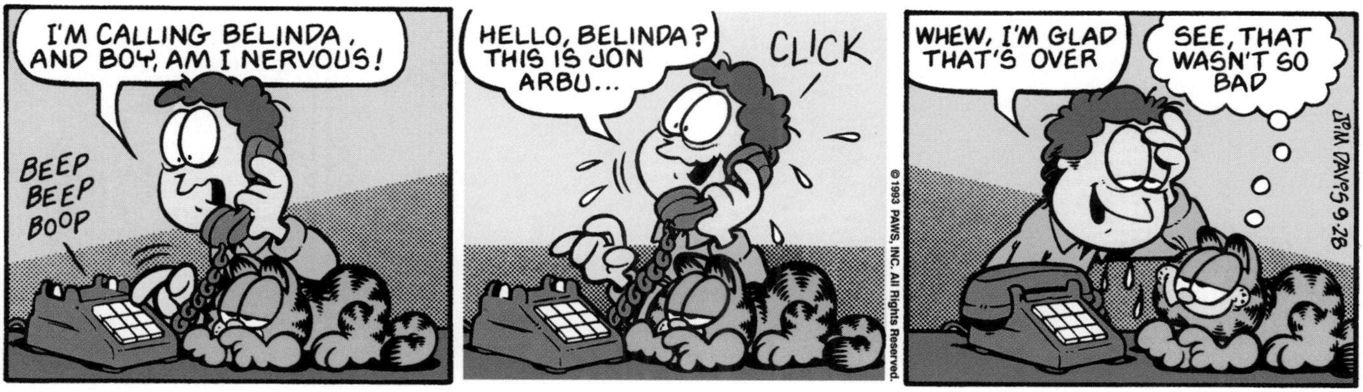
I'M CALLING BELINDA, AND BOY, AM I NERVOUS!
BEEP BEEP BOOP
HELLO, BELINDA? THIS IS JON ARBU...
CLICK
© 1993 PAWS, INC. All Rights Reserved.
WHEW, I'M GLAD THAT'S OVER
SEE, THAT WASN'T SO BAD
JIM DAVIS 9-28

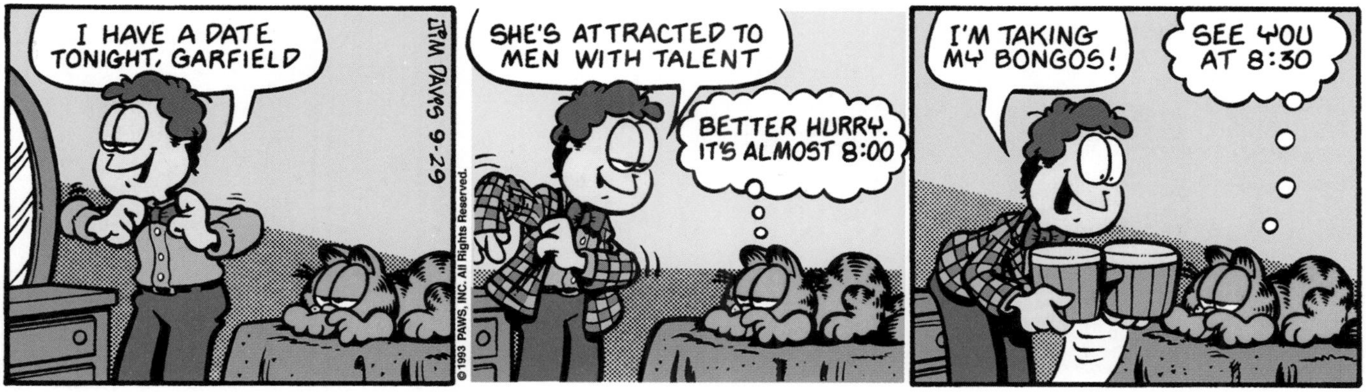
I HAVE A DATE TONIGHT, GARFIELD
JIM DAVIS 9-29
© 1993 PAWS, INC. All Rights Reserved.
SHE'S ATTRACTED TO MEN WITH TALENT
BETTER HURRY. IT'S ALMOST 8:00
I'M TAKING MY BONGOS!
SEE YOU AT 8:30

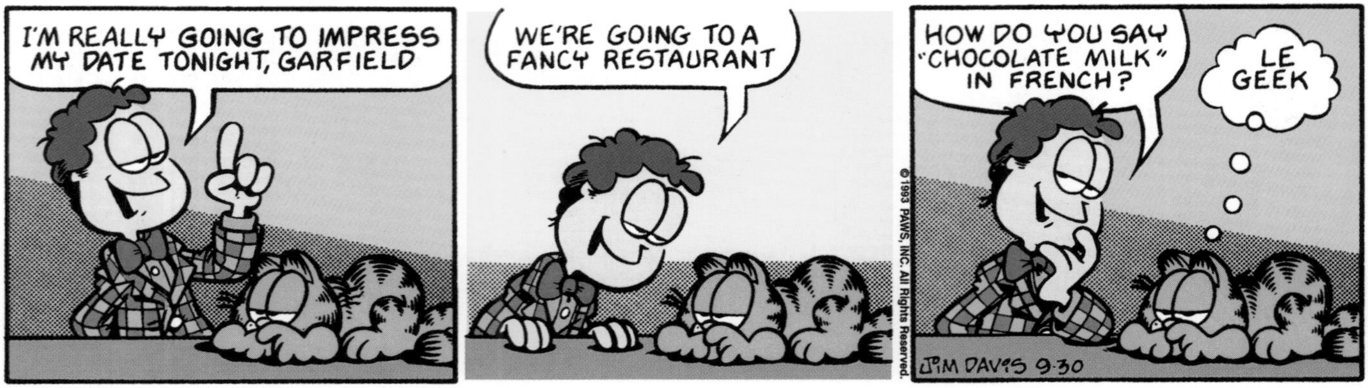
I'M REALLY GOING TO IMPRESS MY DATE TONIGHT, GARFIELD
WE'RE GOING TO A FANCY RESTAURANT
HOW DO YOU SAY "CHOCOLATE MILK" IN FRENCH?
LE GEEK
© 1993 PAWS, INC. All Rights Reserved.
JIM DAVIS 9-30

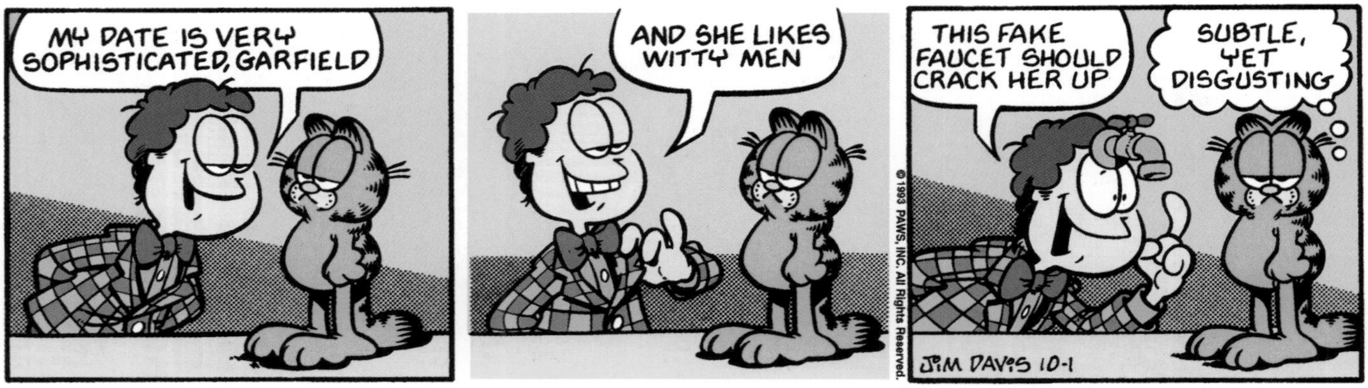
MY DATE IS VERY SOPHISTICATED, GARFIELD
AND SHE LIKES WITTY MEN
THIS FAKE FAUCET SHOULD CRACK HER UP
SUBTLE, YET DISGUSTING
© 1993 PAWS, INC. All Rights Reserved.
JIM DAVIS 10-1

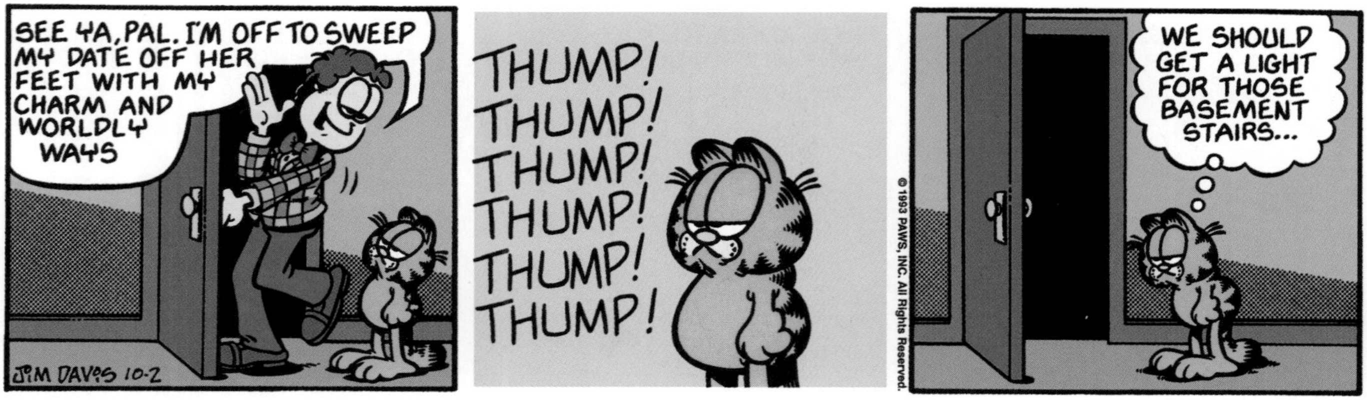
SEE YA, PAL. I'M OFF TO SWEEP MY DATE OFF HER FEET WITH MY CHARM AND WORLDLY WAYS
JIM DAVIS 10-2
THUMP! THUMP! THUMP! THUMP! THUMP! THUMP!
WE SHOULD GET A LIGHT FOR THOSE BASEMENT STAIRS...
© 1993 PAWS, INC. All Rights Reserved.

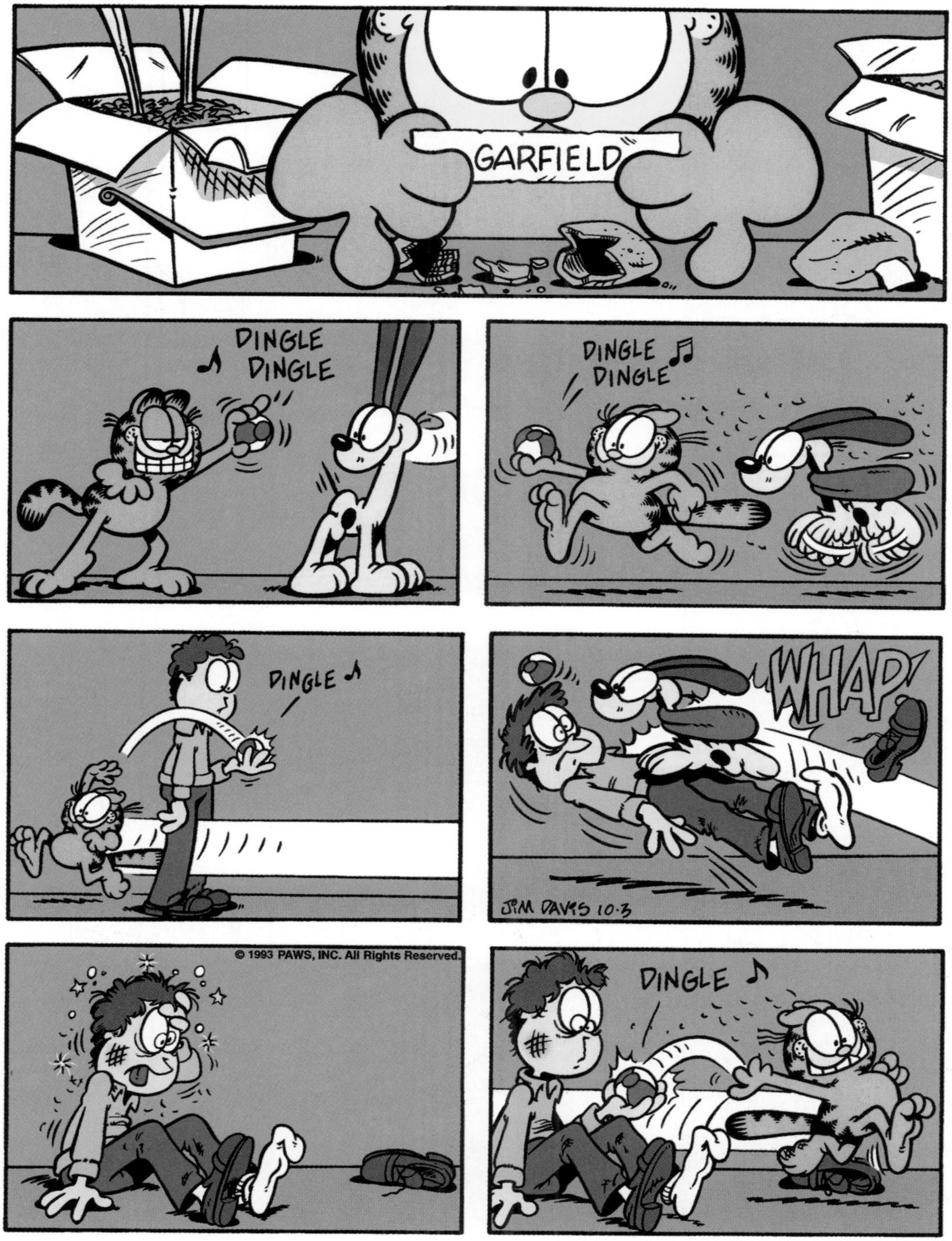
GARFIELD
DINGLE DINGLE
DINGLE DINGLE
DINGLE
WHAP!
JIM DAVIS 10-3
© 1993 PAWS, INC. All Rights Reserved.
DINGLE

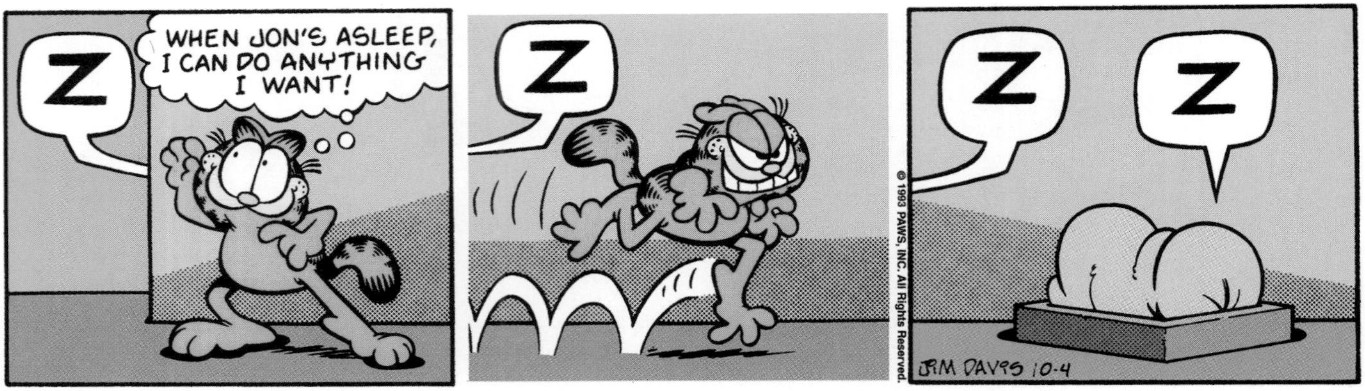
Z
WHEN JON'S ASLEEP, I CAN DO ANYTHING I WANT!
Z
© 1993 PAWS, INC. All Rights Reserved.
Z
Z
JIM DAVIS 10-4

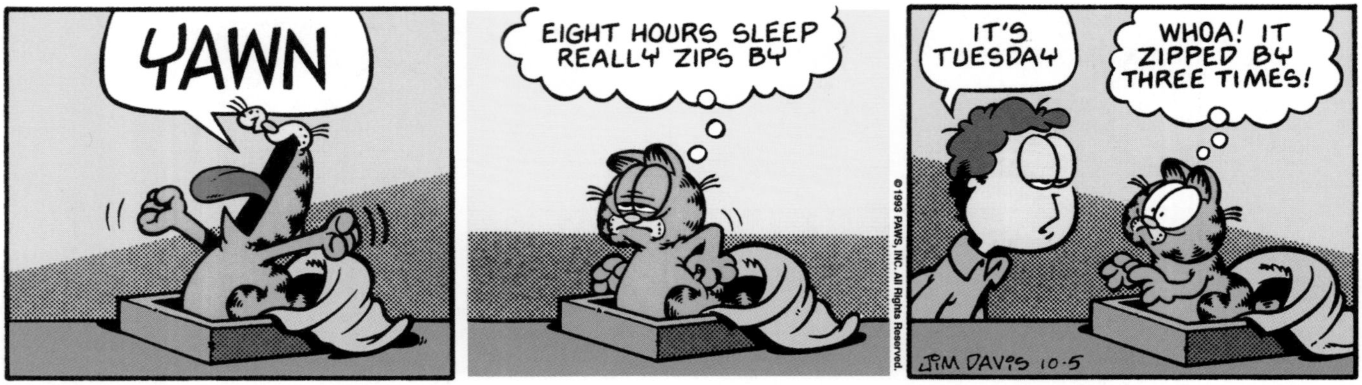
YAWN
EIGHT HOURS SLEEP REALLY ZIPS BY
© 1993 PAWS, INC. All Rights Reserved.
IT'S TUESDAY
WHOA! IT ZIPPED BY THREE TIMES!
JIM DAVIS 10-5

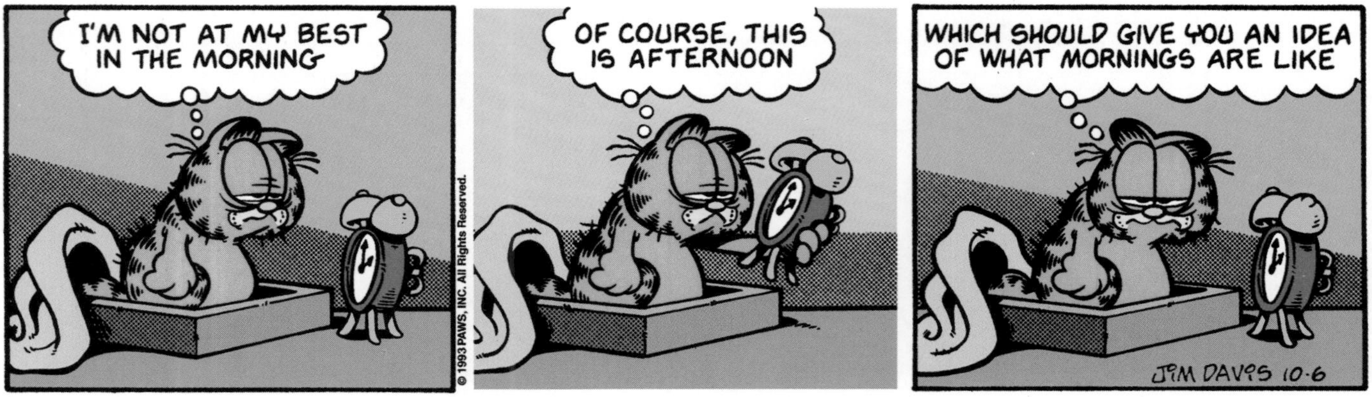
I'M NOT AT MY BEST IN THE MORNING
© 1993 PAWS, INC. All Rights Reserved.
OF COURSE, THIS IS AFTERNOON
WHICH SHOULD GIVE YOU AN IDEA OF WHAT MORNINGS ARE LIKE
JIM DAVIS 10-6

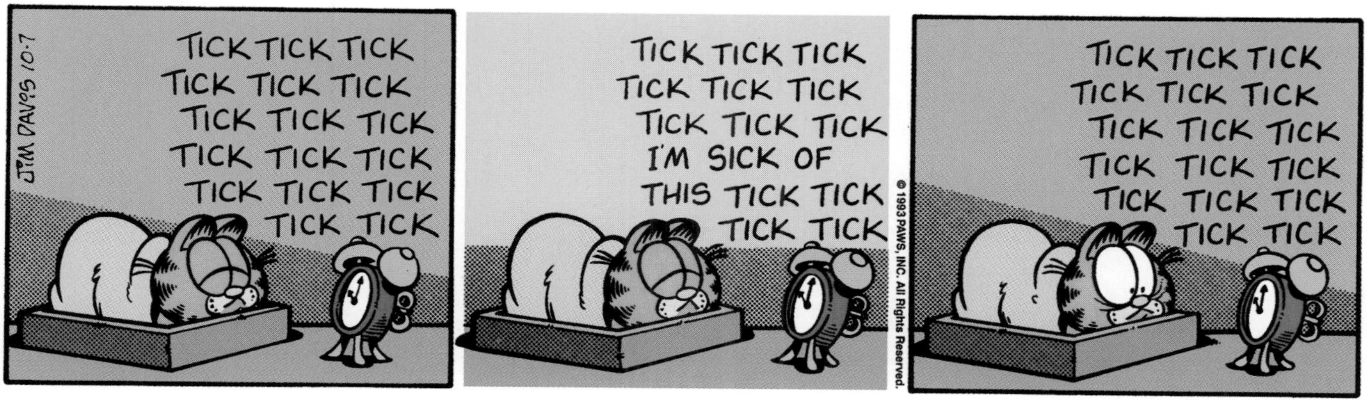
JIM DAVIS 10-7
TICK TICK TICK TICK TICK TICK TICK TICK TICK TICK TICK TICK TICK TICK TICK TICK TICK
TICK TICK TICK TICK TICK TICK TICK TICK TICK I'M SICK OF THIS TICK TICK TICK TICK
© 1993 PAWS, INC. All Rights Reserved.
TICK TICK TICK TICK TICK TICK TICK TICK TICK TICK TICK TICK TICK TICK TICK TICK TICK

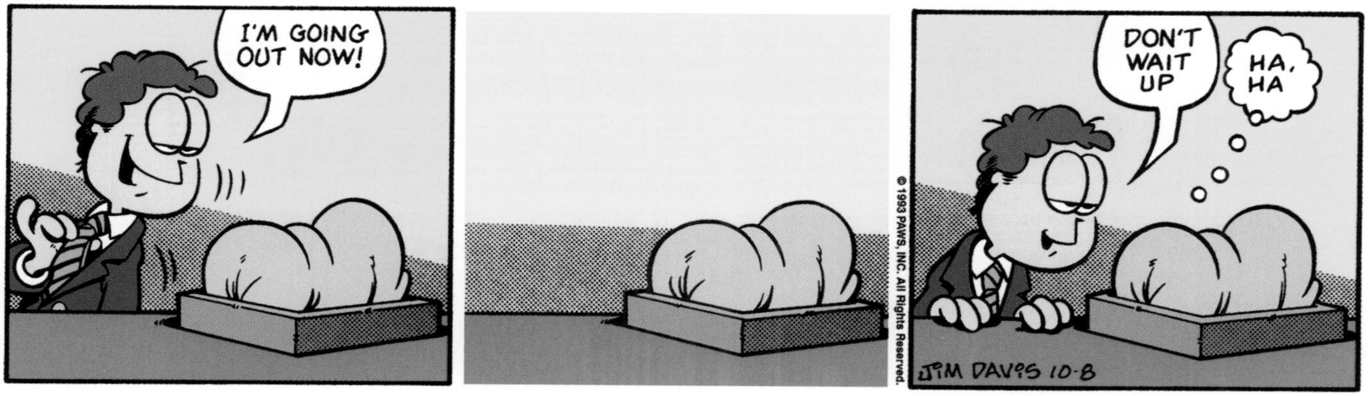
I'M GOING OUT NOW!
© 1993 PAWS, INC. All Rights Reserved.
DON'T WAIT UP
HA, HA
JIM DAVIS 10-8

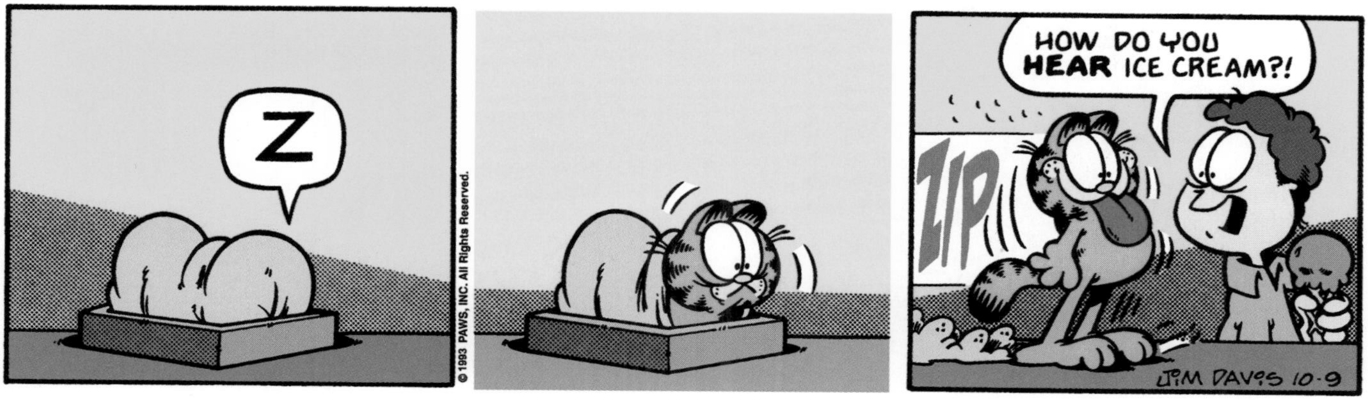
Z
© 1993 PAWS, INC. All Rights Reserved.
ZIP
HOW DO YOU HEAR ICE CREAM?!
JIM DAVIS 10-9

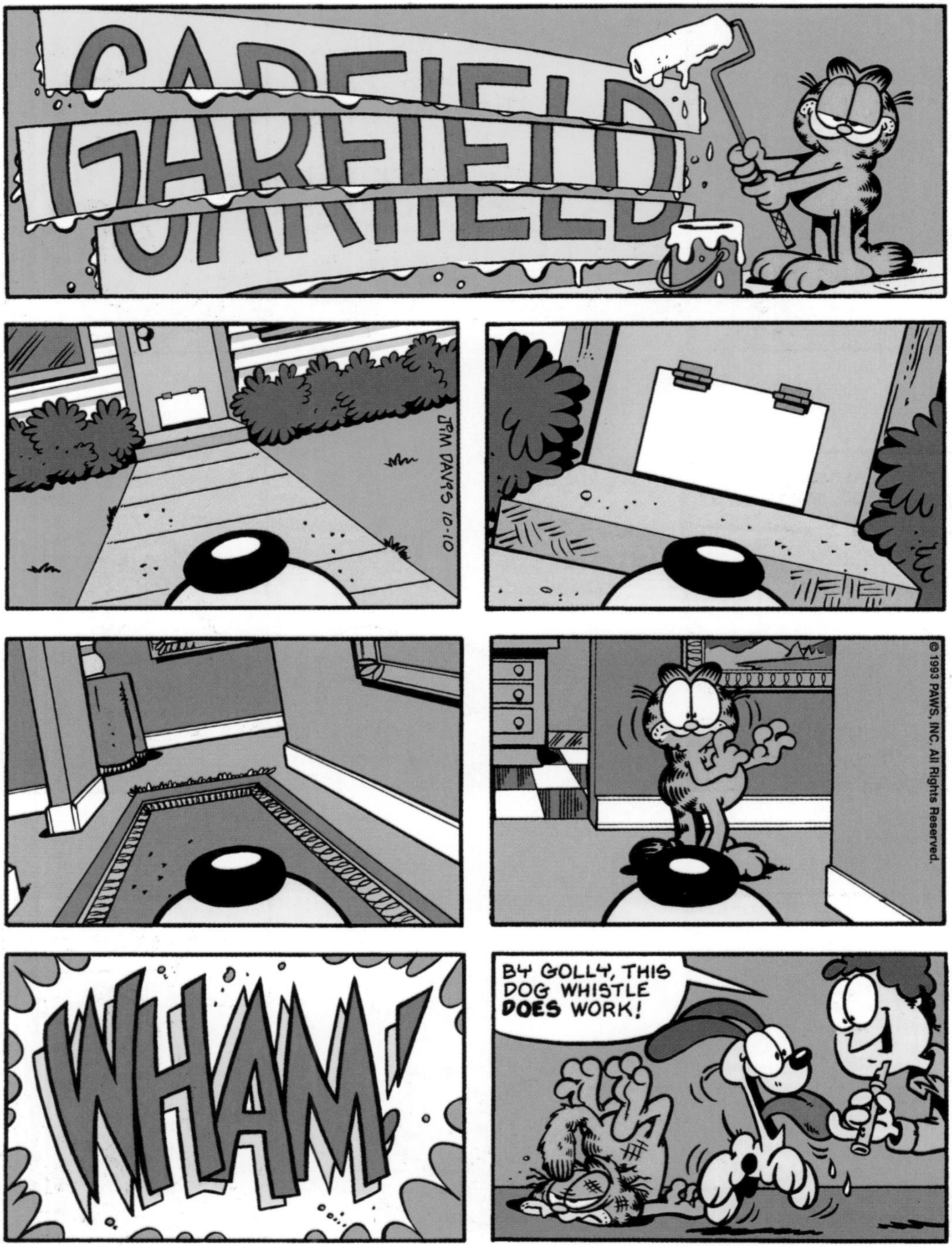
GARFIELD
GARFIELD
GARFIELD
JIM DAVIS 10-10
© 1993 PAWS, INC. All Rights Reserved.
WHAM!
BY GOLLY, THIS DOG WHISTLE **DOES** WORK!

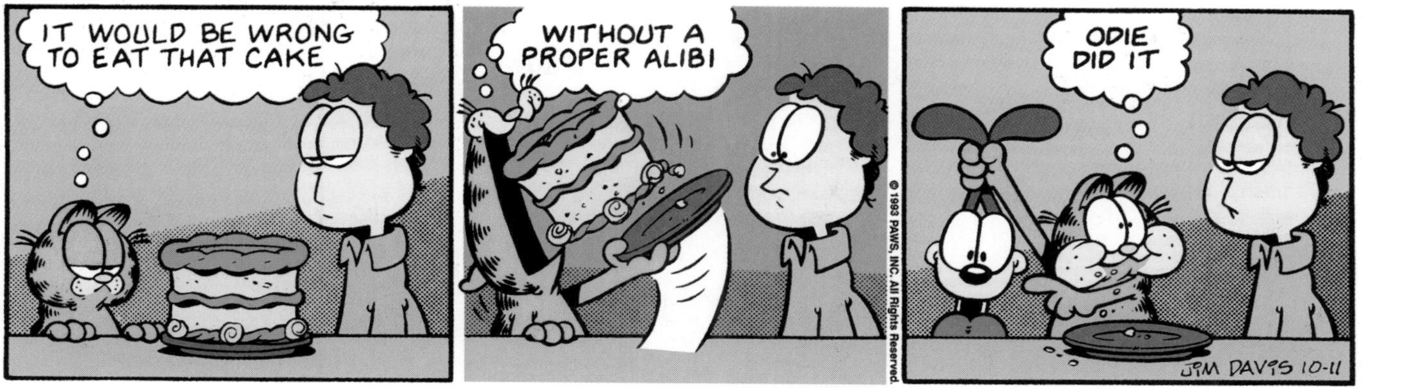
IT WOULD BE WRONG TO EAT THAT CAKE
WITHOUT A PROPER ALIBI
ODIE DID IT
© 1993 PAWS, INC. All Rights Reserved.
JIM DAVIS 10-11

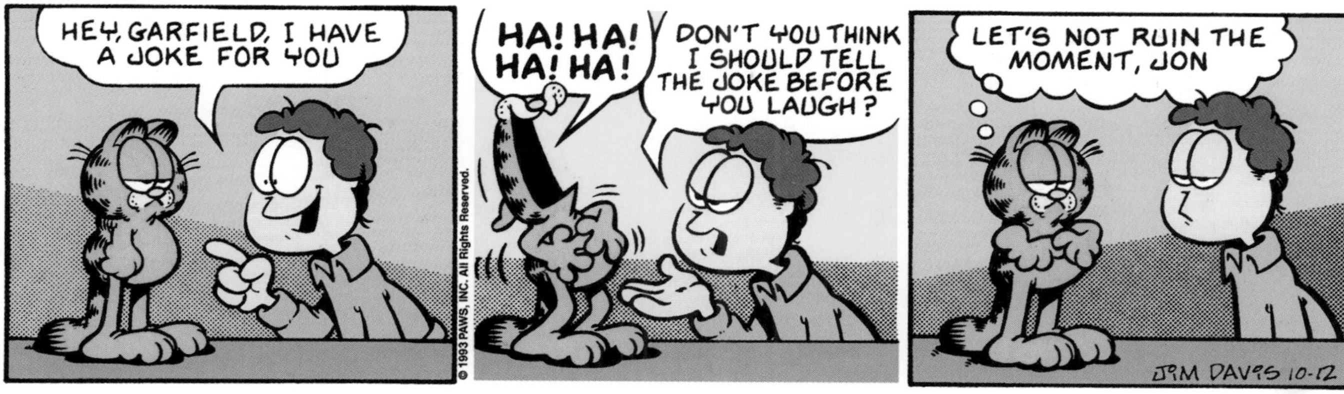
HEY, GARFIELD, I HAVE A JOKE FOR YOU
HA! HA! HA! HA!
DON'T YOU THINK I SHOULD TELL THE JOKE BEFORE YOU LAUGH?
LET'S NOT RUIN THE MOMENT, JON
© 1993 PAWS, INC. All Rights Reserved.
JIM DAVIS 10-12

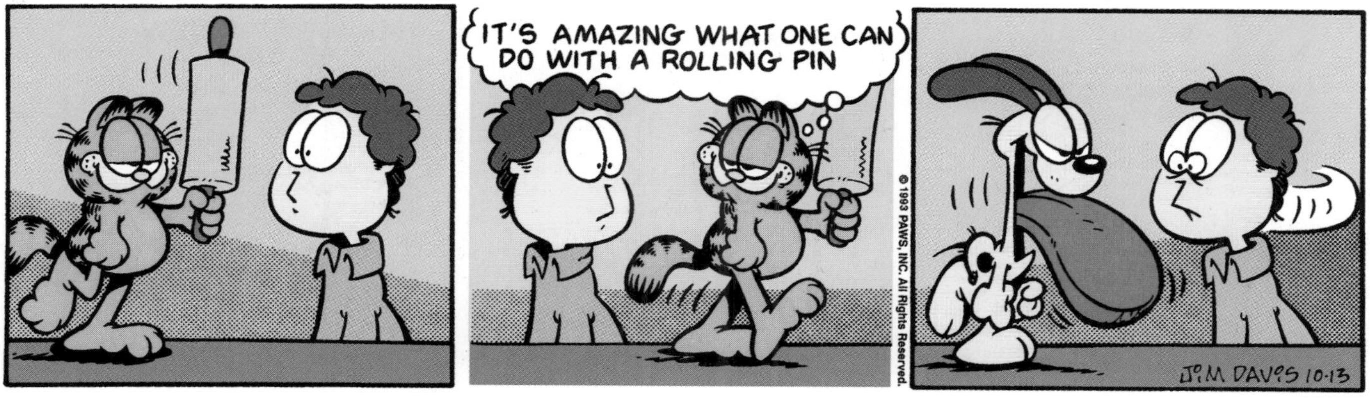
IT'S AMAZING WHAT ONE CAN DO WITH A ROLLING PIN
© 1993 PAWS, INC. All Rights Reserved.
JIM DAVIS 10-13

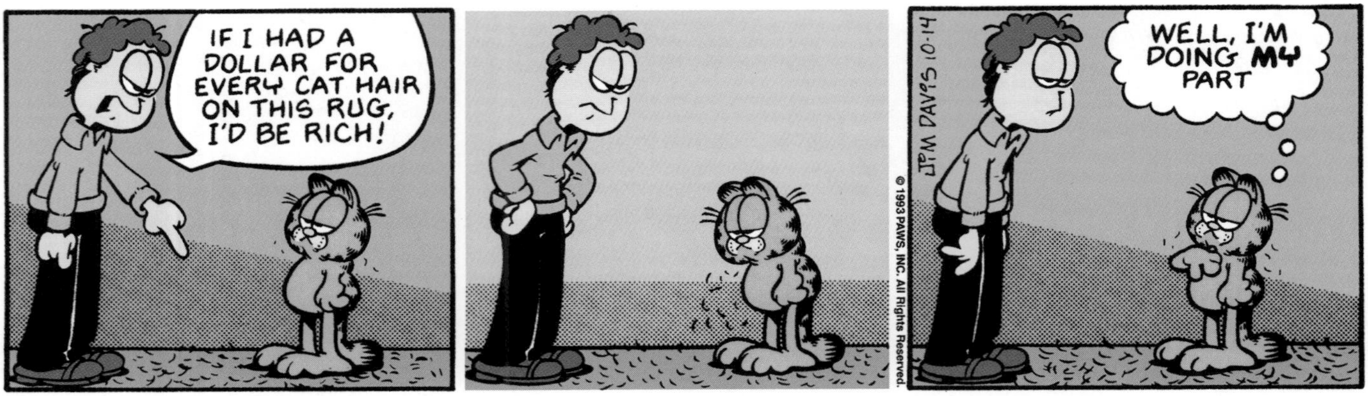
IF I HAD A DOLLAR FOR EVERY CAT HAIR ON THIS RUG, I'D BE RICH!
WELL, I'M DOING MY PART
JIM DAVIS 10-14
© 1993 PAWS, INC. All Rights Reserved.

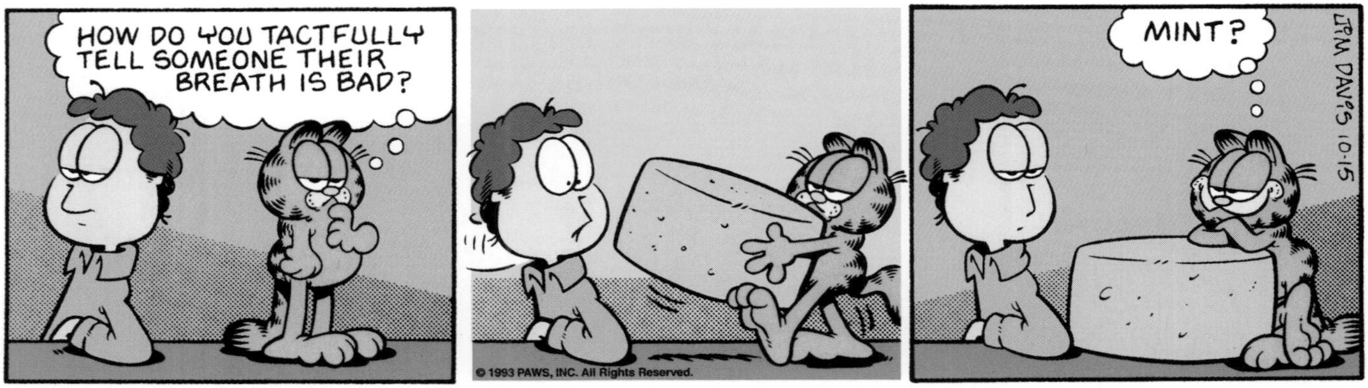
HOW DO YOU TACTFULLY TELL SOMEONE THEIR BREATH IS BAD?
MINT?
JIM DAVIS 10-15
© 1993 PAWS, INC. All Rights Reserved.

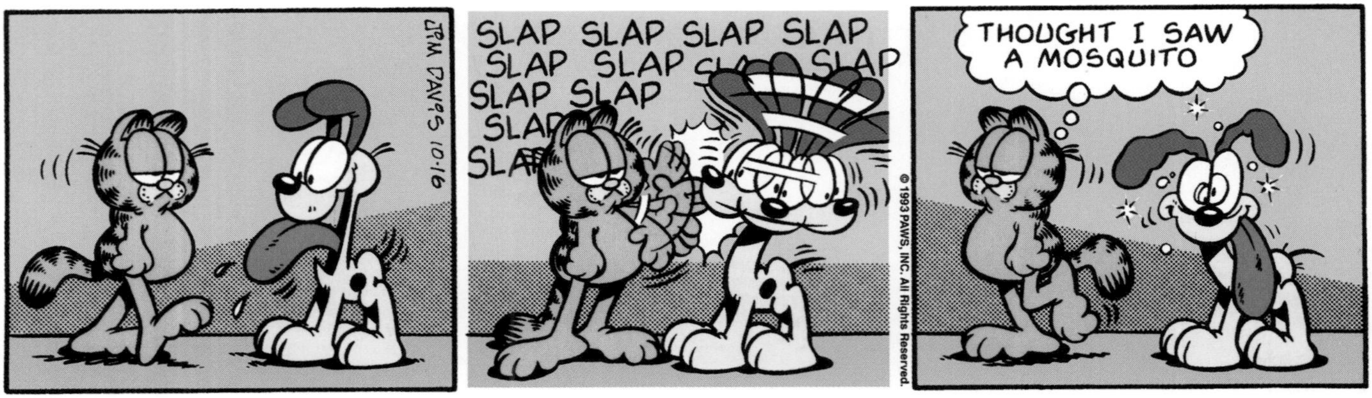
JIM DAVIS 10-16
SLAP SLAP SLAP SLAP
SLAP SLAP SLAP
SLAP SLAP
THOUGHT I SAW A MOSQUITO
© 1993 PAWS, INC. All Rights Reserved.

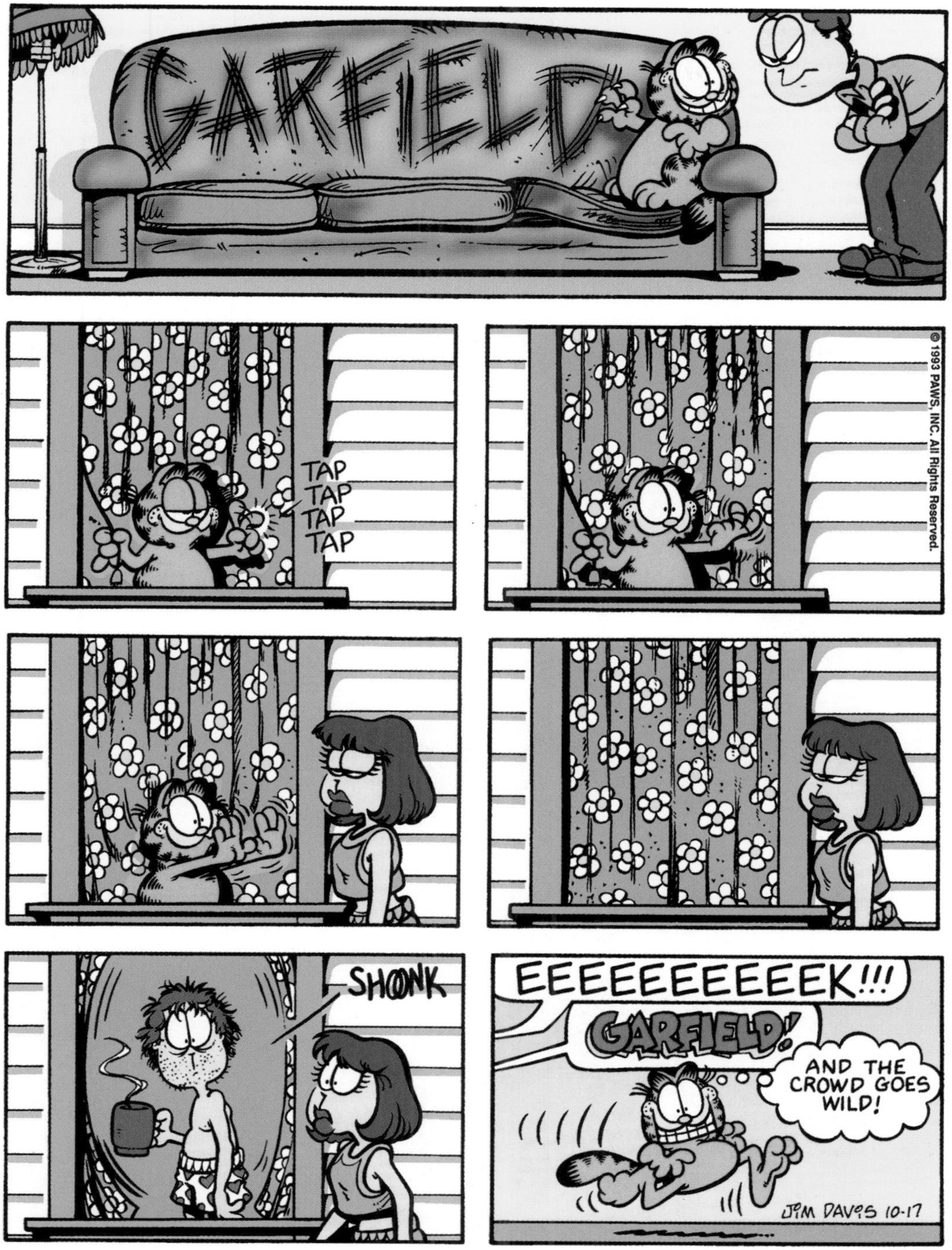
GARFIELD
TAP TAP TAP TAP
© 1993 PAWS, INC. All Rights Reserved.
SHOONK
EEEEEEEEEEK!!!
GARFIELD!
AND THE CROWD GOES WILD!
JIM DAVIS 10-17

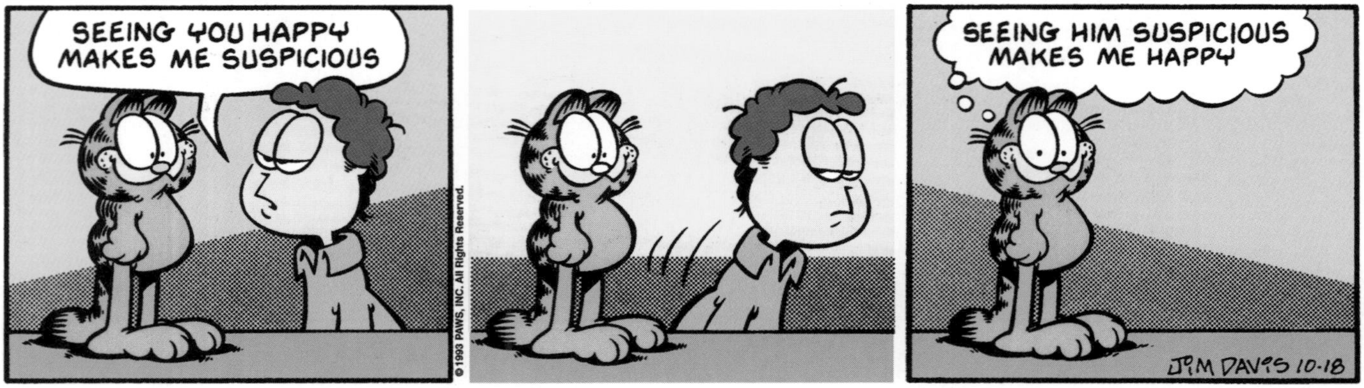
SEEING YOU HAPPY MAKES ME SUSPICIOUS
© 1993 PAWS, INC. All Rights Reserved.
SEEING HIM SUSPICIOUS MAKES ME HAPPY
JIM DAVIS 10-18

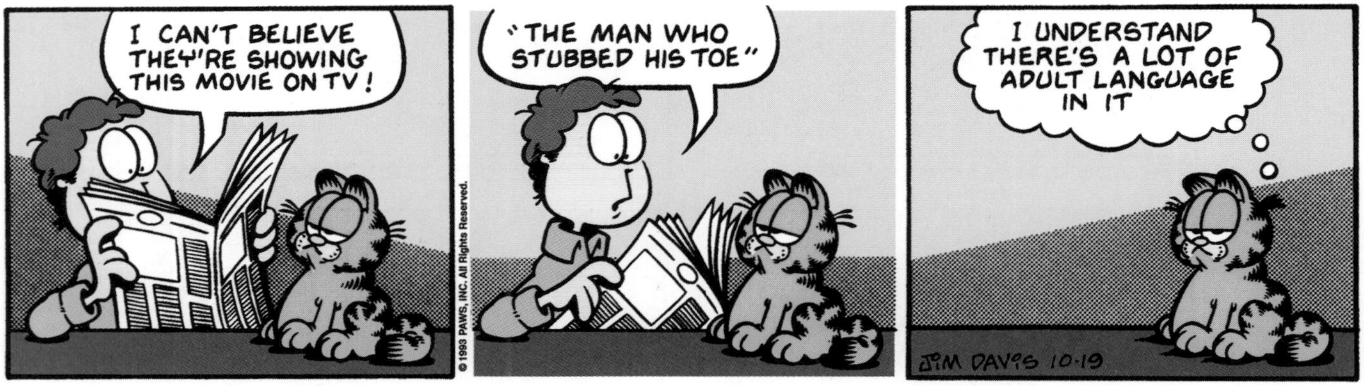
I CAN'T BELIEVE THEY'RE SHOWING THIS MOVIE ON TV!
© 1993 PAWS, INC. All Rights Reserved.
"THE MAN WHO STUBBED HIS TOE"
I UNDERSTAND THERE'S A LOT OF ADULT LANGUAGE IN IT
JIM DAVIS 10-19

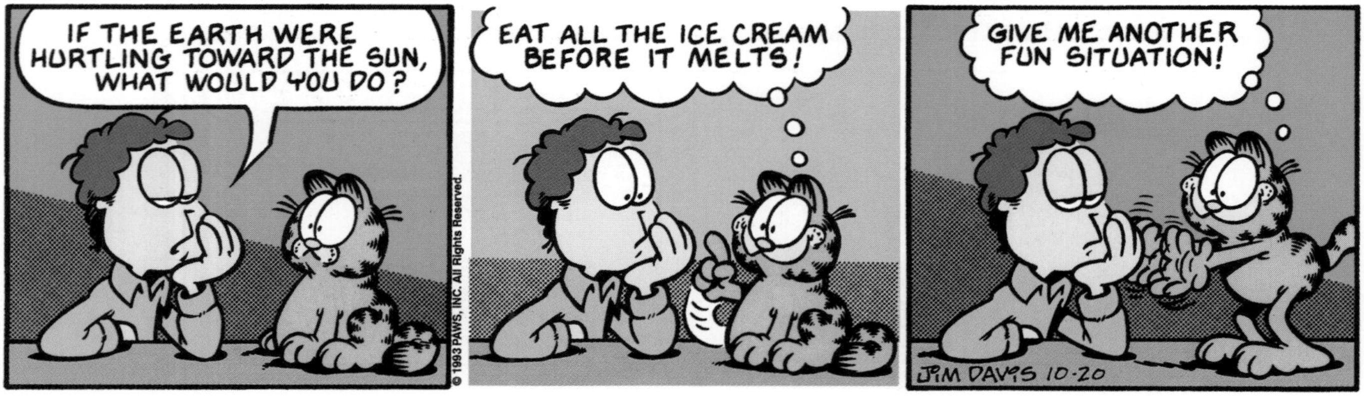
IF THE EARTH WERE HURTLING TOWARD THE SUN, WHAT WOULD YOU DO?
© 1993 PAWS, INC. All Rights Reserved.
EAT ALL THE ICE CREAM BEFORE IT MELTS!
GIVE ME ANOTHER FUN SITUATION!
JIM DAVIS 10-20

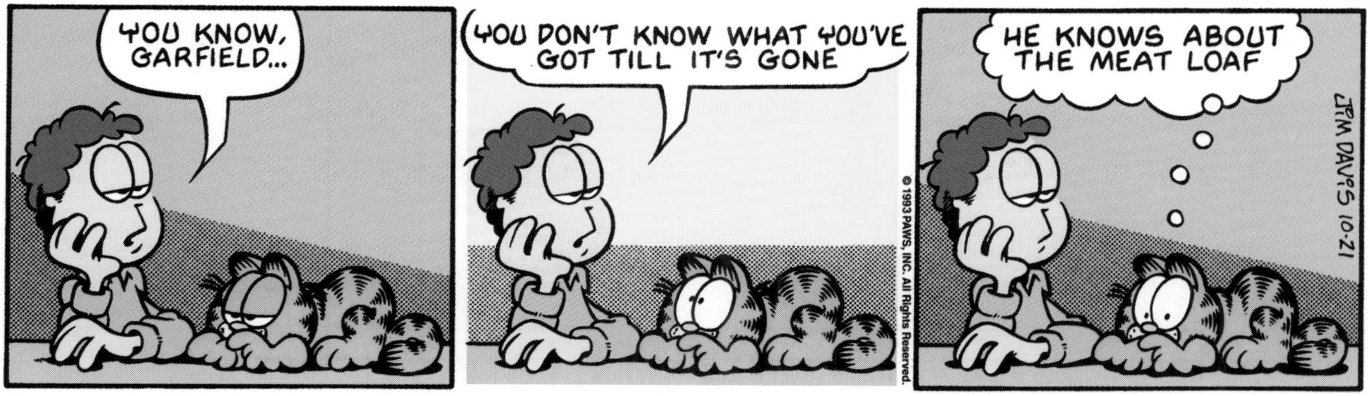
YOU KNOW, GARFIELD...
YOU DON'T KNOW WHAT YOU'VE GOT TILL IT'S GONE
HE KNOWS ABOUT THE MEAT LOAF
JIM DAVIS 10-21
© 1993 PAWS, INC. All Rights Reserved.

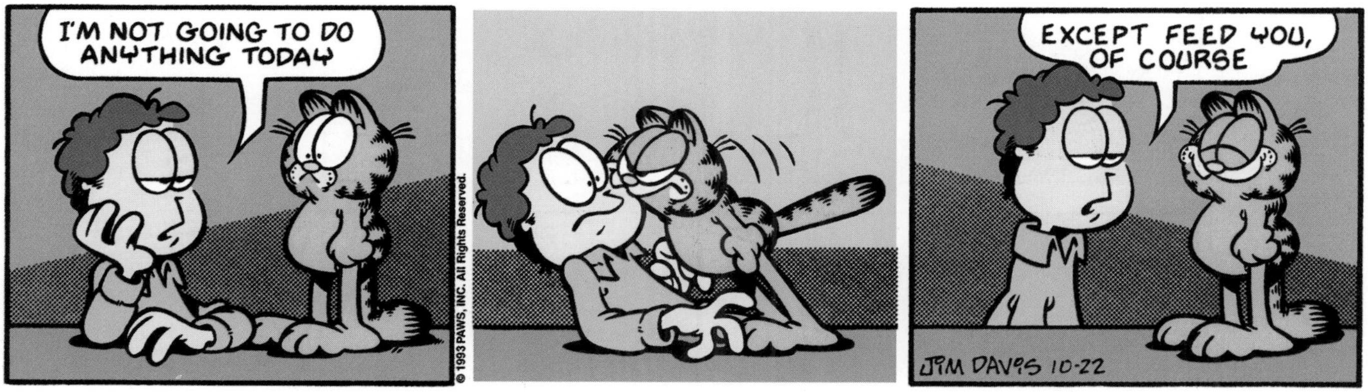
I'M NOT GOING TO DO ANYTHING TODAY
EXCEPT FEED YOU, OF COURSE
JIM DAVIS 10-22
© 1993 PAWS, INC. All Rights Reserved.

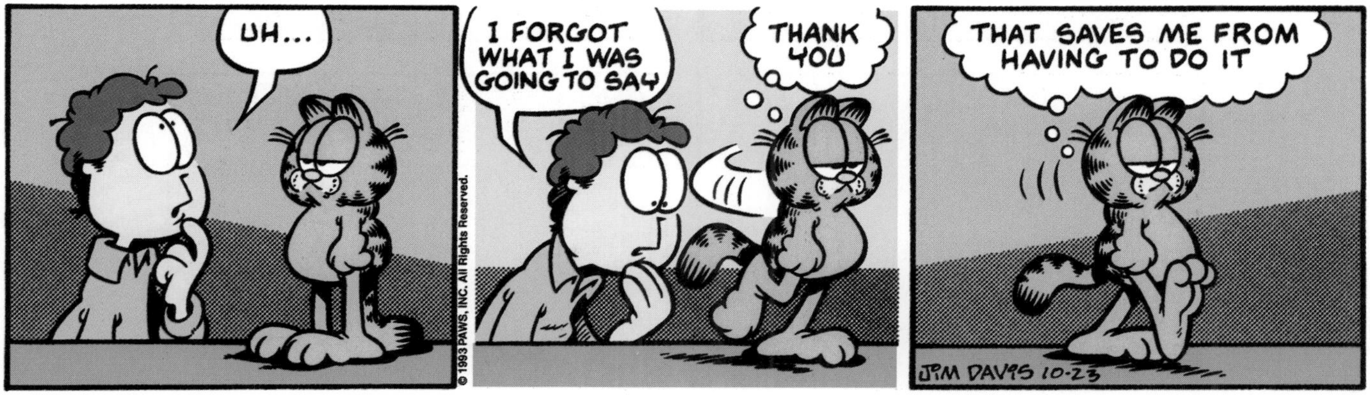
UH...
I FORGOT WHAT I WAS GOING TO SAY
THANK YOU
THAT SAVES ME FROM HAVING TO DO IT
JIM DAVIS 10-23
© 1993 PAWS, INC. All Rights Reserved.

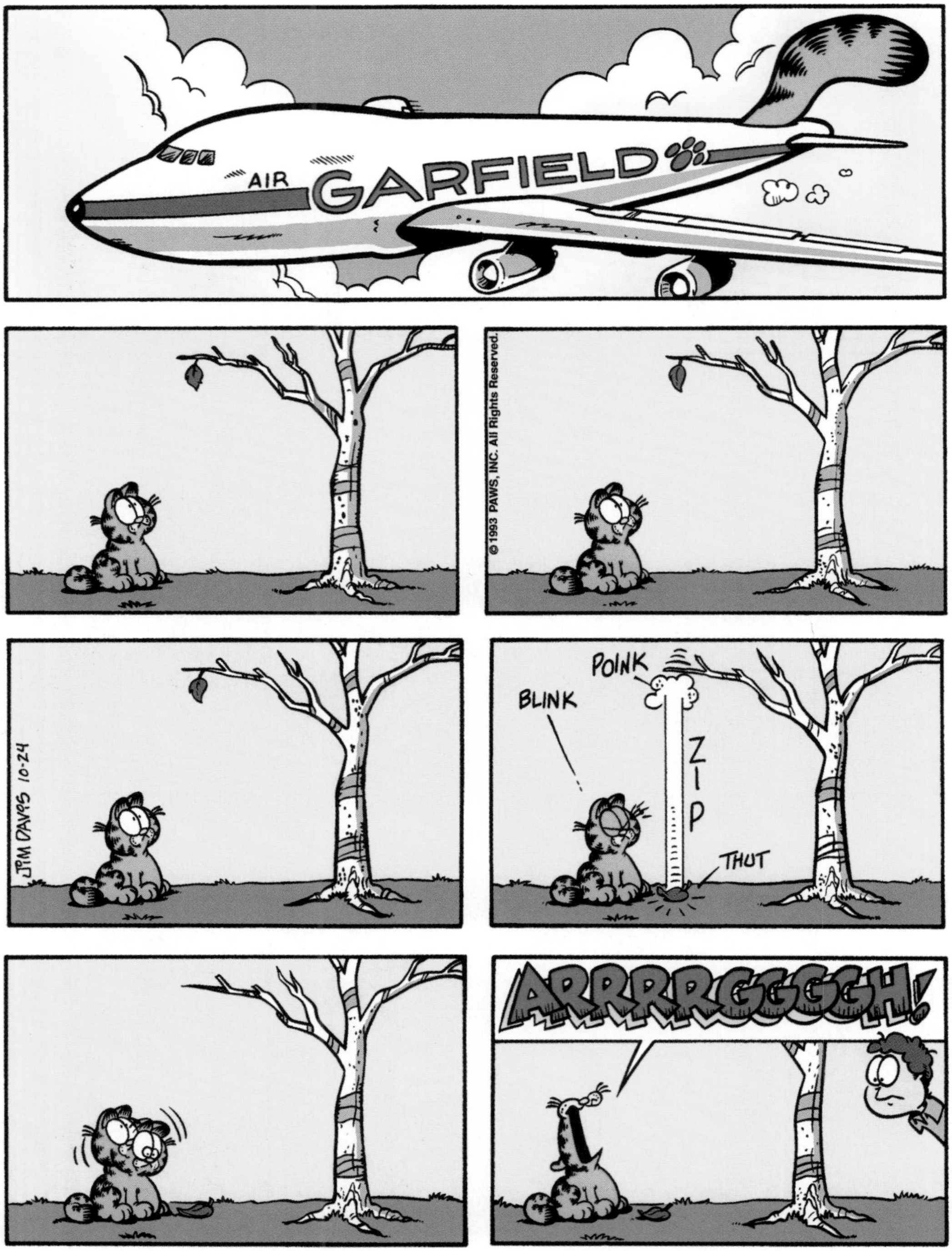
AIR GARFIELD
© 1993 PAWS, INC. All Rights Reserved.
JIM DAVIS 10-24
POINK
BLINK
ZIP
THUT
ARRRRGGGGH!

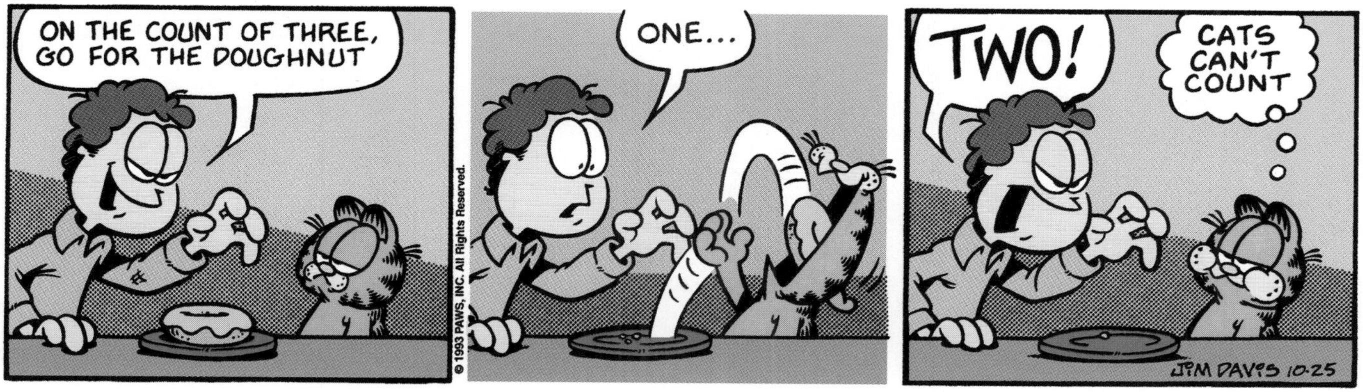
ON THE COUNT OF THREE, GO FOR THE DOUGHNUT
© 1993 PAWS, INC. All Rights Reserved.
ONE...
TWO!
CATS CAN'T COUNT
JIM DAVIS 10-25

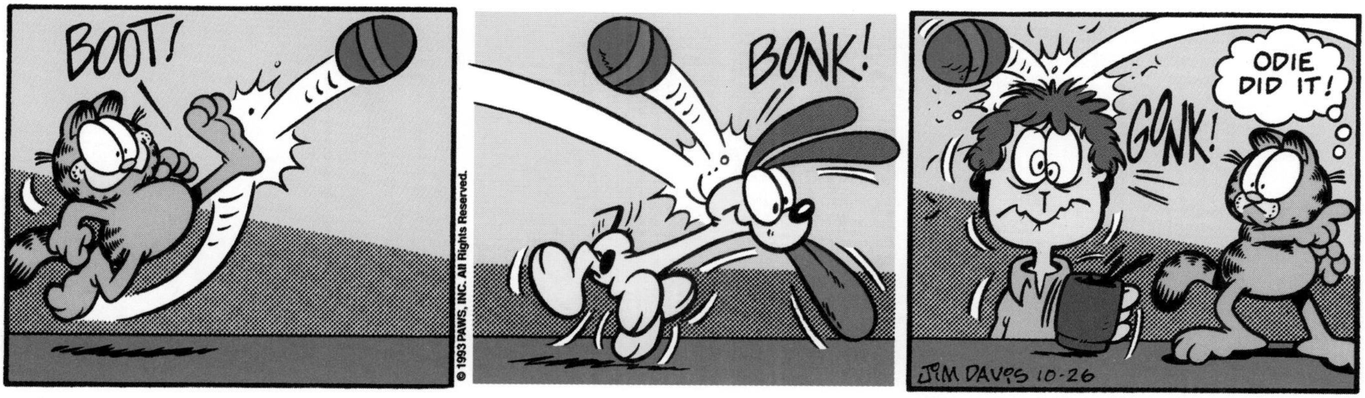
BOOT!
© 1993 PAWS, INC. All Rights Reserved.
BONK!
GONK!
ODIE DID IT!
JIM DAVIS 10-26

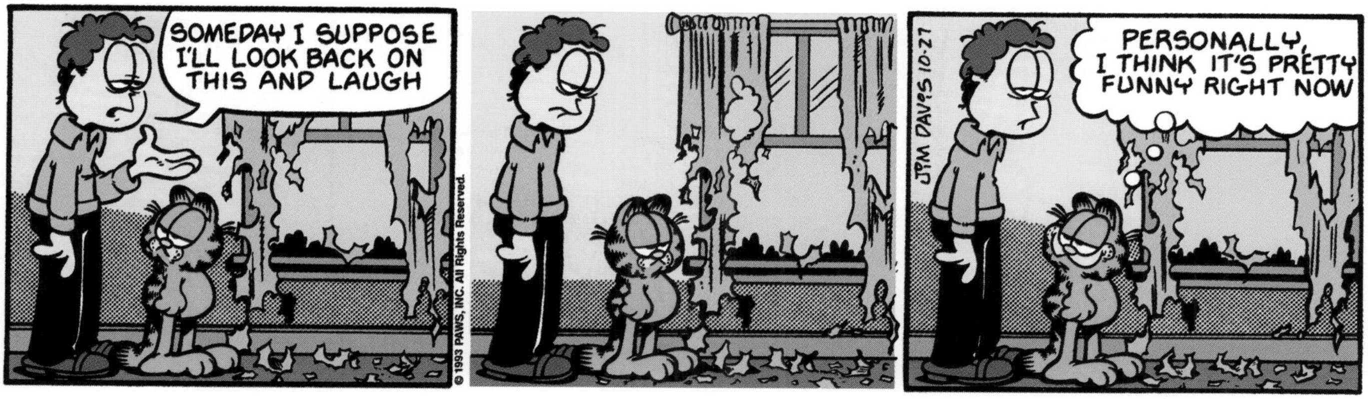
SOMEDAY I SUPPOSE I'LL LOOK BACK ON THIS AND LAUGH
© 1993 PAWS, INC. All Rights Reserved.
JIM DAVIS 10-27
PERSONALLY, I THINK IT'S PRETTY FUNNY RIGHT NOW

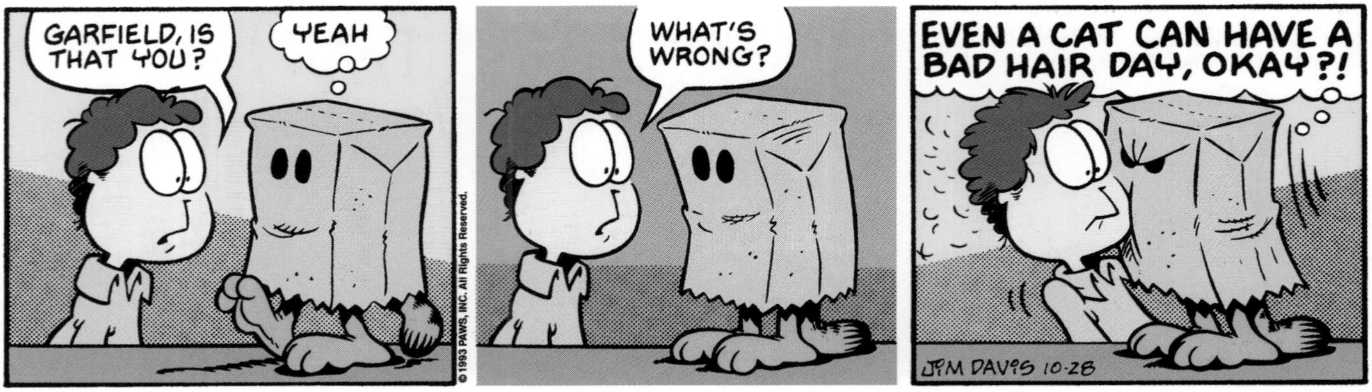
GARFIELD, IS THAT YOU?
YEAH
WHAT'S WRONG?
EVEN A CAT CAN HAVE A BAD HAIR DAY, OKAY?!
© 1993 PAWS, INC. All Rights Reserved.
JIM DAVIS 10-28

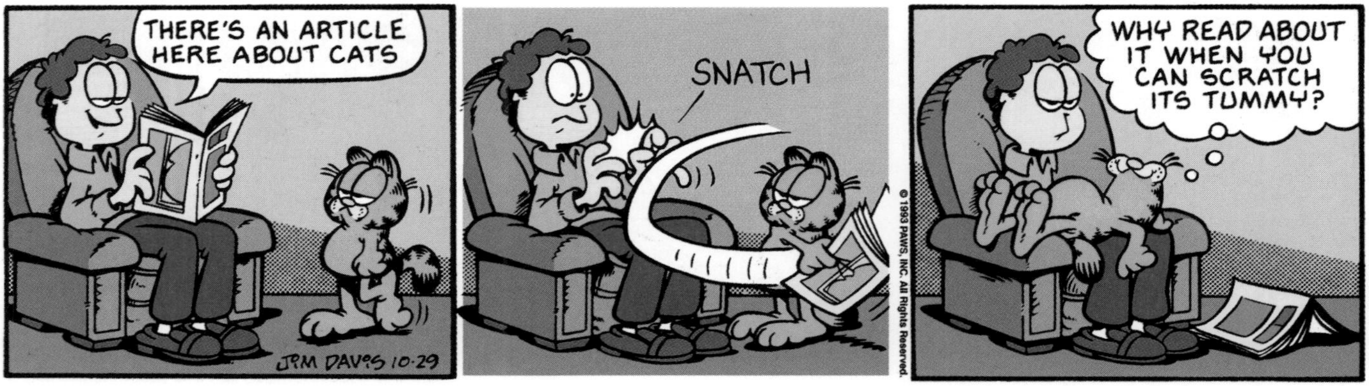
THERE'S AN ARTICLE HERE ABOUT CATS
JIM DAVIS 10-29
SNATCH
WHY READ ABOUT IT WHEN YOU CAN SCRATCH ITS TUMMY?
© 1993 PAWS, INC. All Rights Reserved.

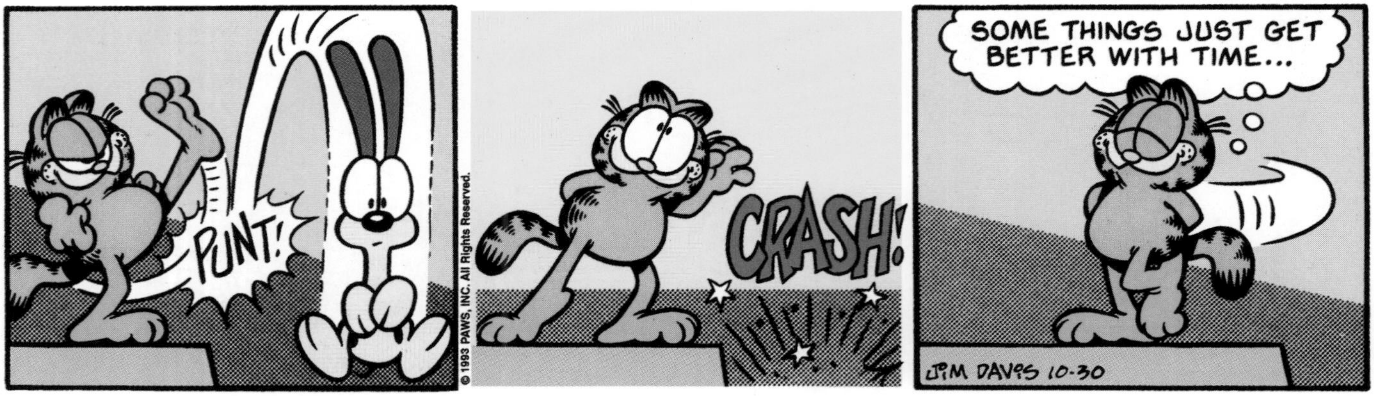
PUNT!
© 1993 PAWS, INC. All Rights Reserved.
CRASH!
SOME THINGS JUST GET BETTER WITH TIME...
JIM DAVIS 10-30

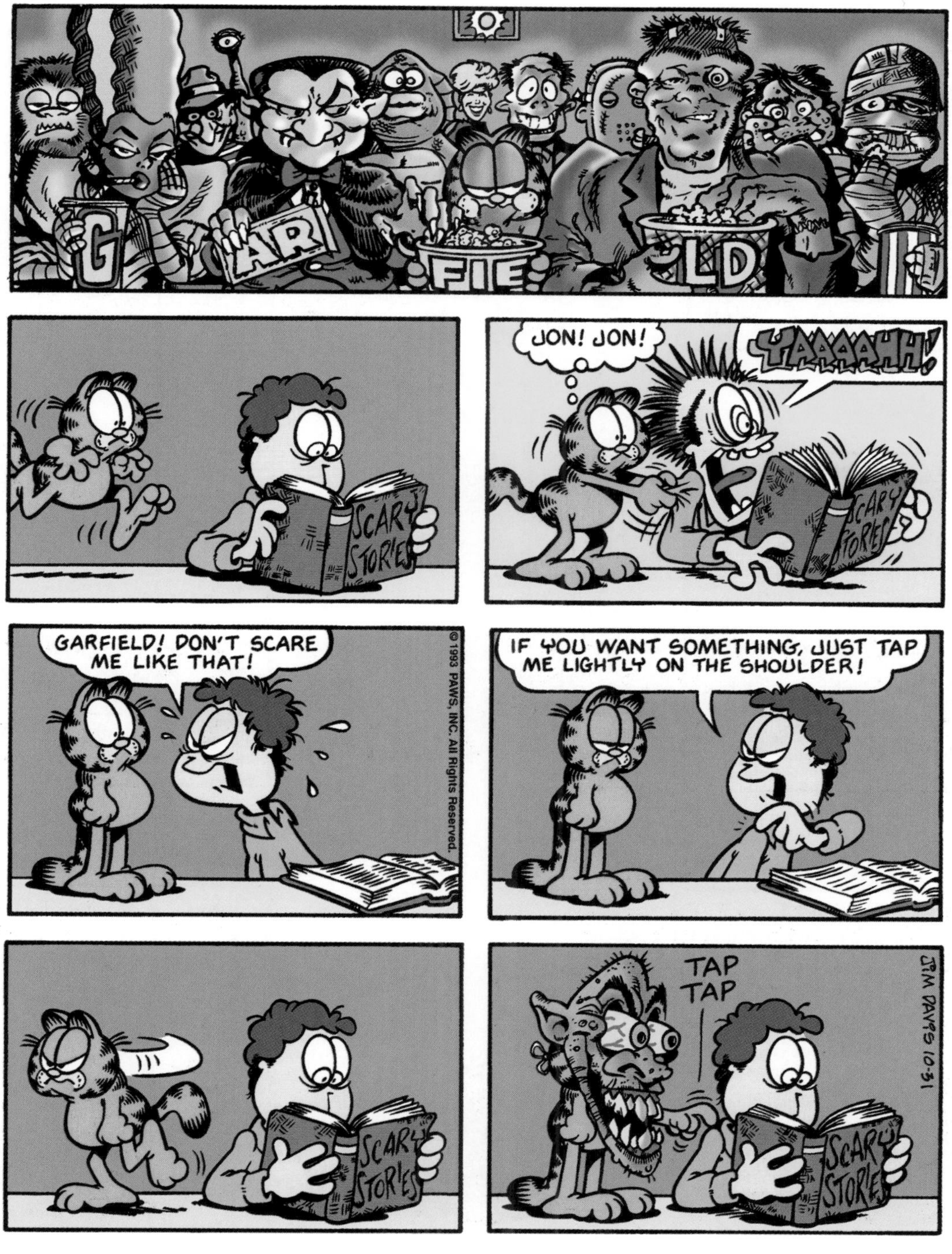
G AR FIE LD
SCARY STORIES
JON! JON!
YAAAAHH!
SCARY STORIES
GARFIELD! DON'T SCARE ME LIKE THAT!
© 1993 PAWS, INC. All Rights Reserved.
IF YOU WANT SOMETHING, JUST TAP ME LIGHTLY ON THE SHOULDER!
SCARY STORIES
TAP TAP
SCARY STORIES
JIM DAVIS 10-31

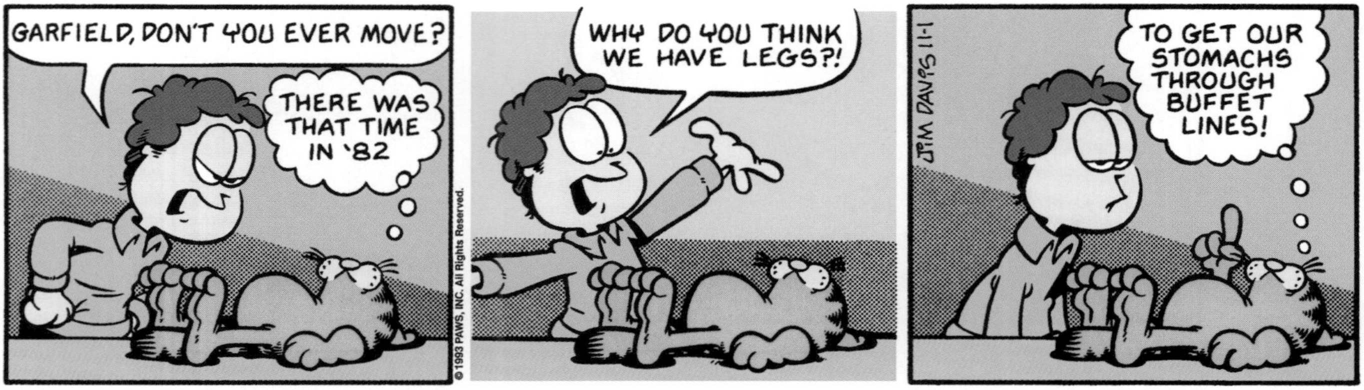
GARFIELD, DON'T YOU EVER MOVE?
THERE WAS THAT TIME IN '82
WHY DO YOU THINK WE HAVE LEGS?!
TO GET OUR STOMACHS THROUGH BUFFET LINES!
JIM DAVIS 11-1
© 1993 PAWS, INC. All Rights Reserved.

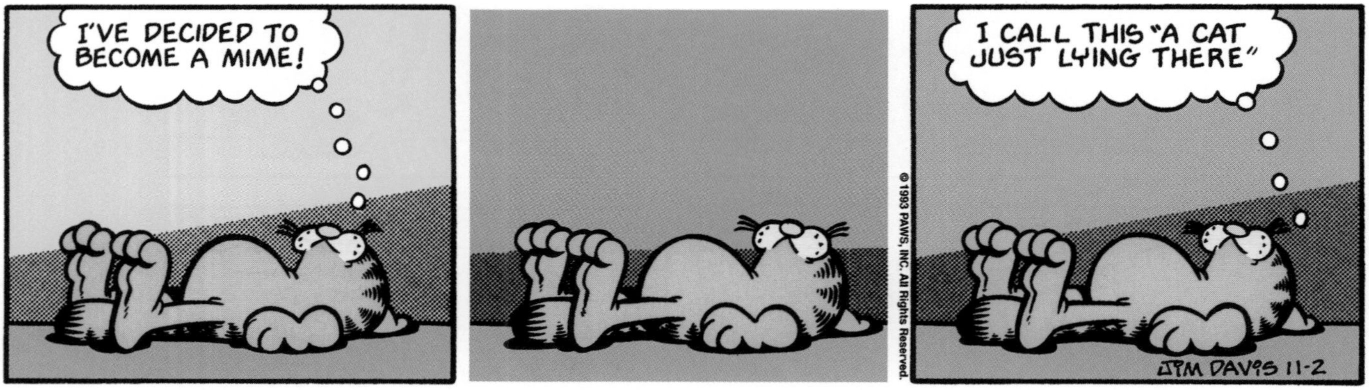
I'VE DECIDED TO BECOME A MIME!
I CALL THIS "A CAT JUST LYING THERE"
JIM DAVIS 11-2
© 1993 PAWS, INC. All Rights Reserved.

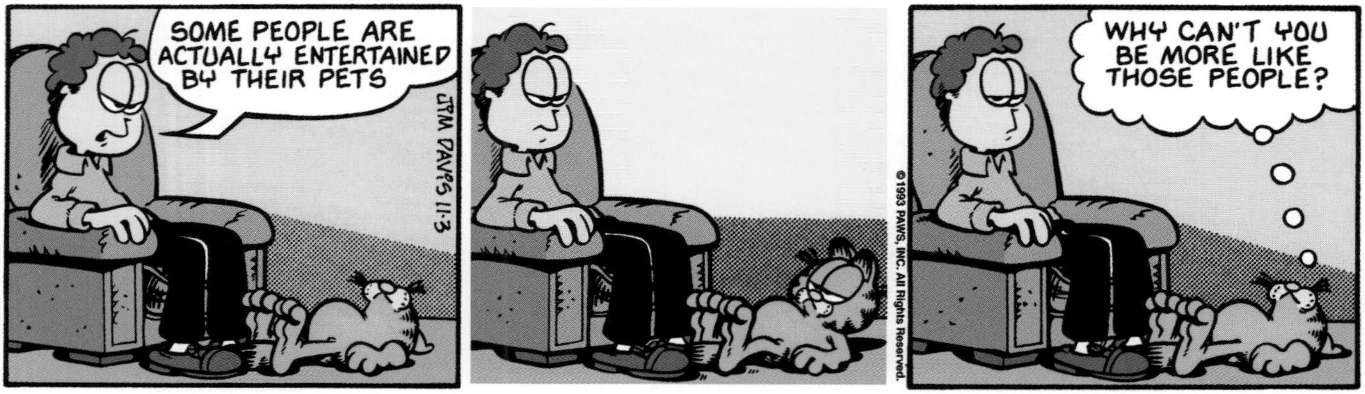
SOME PEOPLE ARE ACTUALLY ENTERTAINED BY THEIR PETS
WHY CAN'T YOU BE MORE LIKE THOSE PEOPLE?
JIM DAVIS 11-3
© 1993 PAWS, INC. All Rights Reserved.

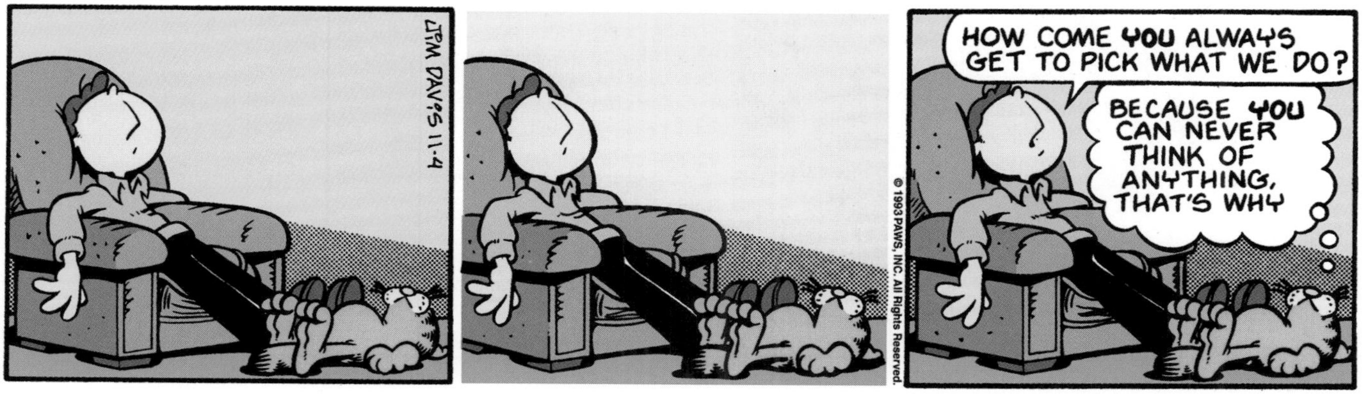
JIM DAVIS 11-4
© 1993 PAWS, INC. All Rights Reserved.
HOW COME YOU ALWAYS GET TO PICK WHAT WE DO?
BECAUSE YOU CAN NEVER THINK OF ANYTHING, THAT'S WHY

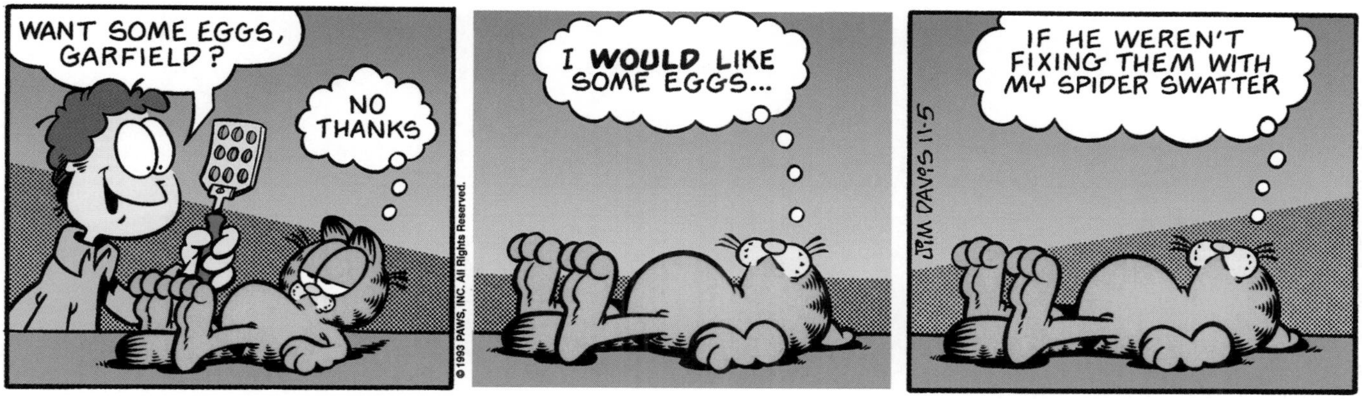
WANT SOME EGGS, GARFIELD?
NO THANKS
© 1993 PAWS, INC. All Rights Reserved.
I WOULD LIKE SOME EGGS...
JIM DAVIS 11-5
IF HE WEREN'T FIXING THEM WITH MY SPIDER SWATTER

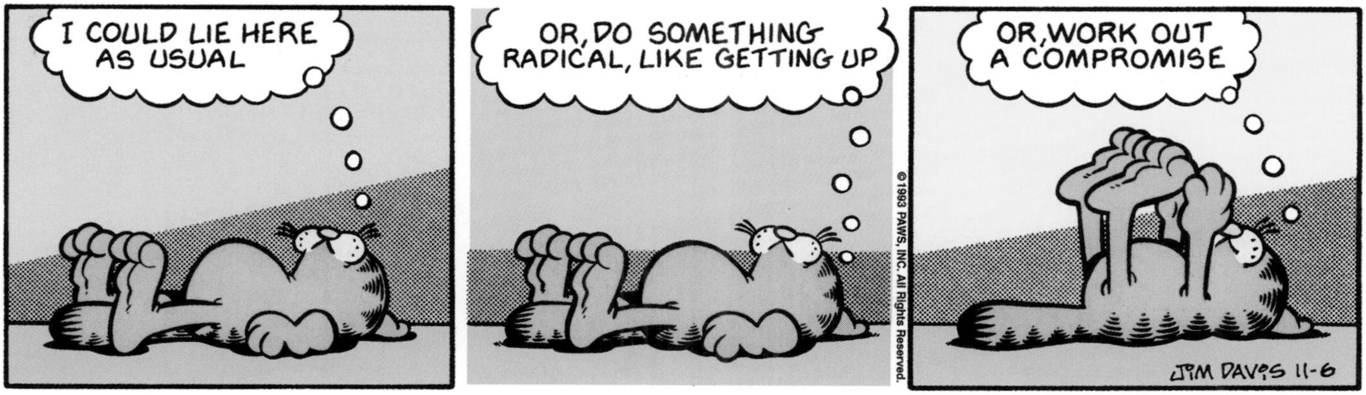
I COULD LIE HERE AS USUAL
OR, DO SOMETHING RADICAL, LIKE GETTING UP
© 1993 PAWS, INC. All Rights Reserved.
OR, WORK OUT A COMPROMISE
JIM DAVIS 11-6

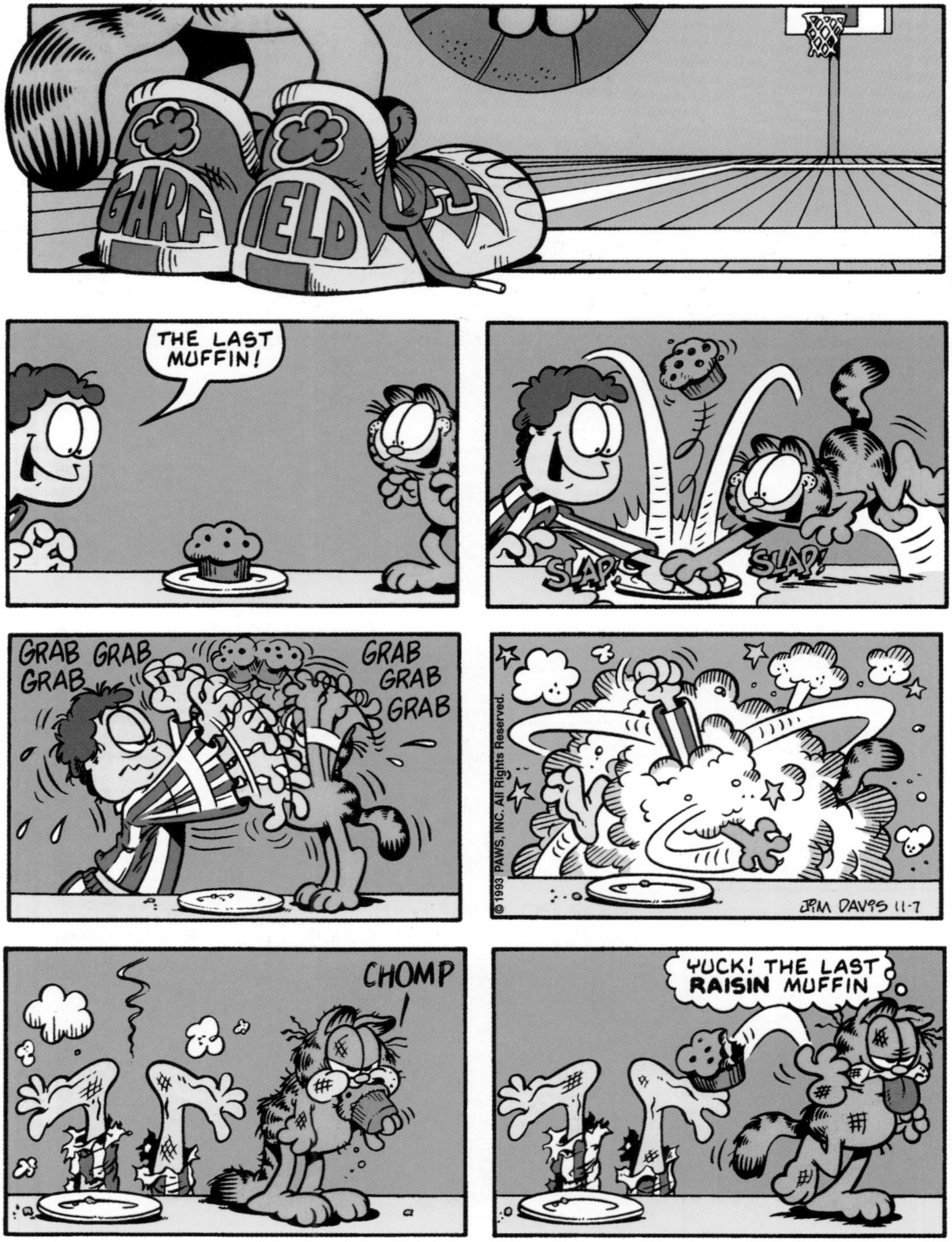
GARFIELD
THE LAST MUFFIN!
SLAP!
SLAP!
GRAB GRAB GRAB
GRAB GRAB GRAB
© 1993 PAWS, INC. All Rights Reserved.
JIM DAVIS 11-7
CHOMP
YUCK! THE LAST RAISIN MUFFIN

FETCH THE INVISIBLE BALL, ODIE!
THAT SHOULD KEEP HIM BUSY
JIM DAVIS 11-8
© 1993 PAWS, INC. All Rights Reserved.

GASP!
GARFI
AAARRRRGGGHHHHH
THUD!
GARFI
© 1993 PAWS, INC. All Rights Reserved.
GARFIELD, I JUST FED YOU A HALF HOUR AGO
DO YOU KNOW HOW LONG THAT IS IN CAT MINUTES?
GARF
JIM DAVIS 11-9

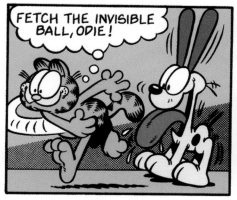

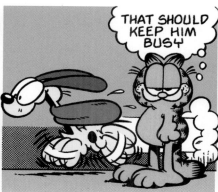

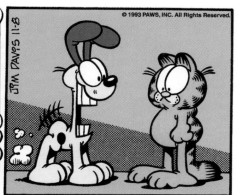

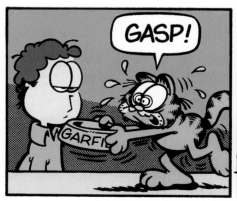

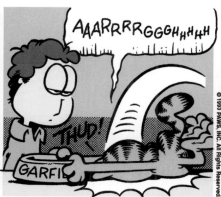

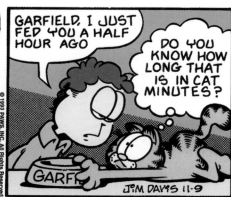

GARFIELD PRODUCTS YOU WON'T BE SEEING...

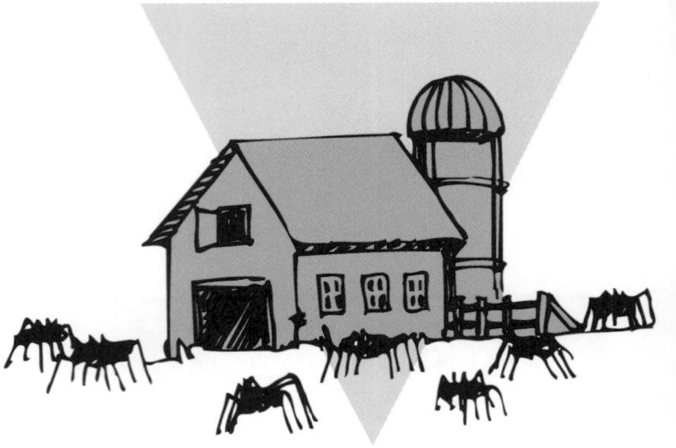

GARFIELD'S
TARANTULA FARM

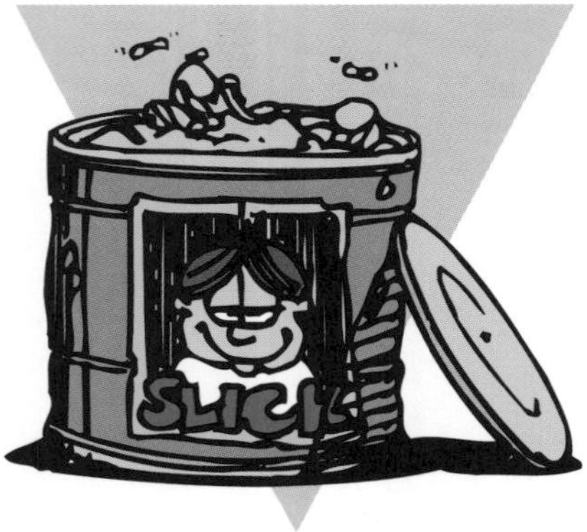
SLICK

GARFIELD'S
STYLING LARD

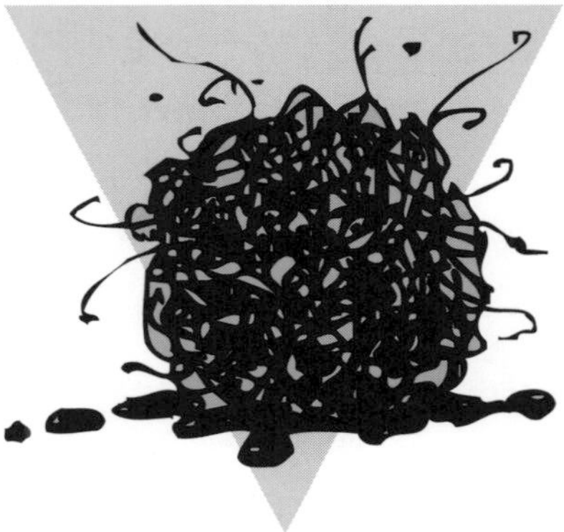

GARFIELD'S
"HAIRBALL O' FUN"

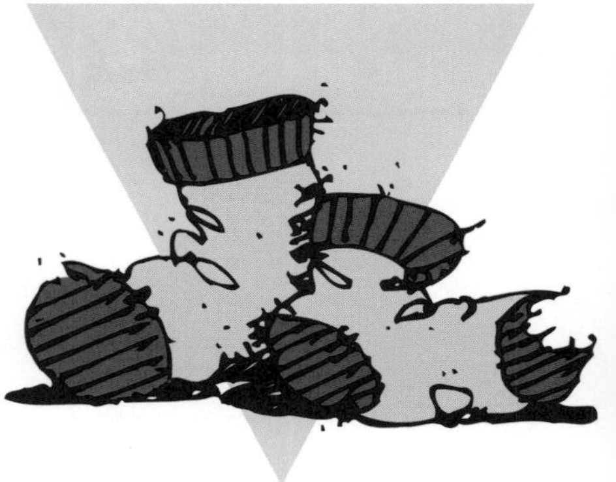

GARFIELD'S
EDIBLE SWEAT SOCKS

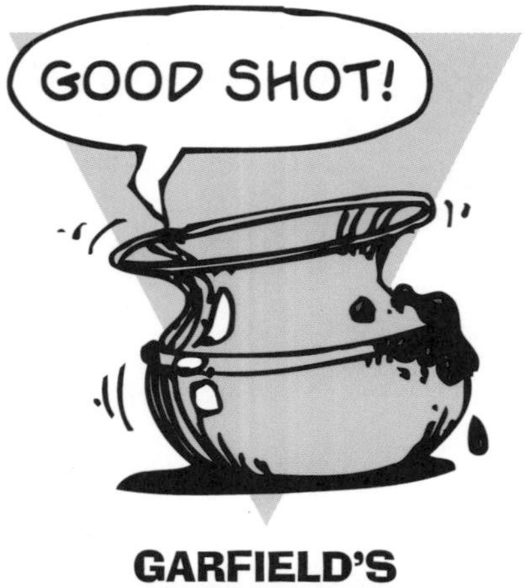
GOOD SHOT!

GARFIELD'S
TALKING SPITTOON

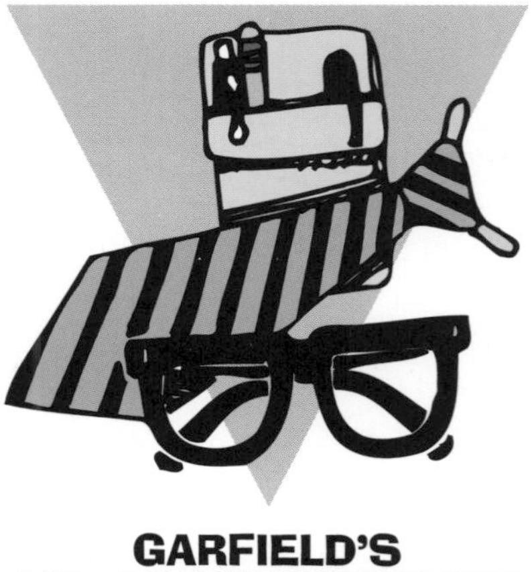

GARFIELD'S
"JR. ACCOUNTANT" KIT

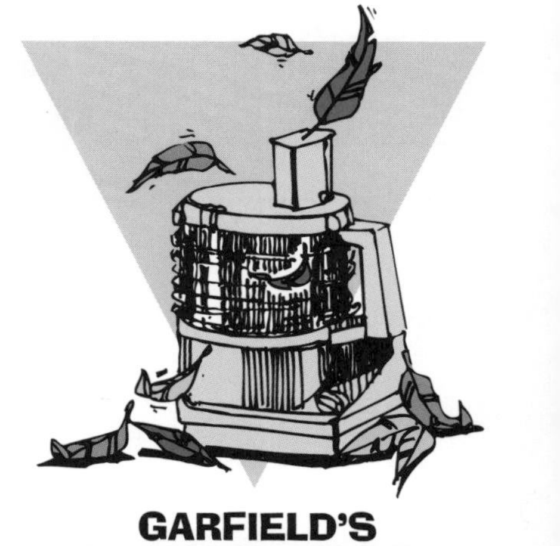

GARFIELD'S
BIRD PROCESSOR

Garfield
dishes
it out

BY JIM DAVIS

Ballantine Books • New York

GARFIELD'S TOP TEN COUNTRY PET TUNES

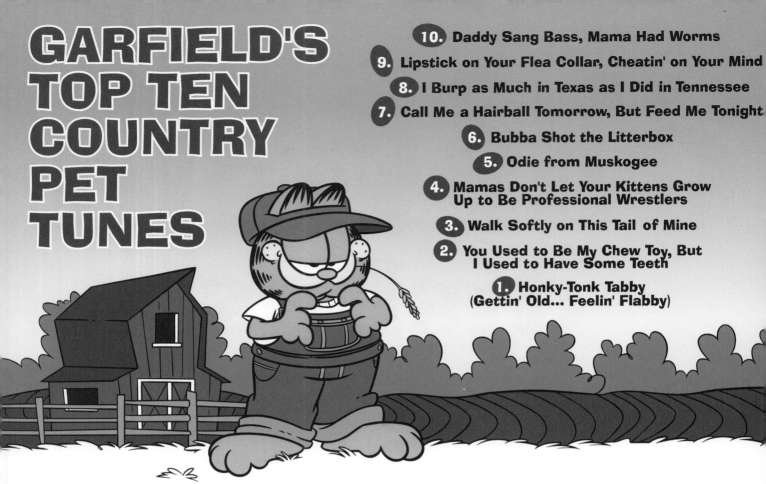

10. Daddy Sang Bass, Mama Had Worms
9. Lipstick on Your Flea Collar, Cheatin' on Your Mind
8. I Burp as Much in Texas as I Did in Tennessee
7. Call Me a Hairball Tomorrow, But Feed Me Tonight
6. Bubba Shot the Litterbox
5. Odie from Muskogee
4. Mamas Don't Let Your Kittens Grow Up to Be Professional Wrestlers
3. Walk Softly on This Tail of Mine
2. You Used to Be My Chew Toy, But I Used to Have Some Teeth
1. Honky-Tonk Tabby (Gettin' Old... Feelin' Flabby)

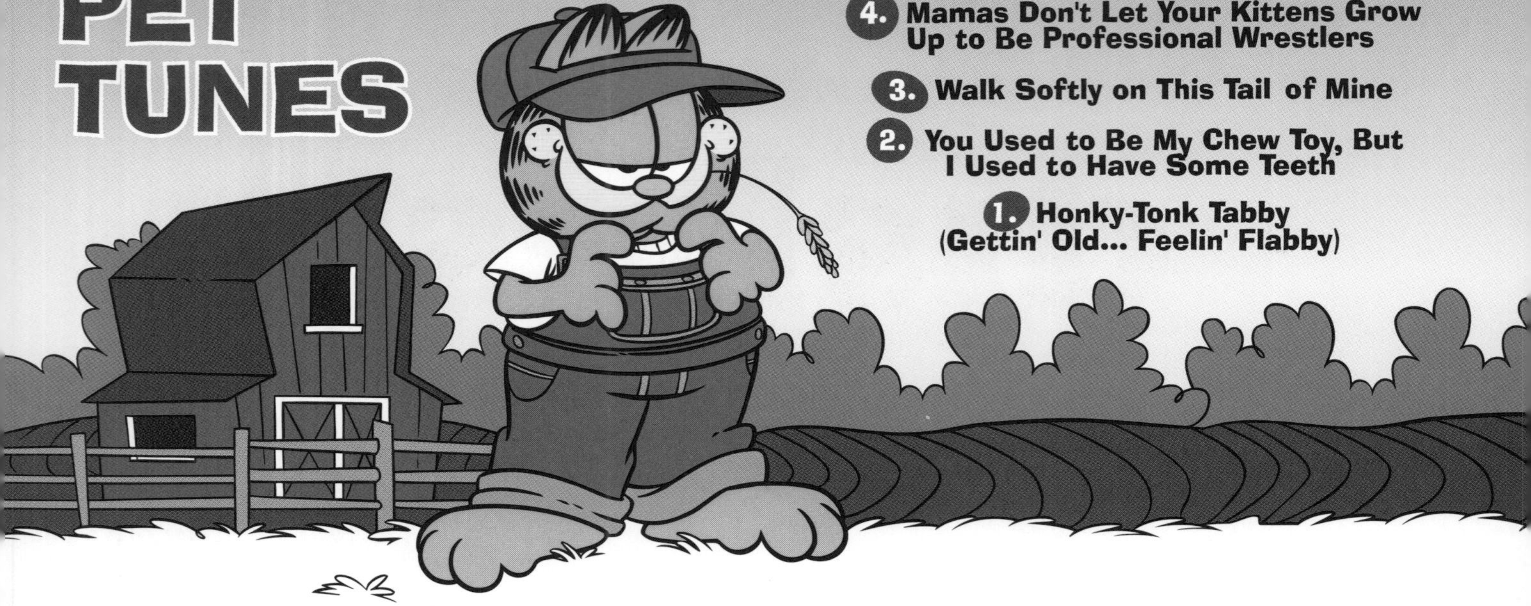

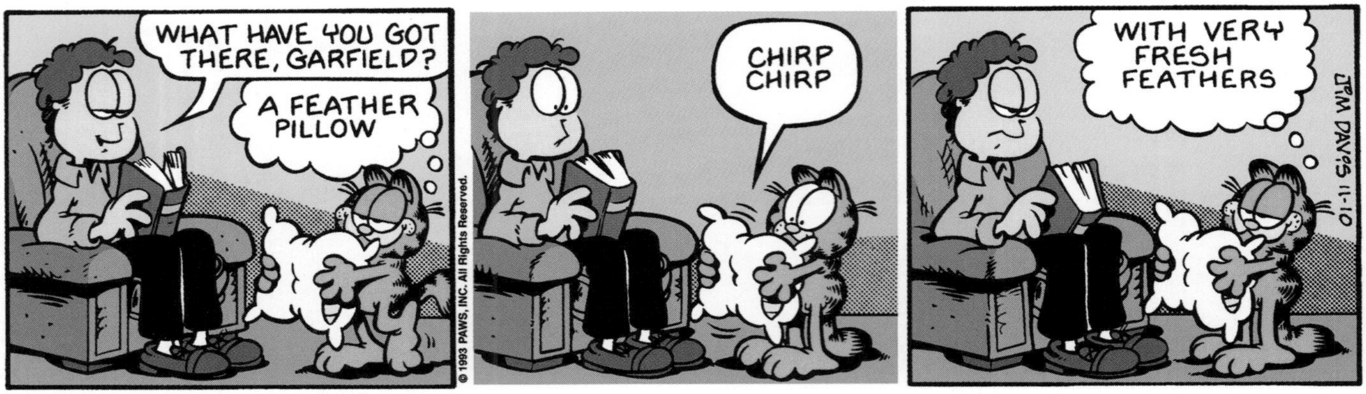
WHAT HAVE YOU GOT THERE, GARFIELD?
A FEATHER PILLOW
CHIRP CHIRP
WITH VERY FRESH FEATHERS
JIM DAVIS 11-10

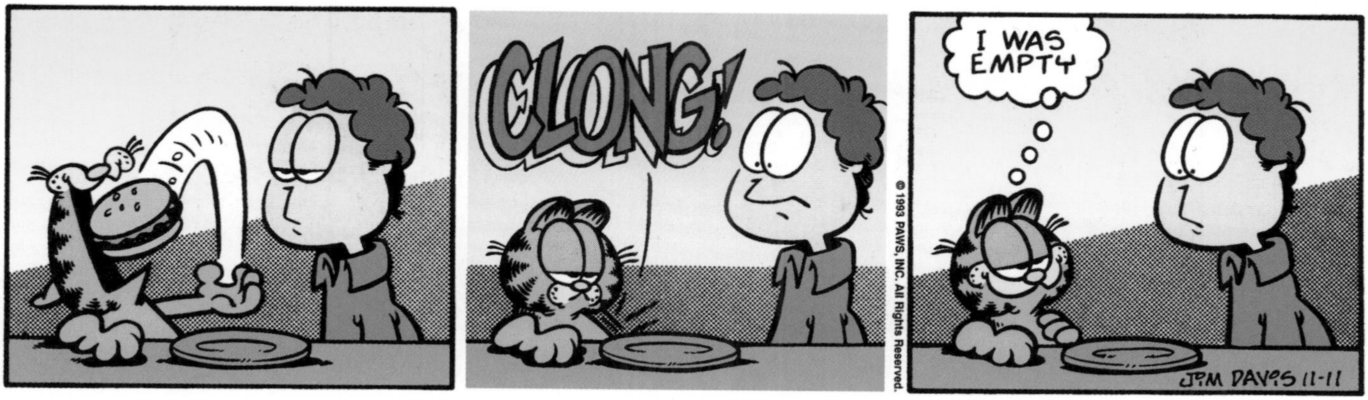
CLONG!
I WAS EMPTY
JIM DAVIS 11-11

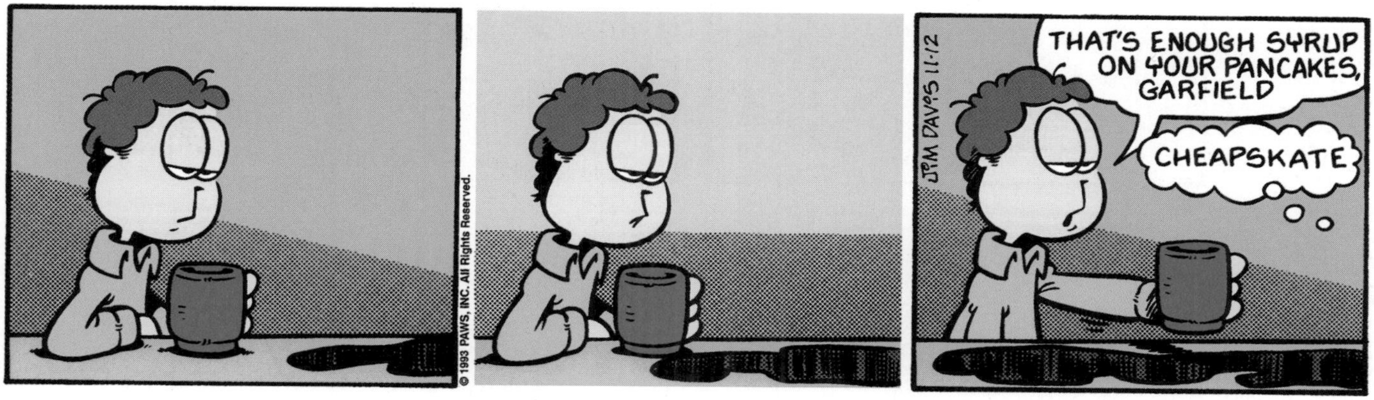
JIM DAVIS 11-12
THAT'S ENOUGH SYRUP ON YOUR PANCAKES, GARFIELD
CHEAPSKATE

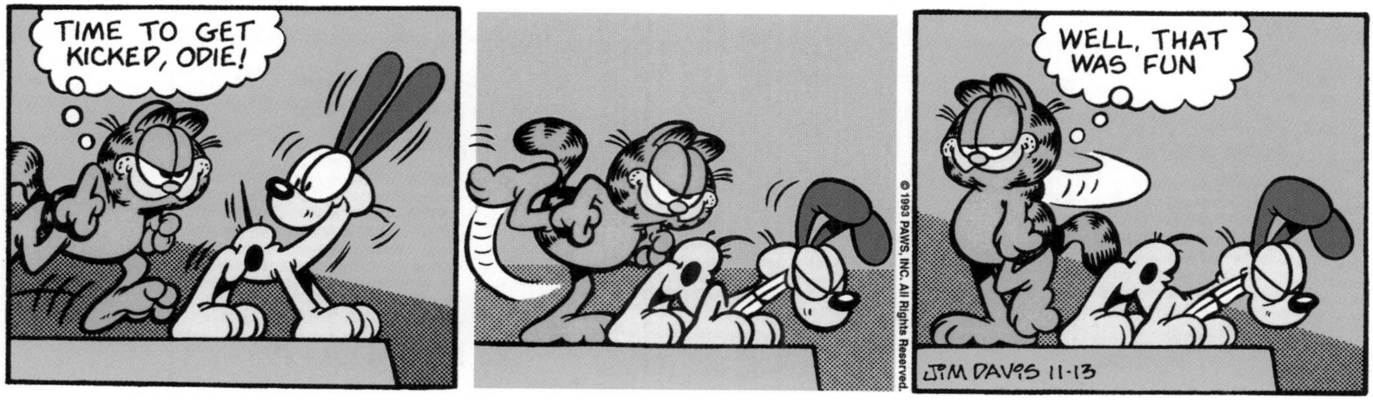
TIME TO GET KICKED, ODIE!
WELL, THAT WAS FUN
JIM DAVIS 11-13

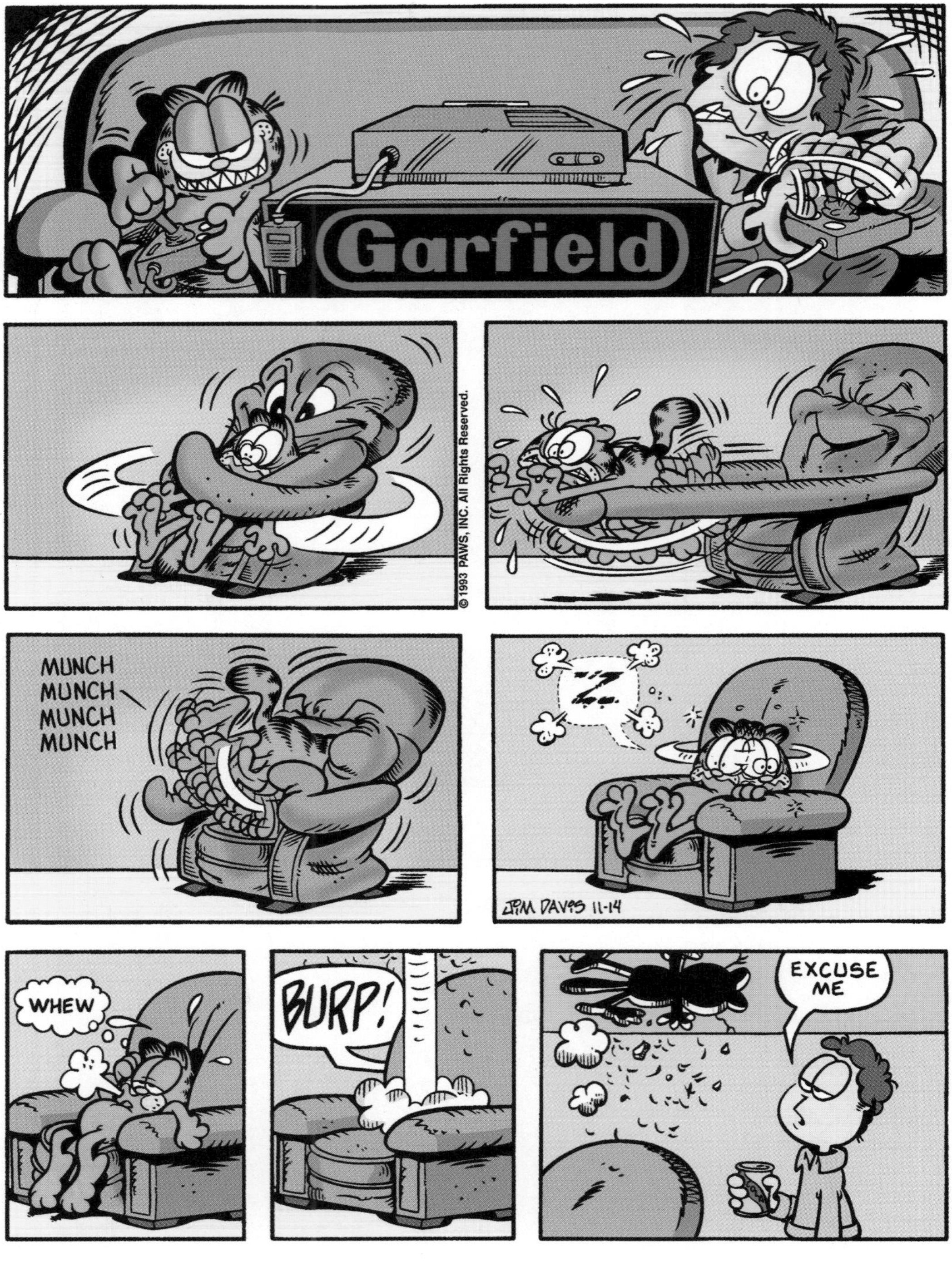
Garfield
© 1993 PAWS, INC. All Rights Reserved.
MUNCH MUNCH MUNCH MUNCH
JIM DAVIS 11-14
WHEW
BURP!
EXCUSE ME

I CAN'T DECIDE WHAT TO WATCH
CLICK CLICK CLICK
CLICK CLICK CLICK CLICK
WHICH IS PRETTY ENTERTAINING
CLICK CLICK CLICK
© 1993 PAWS, INC. All Rights Reserved.
JIM DAVIS 11-15

DO YOU WATCH TOO MUCH TELEVISION?
WAY, WAY TOO MUCH?
IF SO, THANK YOU FROM THE BOTTOM OF OUR HEARTS
YOU'RE WELCOME
© 1993 PAWS, INC. All Rights Reserved.
JIM DAVIS 11-16

ARF! ARF!
WHAT IS IT, BOY?
DID TIMMY FALL DOWN THE WELL AGAIN?
ARF!
LEAVE HIM DOWN THERE
LEAD ME TO HIM!
ARF!
GOOD THINKING! YOU CAN TOSS THE DOG IN TOO!
© 1993 PAWS, INC. All Rights Reserved.
JIM DAVIS 11-17

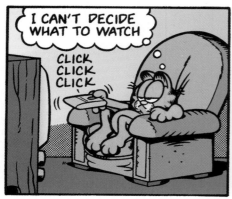

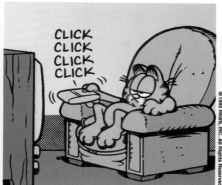

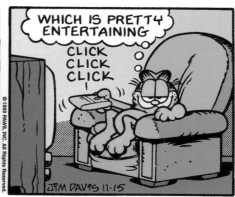

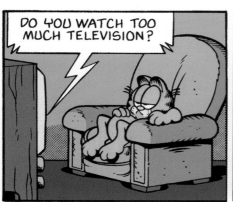

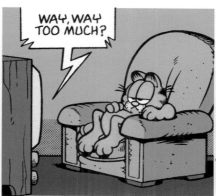

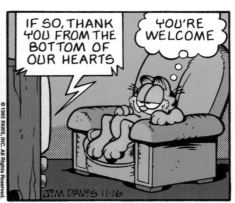

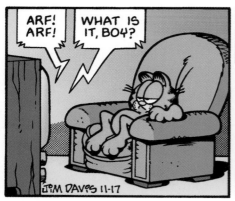

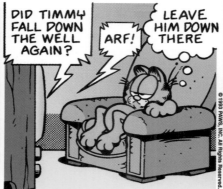

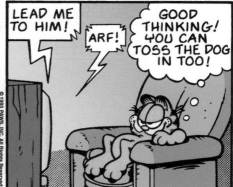

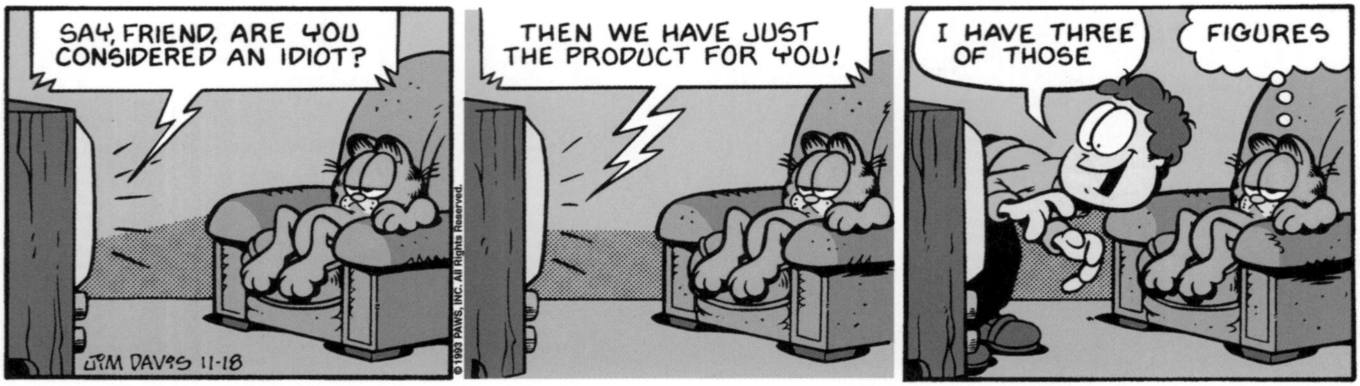
SAY, FRIEND, ARE YOU CONSIDERED AN IDIOT?
JIM DAVIS 11-18
© 1993 PAWS, INC. All Rights Reserved.
THEN WE HAVE JUST THE PRODUCT FOR YOU!
I HAVE THREE OF THOSE
FIGURES

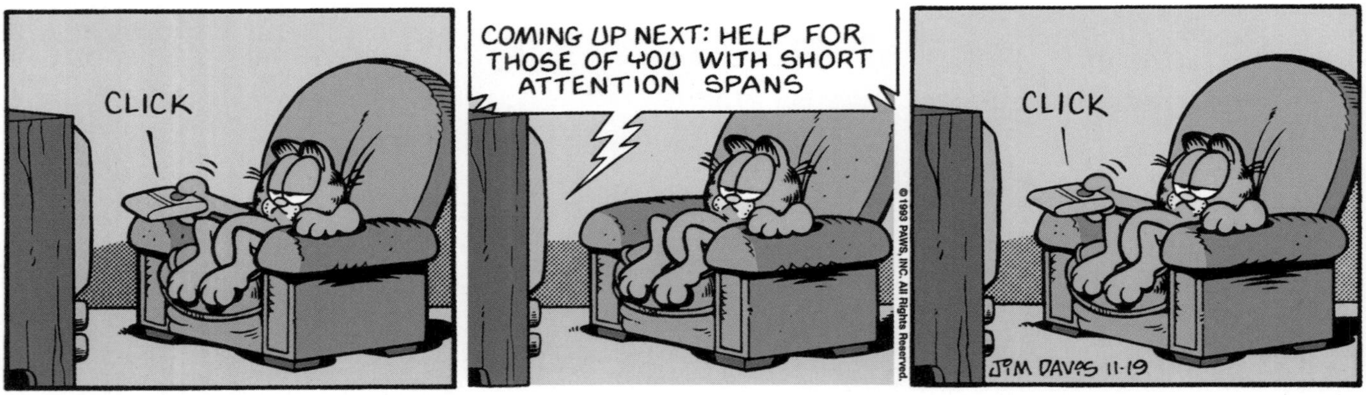
CLICK
COMING UP NEXT: HELP FOR THOSE OF YOU WITH SHORT ATTENTION SPANS
© 1993 PAWS, INC. All Rights Reserved.
CLICK
JIM DAVIS 11-19

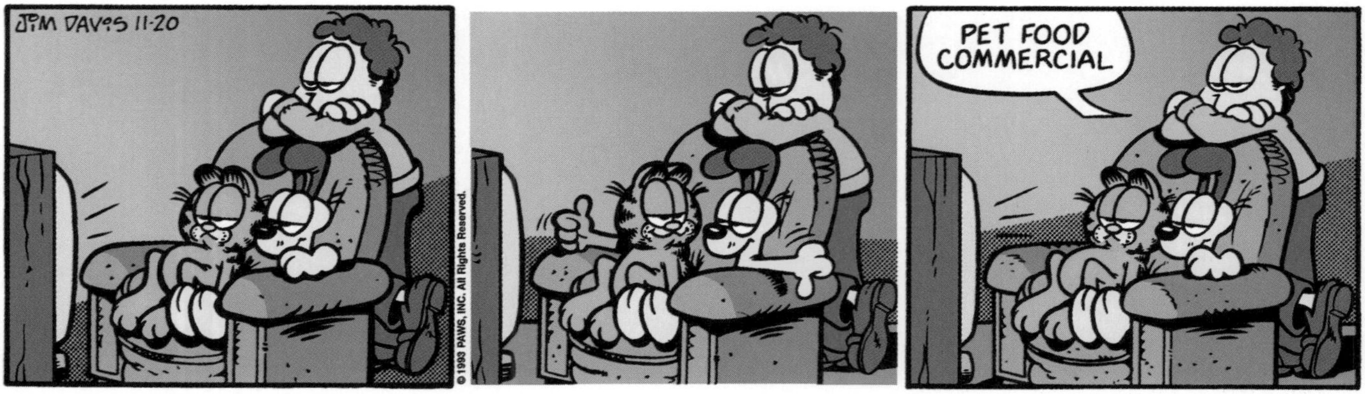
JIM DAVIS 11-20
© 1993 PAWS, INC. All Rights Reserved.
PET FOOD COMMERCIAL

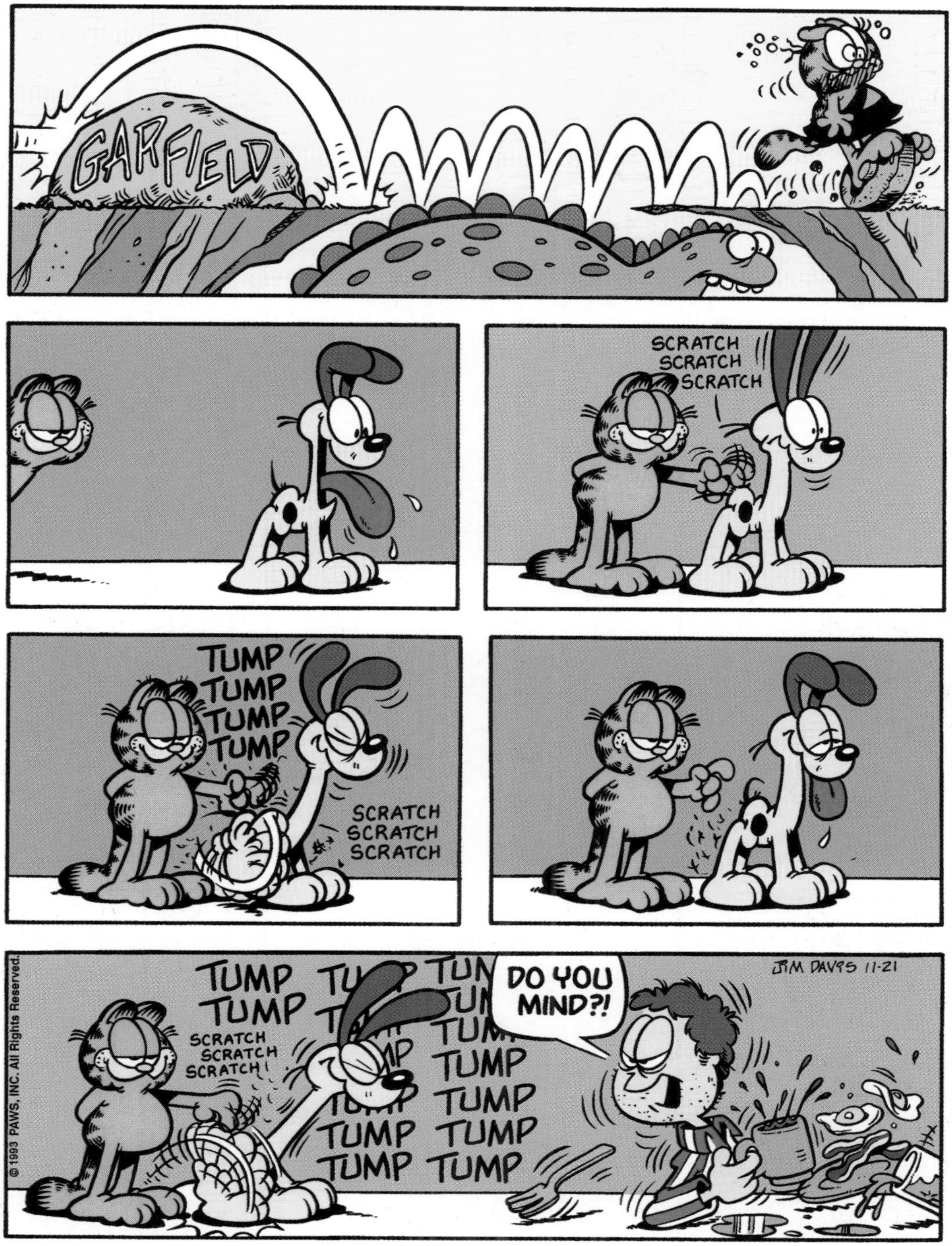
GARFIELD
SCRATCH
SCRATCH
SCRATCH
TUMP
TUMP
TUMP
TUMP
TUMP
SCRATCH
SCRATCH
SCRATCH
TUMP
TUMP
SCRATCH
SCRATCH
SCRATCH
TUMP TUMP TUMP TUMP
TUMP TUMP TUMP
DO YOU MIND?!
JIM DAVIS 11-21

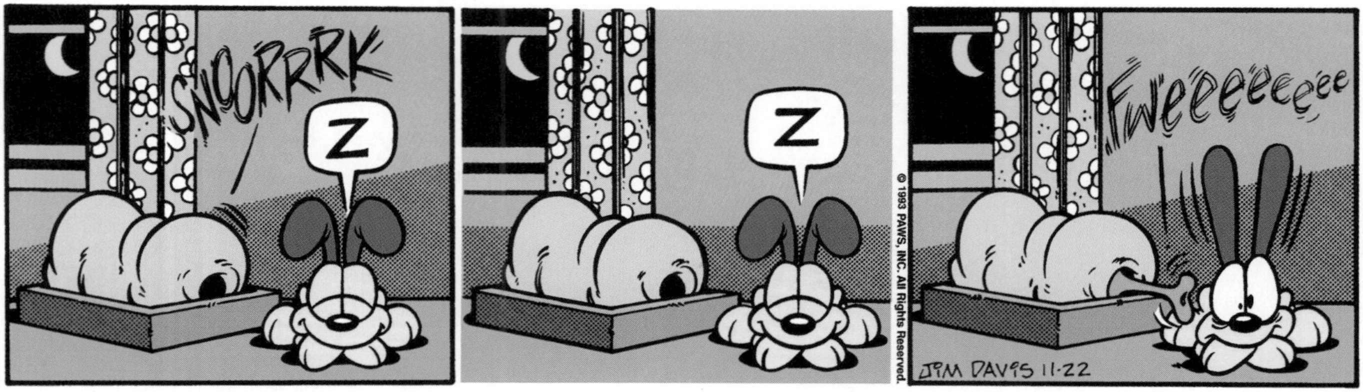
SNOORRRK
Z
Z
Fweeeeeeee
© 1993 PAWS, INC. All Rights Reserved.
JIM DAVIS 11-22

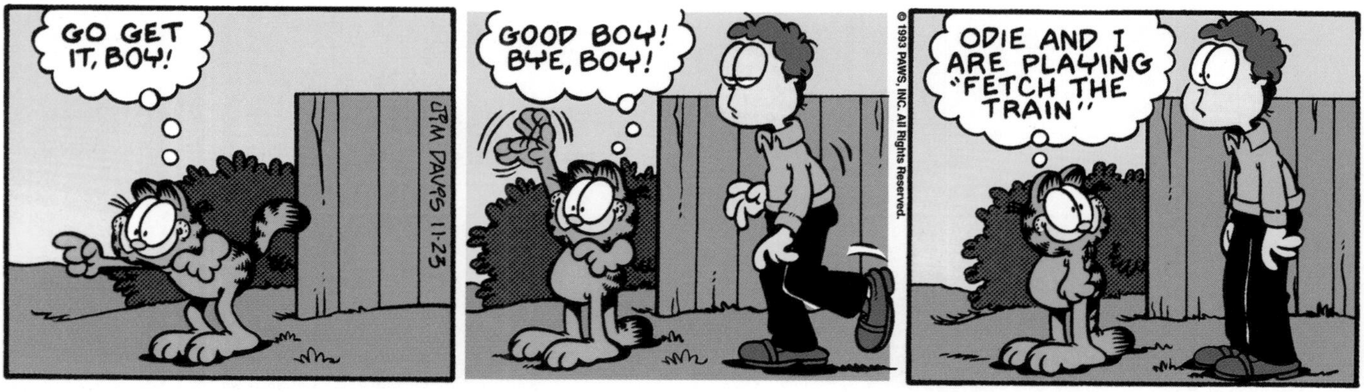
GO GET IT, BOY!
JIM DAVIS 11-23
GOOD BOY! BYE, BOY!
© 1993 PAWS, INC. All Rights Reserved.
ODIE AND I ARE PLAYING "FETCH THE TRAIN"

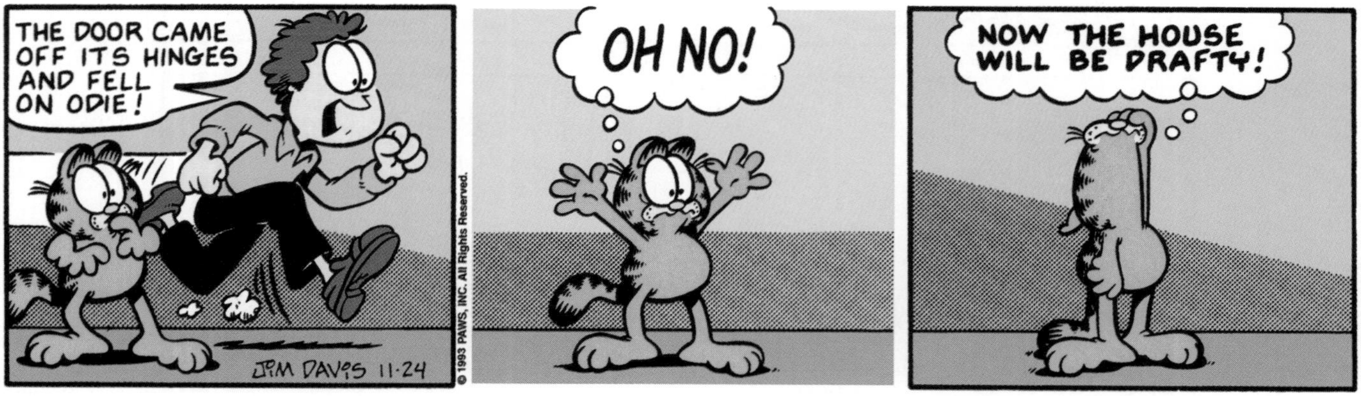
THE DOOR CAME OFF ITS HINGES AND FELL ON ODIE!
JIM DAVIS 11-24
© 1993 PAWS, INC. All Rights Reserved.
OH NO!
NOW THE HOUSE WILL BE DRAFTY!

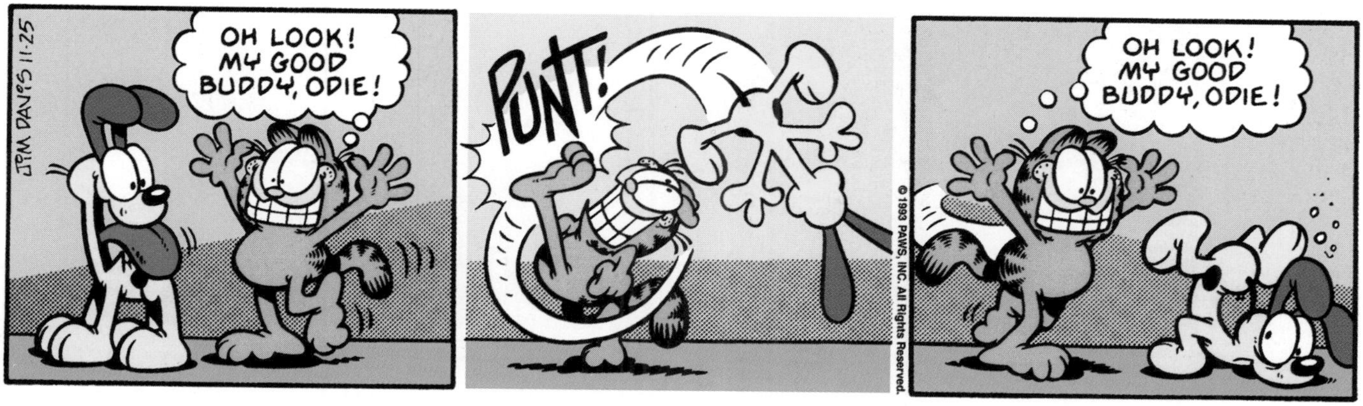
JIM DAVIS 11-25
OH LOOK! MY GOOD BUDDY, ODIE!
PUNT!
© 1993 PAWS, INC. All Rights Reserved.
OH LOOK! MY GOOD BUDDY, ODIE!

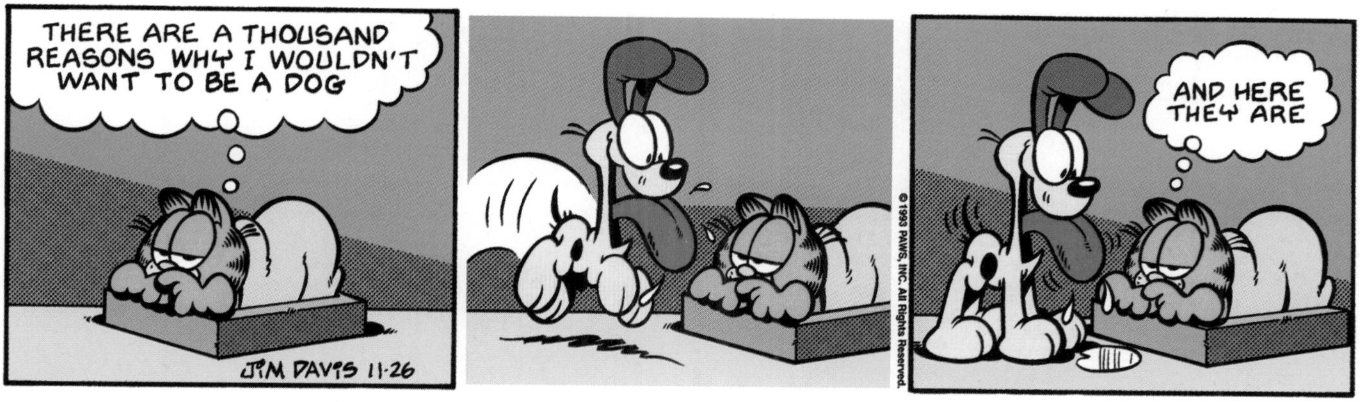
THERE ARE A THOUSAND REASONS WHY I WOULDN'T WANT TO BE A DOG
JIM DAVIS 11-26
© 1993 PAWS, INC. All Rights Reserved.
AND HERE THEY ARE

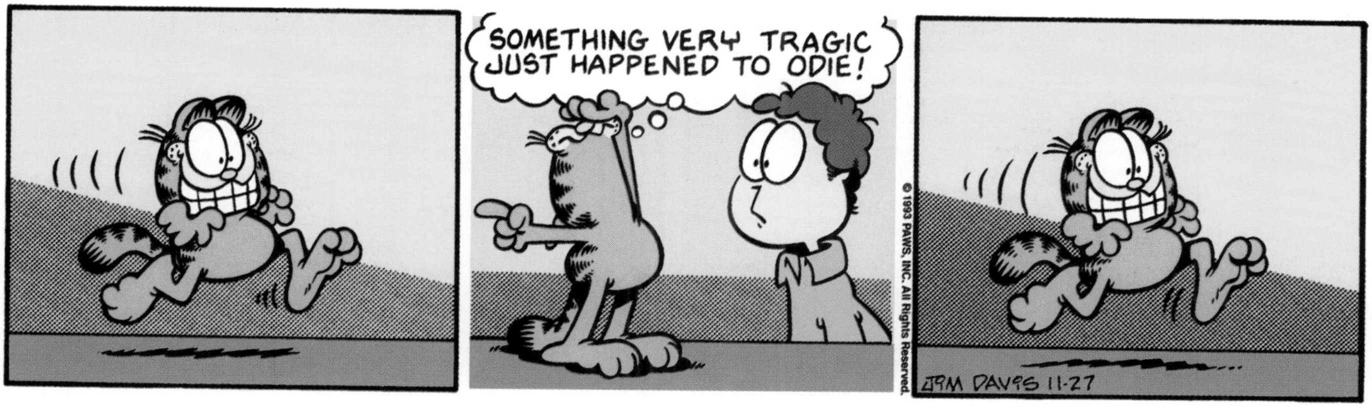
SOMETHING VERY TRAGIC JUST HAPPENED TO ODIE!
© 1993 PAWS, INC. All Rights Reserved.
JIM DAVIS 11-27

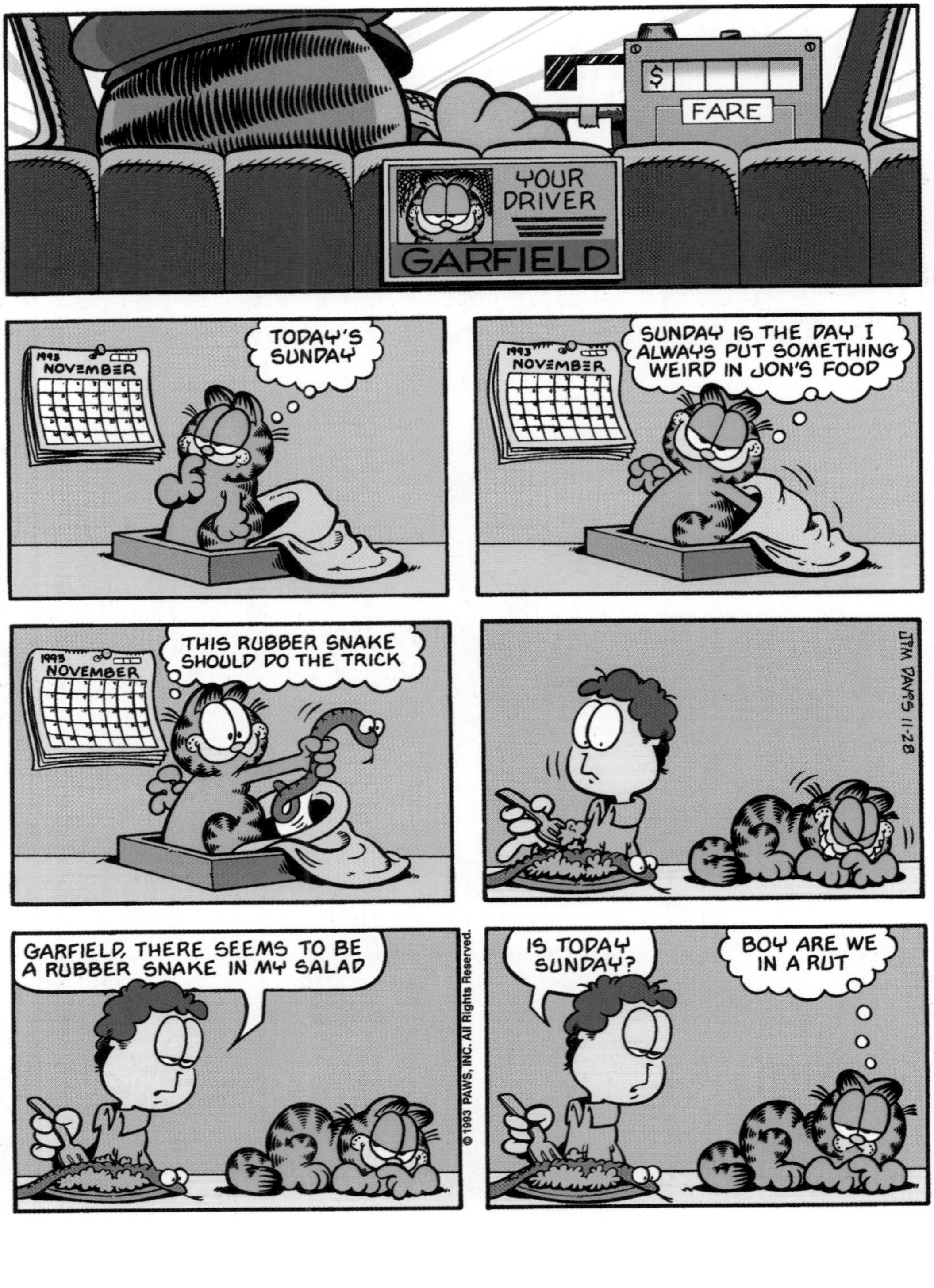
$
FARE
YOUR DRIVER
GARFIELD
1993 NOVEMBER
TODAY'S SUNDAY
SUNDAY IS THE DAY I ALWAYS PUT SOMETHING WEIRD IN JON'S FOOD
THIS RUBBER SNAKE SHOULD DO THE TRICK
JIM DAVIS 11-28
GARFIELD, THERE SEEMS TO BE A RUBBER SNAKE IN MY SALAD
IS TODAY SUNDAY?
BOY ARE WE IN A RUT

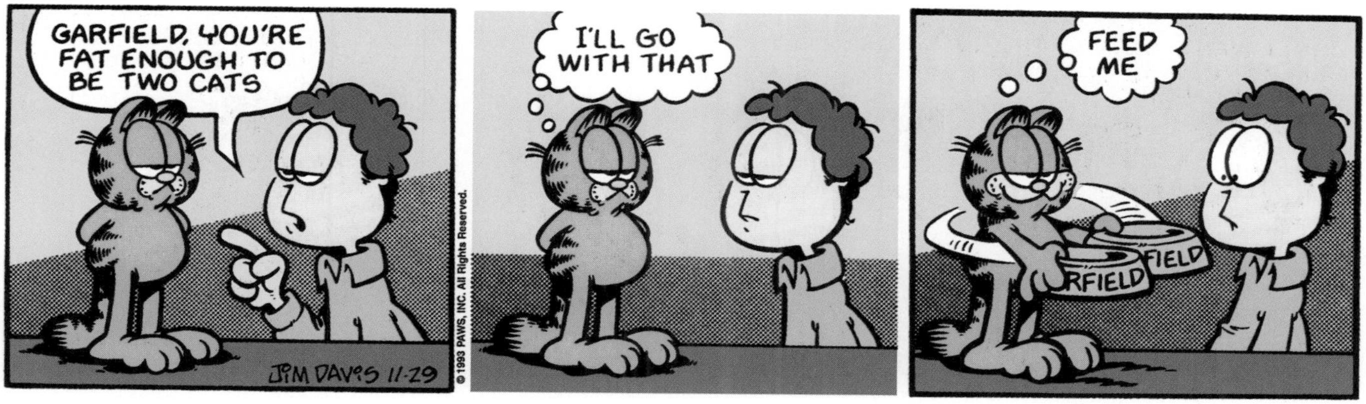
GARFIELD, YOU'RE FAT ENOUGH TO BE TWO CATS
JIM DAVIS 11-29
© 1993 PAWS, INC. All Rights Reserved.
I'LL GO WITH THAT
FEED ME
RFIELD
FIELD

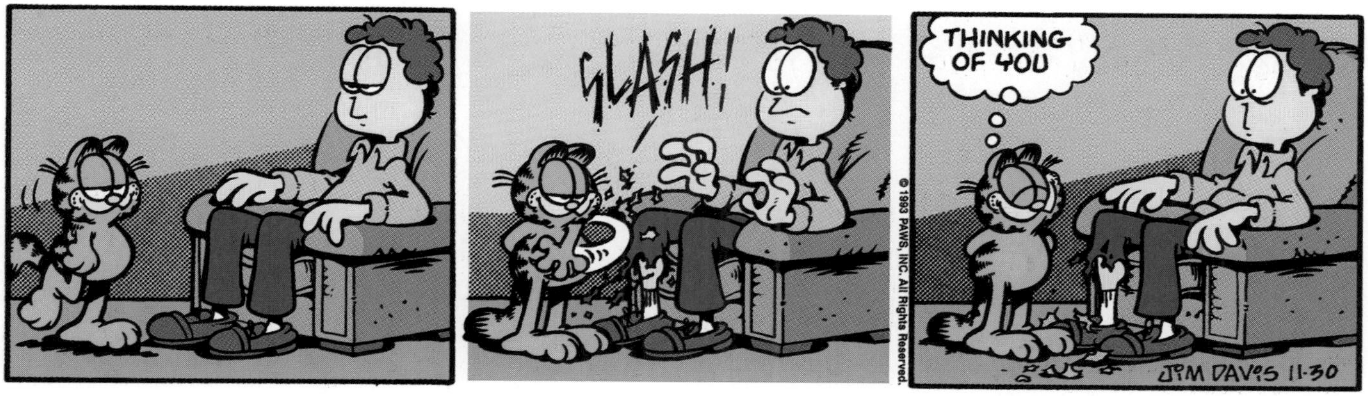
SLASH!
© 1993 PAWS, INC. All Rights Reserved.
THINKING OF YOU
JIM DAVIS 11-30

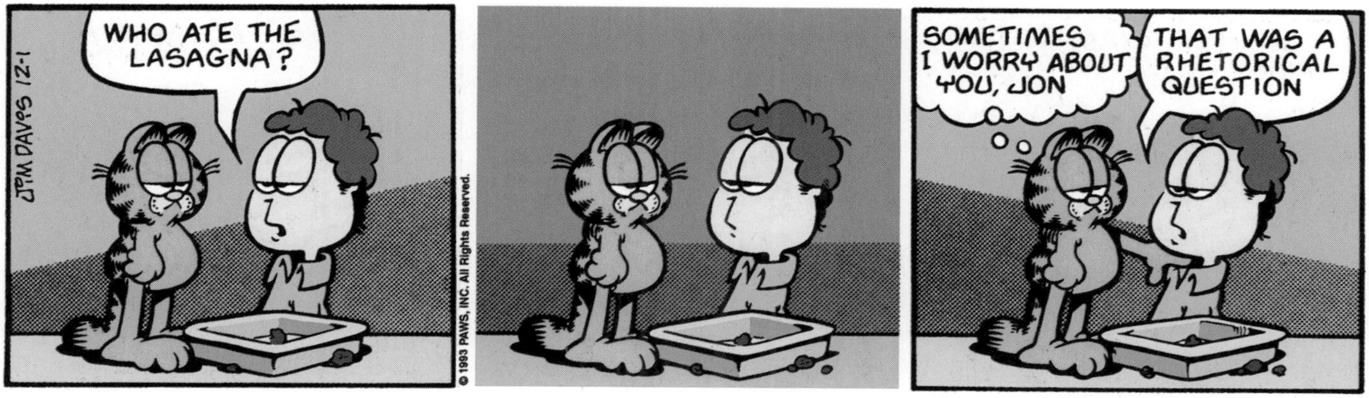
JIM DAVIS 12-1
WHO ATE THE LASAGNA?
© 1993 PAWS, INC. All Rights Reserved.
SOMETIMES I WORRY ABOUT YOU, JON
THAT WAS A RHETORICAL QUESTION

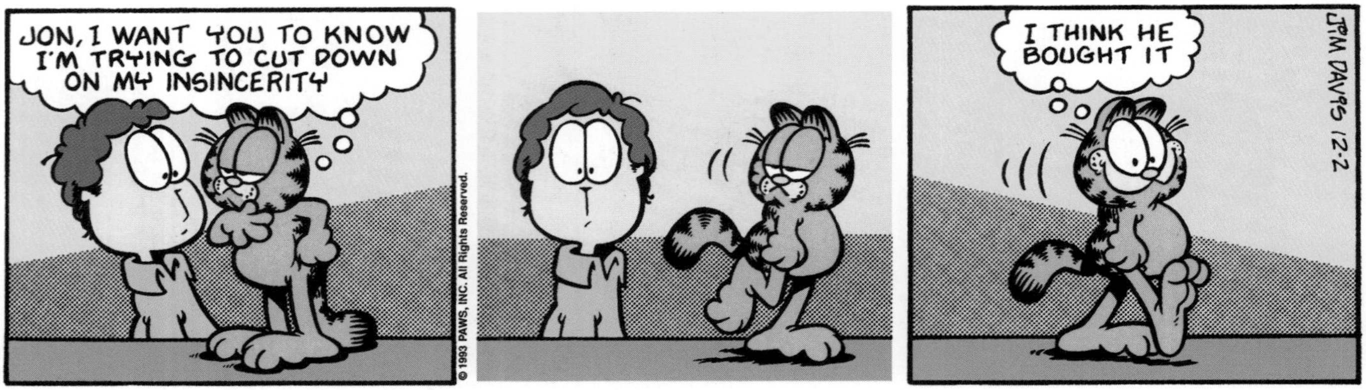
JON, I WANT YOU TO KNOW I'M TRYING TO CUT DOWN ON MY INSINCERITY
© 1993 PAWS, INC. All Rights Reserved.
I THINK HE BOUGHT IT
JIM DAVIS 12-2

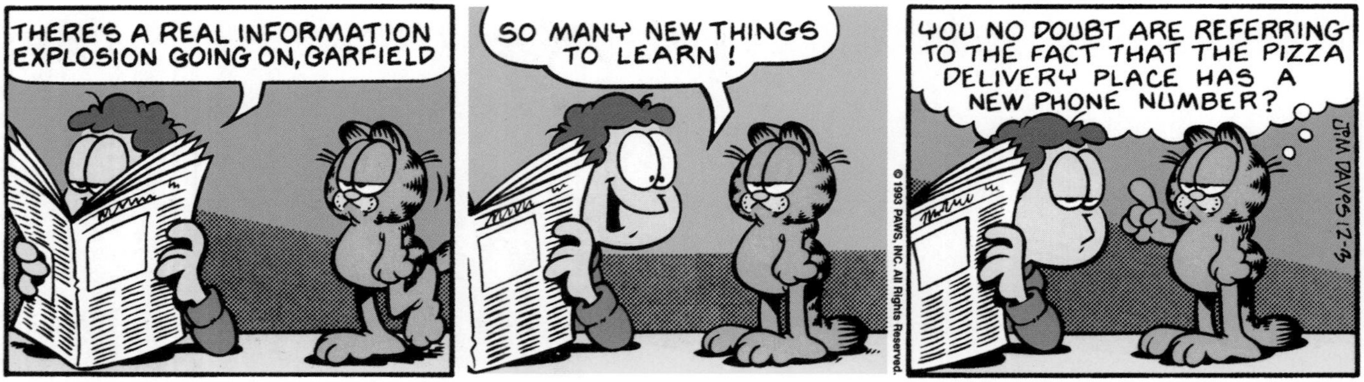
THERE'S A REAL INFORMATION EXPLOSION GOING ON, GARFIELD
SO MANY NEW THINGS TO LEARN!
© 1993 PAWS, INC. All Rights Reserved.
YOU NO DOUBT ARE REFERRING TO THE FACT THAT THE PIZZA DELIVERY PLACE HAS A NEW PHONE NUMBER?
JIM DAVIS 12-3

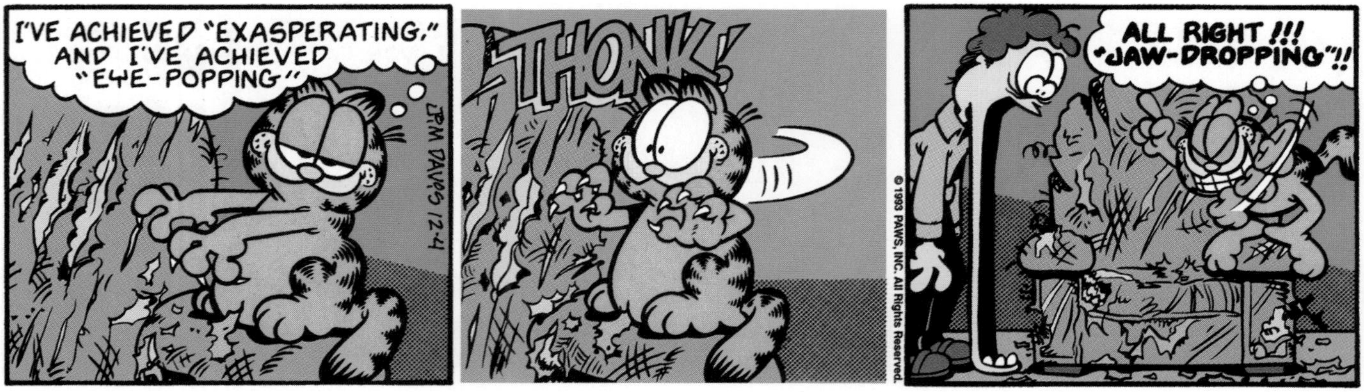
I'VE ACHIEVED "EXASPERATING," AND I'VE ACHIEVED "EYE-POPPING"
JIM DAVIS 12-4
THONK!
© 1993 PAWS, INC. All Rights Reserved.
ALL RIGHT!!! "JAW-DROPPING"!!

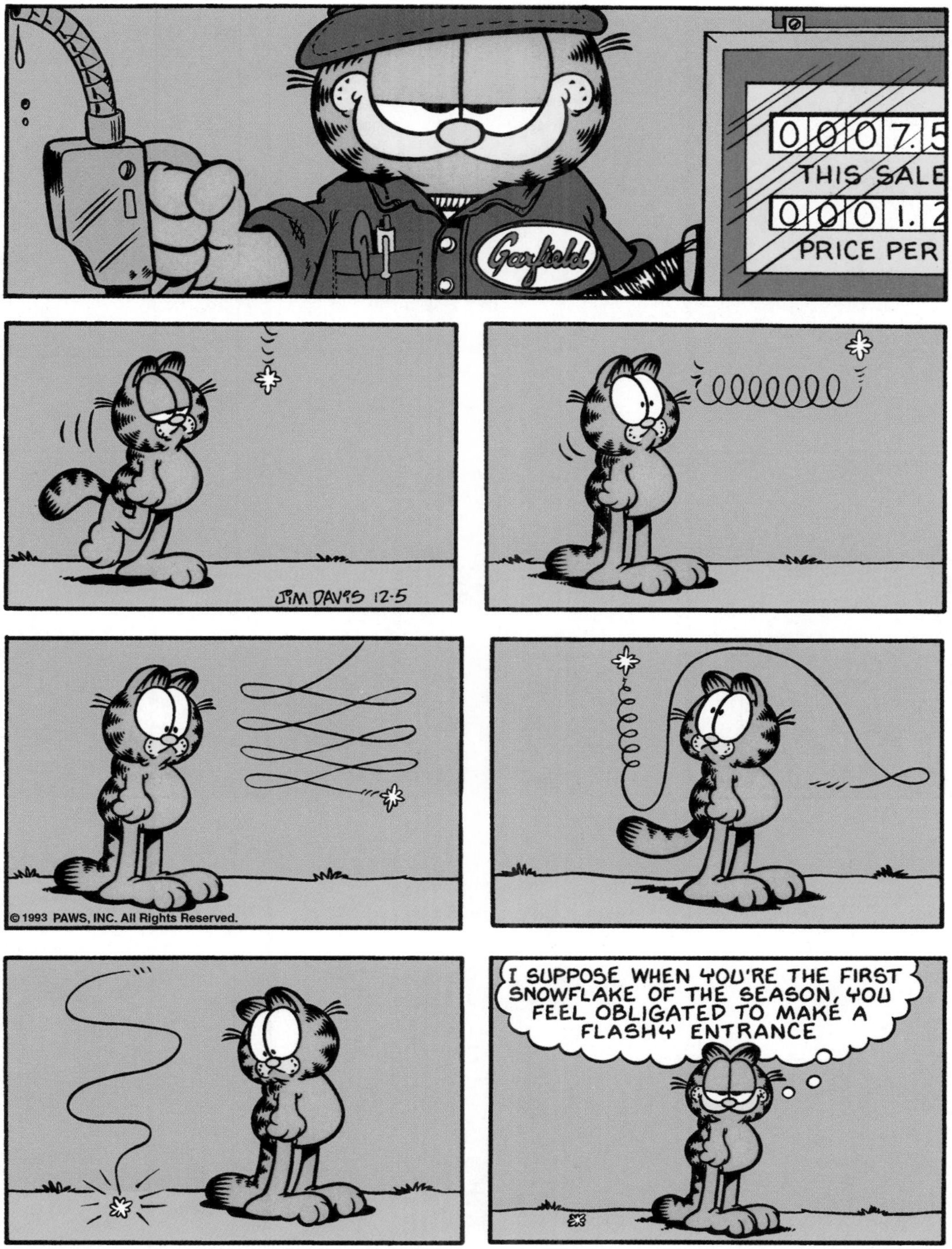

0007.5
THIS SALE
0001.2
PRICE PER
Garfield
JIM DAVIS 12-5
© 1993 PAWS, INC. All Rights Reserved.
I SUPPOSE WHEN YOU'RE THE FIRST SNOWFLAKE OF THE SEASON, YOU FEEL OBLIGATED TO MAKE A FLASHY ENTRANCE

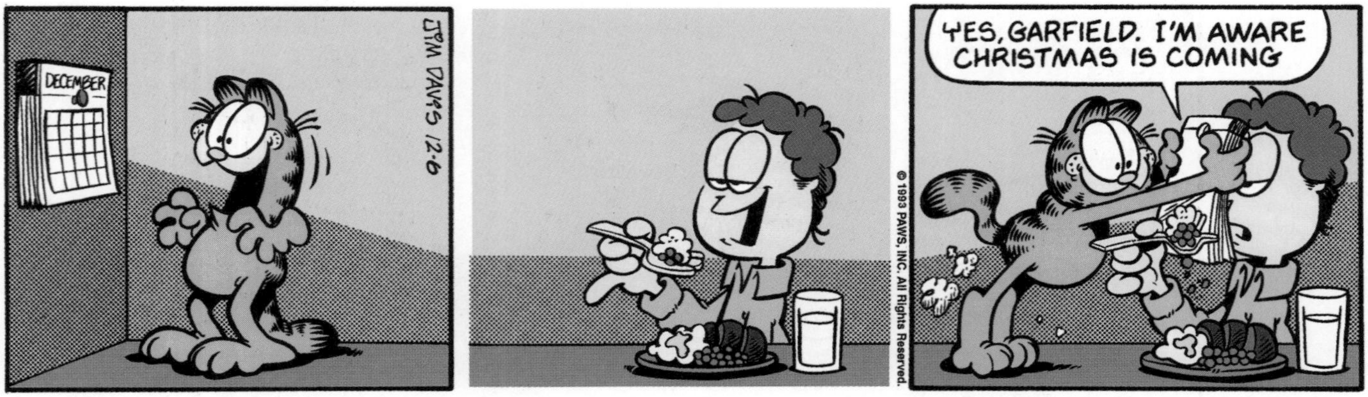
DECEMBER
JIM DAVIS 12-6
© 1993 PAWS, INC. All Rights Reserved.
YES, GARFIELD. I'M AWARE CHRISTMAS IS COMING

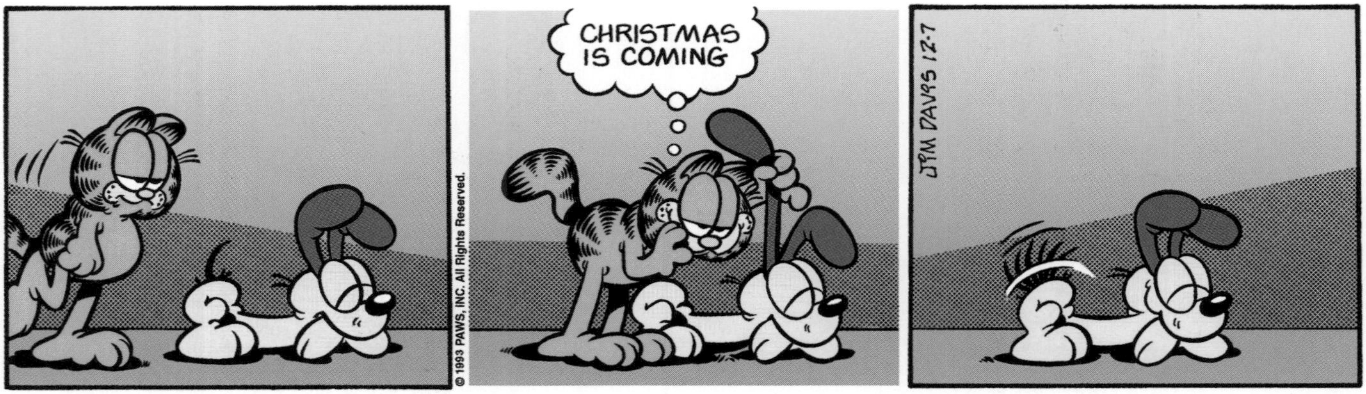
© 1993 PAWS, INC. All Rights Reserved.
CHRISTMAS IS COMING
JIM DAVIS 12-7

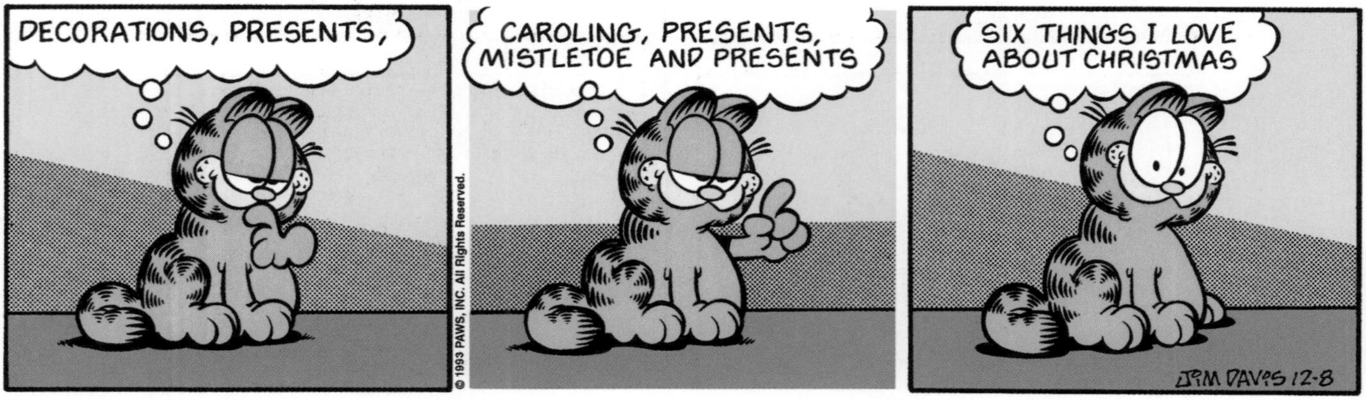
DECORATIONS, PRESENTS,
© 1993 PAWS, INC. All Rights Reserved.
CAROLING, PRESENTS, MISTLETOE AND PRESENTS
SIX THINGS I LOVE ABOUT CHRISTMAS
JIM DAVIS 12-8

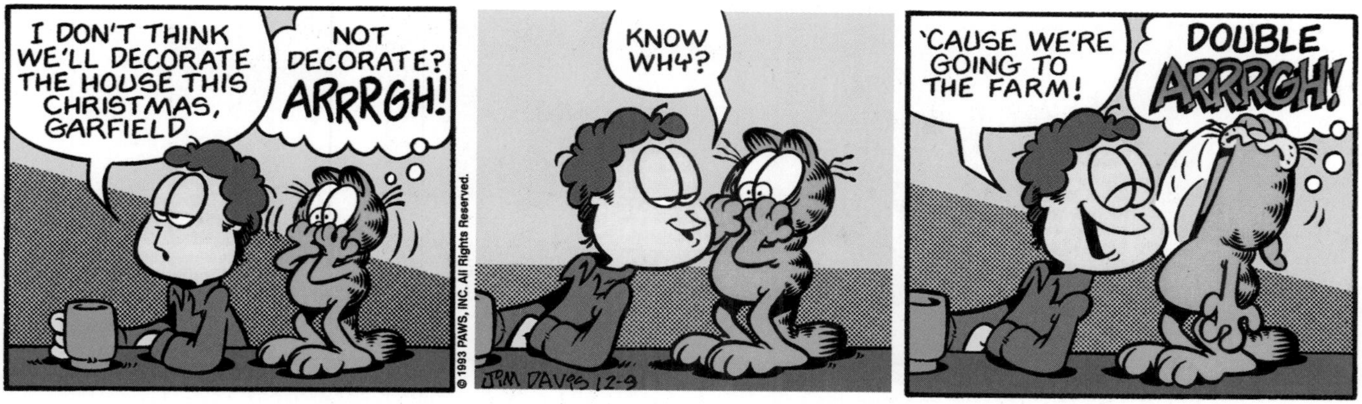
I DON'T THINK WE'LL DECORATE THE HOUSE THIS CHRISTMAS, GARFIELD
NOT DECORATE? ARRRGH!
© 1993 PAWS, INC. All Rights Reserved.
KNOW WHY?
JIM DAVIS 12-9
'CAUSE WE'RE GOING TO THE FARM!
DOUBLE ARRRGH!

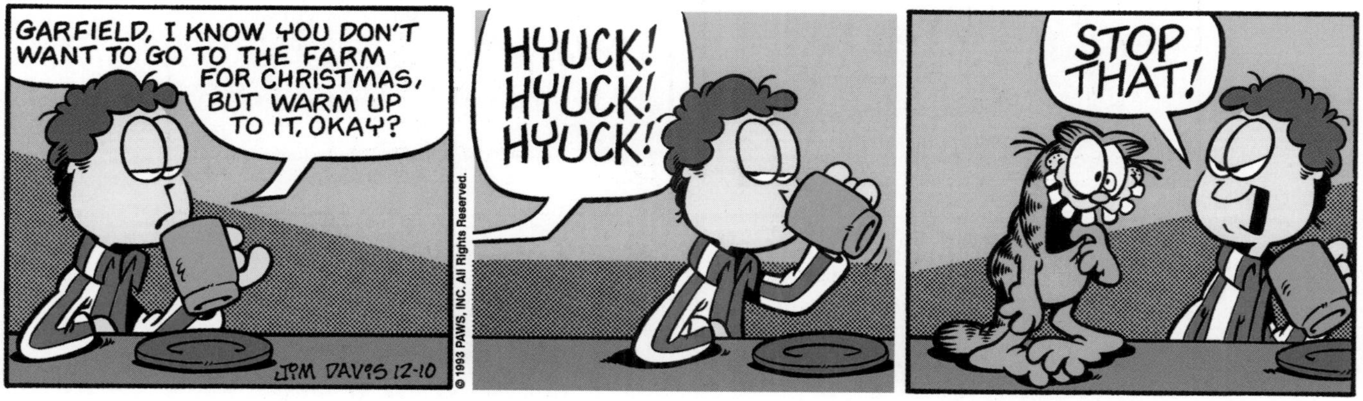
GARFIELD, I KNOW YOU DON'T WANT TO GO TO THE FARM FOR CHRISTMAS, BUT WARM UP TO IT, OKAY?
JIM DAVIS 12-10
© 1993 PAWS, INC. All Rights Reserved.
HYUCK! HYUCK! HYUCK!
STOP THAT!

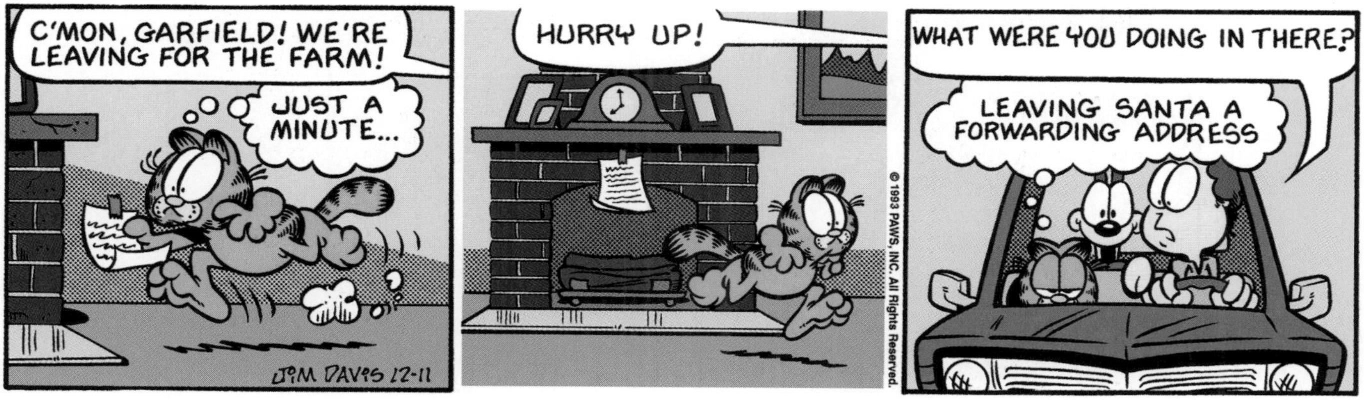
C'MON, GARFIELD! WE'RE LEAVING FOR THE FARM!
JUST A MINUTE...
JIM DAVIS 12-11
HURRY UP!
© 1993 PAWS, INC. All Rights Reserved.
WHAT WERE YOU DOING IN THERE?
LEAVING SANTA A FORWARDING ADDRESS

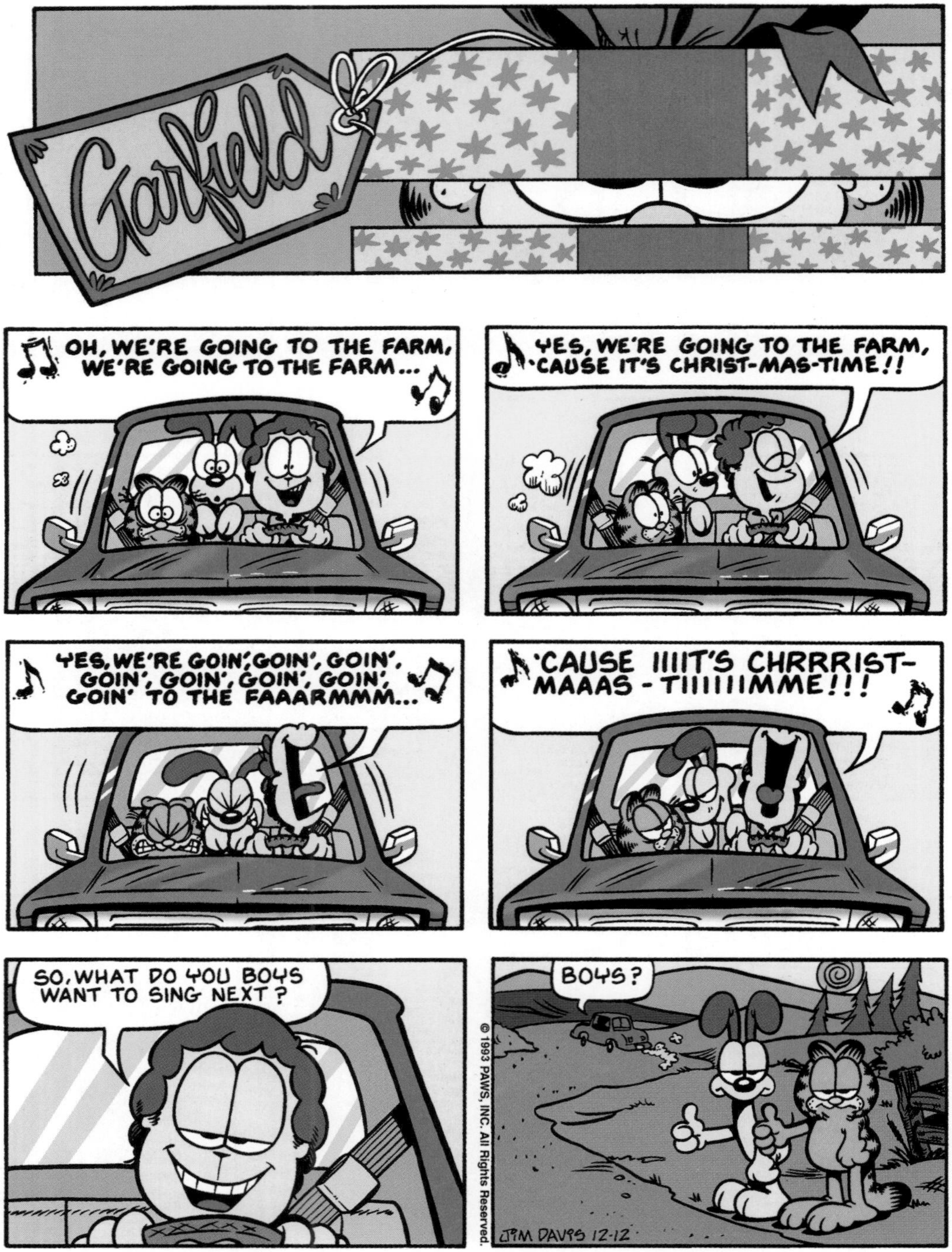
Garfield
OH, WE'RE GOING TO THE FARM, WE'RE GOING TO THE FARM...
YES, WE'RE GOING TO THE FARM, 'CAUSE IT'S CHRIST-MAS-TIME!!
YES, WE'RE GOIN', GOIN', GOIN', GOIN', GOIN', GOIN', GOIN', GOIN' TO THE FAAARMMM...
'CAUSE IIIIT'S CHRRRIST-MAAAS - TIIIIIIMME!!!
SO, WHAT DO YOU BOYS WANT TO SING NEXT?
BOYS?
JIM DAVIS 12-12

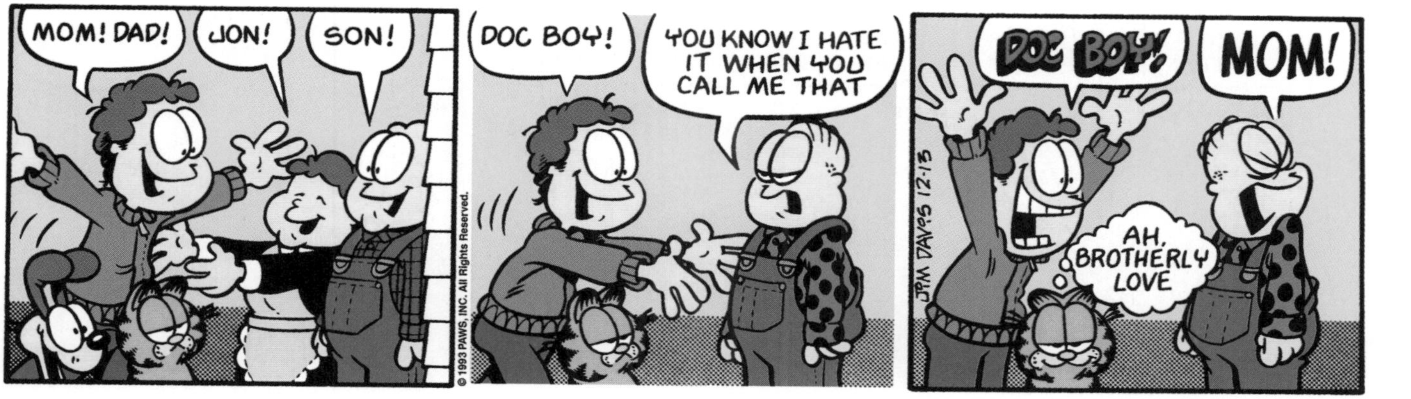
MOM! DAD!
JON!
SON!
DOC BOY!
YOU KNOW I HATE IT WHEN YOU CALL ME THAT
© 1993 PAWS, INC. All Rights Reserved.
DOC BOY!
MOM!
AH, BROTHERLY LOVE
JPM DAVPS 12·13

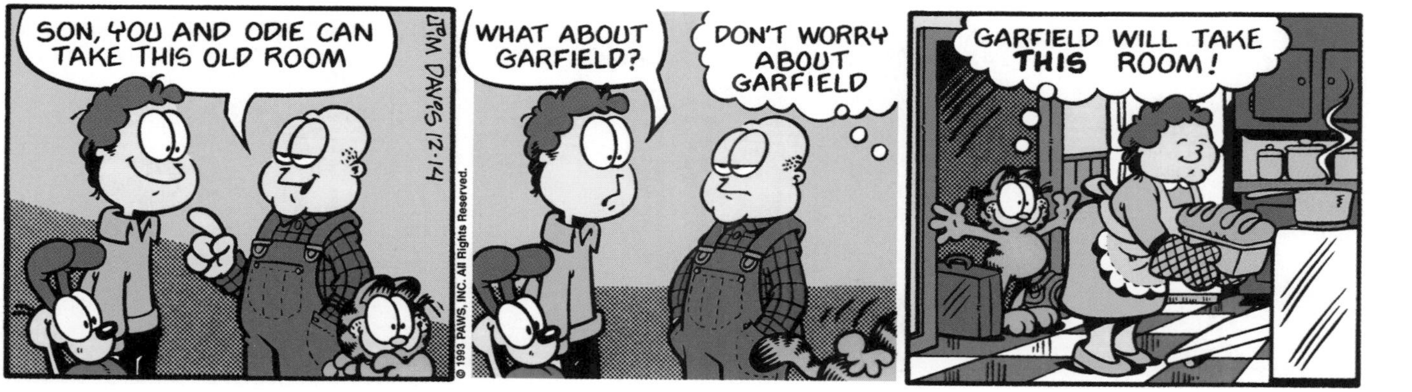
SON, YOU AND ODIE CAN TAKE THIS OLD ROOM
JPM DAVPS 12·14
© 1993 PAWS, INC. All Rights Reserved.
WHAT ABOUT GARFIELD?
DON'T WORRY ABOUT GARFIELD
GARFIELD WILL TAKE THIS ROOM!

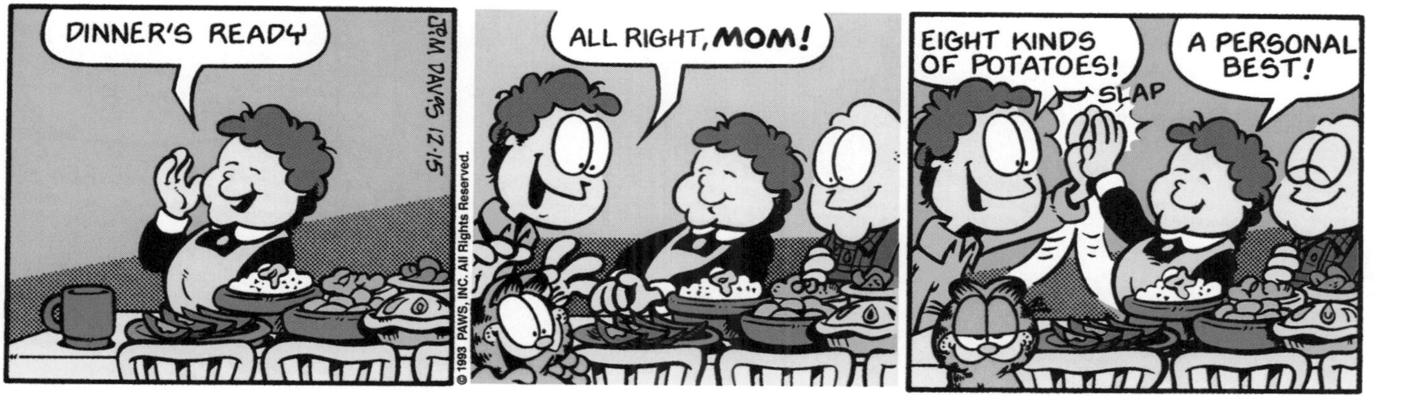
DINNER'S READY
JPM DAVPS 12·15
© 1993 PAWS, INC. All Rights Reserved.
ALL RIGHT, MOM!
EIGHT KINDS OF POTATOES!
SLAP
A PERSONAL BEST!

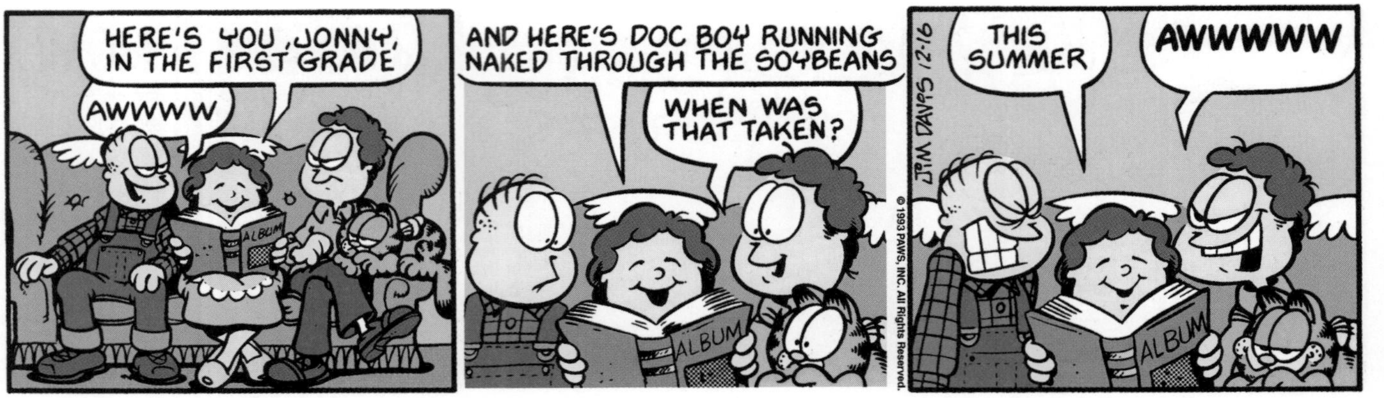
HERE'S YOU, JONNY, IN THE FIRST GRADE
AWWWW
AND HERE'S DOC BOY RUNNING NAKED THROUGH THE SOYBEANS
WHEN WAS THAT TAKEN?
THIS SUMMER
AWWWWW
JIM DAVIS 12-16
© 1993 PAWS, INC. All Rights Reserved.

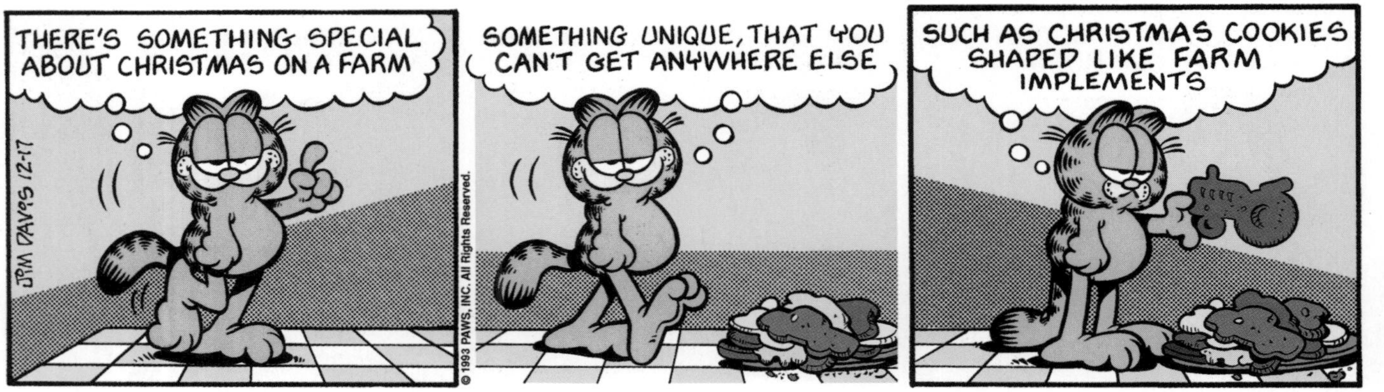
THERE'S SOMETHING SPECIAL ABOUT CHRISTMAS ON A FARM
SOMETHING UNIQUE, THAT YOU CAN'T GET ANYWHERE ELSE
SUCH AS CHRISTMAS COOKIES SHAPED LIKE FARM IMPLEMENTS
JIM DAVIS 12-17
© 1993 PAWS, INC. All Rights Reserved.

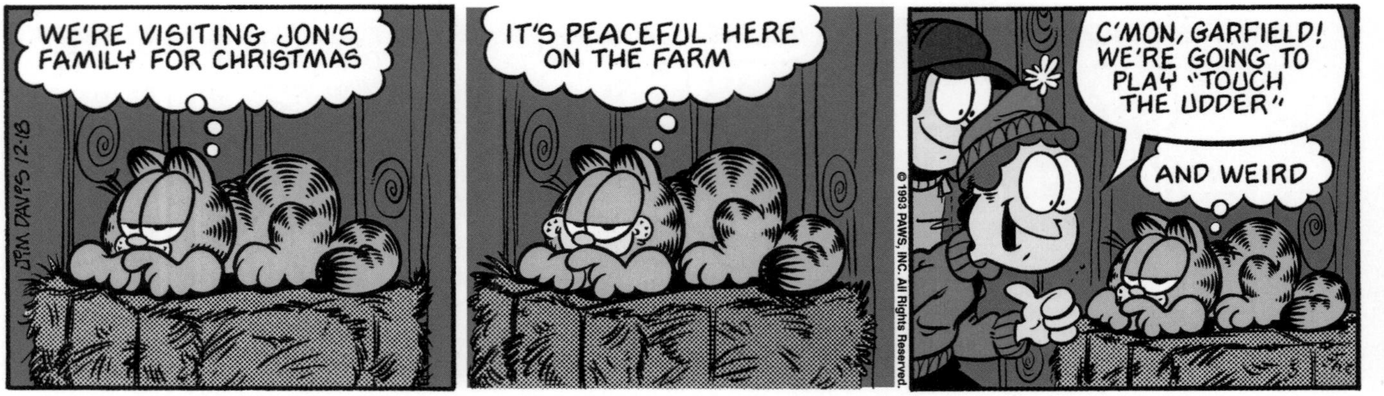
WE'RE VISITING JON'S FAMILY FOR CHRISTMAS
IT'S PEACEFUL HERE ON THE FARM
C'MON, GARFIELD! WE'RE GOING TO PLAY "TOUCH THE UDDER"
AND WEIRD
JIM DAVIS 12-18
© 1993 PAWS, INC. All Rights Reserved.

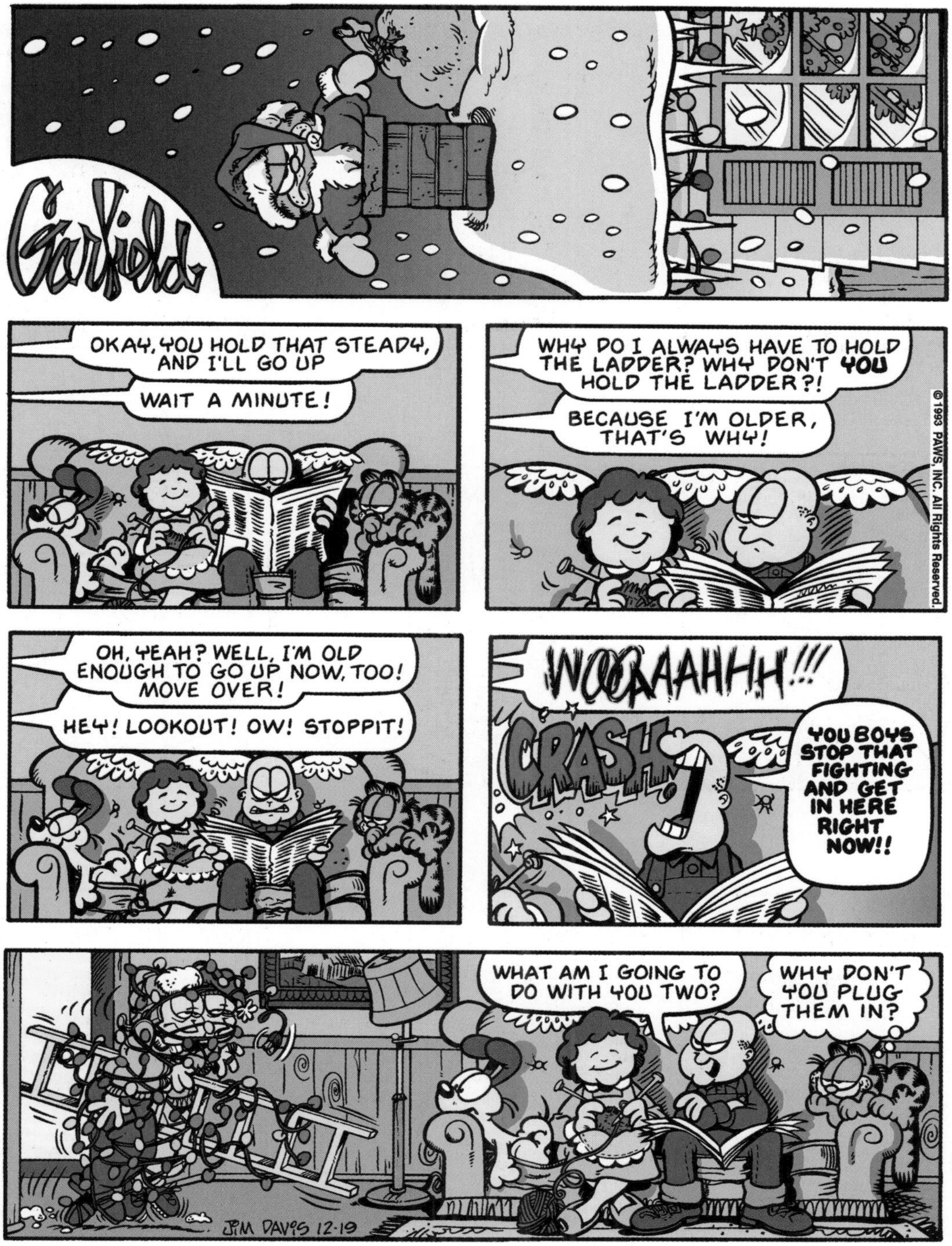
Garfield
OKAY, YOU HOLD THAT STEADY, AND I'LL GO UP
WAIT A MINUTE!
WHY DO I ALWAYS HAVE TO HOLD THE LADDER? WHY DON'T YOU HOLD THE LADDER?!
BECAUSE I'M OLDER, THAT'S WHY!
© 1993 PAWS, INC. All Rights Reserved.
OH, YEAH? WELL, I'M OLD ENOUGH TO GO UP NOW, TOO! MOVE OVER!
HEY! LOOKOUT! OW! STOPPIT!
WOOAAAHHH!!!
CRASH
YOU BOYS STOP THAT FIGHTING AND GET IN HERE RIGHT NOW!!
WHAT AM I GOING TO DO WITH YOU TWO?
WHY DON'T YOU PLUG THEM IN?
JIM DAVIS 12-19

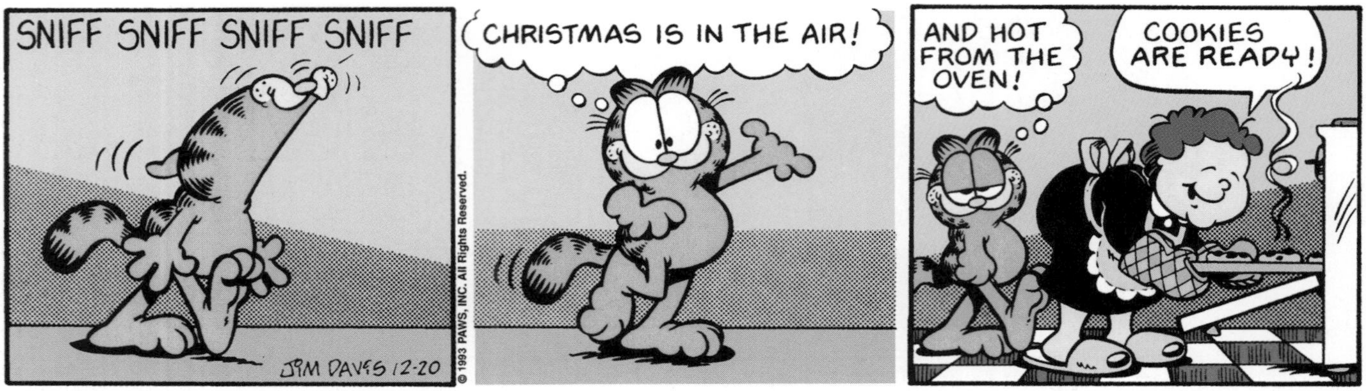
SNIFF SNIFF SNIFF SNIFF
JIM DAVIS 12-20
© 1993 PAWS, INC. All Rights Reserved.
CHRISTMAS IS IN THE AIR!
AND HOT FROM THE OVEN!
COOKIES ARE READY!

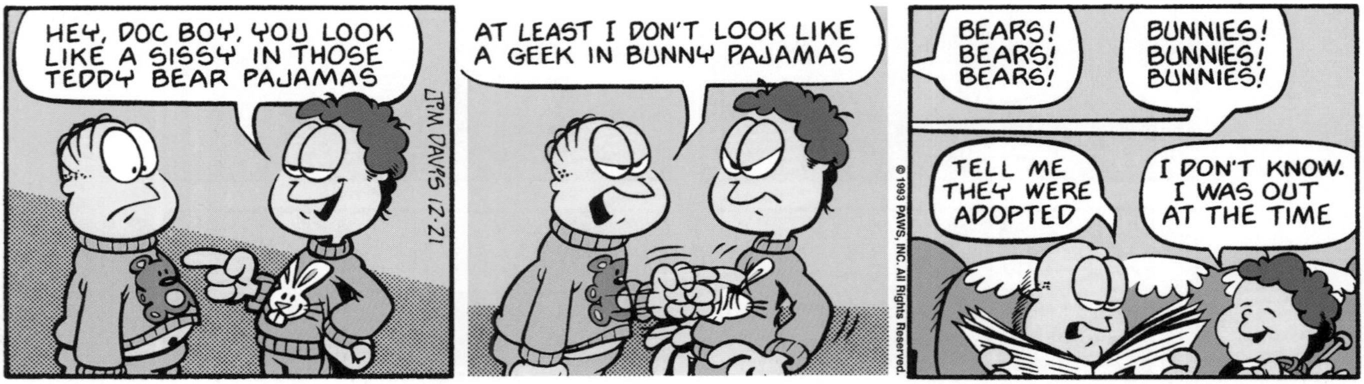
HEY, DOC BOY, YOU LOOK LIKE A SISSY IN THOSE TEDDY BEAR PAJAMAS
JIM DAVIS 12-21
AT LEAST I DON'T LOOK LIKE A GEEK IN BUNNY PAJAMAS
BEARS! BEARS! BEARS!
BUNNIES! BUNNIES! BUNNIES!
TELL ME THEY WERE ADOPTED
I DON'T KNOW. I WAS OUT AT THE TIME
© 1993 PAWS, INC. All Rights Reserved.

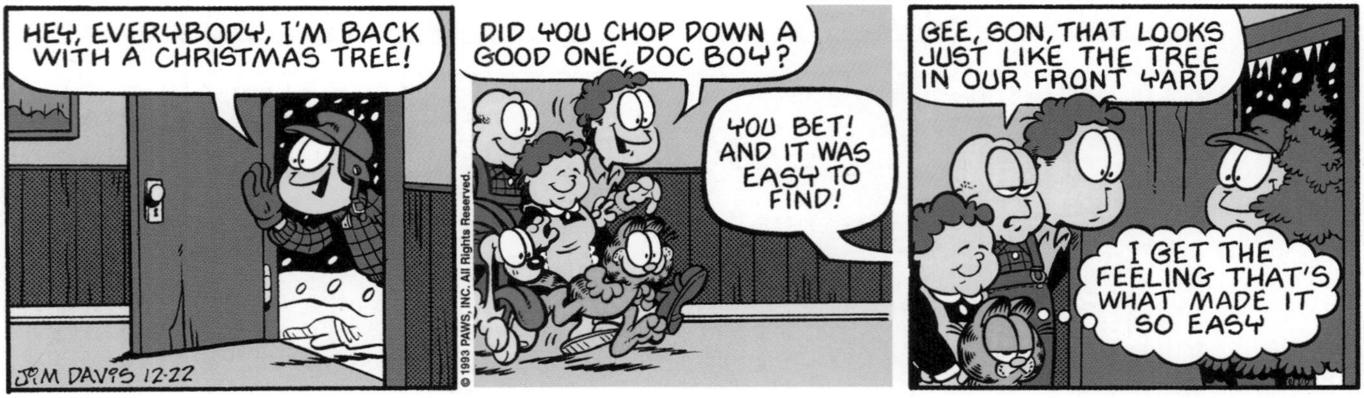
HEY, EVERYBODY, I'M BACK WITH A CHRISTMAS TREE!
JIM DAVIS 12-22
© 1993 PAWS, INC. All Rights Reserved.
DID YOU CHOP DOWN A GOOD ONE, DOC BOY?
YOU BET! AND IT WAS EASY TO FIND!
GEE, SON, THAT LOOKS JUST LIKE THE TREE IN OUR FRONT YARD
I GET THE FEELING THAT'S WHAT MADE IT SO EASY

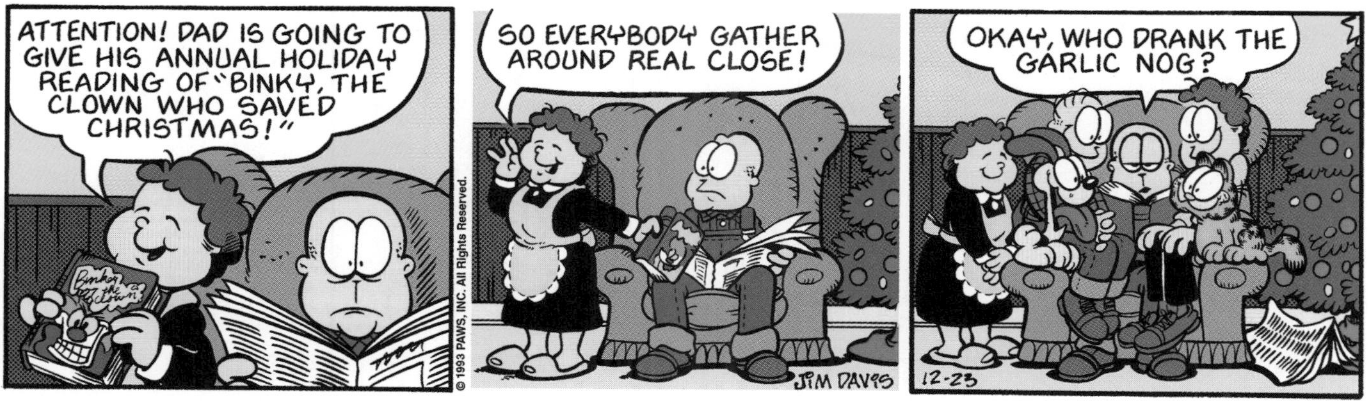
ATTENTION! DAD IS GOING TO GIVE HIS ANNUAL HOLIDAY READING OF "BINKY, THE CLOWN WHO SAVED CHRISTMAS!"
© 1993 PAWS, INC. All Rights Reserved.
SO EVERYBODY GATHER AROUND REAL CLOSE!
JIM DAVIS
OKAY, WHO DRANK THE GARLIC NOG?
12-23

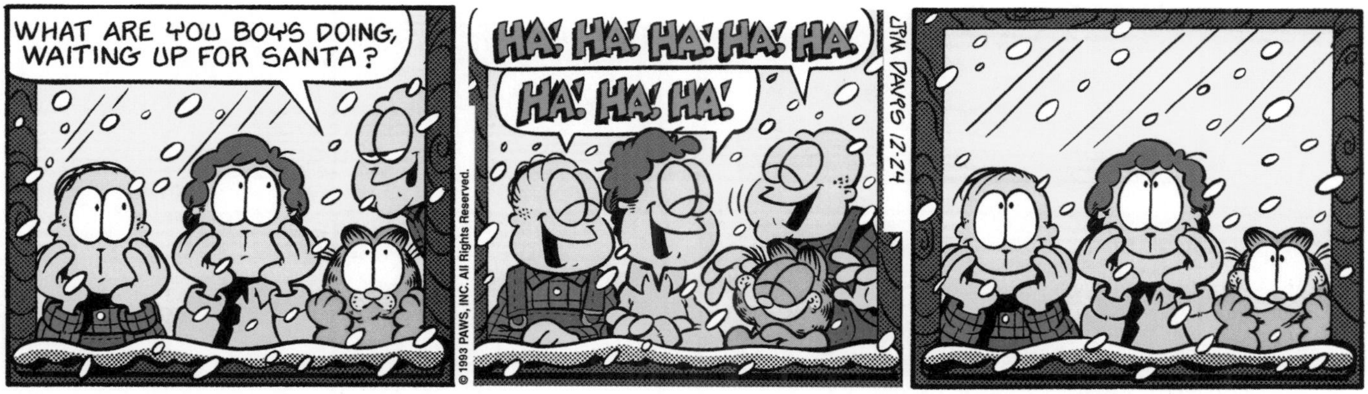
WHAT ARE YOU BOYS DOING, WAITING UP FOR SANTA?
© 1993 PAWS, INC. All Rights Reserved.
HA! HA! HA! HA! HA!
HA! HA! HA!
JIM DAVIS 12-24

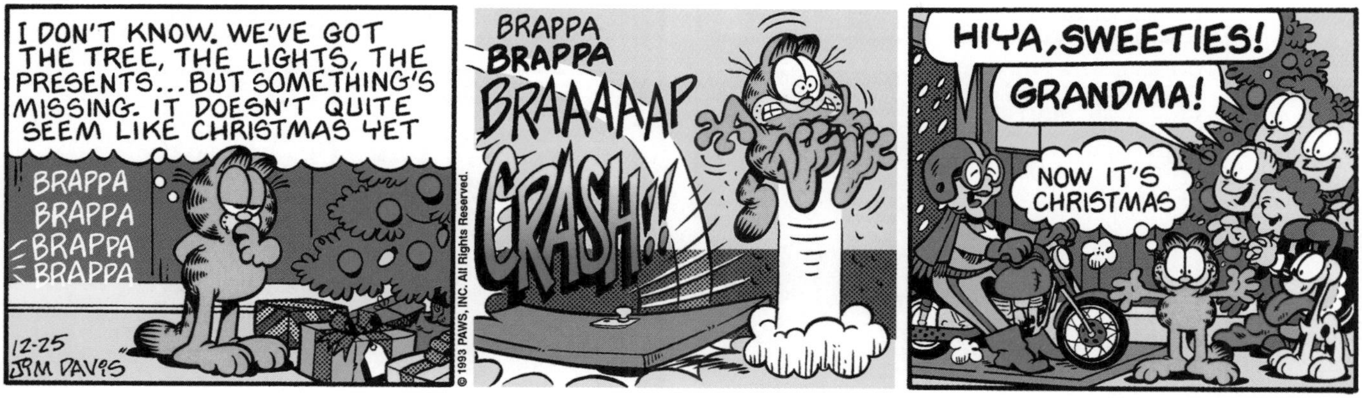
I DON'T KNOW. WE'VE GOT THE TREE, THE LIGHTS, THE PRESENTS... BUT SOMETHING'S MISSING. IT DOESN'T QUITE SEEM LIKE CHRISTMAS YET
BRAPPA
BRAPPA
BRAPPA
BRAPPA
BRAPPA
12-25
JIM DAVIS
© 1993 PAWS, INC. All Rights Reserved.
BRAPPA
BRAPPA
BRAAAAAP
CRASH!!
HIYA, SWEETIES!
GRANDMA!
NOW IT'S CHRISTMAS

Jon
Odie
Arlene
Mom
XOXO
love,
Garfield
Happy Holidays
GOOD-BYE, CHRISTMAS
GOOD-BYE, CHRISTMAS TREE...
GOOD-BYE, LIGHTS. GOOD-BYE, TINSEL...
GOOD-BYE, PRESENTS. GOOD-BYE, WRAPPING PAPER...
GOOD-BYE, MISTLETOE...
HE-LLOOOOO LEFTOVERS!!!
JPM DAVPS 12-26

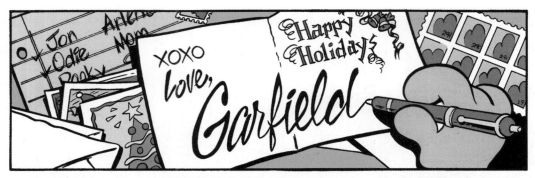

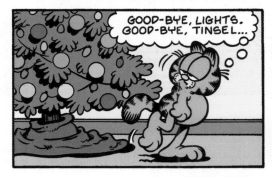

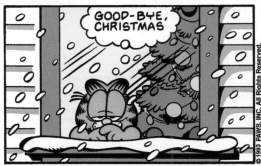

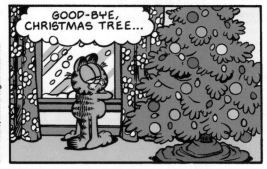

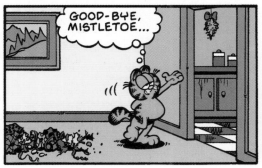

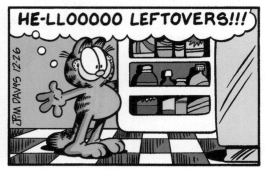

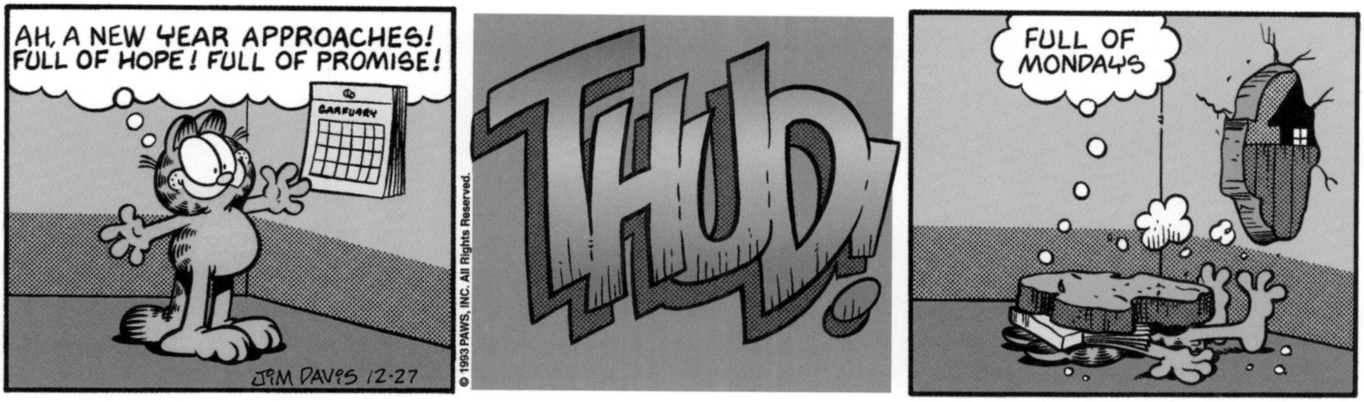
AH, A NEW YEAR APPROACHES! FULL OF HOPE! FULL OF PROMISE!
GARFUARY
JIM DAVIS 12-27
© 1993 PAWS, INC. All Rights Reserved.
THUD!
FULL OF MONDAYS

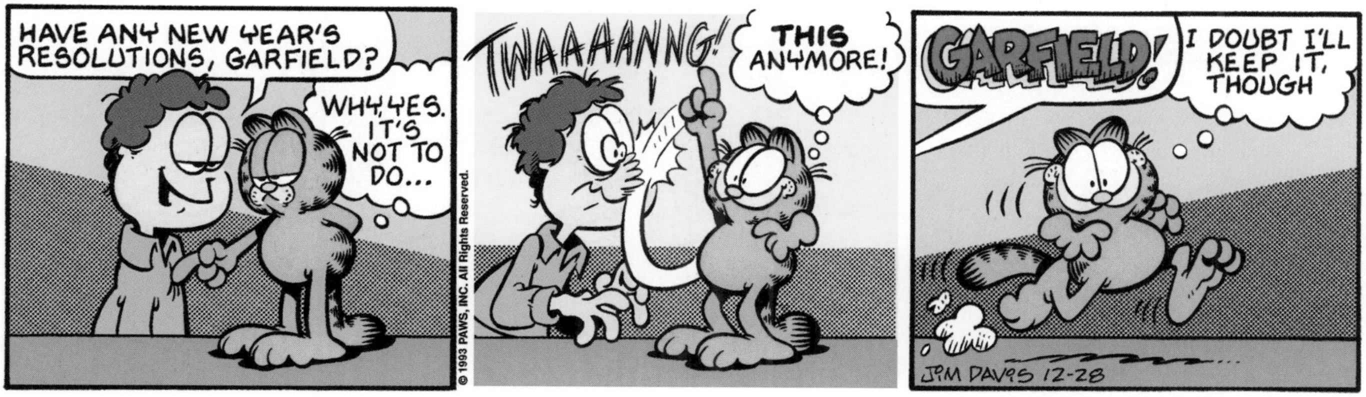
HAVE ANY NEW YEAR'S RESOLUTIONS, GARFIELD?
WHY, YES. IT'S NOT TO DO...
© 1993 PAWS, INC. All Rights Reserved.
TWAAAANNG!
THIS ANYMORE!
GARFIELD!
I DOUBT I'LL KEEP IT, THOUGH
JIM DAVIS 12-28

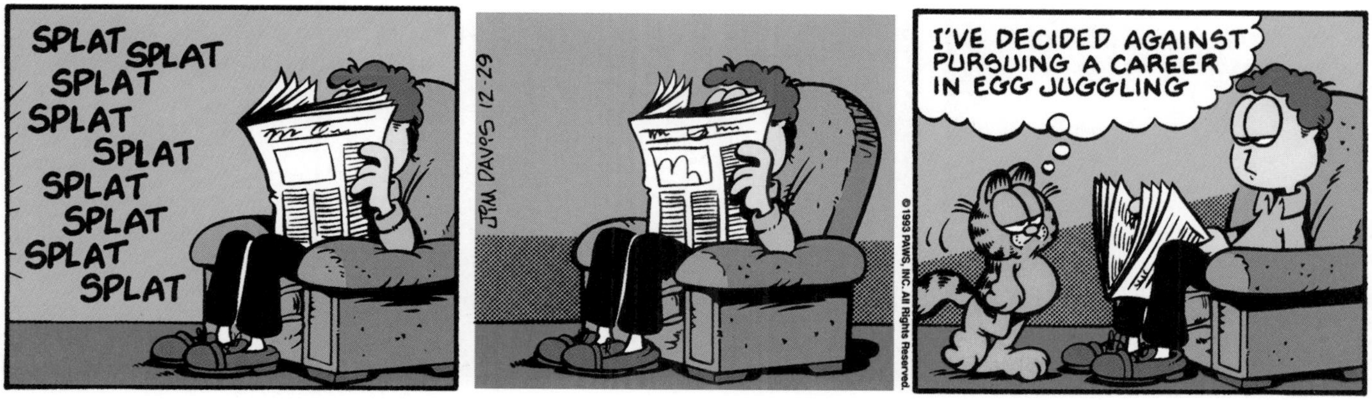
SPLAT SPLAT SPLAT SPLAT SPLAT SPLAT SPLAT SPLAT SPLAT
JIM DAVIS 12-29
© 1993 PAWS, INC. All Rights Reserved.
I'VE DECIDED AGAINST PURSUING A CAREER IN EGG JUGGLING

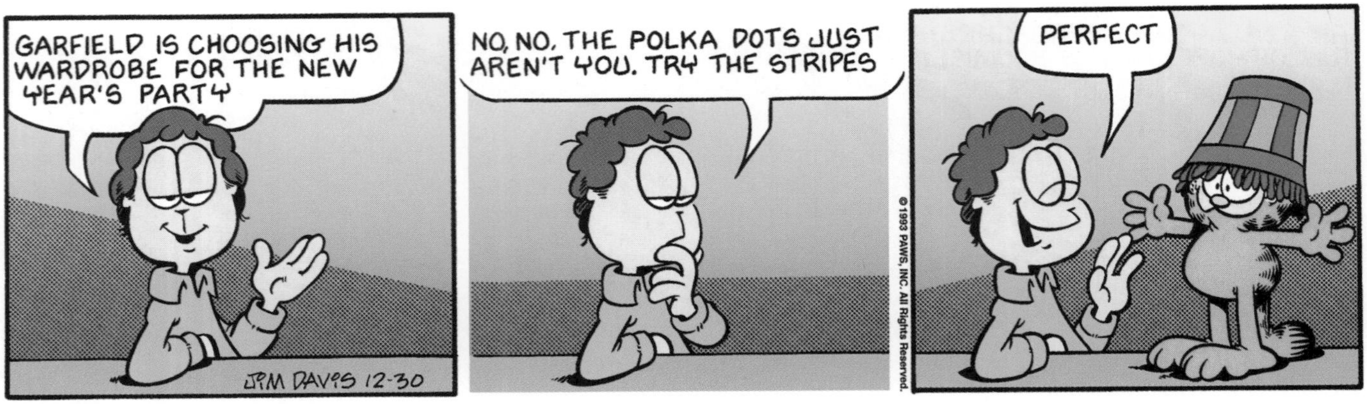
GARFIELD IS CHOOSING HIS WARDROBE FOR THE NEW YEAR'S PARTY
NO, NO, THE POLKA DOTS JUST AREN'T YOU. TRY THE STRIPES
PERFECT
JIM DAVIS 12-30
© 1993 PAWS, INC. All Rights Reserved.

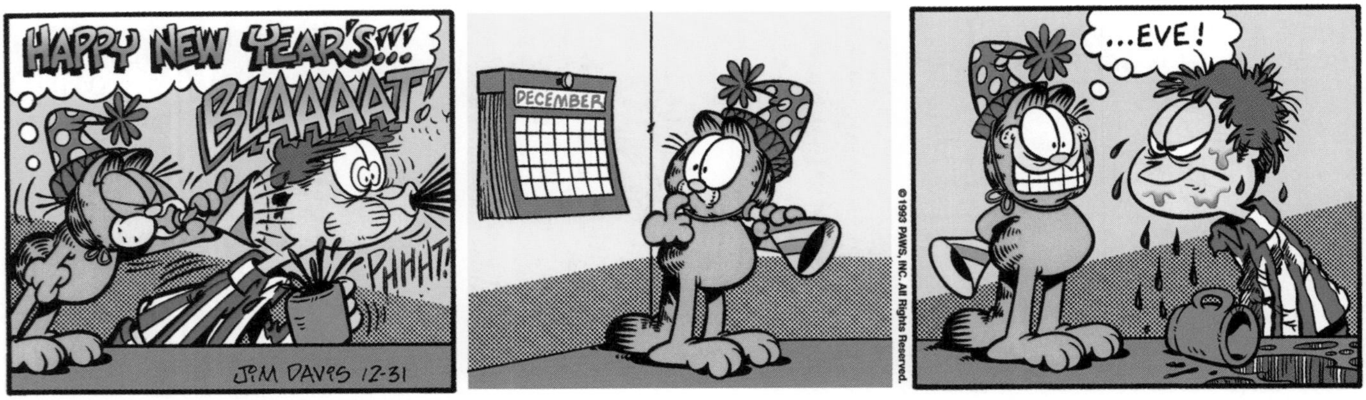
HAPPY NEW YEAR'S!!!
BLAAAAT!
PHHHT!
DECEMBER
...EVE!
JIM DAVIS 12-31
© 1993 PAWS, INC. All Rights Reserved.

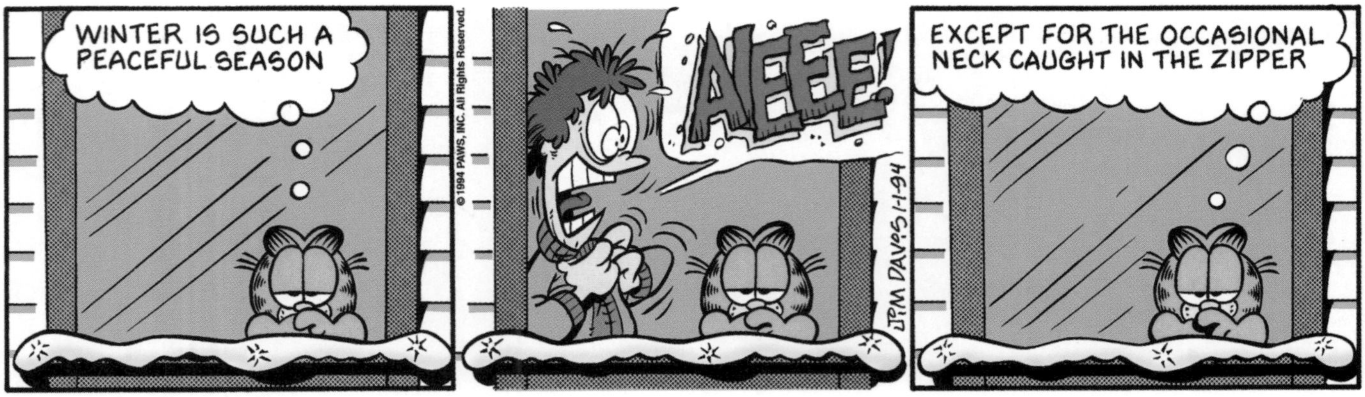
WINTER IS SUCH A PEACEFUL SEASON
AIEEE!
EXCEPT FOR THE OCCASIONAL NECK CAUGHT IN THE ZIPPER
JIM DAVIS 1-1-94
© 1994 PAWS, INC. All Rights Reserved.

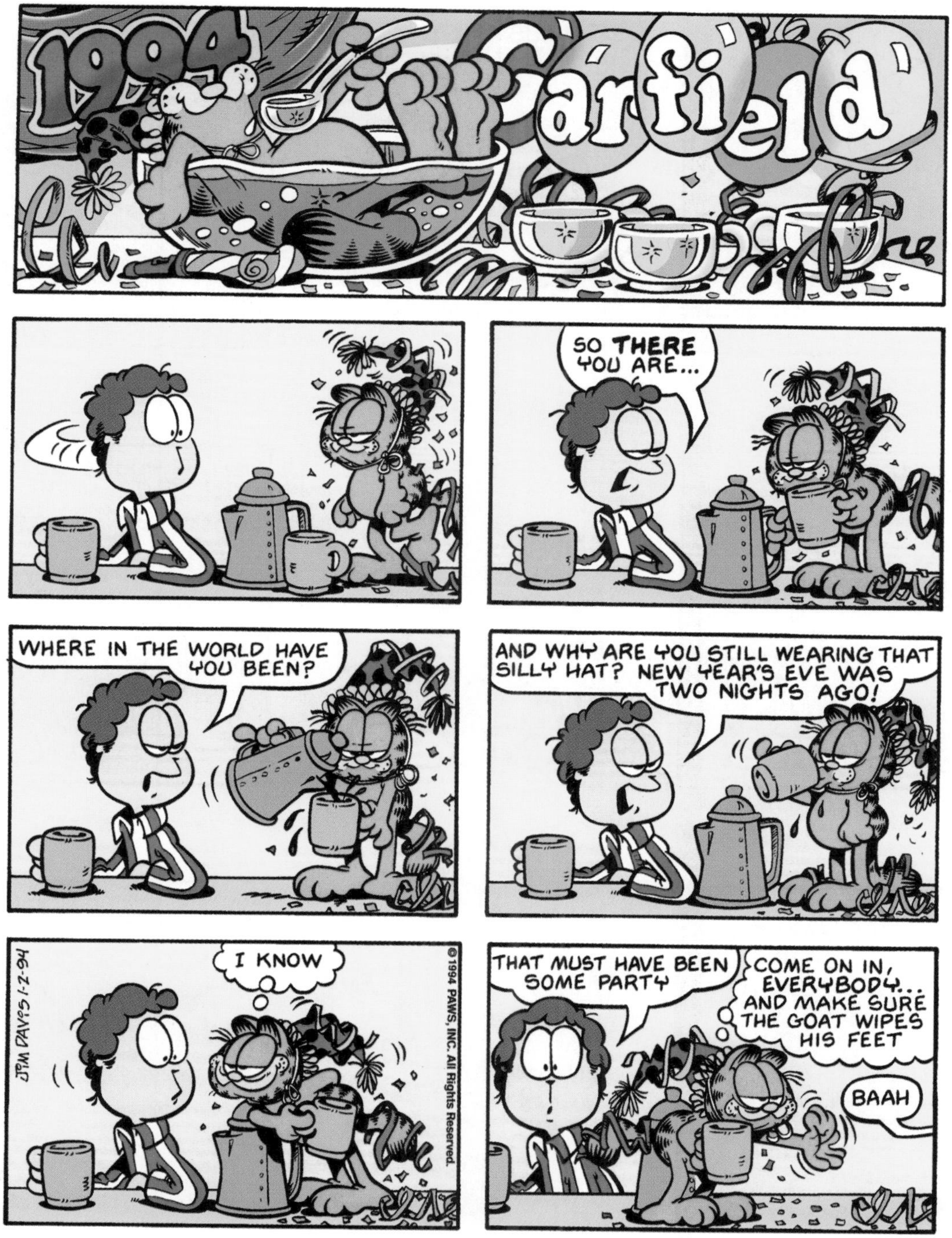
1994
Garfield
SO THERE YOU ARE...
WHERE IN THE WORLD HAVE YOU BEEN?
AND WHY ARE YOU STILL WEARING THAT SILLY HAT? NEW YEAR'S EVE WAS TWO NIGHTS AGO!
JPM DAVPS 1-2-94
© 1994 PAWS, INC. All Rights Reserved.
I KNOW
THAT MUST HAVE BEEN SOME PARTY
COME ON IN, EVERYBODY... AND MAKE SURE THE GOAT WIPES HIS FEET
BAAH

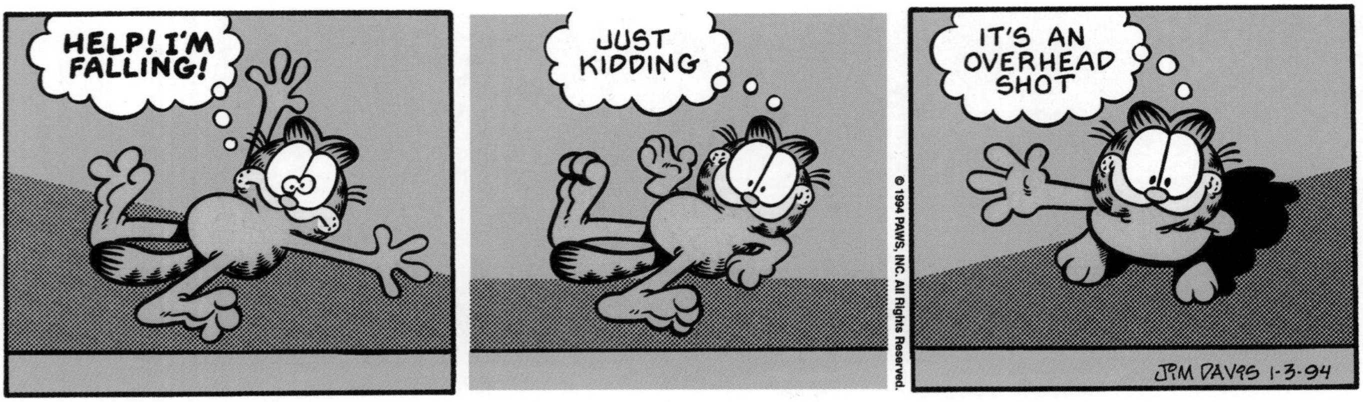
HELP! I'M FALLING!
JUST KIDDING
IT'S AN OVERHEAD SHOT
© 1994 PAWS, INC. All Rights Reserved.
JIM DAVIS 1-3-94

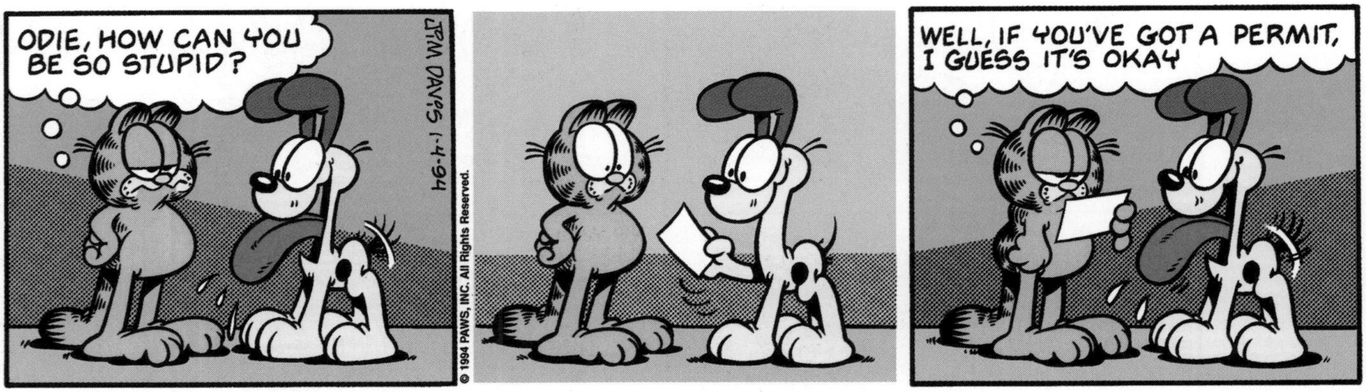
ODIE, HOW CAN YOU BE SO STUPID?
JIM DAVIS 1-4-94
© 1994 PAWS, INC. All Rights Reserved.
WELL, IF YOU'VE GOT A PERMIT, I GUESS IT'S OKAY

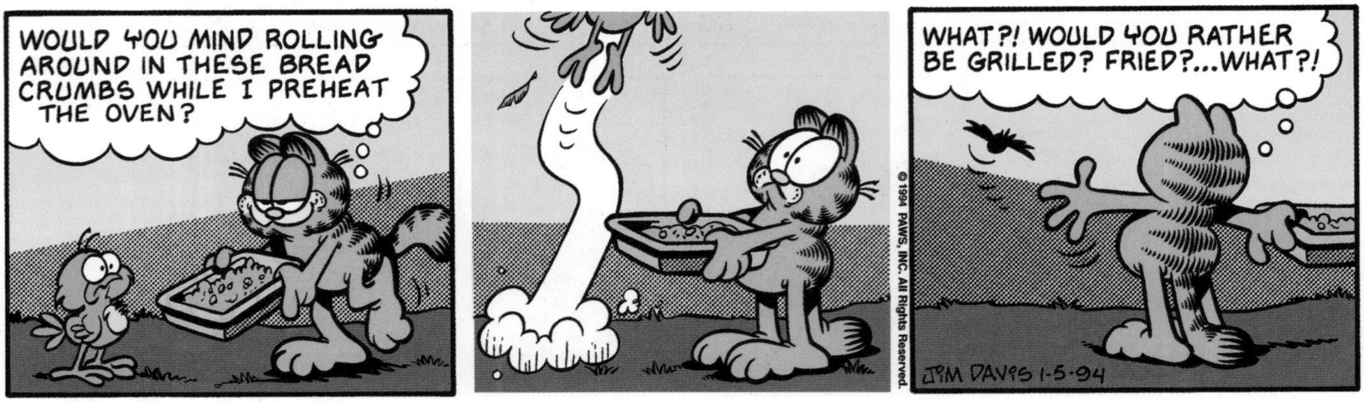
WOULD YOU MIND ROLLING AROUND IN THESE BREAD CRUMBS WHILE I PREHEAT THE OVEN?
© 1994 PAWS, INC. All Rights Reserved.
WHAT?! WOULD YOU RATHER BE GRILLED? FRIED?...WHAT?!
JIM DAVIS 1-5-94

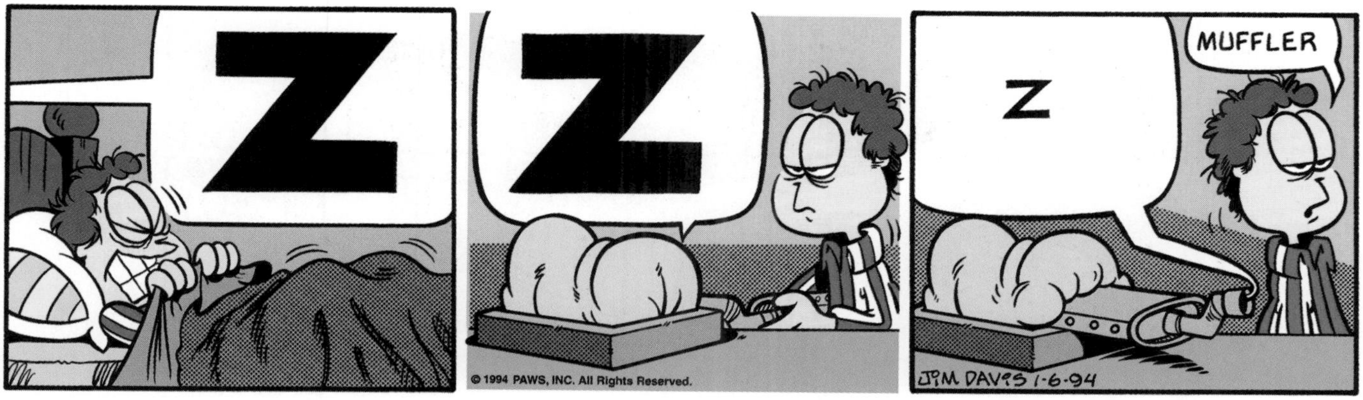
Z
Z
Z
MUFFLER
© 1994 PAWS, INC. All Rights Reserved.
JIM DAVIS 1-6-94

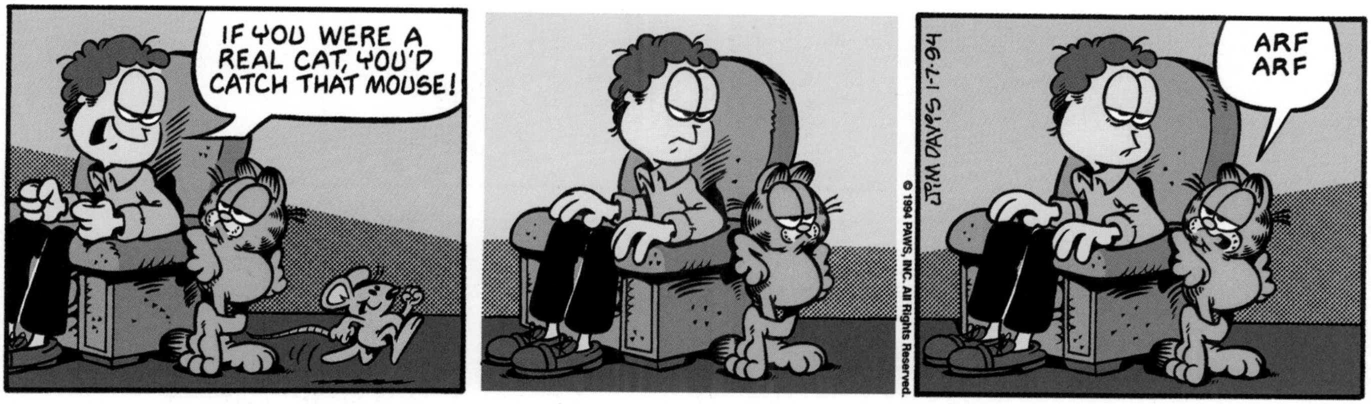
IF YOU WERE A REAL CAT, YOU'D CATCH THAT MOUSE!
© 1994 PAWS, INC. All Rights Reserved.
JIM DAVIS 1-7-94
ARF ARF

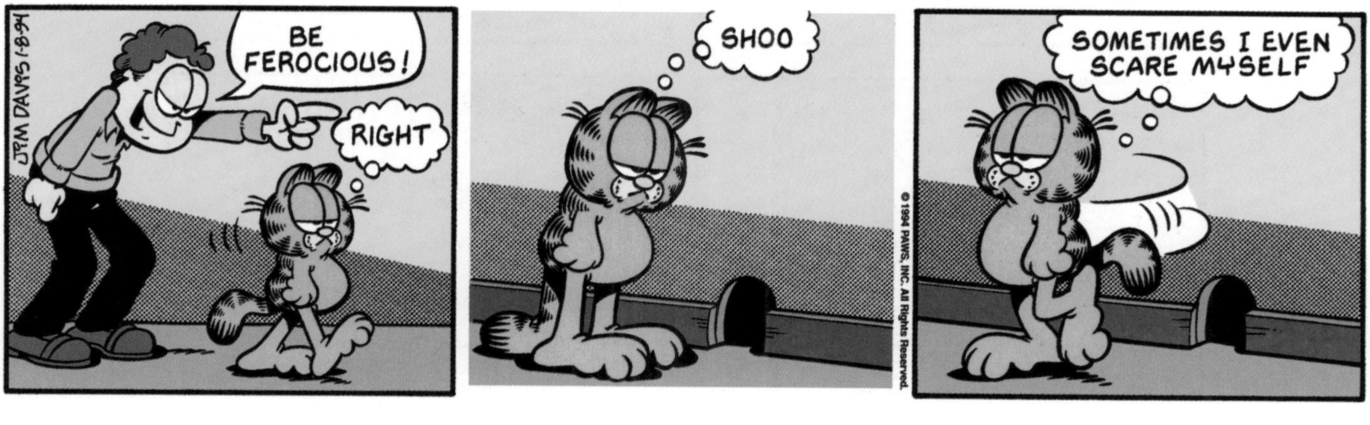
JIM DAVIS 1-8-94
BE FEROCIOUS!
RIGHT
SHOO
© 1994 PAWS, INC. All Rights Reserved.
SOMETIMES I EVEN SCARE MYSELF

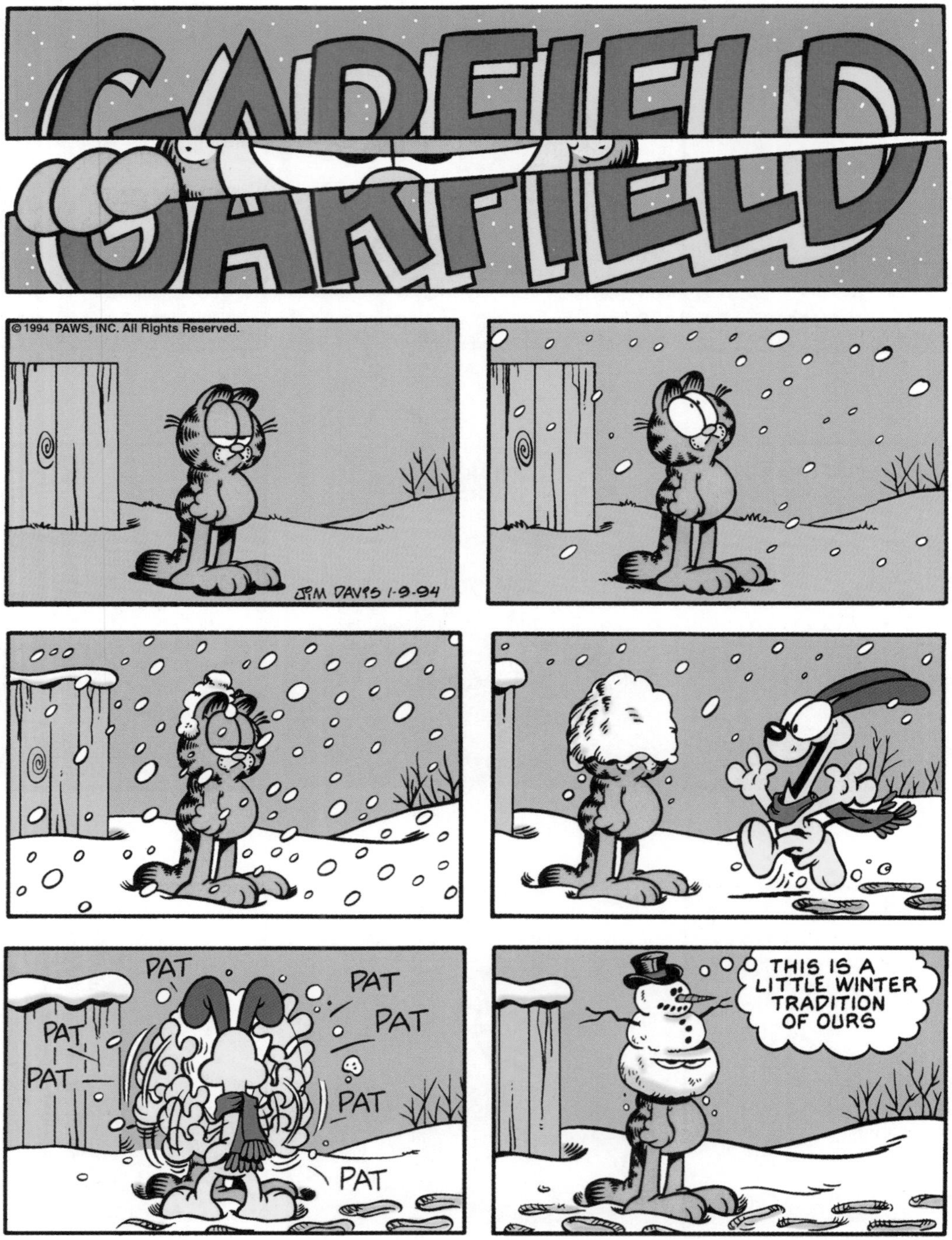
GARFIELD
© 1994 PAWS, INC. All Rights Reserved.
JIM DAVIS 1-9-94
PAT
PAT
PAT
PAT
PAT
PAT
PAT
THIS IS A LITTLE WINTER TRADITION OF OURS

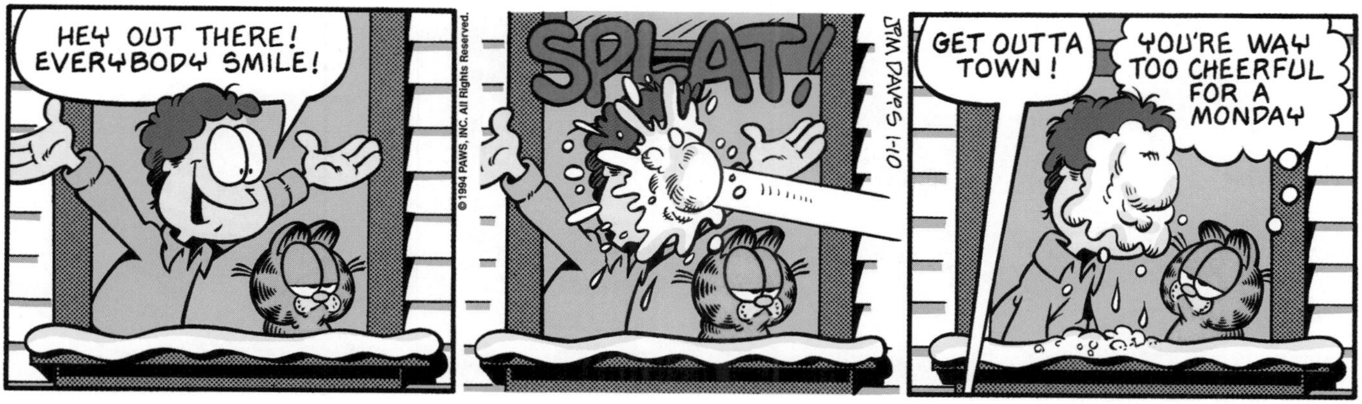
HEY OUT THERE! EVERYBODY SMILE!
© 1994 PAWS, INC. All Rights Reserved.
SPLAT!
JIM DAVIS 1-10
GET OUTTA TOWN!
YOU'RE WAY TOO CHEERFUL FOR A MONDAY

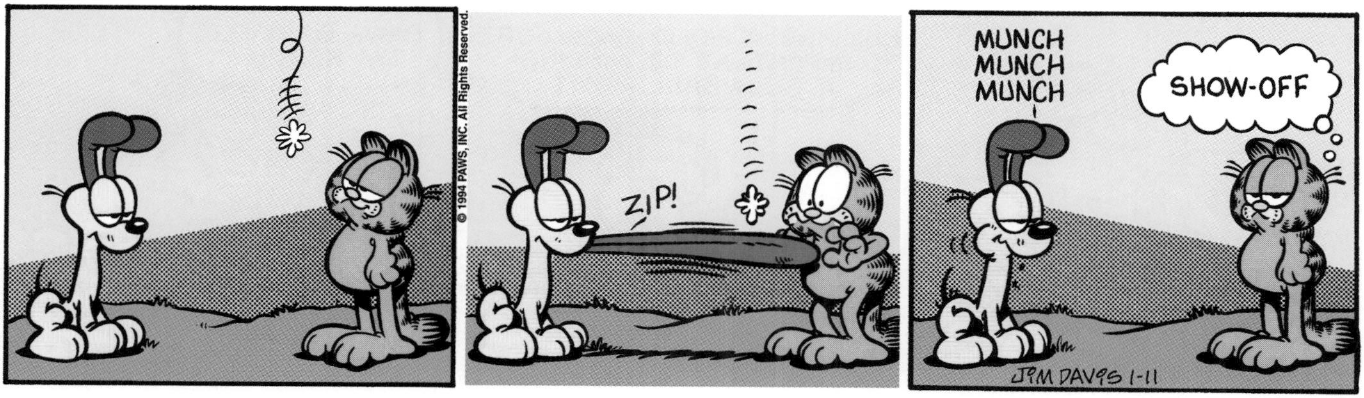
© 1994 PAWS, INC. All Rights Reserved.
ZIP!
MUNCH MUNCH MUNCH
SHOW-OFF
JIM DAVIS 1-11

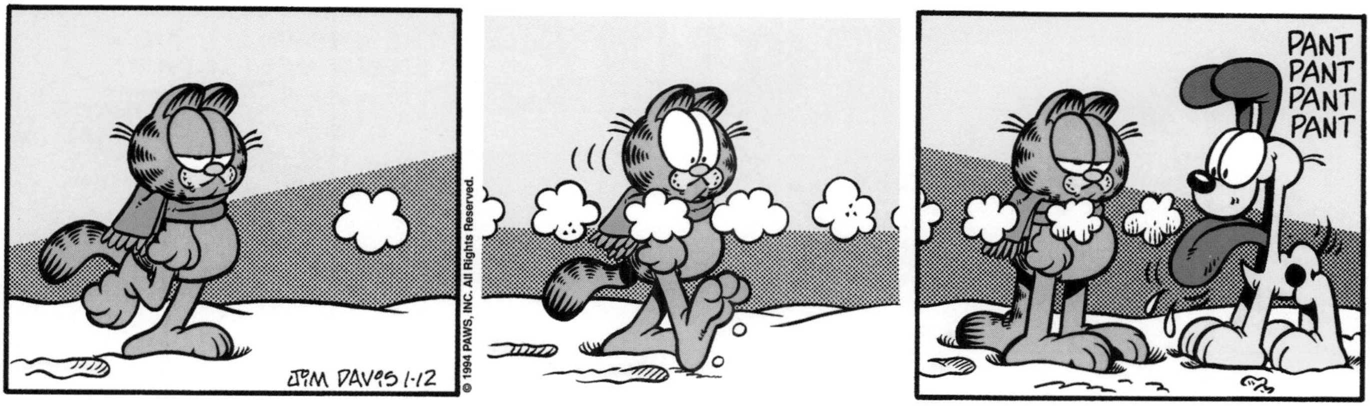
JIM DAVIS 1-12
© 1994 PAWS, INC. All Rights Reserved.
PANT PANT PANT PANT

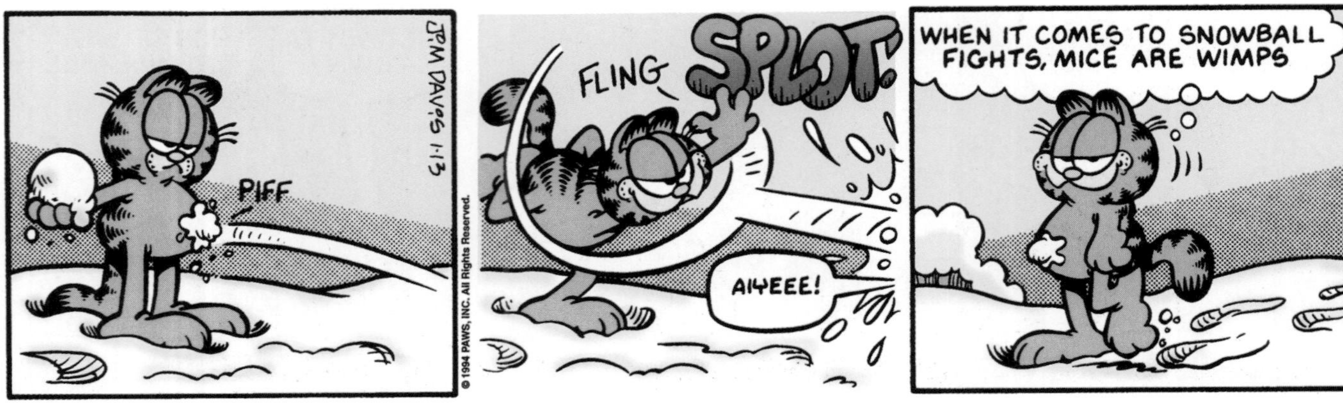
JIM DAVIS 1-13
PIFF
© 1994 PAWS, INC. All Rights Reserved.
FLING
SPLOT!
AIYEEE!
WHEN IT COMES TO SNOWBALL FIGHTS, MICE ARE WIMPS

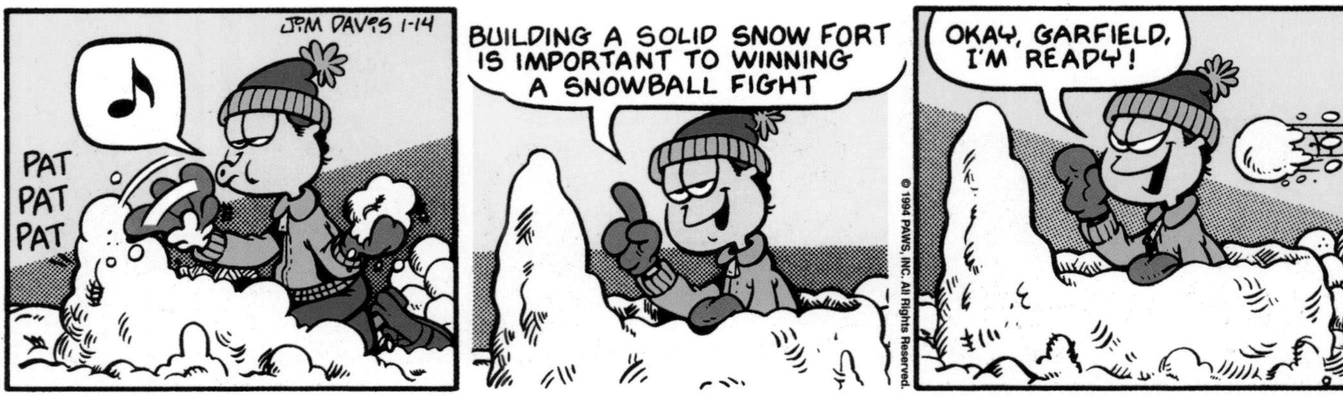
JIM DAVIS 1-14
♪
PAT PAT PAT
BUILDING A SOLID SNOW FORT IS IMPORTANT TO WINNING A SNOWBALL FIGHT
© 1994 PAWS, INC. All Rights Reserved.
OKAY, GARFIELD, I'M READY!

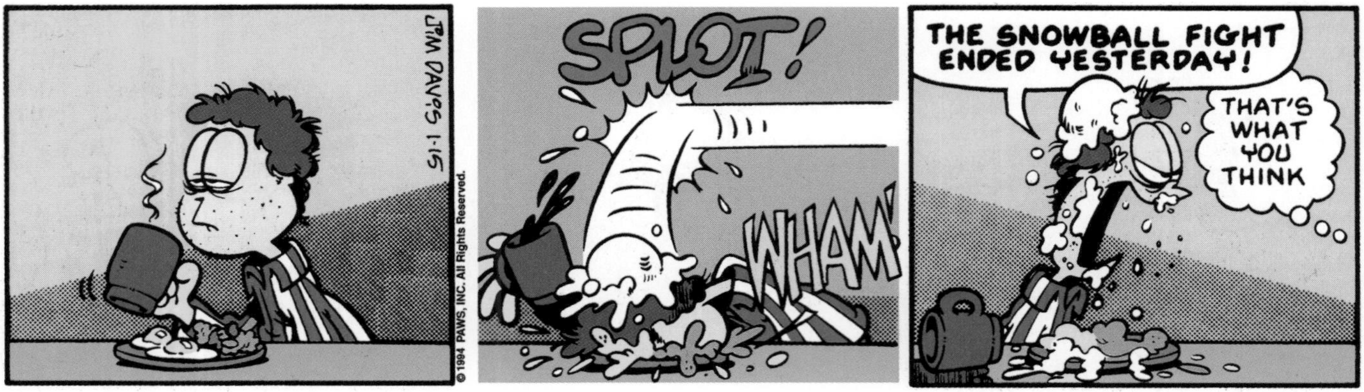
JIM DAVIS 1-15
© 1994 PAWS, INC. All Rights Reserved.
SPLOT!
WHAM!
THE SNOWBALL FIGHT ENDED YESTERDAY!
THAT'S WHAT YOU THINK

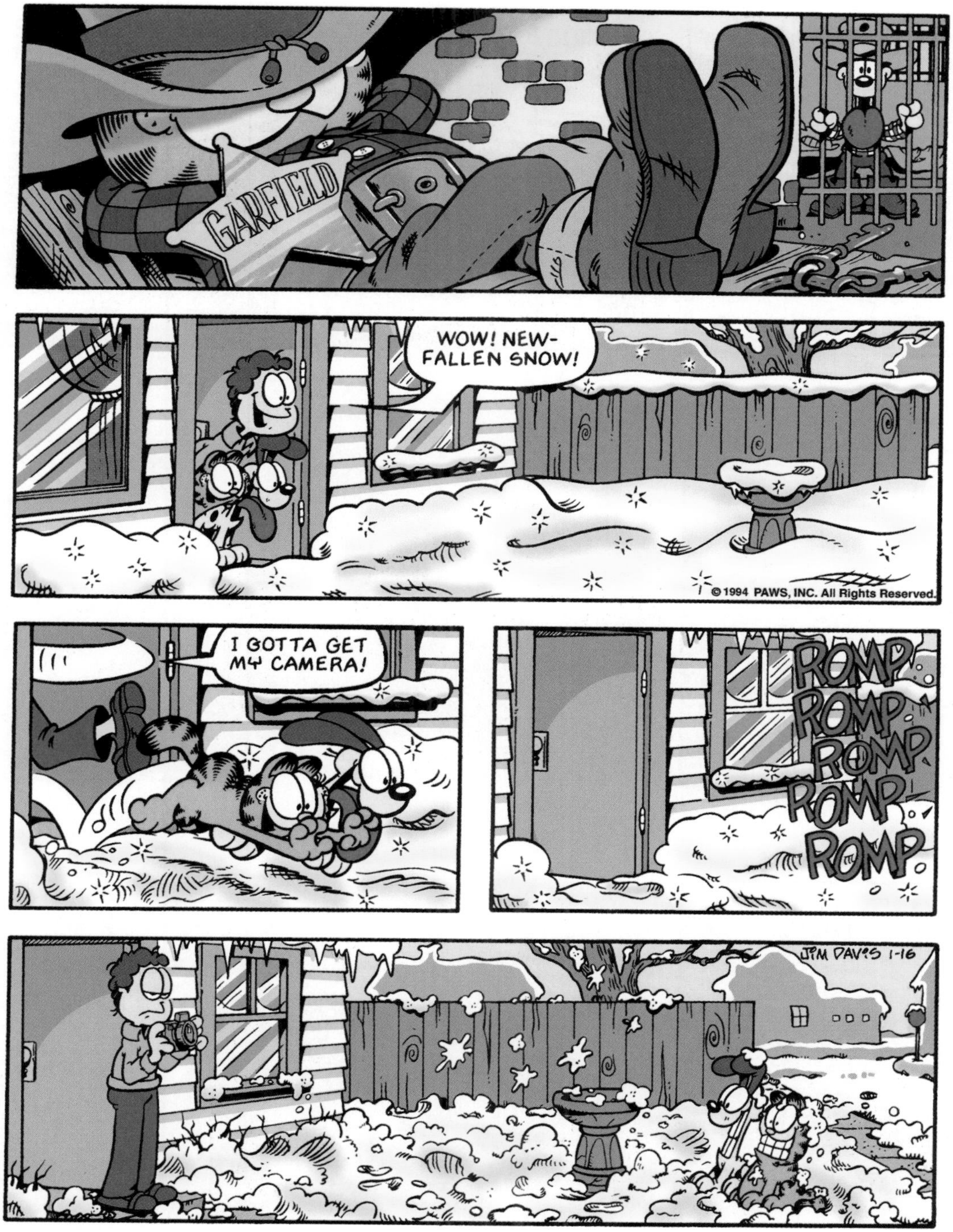
GARFIELD
WOW! NEW-FALLEN SNOW!
© 1994 PAWS, INC. All Rights Reserved.
I GOTTA GET MY CAMERA!
ROMP ROMP ROMP ROMP ROMP
JIM DAVIS 1-16

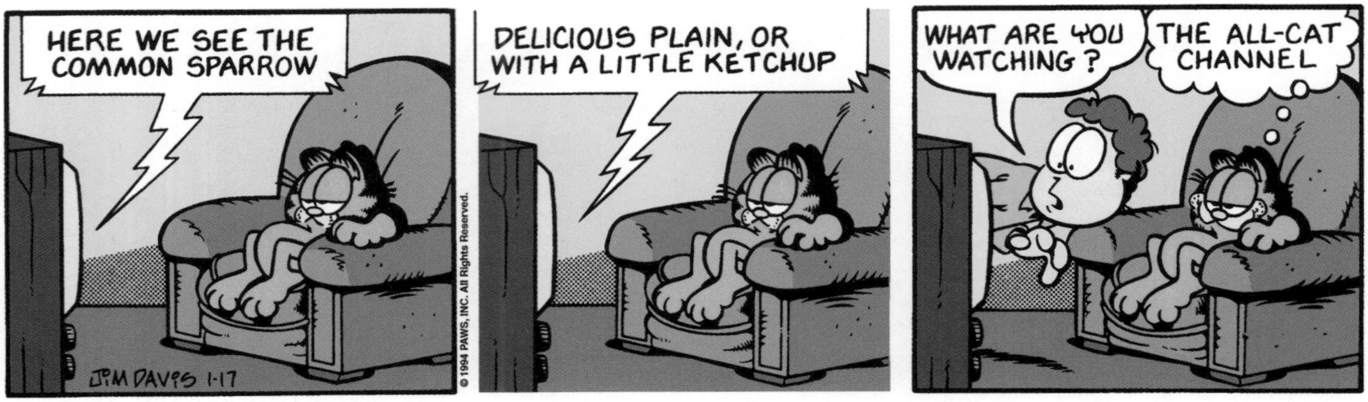
HERE WE SEE THE COMMON SPARROW
JIM DAVIS 1-17
© 1994 PAWS, INC. All Rights Reserved.
DELICIOUS PLAIN, OR WITH A LITTLE KETCHUP
WHAT ARE YOU WATCHING?
THE ALL-CAT CHANNEL

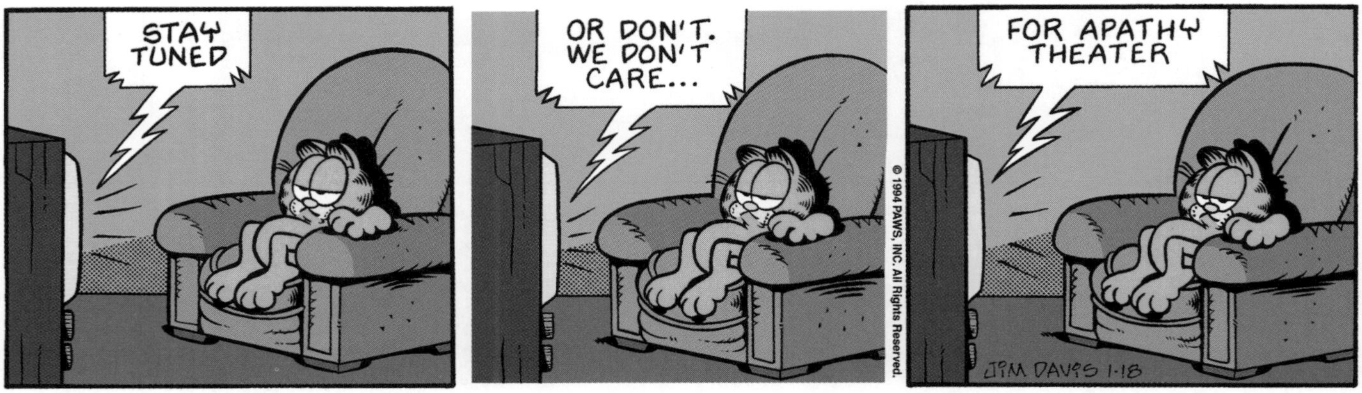
STAY TUNED
OR DON'T. WE DON'T CARE...
© 1994 PAWS, INC. All Rights Reserved.
FOR APATHY THEATER
JIM DAVIS 1-18

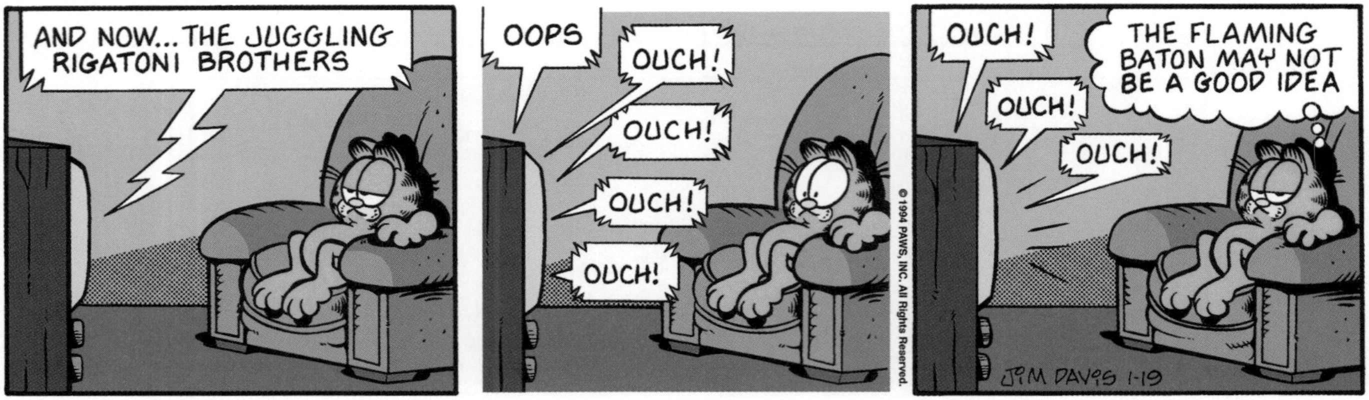
AND NOW... THE JUGGLING RIGATONI BROTHERS
OOPS
OUCH!
OUCH!
OUCH!
OUCH!
© 1994 PAWS, INC. All Rights Reserved.
OUCH!
OUCH!
OUCH!
THE FLAMING BATON MAY NOT BE A GOOD IDEA
JIM DAVIS 1-19

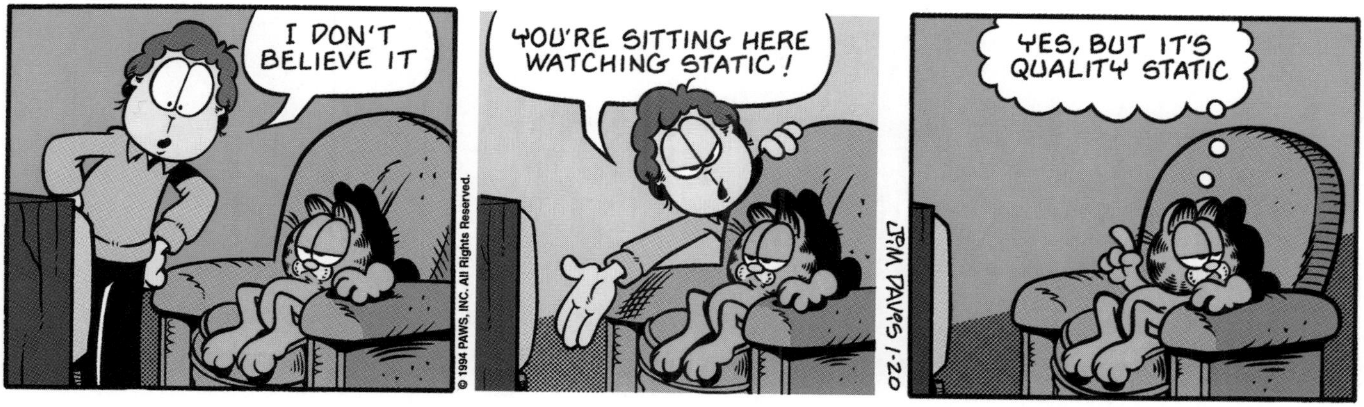
I DON'T BELIEVE IT
© 1994 PAWS, INC. All Rights Reserved.
YOU'RE SITTING HERE WATCHING STATIC!
JIM DAVIS 1-20
YES, BUT IT'S QUALITY STATIC

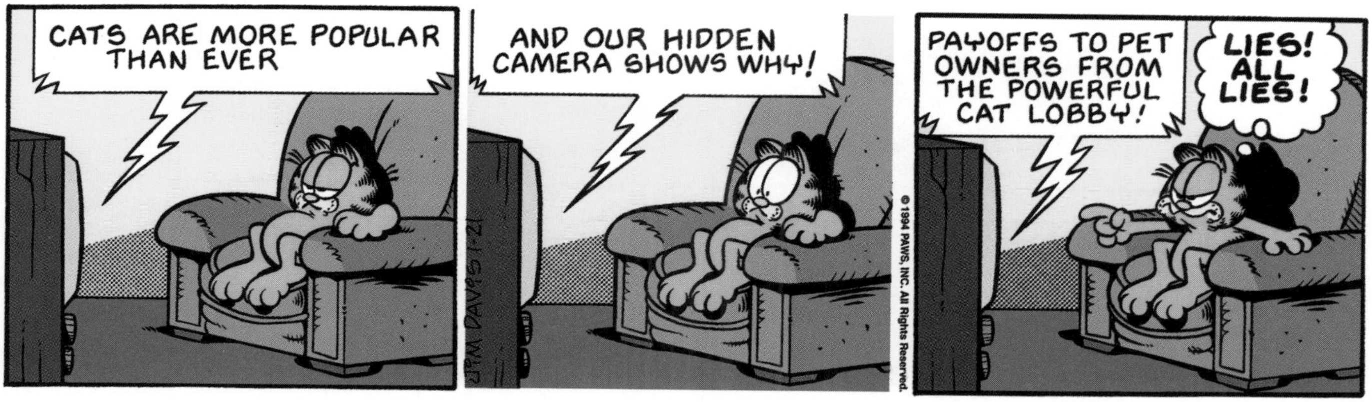
CATS ARE MORE POPULAR THAN EVER
JIM DAVIS 1-21
AND OUR HIDDEN CAMERA SHOWS WHY!
© 1994 PAWS, INC. All Rights Reserved.
PAYOFFS TO PET OWNERS FROM THE POWERFUL CAT LOBBY!
LIES! ALL LIES!

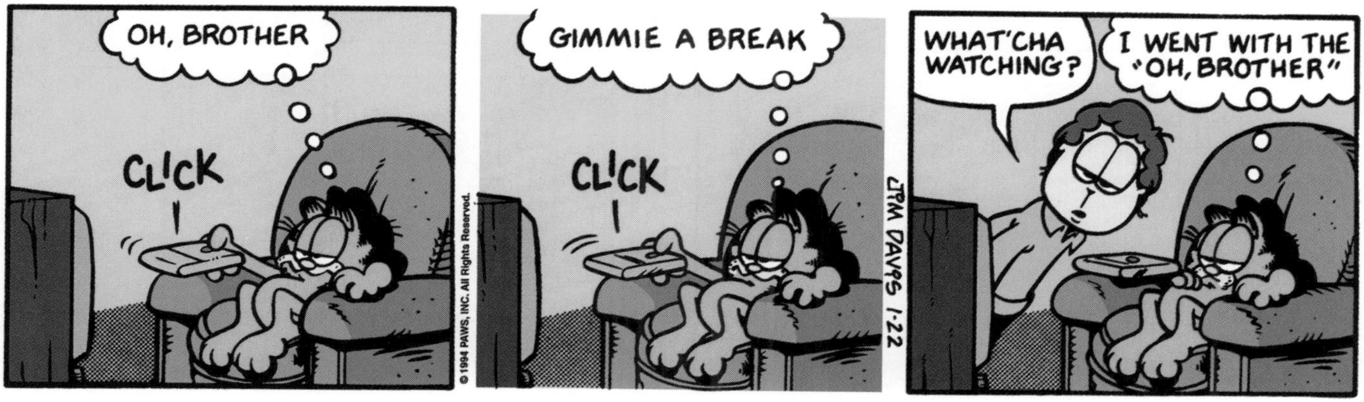
OH, BROTHER
CLICK
© 1994 PAWS, INC. All Rights Reserved.
GIMMIE A BREAK
CLICK
JIM DAVIS 1-22
WHAT'CHA WATCHING?
I WENT WITH THE "OH, BROTHER"

GARFIELD
Z
JIM DAVIS 1-23
WHAM!!
FLIP
FLIP
FLIP
FLIP
FLIP
FLIP
FLIP
ZZZZZZZZZZZZZZZZ
FLIP
FLIP
FLIP
FLIP
FLIP
FLIP
FLIP
?
© 1994 PAWS, INC. All Rights Reserved.
FLIP
FLIP
FLIP
FLIP
FLIP

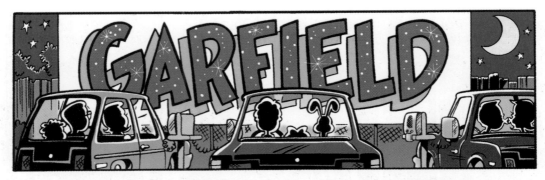

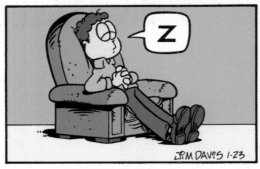

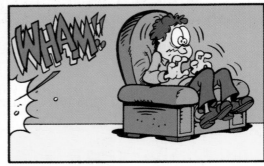

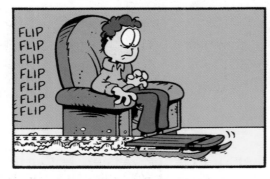

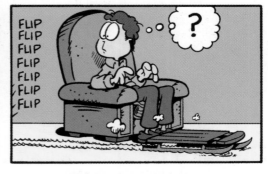

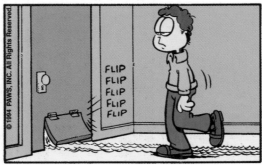

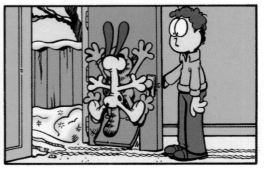

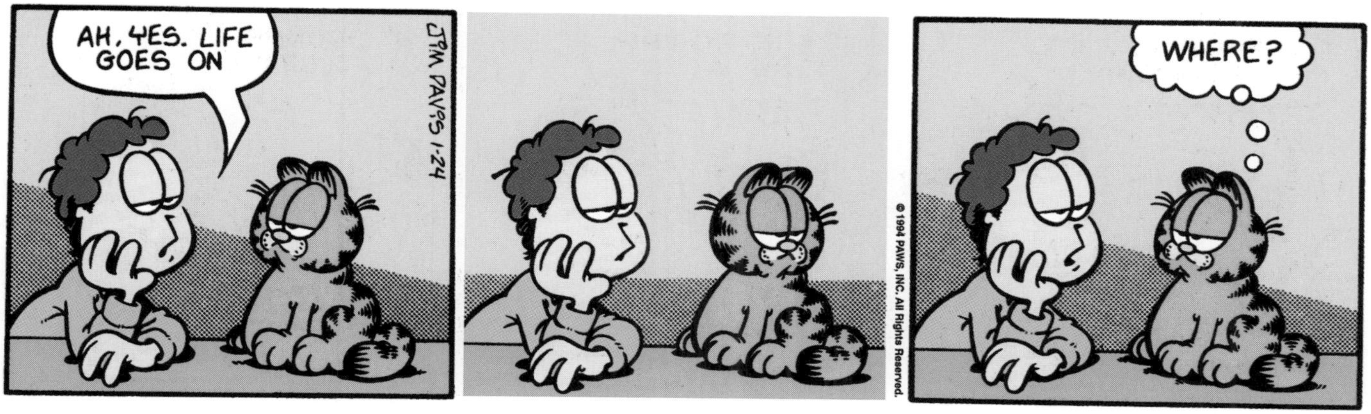
AH, YES. LIFE GOES ON
JIM DAVIS 1-24
© 1994 PAWS, INC. All Rights Reserved.
WHERE?

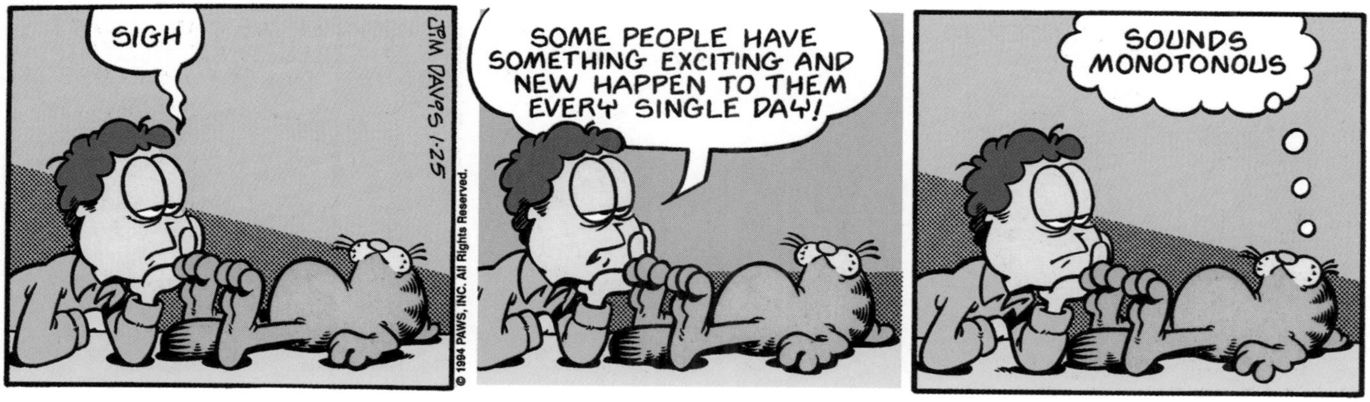
SIGH
JIM DAVIS 1-25
© 1994 PAWS, INC. All Rights Reserved.
SOME PEOPLE HAVE SOMETHING EXCITING AND NEW HAPPEN TO THEM EVERY SINGLE DAY!
SOUNDS MONOTONOUS

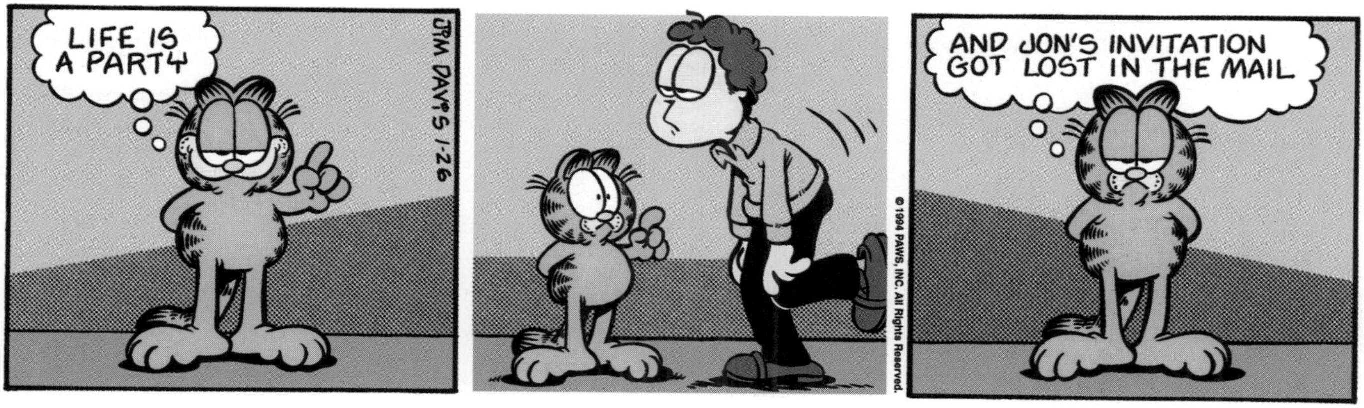
LIFE IS A PARTY
JIM DAVIS 1-26
© 1994 PAWS, INC. All Rights Reserved.
AND JON'S INVITATION GOT LOST IN THE MAIL

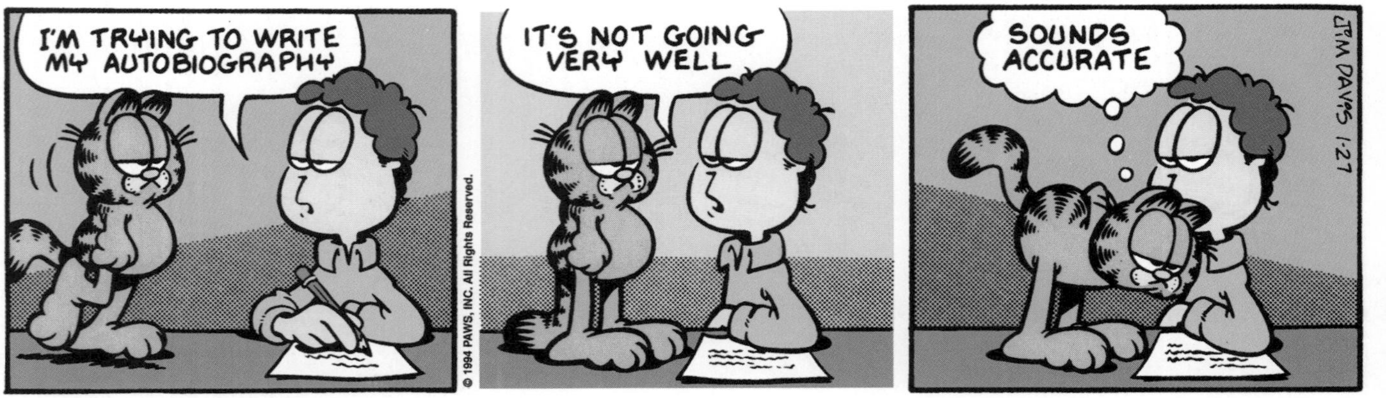
I'M TRYING TO WRITE MY AUTOBIOGRAPHY
© 1994 PAWS, INC. All Rights Reserved.
IT'S NOT GOING VERY WELL
SOUNDS ACCURATE
JIM DAVIS 1-27

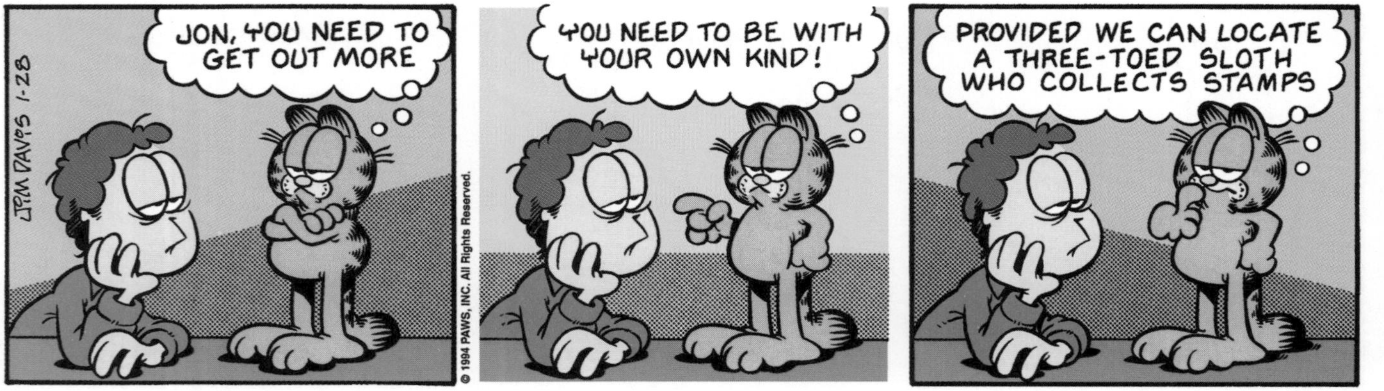
JIM DAVIS 1-28
JON, YOU NEED TO GET OUT MORE
© 1994 PAWS, INC. All Rights Reserved.
YOU NEED TO BE WITH YOUR OWN KIND!
PROVIDED WE CAN LOCATE A THREE-TOED SLOTH WHO COLLECTS STAMPS

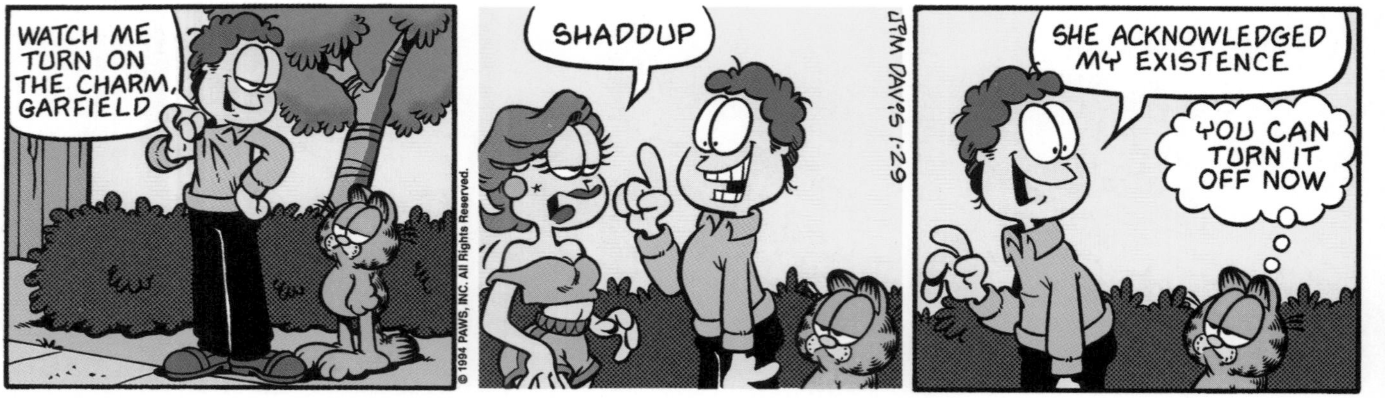
WATCH ME TURN ON THE CHARM, GARFIELD
© 1994 PAWS, INC. All Rights Reserved.
SHADDUP
JIM DAVIS 1-29
SHE ACKNOWLEDGED MY EXISTENCE
YOU CAN TURN IT OFF NOW

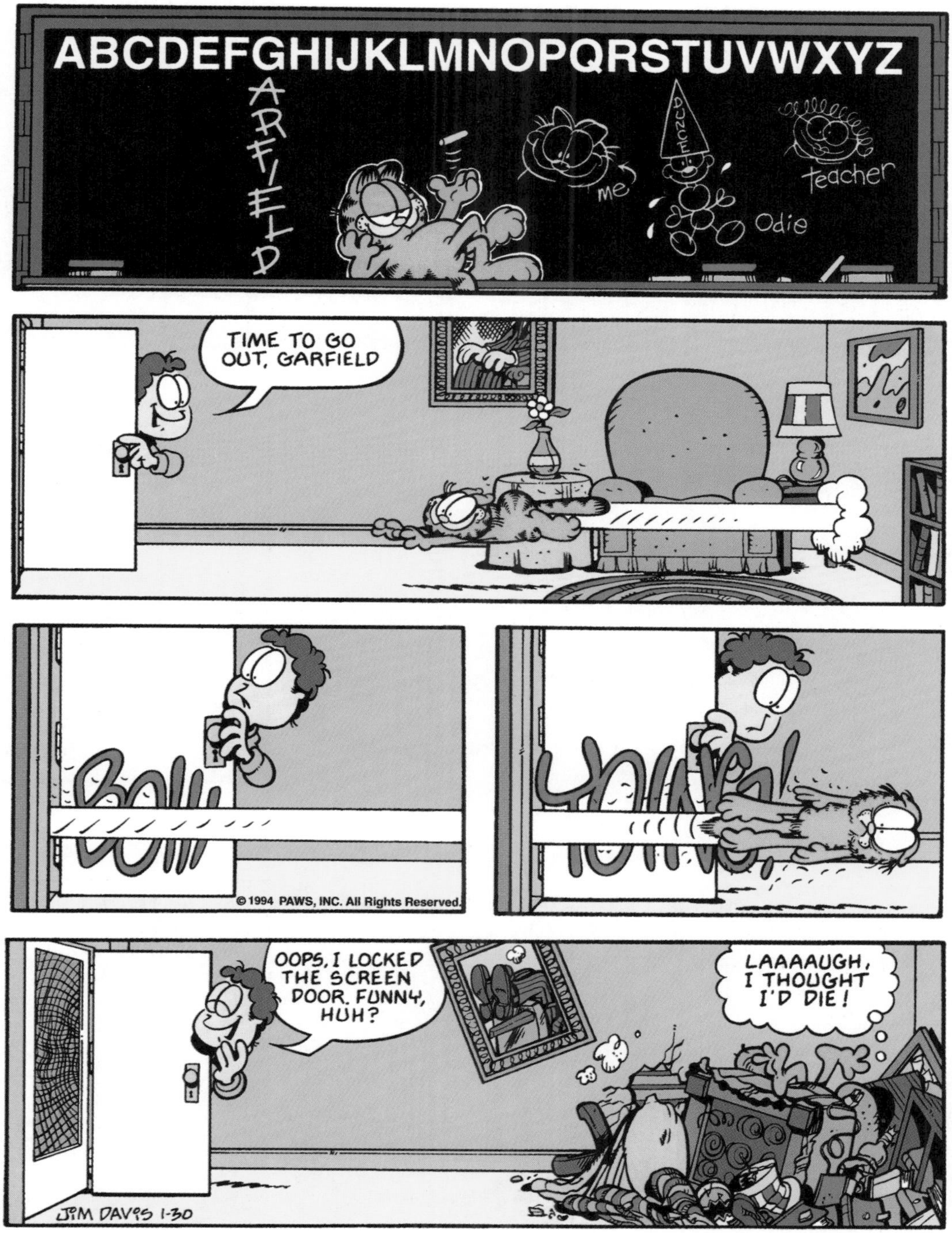
ABCDEFGHIJKLMNOPQRSTUVWXYZ
GARFIELD
me
DUNCE
Odie
teacher
TIME TO GO OUT, GARFIELD
BOIIII
YOING!
© 1994 PAWS, INC. All Rights Reserved.
OOPS, I LOCKED THE SCREEN DOOR. FUNNY, HUH?
LAAAAUGH, I THOUGHT I'D DIE!
JIM DAVIS 1-30

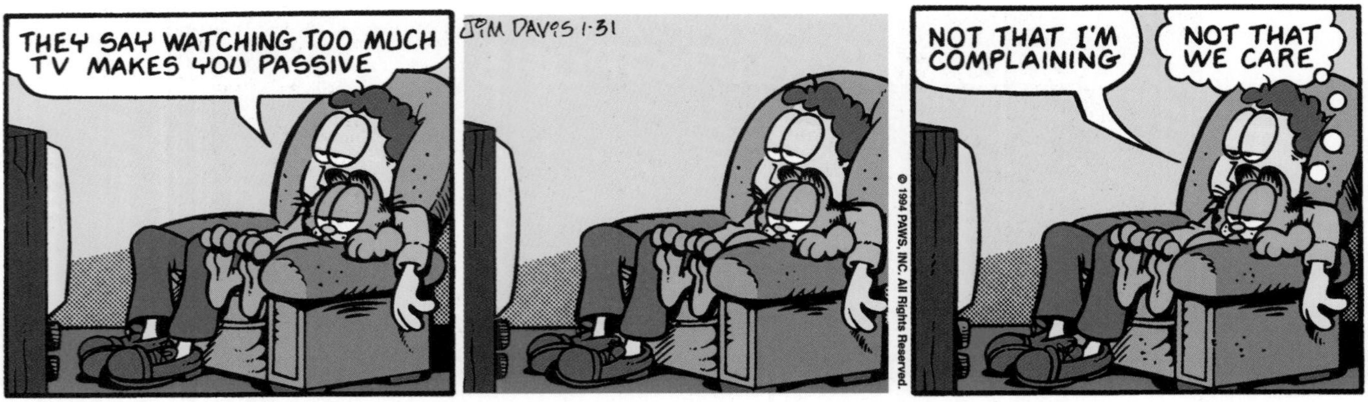
THEY SAY WATCHING TOO MUCH TV MAKES YOU PASSIVE
JIM DAVIS 1-31
© 1994 PAWS, INC. All Rights Reserved.
NOT THAT I'M COMPLAINING
NOT THAT WE CARE

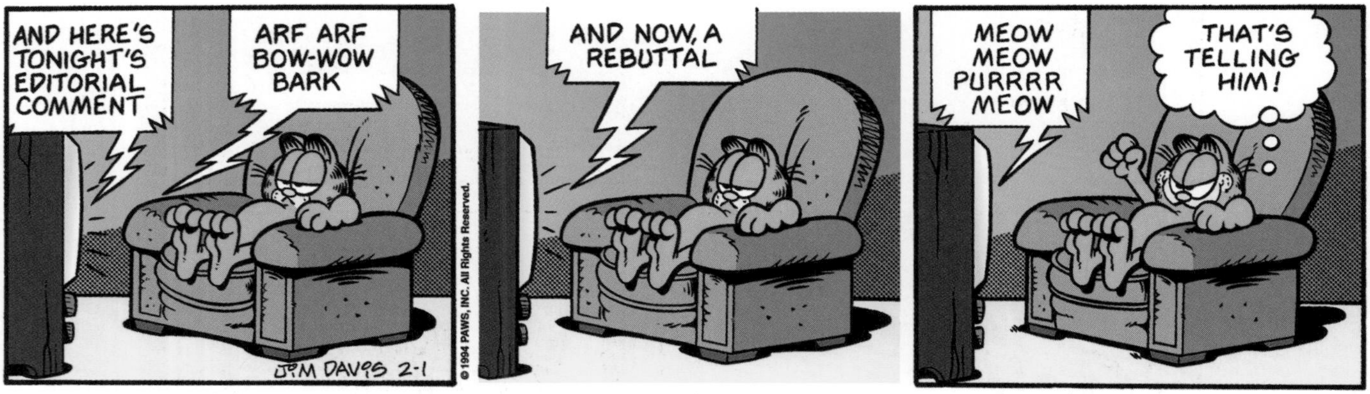
AND HERE'S TONIGHT'S EDITORIAL COMMENT
ARF ARF BOW-WOW BARK
JIM DAVIS 2-1
© 1994 PAWS, INC. All Rights Reserved.
AND NOW, A REBUTTAL
MEOW MEOW PURRRR MEOW
THAT'S TELLING HIM!

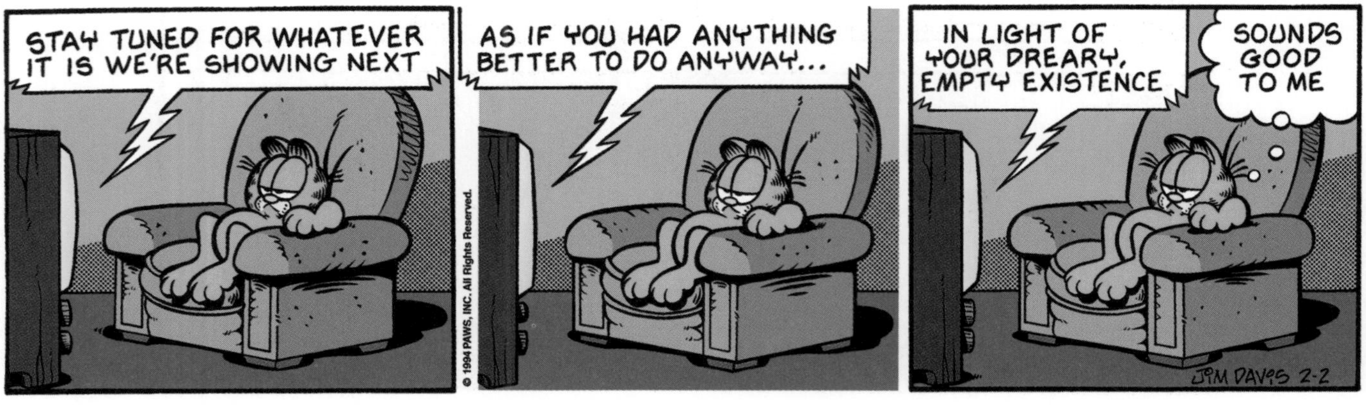
STAY TUNED FOR WHATEVER IT IS WE'RE SHOWING NEXT
© 1994 PAWS, INC. All Rights Reserved.
AS IF YOU HAD ANYTHING BETTER TO DO ANYWAY...
IN LIGHT OF YOUR DREARY, EMPTY EXISTENCE
SOUNDS GOOD TO ME
JIM DAVIS 2-2

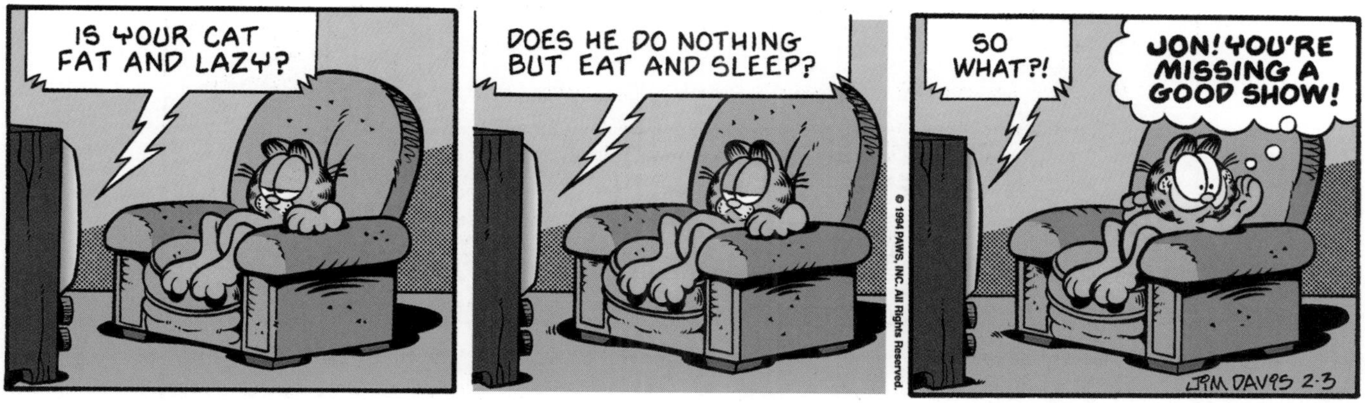
IS YOUR CAT FAT AND LAZY?
DOES HE DO NOTHING BUT EAT AND SLEEP?
© 1994 PAWS, INC. All Rights Reserved.
SO WHAT?!
JON! YOU'RE MISSING A GOOD SHOW!
JIM DAVIS 2-3

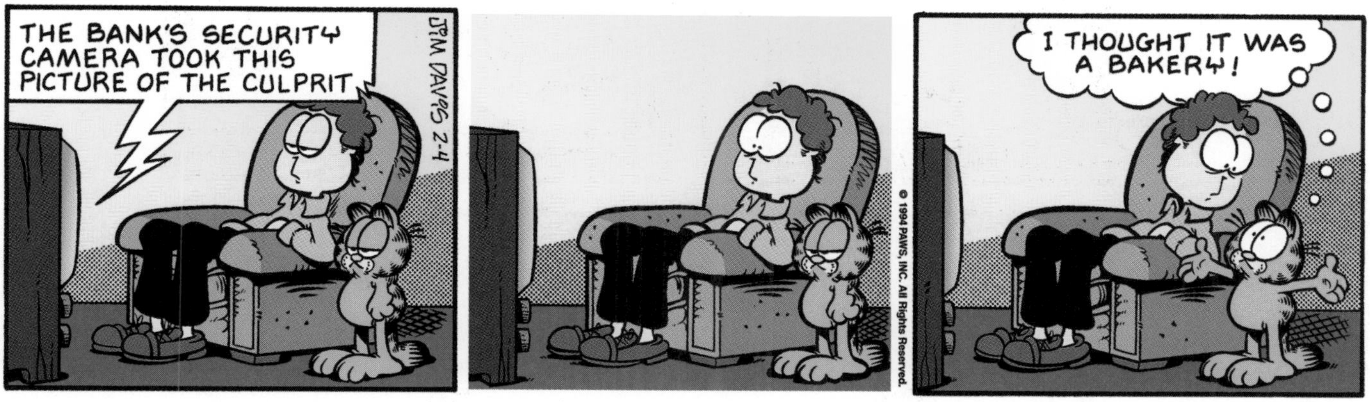
THE BANK'S SECURITY CAMERA TOOK THIS PICTURE OF THE CULPRIT
JIM DAVIS 2-4
© 1994 PAWS, INC. All Rights Reserved.
I THOUGHT IT WAS A BAKERY!

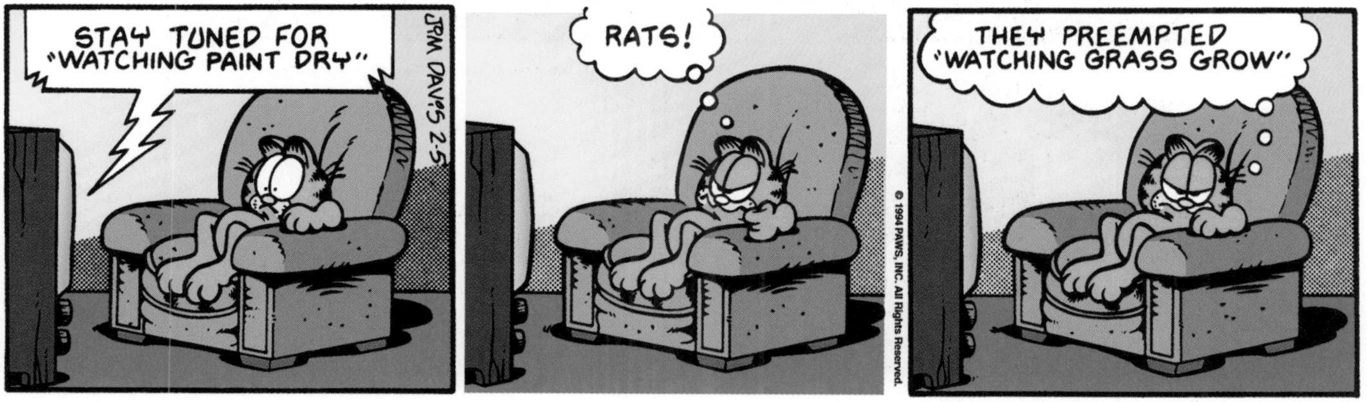
STAY TUNED FOR "WATCHING PAINT DRY"
JIM DAVIS 2-5
RATS!
© 1994 PAWS, INC. All Rights Reserved.
THEY PREEMPTED "WATCHING GRASS GROW"

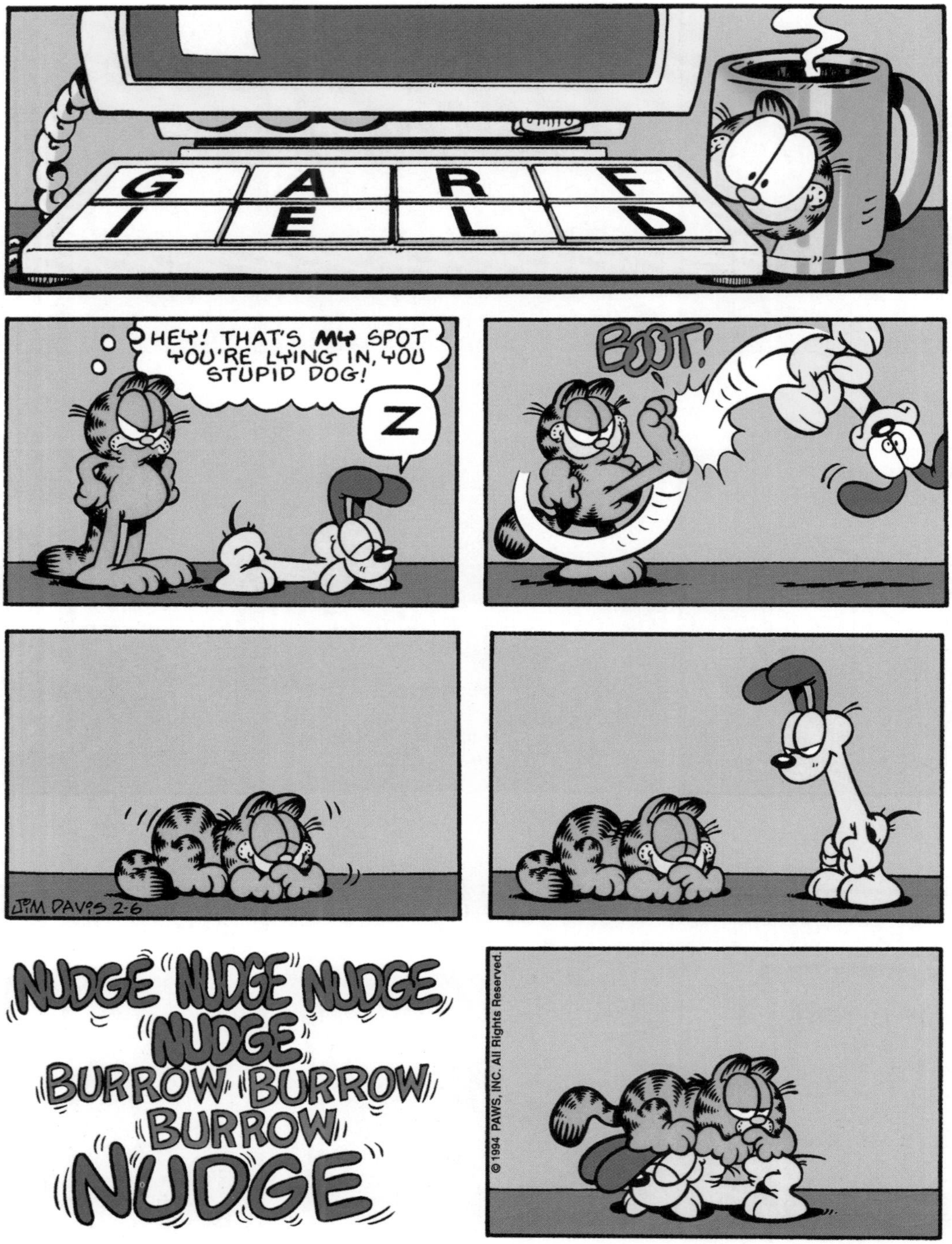
GARFIELD
HEY! THAT'S MY SPOT YOU'RE LYING IN, YOU STUPID DOG!
Z
BOOT!
JIM DAVIS 2-6
NUDGE NUDGE NUDGE
NUDGE
BURROW BURROW
BURROW
NUDGE

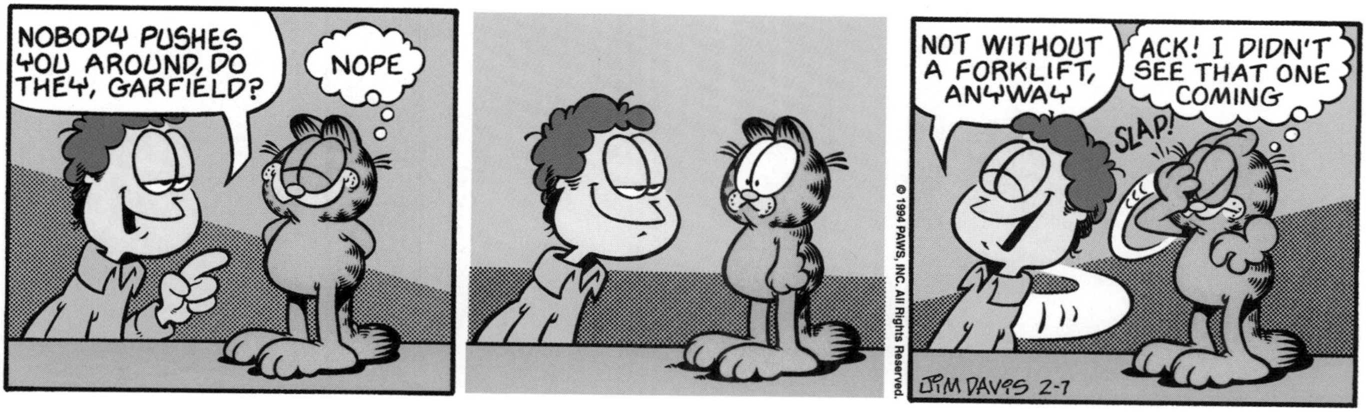
NOBODY PUSHES YOU AROUND, DO THEY, GARFIELD?
NOPE
NOT WITHOUT A FORKLIFT, ANYWAY
ACK! I DIDN'T SEE THAT ONE COMING
SLAP!
© 1994 PAWS, INC. All Rights Reserved.
JIM DAVIS 2-7

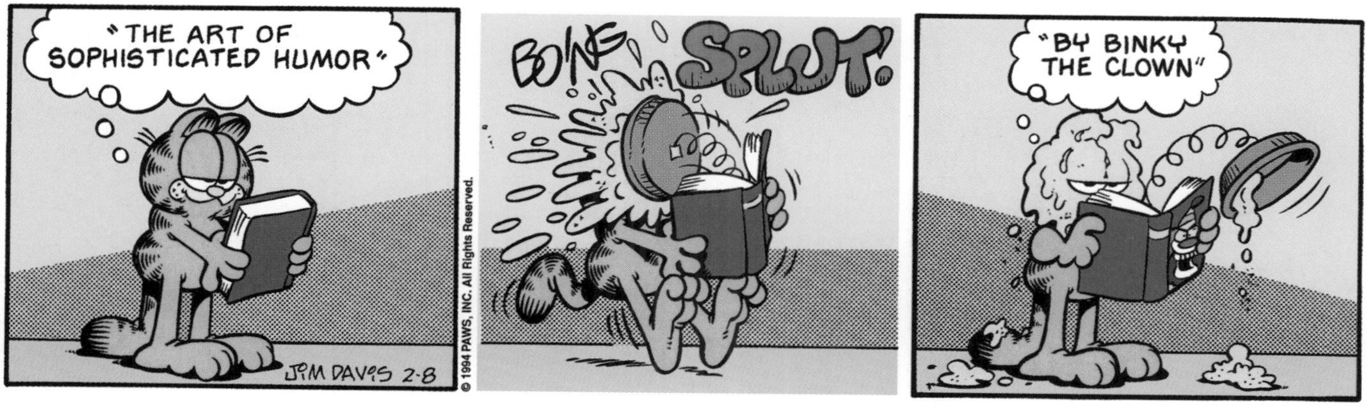
"THE ART OF SOPHISTICATED HUMOR"
JIM DAVIS 2-8
© 1994 PAWS, INC. All Rights Reserved.
BOING
SPLUT!
"BY BINKY THE CLOWN"

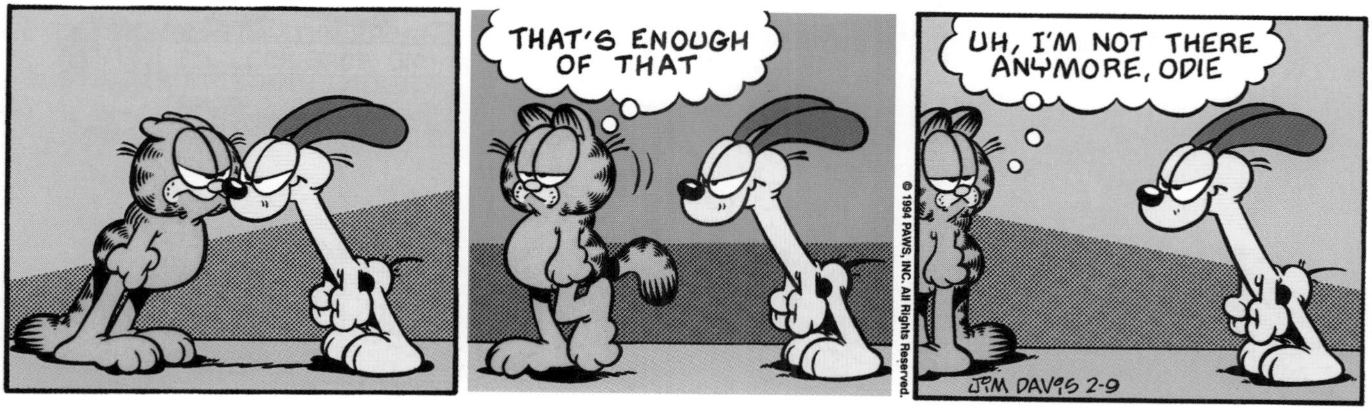
THAT'S ENOUGH OF THAT
© 1994 PAWS, INC. All Rights Reserved.
UH, I'M NOT THERE ANYMORE, ODIE
JIM DAVIS 2-9

JIM DAVIS 2-10
YAWN
GARFIELD
GARFIE
-GULP!
© 1994 PAWS, INC. All Rights Reserved.
YAWN
I HAVEN'T SEEN HIS FACE IN TWO DAYS
GARFIELD

JIM DAVIS 2-11
© 1994 PAWS, INC. All Rights Reserved.
I WAS READING THAT
NOBODY CARES ABOUT YOUR PAST, JON

SEE, YOU ROLL THE SOCKS UP LIKE THIS
JIM DAVIS 2-12
HERE, YOU TRY IT
© 1994 PAWS, INC. All Rights Reserved.
YOU'RE NOT WITH ME ON THIS
NOW, LET'S DO THE UNDERWEAR

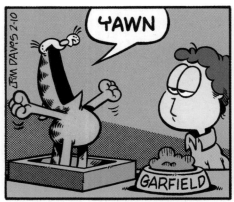

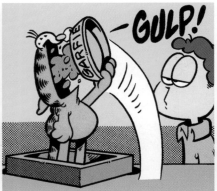

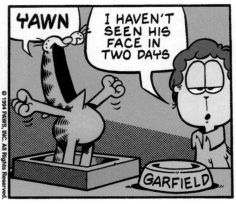

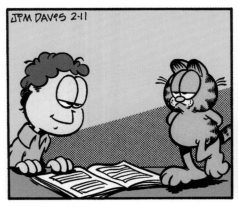

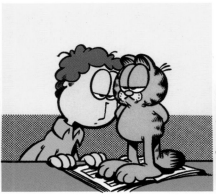

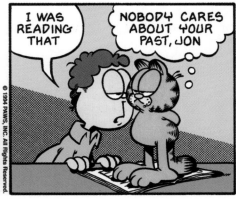

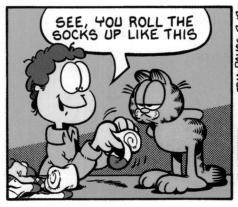

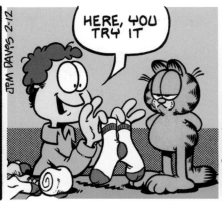

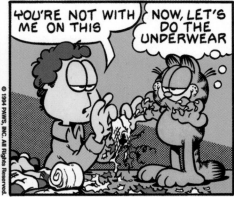

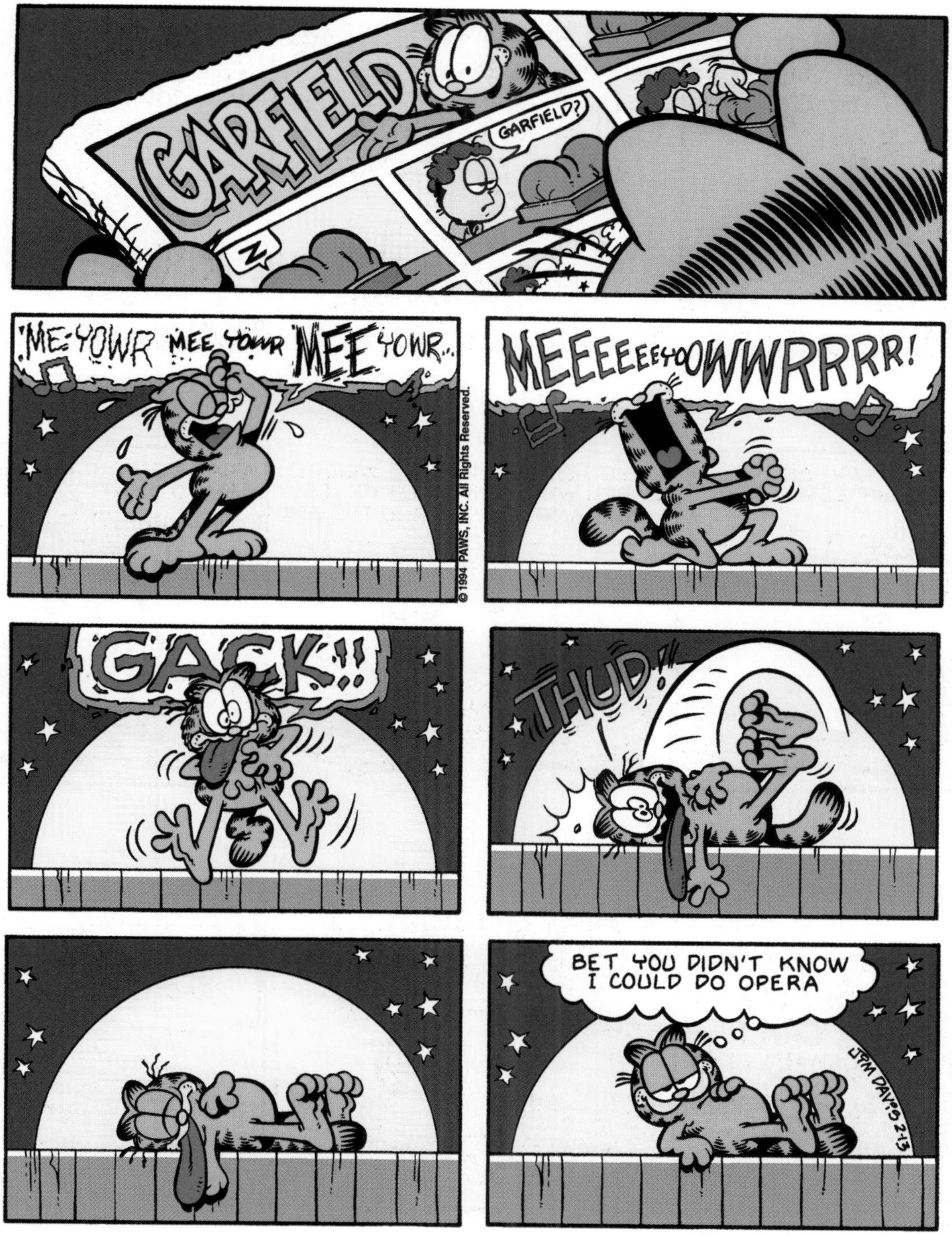
GARFIELD
GARFIELD?
Z
ME-YOWR MEE YOWR MEE YOWR...
© 1994 PAWS, INC. All Rights Reserved.
MEEEEEEYOOWWRRRRR!
GACK!!
THUD!
BET YOU DIDN'T KNOW I COULD DO OPERA
JPM DAVIS 2-13

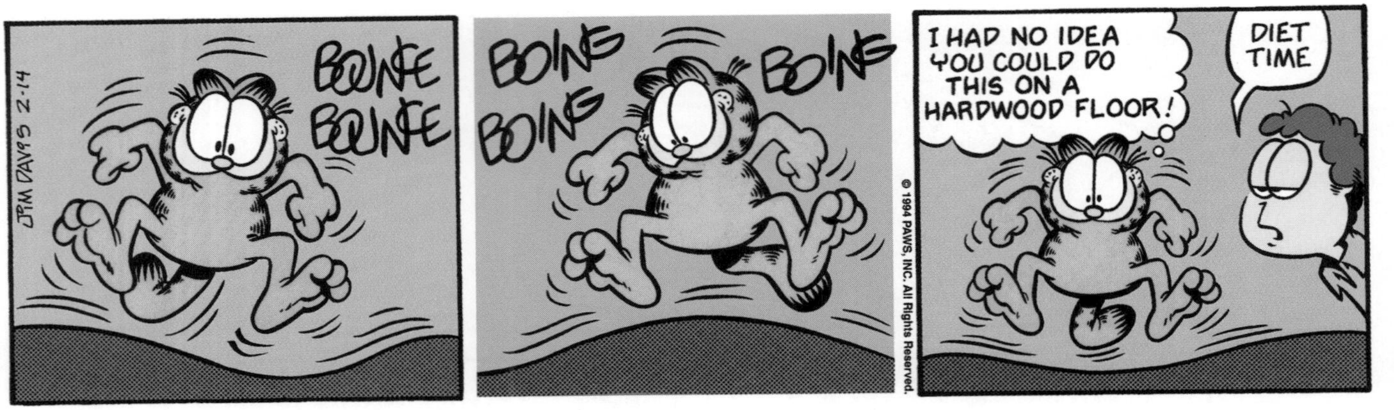
JIM DAVIS 2·14
BOUNCE BOUNCE
BOING BOING BOING
I HAD NO IDEA YOU COULD DO THIS ON A HARDWOOD FLOOR!
DIET TIME
© 1994 PAWS, INC. All Rights Reserved.

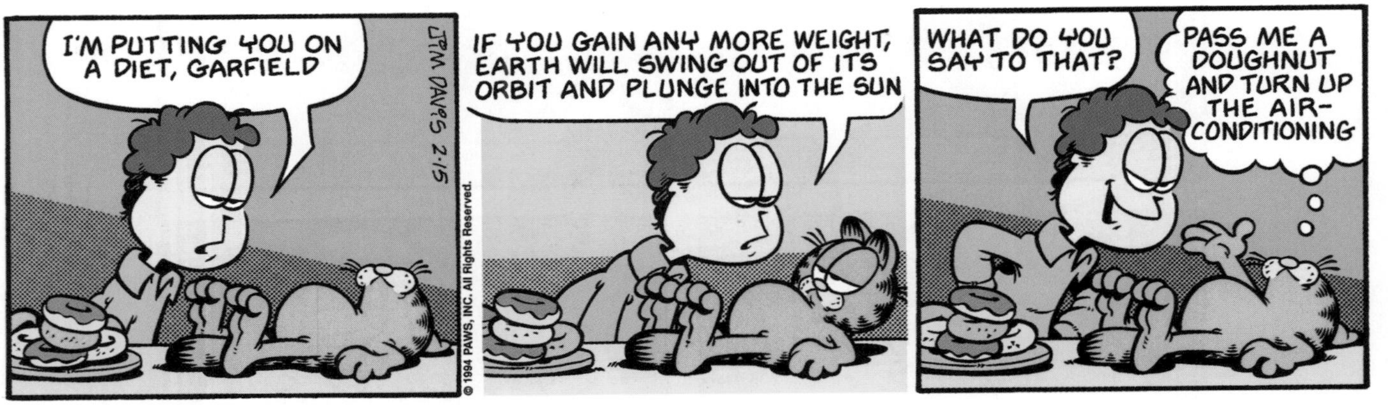
I'M PUTTING YOU ON A DIET, GARFIELD
JIM DAVIS 2·15
© 1994 PAWS, INC. All Rights Reserved.
IF YOU GAIN ANY MORE WEIGHT, EARTH WILL SWING OUT OF ITS ORBIT AND PLUNGE INTO THE SUN
WHAT DO YOU SAY TO THAT?
PASS ME A DOUGHNUT AND TURN UP THE AIR-CONDITIONING

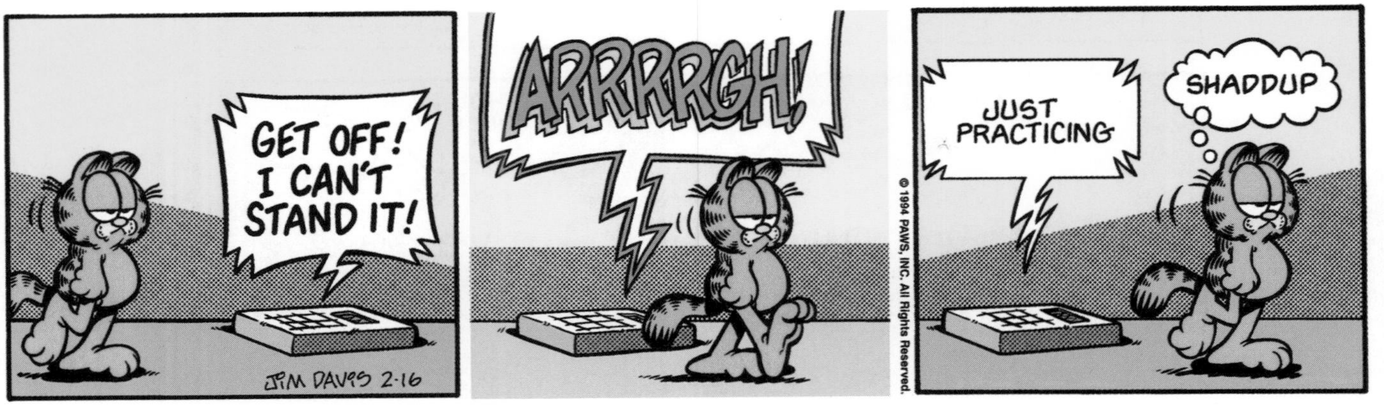
GET OFF! I CAN'T STAND IT!
JIM DAVIS 2·16
ARRRRRGH!
JUST PRACTICING
SHADDUP
© 1994 PAWS, INC. All Rights Reserved.

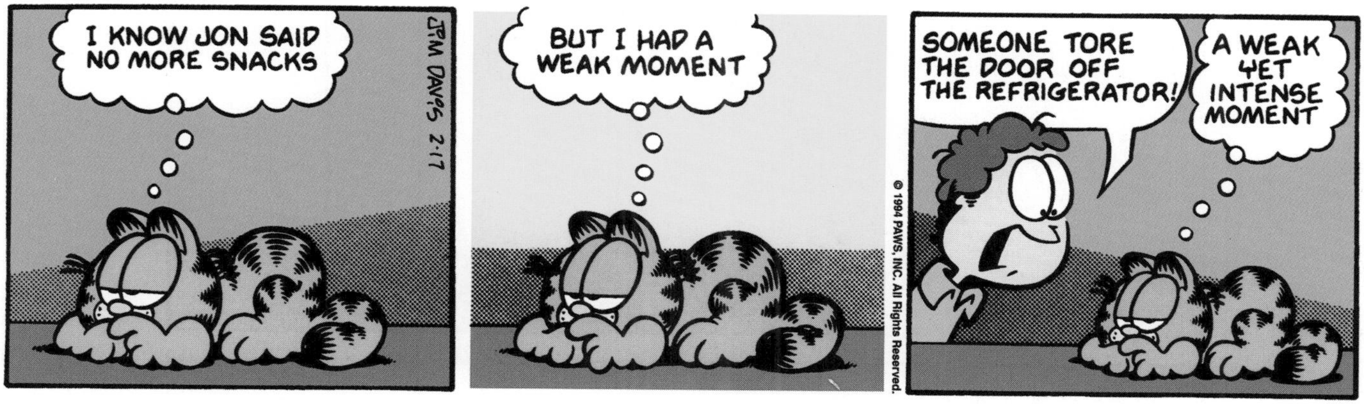
I KNOW JON SAID NO MORE SNACKS
JIM DAVIS 2-17
BUT I HAD A WEAK MOMENT
SOMEONE TORE THE DOOR OFF THE REFRIGERATOR!
A WEAK YET INTENSE MOMENT

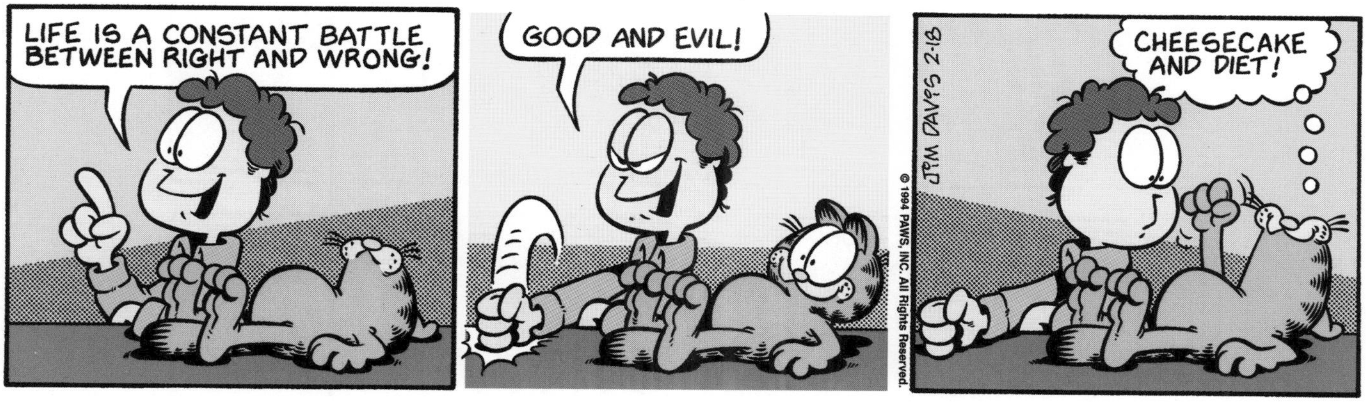
LIFE IS A CONSTANT BATTLE BETWEEN RIGHT AND WRONG!
GOOD AND EVIL!
JIM DAVIS 2-18
CHEESECAKE AND DIET!

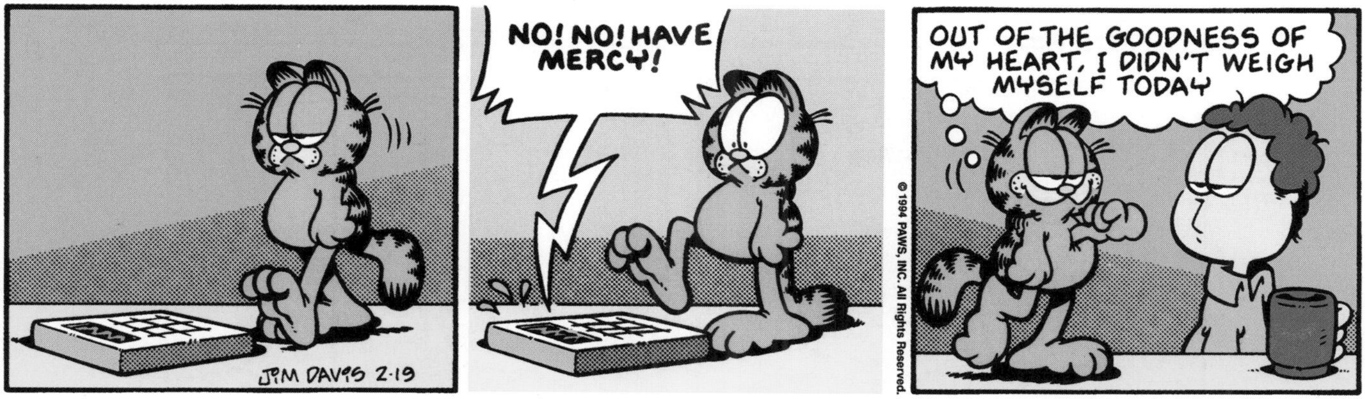
JIM DAVIS 2-19
NO! NO! HAVE MERCY!
OUT OF THE GOODNESS OF MY HEART, I DIDN'T WEIGH MYSELF TODAY

Garfield
BRINNNG!
'MORNING, GARFIELD
'MORNING, JON
© 1994 PAWS, INC. All Rights Reserved.
'MORNING, POOKY
CRUNCH CRUNCH
'MORNING, ODIE
I GOTTA GET OFF THIS DIET
JIM DAVIS 2-20

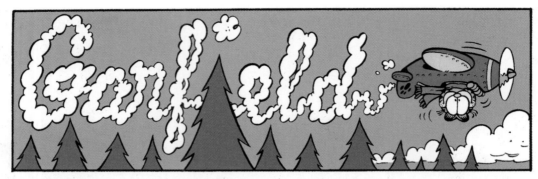

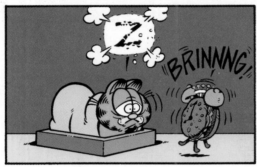

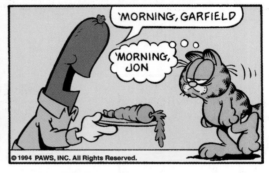

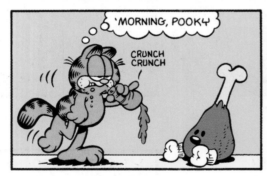

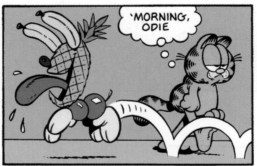

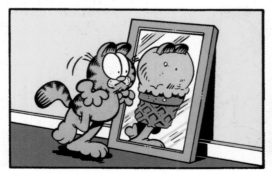

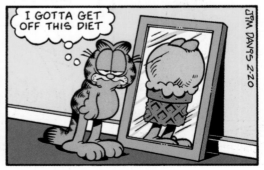

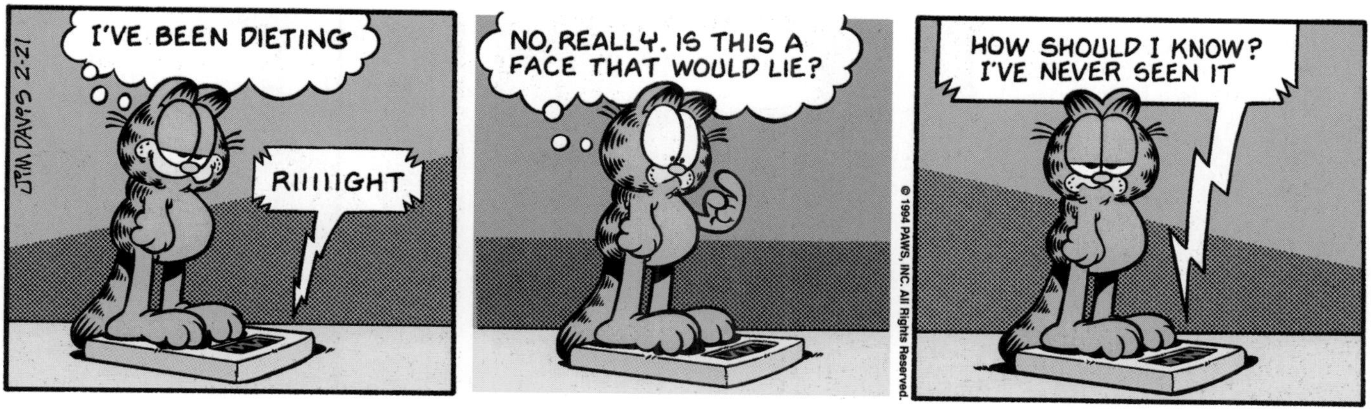
JIM DAVIS 2-21
I'VE BEEN DIETING
RIIIIIGHT
NO, REALLY. IS THIS A FACE THAT WOULD LIE?
HOW SHOULD I KNOW? I'VE NEVER SEEN IT
© 1994 PAWS, INC. All Rights Reserved.

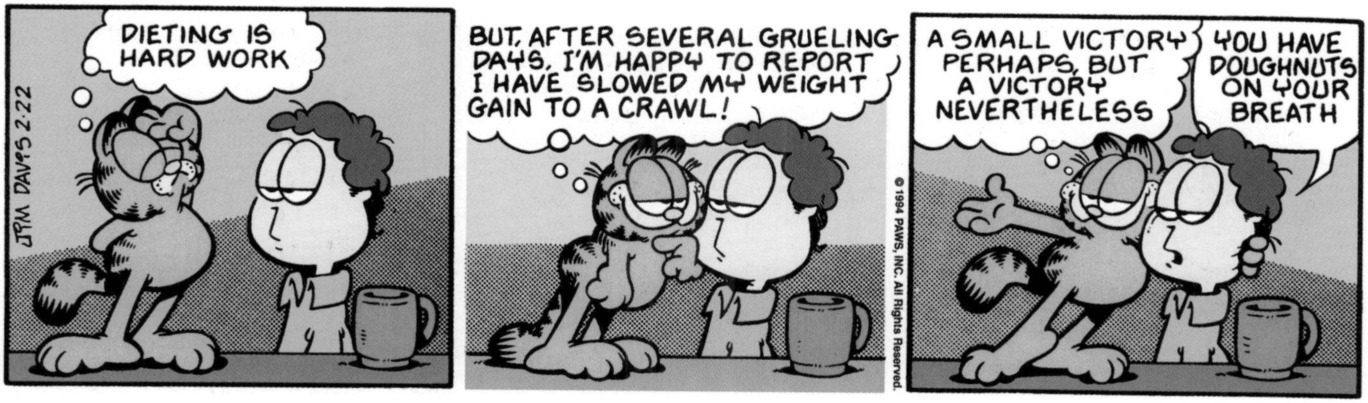
JIM DAVIS 2-22
DIETING IS HARD WORK
BUT, AFTER SEVERAL GRUELING DAYS, I'M HAPPY TO REPORT I HAVE SLOWED MY WEIGHT GAIN TO A CRAWL!
A SMALL VICTORY PERHAPS, BUT A VICTORY NEVERTHELESS
YOU HAVE DOUGHNUTS ON YOUR BREATH
© 1994 PAWS, INC. All Rights Reserved.

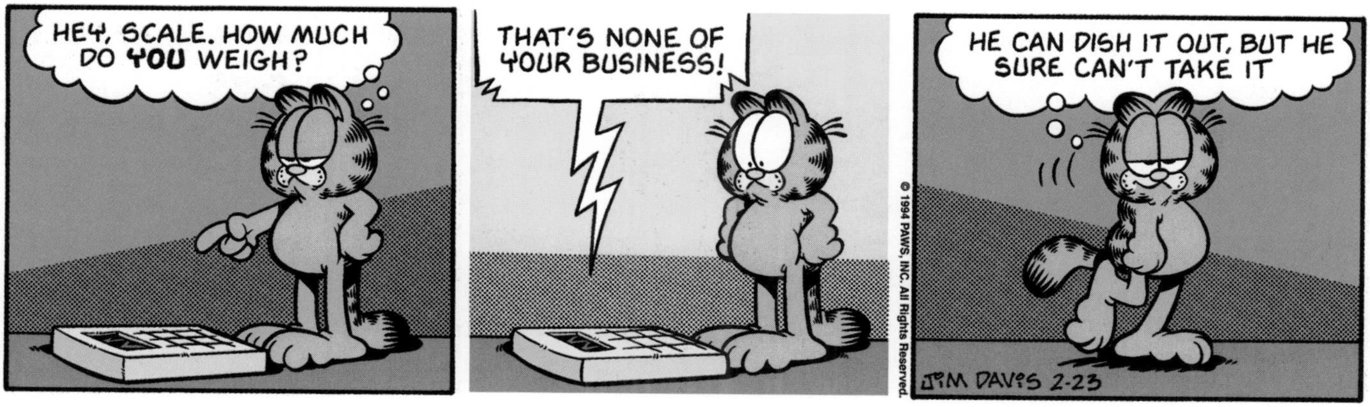
HEY, SCALE. HOW MUCH DO **YOU** WEIGH?
THAT'S NONE OF YOUR BUSINESS!
HE CAN DISH IT OUT, BUT HE SURE CAN'T TAKE IT
JIM DAVIS 2-23
© 1994 PAWS, INC. All Rights Reserved.

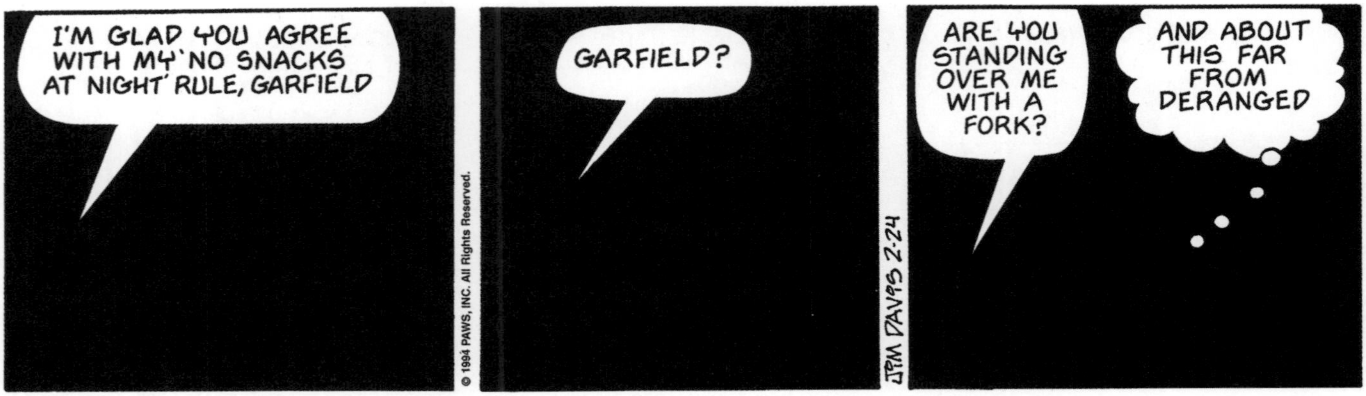
I'M GLAD YOU AGREE WITH MY 'NO SNACKS AT NIGHT' RULE, GARFIELD
GARFIELD?
ARE YOU STANDING OVER ME WITH A FORK?
AND ABOUT THIS FAR FROM DERANGED
© 1994 PAWS, INC. All Rights Reserved.
JIM DAVIS 2-24

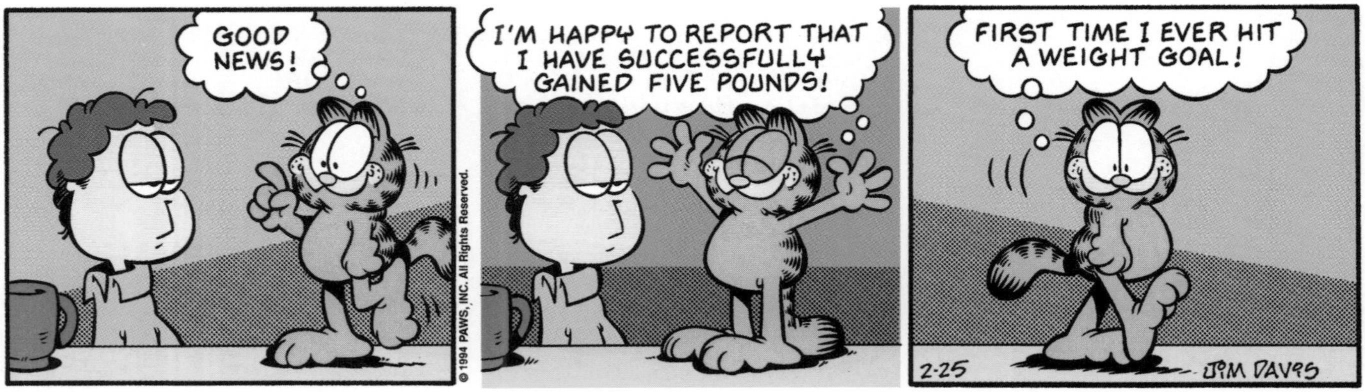
GOOD NEWS!
I'M HAPPY TO REPORT THAT I HAVE SUCCESSFULLY GAINED FIVE POUNDS!
FIRST TIME I EVER HIT A WEIGHT GOAL!
© 1994 PAWS, INC. All Rights Reserved.
2-25
JIM DAVIS

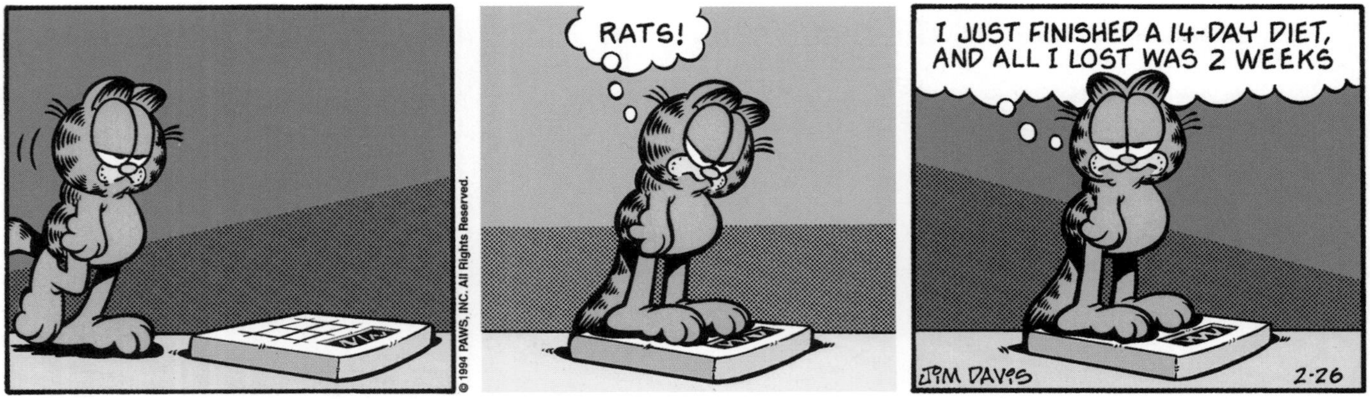
RATS!
I JUST FINISHED A 14-DAY DIET, AND ALL I LOST WAS 2 WEEKS
© 1994 PAWS, INC. All Rights Reserved.
JIM DAVIS
2-26

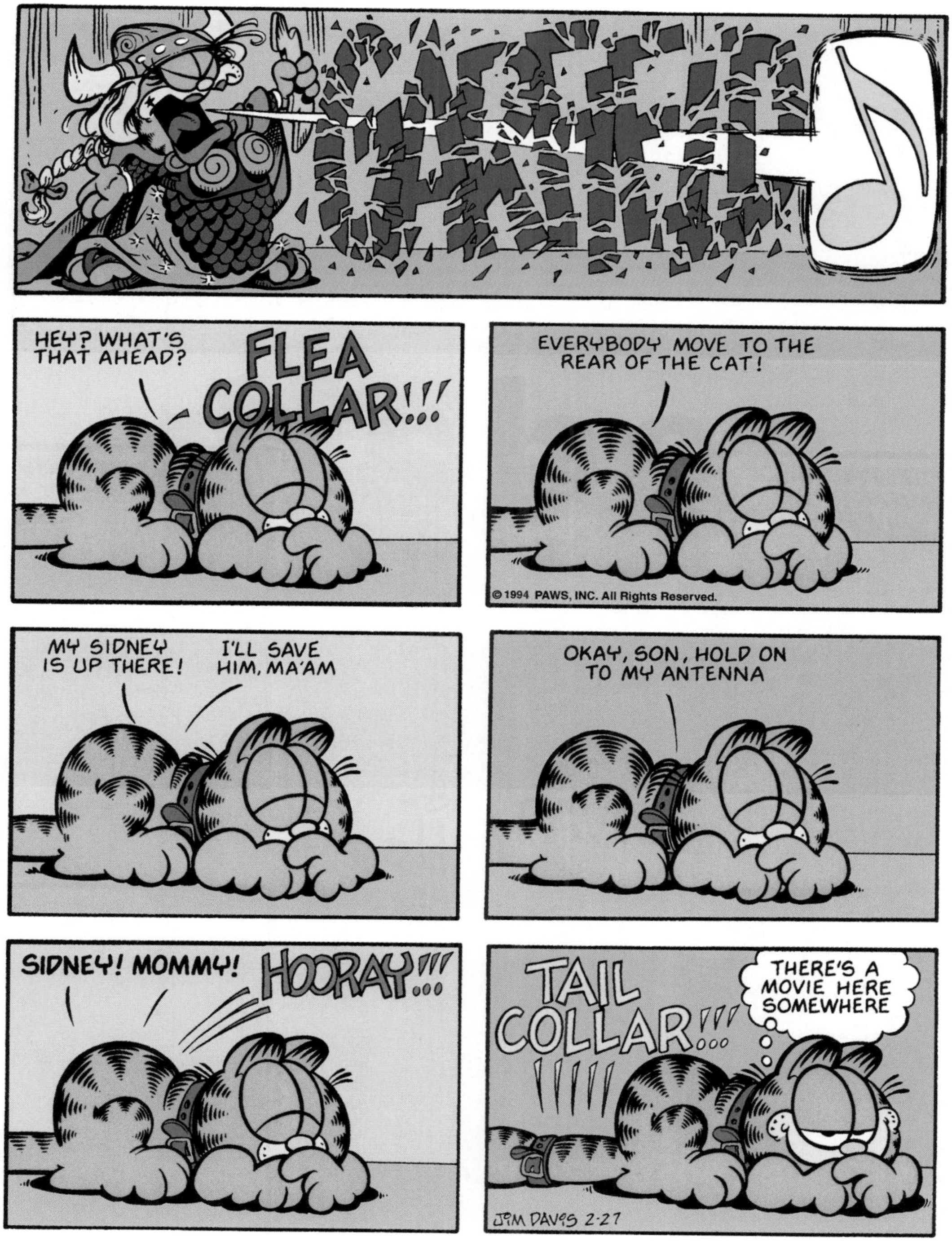
HEY? WHAT'S THAT AHEAD?
FLEA COLLAR!!!
EVERYBODY MOVE TO THE REAR OF THE CAT!
© 1994 PAWS, INC. All Rights Reserved.
MY SIDNEY IS UP THERE!
I'LL SAVE HIM, MA'AM
OKAY, SON, HOLD ON TO MY ANTENNA
SIDNEY! MOMMY!
HOORAY!!!
TAIL COLLAR!!!
THERE'S A MOVIE HERE SOMEWHERE
JIM DAVIS 2-27

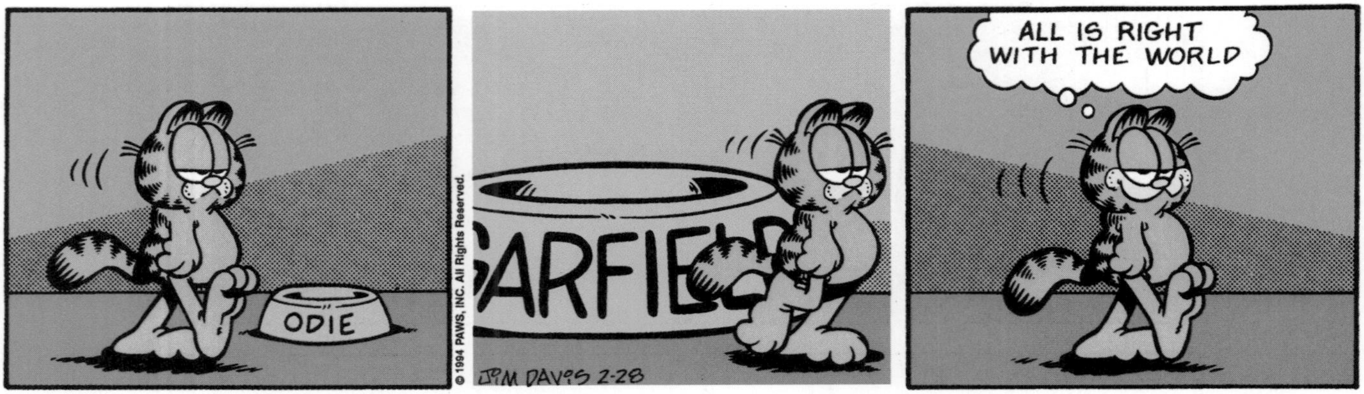
ODIE
GARFIELD
© 1994 PAWS, INC. All Rights Reserved.
JIM DAVIS 2-28
ALL IS RIGHT WITH THE WORLD

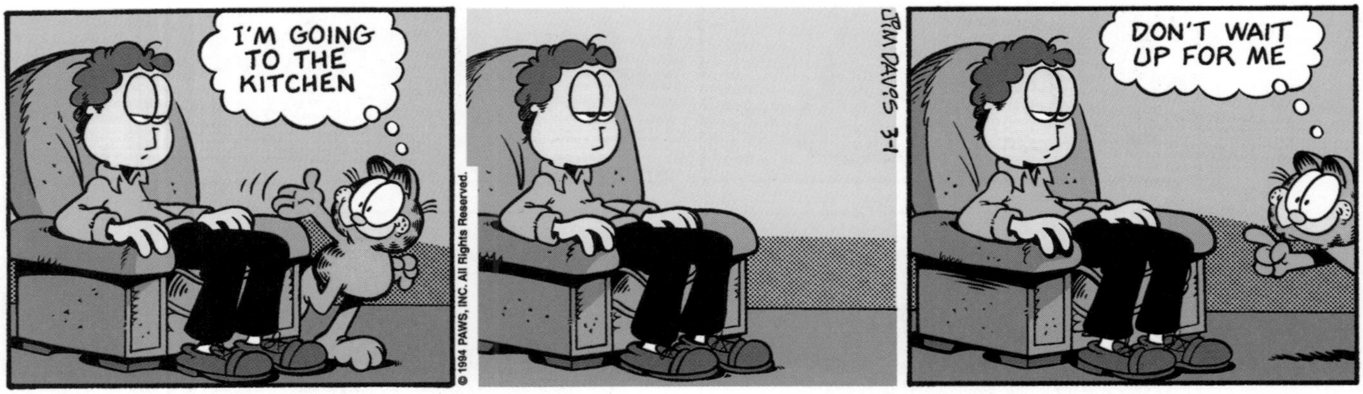
I'M GOING TO THE KITCHEN
© 1994 PAWS, INC. All Rights Reserved.
JIM DAVIS 3-1
DON'T WAIT UP FOR ME

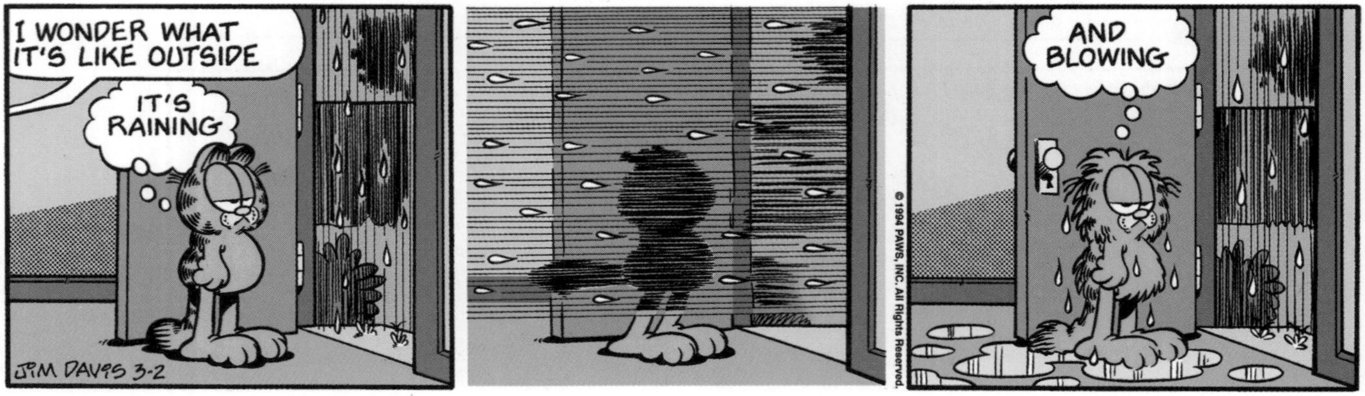
I WONDER WHAT IT'S LIKE OUTSIDE
IT'S RAINING
JIM DAVIS 3-2
© 1994 PAWS, INC. All Rights Reserved.
AND BLOWING

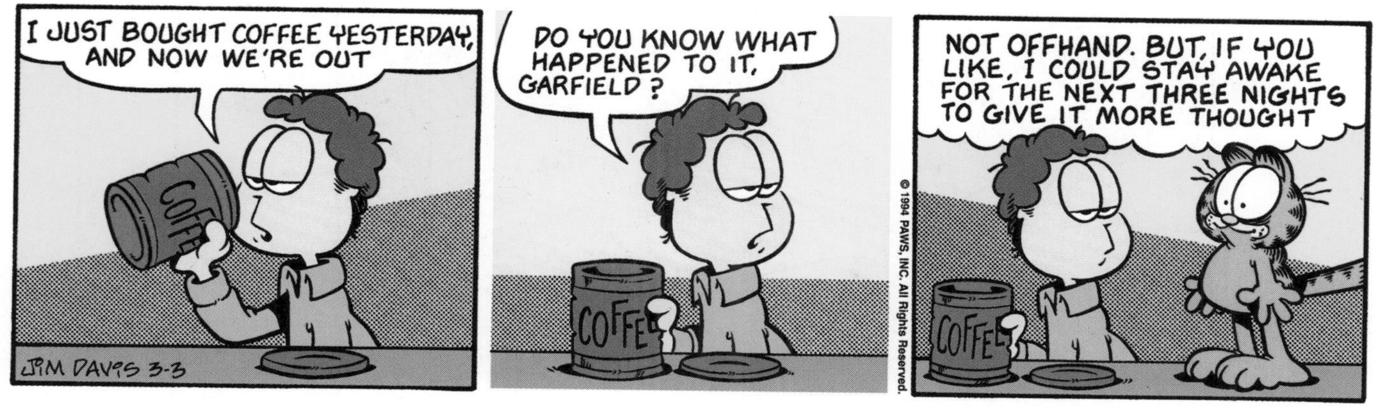
I JUST BOUGHT COFFEE YESTERDAY, AND NOW WE'RE OUT
JIM DAVIS 3-3
DO YOU KNOW WHAT HAPPENED TO IT, GARFIELD ?
© 1994 PAWS, INC. All Rights Reserved.
NOT OFFHAND. BUT, IF YOU LIKE, I COULD STAY AWAKE FOR THE NEXT THREE NIGHTS TO GIVE IT MORE THOUGHT

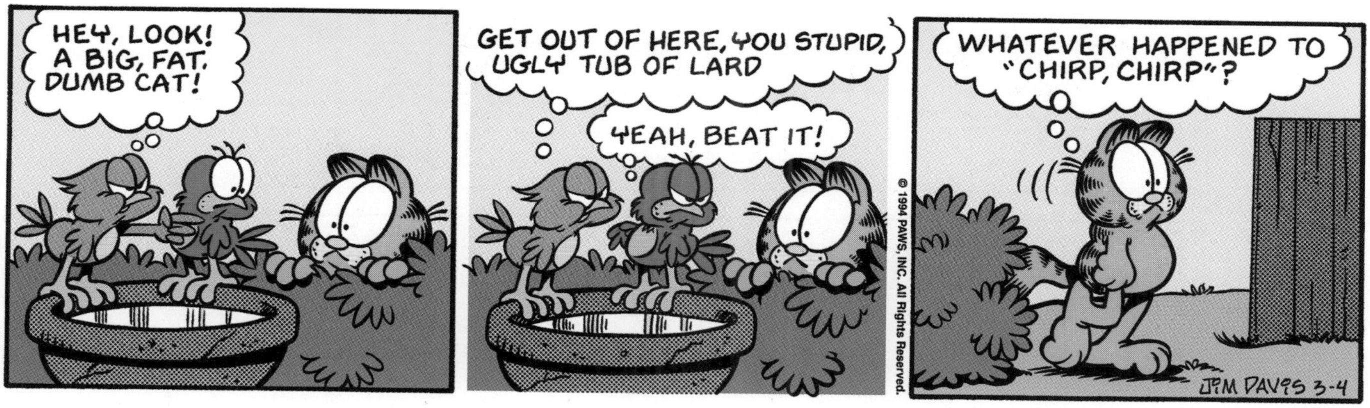
HEY, LOOK! A BIG, FAT, DUMB CAT!
GET OUT OF HERE, YOU STUPID, UGLY TUB OF LARD
YEAH, BEAT IT!
© 1994 PAWS, INC. All Rights Reserved.
WHATEVER HAPPENED TO "CHIRP, CHIRP"?
JIM DAVIS 3-4

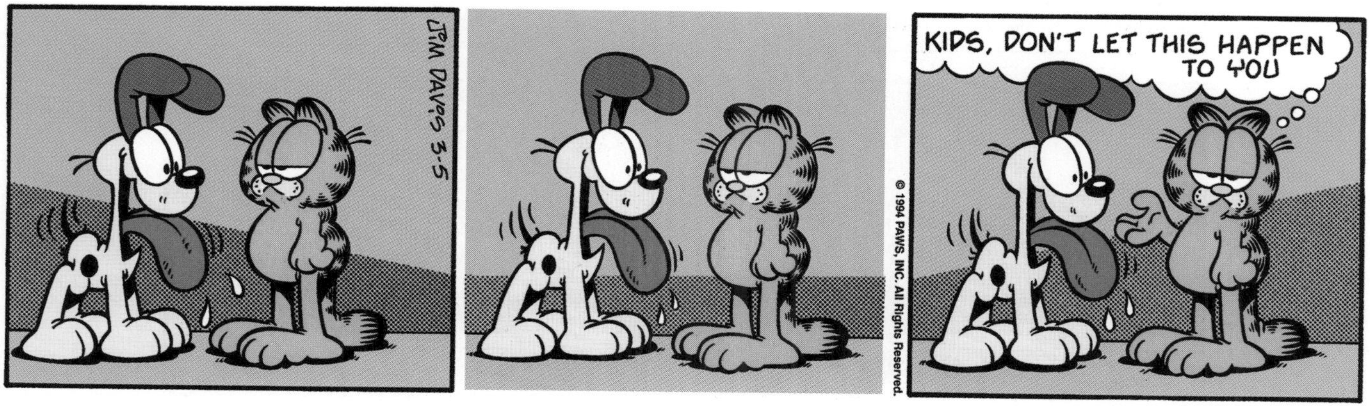
JIM DAVIS 3-5
© 1994 PAWS, INC. All Rights Reserved.
KIDS, DON'T LET THIS HAPPEN TO YOU

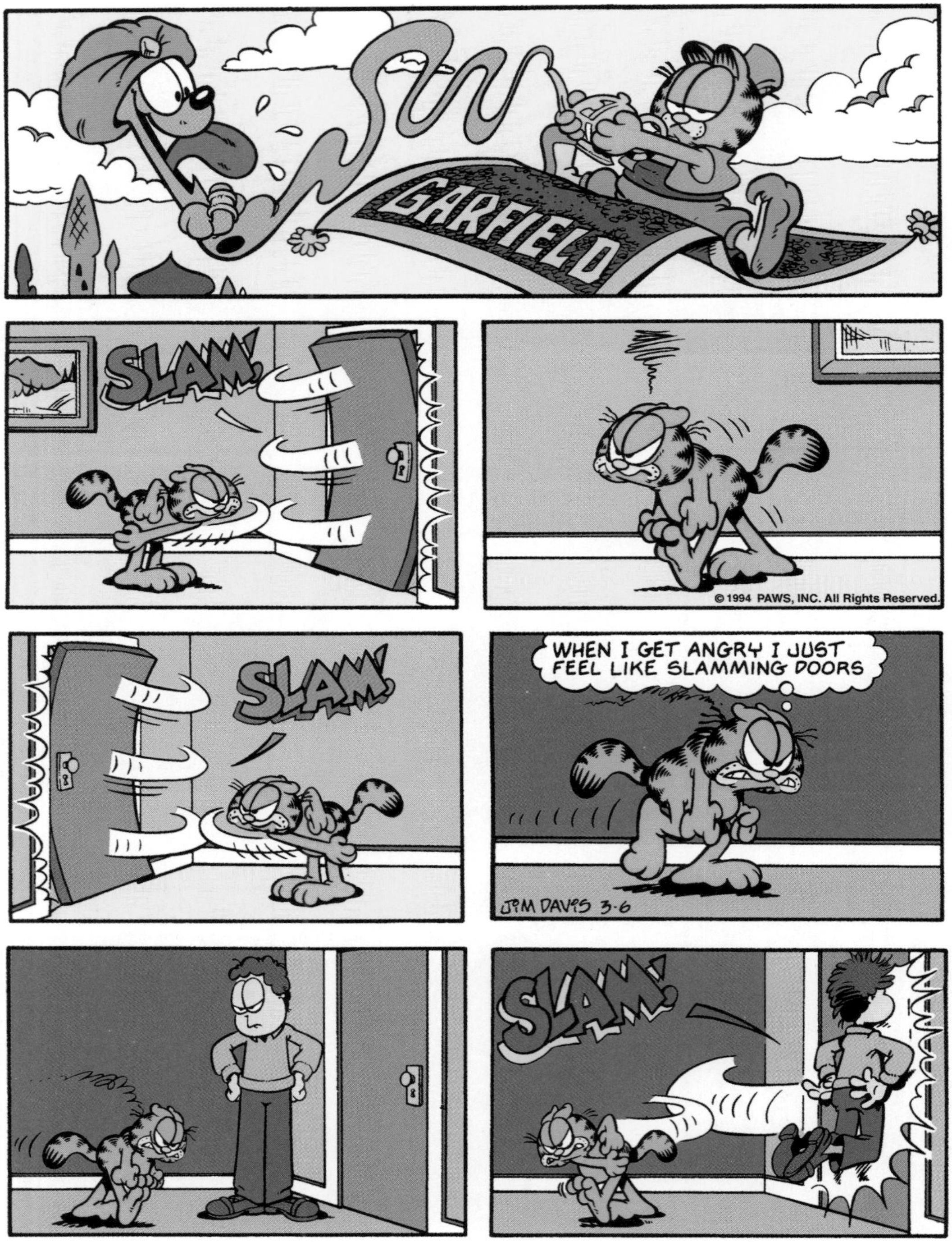
GARFIELD
SLAM!
© 1994 PAWS, INC. All Rights Reserved.
SLAM!
WHEN I GET ANGRY I JUST FEEL LIKE SLAMMING DOORS
JIM DAVIS 3-6
SLAM!

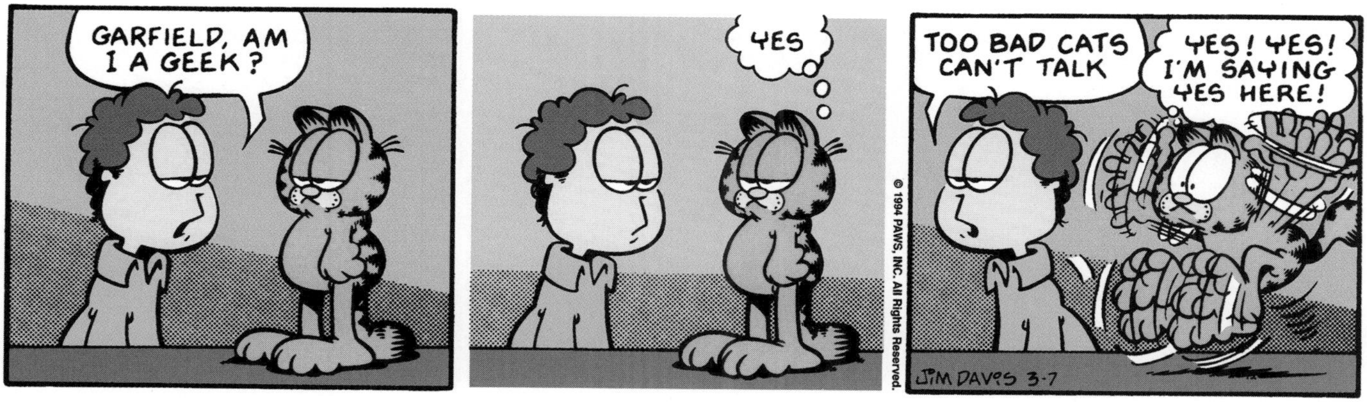
GARFIELD, AM I A GEEK?
YES
© 1994 PAWS, INC. All Rights Reserved.
TOO BAD CATS CAN'T TALK
YES! YES! I'M SAYING YES HERE!
JIM DAVIS 3-7

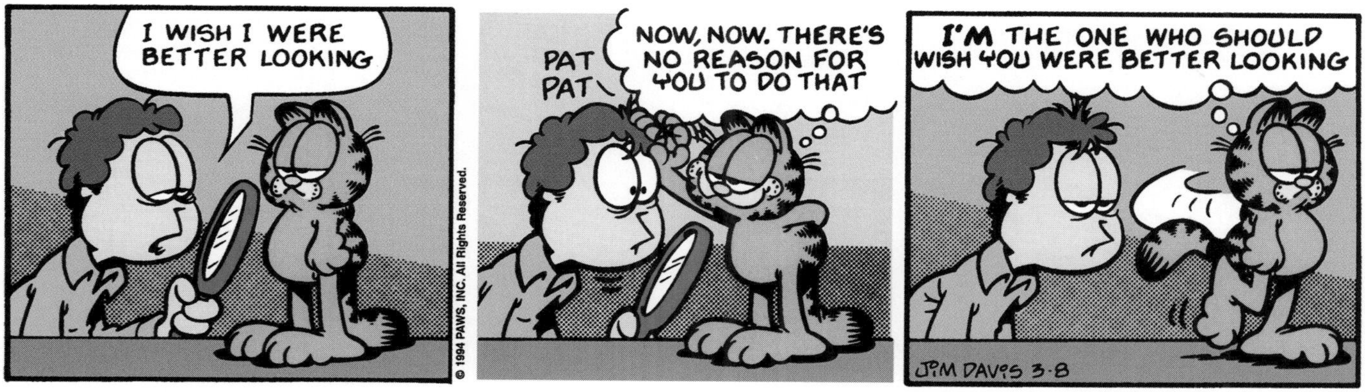
I WISH I WERE BETTER LOOKING
© 1994 PAWS, INC. All Rights Reserved.
PAT PAT
NOW, NOW. THERE'S NO REASON FOR YOU TO DO THAT
I'M THE ONE WHO SHOULD WISH YOU WERE BETTER LOOKING
JIM DAVIS 3-8

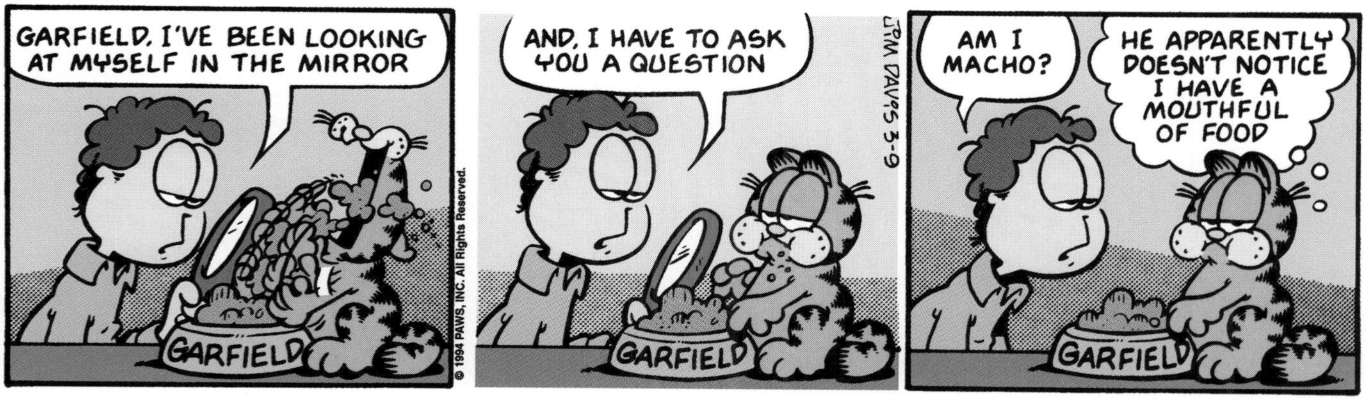
GARFIELD, I'VE BEEN LOOKING AT MYSELF IN THE MIRROR
GARFIELD
© 1994 PAWS, INC. All Rights Reserved.
AND, I HAVE TO ASK YOU A QUESTION
GARFIELD
JIM DAVIS 3-9
AM I MACHO?
HE APPARENTLY DOESN'T NOTICE I HAVE A MOUTHFUL OF FOOD
GARFIELD

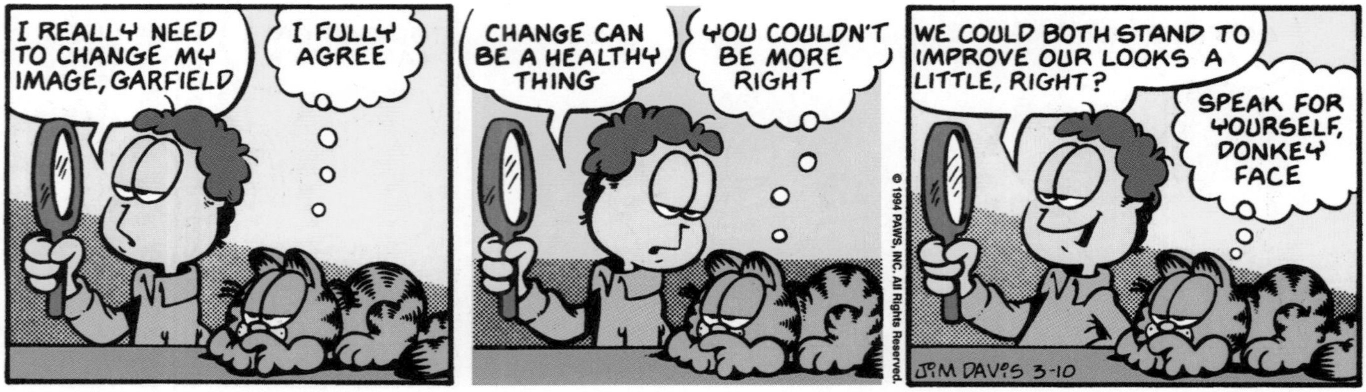
I REALLY NEED TO CHANGE MY IMAGE, GARFIELD
I FULLY AGREE
CHANGE CAN BE A HEALTHY THING
YOU COULDN'T BE MORE RIGHT
WE COULD BOTH STAND TO IMPROVE OUR LOOKS A LITTLE, RIGHT?
SPEAK FOR YOURSELF, DONKEY FACE
JIM DAVIS 3-10
© 1994 PAWS, INC. All Rights Reserved.

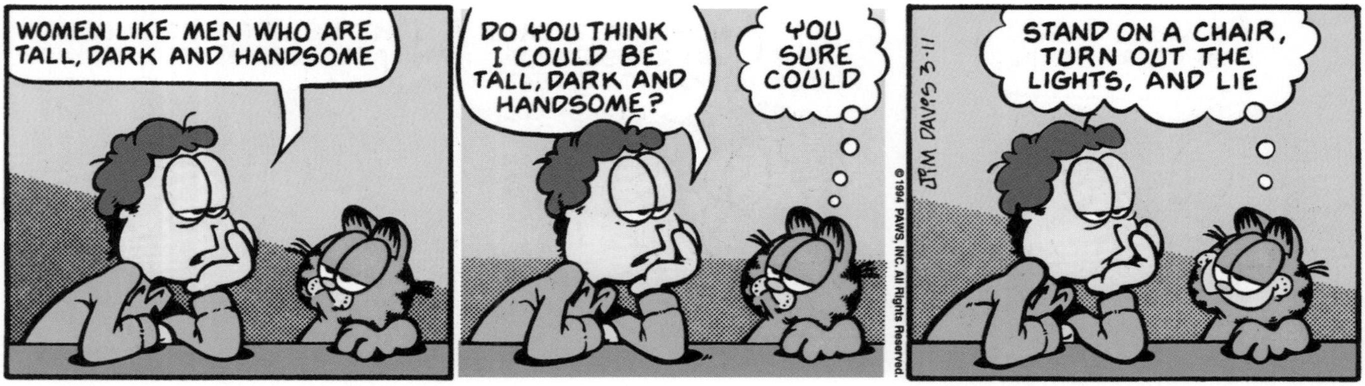
WOMEN LIKE MEN WHO ARE TALL, DARK AND HANDSOME
DO YOU THINK I COULD BE TALL, DARK AND HANDSOME?
YOU SURE COULD
STAND ON A CHAIR, TURN OUT THE LIGHTS, AND LIE
JIM DAVIS 3-11
© 1994 PAWS, INC. All Rights Reserved.

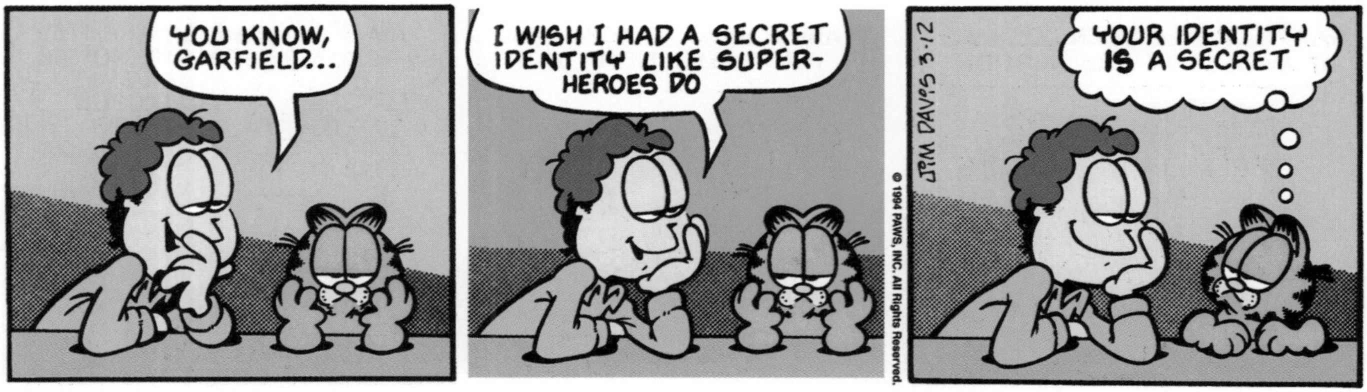
YOU KNOW, GARFIELD...
I WISH I HAD A SECRET IDENTITY LIKE SUPER-HEROES DO
YOUR IDENTITY **IS** A SECRET
JIM DAVIS 3-12
© 1994 PAWS, INC. All Rights Reserved.

GARF
IELD
Z
YANK!
WHIRRRRRR
JIM DAVIS 3-13
© 1994 PAWS, INC. All Rights Reserved.
Z
STOMP!
B-D-D-D-D-D-D

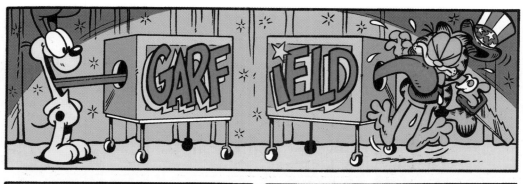

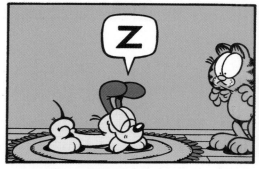

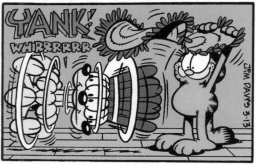

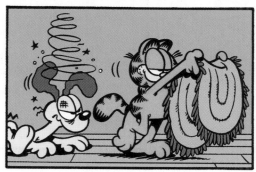

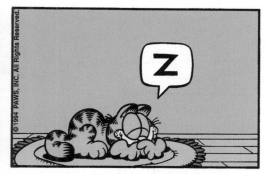

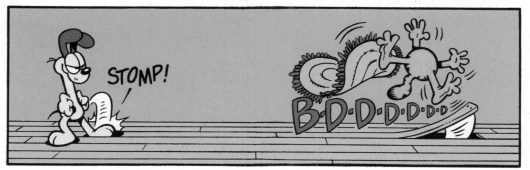

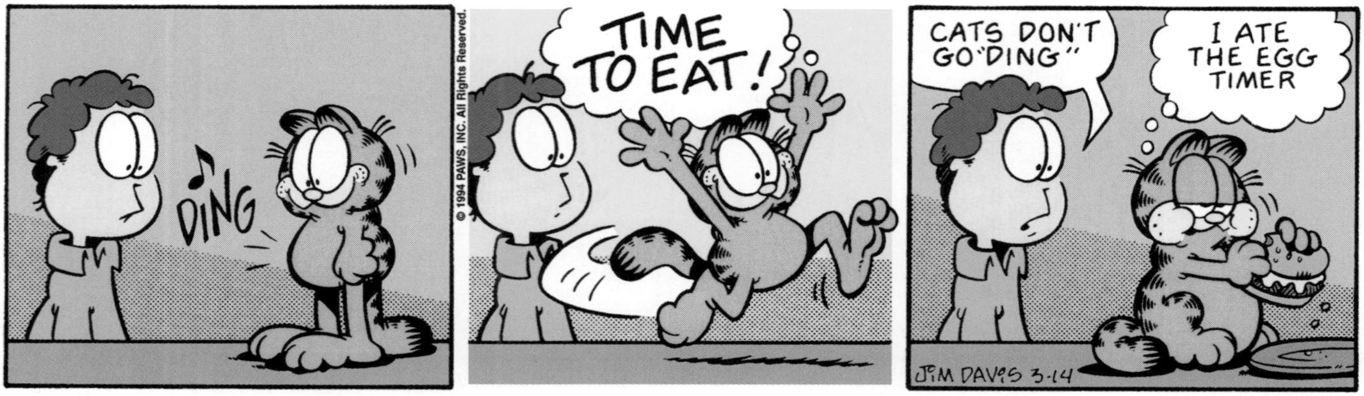
DING
TIME TO EAT!
CATS DON'T GO "DING"
I ATE THE EGG TIMER
JIM DAVIS 3-14

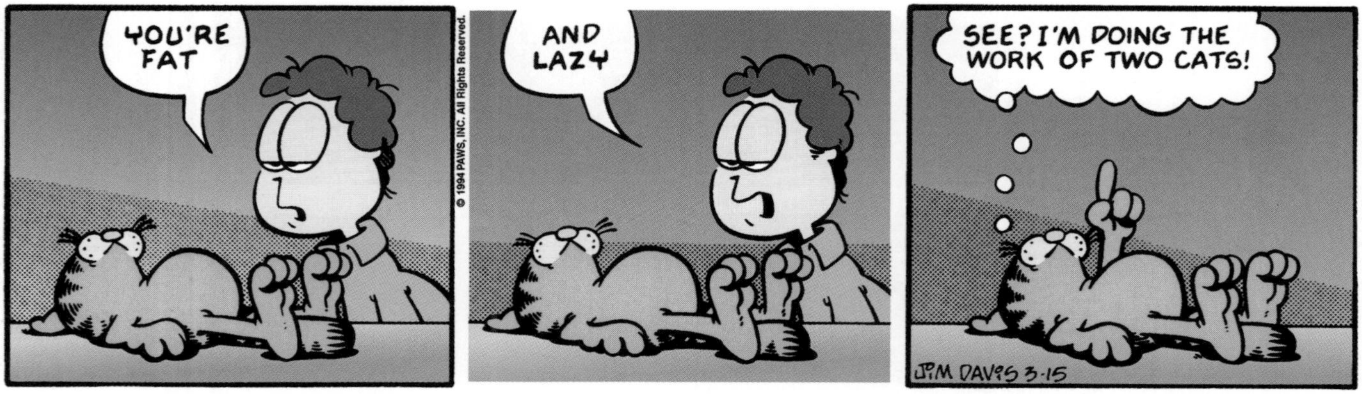
YOU'RE FAT
AND LAZY
SEE? I'M DOING THE WORK OF TWO CATS!
JIM DAVIS 3-15

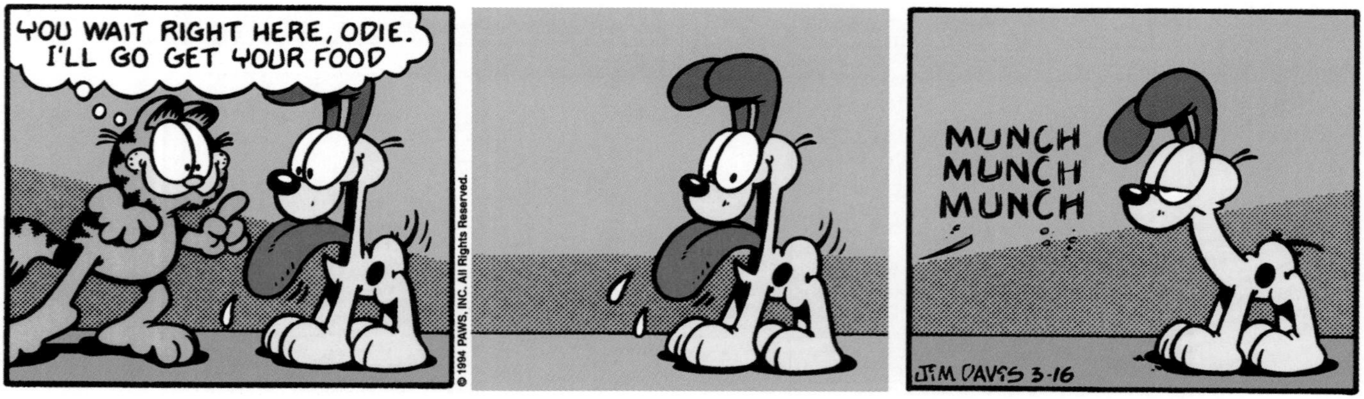
YOU WAIT RIGHT HERE, ODIE. I'LL GO GET YOUR FOOD
MUNCH
MUNCH
MUNCH
JIM DAVIS 3-16

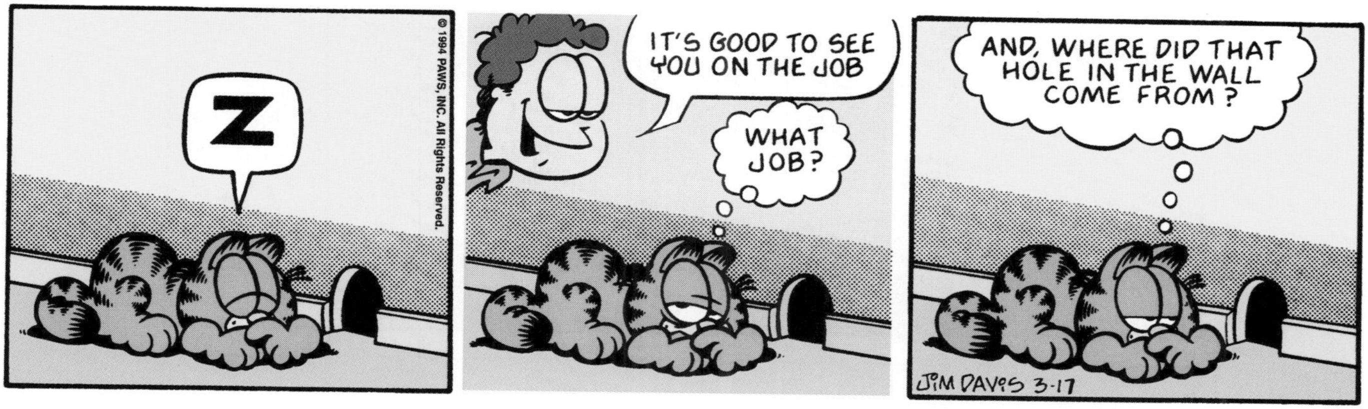
Z
© 1994 PAWS, INC. All Rights Reserved.
IT'S GOOD TO SEE YOU ON THE JOB
WHAT JOB?
AND, WHERE DID THAT HOLE IN THE WALL COME FROM?
JIM DAVIS 3-17

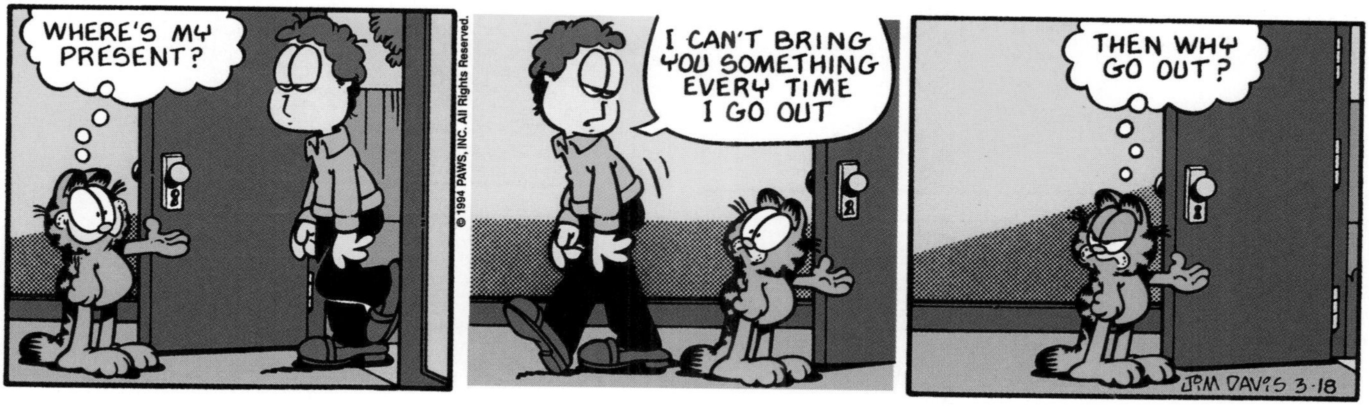
WHERE'S MY PRESENT?
© 1994 PAWS, INC. All Rights Reserved.
I CAN'T BRING YOU SOMETHING EVERY TIME I GO OUT
THEN WHY GO OUT?
JIM DAVIS 3-18

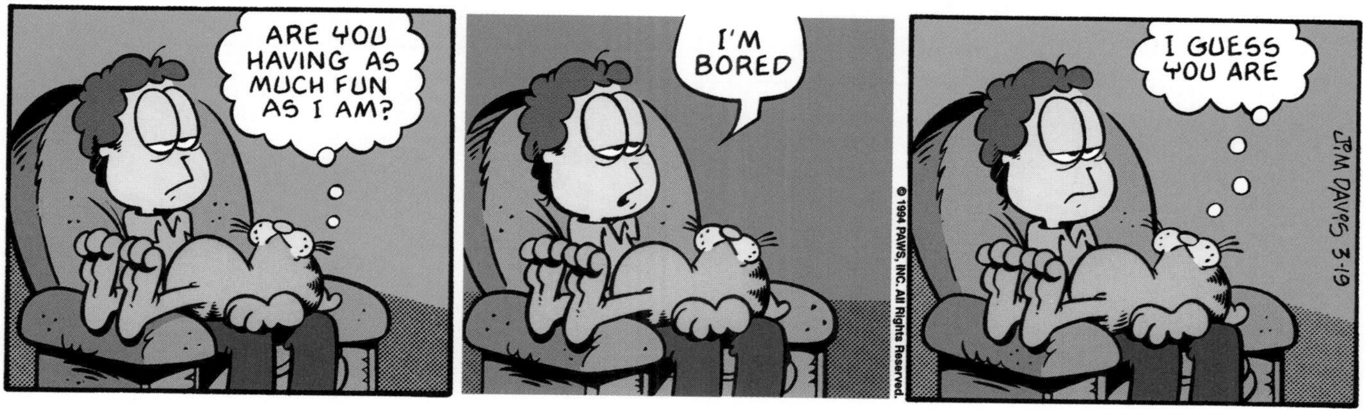
ARE YOU HAVING AS MUCH FUN AS I AM?
I'M BORED
© 1994 PAWS, INC. All Rights Reserved.
I GUESS YOU ARE
JIM DAVIS 3-19

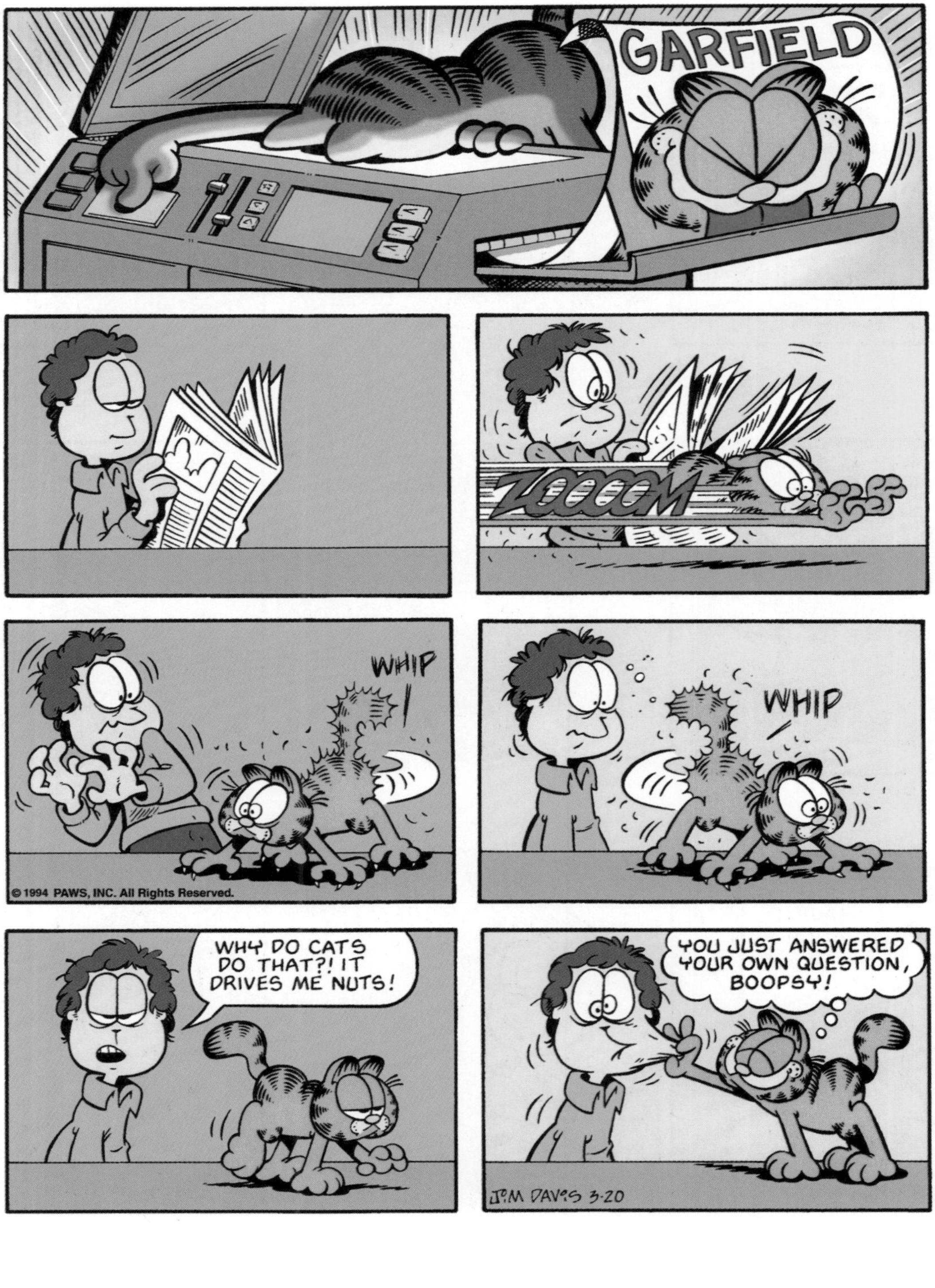
GARFIELD
ZOOOOM
WHIP
WHIP
WHY DO CATS DO THAT?! IT DRIVES ME NUTS!
YOU JUST ANSWERED YOUR OWN QUESTION, BOOPSY!
JIM DAVIS 3-20

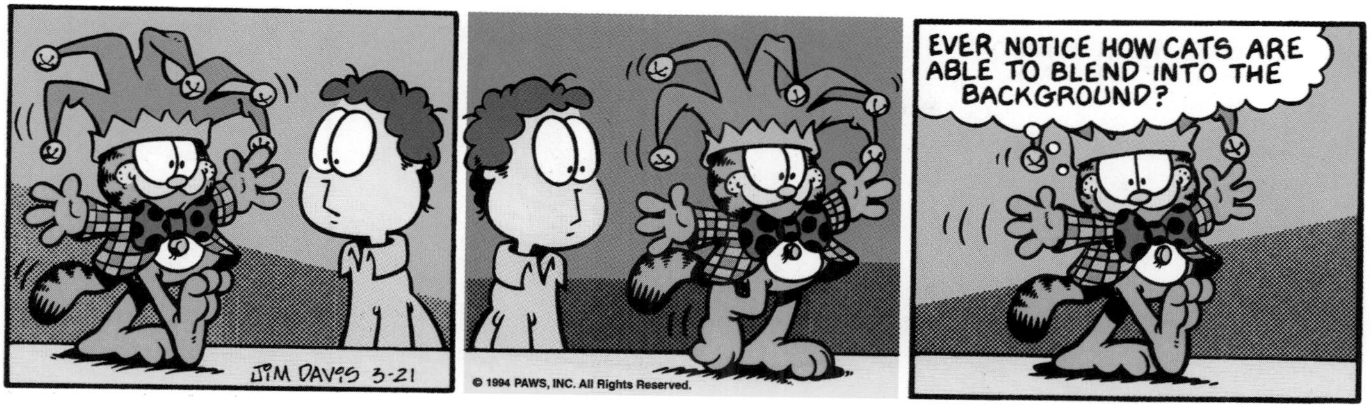
JIM DAVIS 3-21
© 1994 PAWS, INC. All Rights Reserved.
EVER NOTICE HOW CATS ARE ABLE TO BLEND INTO THE BACKGROUND?

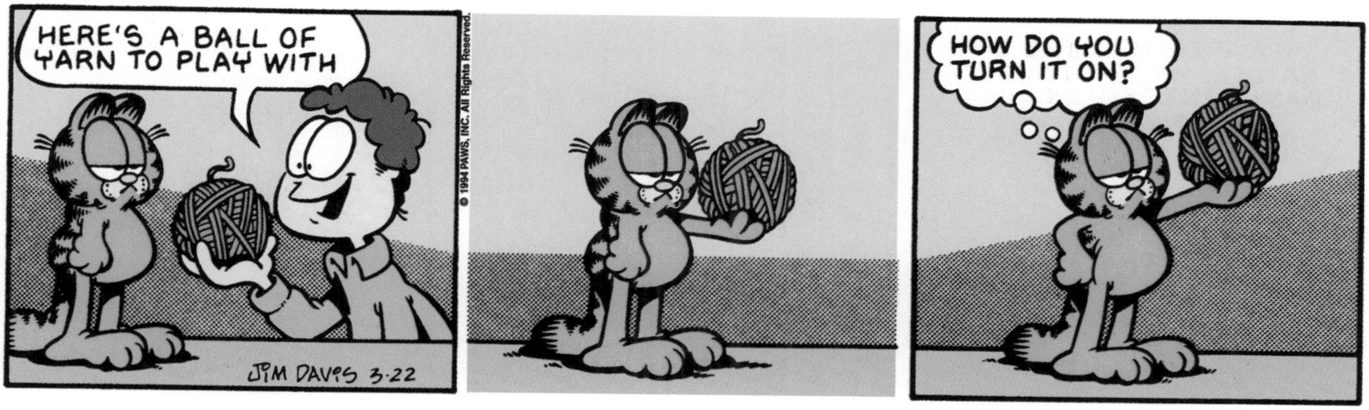
HERE'S A BALL OF YARN TO PLAY WITH
JIM DAVIS 3-22
© 1994 PAWS, INC. All Rights Reserved.
HOW DO YOU TURN IT ON?

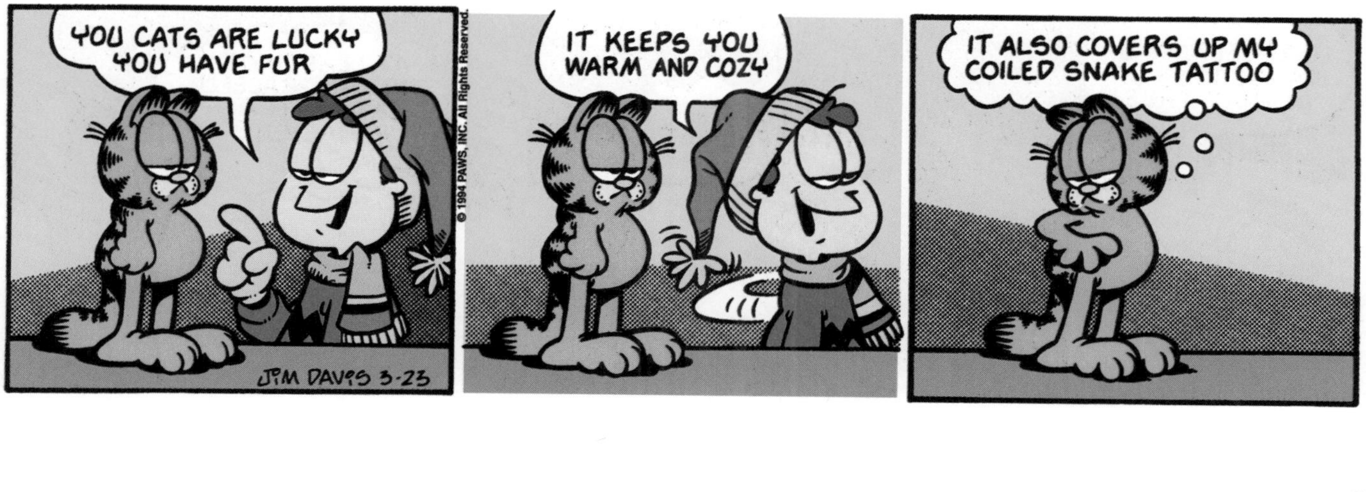
YOU CATS ARE LUCKY YOU HAVE FUR
JIM DAVIS 3-23
© 1994 PAWS, INC. All Rights Reserved.
IT KEEPS YOU WARM AND COZY
IT ALSO COVERS UP MY COILED SNAKE TATTOO

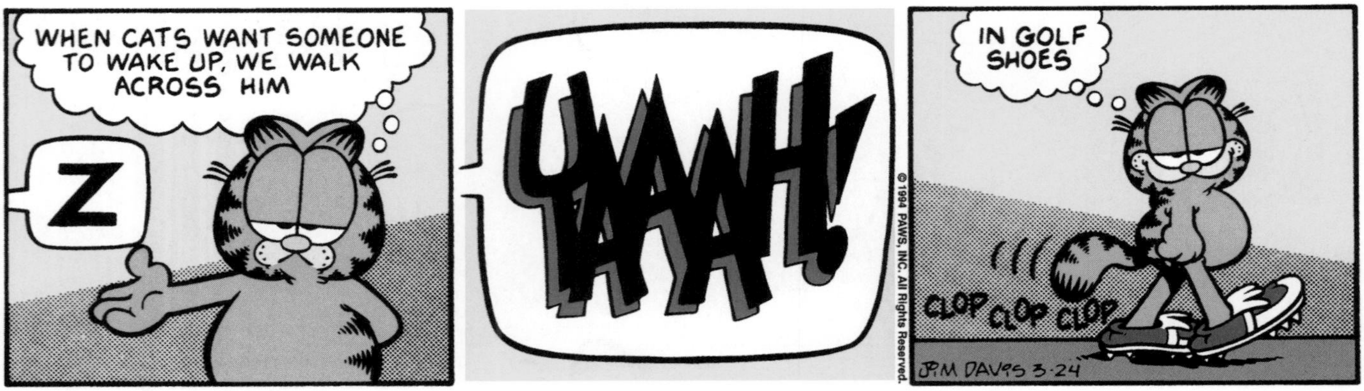
WHEN CATS WANT SOMEONE TO WAKE UP, WE WALK ACROSS HIM
Z
UWAAH!
© 1994 PAWS, INC. All Rights Reserved.
IN GOLF SHOES
CLOP CLOP CLOP
JIM DAVIS 3-24

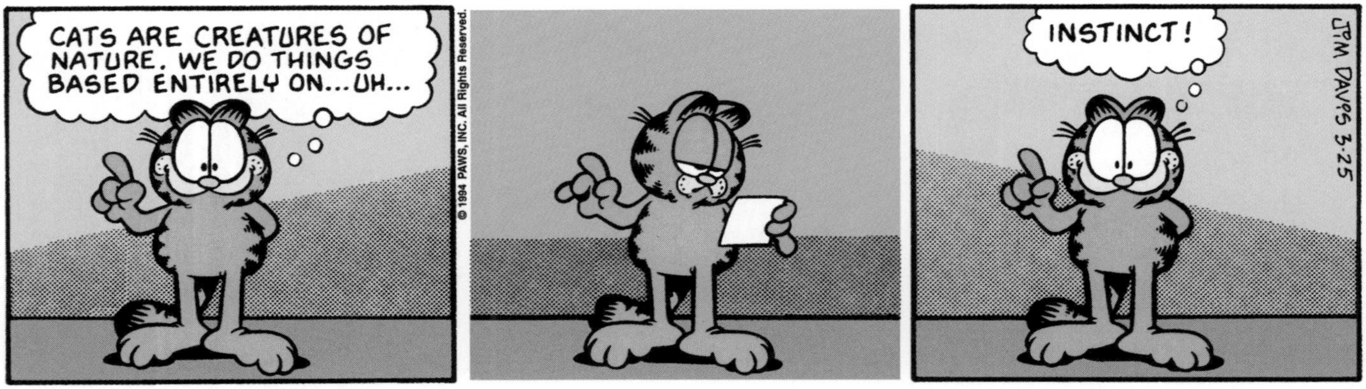
CATS ARE CREATURES OF NATURE. WE DO THINGS BASED ENTIRELY ON... UH...
© 1994 PAWS, INC. All Rights Reserved.
INSTINCT!
JIM DAVIS 3-25

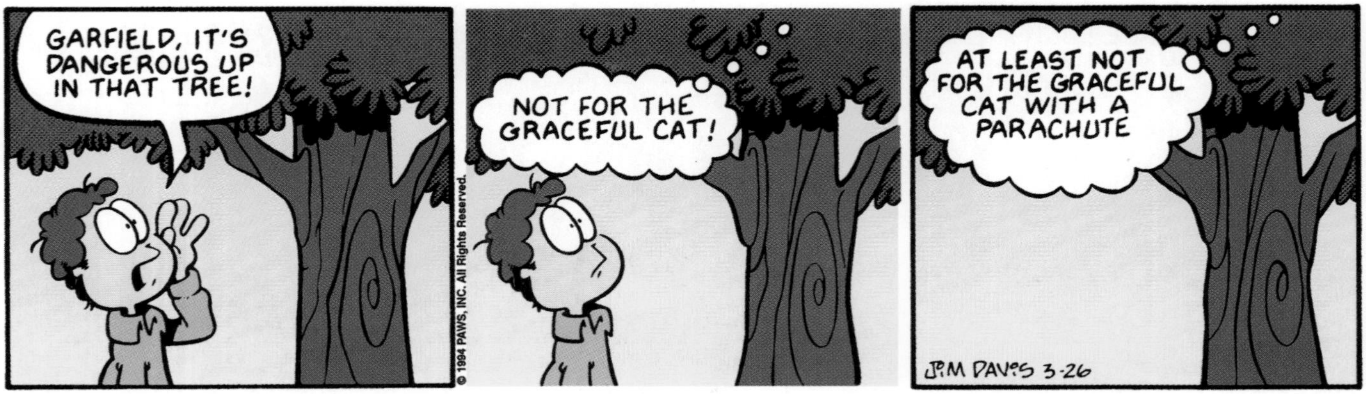
GARFIELD, IT'S DANGEROUS UP IN THAT TREE!
© 1994 PAWS, INC. All Rights Reserved.
NOT FOR THE GRACEFUL CAT!
AT LEAST NOT FOR THE GRACEFUL CAT WITH A PARACHUTE
JIM DAVIS 3-26

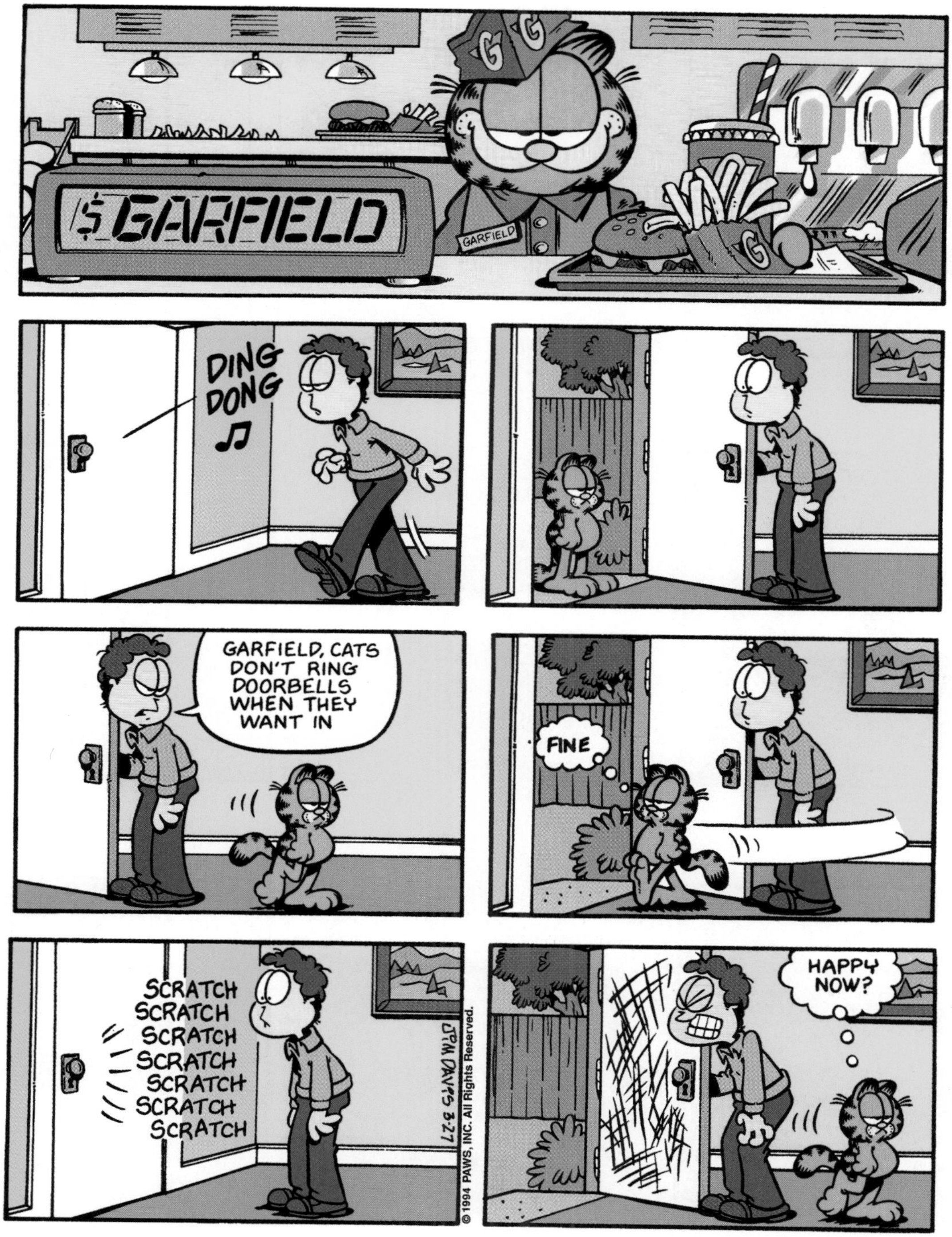
$ GARFIELD
GARFIELD
DING DONG
GARFIELD, CATS DON'T RING DOORBELLS WHEN THEY WANT IN
FINE
SCRATCH
SCRATCH
SCRATCH
SCRATCH
SCRATCH
SCRATCH
SCRATCH
HAPPY NOW?

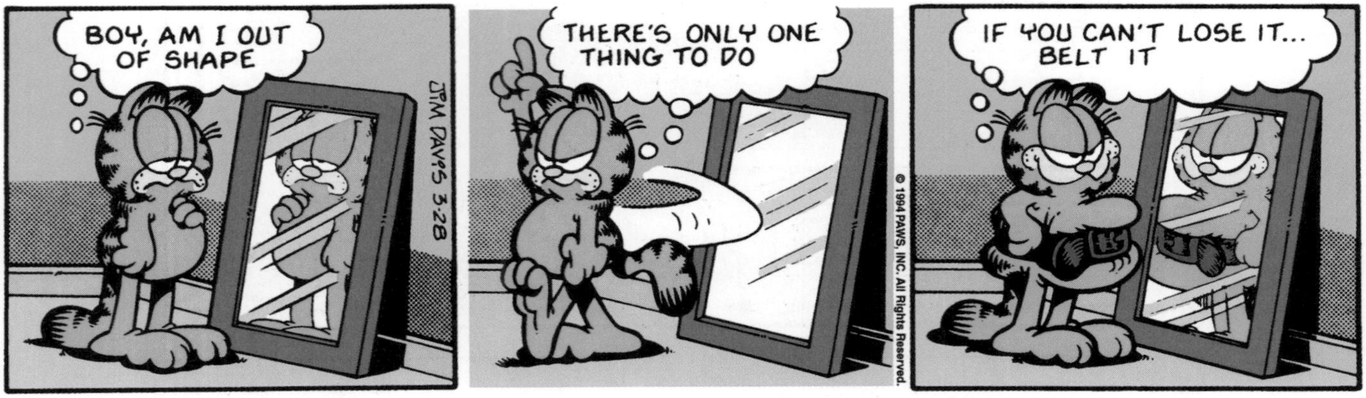
BOY, AM I OUT OF SHAPE
JIM DAVIS 3-28
THERE'S ONLY ONE THING TO DO
© 1994 PAWS, INC. All Rights Reserved.
IF YOU CAN'T LOSE IT... BELT IT

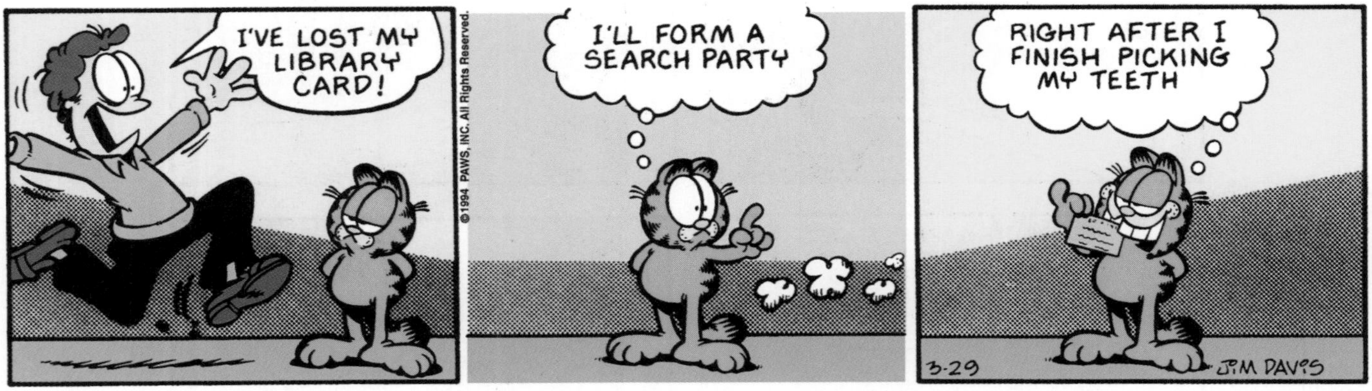
I'VE LOST MY LIBRARY CARD!
© 1994 PAWS, INC. All Rights Reserved.
I'LL FORM A SEARCH PARTY
RIGHT AFTER I FINISH PICKING MY TEETH
3-29
JIM DAVIS

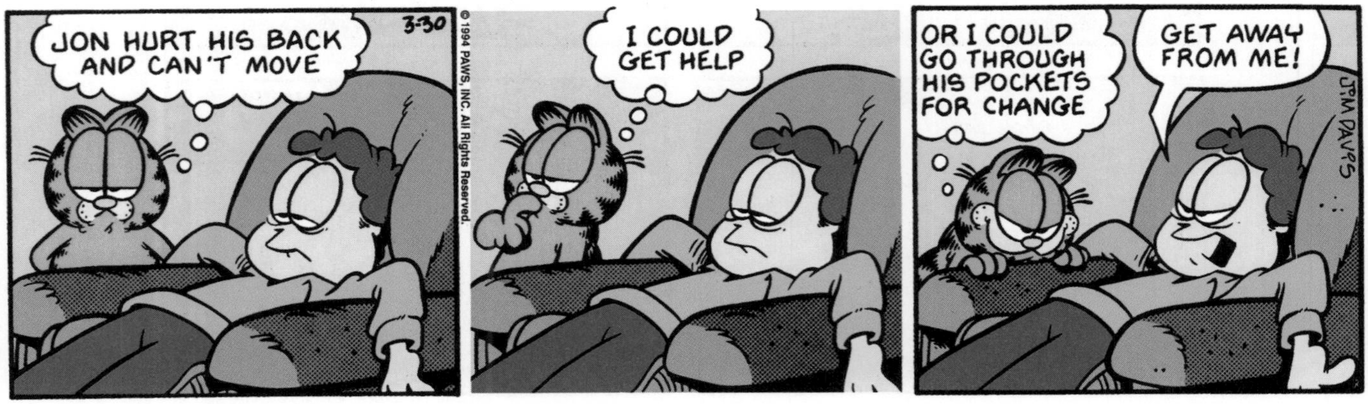
JON HURT HIS BACK AND CAN'T MOVE
3-30
© 1994 PAWS, INC. All Rights Reserved.
I COULD GET HELP
OR I COULD GO THROUGH HIS POCKETS FOR CHANGE
GET AWAY FROM ME!
JIM DAVIS

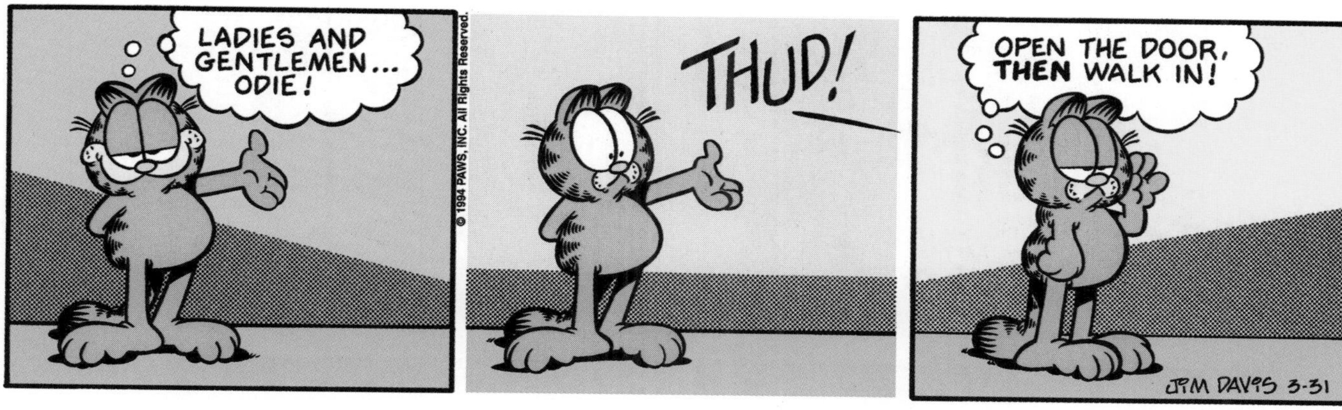
LADIES AND GENTLEMEN... ODIE!
© 1994 PAWS, INC. All Rights Reserved.
THUD!
OPEN THE DOOR, **THEN** WALK IN!
JIM DAVIS 3-31

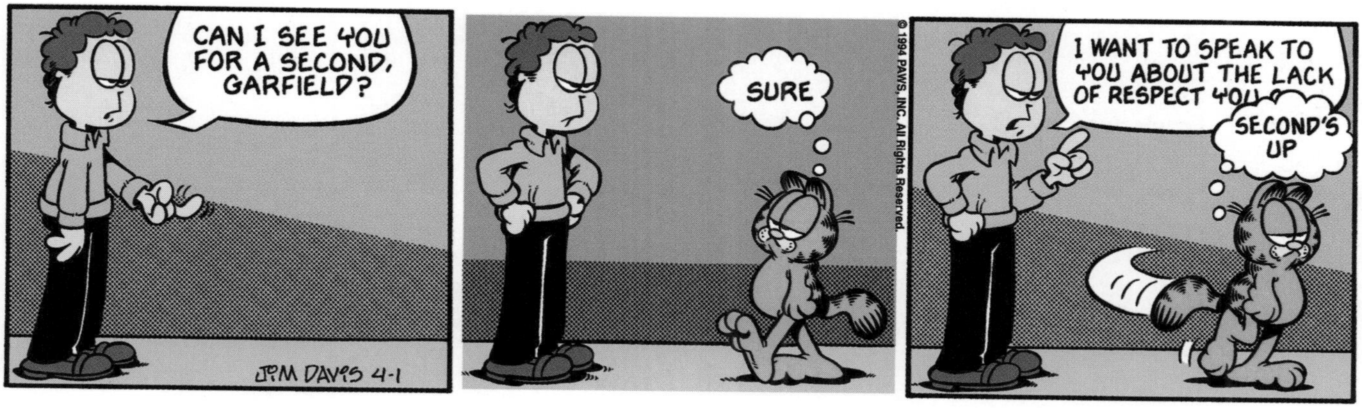
CAN I SEE YOU FOR A SECOND, GARFIELD?
JIM DAVIS 4-1
SURE
© 1994 PAWS, INC. All Rights Reserved.
I WANT TO SPEAK TO YOU ABOUT THE LACK OF RESPECT
SECOND'S UP

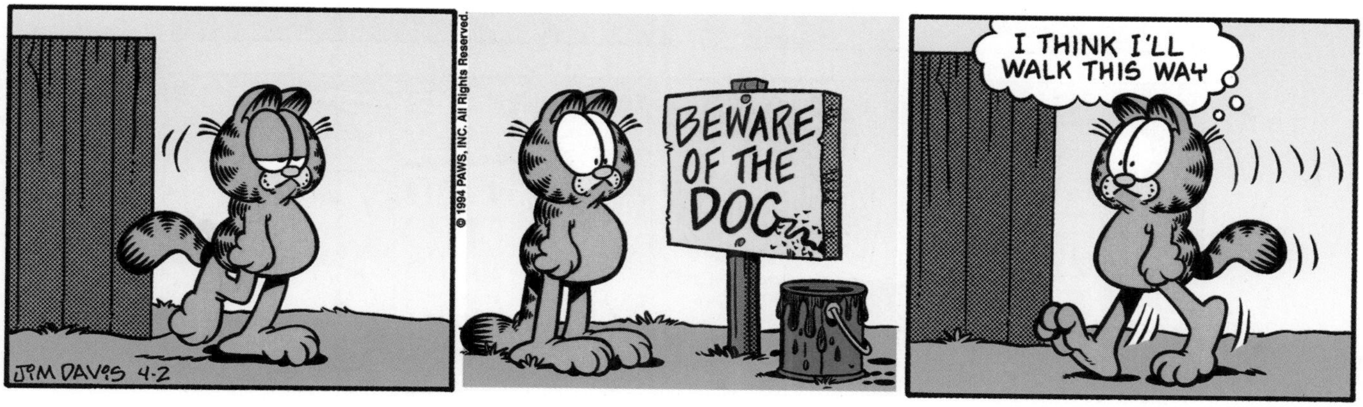
JIM DAVIS 4-2
© 1994 PAWS, INC. All Rights Reserved.
BEWARE OF THE DOG
I THINK I'LL WALK THIS WAY

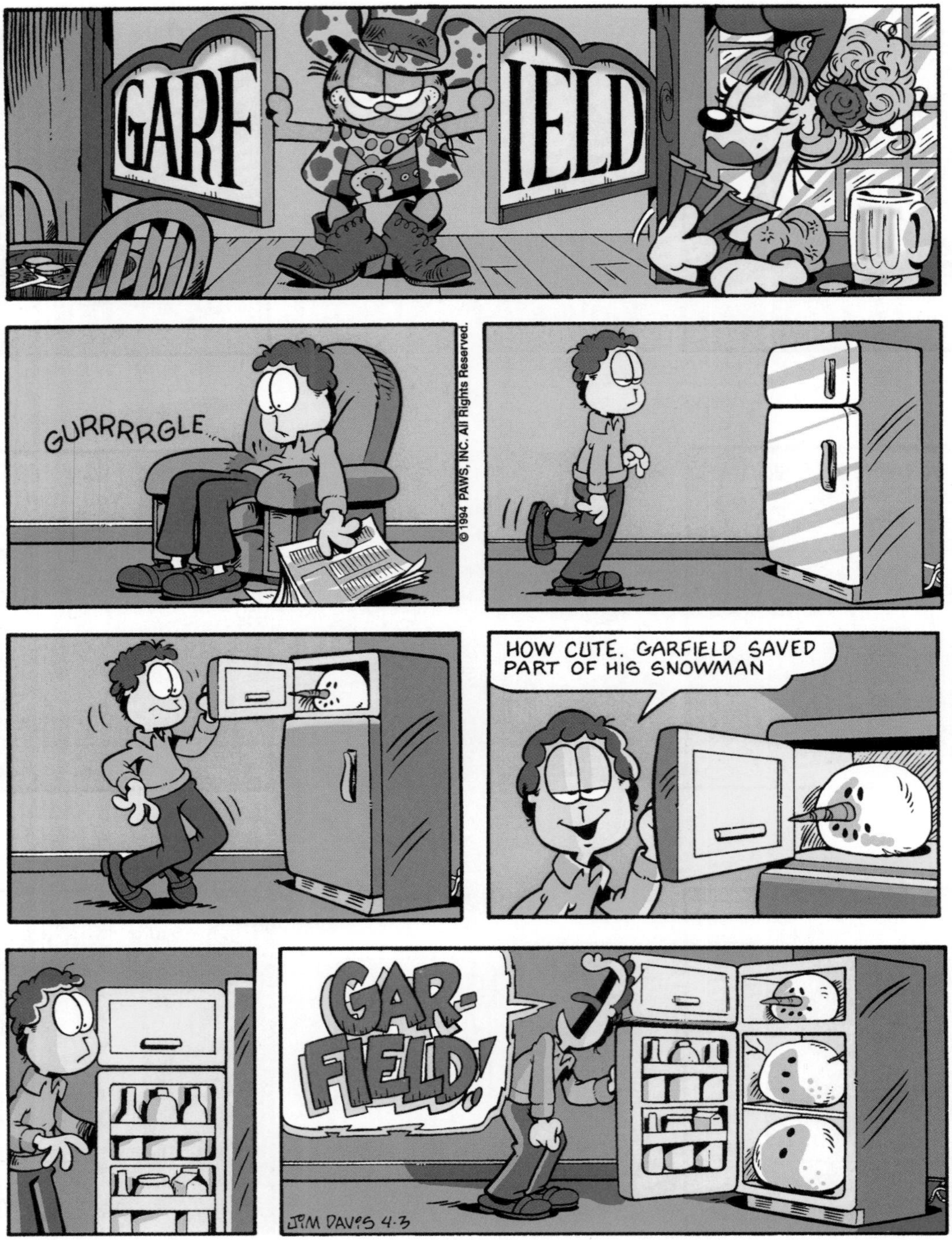
GARF
IELD
© 1994 PAWS, INC. All Rights Reserved.
GURRRRGLE...
HOW CUTE. GARFIELD SAVED PART OF HIS SNOWMAN
GAR-FIELD!
JIM DAVIS 4-3

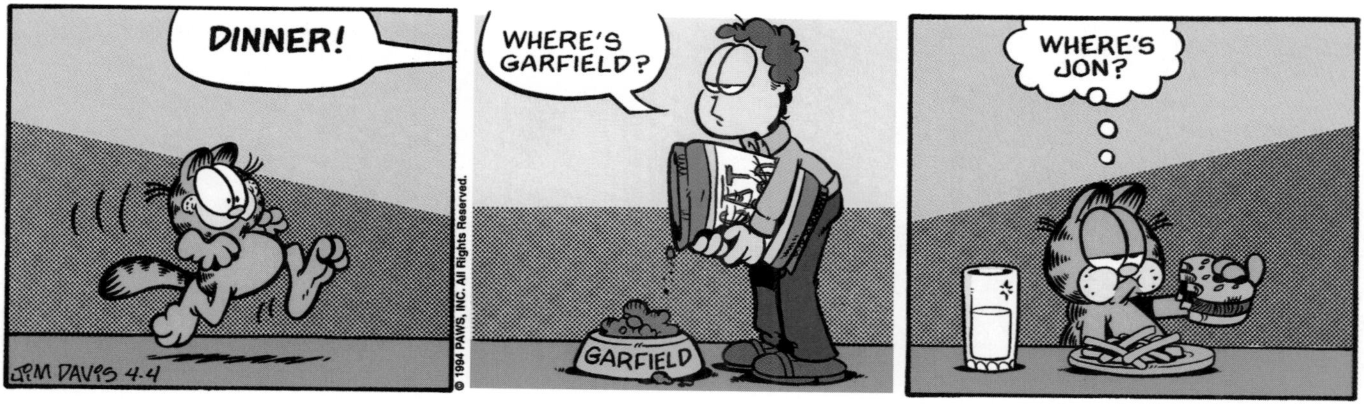
DINNER!
JIM DAVIS 4-4
© 1994 PAWS, INC. All Rights Reserved.
WHERE'S GARFIELD?
GARFIELD
WHERE'S JON?

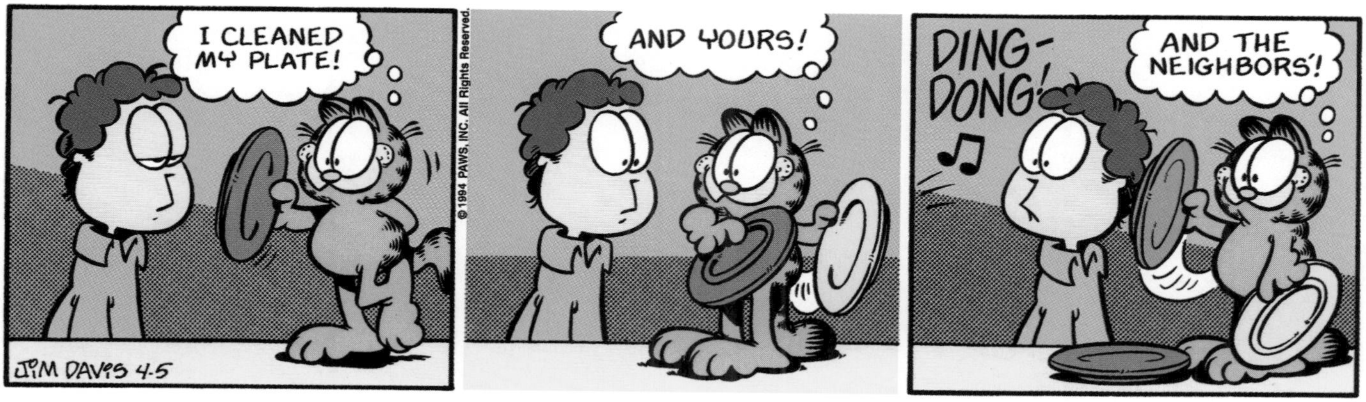
I CLEANED MY PLATE!
JIM DAVIS 4-5
© 1994 PAWS, INC. All Rights Reserved.
AND YOURS!
DING-DONG!
AND THE NEIGHBORS'!

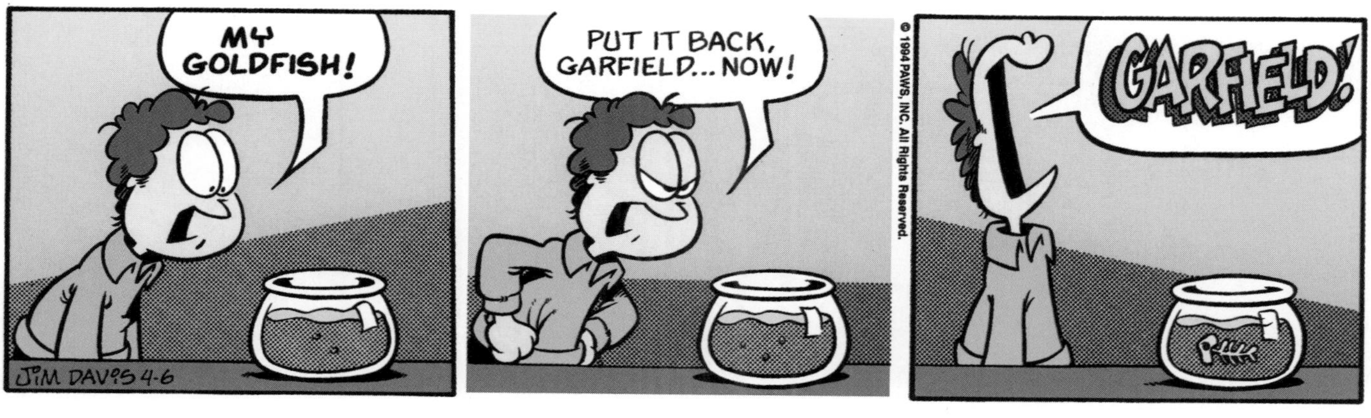
MY GOLDFISH!
JIM DAVIS 4-6
PUT IT BACK, GARFIELD... NOW!
© 1994 PAWS, INC. All Rights Reserved.
GARFIELD!

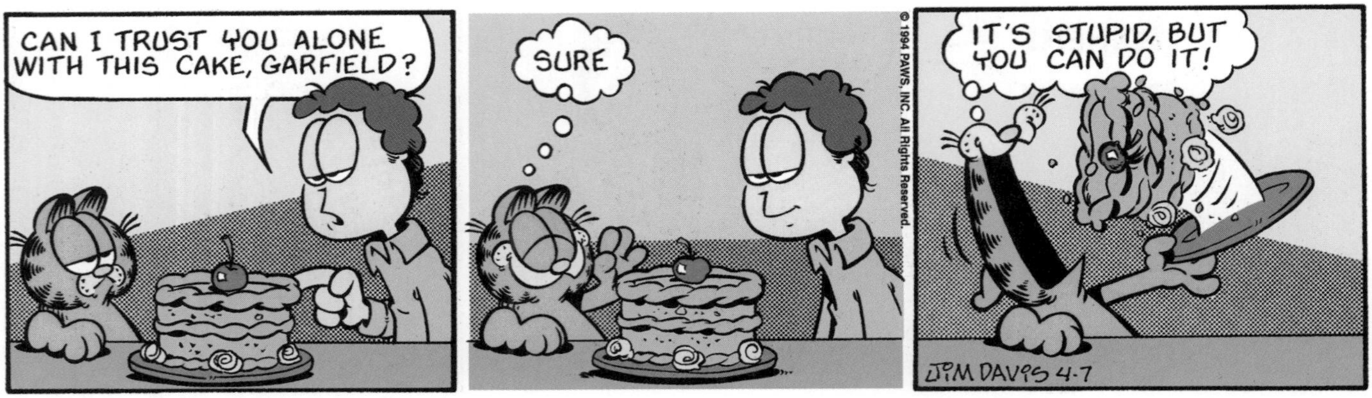
CAN I TRUST YOU ALONE WITH THIS CAKE, GARFIELD?
SURE
© 1994 PAWS, INC. All Rights Reserved.
IT'S STUPID, BUT YOU CAN DO IT!
JIM DAVIS 4-7

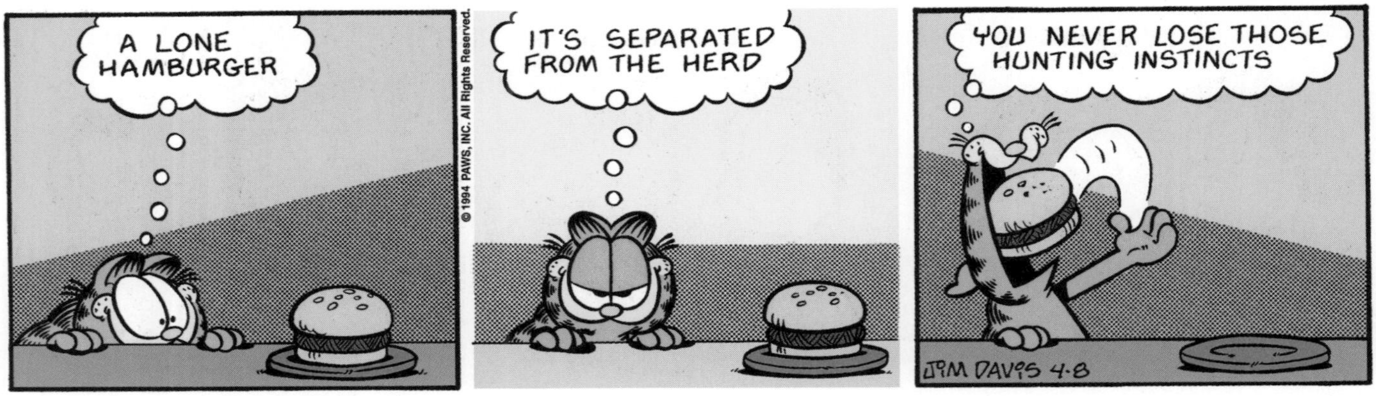
A LONE HAMBURGER
© 1994 PAWS, INC. All Rights Reserved.
IT'S SEPARATED FROM THE HERD
YOU NEVER LOSE THOSE HUNTING INSTINCTS
JIM DAVIS 4-8

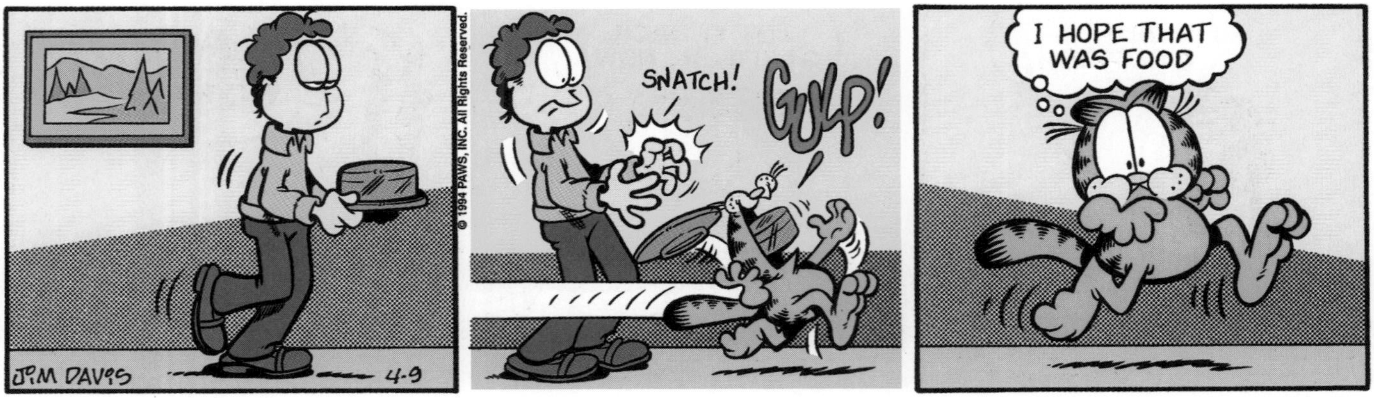
JIM DAVIS 4-9
© 1994 PAWS, INC. All Rights Reserved.
SNATCH!
GULP!
I HOPE THAT WAS FOOD

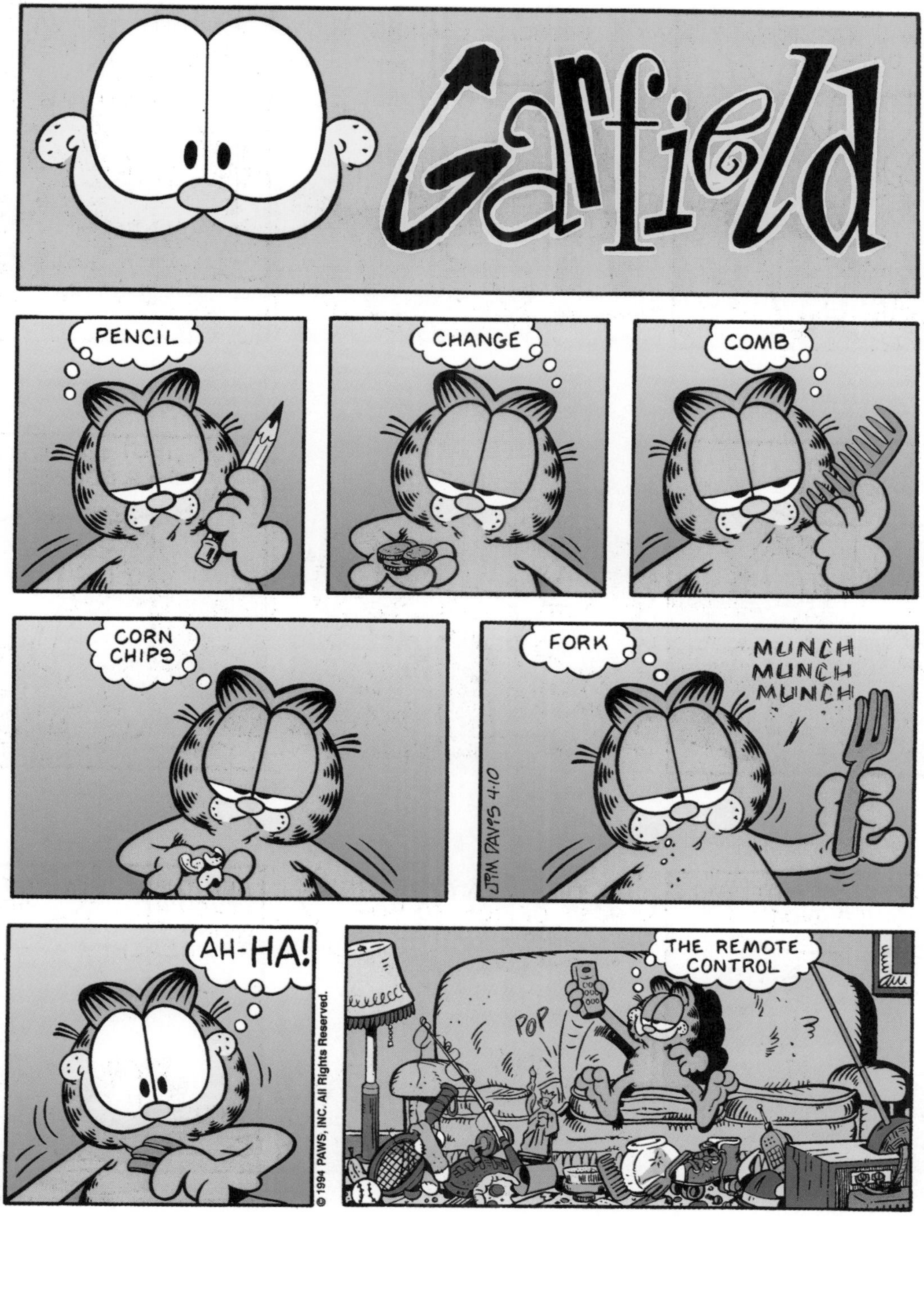
Garfield
PENCIL
CHANGE
COMB
CORN CHIPS
FORK
MUNCH MUNCH MUNCH
JIM DAVIS 4-10
AH-HA!
© 1994 PAWS, INC. All Rights Reserved.
THE REMOTE CONTROL
POP

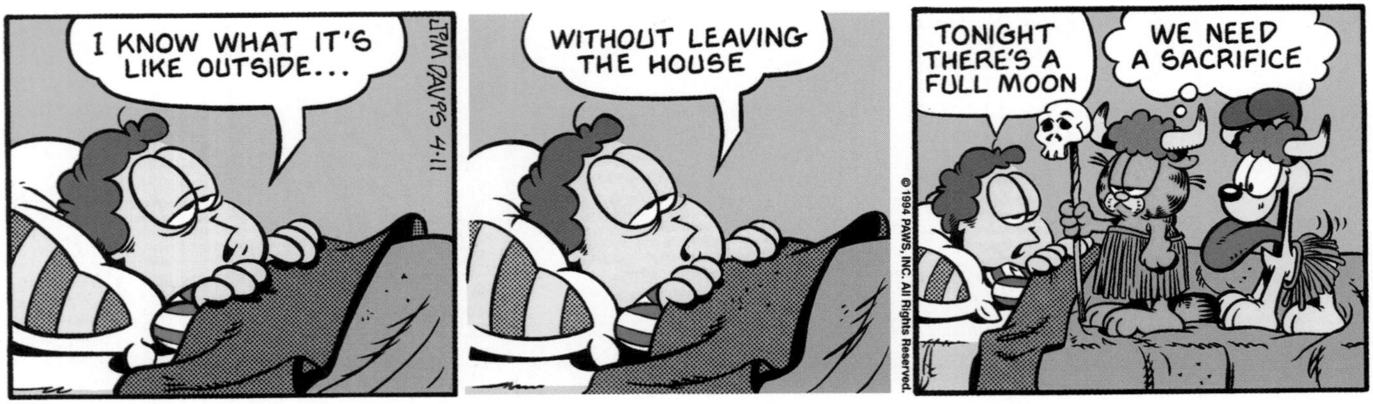
I KNOW WHAT IT'S LIKE OUTSIDE...
JIM DAVIS 4-11
WITHOUT LEAVING THE HOUSE
TONIGHT THERE'S A FULL MOON
WE NEED A SACRIFICE
© 1994 PAWS, INC. All Rights Reserved.

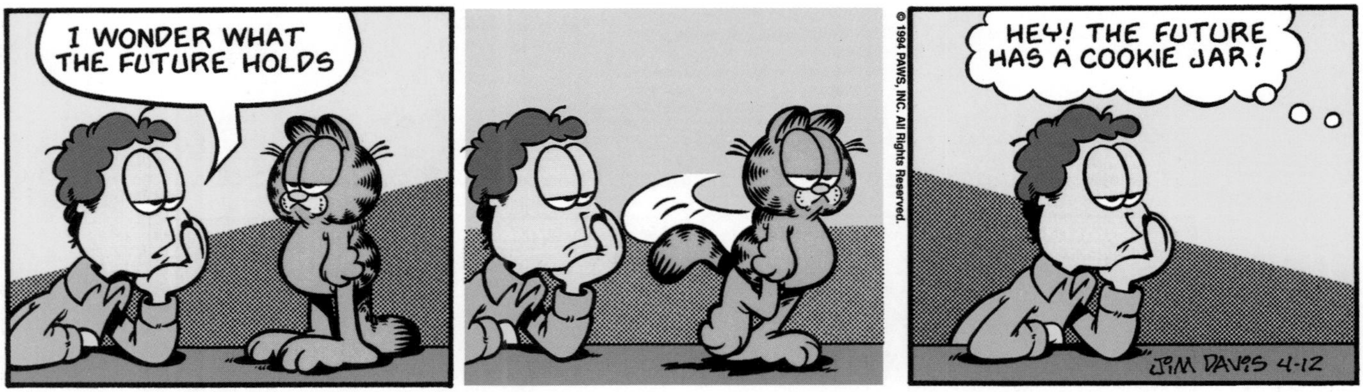
I WONDER WHAT THE FUTURE HOLDS
© 1994 PAWS, INC. All Rights Reserved.
HEY! THE FUTURE HAS A COOKIE JAR!
JIM DAVIS 4-12

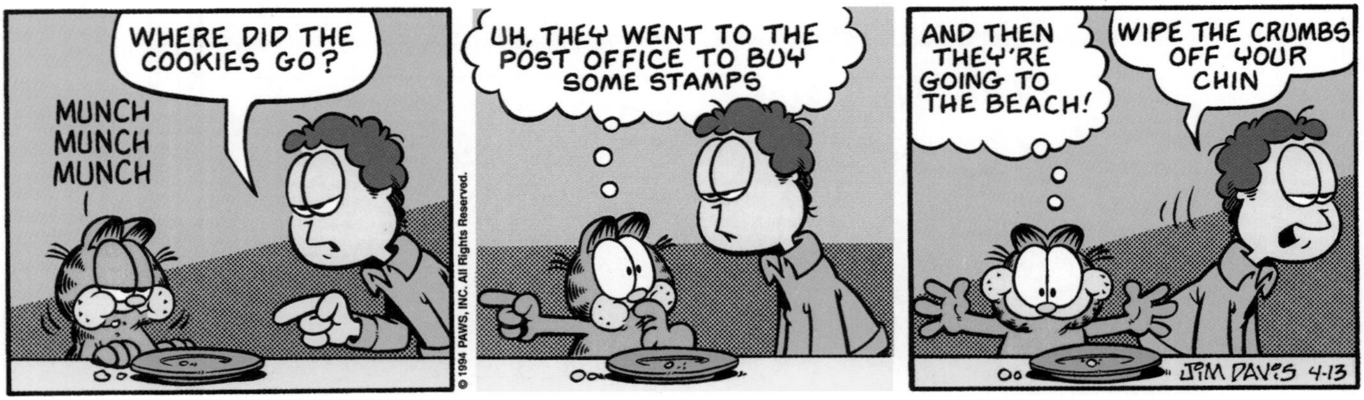
MUNCH MUNCH MUNCH
WHERE DID THE COOKIES GO?
© 1994 PAWS, INC. All Rights Reserved.
UH, THEY WENT TO THE POST OFFICE TO BUY SOME STAMPS
AND THEN THEY'RE GOING TO THE BEACH!
WIPE THE CRUMBS OFF YOUR CHIN
JIM DAVIS 4-13

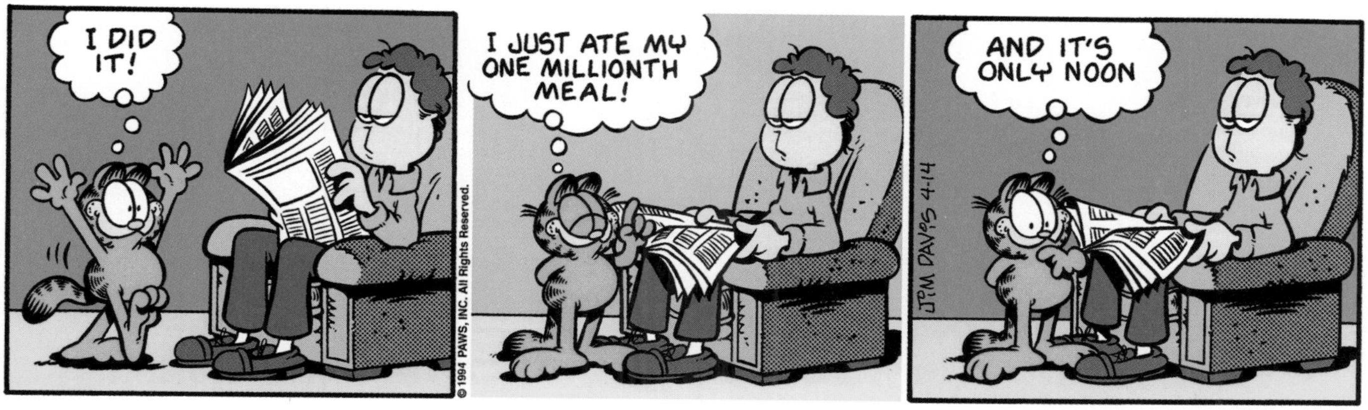
I DID IT!
I JUST ATE MY ONE MILLIONTH MEAL!
AND IT'S ONLY NOON
JIM DAVIS 4-14
© 1994 PAWS, INC. All Rights Reserved.

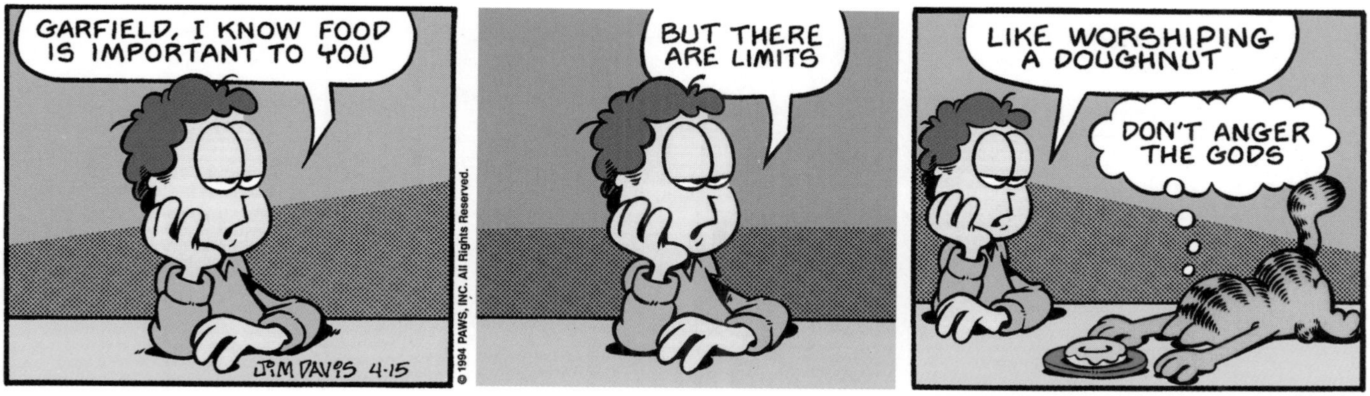
GARFIELD, I KNOW FOOD IS IMPORTANT TO YOU
JIM DAVIS 4-15
BUT THERE ARE LIMITS
LIKE WORSHIPING A DOUGHNUT
DON'T ANGER THE GODS
© 1994 PAWS, INC. All Rights Reserved.

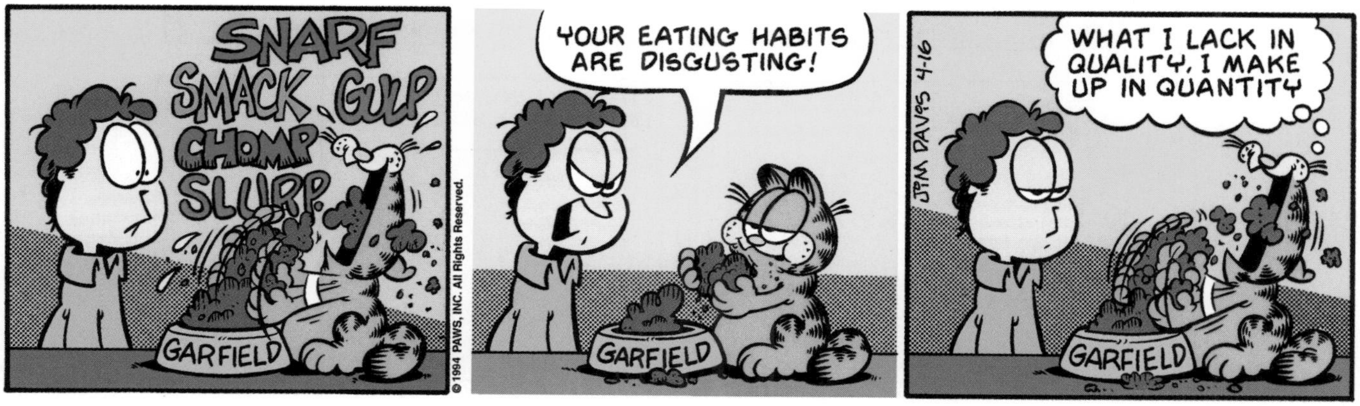
SNARF
SMACK
GULP
CHOMP
SLURP
GARFIELD
YOUR EATING HABITS ARE DISGUSTING!
GARFIELD
WHAT I LACK IN QUALITY, I MAKE UP IN QUANTITY
JIM DAVIS 4-16
GARFIELD
© 1994 PAWS, INC. All Rights Reserved.

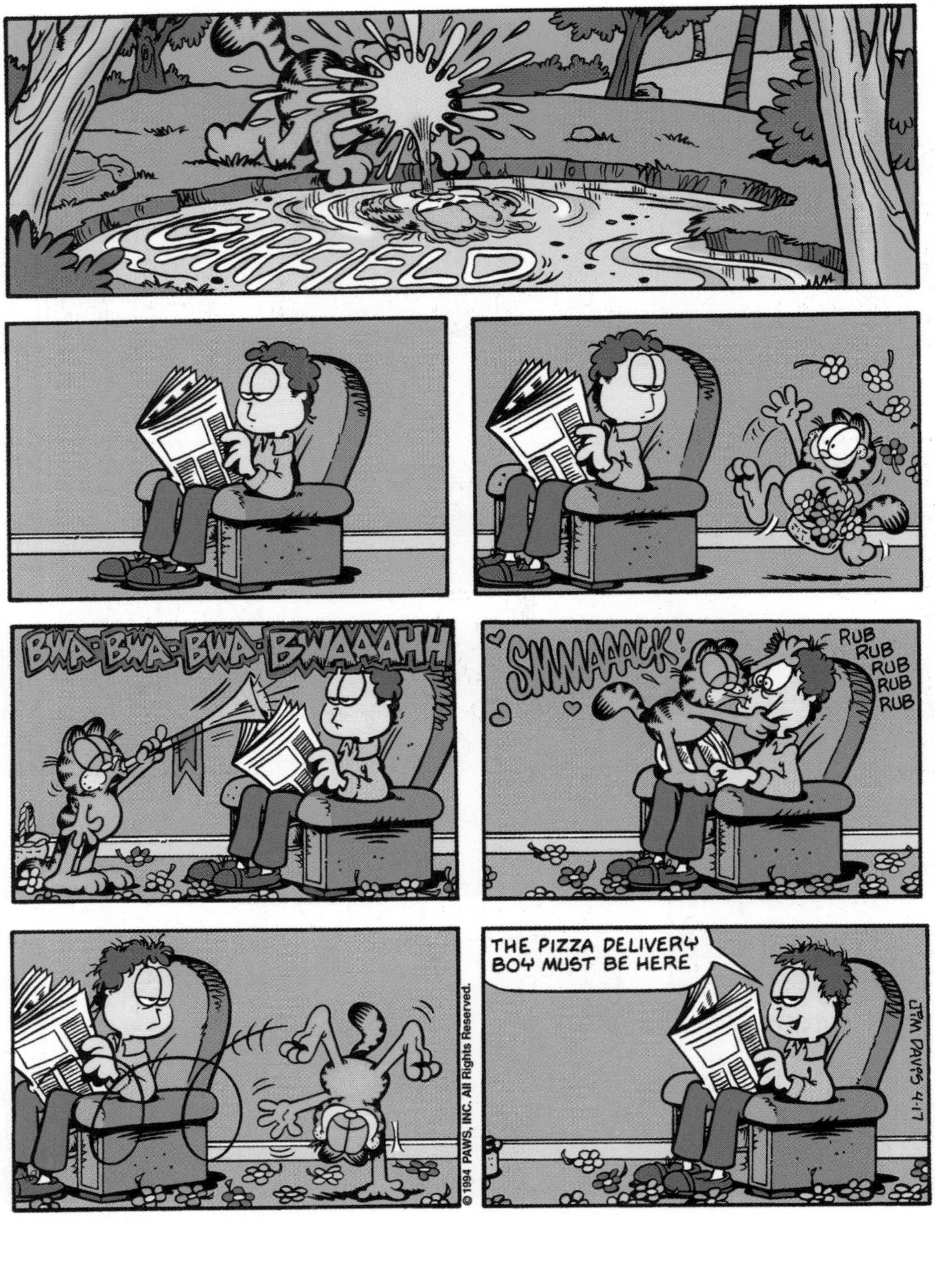
GARFIELD
BWA-BWA-BWA-BWAAAHH
SMMAAACK!
RUB RUB RUB RUB RUB
THE PIZZA DELIVERY BOY MUST BE HERE
JIM DAVIS 4-17

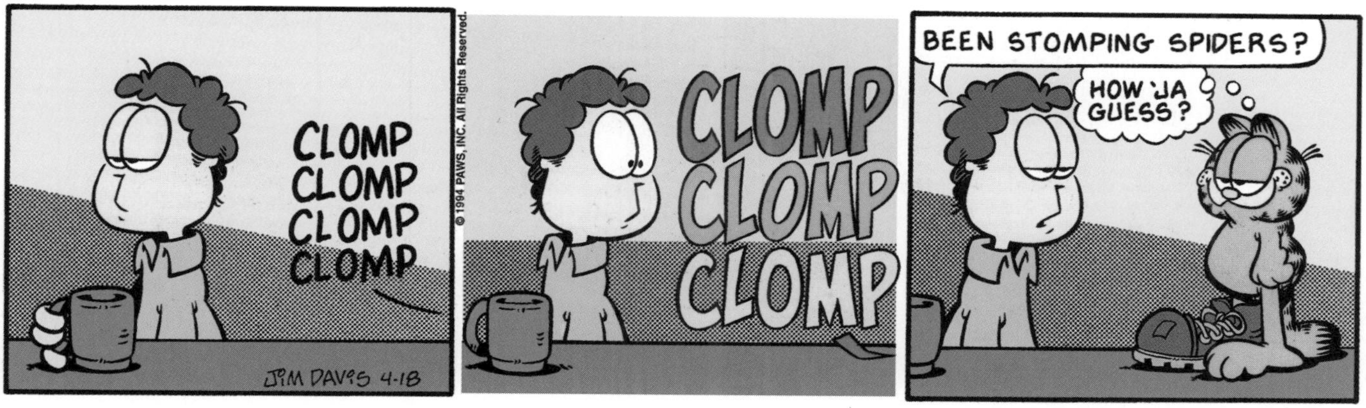
CLOMP
CLOMP
CLOMP
CLOMP
JIM DAVIS 4-18
© 1994 PAWS, INC. All Rights Reserved.
CLOMP
CLOMP
CLOMP
BEEN STOMPING SPIDERS?
HOW 'JA GUESS?

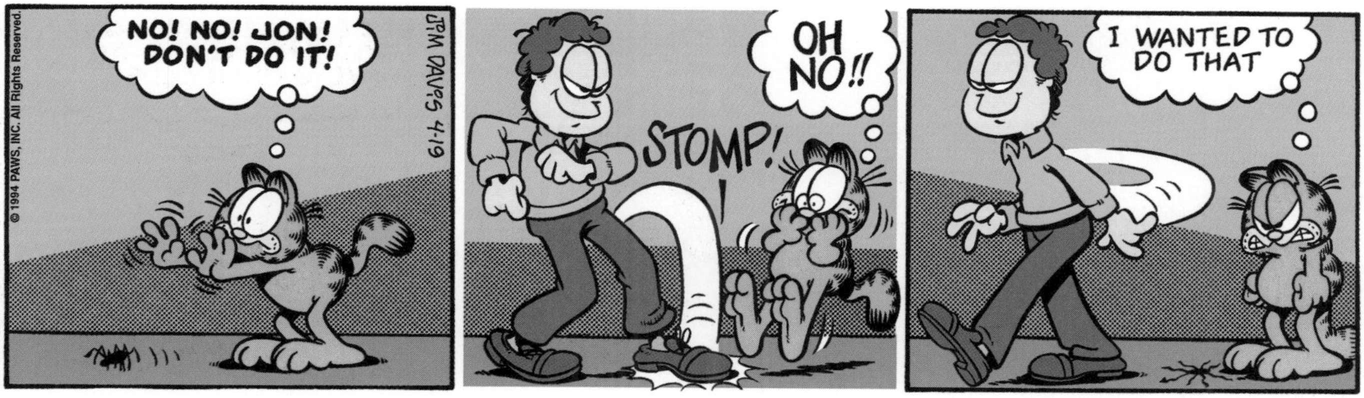
© 1994 PAWS, INC. All Rights Reserved.
NO! NO! JON! DON'T DO IT!
JIM DAVIS 4-19
STOMP!
OH NO!!
I WANTED TO DO THAT

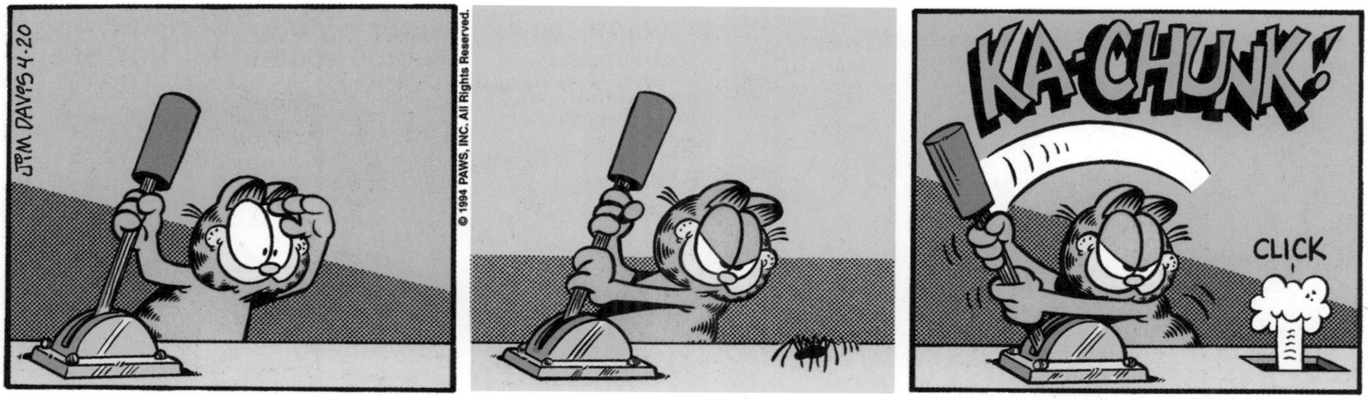
JIM DAVIS 4-20
© 1994 PAWS, INC. All Rights Reserved.
KA-CHUNK!
CLICK

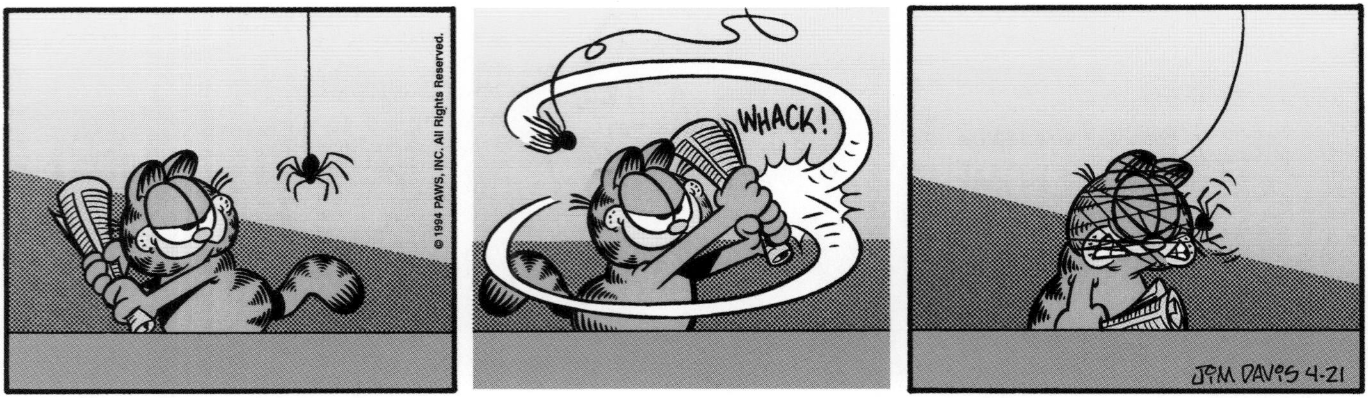
© 1994 PAWS, INC. All Rights Reserved.
WHACK!
JIM DAVIS 4-21

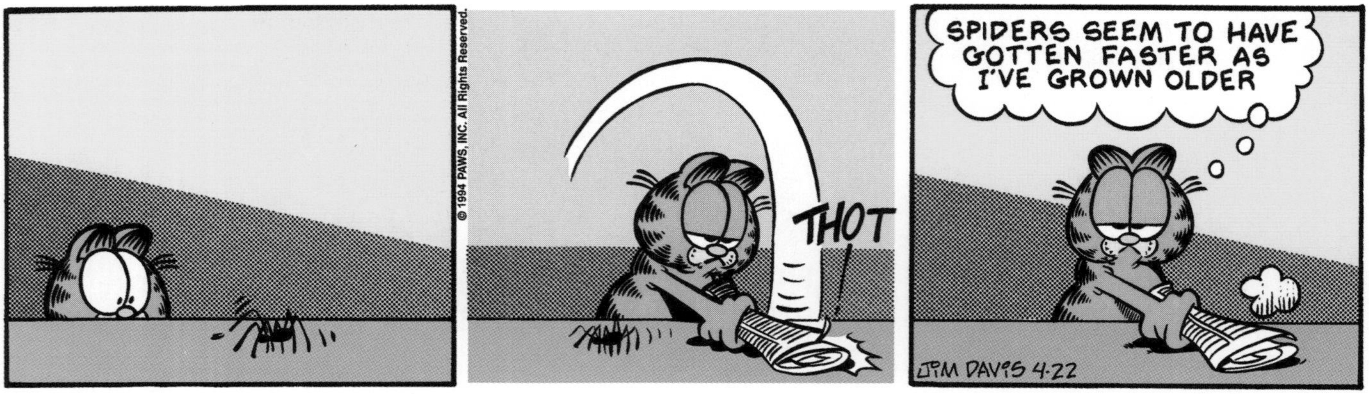
© 1994 PAWS, INC. All Rights Reserved.
THOT
SPIDERS SEEM TO HAVE GOTTEN FASTER AS I'VE GROWN OLDER
JIM DAVIS 4-22

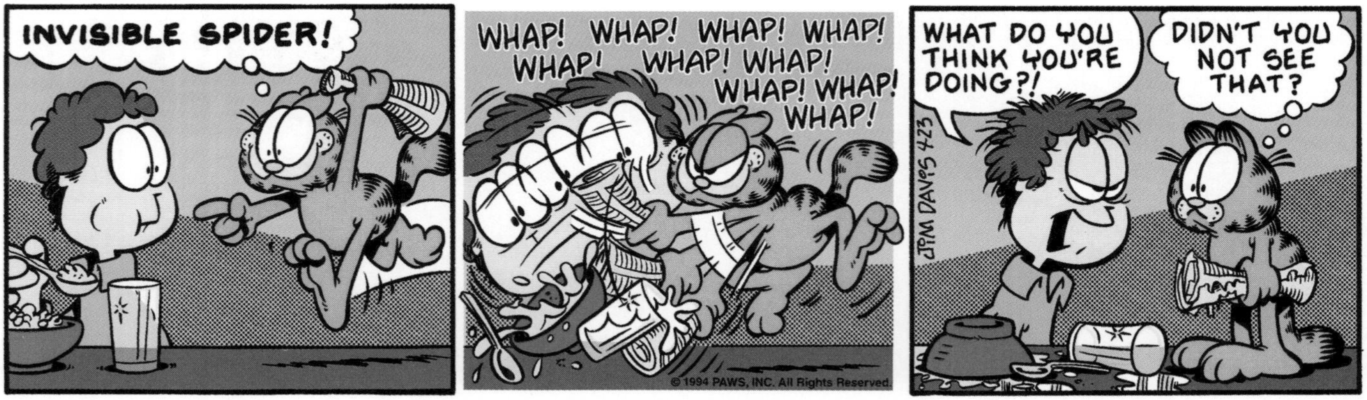
INVISIBLE SPIDER!
WHAP! WHAP! WHAP! WHAP! WHAP! WHAP! WHAP! WHAP! WHAP! WHAP!
© 1994 PAWS, INC. All Rights Reserved.
WHAT DO YOU THINK YOU'RE DOING?!
DIDN'T YOU NOT SEE THAT?
JIM DAVIS 4-23

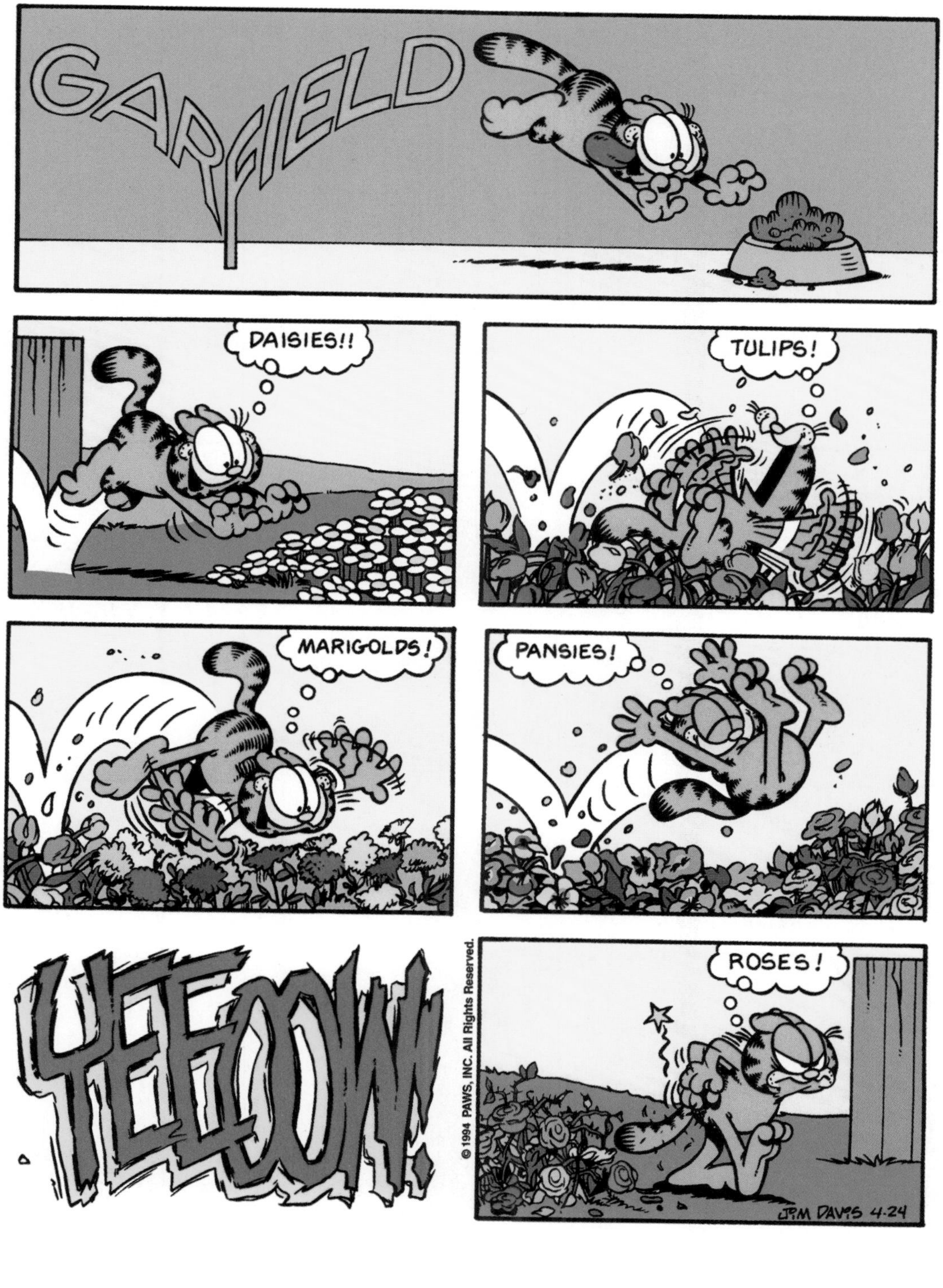
GARFIELD
DAISIES!!
TULIPS!
MARIGOLDS!
PANSIES!
YEEOOW!
© 1994 PAWS, INC. All Rights Reserved.
ROSES!
JIM DAVIS 4-24

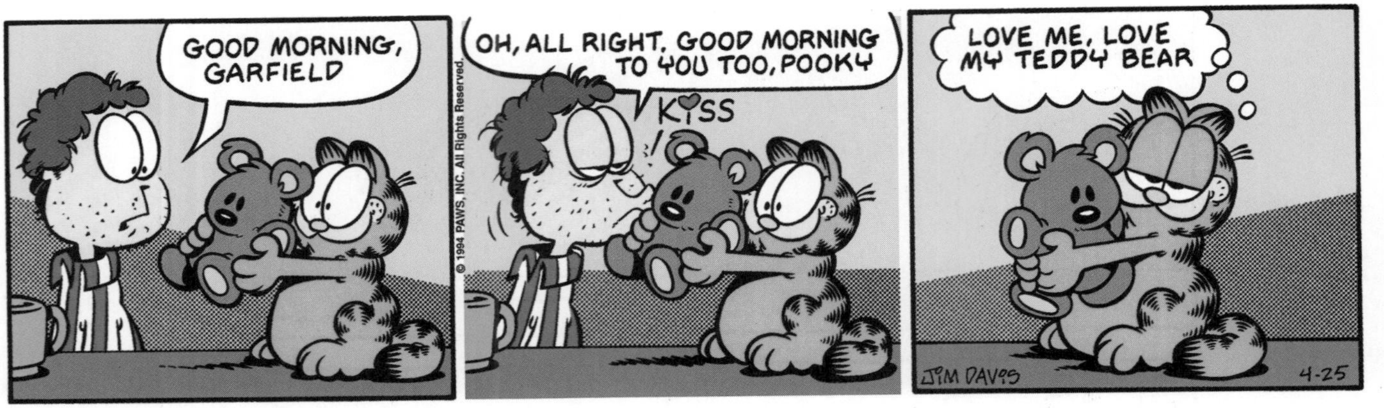
GOOD MORNING, GARFIELD
© 1994 PAWS, INC. All Rights Reserved.
OH, ALL RIGHT. GOOD MORNING TO YOU TOO, POOKY
KISS
LOVE ME, LOVE MY TEDDY BEAR
JIM DAVIS 4-25

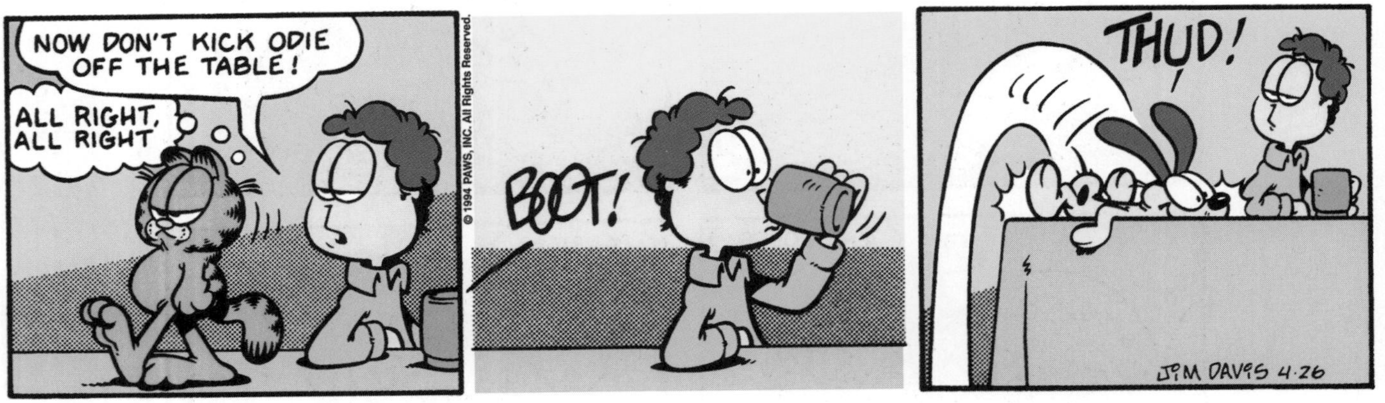
NOW DON'T KICK ODIE OFF THE TABLE!
ALL RIGHT, ALL RIGHT
© 1994 PAWS, INC. All Rights Reserved.
BOOT!
THUD!
JIM DAVIS 4-26

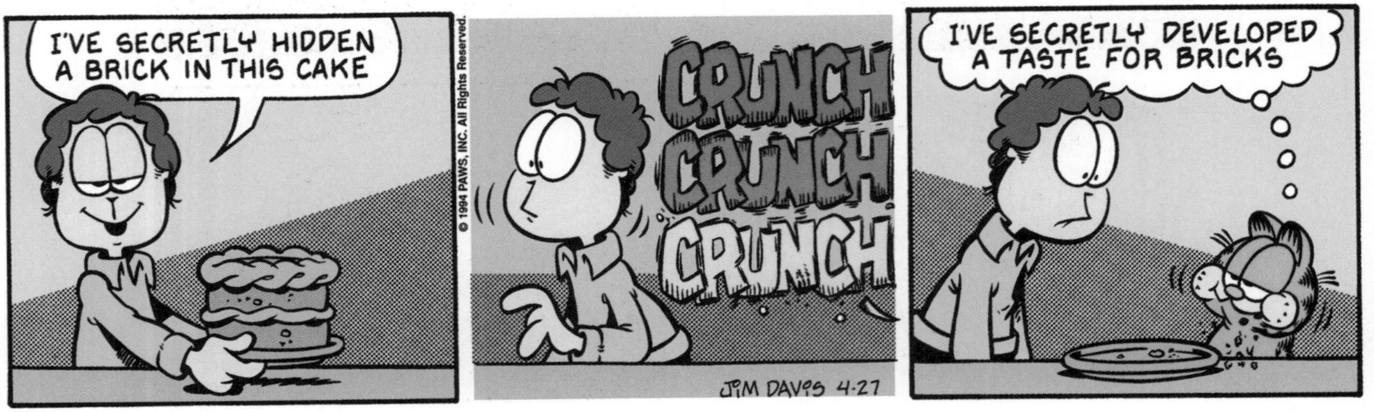
I'VE SECRETLY HIDDEN A BRICK IN THIS CAKE
© 1994 PAWS, INC. All Rights Reserved.
CRUNCH
CRUNCH
CRUNCH
JIM DAVIS 4-27
I'VE SECRETLY DEVELOPED A TASTE FOR BRICKS

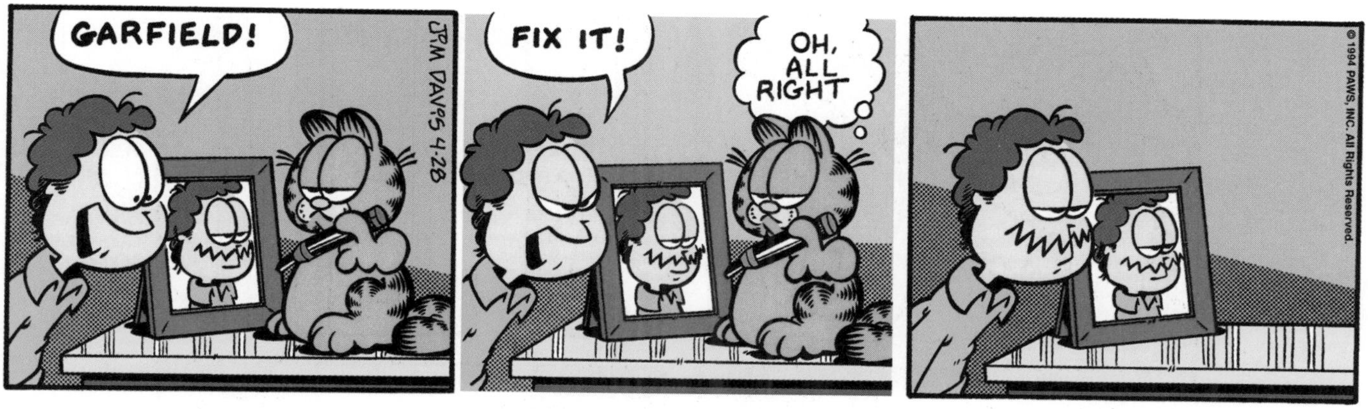
GARFIELD!
JIM DAVIS 4-28
FIX IT!
OH, ALL RIGHT
© 1994 PAWS, INC. All Rights Reserved.

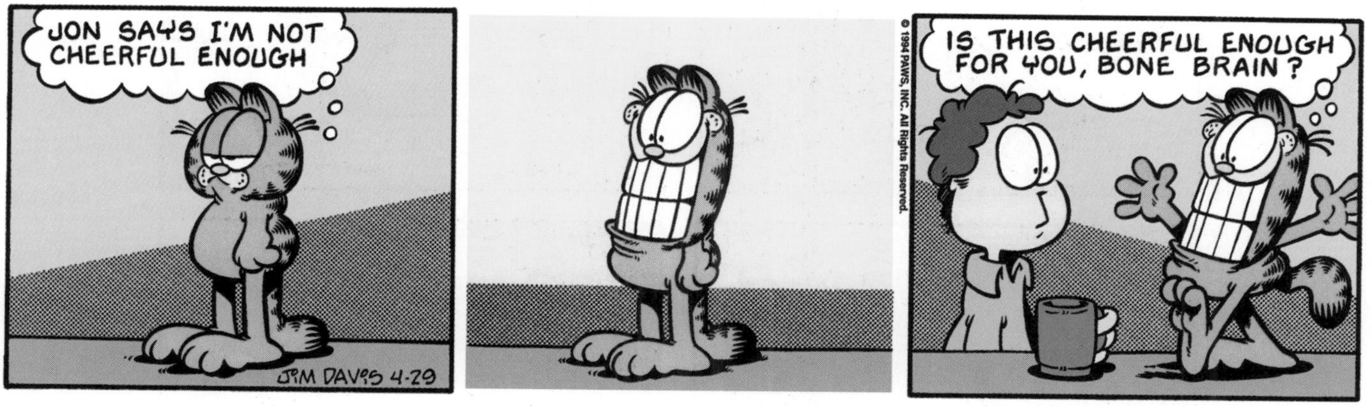
JON SAYS I'M NOT CHEERFUL ENOUGH
JIM DAVIS 4-29
© 1994 PAWS, INC. All Rights Reserved.
IS THIS CHEERFUL ENOUGH FOR YOU, BONE BRAIN?

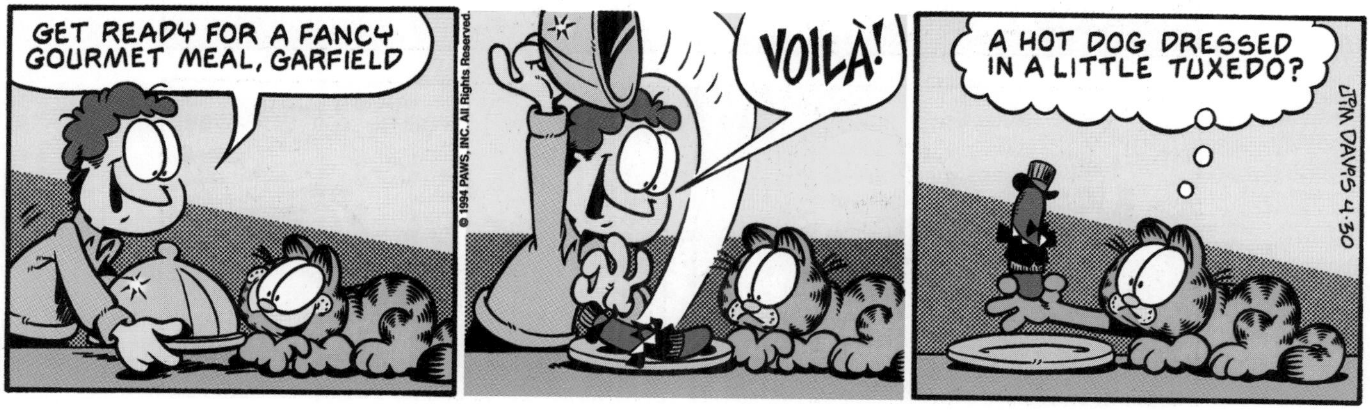
GET READY FOR A FANCY GOURMET MEAL, GARFIELD
© 1994 PAWS, INC. All Rights Reserved.
VOILÀ!
A HOT DOG DRESSED IN A LITTLE TUXEDO?
JIM DAVIS 4-30

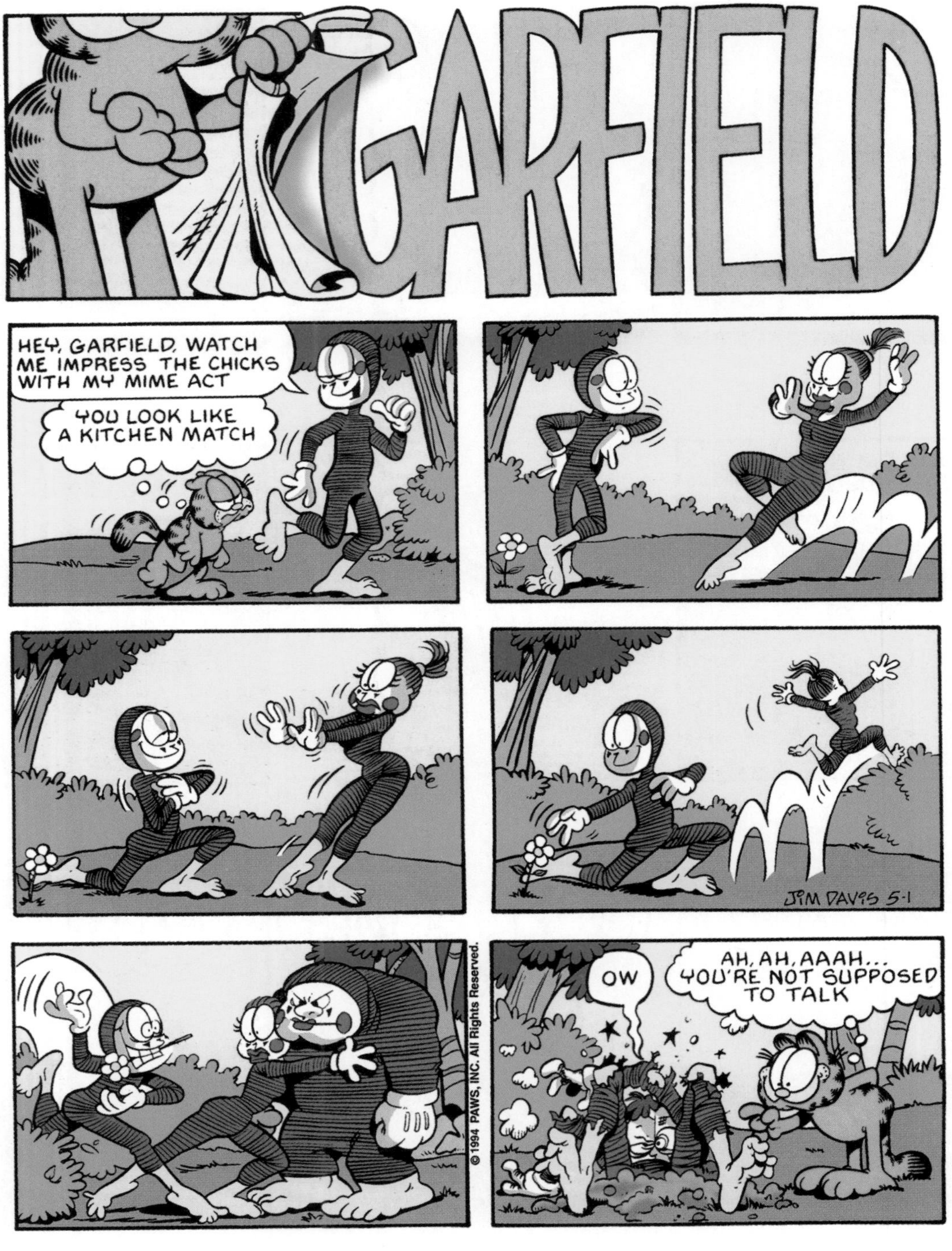
GARFIELD
HEY, GARFIELD, WATCH ME IMPRESS THE CHICKS WITH MY MIME ACT
YOU LOOK LIKE A KITCHEN MATCH
JIM DAVIS 5-1
© 1994 PAWS, INC. All Rights Reserved.
OW
AH, AH, AAAH... YOU'RE NOT SUPPOSED TO TALK

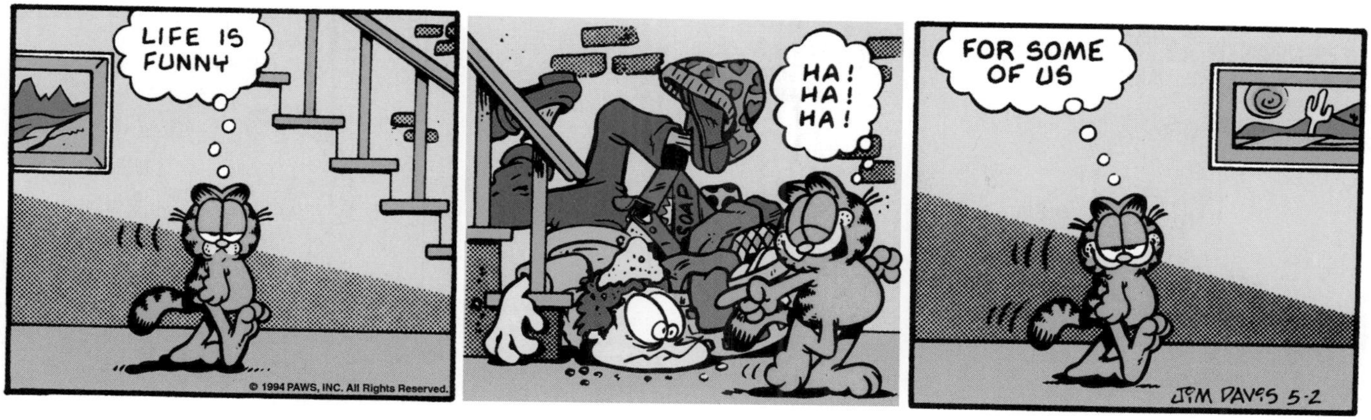
LIFE IS FUNNY
© 1994 PAWS, INC. All Rights Reserved.
HA! HA! HA!
SOAP
FOR SOME OF US
JIM DAVIS 5-2

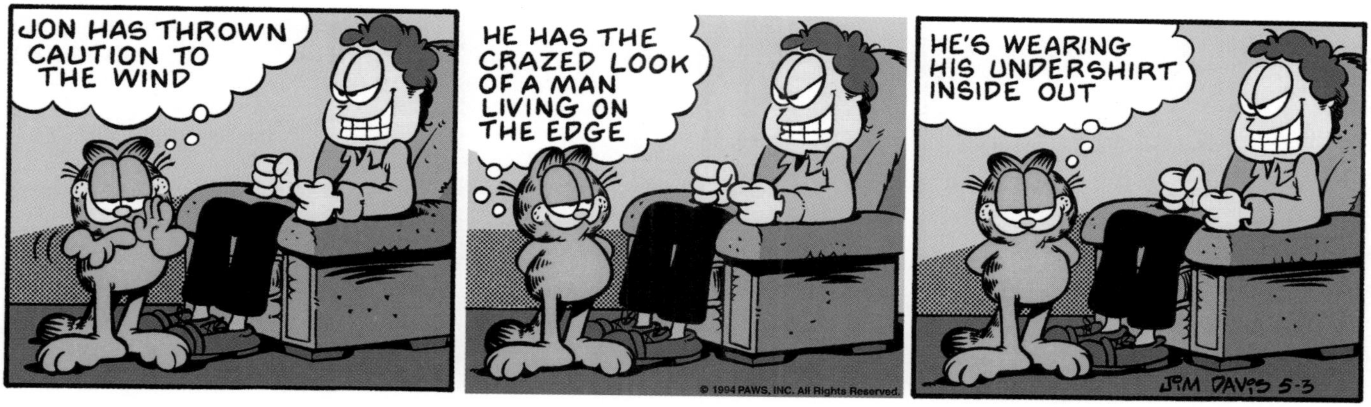
JON HAS THROWN CAUTION TO THE WIND
HE HAS THE CRAZED LOOK OF A MAN LIVING ON THE EDGE
© 1994 PAWS, INC. All Rights Reserved.
HE'S WEARING HIS UNDERSHIRT INSIDE OUT
JIM DAVIS 5-3

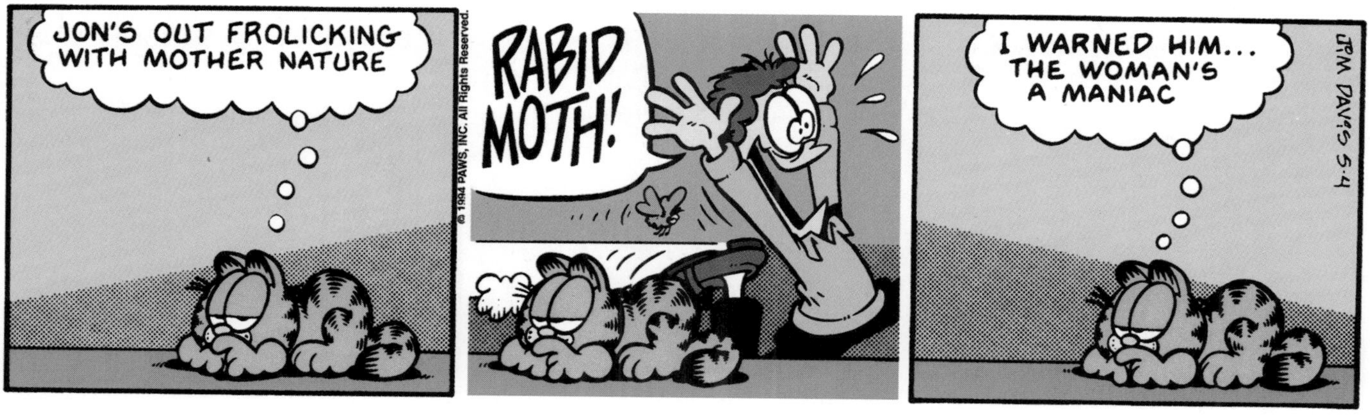
JON'S OUT FROLICKING WITH MOTHER NATURE
© 1994 PAWS, INC. All Rights Reserved.
RABID MOTH!
I WARNED HIM... THE WOMAN'S A MANIAC
JIM DAVIS 5-4

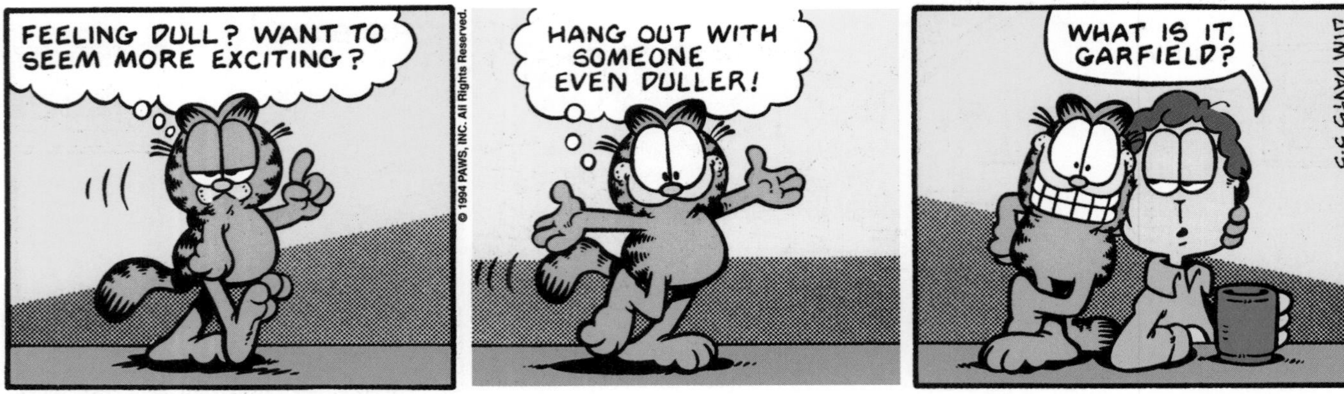
FEELING DULL? WANT TO SEEM MORE EXCITING?
HANG OUT WITH SOMEONE EVEN DULLER!
WHAT IS IT, GARFIELD?
JIM DAVIS 5-5
© 1994 PAWS, INC. All Rights Reserved.

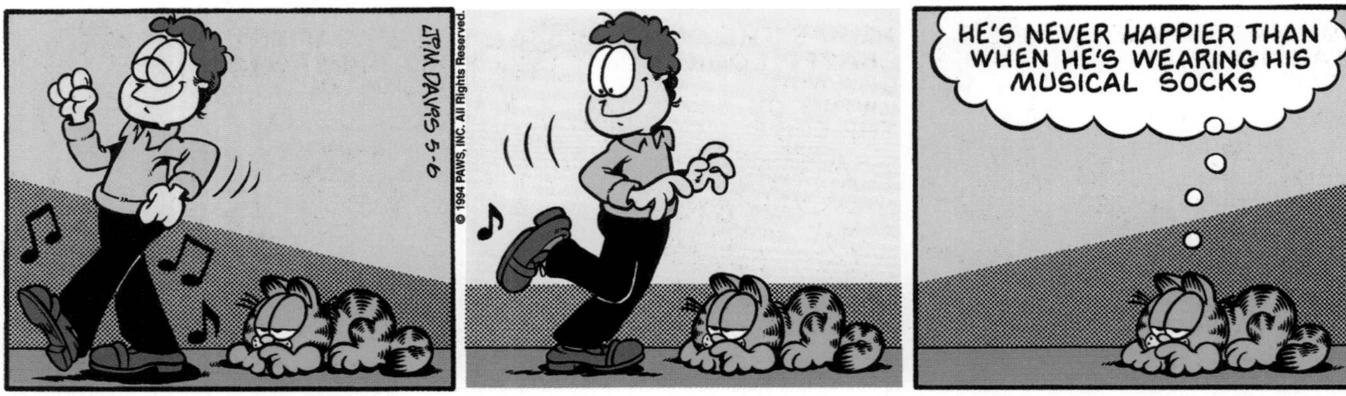
JIM DAVIS 5-6
© 1994 PAWS, INC. All Rights Reserved.
HE'S NEVER HAPPIER THAN WHEN HE'S WEARING HIS MUSICAL SOCKS

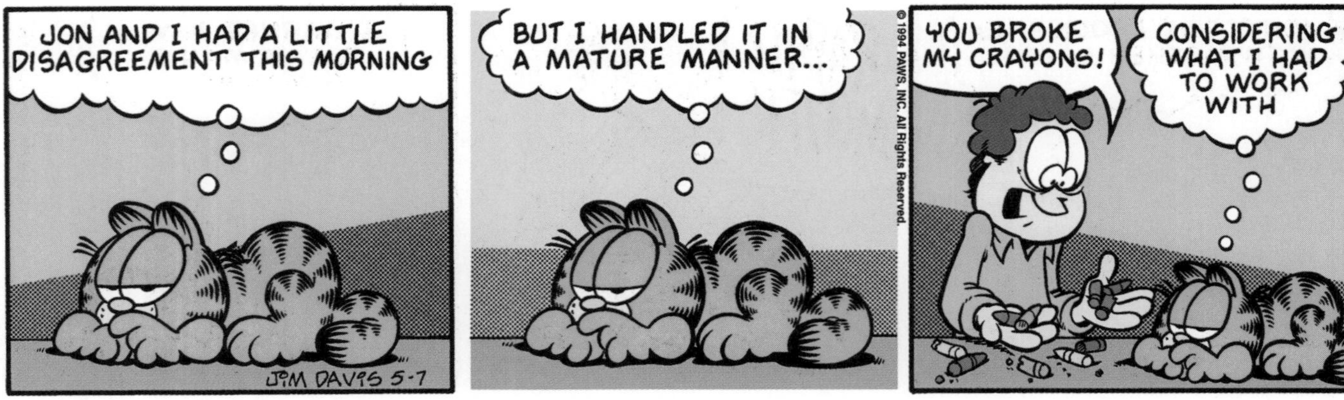
JON AND I HAD A LITTLE DISAGREEMENT THIS MORNING
JIM DAVIS 5-7
BUT I HANDLED IT IN A MATURE MANNER...
© 1994 PAWS, INC. All Rights Reserved.
YOU BROKE MY CRAYONS!
CONSIDERING WHAT I HAD TO WORK WITH

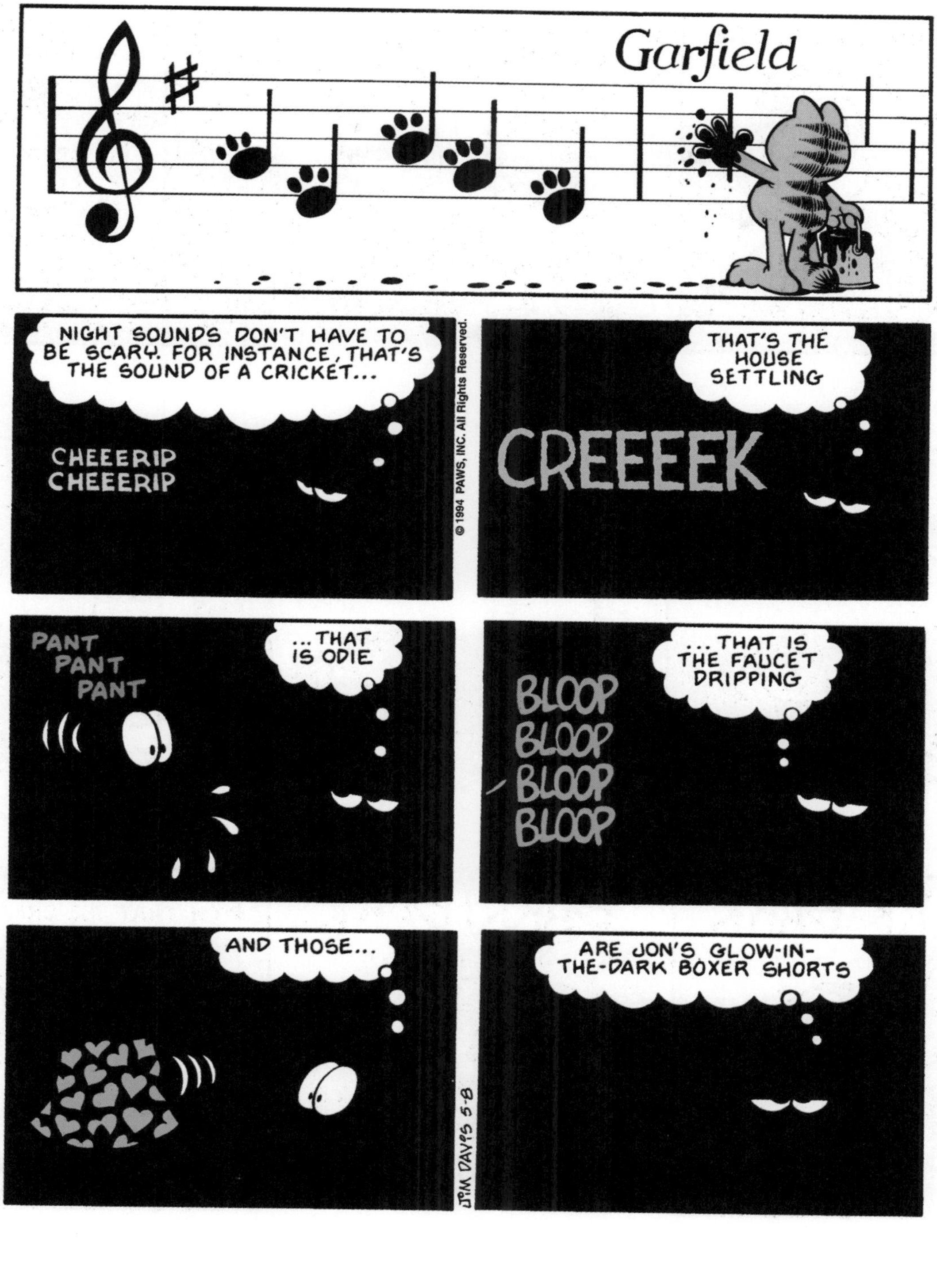

Garfield
NIGHT SOUNDS DON'T HAVE TO BE SCARY. FOR INSTANCE, THAT'S THE SOUND OF A CRICKET...
CHEEERIP CHEEERIP
© 1994 PAWS, INC. All Rights Reserved.
THAT'S THE HOUSE SETTLING
CREEEEK
PANT PANT PANT
...THAT IS ODIE
...THAT IS THE FAUCET DRIPPING
BLOOP BLOOP BLOOP BLOOP
AND THOSE...
ARE JON'S GLOW-IN-THE-DARK BOXER SHORTS
JIM DAVIS 5-8

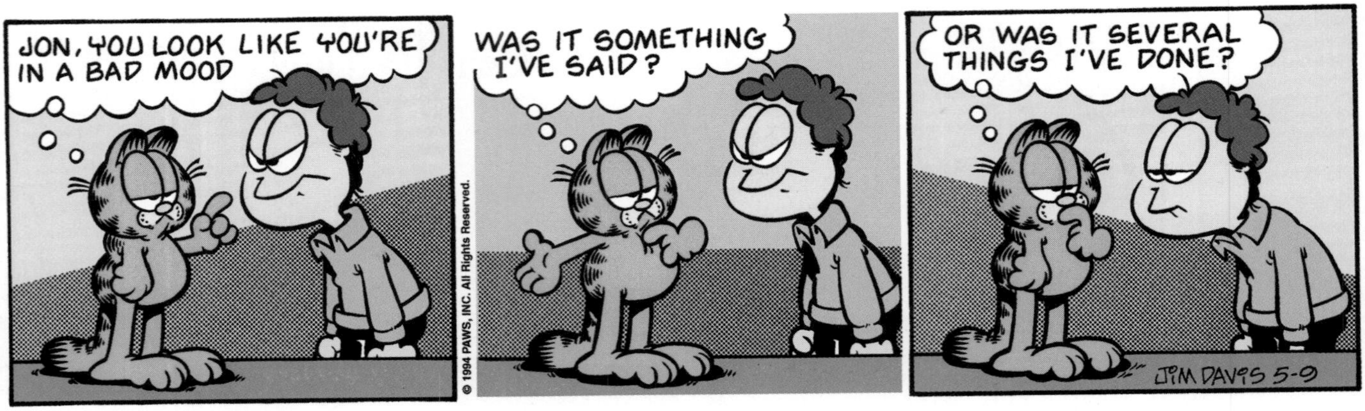
JON, YOU LOOK LIKE YOU'RE IN A BAD MOOD
WAS IT SOMETHING I'VE SAID?
OR WAS IT SEVERAL THINGS I'VE DONE?
© 1994 PAWS, INC. All Rights Reserved.
JIM DAVIS 5-9

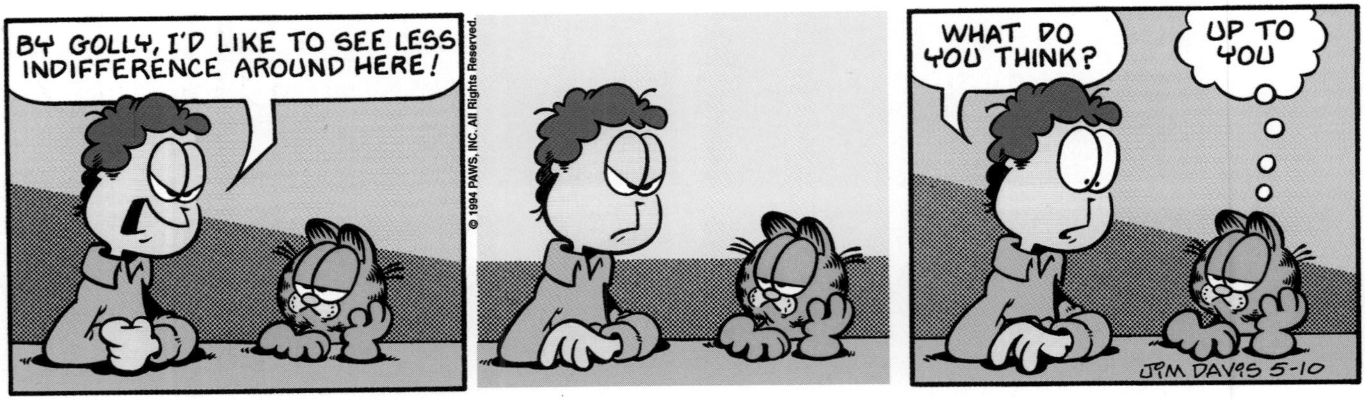
BY GOLLY, I'D LIKE TO SEE LESS INDIFFERENCE AROUND HERE!
© 1994 PAWS, INC. All Rights Reserved.
WHAT DO YOU THINK?
UP TO YOU
JIM DAVIS 5-10

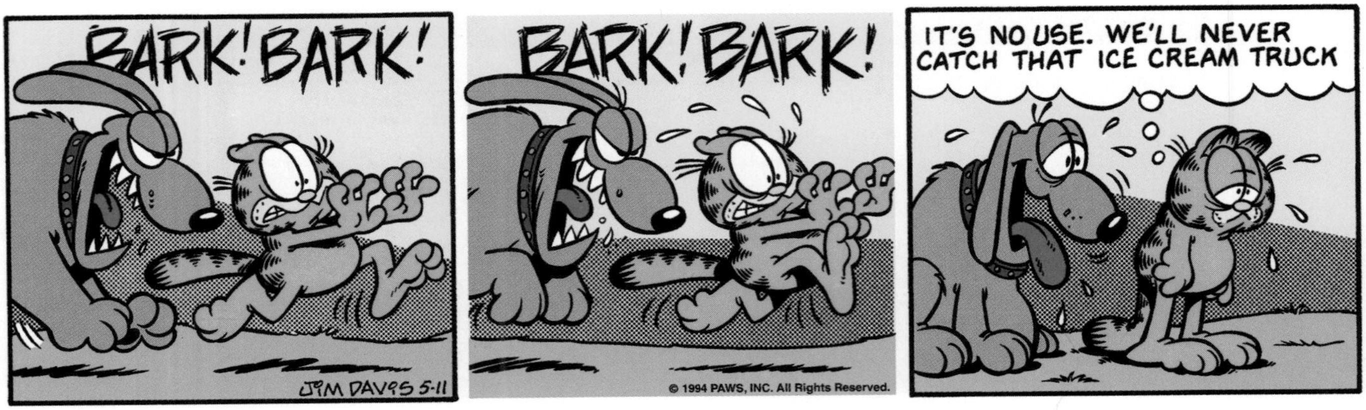
BARK! BARK!
JIM DAVIS 5-11
BARK! BARK!
© 1994 PAWS, INC. All Rights Reserved.
IT'S NO USE. WE'LL NEVER CATCH THAT ICE CREAM TRUCK

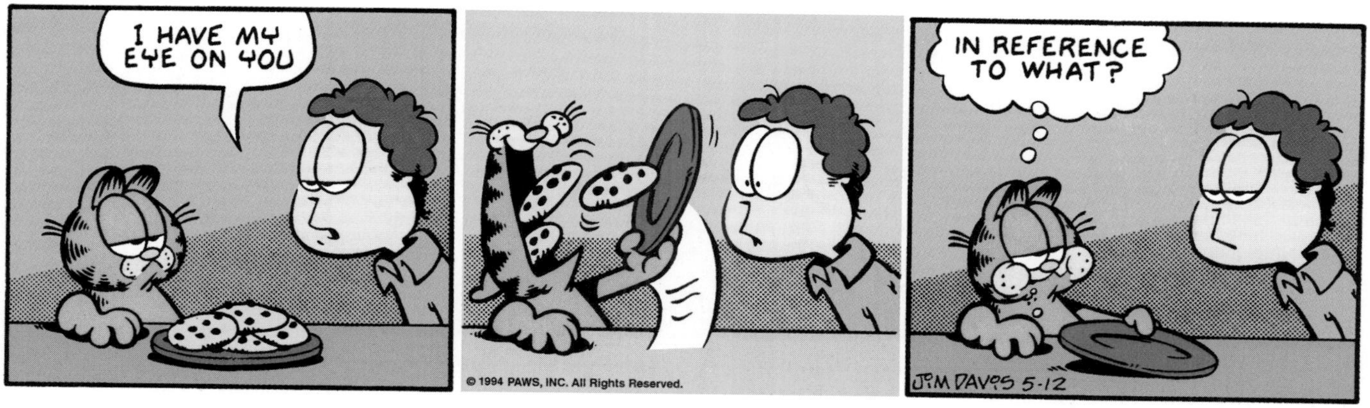
I HAVE MY EYE ON YOU
IN REFERENCE TO WHAT?
© 1994 PAWS, INC. All Rights Reserved.
JIM DAVIS 5-12

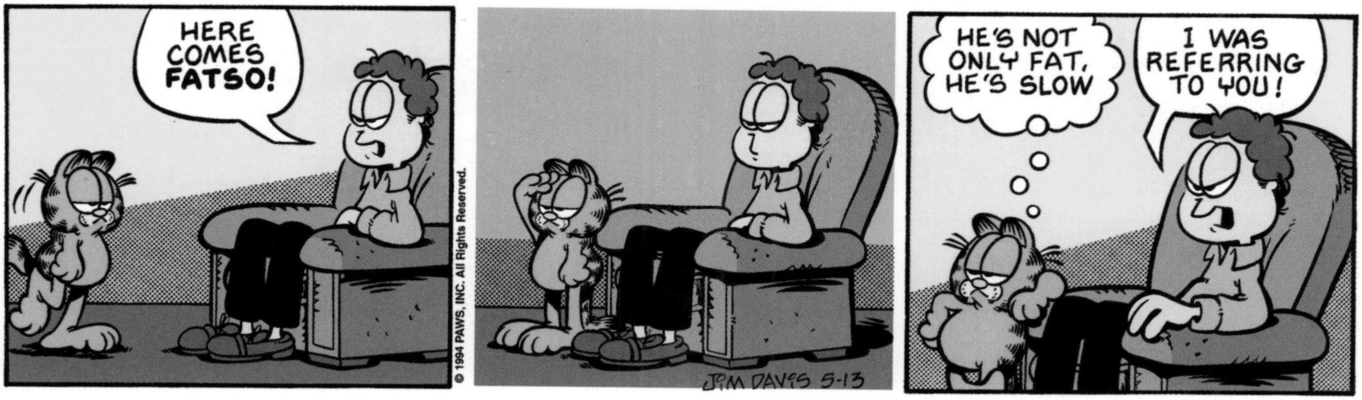
HERE COMES FATSO!
HE'S NOT ONLY FAT, HE'S SLOW
I WAS REFERRING TO YOU!
© 1994 PAWS, INC. All Rights Reserved.
JIM DAVIS 5-13

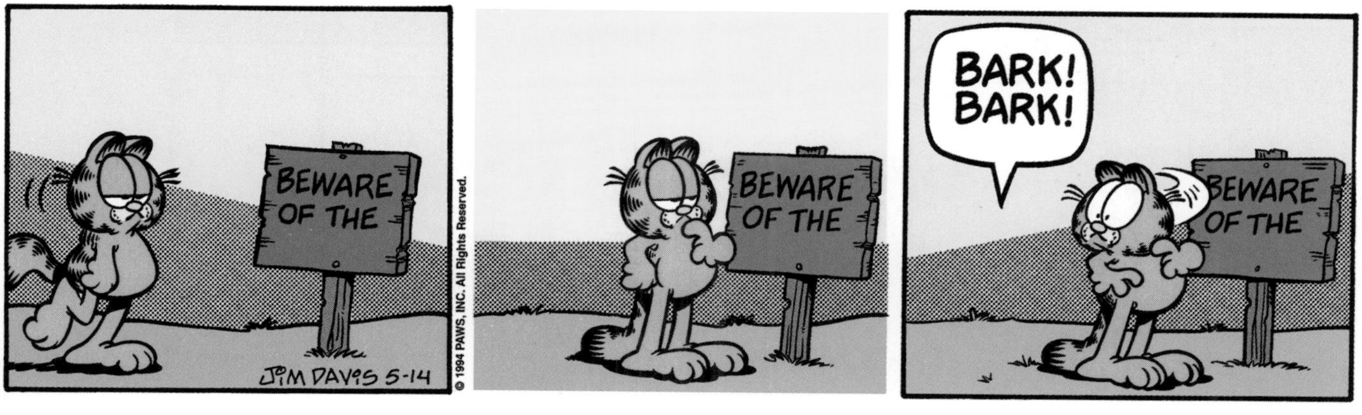
BEWARE OF THE
BARK! BARK!
© 1994 PAWS, INC. All Rights Reserved.
JIM DAVIS 5-14

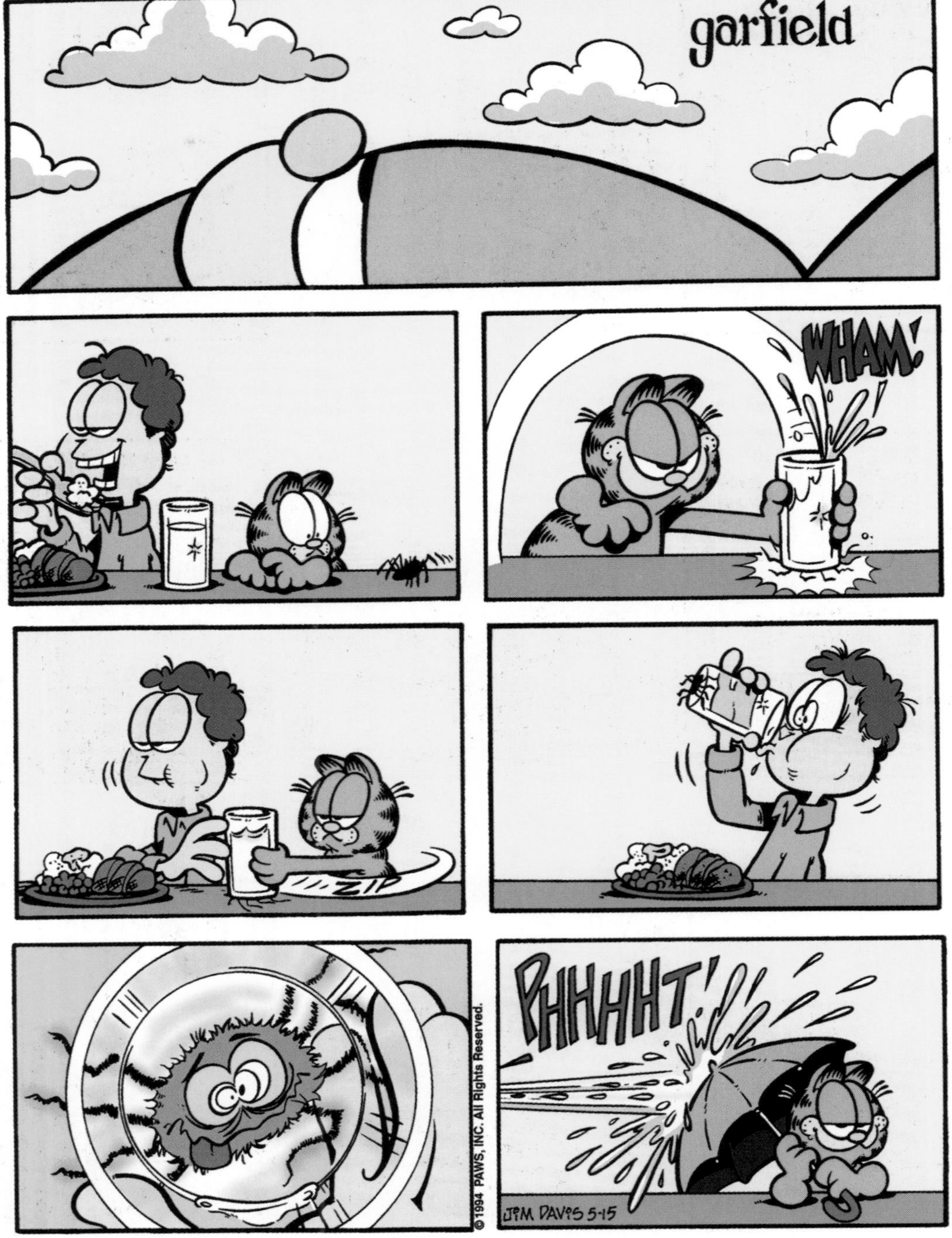
garfield
WHAM!
ZIP
PHHHHT!
JIM DAVIS 5-15

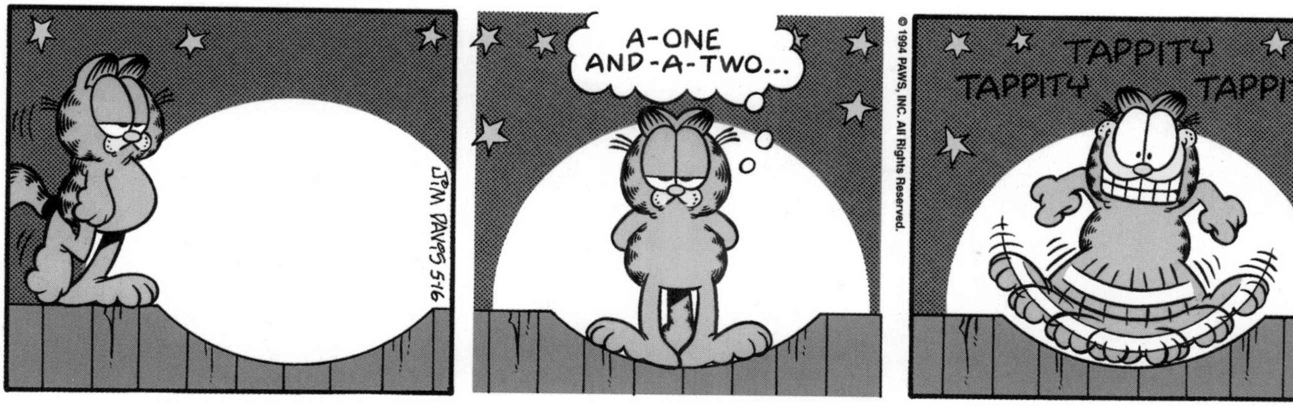
JIM DAVIS 5-16
A-ONE AND-A-TWO...
© 1994 PAWS, INC. All Rights Reserved.
TAPPITY
TAPPITY
TAPPITY

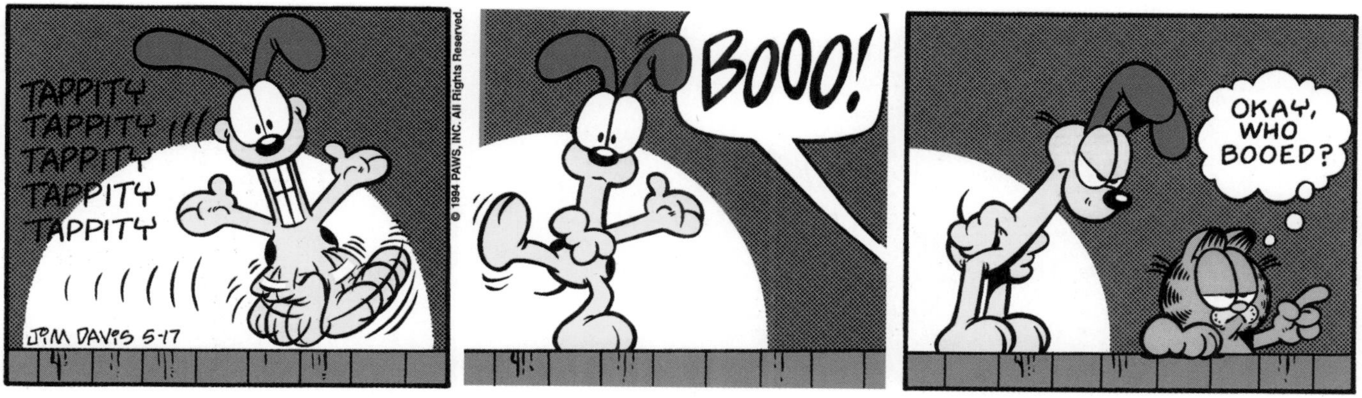
TAPPITY
TAPPITY
TAPPITY
TAPPITY
TAPPITY
JIM DAVIS 5-17
© 1994 PAWS, INC. All Rights Reserved.
BOOO!
OKAY, WHO BOOED?

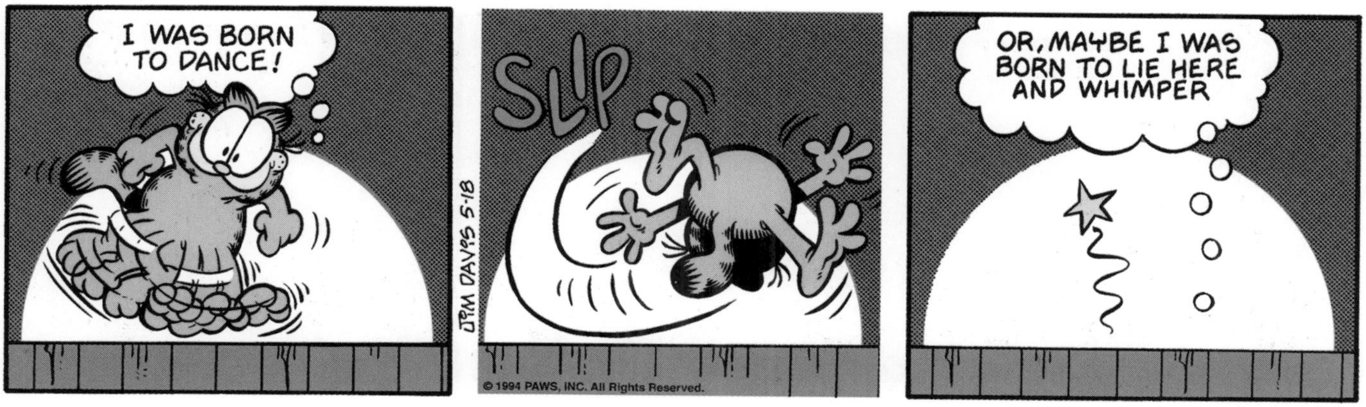
I WAS BORN TO DANCE!
JIM DAVIS 5-18
SLIP
© 1994 PAWS, INC. All Rights Reserved.
OR, MAYBE I WAS BORN TO LIE HERE AND WHIMPER

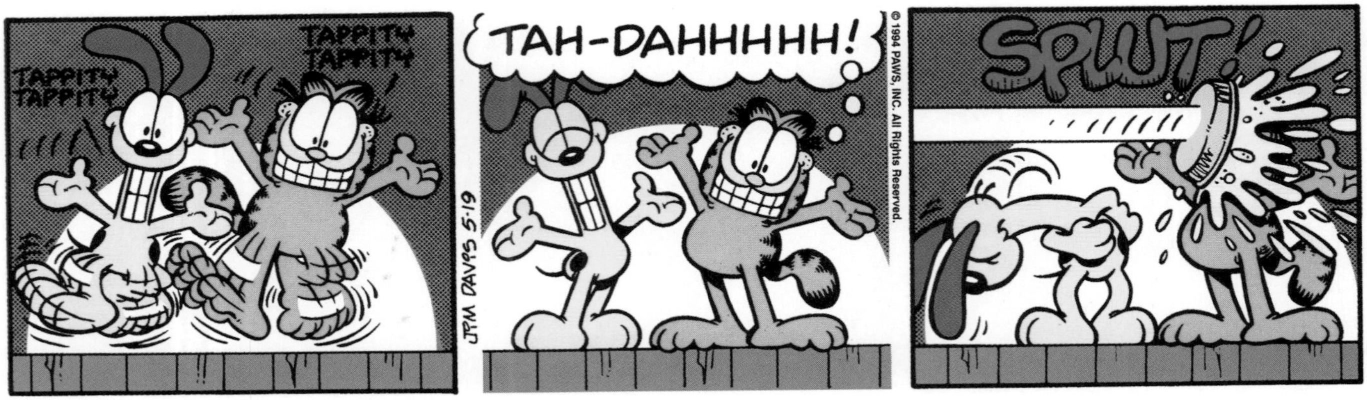
TAPPITY TAPPITY
TAPPITY TAPPITY
JIM DAVIS 5-19
TAH-DAHHHHH!
© 1994 PAWS, INC. All Rights Reserved.
SPLUT!

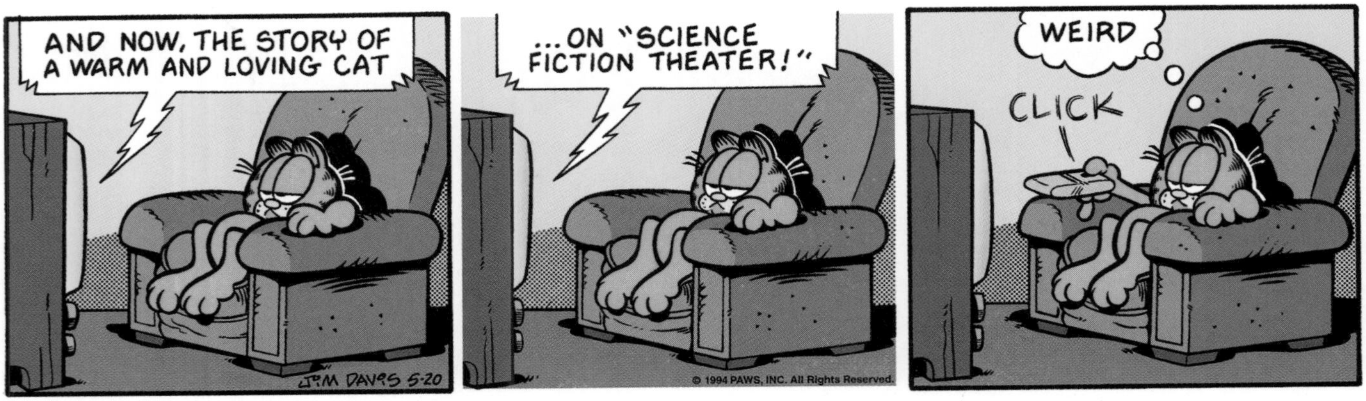
AND NOW, THE STORY OF A WARM AND LOVING CAT
JIM DAVIS 5-20
...ON "SCIENCE FICTION THEATER!"
© 1994 PAWS, INC. All Rights Reserved.
WEIRD
CLICK

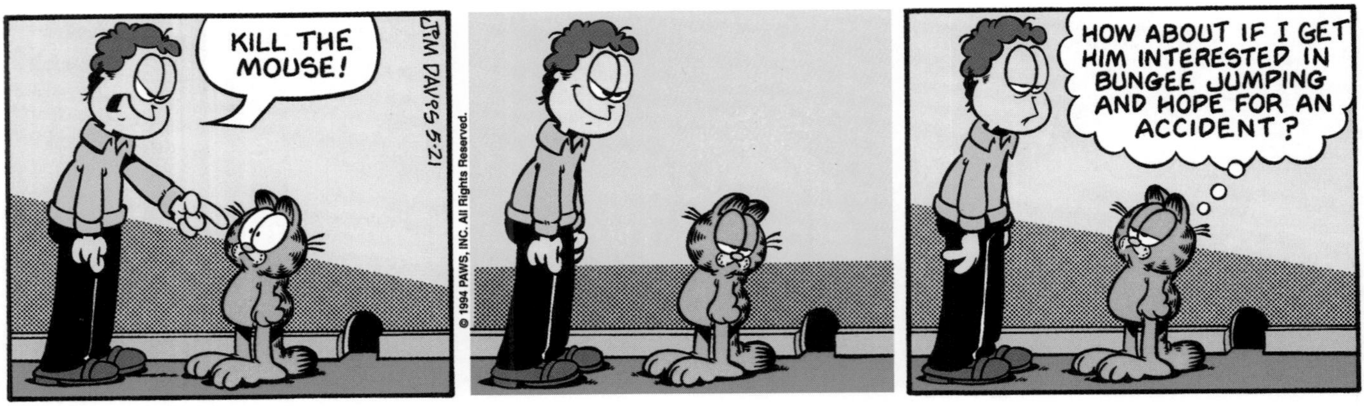
KILL THE MOUSE!
JIM DAVIS 5-21
© 1994 PAWS, INC. All Rights Reserved.
HOW ABOUT IF I GET HIM INTERESTED IN BUNGEE JUMPING AND HOPE FOR AN ACCIDENT?

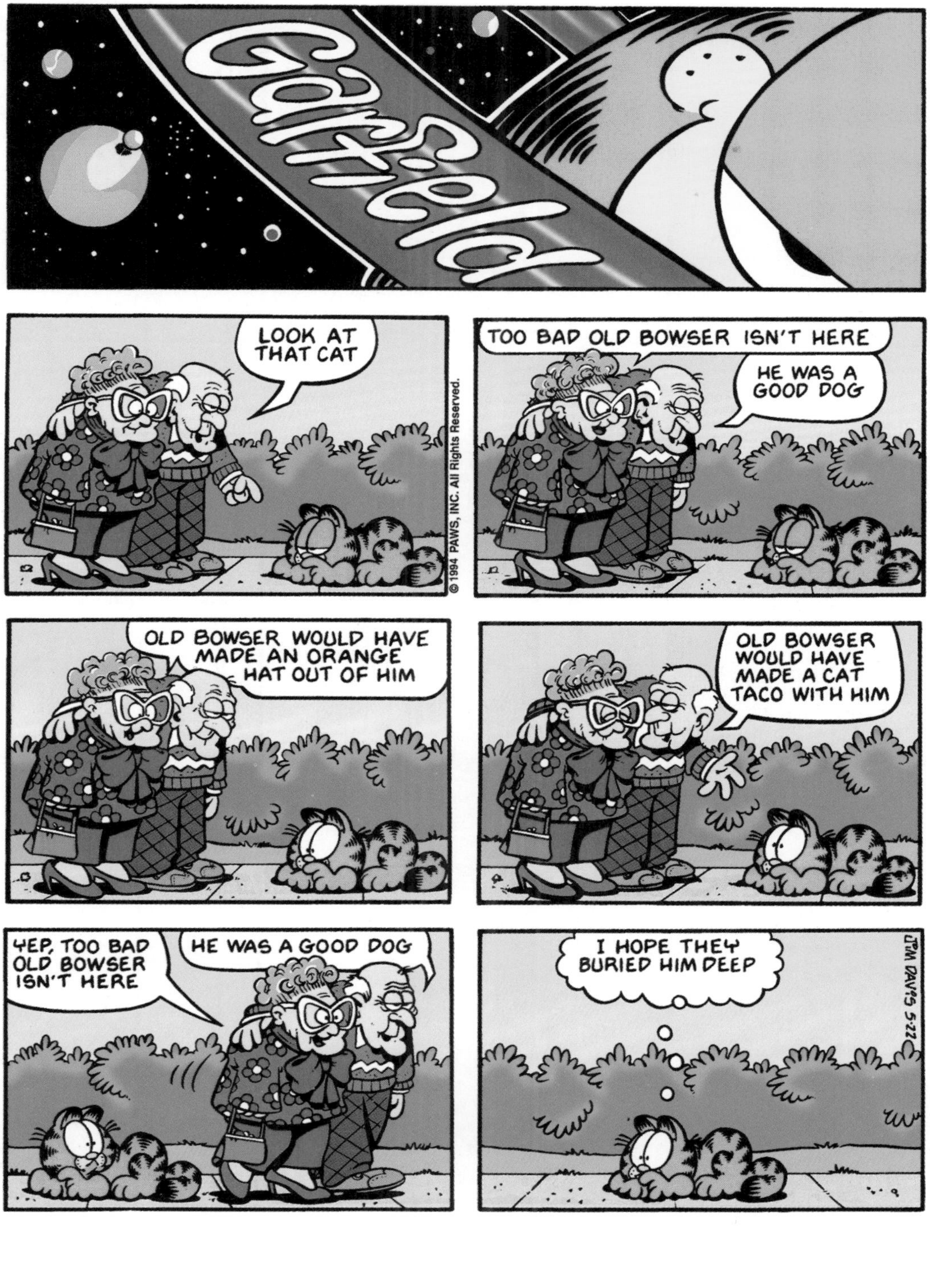
Garfield
LOOK AT THAT CAT
TOO BAD OLD BOWSER ISN'T HERE
HE WAS A GOOD DOG
OLD BOWSER WOULD HAVE MADE AN ORANGE HAT OUT OF HIM
OLD BOWSER WOULD HAVE MADE A CAT TACO WITH HIM
YEP, TOO BAD OLD BOWSER ISN'T HERE
HE WAS A GOOD DOG
I HOPE THEY BURIED HIM DEEP
JPM DAV95 5-22

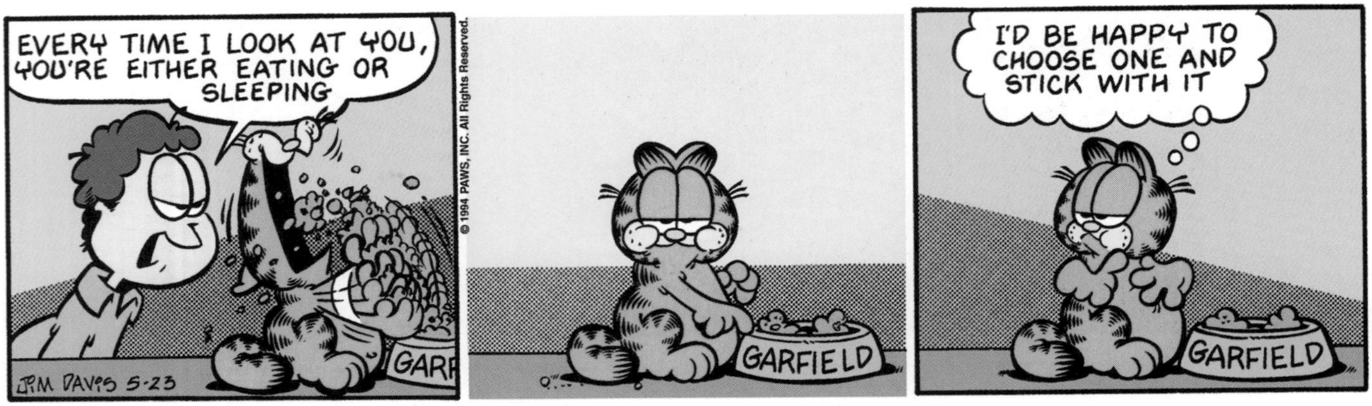

EVERY TIME I LOOK AT YOU, YOU'RE EITHER EATING OR SLEEPING
JIM DAVIS 5-23
© 1994 PAWS, INC. All Rights Reserved.
GARFIELD
I'D BE HAPPY TO CHOOSE ONE AND STICK WITH IT
GARFIELD

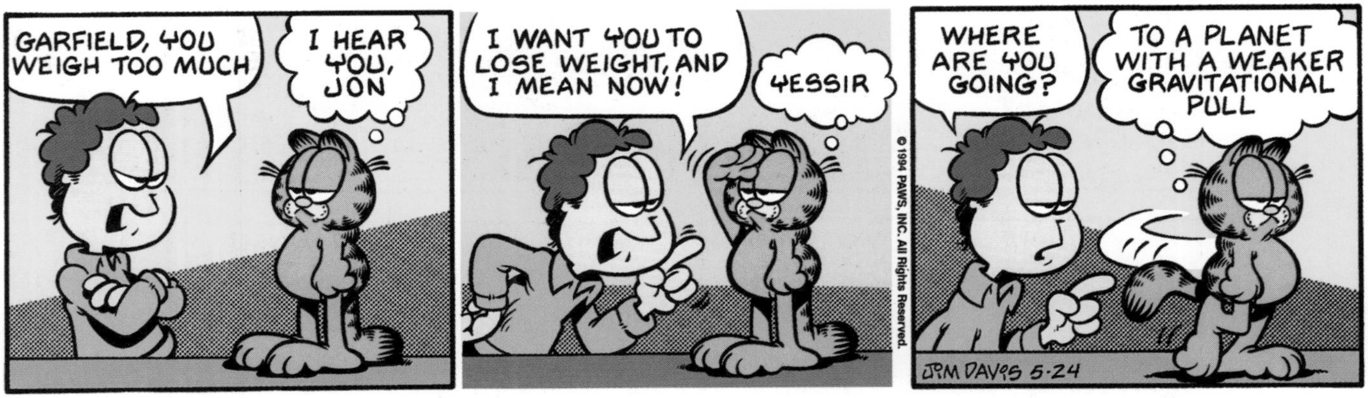

GARFIELD, YOU WEIGH TOO MUCH
I HEAR YOU, JON
I WANT YOU TO LOSE WEIGHT, AND I MEAN NOW!
YESSIR
© 1994 PAWS, INC. All Rights Reserved.
WHERE ARE YOU GOING?
TO A PLANET WITH A WEAKER GRAVITATIONAL PULL
JIM DAVIS 5-24

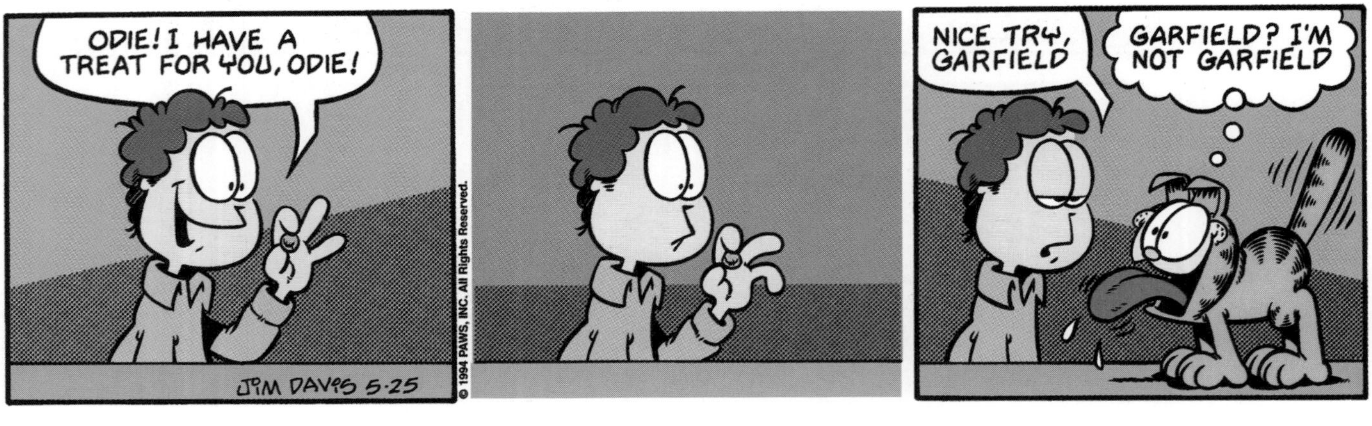

ODIE! I HAVE A TREAT FOR YOU, ODIE!
JIM DAVIS 5-25
© 1994 PAWS, INC. All Rights Reserved.
NICE TRY, GARFIELD
GARFIELD? I'M NOT GARFIELD

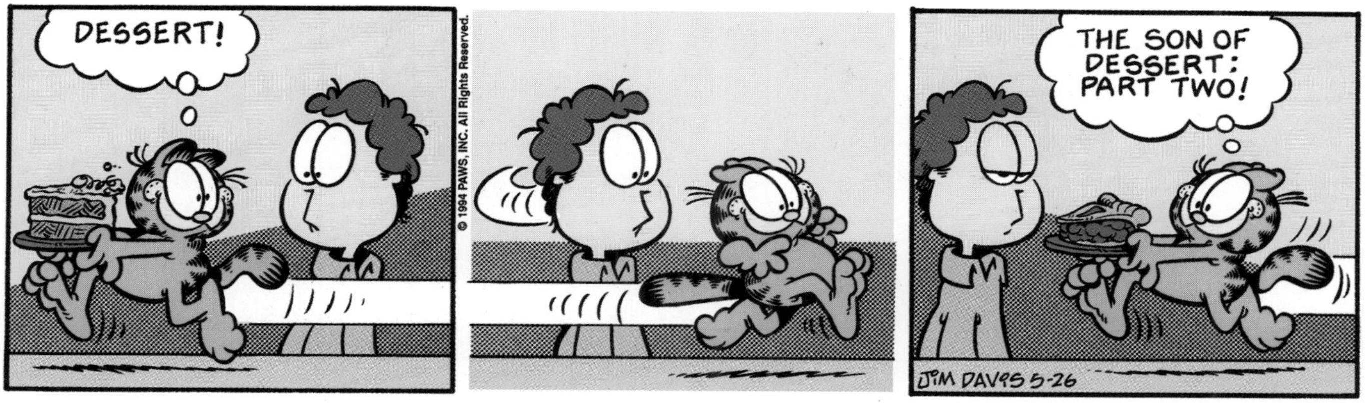
DESSERT!
© 1994 PAWS, INC. All Rights Reserved.
THE SON OF DESSERT: PART TWO!
JIM DAVIS 5-26

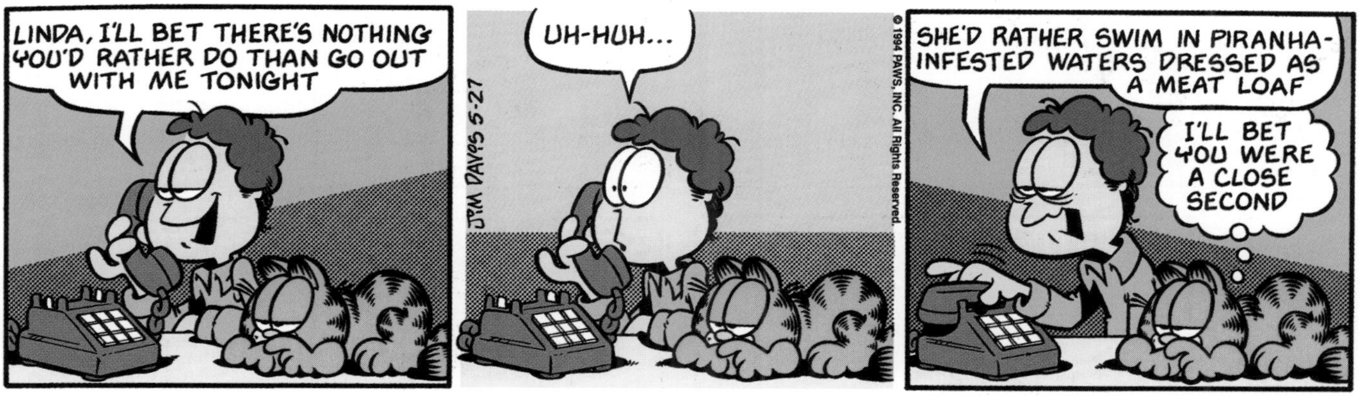
LINDA, I'LL BET THERE'S NOTHING YOU'D RATHER DO THAN GO OUT WITH ME TONIGHT
JIM DAVIS 5-27
UH-HUH...
© 1994 PAWS, INC. All Rights Reserved.
SHE'D RATHER SWIM IN PIRANHA-INFESTED WATERS DRESSED AS A MEAT LOAF
I'LL BET YOU WERE A CLOSE SECOND

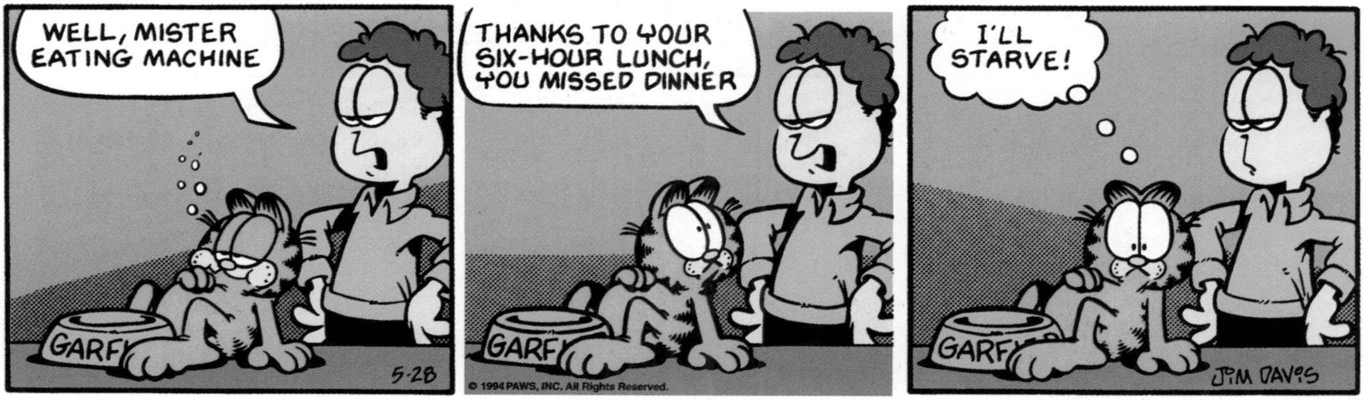
WELL, MISTER EATING MACHINE
GARF
5-28
THANKS TO YOUR SIX-HOUR LUNCH, YOU MISSED DINNER
GARF
© 1994 PAWS, INC. All Rights Reserved.
I'LL STARVE!
GARF
JIM DAVIS

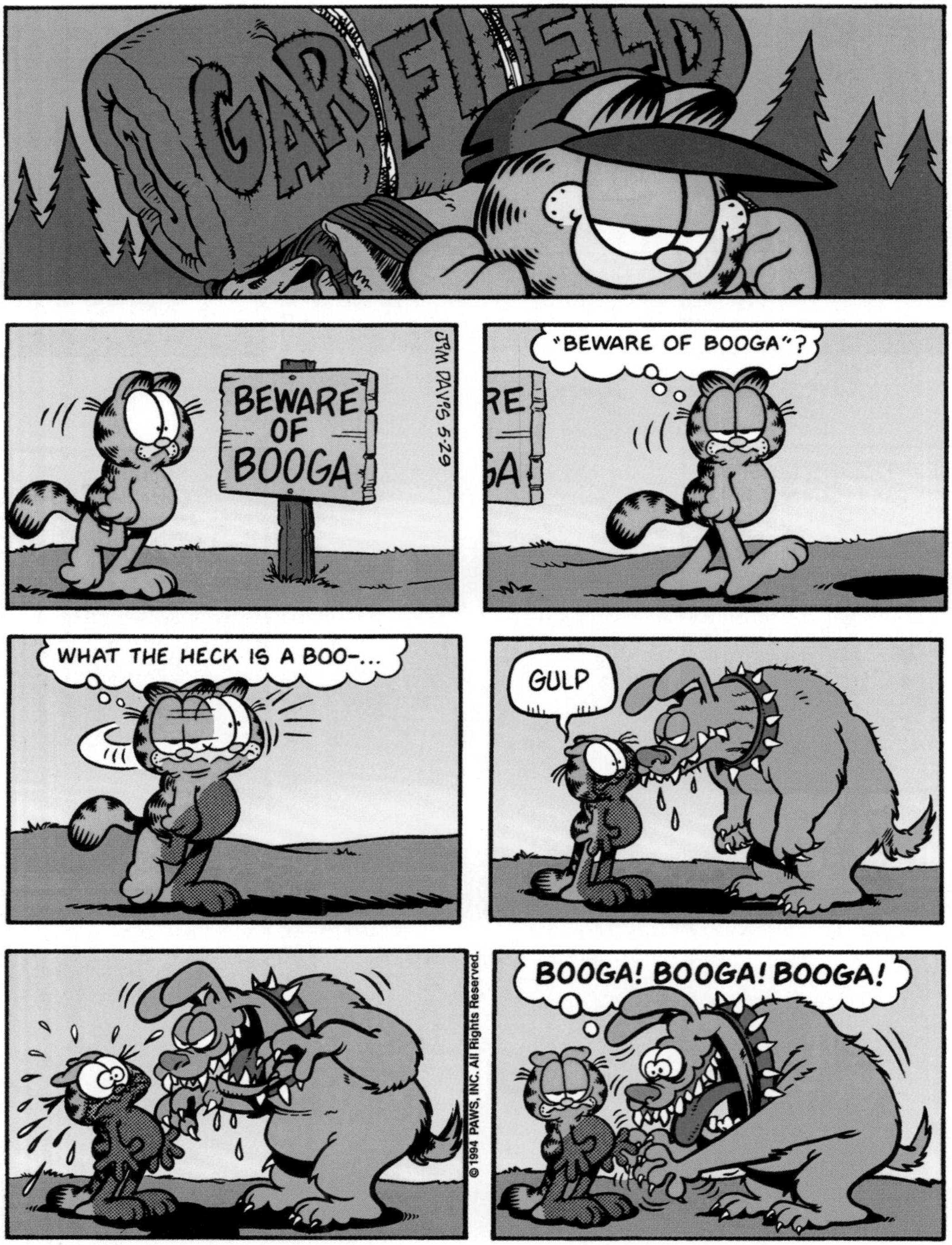
GARFIELD
BEWARE OF BOOGA
JIM DAVIS 5-29
"BEWARE OF BOOGA"?
WHAT THE HECK IS A BOO-...
GULP
BOOGA! BOOGA! BOOGA!
© 1994 PAWS, INC. All Rights Reserved.

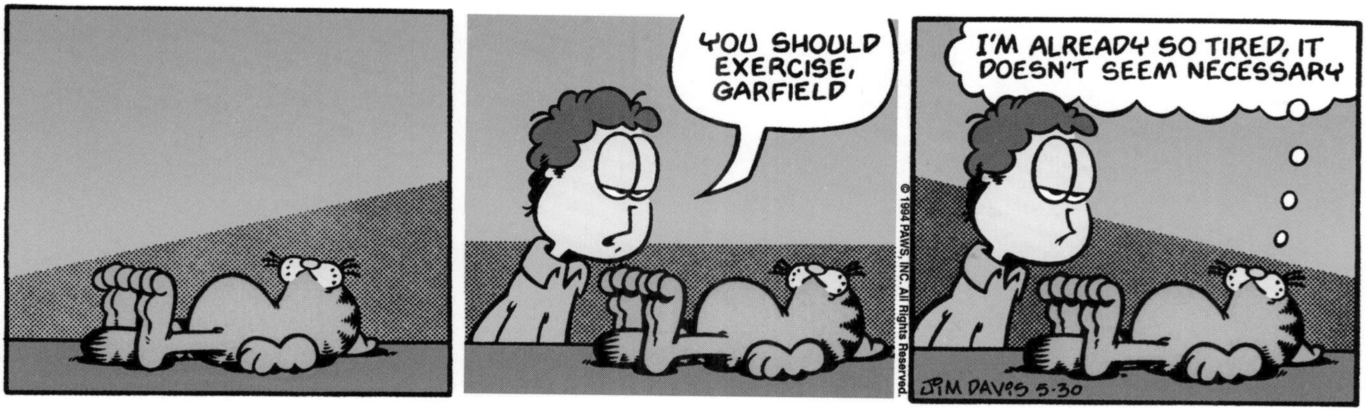
YOU SHOULD EXERCISE, GARFIELD
I'M ALREADY SO TIRED, IT DOESN'T SEEM NECESSARY
© 1994 PAWS, INC. All Rights Reserved.
JIM DAVIS 5-30

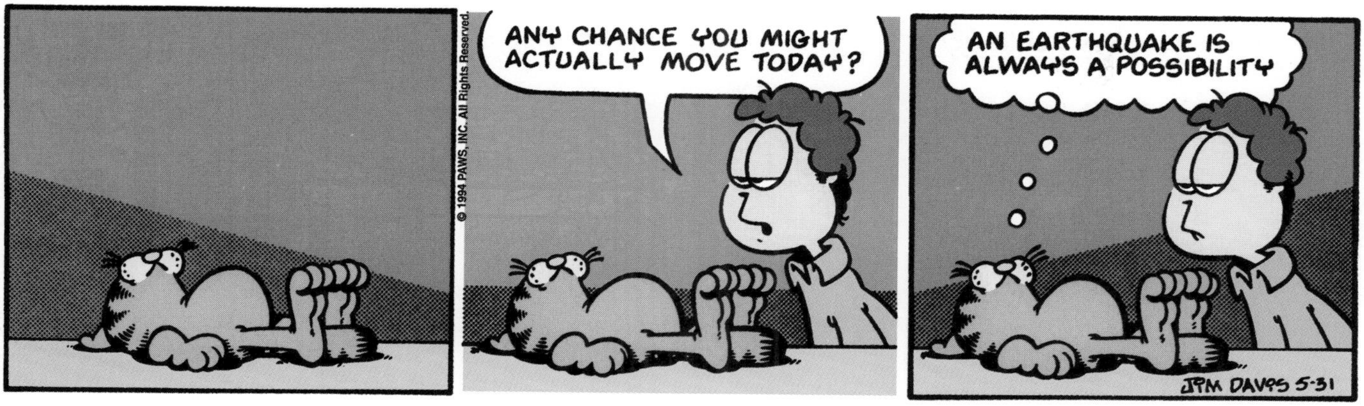
© 1994 PAWS, INC. All Rights Reserved.
ANY CHANCE YOU MIGHT ACTUALLY MOVE TODAY?
AN EARTHQUAKE IS ALWAYS A POSSIBILITY
JIM DAVIS 5-31

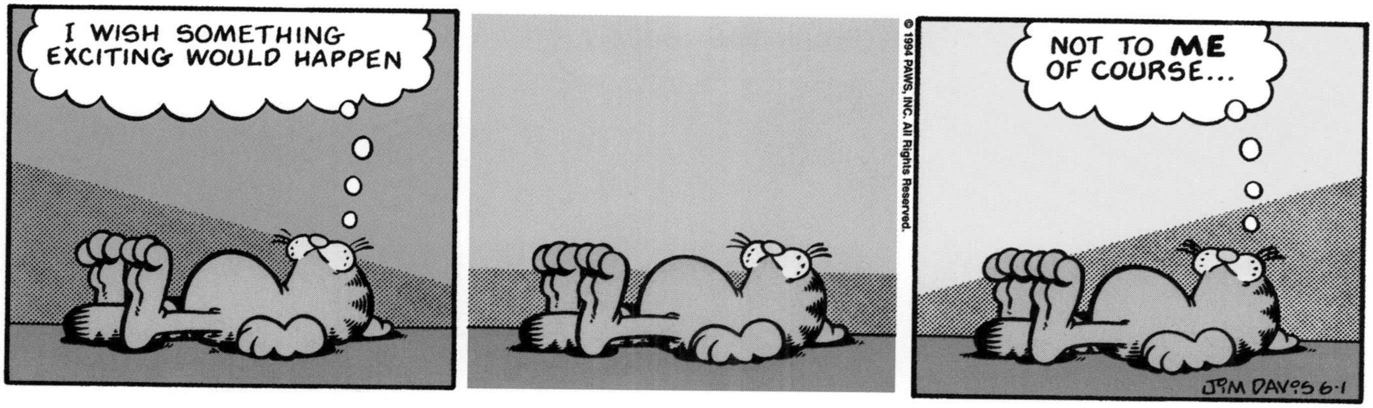
I WISH SOMETHING EXCITING WOULD HAPPEN
© 1994 PAWS, INC. All Rights Reserved.
NOT TO **ME** OF COURSE...
JIM DAVIS 6-1

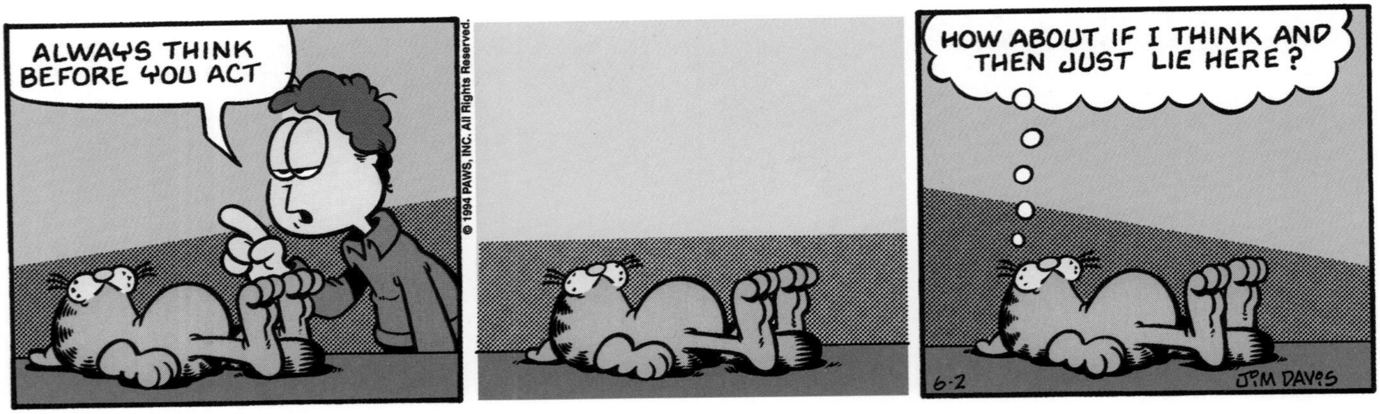
ALWAYS THINK BEFORE YOU ACT
© 1994 PAWS, INC. All Rights Reserved.
HOW ABOUT IF I THINK AND THEN JUST LIE HERE?
6-2
JIM DAVIS

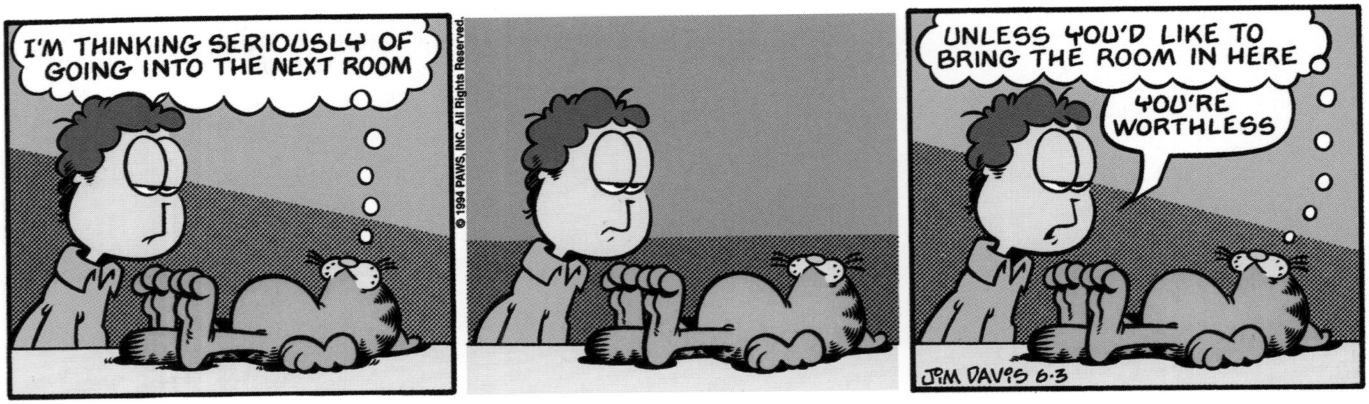
I'M THINKING SERIOUSLY OF GOING INTO THE NEXT ROOM
© 1994 PAWS, INC. All Rights Reserved.
UNLESS YOU'D LIKE TO BRING THE ROOM IN HERE
YOU'RE WORTHLESS
JIM DAVIS 6-3

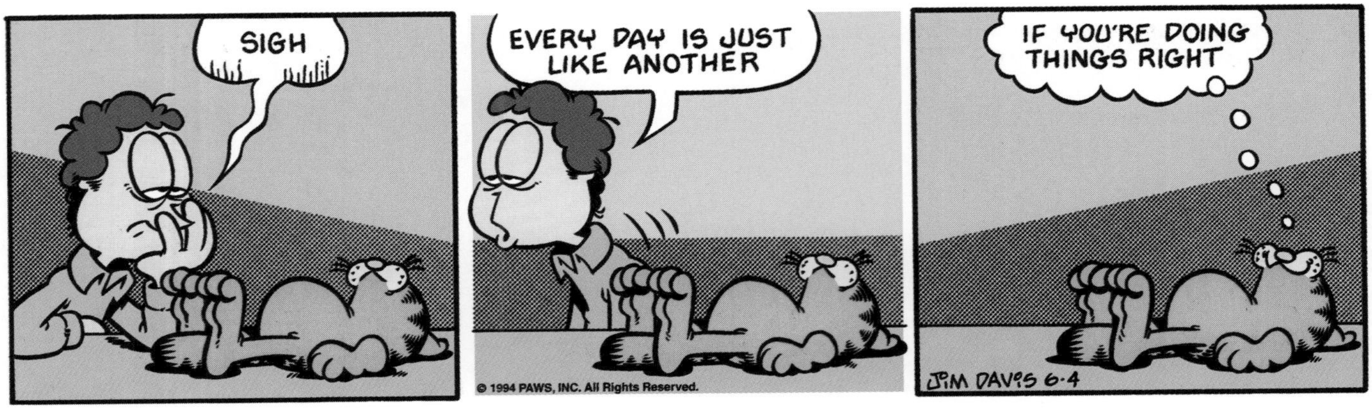
SIGH
EVERY DAY IS JUST LIKE ANOTHER
© 1994 PAWS, INC. All Rights Reserved.
IF YOU'RE DOING THINGS RIGHT
JIM DAVIS 6-4

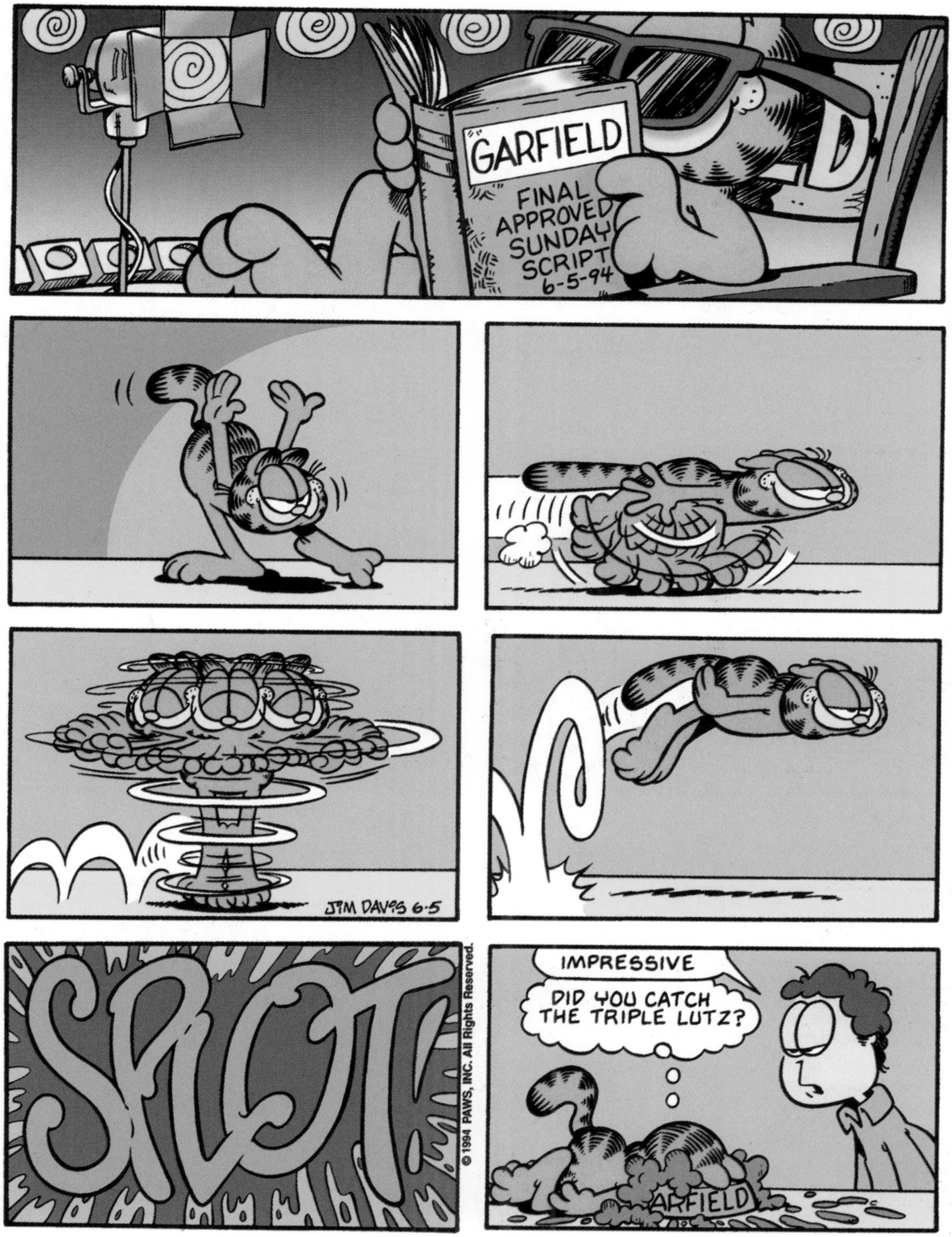
GARFIELD
FINAL APPROVED SUNDAY SCRIPT 6-5-94
JIM DAVIS 6-5
SPLOT!
IMPRESSIVE
DID YOU CATCH THE TRIPLE LUTZ?
GARFIELD

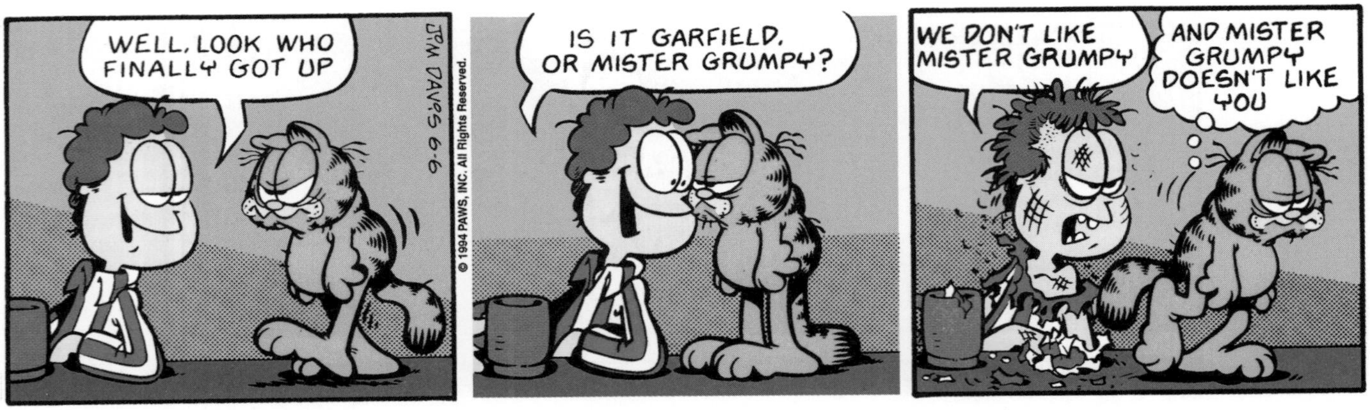
WELL, LOOK WHO FINALLY GOT UP
JIM DAVIS 6-6
© 1994 PAWS, INC. All Rights Reserved.
IS IT GARFIELD, OR MISTER GRUMPY?
WE DON'T LIKE MISTER GRUMPY
AND MISTER GRUMPY DOESN'T LIKE YOU

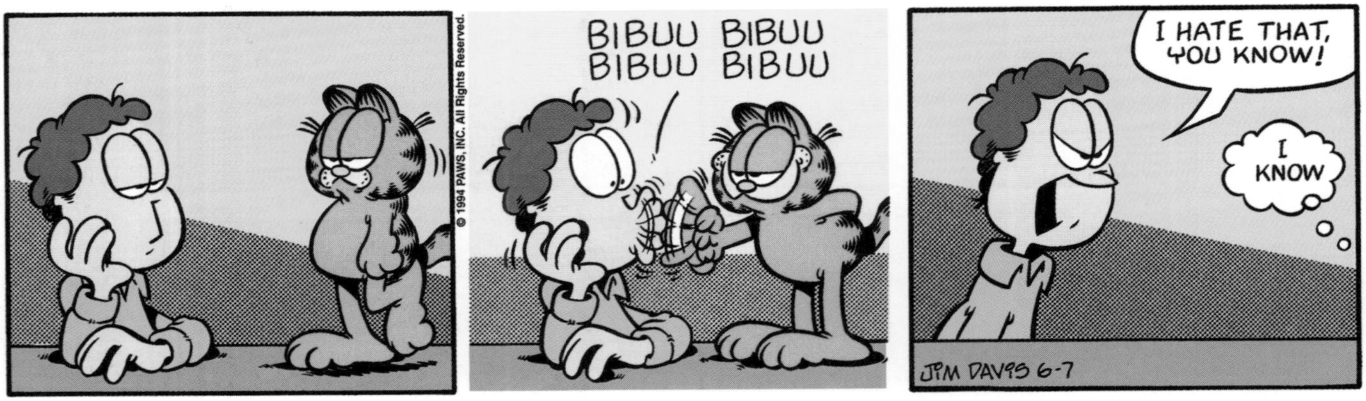
© 1994 PAWS, INC. All Rights Reserved.
BIBUU BIBUU BIBUU BIBUU
I HATE THAT, YOU KNOW!
I KNOW
JIM DAVIS 6-7

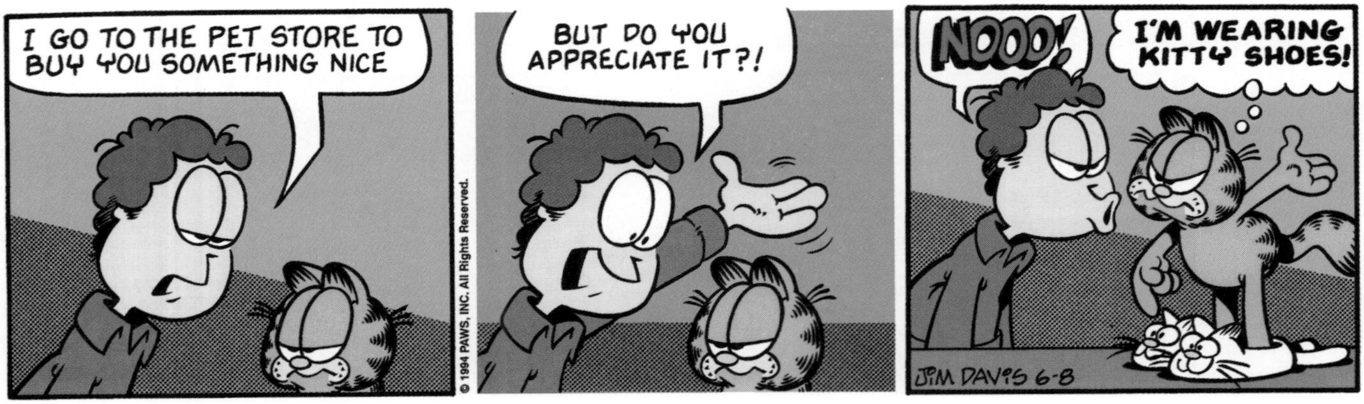
I GO TO THE PET STORE TO BUY YOU SOMETHING NICE
© 1994 PAWS, INC. All Rights Reserved.
BUT DO YOU APPRECIATE IT?!
NOOO!
I'M WEARING KITTY SHOES!
JIM DAVIS 6-8

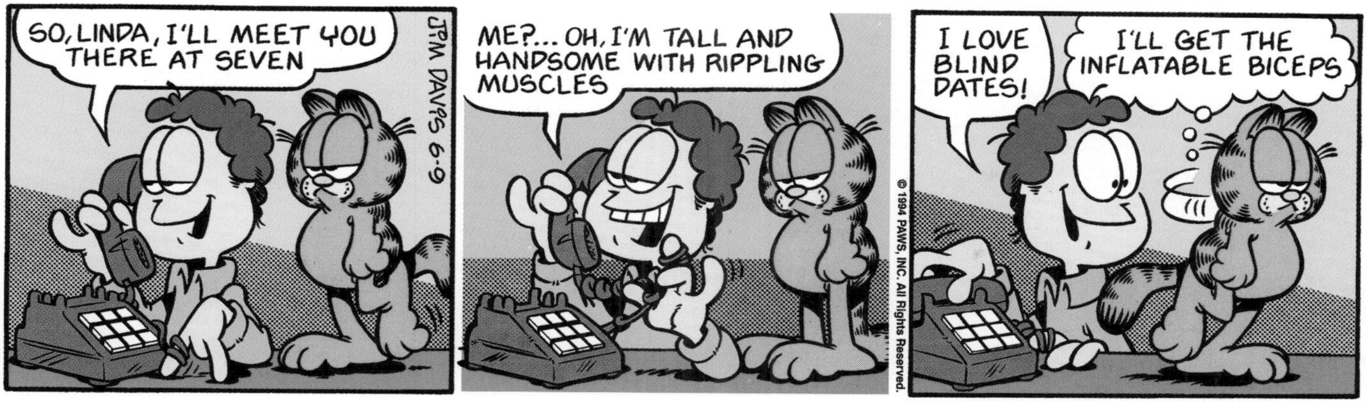
SO, LINDA, I'LL MEET YOU THERE AT SEVEN
ME?... OH, I'M TALL AND HANDSOME WITH RIPPLING MUSCLES
© 1994 PAWS, INC. All Rights Reserved.
I LOVE BLIND DATES!
I'LL GET THE INFLATABLE BICEPS

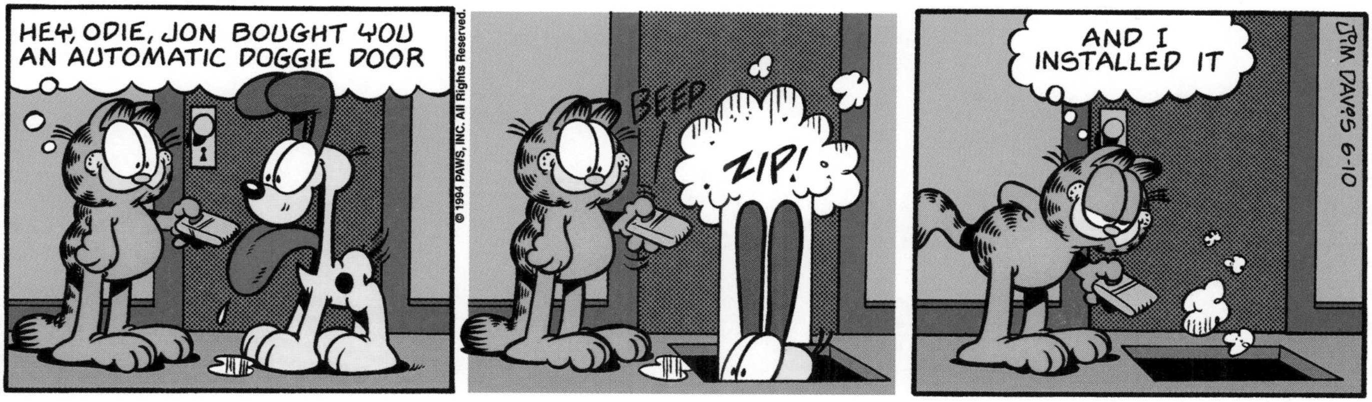
HEY, ODIE, JON BOUGHT YOU AN AUTOMATIC DOGGIE DOOR
© 1994 PAWS, INC. All Rights Reserved.
BEEP
ZIP!
AND I INSTALLED IT

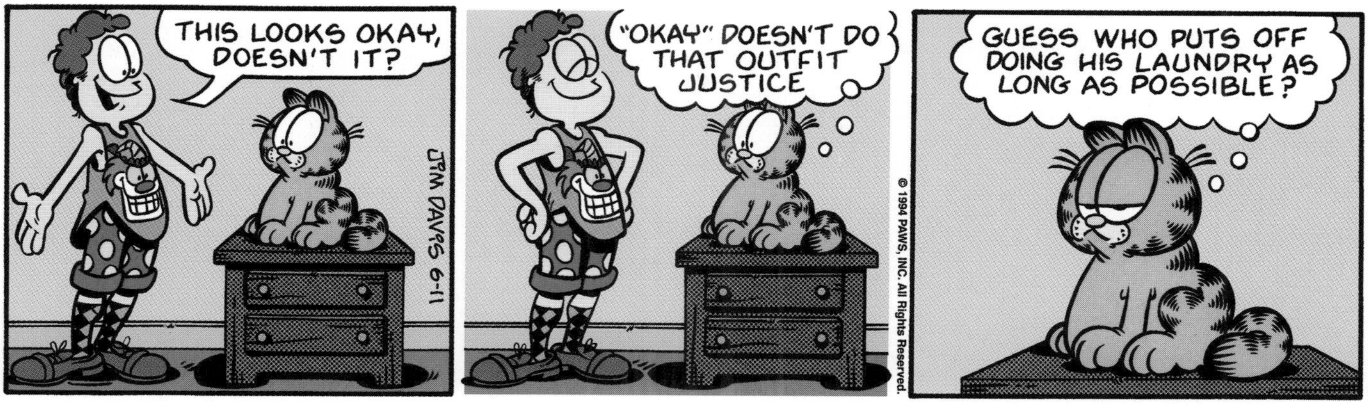
THIS LOOKS OKAY, DOESN'T IT?
"OKAY" DOESN'T DO THAT OUTFIT JUSTICE
© 1994 PAWS, INC. All Rights Reserved.
GUESS WHO PUTS OFF DOING HIS LAUNDRY AS LONG AS POSSIBLE?

GARFIELD'S PARALLEL UNIVERSE

NIGHT IS DAY
AND BLACK IS WHITE...
BEHOLD A WORLD
OF INVERTED SIGHT!

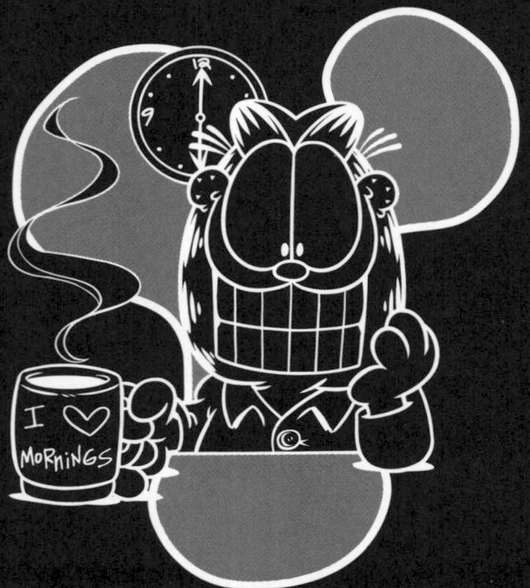
I ♥ MORNINGS

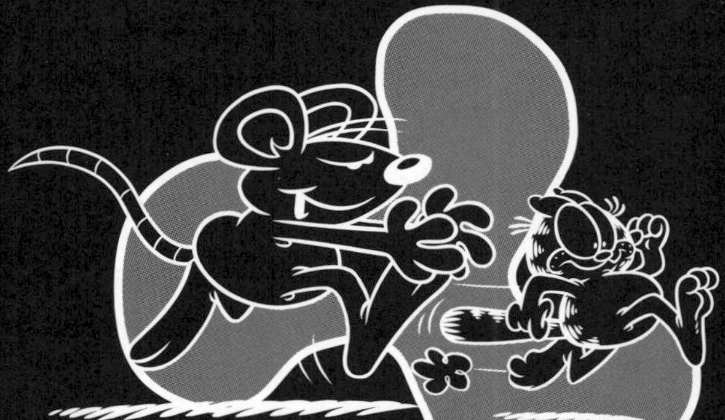

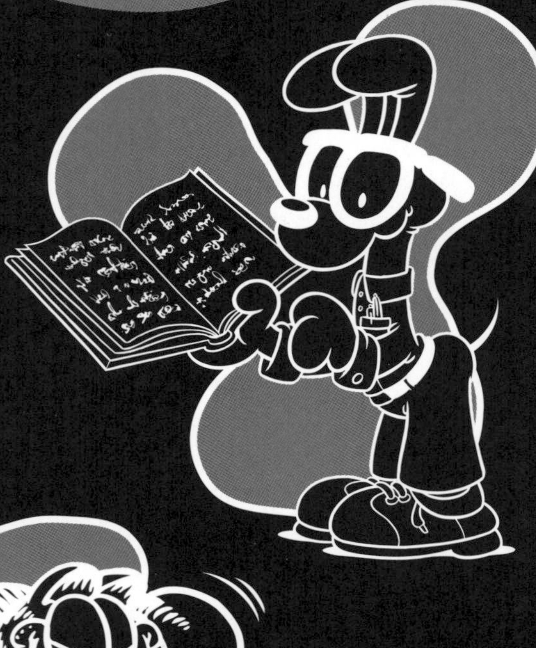

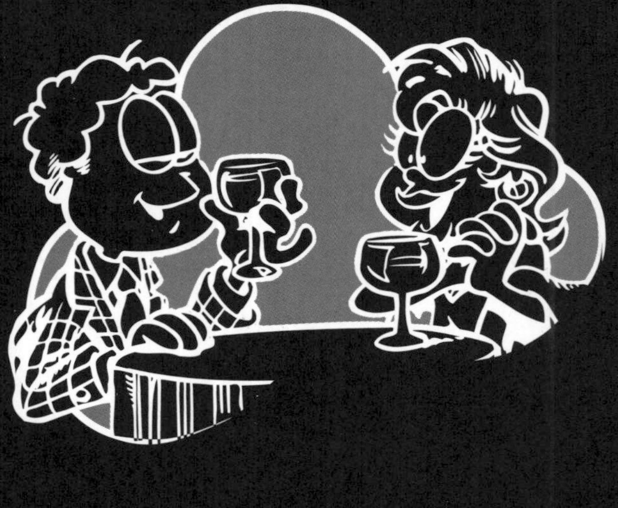

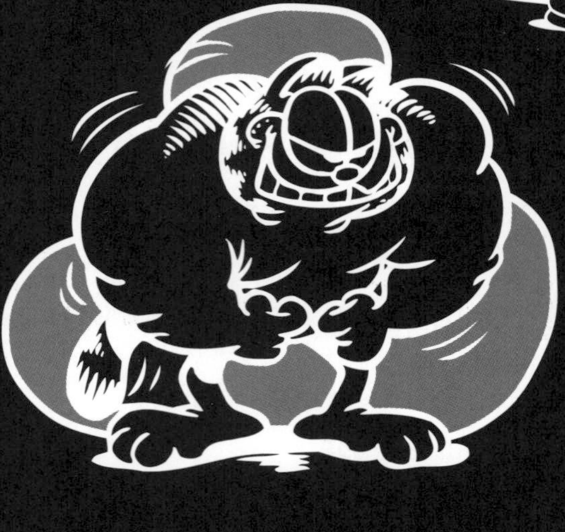

STRIPS, SPECIALS, OR BESTSELLING BOOKS . . .

GARFIELD'S ON EVERYONE'S MENU.

Don't miss even one episode in the Tubby Tabby's hilarious series!

 **New larger, full-color format!**